DRESS ACCESSORIES

c 1150 – *c* 1450

DEDICATION

The authors dedicate this volume to
Brian Spencer, former senior keeper of
the Medieval Department,
Museum of London, in grateful
recognition of his wisdom and kindness
generously given over many years
(GE & FP)

Front Cover: Buckle maker, German, *c.*1425, after
Nuremberg Hausbuch (Treue et al.
1965, pl 49)

Back cover: Amber waste from bead-making, 14th-
century, BC72 site

Half-title (i)   Woman preening, with a mirror, after
14th-century MS (private collection)

===== MUSEUM OF LONDON =====

MEDIEVAL FINDS FROM EXCAVATIONS IN LONDON: 3

DRESS ACCESSORIES

*c.*1150 – *c.*1450

Geoff Egan and Frances Pritchard

with contributions by
Justine Bayley, Mike Heyworth, Rose Johnson, Peter Stott and others

Principal illustrators:
Susan Mitford and Nick Griffiths

LONDON: HMSO

First published 1991

ISBN 0 11 290444 0

British Library Cataloguing in Publication Data
A CIP catalogue record for this book is available from the British Library

HMSO publications are available from:
HMSO Publications Centre
(Mail and telephone orders only)
PO Box 276, London, SW8 5DT
Telephone orders 071–873 9090
General enquiries 071–873 0011
(queuing system in operation for both numbers)

HMSO Bookshops

49 High Holborn, London, WC1V 6HB 071–873 0011 (Counter service only)
258 Broad Street, Birmingham, B1 2HE 021–643 3740
Southey House, 33 Wine Street, Bristol, BS1 2BQ (0272) 264306
9–21 Princess Street, Manchester, M60 8AS 061–834 7201
80 Chichester Street, Belfast, BT1 4JY (0232) 238451
71 Lothian Road, Edinburgh, EH3 9AZ 031–228 4181

HMSO's Accredited Agents
(see Yellow Pages)

and through good booksellers

Erratum:
BIG82 acc. no. 3159 appears as nos. 498 and 743: the
first entry should be ignored.

*Publication of this book has been assisted by a grant from the
City of London Archaeological Trust, which is gratefully acknowledged.*

Printed in the United Kingdom for HMSO
Dd 240092   9/91   C13

Contents

Introduction

This is the third of the thematic volumes on medieval finds from excavations in the City of London. This work was undertaken by the Department of Urban Archaeology, Museum of London (up to 1973 by its predecessor, the Field Archaeology Section of the Guildhall Museum), during redevelopment in the 1970s and early 1980s. It takes for its subject dress accessories and toilet items from the three-hundred year period *c*.1150 to *c*.1450.

As in the two previous volumes (*Knives and Scabbards*, Cowgill et al. 1987; *Shoes and Pattens*, Grew and de Neergaard 1988) the emphasis is on finds from the waterfront area. Here foreshore deposits and dumps of rubbish put down in reclaiming new land from the River Thames have preserved metals and organic materials in exceptionally good condition compared with items recovered on most inland sites. Some other objects, which provide significant information either in their own right or about those recovered from the waterfront sites, have been included from other City excavations or from other sources. Notable among the latter are the Museum of London's established (pre – 1975) and more recent collections (MoL in text), as well as some private collections of London material. Further comparanda from outside London are mentioned where appropriate, though they receive less detailed treatment.

The great diversity in form and manufacturing techniques evident in the 1784 dress accessories described in this book necessitates a different approach from the highly synthesised typology used in *Shoes and Pattens*. Girdles and fittings for them take up a large part of the volume. This reflects the wide variety available during the period considered of items which in many cases gave a modest opportunity for fashionable self expression. Variety and standardisation can each be emphasised within many of the basic categories – the extremes being found respectively among the mounts and the lace chapes.

Some categories of finds described here are already well represented in museum collections, but the close dating for the site sequences from which the very large number of stratified objects included here were excavated provides, virtually for the first time, an accurate chronological framework. Associated groups of finds (from the same series of reclamation-dump deposits etc) can be reassembled from the stratigraphic information given below (pp 3–12). The further inferences (typological, patterns of use in alloys, degree of ornamentation, earliest/latest occurrence, etc) that can reasonably be drawn from this may be of interest in their own right, or particular categories and whole assemblages may be compared with finds from other excavations, whether in London or elsewhere. A further strength of the collection described here is its sheer size. Over 1750 well preserved and closely dated objects offer the opportunity for statistical analysis of a type which hitherto has only been available for those studying ancient ceramics. It seems unlikely at present that any other series of dress accessories of comparable date anywhere in the country could provide such an extensive database. A number of statistical inferences are made in this volume, but there will be readers who will wish to reinterpret, dissect and reassemble the raw data, and to use selected information to set against other medieval assemblages. To make such analysis possible, but at the same time to prevent the book exceeding reasonable bounds of length and cost, representative objects, rather than every single item, are illustrated. In deciding on terminology, which dimensions, and the level of detail to include in the catalogue descriptions of each object, therefore, a balance has been sought between burdening the text with minutiae and providing adequate data to characterise various traits to help researchers. The objects have been considered not only from the point of view of the original users, but also from that of the manufacturer as well. The tenacity of some traditions in manufacture has been identified, though it will probably need far more examples to be assessed in this way before, for example, the products of a particular workshop can be confidently identified among these and other finds.

The chapters dealing with the different categories of accessories begin with girdles and buckles – basic articles of dress which the overwhelming majority of Londoners would have worn. These are followed by other girdle fittings – strap-ends, mounts etc – which were also very common, but were in less universal usage. Different means of securing clothes around the body – brooches, buttons and lace chapes – are discussed next, followed by hair accessories and more purely decorative categories. Purses, which were worn suspended from the girdle, are followed by toilet articles, some of which were carried around on the person while others probably did not leave the home.

Comparison of the recently excavated assemblages with the London Museum Medieval Catalogue (Ward–Perkins 1940), where it covers the same categories (the Guildhall Museum Catalogue of 1908 includes very few corresponding items), and with the collections of the former London and Guildhall Museums, shows that the splendid series of dress accessories assembled prior to 1975 (when the two collections were united in the Museum of London) must have been acquired on a highly selective basis. Not only are the majority of these items from the two former museums complete, a far greater proportion than emerges in the excavated groups are highly decorative. Some categories among the recently excavated accessories in cheap alloys, notably items of lead/tin, were not included in the two catalogues mentioned above (the few lead-alloy medieval rings in the national collection were similarly omitted from the British Museum's catalogue of finger rings). A few categories, like spangles, medieval buttons and needlecases, are completely absent from the old London collections. Conversely, most of the more expensive items that were published are not represented among the material excavated during the 1970s and early 1980s. Apart from four thin finger rings and a handful of gilded items there is no gold among these finds, and the few silver objects have a metal content that together would barely amount to that of six and a half contemporary pennies.

Recent acquisitions by the Museum of London have considerably extended the range of the established collections; selectivity on the basis of completeness continues, though other items of particular interest are collected, and items of new forms tend to be acquired in preference to those of types already represented. The recorded contexts of the excavated assemblages that are the subject of the present volume provide the most reliable basis available for dating. Although high-class items are very scarce, the relative popularity of everyday forms can begin to be established from duplicate items, as can recurrent patterns of wear and breakage. In terms of published material, the assemblages presented here transform the picture of the importance of accessories of lead and tin alloys. A few design elements which recur on different categories of fittings towards the end of the period under consideration may point towards some notion of ensuite accessories for dress (fig 157), perhaps ultimately deriving from armorial devices of aristocratic parade items. There are several juxtapositions of different strap fittings found together still in place, which would probably never have occurred to the researcher. (See on Combinations of Diverse Strap Fittings and Possible Ensuite Items).

Detailed analysis of the metallic content of a large number of the objects described has been undertaken by the staff of the Ancient Monuments Laboratory (initially by Paul Wilthew and subsequently by Mike Heyworth, both working under the supervision of Justine Bayley). It is particularly pleasing that the Historic Buildings and Monuments Commission (England) has funded this important aspect of the research. The results for the first time establish some parameters for the study of other assemblages of similar late-medieval metalwork.

Some of the methods of manufacture appear remarkably labour-intensive to the present-day observer. Several items have been assembled from different elements (occasionally using diverse alloys) where there is no apparent decorative or functional advantage over using a single piece of metal. Punched decoration was sometimes added to cast fittings (eg nos. 1714–16), and there are instances where elements of the ornamentation were continued onto part of an object which would not have been visible (eg nos. 473 & 475). This seems to emphasise a basic difference in outlook between the medieval and the latter-day production worker (compare the large proportion of metal that had to be recycled following each casting as evidenced by the item at the bottom in fig 153 – see p 239 – this may well be an extreme instance). A remarkable copper-alloy buckle (no. 39), manufactured by a combination of labour-intensive techniques where a single casting would have sufficed, seems, when compared with the other buckles listed here, to have been as anomalous in its own time as it would be today.

It may come as a surprise to those familiar only with the idealised view of medieval production propounded by William Morris and others, that poor workmanship, inadequate materials, and designs that are every bit as banal and repetitive as those seen in modern seaside souvenirs were current in medieval London. It is quite clear that in the 14th-century copper-alloy buckles were being cast in batches of over one hundred at a time, and by the 15th century mass-production of cheap trinkets in the basest alloys for the demands of a flourishing popular market was firmly established. It would, of course, be misleading to characterise the entire subject matter of this volume as cheap and nasty – though some of these objects certainly were. There are many plain and decorative items, which, as wear on them shows, were capable of serving their intended purpose perfectly adequately over a long period. Some accessories were used until they wore out; others were repaired – in some instances by methods that are by any criterion amateurish. Evidence for repairs has been observed largely on what appear to be better-quality fittings rather than the cheapest of the range. A very few objects, like three armorial mounts (no. 933 – these were surely specially commissioned) and a silver-gilt mirror case (no. 1718), stand out because they combine highly skilled workmanship with effective design.

Exotic materials, notably among the beads, hint at some of the international trade links attested by documentary sources. Bead manufacture in London from raw jet and amber (the former material was certainly and the latter was probably available in England) is complemented by waste pieces of Mediterranean red coral in the same assemblages. Although several parallels among metal girdle fittings and brooches have been traced with objects excavated on the Continent, it is not possible at this stage to say whether this represents trade in either direction or a common international style. The manufacture in London of sheet-copper mounts and various cast buckles and strap loops of copper-alloy, and also of sheet-iron items with tin coating is attested by a limited amount of industrial waste. The main excavated waterfront groups discussed here do not include any moulds for metal items, though there are examples of both clay and stone from inland and more recent waterfront sites, and they also appear among chance finds from the City. A future volume will, it is hoped, make available the large amount of new information on manufacture – some of which is still being recovered from the ground at the time of writing.

Many of the motifs and methods of manufacture that are found in these dress fittings can be paralleled at a general level in the jewellery of non-industrial societies from the ancient world to the present (cf Gerlach 1971, passim). Nevertheless, these London assemblages possess a character that specifically and unmistakably ties them to the high middle ages of north-west Europe. It is too early to put this in perspective, with so much important material unpublished from recent excavations in this country (including further large groups from subsequent fieldwork in the City of London) and on the Continent. The remarkable finds from Meols in Merseyside, published in the middle of the last century (Hume 1863), provide the most extensive series of parallels available so far. Comparisons with assemblages excavated in Bristol and Beverley, and from the Bedern site in York, should soon be possible, and it will be particularly useful in the longer term to try to identify any regional variations.

It seems remarkable in a period when limited social provision meant that life for the urban poor was far from easy, that so many items of metal were discarded apparently without being reused or recycled. The extensive retrieval activity on urban rubbish dumps in many third-world countries today shows that the unpleasantness of the task does not prevent it being a major source of day-to-day income for the deprived. Perhaps those to whom metal scraps would have provided some useful income did not have access to the dumps. It is impossible to know the precise circumstances of the accumulation of material dumped to make up the newly reclaimed land along London's waterfront in the high medieval period, but the failure of contemporaries to recover so many reusable or recyclable items is the good fortune of today's researchers.

All London waterfront sites seem to be prolific in finds if appropriate retrieval methods are used. On sites in the 1970s only hand collection took place. At Billingsgate (BIG82) a certain amount of sieving and metal detecting was undertaken by the Department of Urban Archaeology's staff. The use of metal detectors in the skilled hands of members of the Society of Thames Mudlarks under the direction of the Department of Urban Archaeology was the principal factor in the recovery of virtually all of the metal items included in this volume from the watching briefs at Swan Lane and Billingsgate. It is sobering to look at the SWA81 and BWB83 items, some 68 per cent of the catalogued objects listed here (from all categories and materials), and to consider which parts of this study – including some of the most outstanding individual items as well as entire categories of objects (eg shield-shaped strap-ends nos. 732–742) – could not have been written without this fruitful cooperation in the recovery of groups of finds for the Museum of London.

As much as any of the individual points touched on above, the fascination of this extensive series of finds lies in the range of items within basic categories. The dress accessories used in medieval London were demonstrably far more varied than these recent discoveries alone are able to indicate. The picture this volume provides is by no means a complete one, but its aim is to bring the everyday variety of this aspect of medieval life into a sharper focus, within a more detailed chronological framework.

Conventions used in the text

For all catalogued items, the first number (the *catalogue number*) is in a running sequence indicating the position in the category lists in this volume. Then comes the *site code*, which is followed by the *accession number* (unique within each site), the *context number* (layer number) in brackets, and the *ceramic phase number*:– eg "**18** SWA81 36 (2103) 12" is item number 18 in this volume, which is accession no. 36 from the Swan Lane site, found in layer 2103, which has

been assigned to ceramic phase 12. (For dates assigned to ceramic phases, see p00).

Only objects excavated at the London sites listed at the end of this section are included in the numbered series. Where two or more items that are essentially similar or part of a single article have been given the same accession number, they are here given the same catalogue number, otherwise each different item has a separate number in the catalogue series.

Occasionally different items on a single object are discussed under different category headings – eg *girdles* with *mounts* and a *buckle* – here each item is separately numbered, and there is appropriate cross referencing.

Abbreviations

acc. no.	– accession number
AML	– analysis by Ancient Monuments Laboratory, HBMC(E)
BM, MLA	– British Museum, Dept. of Medieval & Later Antiquities
c	– chapter (in Statutes)
c.	– circa
d	– diameter
DUA	– Department of Urban Archaeology (Museum of London)
estd	– estimated
h	– height
HBMC(E)	– Historic Buildings and Monuments Commission (England)
l	– length
lead-tin	– lead and tin* (analysed items only)
lead/tin	– lead and/or tin
MLC	– analysis by Museum of London Conservation Dept.
MoL	– Museum of London
nd	– no date
RAK	– XRF analysis at Royal Armouries, HM Tower of London, by Roger Turner of Kevex Ltd
th	– thickness
w	– width
XRF	– x-ray fluorescence analysis

* Since the non-quantitative spot tests used by the Museum of London Conservation Dept can detect the presence of very small quantities of a metal, some items described as 'lead-tin (MLC)' may contain less lead than others described as 'tin (AML)' – the latter indicates a lead content of *c.*5% or less. In this book 'pewter' is used only of items so designated by Mike Heyworth as a result of analysis at the Ancient Monuments Laboratory (see fig 262).

Site codes

BC72   – Baynard House, Queen Victoria Street ('Baynard Castle Dock'), 1972

BIG82   – Billingsgate lorry park, Lower Thames Street, 1982

BOY86   – City of London Boys' School, 1986

BWB83   – Billingsgate lorry park, watching brief, 1983

CUS73   – Old Custom House, Lower Thames Street, 1973

GAG87   – Guildhall Art Gallery, 1987

LUD82   – Ludgate Hill, 1982

MIL72   – 10 Milk Street, 1972

MLK76   – 1–6 Milk Street, 1976

OPT81   – 2–3 Copthall Avenue, 1981

SH74   – Seal House, 106–108 Upper Thames Street, 1974

SM75   – St Magnus Church, Lower Thames Street, 1975

SUN86   – Sunlight Wharf, Upper Thames Street, 1986

SWA81   – Swan Lane, 95–103 Upper Thames Street, 1981

TEX88   – Thames Exchange, Upper Thames Street, 1988 .

TL74   – Trig Lane, Upper Thames Street, 1974

WAY83   – 10–13 Ludgate Broadway, 1983

For detailed location of objects from the BIG82, BWB83, SWA81 and TL74 sites within the sequences, see section on Context and Dating of the Finds (figs 2–5).

Ceramic phase dates

6   *c*.1150 – *c*.1200
7   *c*.1200 – *c*.1230
8   *c*.1230 – *c*.1260
9   *c*.1270 – *c*.1350
10 *c*.1330 – *c*.1380
11 *c*.1350 – *c*.1400
12 *c*.1400 – *c*.1450

Drawing conventions

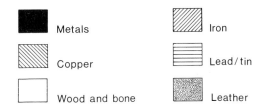

Metals   Iron

Copper   Lead/tin

Wood and bone   Leather

All the numbered objects in the catalogue from the sites listed above, together with detailed archive reports and associated information, are stored at the Museum of London, where they can be examined by prior arrangement. Details of comparative items published here from private collections are held by the Medieval Department of the Museum of London; appropriate enquiries can be answered at the Museum or passed on to the owners.

Dating and Context of the Finds

As in the earlier volumes of this series, the overwhelming majority of the 1784 catalogued finds included were recovered on sites adjacent to the River Thames, both from the dumped fills, mainly of highly organic refuse, deposited for land reclamation, and from the more mixed gravel and silt foreshores that accumulated against the successive medieval revetments. The dumps, which were up to 2m deep, eventually formed almost 100m of new land – virtually all of the block to the south of modern Upper and Lower Thames Streets – as reclamation from the river progressed through the three centuries of the later middle ages with which this volume is concerned (c.1150 – c.1450). A few other selected finds, including some discarded in the City Ditch near Ludgate, have been included from inland sites, but by and large the preservation of metal and leather in soils away from the waterfront is poor, and within the present categories the finds assemblages from inland sites have only very exceptionally approached the diversity and proliferation of those retrieved beside the Thames. Without the waterfront material it would have been quite impossible (even if the finds from more recent excavations had also been considered) to produce the kind of synthesis that is presented here. Notably absent from recent excavations in the City are later-medieval assemblages from domestic and other more specific contexts. Horizontal deposits, such as floors, that could be attributed to the 14th or 15th centuries have virtually all been removed in the City of London by subsequent activity. The cut features that have survived – foundations, rubbish pits and wells – have generally proved disappointingly unproductive of material in categories appropriate for inclusion in this and the preceding volumes in the series. Indeed, but for the waterfront assemblages, the surviving material culture from medieval London – with the exception of ceramics and, less directly, the various structural remains – would give little indication that this was the most important city of the realm and the thriving market for the consumption of goods of all kinds that documentary sources attest.

The freshness of breaks in many pottery sherds found in the organic dumps, and the unadvanced state of decomposition of some of the plant material there – reeds and moss, for example – suggest that much of the refuse was very recently discarded when deposited. Most of this was presumably domestic rubbish and stable sweepings, perhaps with some pit-clearance material. The pottery from foreshore deposits (which often include some organic material similar to that in the dumps, presumably deriving from the same sources) is sometimes more abraded, and occasionally markedly more so. This abrasion probably represents tidal action during the accumulation of the foreshore against the wharves. The mechanisms of the movement of material in the river by the action of the water are highly complex, and depend on ephemeral factors in each immediate area at different states of the tide and according to the amplitude of the river at any season. Nevertheless, most of the pottery here too appears quite fresh, and the ceramic phasing assigned to the latest sherds accords well with coin and other dating and the wider sequences. No significantly higher degree of abrasion has so far been noted on the metal objects from foreshores compared with those from the reclamation dumps, though corrosion in very gravelly deposits of the former can be more advanced. The relatively high density of many of the metal objects may well mean that they were less liable to tidal movement than pottery (though the shape and thinness of some of the lead/tin brooches etc could have rendered these more mobile in the water than might at first sight be supposed). The heavier objects are likely to have settled where they fell, while the matrix of the foreshore moved around them (cf the effect of gold panning). Future studies may further elucidate these points.

There are a few earlier finds among the later medieval deposits – the odd Saxon or Roman objects usually stand out. There is always the possibility that a slightly earlier medieval object may have been kept for some time as an heirloom before it was discarded, or that it ended up in a

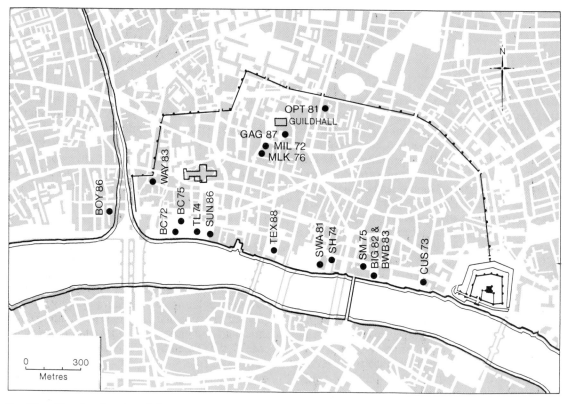

1   City of London, location of sites mentioned in the text

dump with predominantly later material for other reasons. This can be difficult to pinpoint in the present state of knowledge, particularly with scarcer items, but wider considerations may sometimes indicate instances where this could have happened (eg mirror case no. 1718, dated by the style of the decoration). Very occasionally an object appears from all the available information to be intrusive from a later period (eg buckle no. 473). This kind of anomaly may be attributable to a variety of factors – including errors in excavation or subsequent documentation, or an object may be a very early, so far isolated, instance of a category which later became more common. Any special factors to be taken into account are detailed in the discussion of each site given below. The overwhelming majority of the finds presented here are from well-dated deposits, however, and are thought to have been discarded within a generation or so of manufacture. For further discussion of the context of waterfront finds with particular reference to the

Trig Lane site, see Rhodes 1982B, 85–92. For the locations of the sites see fig 1.

The majority of the extremely varied finds included in this book seem to have been either casually discarded or single losses, though some groups of similar items may have more significance. These include some manufacturing evidence – the bead-making waste of diverse materials from Baynard Castle Dock (BC72) and Trig Lane (TL74) sites (also possibly suggested by two amber items from Swan Lane – SWA81), bone waste from Ludgate Hill (LUD82), and the evidence for casting various copper-alloy belt fittings from Copthall Avenue (OPT81). The large number of similar lead-tin shoe buckles from Trig Lane and the latest groups recovered at Swan Lane may also represent some kind of commercial activity. Most, but not all of these buckles had been well-used by the time they were discarded; some appear broken beyond repair. Since no other categories of dress accessories were found in such large numbers, these particular assemblages could represent an aspect of cobbling (perhaps the retrieval of usable leather from worn shoes in order to patch others – here represented by metal fittings that were at that stage mostly expendable by-products).

The waterfront was one of the principal locations for discarding rubbish of all kinds during the medieval period, both on the wharfside at recognised laystalls and, inevitably (despite the attempts of the City authorities to prevent it), in the River Thames and on the foreshore (Sabine 1937, 32 & 37–40). In the present state of knowledge it is virtually impossible to identify the place of origin within the City of even those groups of waste which represent specific crafts that are known from documentary sources to have been carried out in particular areas. Although beadmaking gave its name to Paternoster Row (first recorded in the early 14th century as Paternoster Street – Harben 1918, 459) just to the north of St Paul's Cathedral, and the Trig Lane/Baynard Castle area is the closest part of the waterfront to this, the possible link with the excavated bead-manufacturing waste remains very tenuous, as it is unlikely that any craft was entirely restricted to one area of the City. Single, scattered workshops could easily have produced each of the assemblages of waste that have been recovered.

The finds from one series of late 14th-century dump deposits at the BC72 site have already been singled out in the course of earlier research by the virtue of some unusual aspects of the assemblage of shoes they produced (rather than being patched, these particular shoes were discarded when they started to become worn) compared with others recovered from London sites (Grew and de Neergaard 1988, 90); the 16 or more used (?)spur straps with varied mounts (nos. 1168–85), and the only horse shoes known with punched marks (Clark 1988, 19 & 21 nos. 8 & 9, fig 7) further reinforce the impression that, although these dumps also produced run-of-the-mill finds such as the bead-manufacturing waste, part of this assemblage differs markedly from the others along the waterfront. A milieu that had so many different highly decorated spurs for disposal must have been an extremely affluent one. It remains to be seen whether any specific connection can be established (for example, linking these objects with the nearby Great Wardrobe). The large number of iron (as opposed to lead-tin) plain circular shoe buckles from this site is also in contrast to other assemblages so far analysed, though the significance is far from clear. Another notable assemblage of leatherwork and metal fittings that is in some ways comparable, also including horse equipment which hints at a military milieu, came from a single late 14th-century deposit at Trig Lane (context 414).

The dating of the deposits at the waterfront sites depends in the first instance on coins, supplemented where possible by dendrochronology. This has permitted key changes in the ceramic sequence to be assigned approximate dates (principally the work of Alan Vince). The *ceramic phases* thus defined are the linch pin of the dating assigned in this volume to each of the groups of deposits that together constituted a reclamation dump or foreshore etc. A brief summary of the dated sequence proposed for each of the major sites is given below. Post-excavation analysis methods differed from site to site so that groupings and interpretation may not correspond precisely between the proposed sequences.

Ceramic phasing with defining pottery fabrics

phase 6	*c*.1150 – *c*.1200	shelly sandy ware
phase 7	*c*.1200 – *c*.1230	London/Rouen wares
phase 8	*c*.1230 – *c*.1260	Kingston ware
phase 9	*c*.1270 – *c*.1350	Mill Green ware
phase 10	*c*.1330 – *c*.1380	late medieval Hertfordshire glazed ware
phase 11	*c*.1350 – *c*.1400	Cheam ware
phase 12	*c*.1400 – *c*.1450	coarse border ware/ bifid rims

For further details, see Vince 1985, 25–93.

Analysis of the complicated site records has progressed, in some cases significantly, beyond the point reached when the first of the volumes in this series was written. The slightly simplified site plans (figs 2–5) for four of the major excavations can be used in conjunction with the lists below of individual contexts and the discussion of each site to pinpoint the location in the sequence at which a specific find was discovered. All the contexts – the individual recorded layers – which comprise a single foreshore or a reclamation dump at these sites have been assigned a *group number*; these groups are the key components in the analysis of each site sequence.

For example, (method for BWB83 and SWA81 sites) the buckle that is catalogue no. 314 in this book (SWA81 accession no. 530) is from context 2040 of group 74; group 74 can be located on the Swan-Lane site plan (fig 4). From the plan, it can be seen that the buckle was found in a ceramic-phase 9 reclamation dump associated with the second of a sequence of three successive revetments constructed during the period that defined as ceramic phase 9 (*c*.1270 – *c*.1350). The group-74 dump is likely to have been deposited at some time in the middle of this period – it might be taken to date from the first quarter of the 14th century, but in this particular instance tokens of a type thought not to have been issued after 1279, found in some of the group-74 deposits, provide a firmer and slightly earlier date. Where a particular group is part of a sequence within a single ceramic phase and no further dating evidence is available, there is at present no way of telling how early or late within the phase each of the successive programmes of reclamation and revetment construction took place. As a second example (method for BIG82 and TL74 sites), brooch no. 1363, TL74 accession no. 2551, is from Trig Lane site, context 368, which is assigned in the list below to a dump from group 15 (ie it is associated with structure 15) of ceramic phase 12 (*c*.1400 – *c*.1450). The site plan (fig 5) shows that structure 15 is a river wall, dated to 1440+ by dendrochronology. The deposition of the brooch in the associated dump can thus be dated to the 1440s, later than some of the other items from ceramic phase 12 at this site. It is possible to take all this one stage further, to examine the dating evidence for the other brooches of the same kind. The three similar brooches (nos. 1360–62) found in ceramic-phase 12 deposits at the Swan Lane site came from a foreshore in front of a revetment dated by dendrochronology to *c*.1394+, and from the overlying dumps (associated with the next programme of reclamation) which appear from coin evidence to date to 1422+. This begins to establish the period when brooches of this kind were in fashion. This level of information is not yet available for all sites, much less for all contexts that produced finds; as research progresses further details can be expected to be added, and minor alterations made.

The Sites

This section is intended to provide a brief background to all the City of London sites mentioned in this book. There is also detailed information, where this is available, on the sequences at those sites which were most productive of finds, for researchers interested in following up the contexts of specific items. Only contexts which produced finds discussed in this book are listed.

BC72: Baynard House, Queen Victoria Street 'Baynard Castle Dock' (site supervisor *P Marsden*)
Two extensive groups of dump deposits, attributed to ceramic phase 11, associated with a stone-walled dock known as the 'East Watergate' (Webster and Cherry 1973, 162–63; Vince in Cowgill et al. 1987, 2). The finds assemblage from one dump group (contexts 55, 79, 83, 88, 88/1, 89 and 150) stands out for the high-class milieu to which (by implication of internal evidence – see p 3) some of the objects relate – though there are also everyday items from these same deposits.

BIG82: Billingsgate lorry park, Lower Thames Street – fig 2 (site supervisor *S Roskams*)
Finds from a detailed sequence of dumps and foreshores of ceramic phases 6 to 8 (Youngs et al. 1983, 191–92, cf Vince in Cowgill et al. 1987, 3). Dating is provided by coins, pottery and dendrochronology. Some sieving and also metal detecting was undertaken by site staff not previously experienced in the latter method (the Society of Thames Mudlarks was not involved during the controlled excavation here); these efforts at their most intensive covered about a quarter of the volume of material excavated, but they were abandoned in the face of limited resources for completing the excavation. After the formal excavation was completed and access to the site had been denied to archaeologists, a number of finds were recovered from the spoil heaps by members of the public. Because in some areas water-lain deposits appeared to have accumulated over land-reclamation dumps, and some deposits defined as foreshores included extensive organic etc dump-type material (perhaps rubbish discarded in the river), it is difficult to categorise each context firmly as either reclamation dump or foreshore. The group-8 revetments and possibly others may have been replaced at least once, resulting in a complicated structural sequence; interpretation may change as a result of further analysis.

For the subsequent watching brief covering the remaining five sixths of the redevelopment site and the later part of the sequence, see BWB83 below.

For ceramic phasing see individual catalogue items.

Note – where there is no structure having exactly the same number as the group, the deposit may relate to any of the structures with a number corresponding to that before the comma.

Contexts which have no type designated, or which do not appear in the following list and which have been phased as part of the relevant groups (see fig 2) need to have the precise nature

of their association with the reclamation sequence clarified by further post-excavation work.

f = foreshore
d = dump

context	group	type	context	group	type
2171	12		3511	10,2	f
2196	12		3521	10,2	f
2243	12		3529	8,1	d
2284	12		3561	8,1	d
2498	13		3562	8,1	d
2506	11		3807	11	

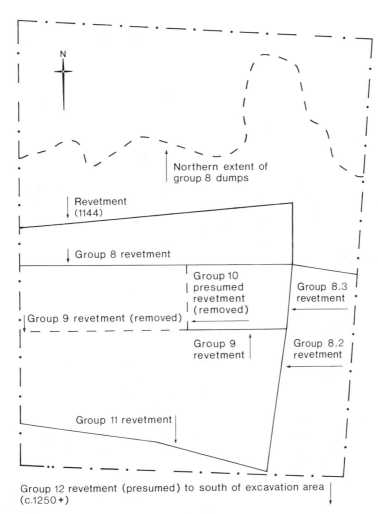

N

Northern extent of
group 8 dumps

Revetment
(1144)

Group 8 revetment

Group 10
presumed
revetment
(removed)

Group 8.3
revetment

Group 9 revetment (removed)

Group 9
revetment

Group 8.2
revetment

Group 11 revetment

Group 12 revetment (presumed) to south of excavation area
(c.1250+)

2 Billingsgate lorry park site (BIG82) – schematic plan

2514	12		4012	9,2	d
2516	12		4064	8,1	d
2544	12		4086	11	
2591	12		4100	10,1	d
2596	12		4103	10,1	d
2636	11		4105	10,1	d
2745	12		4178	8,1	d
2831	12		4201	11	
2853	12		4449	10,1	d
2879	11,4		4533	8,11	d
2888	12		4761	7,10	
2898	11		5020	8,2	d
2914	12		5066	8	
2972	11		5113	8,2	
3071	11		5221	9,2	d
3135	11		5222	9,2	d
3204	11		5224	9,2	d
3212	9,2	d	5277	9,2	d
3232	11		5363	8,2	d
3267	9,2	d	5364	8,2	d
3367	8,1	d	5400	8,2	d
3394	10,2	f	6219	8,1	
3405	11,4		6220	8,1	d
3506	9,2	d	6974	11,4	

BOY86: City of London Boys' School (site supervisor *C Spence*)

Included for comparanda: late-medieval sequence of dumps continuing into the (?)late 15th century. Metal detecting by Society of Thames Mudlarks.

BWB83: Billingsgate lorry park, watching brief – fig 3 (site supervisor *G Egan*)

Extensive finds from ceramic phases 6 to 12 (mainly 9 to 12). Access was initially severely constrained by the developers until most of the structural sequence had been removed. Very limited detailed recording of dumps and traces of revetments etc in at least three adjacent properties provided a sketchy basic sequence in some parts of the site, but the majority of the finds came from foreshores and deeper riverine deposits (some already disturbed when examined), after all structural features had been removed. For these reasons dating must be considered much more rough-and-ready than for other sites. Most of the finds have been assigned to ceramic phase 11 (although individual groups within this broad category appear to be assignable to ceramic phase 10, their locations do not readily combine to produce a coherent overall sequence as on the other waterfront sites – because of the constraints during recording, major features such as inlets may not have been identified; similarly the division between deposits of ceramic phases 11 and 12 is not clear-cut).

In broad terms the sequence is coherent, and a northern limit for deposits attributed to each ceramic phase is indicated in fig 3. In this watching brief the dating for some objects may have been attributed to a later phase than would have been the case had more detailed recording been possible. On the positive side, the very extensive assemblages of finds recovered were the result of metal detecting by the Society of Thames Mudlarks. For the earlier part of the sequence at the site see BIG82 above.

In the following table bracketed context numbers indicate deposits that were disturbed before retrieval took place; there is the possibility of contamination by earlier or occasionally later items among finds recovered from these deposits.

d = dump
f = foreshore
m = mixed dump and foreshore

context	group(s)	type	ceramic phase
(4)	57/59	m	11
(16)	57/59	m	11
(17)	45/47	m	12
(108)	17	f	101
(109)	44	f	11
(110)	28/31/33	m	11
(112)	28/31/33	m	11
(113)	31	d	11
117	31	d	11
(119)	41	d	11
124	50	f	9
125	41	d	11
(126)	41	d	11
(128)	unassigned		
(129)	41	d	11
131	41	?d	11
(136)	unphased	?d	?11
(137)	unphased	?d	?11
(138)	unphased	?d	?11
142	41	d	11
144	42	f	11
(147)	36/38	m	11
149	36	f	11
150	38	d	11
151	36	f	11
154	57	f	11
155	59	d	11
156	59	d	11
157	38	d	11
(204)	57/59	m	11
(207)	57/59	m	11
(219)	9/11	m	9
(222)	9/11	m	9

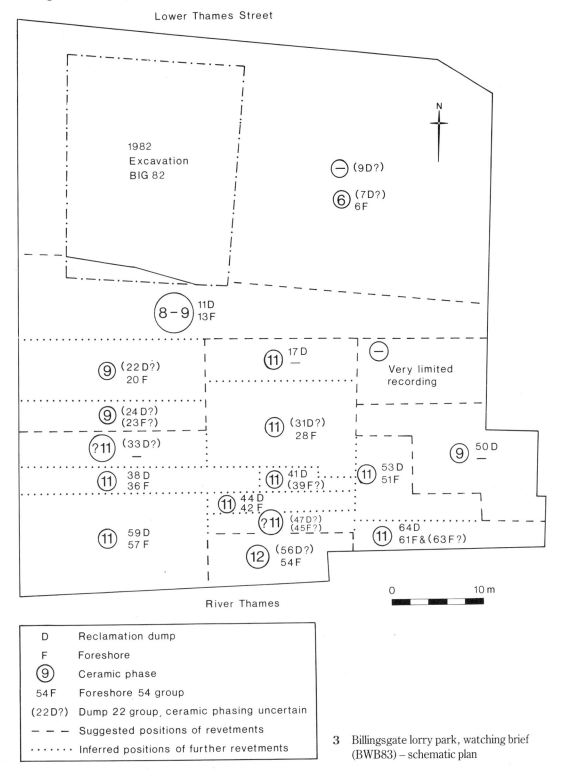

Lower Thames Street

N

1982
Excavation
BIG 82

⊖ (9D?)

⑥ (7D?)
6 F

⑧-⑨ 11D
13 F

⑪ 17 D
—

⊖

Very limited
recording

⑨ (22D?)
20 F

⑨ (24D?)
(23F?)

⑪ (31D?)
28 F

?⑪ (33D?)
—

⑨ 50 D
—

⑪ 38 D
36 F

⑪ 41 D
(39F?)

⑪ 53 D
51 F

⑪ 44 D
42 F

?⑪ (47D?)
(45F?)

⑪ 64 D
61F & (63F?)

⑪ 59 D
57 F

⑫ (56D?)
54 F

River Thames

0   10 m

D	Reclamation dump
F	Foreshore
⑨	Ceramic phase
54 F	Foreshore 54 group
(22D?)	Dump 22 group, ceramic phasing uncertain
– – –	Suggested positions of revetments
· · · · · ·	Inferred positions of further revetments

3 Billingsgate lorry park, watching brief
(BWB83) – schematic plan

(247)	unassigned				345	61	f	11
256	45	f	11		(346)	61/62/64	m	11
257	39	f	11		(348)	57/59	m	11
(259)	unassigned		?9		351	53	d	11
(260)	9/11	m			(352)	61/62/64	m	11
(263)	13	f	9		353	57	f	11
(264)	13	f	9		(354)	57/59	m	11
(265)	45/47/57/59	m	12		(355)	61/62/64	m	11
(269)	unassigned		?9		357	61	f	11
(274)	unassigned		?9		(358)	unassigned		
(275)	unassigned		?12		(359)	51/53	m	11
(276)	44	d	11		(361)	51/53	m	11
279	36	f	11		362	48	m	9
282	36	f	11		366	48	f	9
(283)	36	f	11		(367)	48	f	9
(284)	unassigned		?9		(368)	57/59	f	11
(285)	23/33	m	9		369	51	d	11
(286)	42/44	m	11		373	51	f	11
(287)	57	f	11		(376)	61	f	11
(289)	24/26	m	9		377	61	f	11
(290)	23/24/36	m	9		378	61	f	11
291	42	f	11		380	33	d	11
(292)	57/59	m	11		(383)	61/62/64	m	11
293	44	d	11		386	51	f	11
(295)	42/44	m	11		387	61	f	11
(296)	42	m	11		(389)	61/62/64	m	11
297	57	f	11		391	61	f	11
(298)	57/59	m	11		(395)	61/62/64	m	11
(299)	42/44	m	11		396	61	f	11
300	unassigned	m	?11		399	51	f	11
(301)	42/44	m	11		(401)	61/62/64	m	11
303	36	f	11					
(304)	unassigned		?11					
(305)	36/38	f	11					
(306)	28	f	11					
(307)	45/47	m	11					
308	38	f	11					
309	54	f	12					
(310)	unassigned		?12					
313	54	f	12					
(314)	unassigned		?12					
317	36	f	11					
318	28	f	11					
(319)	54	f	12					
324	54	f	12					
325	50	d	9					
326	54	f	12					
(328)	61/62/64	m	11					
329	61	f	11					
(330)	61/62/64	m	11					
332	61	f	11					
(333)	57/59	m	11					
334	61	f	11					
(338)	61/62/64	m	11					
341	61	f	11					
343	53	d	11					

CUS73:   Old Custom House Site, Lower Thames Street (site supervisor *T Tatton-Brown*)
Published by Tatton-Brown (1974, 117–219).
Trenches I–VI, XI–XII and XIV–XV included material of appropriate date for this volume. Each trench has a separate series of context numbers. The foreshores and dumps produced a limited number of finds attributable to ceramic phases 9 and 11.

GAG87:   Guildhall Art Gallery (site supervisor *G Porter*)
For comparanda: inland site with finds evidence and plant from a workshop casting copper-alloy buckles of a form attributed on other sites to ceramic phase 11.

LUD82:   Ludgate Hill (site supervisor *P Rowsome*)
Inland site including the City Ditch. The main Ditch fills have been dated, by a coin of 1302–10 and documentary evidence of development over the former Ditch area by 1340, to the middle part of ceramic phase 9; earlier fills in another area seem to date to the mid 13th century (ceramic phase 8). See Vince in Cowgill et

al. 1987, 4, and Youngs et al. 1983, 194. Finds include waste from bone-bead manufacture in the early 14th-century Ditch fills.

MIL72: 10 Milk Street (site supervisor *N Farrant*)
Inland site; a pit produced one comb included in this volume.

MLK76: 1–6 Milk Street (site supervisors *S Roskams, J Schofield*)
Inland site; a pit produced one of the girdles discussed in this volume.

OPT81: 2–3 Copthall Avenue (site supervisor *C Maloney*)
Inland site, with a few finds deriving from the manufacture of cast copper-alloy strap fittings (ceramic phase 9) – see Pearce et al. 1985.

SH74: Seal House, 106–108 Upper Thames Street (site supervisor *J Schofield*)
Sequence of dumps and foreshores (ceramic phases 6 to 8). The four successive wharves can be dated to 1133+, 1163–92+, and 1193+ by dendrochronology, and to *c*.1250 by pottery. Few finds relevant to this volume.

SM75: St. Magnus Church, Lower Thames Street (site supervisor *J Schofield*)
Small waterfront site. A chain from ceramic phases 6 to 7 is included in this volume.

SUN86: Sunlight Wharf, Upper Thames Street (site supervisor *R Bluer*)
For comparanda: sequence of reclamation dumps and foreshores (ceramic phases 6 to 12 and later). Metal detecting by Society of Thames Mudlarks.

SWA81: Swan Lane, Upper Thames Street – fig 4 (site supervisor *G Egan*)
Small controlled excavation and subsequent extensive watching brief comprising reclamation dumps and foreshores with up to ten successive revetments in three adjacent properties (ceramic phases 6 to 12). Despite watching brief conditions, the helpful contractors (Sir Robert MacAlpine and Sons) permitted prolonged access to the fullest reclamation sequence recorded among the main sites included in this volume. Metal detecting by the Society of Thames Mudlarks produced extensive and varied finds assemblages that can be dated closely (Egan 1985/86, 42–50), though recording of the earliest (ceramic phase 6) and some of the later

(ceramic phase 11) parts of this sequence is limited. The late 13th-century and early 15th-century deposits were especially productive (ceramic phases 9 and 12). The latest two successive dumps date to 1394+ by dendrochronology, and to 1422+ from coin evidence, and the foreshore associated with the former and underlying the latter can be dated to *c*.1400–30 (the absence of coins of the reign of Henry VI is taken to be inconsistent with deposition as late as the 1430s – Vince in Cowgill et al. 1987, 6).

context	group	context	group
161 (dump, phase 9)		2101	102
1280 (dump, phase 9)		2102	95
2000	70	2103	103
2004	85	2105	95
2006	104/106/107	2106	103
2008	(redeposited)	2107	102
2012	93	2108	103
2016	80	2109	102
2017	74	2110	93
2018	74	2111	103
2020	74	2112	103
2023	100	2113	103
2025	(?)74	2114	103
2027	74	2115	102
2028	74	2117	103
2030	74	2126	77
2031	74	2127	74
2032	100	2128	88
2039	74	2132	74
2040	74	2133	67
2046	74	2134	74
2050	74	2135	67
2051	74	2137	74
2052	58	2139	61
2054	100	2141	74
2055	85	2142	61
2057	74	2144	74
2061	74	2145	61
2062	74	2146	74
2063	74	2149	74
2065	85	2150	61
2069	100	2176	24
2070	74	2182	(?)24
2072	74	2187	24
2075	74	2207	26
2078	74	2209	24
2079	74	2257	(?)38
2081	74	2266	42
2082	103	2269	102
2084	103	2270	61
2085	102	2273	55
2097	103	2274	67
2100	103	2279	42

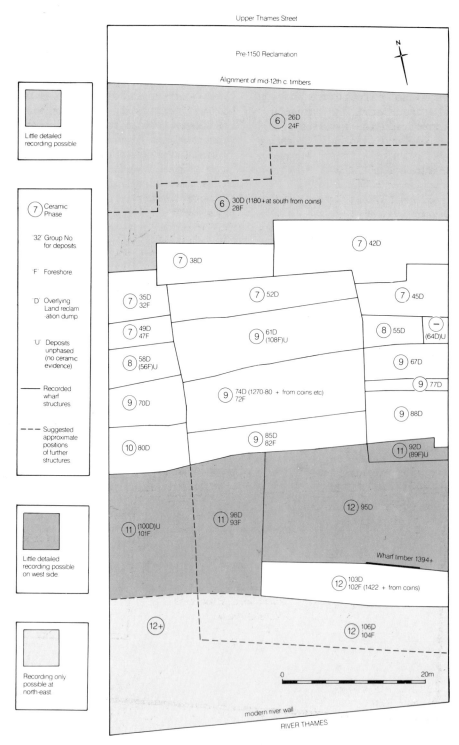

4 Swan Lane site and watching brief (SWA81) – schematic plan

TEX88: Thames Exchange, Upper Thames Street (site co-ordinator *G Milne*, supervisors *C Milne* and *K Tyler*)

For comparanda: extensive site with controlled excavation areas and wider watching brief (ceramic phases 6 to 11, possibly 12). Metal detecting by the Society of Thames Mudlarks. The extensive finds assemblages include evidence from manufacture of cast copper-alloy and lead/tin strap fittings. Details of coin and dendrochronological dating for the very full sequence are not available at the time of writing.

TL74: Trig Lane, Upper Thames Street – fig 5 (site supervisor *G Milne*)

Well-dated sequence of reclamation dumps and foreshores from *c.*1250 to *c.*1440 (ceramic phases 8 to 12). Dating of the 17 revetments/repairs and foreshore structures in three adjacent properties was from dendrochronology, coins and pottery. The field records do not permit specific identification of all contexts as either foreshore or reclamation-dump deposits. Extensive finds from ceramic phases 10 to 12. The structural evidence has been published (Milne and Milne 1982, cf Vince in Cowgill et al. 1987, 6–7). Because all the recorded deposits associated with each major structure (ie the earlier foreshore contexts immediately adjacent and underlying, as well as the later ones accumulating to the south against each revetment, together with the reclamation dumps immediately to the north of the structure) have been put together under one group number, some of the foreshore deposits at this site have in post-excavation analysis been divided between the earlier structural group to the north and the later one to the south. This way of grouping contexts may thus place finds from the same foreshore strata recorded at slightly different points under different group numbers.

5 Trig Lane site (TL74) – schematic plan

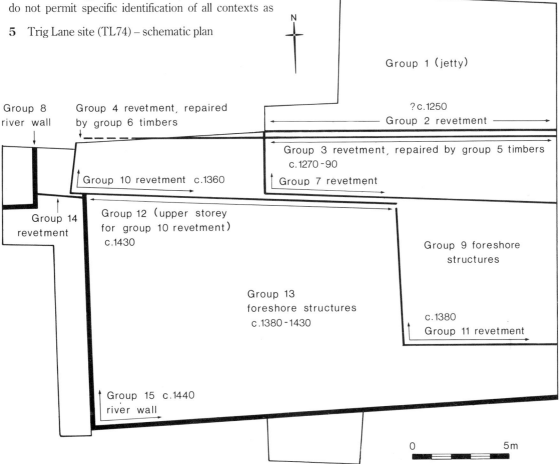

d   = dump
f   = foreshore
accumulated foreshore   = postdating each structure
underlying foreshore   = predating each structure
For ceramic phasing see individual catalogue entries.

context	group	type
	(ie relates to	
	revetment number . . .)	
274	15	d
275	15	d
279	15	d
291	(?)11	d
306	11	d
364	15	d
368	15	d
370	11	d
414	(?)7/11	d
415	11	d
416	10/11/13/15	underlying/
		accumulated f
429	9/11	d/f
431	9/11	d/f
453	11/15	d/accumulated f
1347	7	underlying f
1388	(?)15	underlying f
1457	12	unassigned
1590	2	d
1877	3	d
1942	10	unassigned
1956	10/13	accumulated f
2232	14	d
2332	10	d
2416	2	d
2417	(?)2	d/repair fills
2455	(?)2, + 3 material	d/repair fills
2515	2	d
2525	2	d
2529	2	d
2532	2	d
2608	13	f
2656	10	d

WAY83:   10–13 Ludgate Broadway (site supervisor
P Rowsome)
Inland site; the medieval City Ditch produced one comb
included in this volume.

General observations on the context and dating of the finds

Overall, the finds attributed to ceramic phases 9
to 12 are far more extensive than those consi-

dered to be earlier than *c*.1270. This may in part
be because fewer finds in the categories relevant
to the present series of publications were discarded in either the dumps or the foreshores
during the earlier part of the sequences, but so
far none of the waterfront sites for which the
records have been fully analysed has employed
standard methods of retrieval throughout, using
the same techniques for all the deposits excavated. The Thames Exchange site may in due
course provide a clearer perspective on this
point. At some sites relatively few deposits with
finds have been assigned to ceramic phase 10,
probably because of the chronological overlap
with other phases (see tables 1–4 etc, pp 21–25).
The absence of finds of the 1260s in the present
ceramic dating scheme (between phases 8 and 9)
is an anomaly that needs resolution.

The relative size of the assemblages recovered
can be taken to reflect an increasing affluence in
terms of material culture in the categories considered through the later medieval period. This
accords quite well with the major trend of economic growth at this time, especially during the 13th
century, though there is no clear indication from
the finds of any recession following the Black
Death.

For the future, it may well be possible to define
the extent and nature of change in further categories of objects more closely in the light of these
and other datable finds. The Thames Exchange
site continues, at the time of writing, to produce
new varieties within categories of finds that are
already well-represented in this volume from
deposits attributable to the same ceramic phases.
Varied emphases from site to site in assemblages
attributed to the same ceramic phase may prove
to be subtle indicators of more precise dating than
is yet definable. The objects discarded in any
particular waterfront dump or foreshore may
reflect changing fashions in goods available to
Londoners for only a short parts of a particular
decade (cf discussion p 271, with reference to
brooches nos. 1364–67, and the recovery of
shield-shaped strap-ends nos. 732–42 only at the
Billingsgate watching brief, even though deposits
of the same ceramic phases are well represented
on several other sites included in this book).

Alloy Nomenclature

JUSTINE BAYLEY

Introduction

From Bronze Age times onwards copper was seldom used on its own but was alloyed with one or more other metals to produce a range of alloys with very varied properties. In the past archaeologists have tended to refer to all these copper alloys as 'bronze', but with the advent of widespread compositional analysis this is seen to be misleading as only a proportion of copper-alloy objects are truely bronze, ie an alloy of copper and tin. The composition of a particular object can be precisely defined by quantitative analysis which gives the percentage of each element present. Qualitative analysis identifies the elements present but not the exact amount. As with any other classification, the data provided by the analysis is only a first step and in order that the information may be used it is necessary to develop a terminology which identifies similar objects and groups them together with each group given a name that uniquely identifies it. It is with the choice of where to draw the lines between the different groups and the names to call them that the difficulties begin, as at present there is no single accepted terminology for many of the alloys that were used in antiquity.

Alloy composition

From late Iron Age times onwards copper alloys contained deliberate additions of one or more of the elements tin, zinc and lead. Low levels of other elements were also present but they were accidental inclusions that occurred in the metal ores and were not removed from the metal during smelting or refining operations. These minor and trace elements may suggest a source for the metal or geographical areas of use, as has been done for the Bronze Age (eg Northover 1982, 59), though as yet this is a largely unexplored

topic. Small amounts of the three main alloying elements may also be accidental inclusions deriving from the metal ores or from recycled scrap metal. In defining a nomenclature it is only the deliberate additions that need be considered, as the craftsman making or using the alloy would have been ignorant of the nature, and probably even presence, of most of the minor elements. These impurities would only have been noticed when they adversely affected the properties of the alloy; their presence was most likely to be recorded as low-quality metal rather than as a completely different type of alloy. In grouping analyses slight variations can be ignored as they would not have been discernible to the craftsman making or working the metal.

The craftsmen of antiquity had no means of performing elemental analysis as we do today but they usually had a good idea of the composition of their raw materials. Scrap metal was carefully sorted before it was recycled so that unwanted mixing was largely avoided. They would have relied on the properties of the alloys, their colour, hardness, malleability and ductility, all of which would have indicated to a trained eye the nature of the metal. Some alloys such as those with high levels of lead were well suited to casting, while others which were low in lead could also be wrought and were used to make objects from intermediate products such as sheet and wire. The above discussion indicates that the names given to copper alloys have to reflect the varying amounts of zinc, tin and lead present in them. The alloys of antiquity have zinc contents of up to nearly 30%, tin contents mainly under 15% (but with some alloys with up to 25% tin) and lead levels that go up to around 25%. Occasionally alloys outside this range are found, but not in the form of usuable objects (eg Craddock 1987, 80–82). What is required is a single nomenclature covering the whole range of compositions, one that is equally applicable to objects of all periods so that a single analytically determined composition will bear the same name, irrespective of the date of the object.

The preferred option

The first and in many ways the most satisfactory option is to use modern metallurgical names for alloys, although there are problems as not all the alloys of antiquity are in current use and some extrapolations are necessary. Copper-tin alloys are called bronzes and copper-zinc alloys brasses (although some modern brasses contain far higher zinc levels than any ancient brass). Gunmetal is strictly a bronze with a few per cent of zinc but this definition can be stretched to include all mixed alloys with significant amounts of both zinc and tin. Leaded alloys are those which also contain more than a few per cent of lead. In modern practice the very high lead contents found in some antiquities are not normally used. There is no modern equivalent to the copper-lead alloys of the medieval period but leaded copper is an appropriate and unambiguous term, indicating copper with added lead in the same way that leaded bronze indicates bronze containing lead.

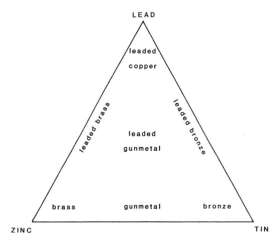

LEAD

leaded copper

leaded brass

leaded gunmetal

leaded bronze

brass   gunmetal   bronze

ZINC   TIN

6   Names for copper alloys

The most satisfactory graphical display of analytical results for copper alloys is on a ternary diagram, an approach pioneered by Bayley and Butcher (1981, 29) for Roman brooches. This depicts the relative proportions of the three alloying elements. The nearer a point representing a particular object is to a corner of the diagram, the higher the proportion of that element present. Figure 6 is a ternary diagram with the alloy names as defined above written in so that their relative compositions are clear: these are the names used in the present catalogue. It should be noted that points that fall close together on the diagram represent approximately the same alloy composition, providing the copper content of the objects is roughly constant. However, the ternary diagram only presents information on the relative proportions of the three major alloying elements present and contains no information on their absolute concentrations. It can show the groupings and spreads of compositions without the need to assign alloy names to individual analyses. Qualitative or semi-quantitative x-ray fluorescence analyses can also be plotted on ternary diagrams; the ratios of peak heights measured can be compared with those of standards of known composition to produce points on the diagram, as has been done by Heyworth (p 389 & 392–3). This approach is helpful as most copper alloys contain detectable amounts of all three alloying elements, although in very different proportions, with the result that a presence/absence analysis is not generally very helpful.

Figure 6 gives no indication of where the boundaries between the different alloys should be drawn, as there are no fixed divisions apart from those defined by the analyst. Often plotting analyses on a ternary diagram brings out clusters in the data, so that sensible boundaries can then be drawn between them. This approach may lack absolute precision (which is after all available in the raw analytical data) but avoids arbitrary boundaries splitting coherent groups of data. The dress accessories data presented here (fig 257) lacks these clusters, the analyses belonging mainly to a continuum that spans the brass-gunmetal area on the ternary diagram, making the brass-gunmetal boundary an arbitrary one.

The empirical approach of drawing lines between clusters is not ideal when attempting to define a universally applicable nomenclature, and so the boundaries shown on fig 7 are suggested instead. Figure 8 shows these superimposed on the ternary diagram. They have been derived

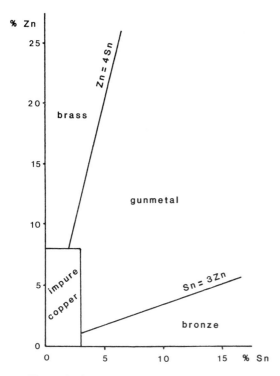

7   Names for low-lead copper alloys

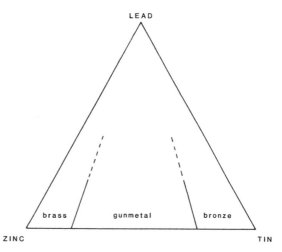

8   Names for copper alloys, (boundaries from fig 7 superimposed on fig 6)

from consideration of alloy properties and made useful and usable divisions when applied to a large body of analyses of Roman metalwork (Bayley, forthcoming). Adding a given percentage of zinc to copper has only half the effect on the alloy's properties compared with the same amount of tin, so the brass-gunmetal-bronze divisions are not symmetrical. As a wide range of compositions is described as gunmetal, subdivisions into zinc-rich and tin-rich gunmetals may sometimes be helpful. Leaded alloys are those with more than 4 per cent lead. Lower levels of lead would have had noticeable effects on the alloy's properties (Craddock 1985, 61–2), but were probably accidental rather than deliberate additions. Some metal was refined to remove even these low lead levels, for example where it was to be mercury gilded (Oddy et al. 1986, 7). Sometimes it is useful to subdivide leaded alloys into those with lesser amounts of the metal which could be wrought, and those with much higher lead concentrations that could only have been cast. In these cases '(leaded)' alloys contain less lead than 'leaded' ones.

The one range of alloys which cannot success-fully be displayed on a ternary diagram are those with low overall levels of additions which, relative to the whole range of copper alloys, are best described as impure copper. These alloys are almost unknown in Roman metalwork but are more frequently found at later periods. In this group are included those alloys with tin under 3%, zinc under 8% and lead under 4%. Normally only one of these elements is present in significant amounts and the copper content is usually around 95%. If it is necessary to display these results alongside those for alloys with larger additions, the method used by Oddy et al. (1986, 22) can be employed. The three variables for the ternary diagram are changed to zinc, lead and tin+copper, though this produces a rather different distribution of points on the diagram to that on fig 6.

Brownsword (1987, 171) also uses ternary diagrams but weights the relative amounts of the three metals present to give better dispersion on the diagram, as he is dealing with only a limited range of compositions. It is therefore essential to check the scales and variables used in all plots before directly comparing them.

Other possibilities

An alternative, though less satisfactory, approach to that outlined above is to use the terminology of antiquity to describe the different copper alloys. There are, however, two main difficulties in this. The first is that different names were used in different periods, reflecting the languages of the time, and the other is the problem of specifically associating the names in use with particular compositions.

If the main objection to the nomenclature already suggested is the anachronism of some of its terms, then the use of Roman terminology to describe medieval metals and vice versa is equally awkward. The second objection to ancient names is, however, a more serious one. In the past alloy names were not used consistently, so that often a single name covered a range of compositions and, conversely, a single alloy could have a number of names, often depending on the use to which it was put or the place it was made. As an example, the term 'brass' is now normally accepted as meaning a copper-zinc alloy with little or no other additions, though in late medieval usage 'brasse' could mean any copper alloy or, very rarely, copper alone with, if anything, a bias towards bronze (Blair et al. 1986, 85). Surprisingly, there is little disagreement between modern analysts on what to call binary alloys such as brass and bronze (in their modern senses); here the anachronistic use of the term 'bronze', which was only introduced into English in the 17th century (Blair et al. 1986, 85), is overlooked. The main problem is with the mixed alloys and it is for these that the term 'latten' has gained a certain measure of popularity with those who analyse medieval metalwork. Cameron (1974, 228) mentions the mid 15th-century instructions for the tomb of Richard Beauchamp, Earl of Warwick, which specify "the finest latten" should be used. By chance this monumental brass survives and has been analysed and shown to contain 8.2% zinc, 3.6% tin and 1.2% lead. This has been used by Brownsword (1987, 170) to suggest that the alloy known as 'latten' in medieval times always had a similar composition and, conversely, that alloys defined above as gunmetals or zinc-rich gunmetals should be known as latten. While neither the composition nor the medieval specification of this particular monument can be questioned, a whole

nomenclature should not be built round a single example. The absence of a consistent correspondence between alloy name and composition in the medieval period has already been mentioned and the same is true of Roman terminology (Bailey 1932, 159). Recent writers are no less confusing as shown by the following contradictory statements about medieval alloy names and the range of compositions they represent.

Brownsword (1988, 2) defines latten as zinc-containing copper alloys which had a more or less golden colour and often contained some tin and/or lead too. Campbell (1987A, 163) says 'metalworkers used . . . a variety of copper alloys, indiscriminately called latten, maslin or brass' and the glossary in the same catalogue defines latten as a 'copper alloy resembling modern brass, but usually containing tin as well as zinc'. Oddy et al. (1986, 6) analysed Romanesque metalwork and they too consider maslin and latten to be similar alloys – but their definition is a quaternary alloy of copper containing at least 1% each of zinc, tin and lead – a very wide range of compositions. Some of the objects they describe as latten also appear in the English Romanesque Art catalogue (Zarnecki et al. 1984) but the alloy names assigned to them are different. A mourning Virgin (no. 231) is described as a brass, which was probably the intention of its maker as it contains some 16% zinc and only 2% tin and under 3% lead. Rather stranger is a doorknocker (no. 266) which is described as bronze but contains 10.3% zinc and only 2.3% tin!

While it is possible to argue that 'latten' is an appropriate term for mixed alloys of medieval date (though the range of compositions included seems to be open to debate), it is not a helpful term in attempting to establish a universal monenclature for the copper alloys of antiquity. 'Gunmetal' at least has a specific modern definition and is no more anachronistic than 'latten' when applied to periods outside the high Middle Ages and thus is to be prefered. Whatever nomenclature is adopted, it is important to define the terms used as, unfortunately, most analysts have their personal preferences and are unlikely to change instantly. A universally applicable nomenclature such as that suggested above should, however, be the aim in the longer term. Where they are dealing with a single period when only a limited range of alloys was used, the whole range of names suggested above may be applied to a subset of the copper alloy compositions of antiquity (eg Oddy et al. 1986) or appropriate historic terms may be used (eg Brownsword 1987). While the original papers carefully define the nomenclature used, other writers drawing on their work will simply copy the alloy names, a practice which is bound to lead to confusion as they are not usually directly comparable. Even where the same name is used for the same alloy (eg brass is universally used to describe a copper-zinc alloy) the levels of additions of other elements permitted may well be different. Oddy et al. (1986, 6) define brass as containing under 1% of both tin and lead, while Brownsword and Pitt (1983, 48) have brasses with over 2% tin, and it is suggested here that even higher tin contents may be acceptable as it is the zinc:tin ratio that is the main criterion, see fig 7 above.

Lead-tin alloys

Lead-tin alloys present fewer problems than copper alloys when it comes to their nomenclature, mainly because the possible range of compositions is limited. At either end of the range are the pure metals, lead and tin, while the alloys of intermediate composition are generally known as pewter. Other elements are rarely present above impurity levels. Most pewter contains more tin than lead but the proportions vary widely from a few per cent up to over 50% lead. The other name that has been applied to these lead-tin alloys is 'solder', which does not describe its composition but its use, joining parts of composite metal objects. Both lead-tin alloys and pure tin were also used to give objects a tin-rich, white coating.

NB – Since non-quantitive spot tests used by the Museum of London Conservation Dept can detect the presence of very small quantities of a metal, some items described in this book as 'lead-tin (MLC)' may contain less lead than others described as 'tin (AML)' – the latter indicates a lead content of *c*.5% or less. In this book 'pewter' is used only of items so designated by Mike Heyworth as a result of analysis at the Ancient Monuments Laboratory (see fig 262). The term 'pewter' in the medieval period covered a wide range of lead-tin alloys (see Hornsby et al. 1989, 15 and Hatcher and Barker 1974, 163–65). (GE)

The Metal Dress Accessories –
some observations

Metals and alloys used

The presentation of detailed information about the catalogued metal accessories allows a number of trends to be identified; only some of the major ones will be discussed in this volume. The simple statistical analysis of similar objects was first undertaken by Hume (1863, 53ff), but the lack of reliable close dating limited the inferences that could be drawn from the material that he published. The evidence given in the present catalogue places this kind of work on a much firmer footing. These London finds can also be compared with others, either trait with trait, item with item, or assemblage with assemblage. (For further discussion of the catalogued items based on analyses by HBMC, see Analysis of the Dress Accessories, p 387–95.)

The large number of girdle- or strap fittings – buckles (479 catalogued items), strap-ends (196 items), and mounts (533 items, similar examples still on straps being counted together as one) comprise over half of the objects included in this book. They show the continuing use in these categories of copper alloys and, to a lesser extent, of iron through the whole of the 300-year period considered here. For the metals used for different categories of the finds through the period covered, see tables 1–7 (p 21, 23, 25, 270, 279, 335 & 390).

Strap fittings in lead/tin alloys first appear in the excavated groups on one leather item from a ceramic-phase 6 deposit (no. 1064, late 12th century – fig 125). Apart from the mounts on this object and in tin coatings, the use of non-ferrous white metals for strap accessories is restricted until the late 14th century to eighteen items from ceramic-phase 9 deposits (c. 1270–c. 1350) – three buckles of simple circular form for shoes (probably from near the beginning of the 1270–1350 period), and fifteen mounts.

Very few, therefore, of the excavated strap fittings made of non-ferrous white metals predate the London Girdlers' Guild's charter of 1321, which sought to ban the use of what were regarded as inferior metals. The charter complained that girdles (ie belts) were garnished (furnished with mounts and buckles) with 'false work, such as lead, pewter and tin, and other false things'. Only 'latten', copper, iron and steel were sanctioned for these fittings. The regulations were intended by the guild to be enforced in all cities and towns throughout the kingdom, and if local officials or searchers sent from London found 'false work . . . the same shall be burned' – ie the strap itself would be destroyed and presumably any metal accessories would be damaged beyond repair (Riley 1868, 155–56). The guild's articles recorded in 1344 again required that no girdler 'shall garnish . . . girdles or garters with any but pure metal, such as latten, or else with iron or steel'. As with the earlier regulations, this was presumably a response to the appearance on the market of what were regarded as inferior metals and alloys on girdles (ibid, 216). The 1344 regulations were apparently still current in 1376 (ibid, 399). A statute of 1391 (15 Ric.II c11) by contrast, recognised that these metals had been in use for some time, and sought to ease the restrictions: 'all girdlers of the realm that work girdles garnished with white metal (*blank metaH*) may work, use and continue their said craft, that is to say, to garnish girdles with white metal as of old times it hath been used, notwithstanding any charters or patents . . . to the contrary' (Statutes of the Realm 1826, 81).

In a case brought in London in 1417 by wardens of the Girdlers' Guild concerning 'three leather girdles harnessed with tin and other false and worthless metals', the straps were judged by the mayor and aldermen to be of good leather, and 'the harnessing of the same was of good and hard metal, and very advantageous for the common people, namely *tyngbasse* with *aurichalcum*, with but little tin intermixed' (the exact nature of the alloy referred to is uncertain, but some kind of debased copper alloy is probably what is meant; Riley 1868, 656–57). By this date, therefore,

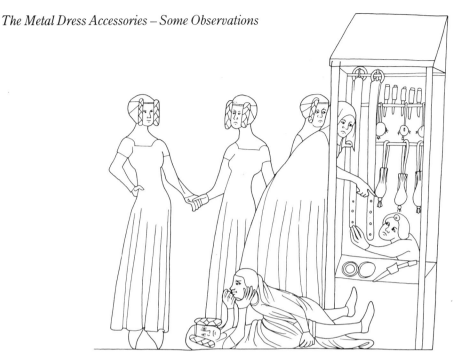

9 Stall with girdles, purses and a cased mirror (after British Library
MS Egerton 1894 f.17)

there was a wider acceptance of alloys which had not been sanctioned by the earlier regulations devised by members of the trade, but which were nevertheless adequate for their intended use on girdles.

This documentary evidence (which is doubtless far from complete) provides valuable corroborative information about the gradual infiltration into the market-place during the 14th and the early 15th centuries of buckles and mounts made of what were regarded, at least by the officials of the Girdlers' Guild with their vested interest in traditional materials, as inferior metals and alloys, though a small number of the earliest excavated lead/tin strap fittings predate these references.

During this period, the supply of lead in England was probably increasing markedly (Salzman 1923, 63; cf Blanchard 1981, 77–79, where a move from 1360 onwards from production centres in Derbyshire to deeper mining in County Durham, the Mendips and Flintshire is identified). The evidence for tin production, in Devon and Cornwall, is less clear at this period (Hatcher and Barker 1974, 41); an increase in Devon's production is not attested until the late 15th century (Greeves 1981, 85).

Many of the lead/tin objects catalogued here would have been described by contemporaries as 'pewter'. Some strap fittings are made of quite pure tin, but they occur in typological categories along with lead/tin items – it is unclear whether or not these fittings were all produced by the same group of workers, and whether any distinction was drawn between the different metals and alloys in the market place.

The early resistance of the Girdlers to the baser metals seems to have been overtaken by a more general acceptance towards the end of the 14th century by those without the same vested interests – not only by the 'common people', who were presumably the main customers for belts with cheap, base-metal accessories, but also by the law-makers and aldermen of the capital. There were, however, clearly still strong feelings on this issue among the Girdlers almost thirty years after the legislation of 1391.

The excavated assemblages reflect these broad developments quite accurately in the gradual rise over the period considered of lead/tin strap fittings, in some categories to predominance over ones of copper alloys and iron (see table 4, p 25). The relatively small numbers overall of definite late 12th- and 13th-century finds in these categories may, however, mean that the extreme sparseness of lead/tin examples from the early part of the period cannot yet be regarded as fully representative. (Pewter spangles, the only lead-tin items categorised here as mounts which seem to have been in wide use before the mid 13th century, have no demonstrable connection with straps). Lead/tin buttons are prominent in the excavated groups much earlier (table 6) than the strap fittings of these metals, and there is great diversity at all periods in the lead/tin alloys used for brooches (table 5). Neither brooches nor buttons include an example of iron. Lead/tin buttons and brooches were probably manufactured from the outset by a separate group of workers from those who made copper-alloy fittings; this division continued when the white-metal workers began to produce buckles and other strap fittings, the rivalry of the two groups being brought out in the documentary evidence cited above.

Although iron and steel were mentioned separately in regulations of the Girdlers' Guild from the early 14th century (see above), no attempt has been made here to differentiate these metals by analysing the buckles. The larger ones, and those which were intended for heavy-duty functions where toughness and resistance to rusting would be especially important (as in horse equipment and armour), might in future be examined scientifically in a programme of analysis similar to that carried out on knife blades (Wilthew in Cowgill et al. 1987, 62–74) to see which are of steel and which are of iron. Investigation along these lines may be carried out when less destructive analytical methods than those readily available at present are further developed.

Some buckles were manufactured in 14th-century London by those who called themselves 'founders' (Veale 1969, 147, citing the Founders' Guild's ordinances of 1365, which seem to imply that these particular buckles – presumably of copper alloy – were for spurs and stirrups). None of the excavated buckles can be identified with certainty as a product of a 'girdler' as opposed to a 'founder' (though some forms correspond with those known on spurs – eg nos. 320–21, fig 48, & no. 482, fig 68). For the wider complexity of arrangements by which craftsmen of different guilds manufactured different categories of copper-alloy objects, see Campbell 1987A, 167.

The origin of the tin-coated sheet-iron mounts, which appear in some numbers in late 14th- and early 15th-century groups, may (as in the early 16th century) have been the eastern part of Germany (Gibbs 1957, 689). Wendy Childs has kindly provided references to a number of ships bringing *plat' alb'* (presumably tin-coated iron sheeting) into London from the Low Countries/lower Rhine area between 1384 and 1449–50 (eg Customs Accounts PRO E122/71/8 m6 for 1389, 1,200 sheets together worth £8, and m26v, 6,000 sheets together worth £32; cf E122/76/34 m8 for 1435–36, which includes 114lbs of *patell 'ferr'*).

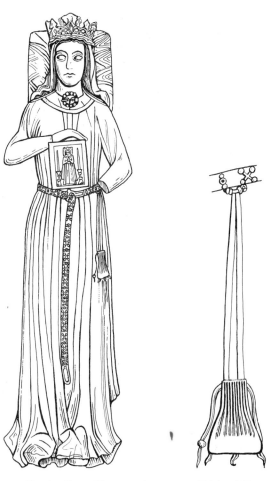

10   Tomb effigy of Berengaria, queen of Richard II (died 1230+) with detail of purse (after Stothard – the tomb is at Espan, N France)

Precious metals are represented among the excavated strap fittings only by eight gilded-copper items (four buckles, two strap-ends and four mounts – almost all attributable to the early part of the period considered – ceramic phases 6 to 8), the group of three high-class, silver-coated armorial mounts from the early 15th century (no. 933), and one contemporary silver-coated ring mount (no. 936). Gilding occurs later on items of other categories, such as brooches – see below on coatings. The noble metals were the jealously guarded preserve of the Goldsmiths Guild, at least in the later, more fully documented part of the period (cf Riley 1868, 397–400, recording investigation into the fraudulent silvering of copper-alloy fittings, and the punishment of a London girdler for his illegal use of the precious metal when he placed silver fittings on a strap, both in 1376). Although the sumptuary law of 1363 (37 Ed.III c8–14) sought to forbid the use of precious metals on belts and in brooches in effect to all except the upper classes, its repeal within a year (38 Ed.III c2) means that it would have had no discernible effect on the recent finds from the appropriate period (ceramic phase 11). The attitudes which led to this statute are, however, part of the wider background of how such objects would have been perceived by some contemporaries. The statute included a requirement that the wearing of girdles (belts) and other apparel even modestly ornamented with silver (*resonablement garniz dargent*) should be restricted to esquires owning land or rents worth at least £500 per year, and to citizens and others having goods and chattels worth at least £1,000 or more – anyone less well-off was forbidden the use of precious metals in the articles of dress specified. The only items among the recent finds for which these attitudes may have had some relevance are a modest silver buckle (no. 211) and a silver brooch (no. 1337 – the other silver brooch included here, no. 1334, is of earlier date).

Buckles

Copper-alloy and iron were used for buckle frames throughout the period considered in this volume, but lead/tin came in for this purpose probably near the beginning of ceramic phase 9 (*c*.1270 – *c*.1350) – see table 1. The relatively small number of iron frames from the earlier part of the sequence is striking, but no explanation has emerged.

Table 1 Buckles – metals used   ( ) = ceramic phases 10–11, * = clasps

Copper	4	4	9		19+4*	3+1* (1)	84+8*	38+3*	178
Iron	1	2	1		24	6 (1)	56+1*	23	115
Lead/tin	-	-	-		3 +1 ?intrusive	-	9	171	184
Total	5	6	10		50 (+1)	10 (2)	159 +1 silver	235	478
Years (AD)	1150	1200	1250		1300	1350	1400	1450	
Ceramic Phase	← 6 →	←7→	←8→		← 9 →	←10→	←11→	←12→	

The distinctive late 14th-/early 15th-century high-quality composite copper-alloy buckles with forked spacers in the plates (nos. 322–30, figs 48–49) appear to imitate a form of strap-end (eg nos. 648, 653 & 672, figs 92–94) from deposits attributed to the late 13th/early 14th century (ceramic phase 9).

The range of decorative forms becomes very wide from ceramic phase 9 (*c*.1270 – *c*.1350)

onwards, and this is sometimes true within particular defined categories of buckle (eg copper-alloy frames nos. 287–302 & 312–18, figs 44 & 46, and lead-tin frames nos. 476–81, fig 66). The use both of relatively pure tin and of a lead-tin alloy ('pewter' in analyses), for example in the frames of the 15th-century category comprising nos. 476–81, makes it difficult to gauge whether those who wore the buckles really drew any

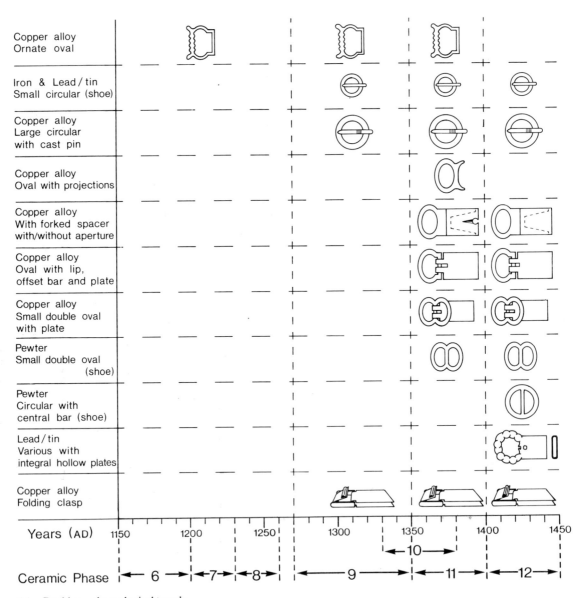

11 Buckles – chronological trends

significant distinction between the metals in these items (the same applies to non-ferrous white-metal mounts). On the other hand, the circular buckles for shoes (nos. 115 etc and 220 etc – figs 39 & 40) that have been analysed all appear to be made of lead-tin (ie 'pewter').

Folding clasps (nos. 551–569, figs 77–78) first appear in deposits attributed to *c.*1270 – *c.*1350, and continue to the end of the period considered in this book. The majority are of copper alloy. The similarity of many of the frames to those of some contemporary buckles (nos. 437–39, fig 61) suggests that both categories were produced by the same manufacturers.

Figure 11 shows the apparent date span of some of the commoner forms of buckles and clasps from the recent excavations (see pp 50–56 for further discussion).

Strap-ends

The earliest strap-ends, from the first half of the 13th century (ceramic phase 7), are of copper alloy – by far the most common metal used for these fittings throughout the entire period considered here. Iron appears in this category in the late 13th/early 14th century, and lead/tin comes in during the late 14th century. Forked spacers are present on composite copper-alloy strap-ends from *c.*1270–*c.*1350 (ceramic phase 9) onwards (eg nos. 648, 653 & 672, figs 92–94); this distinctive method of construction was apparently imitated in buckles from the late 14th century onwards (nos. 322–30, figs 48–49). The ornate lead/tin strap-ends of the early 15th century (nos. 706–13, fig 98) presumably went with the comparably decorative buckles (eg nos. 476–81, fig 66) attributed to the same period.

Figure 12 shows the apparent date span of some of the commoner forms of strap-ends from the recent excavations (see pp 124ff for further discussion).

Mounts

Most of the mounts catalogued here were purely decorative, though some functional categories are included (eyelets nos. 1218–28, strap loops nos. 1229–65, rectangular plates nos. 1202–16 perhaps for connecting lengths of strap, and two forms of hangers for purses etc nos. 1189–98). The strap in colour pl 5E & F, with over 150 mounts still attached, places the large numbers catalogued in some categories in perspective. The extensive variety of the mounts included in this volume is particularly evident in those from

Table 2 Strap ends – metals used   ( ) = ceramic phases 10–11

Copper	-	2	2	36	4 (1) 83	25	153
Iron	-	1	5	4	- 10	1	21
Lead/tin	-	-	-	-	- 4	7	11
Total	-	3	7	40	4 (1) 97	33	185
Years (AD)	1150 1200	1250		1300	1350 ←10→	1400 1450	
Ceramic Phase	← 6 →	←7→ ←8→		← 9 →	←11→	←12→	

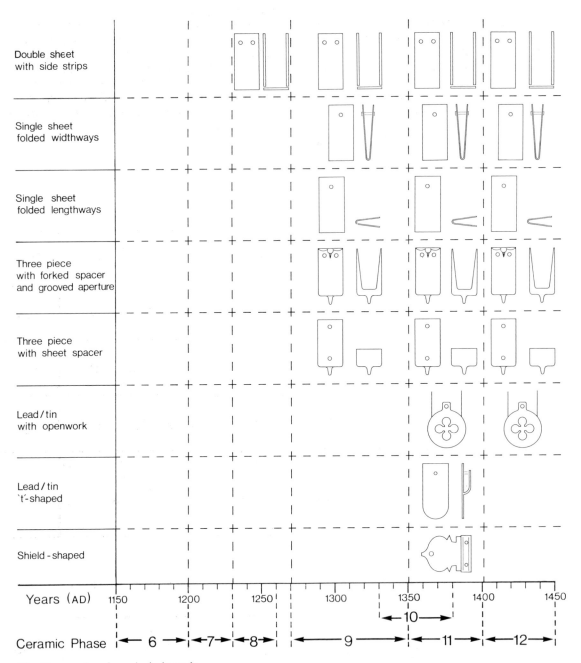

12   Strap ends – chronological trends

late 14th- and early 15th-century deposits (ceramic phases 11 and 12). There are relatively few mounts from prior to the late 13th century, and all but one of these are of copper alloy. The earliest lead/tin mounts for straps are on one object from the late 12th century (no. 1064, fig 125). Late 13th-/early 14th-century deposits produced a few more of lead/tin (eg nos. 824–28, 1065–66, & 1105–06, figs 110, 125 & 128), but the majority come from the late 14th-/early 15th-century deposits. Although several mounts are ornate (including no. 1098 of copper alloy, from the early 13th century, fig 128), the most elaborately decorative examples, comprising both figurative and non-figurative designs, are of lead/tin alloys and of late 14th-/early 15th-century date (eg nos. 1088–92 & 1112–13, figs 126–27 & 129). The large number of varieties of all metals from the last hundred years considered here (*c*.1350–

c.1450), and which are represented in the assemblages only by a single example, are a pointer to a much wider range in use than appears among these recently excavated finds.

Figure 13 shows the apparent date span of some of the commoner forms of mounts from the recent excavations (see pp 162–64 for further discussion).

Table 3 Mounts – metals used
 ( ) = ceramic phases 10–11, * = spangles

	Phase 6	Phase 7	Phase 8	Phase 9	Phase 10	Phase 11	Phase 12	Total
Copper	6	6	5	63	4	185	60	329
Iron	-	-	1	3	1	(2) 22	4	33
Lead/tin	1+1*	3*	6*	15	11	46+2*	35	120
Total	8	9	12	81	16	(2) 255	99	$\overline{482}$
Years (AD)	1150	1200	1250	1300	1350 ←10→	1400	1450	
Ceramic Phase	← 6 →	←7→	←8→	← 9 →	←11→	←12→		

Table 4 Strap fittings of all categories: buckles, strap ends, mounts – totals added from tables 1–3
 ( ) = ceramic phases 10–11

	Phase 6	Phase 7	Phase 8	Phase 9	Phase 10	Phase 11	Phase 12	Total
Total	13	18	29	172	30	(5) 511	367	$\overline{1145}$
Years (AD)	1150	1200	1250	1300	1350 ←10→	1400	1450	
Ceramic Phase	← 6 →	←7→	←8→	← 9 →	←11→	←12→		

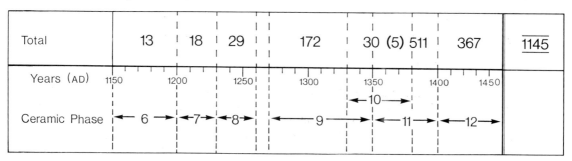

26   *Dress Accessories*

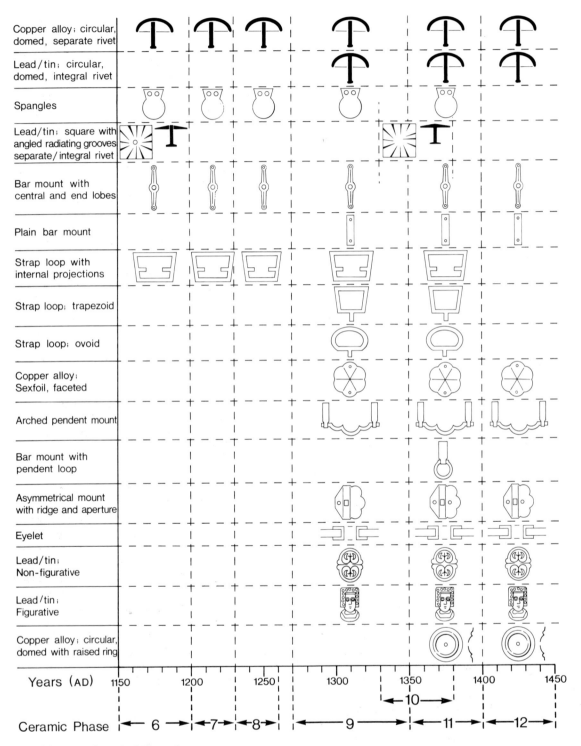

13 Mounts – chronological trends

Coatings

Coatings represented in the excavated fittings are of tin, silver and gold. The first of these is by far the most common. Tin coating was a standard protection for iron items against rusting – a particularly important consideration if an object was going to be exposed to the weather. It also served to give a more shiny appearance, sometimes appearing on copper-alloy items as well as on those of iron, where it seems to have been a regular feature. Tin coating appears on both metals throughout the period covered here. It is definitely present on over 95% of the iron buckles examined, and may well have been removed from some or even all of the others by wear and corrosion. It cannot be traced (MLC) on a few of the plain circular buckles used on shoes (including no. 87, which is still in place) from the BC72 site, or on the majority of the pins tested. The tin coating on mount no. 1201 appears to be restricted to an area defined by its engraved decoration. Tinning was probably used for decorative effect in grooves on a few iron buckle frames (eg nos. 319, 441, & perhaps 399, figs 46, 61 & 56); the pattern would be enhanced once wear had abraded any general coating on the frames (it is most unlikely that tin was applied only to the grooves). Tin coating seems to have been universal for sheet-iron buckle plates, strap-ends and mounts. There is some evidence for the manufacture of the latter items among the recently excavated finds, eg nos. 1290–92 (fig 153) – probably the cutting and shaping of imported sheets that had been coated abroad (see above, p 20). Since the sheets would have had the coating applied while intact, items cut from them would not have been protected from rusting by any tin along their edges. See p 299 for tin coatings.

Only four instances of silver coating have been recognised among the objects described in this volume (all of these are mounts) – on ring mount no. 935 (fig 117), and on three armorial mounts which were found together (no. 933, fig 116), all of which date to the early 15th century. The silver in the latter was used as a mercury amalgam – a technique more familiar in gilding (cf Oddy 1981). The practice of adding a silver coating to base metals could have a fraudulent intention – see p 21.

Most of the gilded copper-alloy strap fittings come from the early part of the period covered in this book – *c*.1150 – *c*.1260 (ceramic phases 6–8). Gilding occurs mainly on objects of purer copper, in which the base metal has a reddish appearance (colour pl 1A, B & D), though gilded strap-end no. 619 (from an early 15th-century deposit, fig 87) is of a yellower alloy, which analysis indicates is brass; see also mount no. 820 (colour pl 1C). The purer copper indicated by the red colour may conform with instructions given in the 12th-century technical treatise of Theophilus, who advocated lead-free copper alloy (*aurichalcum*) for ease of application of a gold coating (Hawthorne and Smith 1979, 145; Oddy et al. 1986, 8). Brooches nos. 1305 and 1319 (figs 160 & 162), pendant no. 1600 (fig 211) and mirror case no. 1718 (colour pl 12C) are the only gilded items among the recent finds other than the strap fittings, most of which these appear to post-date. Oval buckle frames nos. 270–77 (fig 42) hint at a change away from gilding to tin coating during the 13th century for some mass-produced items. Gilding was by no means restricted to fine items – brooch no. 1305 seems to be a very crude object. See p 390 for analyses of gilded items.

The lead/tin mounts on the strap in fig 156 retain traces of a red paint. Colouring by this means may have been quite extensive, though little obvious evidence survives.

Coiled-wire decoration

This appears on several cheap copper-alloy items from the whole period covered by this volume – brooches nos. 1339–41 (fig 164), finger ring no. 1622 (fig 217), hair accessories nos. 1455–57, 1459–60, cf 1467 (figs 195–97 – these include spirals covered with silk), and toilet implements (fig 251, bottom right, see p 378); this decoration also appears on some later cloak fasteners – eg Guildhall Museum Catalogue 1908, 29–30 nos. 415–17 and 420–23, pl XXVI nos. 8, 10, 12, 14–15 and 18 – wrongly described as Roman, but probably of post-medieval date).

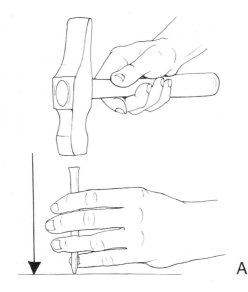

14   Punching and Stamping:
    (A)   punching/stamping tool
    (B)   punched metal
    (C)   stamped metal (thin sheeting)

B

C

15   Punched decoration
    (A)   punched circles on strap plate no. 1215 (2:1)
    (B)   double lines of punched opposed triangles on
          (?)strap-end no. 749 (2:1)
    (C)   punched opposed marks on mirror case
          no. 1715 (2:1)

(A)

(B)

(C)

Secondary decoration

Secondary decoration in the form of tooling occurs on many of the copper-alloy items described in this volume, but only on a very few of the iron and lead/tin ones. The objects which most commonly have such decoration added, after the basic shaping had been completed, are the sheet copper-alloy plates and the frames of buckles, and the plates of strap-ends. It also appears on mounts, brooches, a button, a pendant, pair of tweezers, and mirror cases – all of copper alloy, one mount of tin (no. 1097, fig 127), and three iron buckle frames (nos. 348, 443 & 461, figs 52, 62 & 63).

Thanks are due to Anthony North (Victoria and Albert Museum, Dept of Metalwork) for advice on this subject.

Secondary decoration can be divided into several basic categories:

Punched/stamped – the first term is used where a relatively thick piece of sheeting etc is decorated without the design coming through to the other side (ie the metal is pushed aside), and the second term is used where a quite thin piece of sheeting is altered right through its thickness to the shape of the design on the end of the tool (eg mounts nos. 1049 & 1051, fig 123) – see fig 14A–C. Small stamped or punched motifs are often multiply grouped to produce a continuous pattern or a larger design – see, for example, buckle frame no. 263 (fig 41), buckle plate no. 508 (fig 72), strap-end no. 627 (fig 89), strap plate no. 1215 (fig 15A), and button no. 1403 (fig 179). Relief designs covering an extensive area were produced by pushing or hammering the metal from behind against dies (eg buckle plate no. 500, fig 72) – the technique of repoussé. Repoussé at its finest is represented by silver-gilt mirror case no. 1718 (colour pl 12C), which was probably decorated freehand, raising the higher areas of the

16　Engraving:
  (A)　Engraving tool (left) and enlarged cross section showing removed metal (right)
  (B)　Engraved lines on plate of buckle no. 314 – the lines are slightly hesitant (2:1)
  (C)　Roughly engraved lines on clasp no. 568 (2:1)

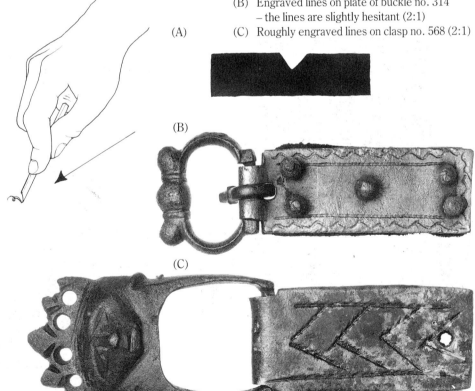

(A)

(B)

(C)

relief with a round-ended tool and finishing the design with a finer one.

It is uncertain precisely how one of the common forms of decoration on sheet copper-alloy objects (buckle plates, brooches, mirror cases, a pair of tweezers no. 1773, fig 253, and pendant no. 1600, fig 211), was produced. The decoration consists of two lines of opposed marks with a small gap between the lines; the marks are usually triangular (fig 15B), but they are more rectangular on buckle plate no. 509, where a different tool was presumably substituted for the usual one. Similar, but more deeply registered marks are found on cast copper-alloy mirror cases; here the means of application could have differed slightly (case no. 1715 also has somewhat rectangular marks, and a longer mark at one end of one of the lines in each pair, as if the tool had

slipped at the start or end of the line – see fig 15C). These marks all appear to have been punched. It looks, from the extremely even spacing between the majority of the paired lines, as if some kind of thin guide (perhaps a wire or a piece of sheeting set on end) might have been placed against the surface to be decorated, so that the punch could follow it along both sides. The marks on each side of the gap, though usually very regularly spaced, are not always in consistently corresponding pairs, so the use of a two-pronged tool is not invariable. On tweezers no. 1773 the lines are parallel but not quite straight (fig 253). On crude buckle plate ro. 502, the marks are very roughly punched, and they clearly show that the tool was moved in a different direction for each line in the pair (fig 72) – the decoration in this instance may have been produced by a different technique from that on the other objects. It is quite possible that no guide was used in making paired lines of punched marks, and that neatly set-out, evenly distanced lines were readily produced freehand by practised workers. This decoration is described in the text as a '(double) line of punched, opposed (triangles)'. It appears on fittings from the late 12th century (eg buckle no. 303, fig 45) to the late 14th century (eg no. 754, fig 104). Compare the single lines of triangles apparently punched along the edges of some bar-mounts (eg no. 1132, fig 133). All the linear tooled motifs seem to have been *engraved* – ie some of the metal was removed,

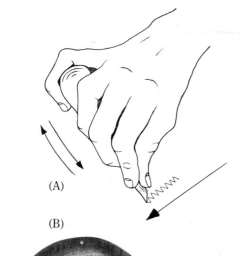

(A)

(B)

17 (A) Engraving zigzags
(B) Engraved zigzags on buckle no. 330 (2:1)

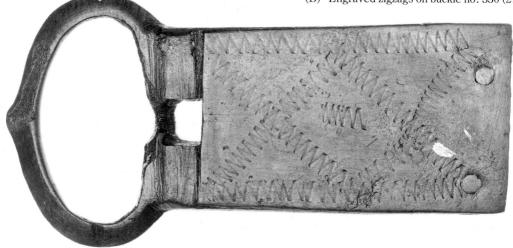

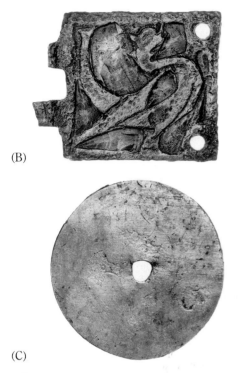

(B)

(C)

(A)

18 (A) Multiple engraving and drilled blind holes on buckle no. 343 (2:1)

(B) Tool marks from cutting away metal for champlevé enamelling on buckle plate no. 530 (2:1)

(C) parallel marks, probably from coarse polishing, on mount no. 777 (2:1)

using a graver (see fig 16A: the more delicate technique of tracing, where the metal is simply pushed aside, seems to be unrepresented among the recent finds). Engraving is a swift process, and is therefore suitable for mass production, while tracing calls for a higher level of skill and a surer hand. For details of these techniques see Maryon (1971, 119–21). Some engraved lines are slightly hesitant (see no. 314, fig 16B); those which are markedly ragged (eg clasp no. 568, fig 16C) are described in the text as 'roughly engraved'.

A few copper-alloy buckle frames have series of short, deeply engraved, contiguous parallel lines – usually three lines together to give a crude, but quite prominent decoration ('multiply engraved' in text) eg buckles nos. 343 & 447 cf 450 (see figs 18A & 62).

A zigzag line could be produced using a walked engraver ('rocked scorper' – the design is sometimes known as 'wriggle work') – see fig 17. This decoration is quite roughly executed on buckle plate no. 517 (fig 73). The intended decorative effect is perfectly clear in most cases (eg buckle plates nos. 313 & 330, figs 46 & 49), but occasionally it is somewhat obscure (eg buckle

plate no. 421 & strap-end no. 670, figs 59 & 93). The technique is used on items from at least the early 13th to the early 15th centuries (early examples are buckle no. 499 & mount no. 1099, colour pl 4A & fig 128).

The plates of two buckles and one folding clasp have circles made with a compass ('compass engraved' in text) – nos. 439, 508 and 551 (figs 61, 72 & 77). The compass engraving accompanies drilled holes on nos. 439 and 551, and punched circles on no. 508. One of the engraved circles on the latter cuts into a rivet – a rare indication that here the secondary decoration was added after the buckle was mounted on the strap (cf strap-end no. 693 for a similar indication – fig 96).

An essay subdividing the toolmarks on prehistoric metalwork (Lowery et al. 1971, 167–82) covers techniques apparently not represented among the medieval objects described in this present volume. Even where there is common ground, it has been found by the present writer to be impossible with many of the items described here to achieve the precise and consistently reliable definition such categorisation requires without the use of a scanning electron microscope (cf Goodburn-Brown 1988, 55–62) or similarly sophisticated equipment. The additional resources this kind of analysis would have demanded have placed such work beyond the scope of the present volume. Maryon's less complicated terms (see above) have therefore been used throughout.

Drilled holes (usually blind holes), sometimes set in patterns, are among the least frequently used of the techniques represented in the assemblages considered. By its nature this method of decoration was appropriate only for relatively thick sheeting (*c.*0.35 – 0.40mm on clasp plate no. 439, cf the plates of clasps nos. 551–52, fig 77), or for cast objects like buckle frame no. 343 (fig 18A) and brooch no. 1317 (fig 162).

Enamelling too is relatively unusual among the assemblages, as might be expected for a technique requiring additional materials. Copper-alloy buckle plate no. 530 is the only instance in this volume in which a champlevé design has clearly been prepared for the application of enamel or niello by cutting away some of the metal (fig 18B). Mounts no. 933 have zigzag engraving to give a rough surface to allow the enamel or niello to adhere (visible on one mount at a point where some of the material has chipped off – see colour pl 2 & fig 116). Fitting no. 727 also retains what are probably traces of enamel (fig 101).

Finishing marks

In addition to tool marks associated with added decoration, many of the cast copper-alloy fittings have file marks from the finishing of areas left uneven from the mould (prominent, for example, on buckle no. 426 – fig 60, and strap-end no. 653 – fig 93). Some circular sheet mounts have marks probably from coarse polishing (nos. 777 etc – fig 18C).

Breakage and repair

Some distinct patterns of breakage and repair can be extrapolated from the large number of buckles and other fittings described in this volume. Several objects can confidently be identified as having been repaired or broken prior to discarding, and there are a number of other possible instances which are far less easy to define. A strap-end which has had the plates joined by wiring them together (no. 634, fig 89) is a very clear instance of a first-aid repair, but it is an isolated example.

Breakage

A broken fitting would in many instances have been discarded. It would be particularly difficult to continue to use a buckle with a broken frame, though a damaged or missing buckle pin might well have been replaced with wire or sheeting that was on hand. A broken sheet plate could quite easily be removed and replaced by another, or if the strap itself became damaged a plate might be transferred to a new one or to a usable part of the old one.

Lead/tin buckles stand out as the group in which damage is more regularly evident than in those of the other metals. Eleven out of the 20 lead/tin frames from the recent excavations that are not standard forms for shoes are in some way broken, and a further five are distorted – ie 80% are damaged, and 55% or more may have been discarded because they had become unusable. The most notable manifestation of this is in the group of lead/tin buckles with integrally cast hollow plates – all six of these from the recent excavations are broken in a variety of different ways (nos. 476–81, fig 66). Large lead-tin frame no. 387 (fig 54) had an internal iron rod along the bar to give it more strength (its present state may be the result either of breakage or corrosion); no. 454, which had no support of this kind, has a broken bar (fig 63), while thick lead-tin frame no. 269 (fig 41) seems to have sustained considerable wear without becoming distorted or damaged. Rectangular frames nos. 455 and 456 have been distorted sideways (fig 63). The 144 lead-tin shoe buckles of standard forms recovered include 35 examples, both the single and double forms, in which the frames or the bars have been bent; in a further seven cases this has resulted in breakage

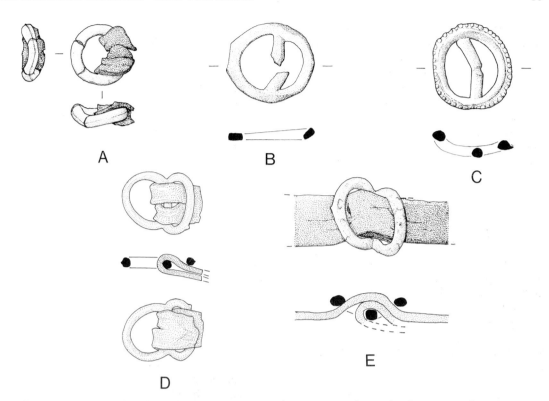

19 Breakage and distortion of lead/tin shoe buckles
(all 1:1)
  (A) distorted and cracked buckle no. 205
  (B) broken and abraded buckle no. 218
  (C) buckle with bent frame and bar, no. 243
  (D) worn buckle with outer loop distorted
       sideways, no. 354
  (E) buckle with both loops distorted sideways,
       no. 356

– see fig 19 (the extensive assemblages of shoe buckles found at the Swan Lane and Trig Lane sites may have been from dumps of cobblers' waste, and may therefore not be representative of shoe buckles discarded by individuals). More than one kind of damage is evident on the shoe buckles: some have suffered strain against the outside edge, which has resulted in a degree of bending of the frames (eg no. 205), in some cases almost to a right angle (eg no. 358). In double-oval buckle no. 373 the (?)outer loop has broken off – this may have been caused by the loose end of the strap being pulled in the opposite direction from that in which it would otherwise have lain (fig 19A). Another form of damage, in buckles with a bar at the centre, is of strain pulling the frame away from the bar, sometimes actually breaking this in the middle (fig 19B; no. 243 combines both forms of damage – fig 19C). One buckle of this form appears to have had the outside edge bent towards the back rather than to the front. Other lead-tin buckles have been distorted sideways, perhaps the result of sustained wear on ill-fitting shoes (see nos. 354 & 356, fig 19D & E).

Damage can be seen to a less marked degree in some of the buckles of other metals. With copper alloys it might have been relatively easy to straighten a slightly bent frame (eg no. 342) without any ill effect, and iron frames seem generally to have been strong enough not to have become distorted in the first place (though no. 410 is broken). Some copper-alloy frames are broken, but this may often be no more than a result of rough treatment at the weak points. Number 301, however, shows evidence of considerable wear prior to breakage, and must have been subject to great strain over a sustained period; no. 391 also shows evidence of long-term wear, but remains intact (figs 44 & 55).

The overall picture of damage being particularly evident on lead/tin buckles is, to a limited extent, a vindication of the claims by the Girdlers' Guild (which had a vested interest in the production of copper-alloy and iron buckles) that the softer base metals were 'inferior' (see pp 18–19).

Repairs

Evidence for repairs is most common among buckle plates and strap-ends (as indicated above, buckle frames are extremely difficult to repair, and while cast pins are probably the original ones in each case, those of wire or sheeting could be either the original feature or a replacement – see p 54). One (?)clasp plate has been repaired by the addition of a piece of sheeting in a different alloy to make good the outside edge (no. 562, colour pl 4B). Less immediately obvious signs of repair or of transfer to a new strap are rivets on buckle plates etc which do not match each other, or they are of different alloys from that of the sheeting of the plates, or iron rivets appearing on copper-alloy fittings (eg buckles nos. 310, 379 & 380, and clasp no. 565 – figs 45, 54 & 78). Further indications are rivets that are crudely applied (eg nos. 499 & 515, colour pl 4A & fig 72), or rivet holes that do not match each other (eg in strap-ends nos. 739 & 769, figs 103–04). The series of buckles with integral bevelled plates (nos. 482–86, fig 68, thought to be from spurs) exhibit several of these traits, suggesting that for this kind of buckle repair was frequently necessary. Occasionally the presence of a rove on only one of several similar rivets on an object hints that here too a repair has been carried out (eg buckle no. 314 and clasps nos. 570–71, figs 46 & 79). Although original rivets were presumably not invariably of the same alloy, or even of the same metal, as the plates, they do match in a large number of what appear to be the better-quality buckles. Amateurishly replaced rivets sometimes use different holes from those for the original

ones (eg buckle no. 326, and strap plate no. 1213 – figs 49 & 141). The plate of buckle no. 317 has an additional hole, which presumably relates to an earlier use for the sheeting. Numbers 502 and 516 (fig 72) are crude folded plates for buckles: these and an irregular fragment of sheeting (no. 1129, the purpose of which is uncertain – held on a strap by tacks, fig 130) are probably also first-aid repairs by owners unskilled in metalworking. Two of the well-made composite copper-alloy buckles with forked spacers (nos. 322 & 326 – figs 48 & 49) have indications of replaced pins, re-riveting, etc. Because they were of good quality, these kinds of buckles were probably regularly retained when the original strap had worn out or broken – ie repair is here likely to be an indication that these fittings were highly regarded rather than of poor quality.

Strap plates, which include some very crude items, seem in a few cases to have been used specifically to secure two lengths of straps together (see no. 1205, fig 141); these ones may have been to repair torn or broken straps (the purpose of some of the better-quality plates is uncertain). Lead-tin strap-end no. 712 (fig 98) has had the broken terminal cut to make it neat again.

Far fewer mounts than buckles have obviously been replaced, but here too a crude or anomalous means of attachment may be an indication that this has happened (eg no. 1196, fig 140).

Lead-tin brooch no. 1344 (colour pl 6E) was found with four of the elements around the edge missing. One or more edge pieces that had broken off accidentally may have been matched by deliberately breaking off others to retain symmetry in the design. Several other lead/tin brooches are broken (eg nos. 1346 & 1364 etc, figs 166 & 171), especially those with integral pins – this is in most cases attributable to the very fragile designs. A few copper-alloy brooches, too, had been broken when they were discarded, but the reasons for this are as obscure as for the broken buckles of similar alloys.

Girdles

Girdles and various other types of belt were made from leather or were woven (usually by manipulating a pack of tablets) from threads of silk, linen or worsted. The sumptuary law of 1363 (statute 37 Ed.III c8–14) seems, from its reference to linen girdles for ploughmen, to imply that these were among the cheapest available. Except for linen which is preserved only occasionally in the damp conditions prevailing along London's waterfront, all these types of thread are represented among the items discussed in this study. Tablet-woven straps were more versatile than those of leather as they were stronger and could be made as one continuous piece, whereas some of the leather straps had to be joined from more than one strip. The number of textile girdles preserved from London is, however, very small, totalling some ten examples (eight of silk, one of worsted and one of silk and worsted), which reflects the tendency of these organic materials to decompose very rapidly after burial in the soil. Occasionally a few fibres remain trapped between a strap-end or buckle plate, and it is probable that more of these could be identified with the aid of an electron-scanning microscope. It is apparent that leather and textile straps were put to similar use, and no type of strap fitting appears to have been associated exclusively with either leather or with tablet-weaving. Because of the limitations of survival, the discussion of the excavated girdles which follows concentrates on examples which illustrate particular points.

As with other dress accessories described in this survey, most come from deposits dating to the 14th and early 15th centuries, and thus their development from 1150 to 1300 can only be illustrated in part from the archaeological record. It is also not always easy to distinguish what function each strap served, particularly as most are fragmentary, with some having been cut up before being discarded. This would have enabled certain of the fittings, especially buckles, to have been recycled (buckle no. 307, for example, is still attached to a strap that has been cut off close to the buckle, possibly in preparation for transfer to a new girdle).

Girdles worn round the waist or hips could be extremely simple, unembellished by mounts of any type. This is demonstrated by a plain leather belt, which was worn by a man who was murdered at Bocksten in southern Sweden at some time during the 14th century. The belt, lacking its buckle and apparently never possessing a strap-end, is 1070mm long and 38–49mm wide (Nockert 1985, 123 fig 103). Pictorial representations also support this impression, and labourers, for example, are depicted in the Luttrell Psalter wearing belts unadorned except for knives and pouches. Thus plain straps are included in this survey, although some may not have been worn as part of dress.

It is not possible to estimate how many of the straps were worn as some form of dress belt, but judging from the size of the buckles and strap-ends it seems unlikely that, apart from sword-belts, any were wider than 60mm for most of the period. It is apparent from visual sources that girdles worn by women became wider during the 15th century than they had been for many centuries, and this was because it became fashionable for girdles to be worn above the natural waistline. The length of a girdle was also subject to the vagaries of fashion, and in the 13th and 14th centuries a girdle often reached almost to the feet of the wearer (figs 10, 20 & 139). The established length of six quarters (1½ yards, c.1.375m) given in the 1344 Girdlers' regulations for silk, worsted and linen from which girdles are to be made (Riley 1868, 216) may, since leather is not included, be a reiteration of the standards for textile production, and not a direct reference to the intended length of girdles: a waist girdle of this length would have reached to little more than knee level. The fragmentary girdles from excavations offer little guidance on this aspect – the longest example, which is incomplete, is only 1040mm in length – although they do occasionally reveal ways in which leather strips were joined to make long girdles, for example by stitching together the overlapping ends (no. 15, fig 22), or by interlacing two leather thongs through two thicknesses of leather (no. 25, fig 29).

Despite the long length of many girdles in the
13th and 14th centuries, slides do not appear to
have been used and the free end either dangled
downwards immediately beside the buckle as, for
example, on the effigies of Berengaria (fig 10) and
a lady in All Saints' Church, Clehonger, Hereford
and Worcester (fig 20), or it was looped round the
girdle beside the buckle or further to one side of
the body. Different ways of looping the end are
portrayed in manuscript illuminations and on effigies and monumental brasses (Hartshorne 1891).
An example is also preserved among the excavated straps (no. 284, fig 43). In addition, a
narrow strip of leather riveted horizontally onto a
strap next to an iron buckle, with a corresponding
strip (which is not preserved) below the buckle
pin (no. 416, fig 58), may have been designed to
take the free end of a strap, or alternatively a
second strap may have passed through it; it is
unlikely to have been worn as a dress belt.

The regulations of the Girdlers' Guild from
1344 indicate that there were at least four, and
perhaps five or more standard widths for girdles
at that time (Riley 1868, 216). Girdles of double,
three times, five times and six times an undefined
width (which may well itself have been in use,
though this is not explicit) are mentioned. It is an
extremely hazardous task in the absence of further details from contemporary sources to try to
relate the archaeological finds to these uncertain
widths – not least because the regulations came
right at the end of ceramic phase 9, and many
objects from the latest decade of that phase (ie
the 1340s) may not have been discarded until the
periods attributed to phases 10 and 11. It may be
possible, by looking at some of the copper-alloy
and iron buckle plates and strap-ends from ceramic phases 10 and 11, especially those of composite form which span the entire width of the
girdle, eventually to extrapolate clusterings of
strap widths, but first attempts indicate that
diversity is as common as clustering. Moreover,
lead/tin fittings were proscribed by the 1344
regulations, and the girdles those metals were
put on may not have respected the Girdlers'
standards. In addition to all these difficulties, a
number of the straps and fittings included in this
study would not have come from girdles, indeed,
some are clearly for spurs. The actual leather of
the excavated girdles will have shrunk on removal
from the soil, (on current treatment the average

20 Stone effigy of a lady from an altar tomb dating to the mid-14th century, All Saints' Church, Clehonger, Hereford and Worcester

shrinkage is 5%), but this will not have been constant for different kinds and thicknesses of leather.

From a preliminary examination of some of the excavated copper-alloy buckle plates and strap-ends, it may in due course be worth considering whether there might have been a series of standard widths for girdles based on *c*.6mm (¼ inch) – the range of strap widths indicated by the appropriate metal fittings included in this volume is from *c*.6 to *c*.50mm. Many of the smarter strap-ends were made to be fitted to girdles 12mm wide (eg nos. 663, 704 & 717), while a waist girdle carved on the stone effigy of Sir John de la Beche, who died in 1306, in St Mary's Church, Aldworth, Berkshire, also has a width of 12mm. At present, however, the diversity of widths makes a possible standard based on a quarter inch no more than an initial hypothesis, which may be considered further if fuller evidence becomes available.

The 1344 regulations also stipulated that no leather below the quality of ox leather should be used for girdles (Riley 1868, 217). In order to test this, a sample of 34 leather straps from deposits dating from the 14th and early 15th centuries (ceramic phases 9 to 12) was examined; these included examples of straps which are not considered to have been worn as girdles. The grain pattern on three examples is too worn for the species to be identified; 28 of the others are probably calf, or cattle where the leather is at least 4mm thick, one is probably pig, another possibly deer, and the remaining example possibly sheep or goat (Glynis Edwards, unpublished Ancient Monuments Laboratory report).

Most leather straps were worn with the grain of the leather on the outside, but there are a few where the position of mounts shows that the suede-like flesh side was worn on the exterior (eg nos. 1131, 1135 & 1186). This is especially characteristic of some of the straps used as spur leathers, which will be discussed in greater detail in a further volume in this series.

Girdles were usually made from a single thickness of leather. The skin was pared down to an even thickness before it was used, generally *c*.2 to 4mm thick. Occasionally where the leather was particularly thin (less than 1mm) the sides were folded inwards with a seam along the centre back which was not always stitched (eg girdle with eyelet mount no. 1223, fig 142; girdle with strap-end no. 710, fig 98). Stirrup leathers were also sometimes folded double in this way (eg on stirrup BIG82 acc. no. 2800, see p 92), and some sword belts may also have been made in this manner (eg no. 13; cf fig 108, with mounts nos. 802 & 1079), but stouter leather was used for these straps. Generally where leather is folded in this fashion to form a strap it can be considered not to have been worn as a part of dress.

Methods of attaching buckles and strap-ends

The end to be fitted to a buckle was treated in a number of different ways. Sometimes it remained the same width as the rest of the girdle and a hole was pierced for the buckle pin. The hole was usually slit lengthways (eg no. 15, fig 22), since this allowed the pin to move and meant that the leather was less likely to tear than if the slit was aligned widthways. There are exceptions to this, for example no. 39 (fig 37) where the unusual form of the buckle pin required the leather to be slit widthways. In addition, a small piece of leather was removed for the buckle pin in some examples. The cut end of the leather was folded over the bar and was riveted, stitched or thonged to the main length of the girdle. On other straps the leather was forked, each tab passing over one side of the bar with the pin lying in between.

Where a buckle has a buckle plate or a forked spacer the girdle was sandwiched in between, extending, more or less, the full length of the metal sheath; the girdle was then held in place by rivets (see p 55). By contrast, the end of a girdle fitted to a strap-end often extended only part of the length of the end (eg nos. 605–607, fig 85, no. 693, fig 96, & no. 705, fig 97) and usually just the rivets at the attachment end were used to secure the girdle.

Stitched decoration

A survey of leatherwork dating from the 10th century to the middle of the 12th century from

(A)

(B)

21 Leather girdle, no. 7, stitched
with silk thread. The dark area
indicates where the strap-end
was originally. (A) front, (B)
reverse (both 1:1), (C) detail of
stitching (4:1)

(C)

Leather straps with vertical awl holes:

catalogue no.	site, acc. no. & context	ceramic phase	fig	dimensions (mm)	no. of rows of awl holes	sewing thread	species of leather
1	MLK76 444 (1080)	6		146×57	4	–	calf
2	CUS73 300 (IV, 55)	9	133	180×7	1	–	–
3	LUD82 307 (1046)	9	133	29×9	1	–	–
4	SWA81 5004 (2047)	9		23×8	2	–	–
5	BC72 3291 (250)	10		72×10	1	–	–
6	BC72 3297 (250)	10		89×36+ (estimated total w 50mm)	4	silk	–
7	BC72 3555 (250)	10	21	103×52	4	silk	calf
8	BC72 3288 (250)	10		130×36+ (estimated total w 60mm)	4	–	calf
9	BC72 3344 (250)	10		126×14+	?4	–	–
10	BC72 3295 (250)	10		90×27+	?4	silk	calf
11	BC72 2550 (83)	11		213×50	4	–	–
12	BC72 2493 (83)	11		225×57	4	–	–
13	BC72 2504 (83)	11		82×32 (both sides folded)	4	–	calf

London has shown that a narrow girdle from an early 12th-century deposit was sewn with a two-strand interlace pattern (Pritchard forthcoming, no. 366, fig 3.125). This form of embroidered decoration, which was probably inspired by tablet weaving, does not occur on any of the later-medieval straps, and stitching on them is generally limited to the edges. There are, however, differences in the way the awl holes were placed.

On a few straps awl holes were positioned widthways and often very close together (three to six holes per 10mm). This includes straps of various widths, the most common being 50mm to 60mm wide, where four rows of holes were pierced, two along each side; these were perhaps sword belts. The earliest example of a strap of this type from London, no. 1, dates to the later 12th century (ceramic phase 6), but they continue to be present in deposits of the late 14th century (ceramic phase 11). A strap with four rows of these awl holes from a late 14th-century deposit

has inward-folding sides meeting in a backseam; it is 32mm wide (no. 13). Three narrow straps, all from deposits dating to no later than the middle of the 14th century (ceramic phases 9 and 10), have just one row of closely spaced awl holes pierced along the centre, and two of these (nos. 2 & 3) have rectangular bar-mounts, which were fitted in place after the straps had been stitched (nos. 1132 & 1133, fig 133). Stitch impressions associated with these holes take the form of continuous lines on both sides of the leather and traces of sewing thread show that this was due to the use of two threads. In both straps where the thread is preserved it is silk (nos. 6 & 7, fig 21). Silk thread is not otherwise preserved as stitching in any of the leather girdles, but this need not mean that its use was circumscribed.

Awl holes for stitching were more often pierced along each side lengthwise or slightly on the diagonal (eg no. 25 fig 29). The stitching appears to have been chiefly decorative and is a common feature of belts even now in the 20th century; it may also have prevented the sides from stretching or laminating. The stitching was not intended to hold together more than one thickness of leather, since girdles were invariably made from leather of a single thickness. Usually the holes pierced the full thickness of the leather, but one strap, 10–11mm wide, has holes which

pierce just the grain face, and here the edge was tunnel-stitched (**no. 14** – BC72 acc. no. 3351). This strap, which was recovered from a deposit dating to the second quarter of the 14th century (ceramic phase 10) and which survives to a length of 122mm, is also unusual in having 19 holes spaced at intervals of 4mm along its centre, presumably for adjusting the fit of the strap.

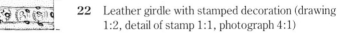

22   Leather girdle with stamped decoration (drawing 1:2, detail of stamp 1:1, photograph 4:1)

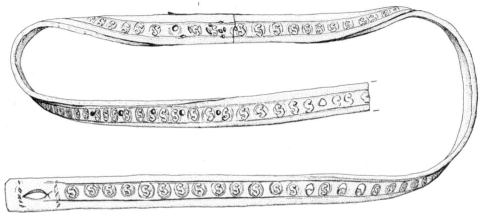

15

Stamped decoration

Methods of decoration which had long been favoured in bookbinding and on sheaths were used on other forms of medieval leatherwork, including girdles. Eight examples of belts impressed with stamped decoration are included in this survey; none of these is from a deposit earlier than the late 14th century (ceramic phase 11) (see p 44). On these girdles from the recent excavations mounts were added only rarely, despite the large number of mounts published in this volume, and as far as can be judged from the short lengths preserved, other fittings such as buckle plates and strap-ends were not always used (eg no. 15 which has no buckle plate, and no. 17 which has no strap-end). However, this was not necessarily typical; a girdle in the Roach-Smith Collection in the British Museum has lead/tin mounts in the form of leafy sprigs alternating with circles enclosing the letter S stamped on the leather (Roach-Smith 1854, 129, no. 641; BM MLA 56, 7–1, 1982), while a strap stamped with a quatrefoil within a lozenge frame which is in the

23 Leather girdle with stamped decoration (drawing 1:2, detail of stamp 1:1, photograph 4:1)

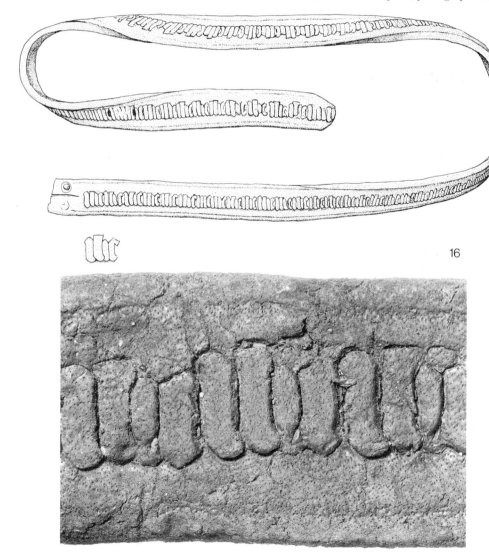

16

collections of the Museum of London preserves its strap-end (fig 84, MoL acc. no. 86.106/1). A girdle which combines stamped with incised decoration (no. 23, fig 28) is discussed under incised decoration.

The area to be decorated was usually marked out with lines, and a die was then impressed into the leather. This is apparent on a belt made from two overlapping strips of leather with a length in excess of 790mm, which is decorated with a series of Ss, each surrounded by a circle of pellets (no. 15, fig 22). This motif was stamped with a die *c.*8mm in diameter between two parallel lines scored in the leather before the belt was sewn

into one long piece. A similar, but not identical, die was used to decorate a strap found in the City Ditch at Aldersgate in the early 1920s, (Ward-Perkins 1940, 193 & 195, fig 60 no. 4), and a third example stamped with Ss, which is in the Roach-Smith Collection, has already been referred to. It appears that these girdles, like those with S-shaped metal mounts (no. 708, fig 98 & no. 1095, fig 127), formed counterparts to collars of Ss and other accessories denoting allegiance to the Lancastrian cause. The practice of stamping the letter S on royal furnishings was in use several decades earlier; Queen Philippa, for example, had her room decorated with silk hangings stamped in gold with the letter S to celebrate the end of her confinement a month after the birth of her fifth son in 1348 (Nicolas 1846, 144; Staniland 1978, 228).

24 Leather girdle with stamped decoration (drawing 1:2, detail of stamp 1:1, photograph 4:1)

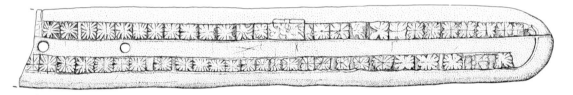

17

25 Leather girdle, no. 18, with stamped decoration (4:1)

On a girdle where the guidelines are indistinct the stamp was less accurately centred (no. 16, fig 23). This girdle, from a late 14th-century deposit (ceramic phase 11), is stamped with the letters 'ihc' (an abbreviation of the name of Jesus), worked from the buckle end. Strap-ends similarly inscribed with 'ihc' in black-letter are known from London (Ward-Perkins 1939, pl XLVII; Ward-Perkins 1940, 270 fig 85 nos. 1, 2 & 6); although there is none from recent excavations, a group of these are dated from the evidence of monumental brasses to between 1390 and 1410 (Ward-Perkins 1939, 127). Girdle accessories inscribed with 'ihc' were apparently being worn in London in the third quarter of the 14th century, since a wealthy citizen, William de Bathe, included a bequest to John Elmede of a 'girdle fastened with *botonet* and clasps with the letters jhc and knife hanging thereto' in 1375 (Cal Wills 1890, 182).

Another belt from a deposit of a similar date is enlivened with a series of small angular quatrefoils stamped with a die 5mm square, arranged in two rows (no. 17, fig 24). The distinctive form of the quatrefoil is reproduced by some mounts (eg fig 107, private collection; and fig 125, no. 1064) and on a strap-end (fig 96, MoL acc. no. 80.65/4).

There are also four straps with stamped decoration from deposits dating to the early 15th century (ceramic phase 12), of which three were recovered from the same context. One example,

19

26 Leather girdle with stamped decoration (drawing 1:2, detail of stamp 1:1, photograph 2:1)

Decorated leather straps:

catalogue no.	site, acc. no. & context	fig	ceramic phase	dimensions (mm)	form of decoration	species of leather
15	BC72 3214 (unstratified)	22	–	790×17 (2 over-lapping pieces)	Ss within a circle of pellets (*stamped*)	calf
16	BC72 2414 (89) & 3017 (150)	23	11	330×19	ihc (*stamped*)	calf/cattle
17	BC72 2553 (83)	24	11	146×20	2 rows of 'quatrefoils' (*stamped*)	calf/cattle
18	TL74 2037 (276)	25	12	122×12	blocks of saltires (*stamped*)	probably calf
19	TL74 1291A (275)	26	12	278×31	latticework (*stamped*)	calf
20	TL74 1291B (275)	27	12	995×43	latticework (*stamped*)	calf/cattle
21	SWA81 4260 (2106)	28	12	164×52	scroll inscribed *tout monn coer* between two talbot dogs & a beaded border (*stamped*)	–
22	BC72 2823 (150)	28	11	58×12	*iudeorum* & a cabled border (*incised & rouletted*)	–
23	BC72 1716 (55)	28	11	67×23	*amen* on a ground of dots (*incised & stamped*)	–
24	BC72 2309/2592 (79)	29	11	308×12	two grooves (*engraved*)	–
25	BC72 2342/2587 (88) & 2590 (79)	29	11	c.1040×31	sexfoils (*punched openwork*)	calf
26	TL74 1388 (3300)	29	12	430×58	sexfoils & a beaded border (*inlaid iron pins*)	–

12mm wide, was stamped with saltire crosses which, when repeated, formed a pattern of interlace (no. 18, fig 25). The other two straps from the same early 15th-century deposit are stamped with latticework. The narrower example was stamped with a die 10mm square consisting of four units of latticework, so that the die only had to be impressed twice across the width of the strap to give four rows of decoration (no. 19, fig 26). Superimposed on this decoration are a series of circular mounts, now very corroded. The second strap is wider and has a finer lattice pattern, which also appears to have been stamped

in blocks of four, but this time with a rectangular die 7×8mm (no. 20, fig 27). There are altogether ten rows of latticework, the die having been stamped five times across the width of the strap. Sometimes the spacing was misjudged, and an eleventh row was added, with the result that some squares were impressed twice with the lines intersecting. As on the other strap with this decoration, circular mounts were secured to the leather with two rivets, and it has a narrow strap-end made from a folded strip of tin-coated iron sheeting. The fourth strap is decorated with a dog on either side of a scroll inscribed in

27 Leather girdle with stamped decoration (drawing 1:2, detail of stamp 1:1, photographs, 1:1 and 4:1)

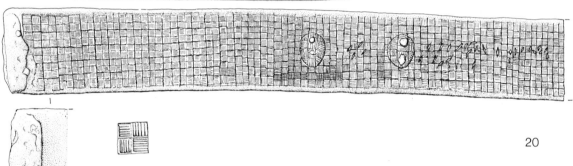

20

black-letter with the amatory motto '*tout monn coer*' (all my heart) within a beaded border which was stamped separately (no. 21, fig 28). Scrolls of lettering were popular on silk textiles produced in the second half of the 14th century and, indeed, a cloth with this form of patterning was recovered from a late 14th-century deposit in the city (Crowfoot et al. forthcoming). It is possible, therefore, that the style of the stamped scroll on this leather girdle was influenced by contemporary textile design.

Incised decoration

Many girdles have single lines incised close to each edge (see eg no. 811, fig 109, no. 852, fig 111, no. 1087, fig 126, no. 1149, fig 134 & no. 1220, fig 142). Sometimes these lines may have acted as a guide for cutting the leather to the correct width or for positioning mounts. Similar incised lines were used as a first step towards engraving a leather girdle or stamping it with a die (eg nos. 15, 17 & 20). The girdle worn by Anne of Bohemia (died 1394) on her effigy in Westminster Abbey is shown stamped with flowers against a background of hatching, and a line forms a border to the decoration on each side.

Lines incised on a leather girdle from a deposit of the late 13th century (ceramic phase 9) are superimposed with a series of small V-shaped incisions spaced at intervals of 1.5mm (no. 1129, fig 130). The incisions only penetrate the grain surface of the leather, and there is no indication that there was any stitching originally.

More elaborate incised decoration occurs on two straps which were recovered from the late 14th-century dock-infill at the BC72 site. Both have inscriptions in black-letter and these are incomplete now. One, inscribed *'iudeorum'* – probably part of the longer legend *'Jesus Nazarenus Rex Judaeorum'* (see brooch no. 1337 p 255), has a cable border along each side which was possibly carried out with a small roulette (no. 22, fig 28). Comparable leather straps inscribed with the names of the three kings (Melchior, Balthasar, and Jasper), and *'ave maria plena gracia'* in the Roach Smith collection have been described as garters (Roach Smith 1854, 130 nos. 644–5; BM MLA 56, 7–1, 1885 and 7).

The other strap, which is 23mm wide, is inscribed *'amen'* against a background of stamped dots (no. 23, fig 28). A ground of stamped dots is likewise a feature of a girdle incised with a lover's posy from Tenter Street, London, which has

been dated to the 15th century (Ward-Perkins 1940, 195, pl XLVI). A comb with the equivalent type of decoration in wood is described under Combs (no. 1745, fig 250).

Engraved decoration

Grooves, rather than incised lines, were occasionally engraved along the length of a girdle. A girdle, 12mm wide, which was recovered from a deposit of the late 14th century (ceramic phase 11), was decorated in this way (no. 24, fig 28). Engraved decoration otherwise appears to have been uncommon on leather straps worn in late-medieval London; this is by contrast to leather shoes, where engraving was a popular means of

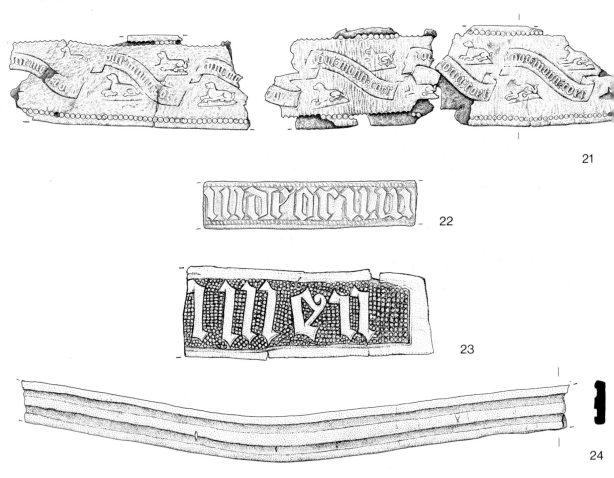

21

22

23

24

28   Leather girdles, no. 21 with stamped decoration, nos. 22–23 with incised and stamped decoration, and no. 24 with linear engraving (no. 21 1:2, nos. 22–24 1:1)

decoration in the 14th century (Grew and de Neergaard 1988, 83–7).

Punched openwork

Another form of decoration was to punch the leather with a metal die, removing a shaped piece to leave an openwork pattern. Only one example of this type of decoration was encountered among the assemblages included in this study and here the openwork is in the form of a sexfoil (no. 25,

fig 29). The strap, 31mm wide, is made from several overlapping strips of leather held together with interlaced thongs, which extend beyond the width of the belt, suggesting that they held further accessories, possibly a sword. Unlike girdle no. 15, the two thicknesses of leather are placed flesh faces together and it appears that the undecorated strips were used for reinforcement. There is a row of stitching along each side, but no sewing thread is preserved in any of the awl holes.

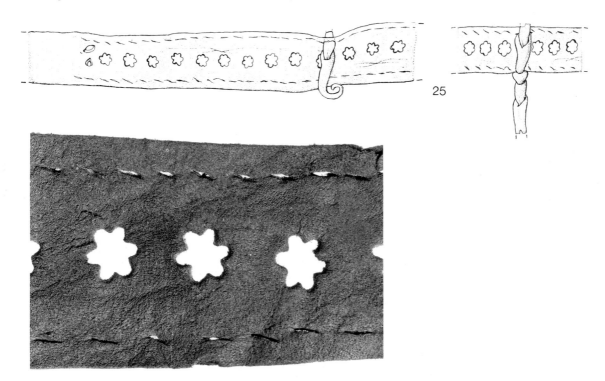

25

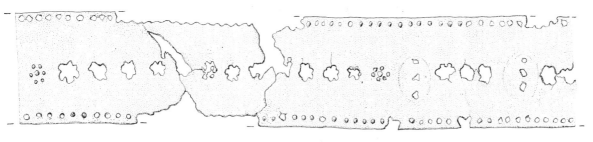

29 Leather girdle no. 25, with punched openwork, and no. 26 with inlaid iron pins (drawings 1:2, detail 1:1, photograph 2:1)

26

Inlaid pins

Part of a strap, 58mm wide, is inlaid with tiny iron pins. These are arranged along the centre of the strap in the form of sexfoils, while on each side is a border comprised of single pins (no. 26, fig 29). This strap, which was recovered from an early 15th-century deposit (ceramic phase 12), appears to be the sole example from recent excavations in London and represents a form of metal ornamentation that is distinct from the more usual mounts. A strap with more ornate decoration of this type, including an inscription in black-letter, was recovered from a deposit in Amsterdam dating to the late 14th or early 15th century (Baart 1977, 93 no. 24). The form of decoration may be compared to patterns made with tin pins on contemporary knife handles (Cowgill et al. 1987, no. 138 pls 4e and 5c).

Tablet-woven girdles

While leather girdles could be dyed, painted, stamped, incised, punched with openwork, engraved or embroidered, tablet-weaving also offered considerable scope for patterning a girdle. This was dictated by the choice of coloured threads, the way the tablets were threaded and how they were manipulated. Technical descriptions of tablet-woven braids, which include a number of girdles, from London deposits of the 14th century and early 15th century are given in the volume on *Textiles and Clothing* (Crowfoot et al. forthcoming), a few observations, however, are noted here.

Braids used as girdles were usually produced in double-faced weaves and skilled weavers adapted the way that girdles were patterned to meet changes in taste. Consequently different styles can be distinguished from among the examples preserved, although none is from a deposit earlier than the 14th century (ceramic phase 9). The chief difference between those of the 14th century and those of the 15th century is that the later girdles tended to imitate expensive fabrics such as velvet, satin and satin damask, whereas in the 14th century coloured stripes and twill effects were more common.

Examples of 14th-century tablet-woven girdles from London include one 8.5mm wide woven in two colours of silk thread to form alternating bands of pink and green, or yellow, running widthways (fig 30). Another girdle, approximately 18mm wide and now very fragmentary, is woven

30 Tablet-woven girdles, top – silk with bar mounts no. 1134 (2:1), and bottom – worsted with buckle no. 325 (1:1)

from silk thread and two colours of worsted thread. Undyed silk and black worsted threads were grouped to form stripes running along the length of the girdle and further patterning of the girdle was carried out by turning the centre tablets in a different sequence from the rest of the pack. In addition, worsted thread dyed red was used for the weft, and this would have been visible only along the edges of the girdle and within the stripe in the centre.

There is also part of a 14th-century girdle tablet-woven from worsted thread preserved in association with its buckle (no. 325, figs 30 & 49).

This is a buckle that is classified here as being among the best quality of those mass-produced in copper alloy. The fact that the girdle is made from worsted thread rather than silk, which would have been more expensive, emphasises the relatively low status of most of the material considered here.

Two other narrow tablet-woven braids from 14th-century deposits (ceramic phase 9 and 10) could originally have been used as girdles. One is a monochrome twill and the other has a lozenge pattern. Braids of similar width were, however, used as spur leathers and as filets for the hair. Examples of the former were recovered from the tombs of Fernando de la Cerda, crown prince of Castile, who died in 1275 (Gómez-Moreno 1946, pl 140; Carretero 1988, 37) and of Sancho IV, king of Castile, who died in 1319 (Museo de Santa Cruz 1984, 136 no. 60). Also, the 'grene knight' in the anonymous 14th-century English poem 'Sir Gawayne and the Grene Knight' is described as wearing 'clene spures . . . Of bright golde, upon silk bordes barred ful ryche' (Ford 1954, 356). Meanwhile, a silken filet from 14th-century London is described under Hair Accessories (no. 1450, fig 192).

Tablet-woven girdles from early 15th-century deposits in London (ceramic phase 12) are made wholly from silk thread. One is 15.5mm wide (fig 31) and the other 28mm. The warp threads are densely crammed together and the tablets appear to have been turned in two packs in a similar sequence on both girdles, to produce a smooth, monochrome surface rather like satin.

Mounts were riveted onto tablet-woven girdles just as on those made from leather (eg fig 30 & nos. 1132–33, fig 133). Beads and gemstones could also be added, as on the spectacular tablet-woven girdle from the tomb of Don Fernando de la Cerda mentioned above.

31 Silk tablet-woven girdle and strap-end no. 618 (4:1). The impression made by the girdle in the metal can be seen.

Buckles

Diversity in form, decoration and material is a feature of buckles from all periods, because these ubiquitous functional accessories present a modest opportunity for fashionable expression at virtually every level of society. The primary classification used below is according to the shape of the frame, and then by metal. Most other aspects of form and decoration are treated as secondary traits, but a few subcategories have been used where subdivision appears a useful aid to defining trends. Such is the variety in the forms of frames that at a detailed level alternative schemes of classification could easily have been used. Some frames of complicated forms are not readily categorised in a simple system. Number 437 (fig 61), for example, could be considered a variation either of oval or of rectangular forms, or a further category could have been devised; to keep things simple, the rectangular characteristics determine its place in the present listing (see also nos. 263–64, fig 41, listed under oval rather than D-shaped frames; there are also difficulties in deciding where a line may reasonably be drawn between rectangular and trapezoidal frames – see nos. 401–03 etc). Other researchers would doubtless have found different solutions. Some of the subcategories reflect biases in the present sample; the groupings would have been formulated in a different way if a more comprehensive survey of medieval buckles had been undertaken.

Within categories the order is according to ceramic phase, and then by the width of the frame (the second dimension – ie approximate strap width). This chronological approach should help with the identification of any further trends in the light of other finds. Buckles which may have lost the plates with which they were originally furnished are listed with those that never had them in the first place; where a parallel is known with a plate, this is indicated. For the difference between circular buckles and annular brooches see pp 64–5.

Thanks are due to Dr Ian and Mrs Alison Goodall for valuable discussion of many points of terminology.

It is extremely difficult to differentiate buckles for horse equipment from those for personal dress, and many of the simpler forms could have been used for both. Horse equipment probably included more buckles in iron than did clothing worn by men and women, but this does not help with the identification of individual examples. Very large frames may be from horse furniture, but large buckles were also used with swords, and occasionally for waist belts in men's and perhaps also women's dress (see fig 34; a large buckle is used on the purse in fig 175). Iron buckles with a frame aperture in excess of 50mm (ie those catering for straps wider than 50mm) are not included below, and will be discussed in a companion volume on horse equipment (Clark forthcoming). Buckles could also be used in completely different contexts – see, for example, the one on a strap around a chest in the mid 15th-century painting *The Prophet Jeremiah* by the master of the Annunciation (reproduced in Wescher 1947, pl 54).

In addition to evidence from funerary monuments and other artistic representations, occasional finds of buckles in association with the remains of individuals permit a few examples to be assigned to male or female dress (eg some of those excavated at the Austin Friars site in Leicester; Clay 1981, 133 & 135 nos. 24–26 & 31–32). Such evidence is very limited, and it would be rash to take it to imply that a particular form was restricted to either sex.

PARTS OF BUCKLES

Frames, which are the most immediately obvious characteristic of buckles, range from plain to very highly decorative. Their shape is used as the principal trait for the categorisation proposed in this volume.

There seems to be little obvious advantage in using, for example, a rectangular design as opposed to a rounded one – fashion was presumably the main consideration in both men's and women's dress. Frames of simple circular, rectangular/square, and D-shapes, in any of the

32 TERMINOLOGY

(Some illustrations combine features which may not be found together.)

<u>Single loop frame</u>

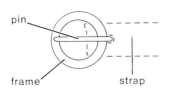

pin

frame

strap

<u>Single loop frame</u>
<u>with central bar</u>

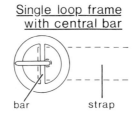

bar   strap

<u>Double loop frame</u>

sheet roller   side   bar   strap

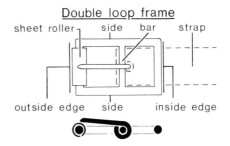

outside edge   side   inside edge

<u>Decorative frames</u>

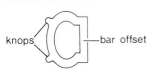

knops   bar offset

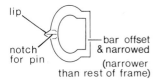

lip

notch
for pin

bar offset
& narrowed
(narrower
than rest of frame)

<u>Frame with folded sheet plate</u>

bar   plate   rivets   strap

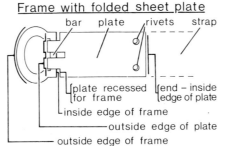

plate recessed
for frame

end – inside
edge of plate

inside edge of frame

outside edge of plate

outside edge of frame

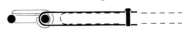

<u>Frame with integral</u>
<u>(rigid) plate</u>

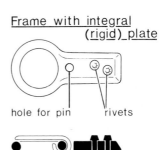

hole for pin   rivets

<u>Double loop frames</u>

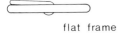

flat frame

angled frame

frame curved
at centre

<u>Pins</u>

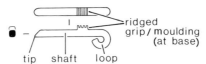

ridged
grip / moulding
(at base)

tip   shaft   loop

transverse ridge

flanges

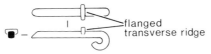

flanged
transverse ridge

collar

combined pin and bar

<u>Sheet plates   (unfolded)</u>

slot for pin   recessed for
frame

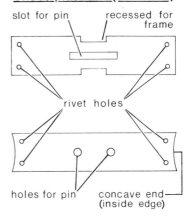

rivet holes

holes for pin   concave end
(inside edge)

33 CATALOGUE SCHEME

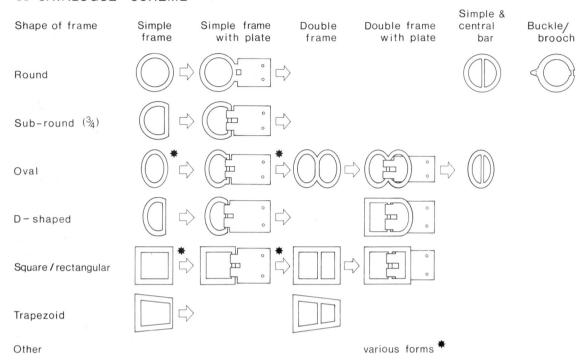

Shape of frame	Simple frame	Simple frame with plate	Double frame	Double frame with plate	Simple & central bar	Buckle/ brooch
Round						
Sub-round (¾)						
Oval						
D-shaped						
Square / rectangular						
Trapezoid						
Other			various forms ✱			

Within each frame type category, folded sheet plates are followed by integral then composite plates
✱ In these categories more decorative subgroups follow the plainer examples

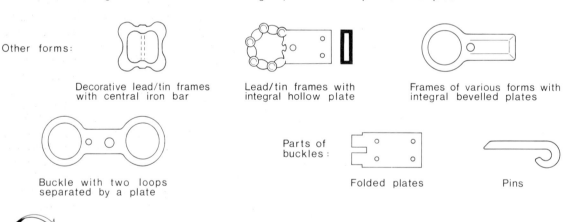

Other forms:

Decorative lead/tin frames with central iron bar

Lead/tin frames with integral hollow plate

Frames of various forms with integral bevelled plates

Buckle with two loops separated by a plate

Parts of buckles:

Folded plates   Pins

Folding strap clasps:

Simple frames ⇨ Composite frames ⇨ Folding ends ⇨ Clasps lacking a folding end ⇨ Plates

 Other clasps

Comparandum: Buckle souvenir (non-functional)

Manufacturing evidence

metals represented, could have been used for a variety of purposes in addition to fastening personal dress. The small, circular frames of iron and lead-tin (with and without a central bar) and also the double-oval frames of lead-tin, all of which were probably for shoes, show how standardised some fittings for a particular function could be – at least from the late 14th century onwards. The one rectangular copper-alloy buckle in place on a shoe upper (no. 448, fig 62) is a reminder that even where standard forms were overwhelmingly preponderant, there could be other, less common fashions – or perhaps transferance from another item as an expediency.

Double frames become commoner towards the later end of the sequence. The earliest, no. 346 (fig 52) is dated to the mid 13th century, but most are from deposits attributed to the late 14th and early 15th centuries. The second loop of the frame would have directed the free end of the strap down against the part that was attached to the bar of the buckle – a somewhat tidier arrangement than with single frames (though the same result might be achieved if a strap-loop was used – see figs 143 & 150, bottom). It would also have provided extra purchase when the strap was fastened or unfastened.

Some double buckles have angled frames – in a few cases this may be the result of distortion from use, though it may have been an original feature in others (the frames of buckles nos. 332 and 333 differ only in having flat and angled profiles – fig 50).

Although they were present in deposits predating the mid 13th century, the sparsity of iron frames compared with copper-alloy ones from the earliest part of the period covered is remarkable. Iron frames were usually relatively plain in form (circular, rectangular or D-shaped). They were often for quite heavy-duty straps, though they include the small-diameter plain-circular examples noted above, which were a standard form in the early 15th century for shoes; the function of the earlier ones of this shape (copper-alloy examples nos. 27–29, fig 36, and nos. 55–58 of iron, fig 38, all of late 13th-/early 14th-century date) is uncertain.

Iron buckles range from very crude ones with rectangular sections (eg the D-shaped stirrup buckle – fig 58), to some extremely elegantly shaped examples on which considerable effort has been expended to produce rounded sections with subtly graded variations (no. 418 is a notable example in this respect – its pin fits neatly into the notch so as to lie flush with the surface of the frame – fig 58).

Frames of simple shapes would be relatively easy for a smith to produce, but a few iron frames are quite ornate (eg no. 319, fig 46); these probably follow fashions which, from the greater numbers recovered, seem to have been more prominent in copper-alloy buckles. D-shaped frame no. 272 has a very narrow bar and a relatively long pin, while the thick frame of no. 395 (fig 56) with its angled profile – both traits were presumably decorative – must have been a particularly difficult form to make.

Double-oval frame no. 376 (fig 53) is the only strap fitting in the entire catalogue that analysis suggests is made of lead unalloyed with tin. The circular leaded bronze frame of no. 40 (fig 36) seems far too malleable to have been usable for most purposes – it may not be a buckle. Several of the lead/tin frames were given an iron bar for strength (eg nos. 473–5, fig 65); in no. 387 an iron rod was set within the non-ferrous metal that made up the visible part of the bar (fig 54).

Rectangular iron frames, particularly the plainer forms, have tended, following Ward-Perkins (1940, 277), to be categorised as harness buckles, but they need not all be for horse equipment (today several different shapes and metals are used for this purpose). Some could have been for men's and women's girdles (a rectangular iron buckle with a central bar was found on the body probably of a girl of 15 to 16 years' age in Leicester – Clay 1981, 138–39 no. 66 fig 50), as well as for armour and sword belts at various levels of society. There are also saddle bags and other kinds of travelling containers to be taken into account. Rectangular buckles with solid rollers (eg no. 428, fig 60) were a specialised form, requiring a high degree of skill to manufacture; these were almost certainly for horse equipment, as later, similar examples suggest. Buckles with a curved profile may have been for armour – see no. 458 (fig 63); several of these frames have rabbets at the corners, and no. 443 (fig 62) has them along both edges.

As would be expected with a hard and resilient metal, there is relatively little evidence among the iron frames of breakage (though see no. 441, fig 61, or of distortion or advanced wear, though the last may sometimes be difficult to distinguish from differential corrosion (see no. 349, fig 52).

A *roller* – a revolving outside edge, either a separate solid rod (only in iron frames in the assemblages published here – eg nos. 428, fig 60, & 441, fig 61), or a sheet cylinder around the frame (eg nos. 315 & 317, fig 46, & no. 432, fig 60) – would permit easier and tighter fastening than a rigid, integral edge, but the presence of rollers on some decorative frames (eg nos. 288, 293 and 301, fig 44) suggests that, as for other parts of buckles, fashion could be a major consideration. An iron frame with a separate, solid roller also of iron was inherently harder to manufacture than the same design cast in copper alloy. Iron buckles with solid rollers include the quite common, robust form of 'horse-harness' buckle referred to above, which is known in a range of sizes (see no. 428, fig 60 – this form lasted for several centuries).

Buckle pins are almost all of copper alloy or iron. In many instances they are of the same metal as the frames, but a significant number of iron frames have pins of copper alloy, and vice-versa (eg no. 38). Only one lead/tin pin survives (buckle no. 480, fig 66, though non-functional buckle pendants like no. 573 had them – fig 80, top right). Frames of the non-ferrous white-metal alloys otherwise have iron-wire pins, some or all of which may be replacements. The only silver item listed under buckles has the frame and pin both of this metal (no. 211, fig 39 – this object could alternatively be a brooch). Drawn-wire pins of copper alloy or more commonly iron were normal on the small buckles of simple, standard shapes used on shoes. They also occur on some medium-sized buckles of copper alloy, where they may be replacements for original cast pins which had become broken (eg nos. 326, 436 & 469 – the latter two have iron pins on copper-alloy frames – figs 49, 61 & 64). Numbers 332 and 333 respectively have iron and copper-alloy pins on frames that are similar in form (fig 50). Cast copper-alloy and, less frequently, wrought-iron pins of all sizes sometimes include ridges or a raised, grooved area on the shaft near the loop (no. 36 has more elaborate decoration, possibly an animal head, at this point – fig 36). Ridges and flanges etc sometimes appear here on the cast or wrought pins of smaller buckles, probably more

for decorative effect than function (eg the iron pin of no. 441, fig 61), and also on some other pins (eg the sheet pin on no. 458, fig 63, and the wire pin on no. 312, fig 46). This feature is also regularly found on the cast pins of more robust, plain buckles of copper alloy and iron, and here it probably was functional. Decoration in this area of the pin also occurs on some open-frame brooches (eg no. 1331, fig 163) – it is possible that the brooches inspired its use on buckles. While this elaboration of the pin would have been visible on a brooch, it would not have been seen on a buckle fastened in the usual modern way – ie with the other end of the strap passing in front of the loop of the pin – though it would have been visible on a waist belt in which the loose end of the strap hung down vertically from the pin (cf fig 10 and Clayton 1979, pl 18). This is possible, for example, with no. 36 (fig 36), though it would probably not have been feasible with a buckle having a shorter aperture, such as no. 399 (fig 56), but it seems most unlikely that the straps for the large, plain-circular buckles would have been worn in this way. This all suggests that the raised area on the shaft of the large, robust buckles like no. 36 etc (see also pins nos. 541, 547 & 549 in fig 75), and perhaps on some smaller ones too, was partly functional rather than purely decorative. It would have provided extra purchase for pressing the pin into the required hole in the strap when this was difficult to secure, or when a particularly tight fit was required – those who have had to struggle with a very full suitcase will recognise the usefulness of such a provision.

Sheet copper-alloy pins are found mainly, but not exclusively, on large- and medium-sized copper-alloy frames. Some are well finished, others are quite crude (eg no. 516, fig 72). Sheet pins are thinner than most cast ones; the former were probably more easily distorted or dislodged. Since sheeting was (like wire) easily worked and probably widely available, it is likely to have been much used for replacing lost pins. The iron-wire pin on copper-alloy buckle no. 439 seems out of place, especially when compared with the copper-wire one on the similar buckle no. 438 (fig 61). The pins on buckles nos. 322 (fig 48) and 469 (fig 64) seem to have been replaced the wrong way round (as has the frame of no. 435 relative to its plate, fig 61). The missing pin for buckle no. 445 would probably have been of a T-shaped form, combined with the bar (see fig 62). The arc-section sheet pin, with its decorative hole, on the unusual buckle no. 39 (fig 37), is, like the frame it serves, in a class of its own.

Buckle plates were found in place on *c*.40% of copper frames, *c*.20% of iron frames, and only one identified as lead/tin (no. 423, with a copper-alloy plate – fig 59). They were presumably lost from an indeterminate number of others (these figures do not include the standard forms of shoe buckles which never had plates).

Plates provided a means of attaching the frame to the strap that was arguably more secure in the long term than folding the leather or textile around the frame and sewing the strap together to hold it in place, as was done with the plain circular frames (riveting was very rarely used for this – see nos. 406 & 416, figs 57 & 58, which are not necessarily from items of dress). Some similar forms of buckle frame are known both with and without plates, eg ornate oval frames nos. 293 and 317 (figs 44 & 46), and rectangular frames nos. 446 and 457 (fig 63). The main stress on the leather or other material of the strap would be distributed by a plate onto a wide area of the fabric around the rivets, while in the case of a folded and sewn strap, much of the strain was concentrated at the fold of the fabric, particularly at the sides. Slight but sustained movement against the frame while in use would, over a period, have tended to weaken the fabric, leading in some instances to the strap tearing right through.

The plates catalogued here had between one and five rivets. One, two or four rivets are most common, and pairs would have been more effective for distributing the stress than arrangements in which a single rivet took most of the strain at a central point (several of the smaller buckles and most of the strap clasps which have a single rivet may not have been intended to be subject to a significant level of strain).

Most copper-alloy and iron plates are of sheet metal, folded around the bar of the buckle frame, with a slot or, much less frequently, two holes for the pin. The plates with holes include some that are quite poorly made (eg nos. 310, fig 45, 514 & 516 fig 72), but there are also some of much better quality (eg no. 314, fig 46). Number 519 may have begun by having holes, which became a slot through wear (fig 73). The thick copper plate

of buckle no. 316 (fig 46) is the only folded one that appears to have been cast. Most plates are of the same basic metal as the frames they accompany, though iron frame no. 422 and lead-tin frame no. 423 (fig 59) have copper-alloy plates. The only lead/tin plates among the finds published here are integral with the frames (nos. 476–81, fig 66). Buckles of copper-alloy sheeting with a curved profile having the plate integral with the frame (nos. 320–21 and parallel, fig 48) and more-robust buckles of copper alloy or iron in which the integral plate is bevelled at the sides (nos. 482–87, figs 68 & 69C) were probably for spurs.

Composite copper-alloy plates consist of two separate pieces of sheeting soldered onto a forked spacer that is integral with the frame. The distinctive, high-quality buckles with this feature (nos. 322–30, figs 48–9) are probably a specifically English form, since precise parallels do not seem to have been found on the Continent (see Fingerlin 1971, 14 & 116). They date from the mid 14th century to at least the early 15th century. Integral lead/tin plates are also hollow, with rivets of the same alloys (these have the only non-ferrous white-metal rivets among the buckles – see nos. 476 & 477, fig 66, & cf strap-ends nos. 714 & 716, fig 99). These integral lead/tin plates may have been inspired by the composite fittings in copper alloy (see buckles nos. 322–30, but the form first appears in copper-alloy strap-ends from *c*.1270 – *c*.1350). The white-metal alloys were sometimes so weak that a strap could be torn out together with the rivet (nos. 478 & 480, fig 66). Whereas many sheet plates were relatively flimsy and therefore liable to distortion (eg nos. 434–36, fig 61), the integral forms – especially the composite ones – were usually much more robust. The sheet plates of several folding clasps and of a few buckle plates are slightly thicker than the average (up to 1mm, as opposed to around 0.4–0.6mm) and, like the sheets in composite plates, they are neatly bevelled at the sides.

Most sheet plates, both for buckles and folding clasps, are recessed at the fold to cater for the frame. Those for buckles are immediately distinguishable from those for clasps (figs 77–78) by the presence of slots or holes for the buckle pin. A few folded strips which look rather like plates, but lack both slots/holes for a pin and recesses for a frame, may be a form of strap-end (nos. 743–58, fig 104; nos. 745, 749, 750, 752, 754 & 756 are decorated on both faces and may have served some other purpose).

Plates provided a flat surface which could be decorated. Though some plates were not ornamented, the possibility was exploited in many copper-alloy and some of the lead/tin examples. The techniques used for surface ornamentation here comprise almost the whole range represented on metalwork in this volume (see p 29ff on Secondary Decoration). The most elaborately decorated buckle plates among the recent finds are of copper-alloy with animal designs (nos. 500 & 530, figs 72 & 73 – probably of late 12th/13th-century date), and of lead/tin with various foliate and linear designs (nos. 475, 479 & 481, figs 65 & 66 – of early 15th-century date). The commonest decoration is quite simple – a single engraved line or pair of lines (eg no. 304, fig 45), or an engraved zigzag (eg no. 499, colour pl 4A) around the sides and edges of the plate. Rivets too could be decorative – their heads were sometimes domed for ornamental effect; in no. 314, one of the more ornate examples, they are somewhat enlarged (fig 46; cf brooch no. 1343, fig 165) – though the great majority were no more than short lengths of wire that would have been barely discernible once in place. Solder has been traced on some rivets; it may have been used to help position them in preparation for striking for permanent fixture. Large, crude rivets can indicate repairs or the transfer of the plate to a different strap (see on Breakage and Repair, p 34).

Although the width of the bar on a buckle is usually an accurate indication of the width of the strap, there are exceptions (see fig 34), and some buckle plates are narrower than the straps to which they were attached (eg nos. 305 & 307, fig 45, & cf no. 446).

Unless otherwise stated, *pins* survive, and are

34 Sculpture of man with large buckle at the waist, *c.*1360, height 0.47m (private collection)

of the same metal as the frame (iron pins are wrought unless stated), *plates* are rectangular and of folded sheeting, *rivets* are present, and of the same metal as the plate, and *roves* are round and of copper alloy. *Rollers* are, by definition, sepa-

35 Measurements for buckles, etc. in the text are given in the following order:
A x B for frame, followed by C x D in brackets for plate.

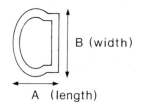

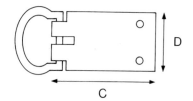

rate. Where two sets of dimensions are given, the first are for the frame, and those following in brackets are for the plate. Where a tin coating is discernible by visual examination or on x-ray plates, this is indicated; no mention means only that no coating is visible; where tests (MLC) for the presence of tin have proved negative, this is stated. Details of cross sections of frames are given in the text only where they are unusual or a particular point is to be made from this information.

Note – *buckles of common forms thought to be for shoes, and rings lacking pins are catalogued in smaller type than the others.*

PLAIN CIRCULAR FRAMES

(strap attached directly to frame)

Circular items with a frame uninterrupted by a constriction for a pin are listed under this present category as buckles, while those with a constriction are included under brooches. (Some of the more elaborate buckle frames have a constriction for a pin on the bar.)

See discussion at the end of this section, and also nos. 211 and 212 for circular items which may either be buckles or brooches.

The late 14th- and early 15th-century buckles in this present category and with frames which are 20mm or less in diameter are probably from shoes – see discussion below. The function of the earlier small buckles is uncertain.

Copper alloy

27 SWA81 acc. no. 3046 (context 2061)
ceramic phase 9
d 9.5mm; pin consists of two layers of sheeting folded around the frame.

28 SWA81 505 (2018) 9 fig 36
d 12.5mm; frame irregular in thickness; iron-wire pin.

29 SWA81 516 (2020) 9
d 14mm; frame irregular in thickness; iron-wire pin.

30 BWB83 5805 (298) 11
d 18mm; frame irregular in thickness; the wire pin is bent by use.

31 BWB83 4569 (285) 11 fig 36
d 24mm

32 BC72 4138 (88) 11 fig 36
d 39.5mm; gunmetal loop, cast brass pin (AML); frame slightly irregular in thickness; pin is worn from frame.

33 BWB83 326 (204) 11
d 39.5mm; cast pin has ridged grip.

34 BC72 90 (25) 11
d 40mm

35 SWA81 8 (84) 11
d 40mm; cast pin has raised knop between two transverse ridges, and is worn by the frame.

36 BWB83 2209 (155) 11 fig 36
d 42mm; cast pin, which has a grip possibly in the form of a very degenerate animal head, is worn and bent from the frame and strap.

37 BWB83 5374 (292) 11
d 47.5mm; very thick frame; cast pin has notched grip, flat tip, and is worn from frame.

38 BWB83 3544 (354) 11 fig 36
d 48mm; copper frame (AML); iron pin is incomplete.

39 BWB83 39 (151) 11 fig 37
d 28mm; the very thick frame has an irregular groove internally; the x-ray photographs show that it was formed by folding a piece of quite thick metal sheeting and then soldering the two narrowed ends together; this part has a constriction for the pin; two side fittings, which are soldered in place, each consist of a pair of conjoined roundels with smooth but irregularly-shaped surfaces; the tapering pin, which is arched in section and has a hole near the loop, has been roughly pushed through the folded leather strap (110×16mm – torn off at other end), and is worn by the frame. The robustness of the frame contrasts with the relatively thin leather strap.

The awkward method of making the frame, and the secondary attachment of the decorative paired roundels (rather than casting in a single operation) are difficult to explain.

This curious object, which is altogether distinct in form and manufacture from the other buckles described here, is the only certain circular single-frame buckle (ie with an associated strap surviving) having a constriction for the pin (taken usually to be a trait of brooches, though cf brooch/buckle no. 212 and D-shaped buckle no. 419).

40 TL74 2695 (368) 12 fig 36
d 19mm; leaded bronze frame (AML); frame has two slight swellings; iron-wire pin is incomplete.

The frame is of a very soft alloy, which would have been unable to withstand any degree of strain on the strap. Possibly not a buckle.

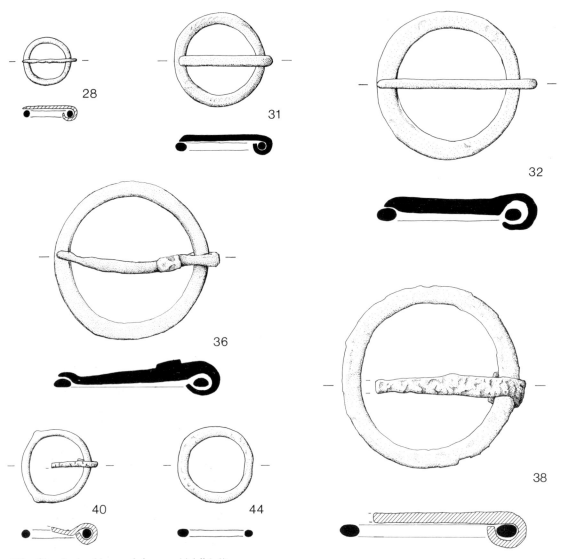

36   Circular buckles, and ring no. 44 (all 1:1)

With the exception of nos. 39 and 40, the buckles listed above suggest two basic groupings – smaller frames from the later 13th/early 14th century, and larger ones from the late 14th century.

The following copper-alloy *rings* (listed in smaller type) are similar in form to the frames of the buckles above, though since they all lack pins they may be parts of other categories of object, such as cheek pieces from snaffle bits for horses (eg Ward-Perkins 1940, 80 type A).

41   BC72   acc. no. 4681   context (250) ceramic phase 10: d 13mm.

42   BC72   4680   (250)   10: fragment; d 42mm.

43   BC72   2120   (80)   10–11: d 41mm.

44   BWB83   2131   (307)   11   fig 36: d 20.5mm; frame irregular in thickness.

45   BWB83   5821   (257)   11: d 22mm; crudely decorated with engraved lines.

46   BC72   4180   (88)   11: d 23mm.

47   BWB83   5822   (298)   11: d 23mm; frame irregular in thickness.

48 BWB83 2649 (330) 11: d 28mm; slightly irregular in thickness.

49 BC72 1818 (55) 11: fragment; d 43mm.

50 SWA81 2396 (2115) 12: d 15mm; irregular in thickness.

51 BWB83 5819 (310) 12: d 22mm.

52 BWB83 5403 (310) 12: d 28mm.

53 BWB83 5820 (275) 12: d 46mm.

Comparandum – copper alloy

54 SWA81 2677 (2108) 12
Distorted ring, d *c*.39mm; a break in the ring differentiates this object from those above; not necessarily from an item of dress.

plain circular frames continued
(with pins unless otherwise stated)

Iron

55 SWA81 1934 (2134) 9 fig 38
d 11mm; tin coating; frame flattish in section.

56 SWA81 683 (2072) 9
d 13mm; no coating visible.

57 BWB83 3111 (290) 9 fig 38
d 38mm; tin coating.

58 BWB83 570 (108) 9
d 46mm; tin coating; frame subrectangular in section and irregular in thickness; pin missing.

59 BC72 4676 (250) 10
frame incomplete; d 12mm; pin missing; no coating visible.

37 Circular buckle, with x-ray photograph (1:1)

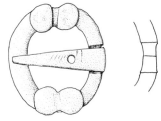

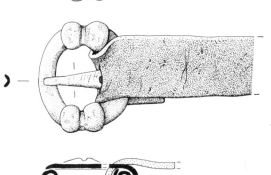

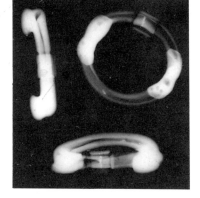

39

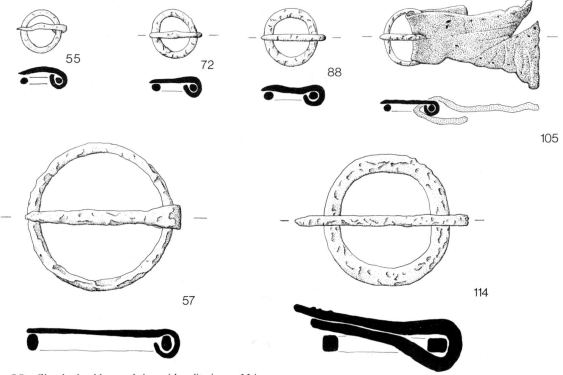

38   Circular buckles, and ring with split pin no. 114
(1:1)

shoe buckles

60 BC72 1670 (55) 11: d 10mm; on shoe; no coating
visible.

61 BC72 1970 (83) 11: d 10mm; on shoe; no coating
visible.

62 BC72 3589 (150) 11: d 10mm; tin coating on pin;
on shoe.

63 BC72 3173 (150) 11: d *c*.10mm; no coating traced
(MLC); on shoe.

64 BC72 3136 (88) 11: d *c*.10.5mm; on shoe; no coating visible.

65 BC72 1554 (55) 11: d 11mm; pin incomplete; tin
coating (MLC); on shoe.

66 BC72 4055 (88) 11: d 11mm; tin coating (MLC).

67 BC72 2899 (150) 11: d 11mm; pin missing; on
shoe.

68 BC72 3810 (150) 11: d 11mm; pin incomplete; tin
coating (MLC); on shoe.

69 BWB83 5167 (157) 11: d 11.5mm; pin missing; no
coating visible.

70 BC72 1650 (55) 11: d *c*.11.5mm; no coating traced
(MLC); on shoe.

71 BC72 1692 (55) 11: d *c*.11.5mm; tin coating
(MLC); on shoe.

72 BC72 2001 (79) 11 fig 38: d 12mm; tin coating
(MLC); pin slightly flattened in section.

73 BC72 1966 (83) 11: d 12mm; tin coating (MLC); on
shoe.

74 BC72 1986 (83) 11: d 12mm; pin missing; on shoe;
no coating visible.

75 BC72 2013 (83) 11: d 12mm; no coating traced
(MLC); on shoe.

76 BC72 2032 (83) 11: d 12mm; on shoe.

77 BC72 2952 (88(1)) 11: d 12mm; on shoe.

78 & 79 BC72 2010/2011 (83) 11: two buckles, both
with tin coating, on an ankle-length boot:
2010) upper buckle: d 12mm
2011) lower buckle: d 12.5mm

80 BC72 2816 (89) 11: d 12.5mm; tin coating (MLC).

81 BC72 3863 (150) 11: distorted; d *c*.12mm; on
shoe.

82 BC72 1636/2 (55) 11: frame damaged; d *c*.13mm;
tin coating (MLC); on strap for shoe.

83 BC72 3227 (150) 11: d *c.*13mm; tin coating (MLC); on shoe.

84 BWB83 751 (306) 11: d 13.5mm; pin missing.

85 BWB83 3371 (308) 11: d 13.5mm; tin coating; pin incomplete.

86 BC72 1732 (55) 11: d 14mm; tin coating (MLC); pin missing; on shoe.

87 BC72 3173 (150) 11: d *c.*14mm; no coating traced (MLC); on shoe.

88 BWB83 5271 (334) 11 fig 38: d 15mm; tin coating.

89 BWB83 4892 (317) 11: d 17mm; tin coating; pin missing.

90 BC72 4757 (255) 11: d 21mm; no coating traced (MLC); pin missing.

91 BWB83 4247 (307) 11: d 23mm; pin missing.

92 BC72 4131 (88) 11: d 26mm; tin coating; frame slightly distorted; pin missing.

93 BC72 4272 (150) 11: d 27.5mm; frame slightly distorted; thinner at one point than elsewhere, perhaps due to wear; tin coating.

94 BWB83 3200 (16) 11: d 37mm; tin coating; pin missing.

95 BWB83 3835 (117) 11: d 39mm; tin coating; pin squarish in section.

96 BWB83 2875 (155) 11: d 39mm; pin missing.

97 BC72 1857 (79) 11: d 46mm; pin missing.

98 BWB83 3442 (298) 11: d 47mm; pin missing.

99 TL74 1308 (368) 12: d 11mm; tin coating (MLC); on shoe.

100 SWA81 799 (2102) 12: d 12mm; tin coating; on leather strap.

101 SWA81 1453 (2113) 12: d 12.5mm; tin coating; pin missing.

102 SWA81 2350 (2102) 12: d 12.5mm; corroded.

103 SWA81 3434 (2102) 12: d 13mm; pin incomplete; tin coating; on leather strap.

104 SWA81 949 (2102) 12: d 13.5mm; tin coating.

105 SWA81 800 (2102) 12 fig 38: d 14mm; tin coating; attached to leather strap 13mm wide, which is folded around frame, with pin through off-central hole.

106 BWB83 3389 (309) 12: d 15mm; frame square in section and irregular in thickness; tin coating.

107 SWA81 2774 (2102) 12: d 15mm; pin incomplete; tin coating.

108 SWA81 5050 (2103) 12: d 15mm; tin coating; pin incomplete; leather from strap survives.

109 SWA81 3030 (2103) 12: Slightly distorted; d 15.5; iron pin incomplete; frame worn by pin.

39 Circular buckles (top row); buckle/brooch and incomplete buckle with plate missing (bottom row); (1:1)

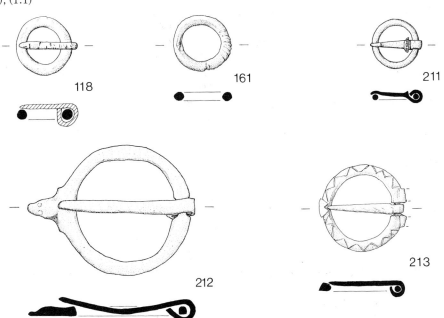

110 SWA81 774 (2097) 12: d 16mm; pin missing; leather survives from strap.

111 SWA81 2775 (2105) 12: d 19.5mm; tin coating; frame square in section and of irregular thickness; pin missing.

112 BWB83 549 (310) 12: d *c*.38mm; tin coating; frame slightly flat in section; pin missing.

113 BWB83 3812 (137) unphased: d 10mm; on shoe.

Comparandum – iron

114 BWB83 4313 (157) 11 fig 38
Ring; d 33mm; tin coating; with split pin.
(function unknown)

Lead-tin

(pins are of iron wire, wear on frame is from the pin, straps are leather)

Nos. 115–17 may not be from shoes; nos. 118–210 almost certainly are.

115 SWA81 1759 (2057) 9
d 15mm; lead-tin (MLC); frame (?)unworn; pin incomplete.

116 SWA81 1760 (2057) 9
as preceding; lead-tin (MLC); leather attached.

117 SWA81 1813 (2081) 9
d 15mm; frame (?)unworn; pin incomplete.

118 BWB83 3420 (307) 11 fig 39: d 14.5mm; frame worn from pin.

119 BWB83 2295 (144) 11: distorted; d *c*.15mm; frame (?)unworn; pin missing.

120 BWB83 3289 (144) 11: distorted; d *c*.15mm; frame (?)unworn; pin missing.

Phase-12 buckles, as preceding items unless stated:

	site	acc. no.	context	diameter	frame	pin	strap
121	TL74	1139	386	13.5mm	?unworn	incomplete	
122	SWA81	1076	2100	14mm	worn & corroded	missing	present
123	SWA81	2880	2106	14mm	worn	incomplete	present
124	TL74	1426C	368	14mm	(obscured)	complete	present
125	TL74	2046	275	14mm		incomplete	missing
126	SWA81	998	2103	14.5mm	worn	incomplete	present
127	SWA81	2991	2101	14.5mm	worn	incomplete	present
128	SWA81	3029	2013	14.5mm	worn	incomplete	missing
129	SWA81	4718	2103	14.5mm	worn	incomplete	present
130	TL74	1426A	368	14.5mm	worn	incomplete	present
131	TL74	1735	368	14.5mm	(obscured)	?missing	on child's shoe
132	BWB83	5405	310	15mm	worn	missing	missing
133	SWA81	649	2084	15mm	worn	slightly bent	missing
134	SWA81	775	2097	15mm	(obscured)	complete	present
135	SWA81	776	2097	15mm	worn	incomplete	present
136	SWA81	792	2085	15mm	possibly worn	incomplete	missing
137	SWA81	811	2097	15mm	worn	missing	missing
138	SWA81	812	2097	15mm	?unworn	missing	missing
139	SWA81	813	2097	15mm	worn	missing	missing
140	SWA81	844A	2113	15mm	worn	incomplete	missing
141	SWA81	895	2111	15mm	worn	incomplete	missing
142	SWA81	896	2111	15mm	worn	incomplete	present
143	SWA81	897	2106	15mm	worn	incomplete	present
144	SWA81	988	2101	15mm	worn	incomplete	present
145	SWA81	990	2101	15mm	?unworn	missing	missing
146	SWA81	993	2103	15mm	?unworn	incomplete	missing
147	SWA81	995	2103	15mm	worn in two areas	complete	missing
148	SWA81	1025	2103	15mm	worn	incomplete	present
149	SWA81	1056	2100	15mm	worn	missing	missing
150	SWA81	1058	2100	15mm	worn	missing	missing

151	SWA81	1073	2101	15mm	(obscured)	complete	present
152	SWA81	1074	2100	15mm	?unworn	missing	present
153	SWA81	1075	2100	15mm	worn	missing	missing
154	SWA81	1474	2113	15mm	worn	incomplete	missing
155	SWA81	1478	2113	15mm	worn	incomplete	missing
156	SWA81	2489	2269	15mm	worn	incomplete	missing
157	SWA81	2490	2269	15mm	unworn	complete	present
158	SWA81	2783	2108	15mm	?unworn	missing	missing
159	SWA81	2784	2108	15mm	worn	missing	missing
160	SWA81	2785	2108	15mm	?worn	incomplete	missing
161	SWA81	2876	2106	15mm	worn	missing	missing
162	SWA81	2878	2106	15mm	worn	complete	missing
163	SWA81	2928	2108	15mm	corroded	incomplete	present
164	SWA81	2943	2109	15mm	slightly worn	missing	missing
165	SWA81	2944	2109	15mm	?unworn	incomplete	missing
166	SWA81	2980	2084	15mm	worn	complete	missing
167	SWA81	3029	2103	15mm	worn	missing	missing
168	SWA81	3088	2069	15mm	worn	incomplete	missing
169	SWA81	3089	2069	15mm	worn	missing	missing
170	SWA81	3406	2082	15mm	worn	incomplete	missing
171	SWA81	4550	2103	15mm	worn	missing	present
172	TL74	622	368	15mm		present	present
173	TL74	1142	275	15mm	(obscured)	incomplete	on shoe
174	TL74	1331	368	15mm	worn	missing	present
175	TL74	1426B	368	15mm	unworn	incomplete	present
176	TL74	1734	368	15mm		incomplete	corroded onto vamp
177	TL74	2045	275	15mm	worn	missing	missing
178	TL74	2085	275	15mm	unworn	incomplete	present
179	TL74	2133	368	15mm	(obscured)	incomplete	present
180	TL74	2177	368	15mm			present
181	TL74	2179	368	15mm	worn		present
182	TL74	2567	275	15mm	worn (found with shoe)	missing	missing
183	TL74	2709	279	15mm		incomplete	missing
184	TL74	2715	275	15mm		present	missing
185	TL74	2716	275	15mm			present
186	TL74	3290	275	15mm	?unworn	missing	missing
187	TL74	3323	368	15mm		?trace	missing
188	SWA81	997	2103	15.5mm	?unworn	incomplete	missing
189	SWA81	2753	2114	15.5mm	corroded	missing	missing
190	TL74	3335	368	15.5mm	unworn	?trace	on shoe
191	TL74	3490	368	15.5mm	unworn	incomplete	present
192	SWA81	874	2101	16mm	worn	missing	present
193	SWA81	2574	2113	16mm	(obscured)	incomplete	present
194	SWA81	2929	2108	16mm	?unworn	missing	missing
195	SWA81	3298	2112	16mm	worn	missing	present

Number 140 is on a knotted strip of leather, together with circular buckle with a central bar no. 245. The frame of no. 161 is worn at several points – the pin seems to have moved relative to the frame during use; no other buckle in this category has such extensive wear marks (fig 39).

Distorted frames, all from ceramic-phase 12 deposits, original diameters estimated to have been c.15mm:
(See fig 19A for no. 205)

				frame	pin	strap
196	BWB83	5865	305	worn	incomplete	missing
197	SWA81	752	2097	worn	incomplete	missing
198	SWA81	843	2101	?unworn	missing	present
199	SWA81	887	2100	worn	incomplete	present
200	SWA81	1479	2113	worn	incomplete	missing
201	SWA81	2395	2115	worn	incomplete	missing
202	SWA81	2491	2269	worn	missing	missing
203	SWA81	2784	2108	worn	missing	missing
204	SWA81	2888	2106	(obscured)	incomplete	present
205	SWA81	2889	2106	?unworn; bent & cracked	incomplete	present
206	SWA81	2990	2101	?unworn	missing	missing
207	SWA81	3030	2103	?unworn	incomplete	missing
208	SWA81	4207	2106	worn	incomplete	present
209	SWA81	4693	2103	worn	incomplete	present
210	TL74	2132	368	unworn	present	present

The preponderance of these standard-form buckles in the early 15th century is very clear (90 examples out of 96, though over 60 of these are from one area of the Swan Lane site, and may represent a special category of waste). Those from deposits attributed to the late 14th century (ceramic phase 11) may be from the very end of that period, while three from late 13th/early 14th-century deposits at the Swan Lane site (nos. 115–17) are apparently distanced by as much as a century from any other lead/tin buckles among the recent finds. This might suggest that their production took quite some time to reach the scale it had attained at the end of the medieval period, or the large numbers at Swan Lane may not be a valid indication of the overall picture. The form continued in use into the post-medieval period. Numbers 122, 141, 173, 174, 177, 179, 180, 183, 187 & 191 have been analysed (MLC).

Silver

211 BWB83 3711 (332) 11 fig 39
Possible buckle; d 12.5mm; cast pin has transverse ridge with beading; weight 0.72 grammes. The pin has apparently been added upside down in contrast to those on other buckles.

This small object is the only item of precious metal listed as a buckle among the recent finds. It is unlikely to have been from a shoe (unless, perhaps, from an exceptionally luxurious one). It could alternatively be a brooch, despite the absence of any constriction for the pin. See p 21 for the possible relevance of the sumptuary law of 1363 to this object.

The differentiation of circular buckles and annular brooches

The function of the copper-alloy and iron items over 30mm in diameter which are listed above as plain-circular buckles seems to have confused researchers for some time. The difficulty appears to have arisen from the identification of similar London finds as 'plain bronze brooches' (Ward-Perkins 1940, 275 and pl LXXVII, nos. 1 & 2, dated to the 13th/14th centuries) based on a comparison made, prior to the full publication of the evidence, with some finds from the Visby mass graves in Sweden. One of the bodies excavated there had what Ward-Perkins describes as 'a brooch on either thigh'. The finds in the graves of the dead from the Battle of Visby (1361) on the island of Gotland, where some bodies were buried in full armour, are a very useful source of information for the usage of certain forms of dress accessories at this period. It is quite clear from the illustrations in the report on the Visby finds that the items Ward-Perkins refers to are in fact buckles. (In his notebooks kept during visits abroad, recently donated to the Museum of London, Ward-Perkins unequivocally describes those from Visby as annular buckles – notebook for trip to Stockholm, p 74. The origin of the subsequent confusion will probably never be known.) Three of those illustrated in the Visby report retain fragments of wide leather straps still in place (Thordeman 1939, 126 fig 120 nos. 19–20 & 22; for other examples, a copper-alloy buckle with leather, found at the waist of the body probably of a woman, and an iron one at the waist of a man's body, see Clay 1981, 133, 135 & 137–38 nos. 24 & 65; cf Jackson 1986, 276–77 fig 7 no. 6 for a further, similar, copper-alloy buckle, which also retains a scrap of leather – found at Hartlepool).

Ward-Perkins (1940, 275) suggested that two objects found at the thigh of one of the bodies at Visby (identified by Thordeman as 'buckles in situ' – op cit 124 fig 117) would have been from a codpiece or hose. Such a function is perhaps possible for very small examples of this form, but the larger ones at Visby that are being described would have been used on belts – perhaps for a sword, or possibly for armour. The wide distribution of similar buckles in England is probably consistent with regular usage on waist belts (girdles).

A circular frame may seem unsuitable for a broad strap, but the Visby evidence shows that the slight bunching of the leather at the curve did not prevent them being used in this way (cf no. 39), just like the more familiar small circular shoe buckles listed above. The blunt tips of the pins for several of these large buckles (see no. 37, and buckle pins nos. 538, 541 & 549, fig 75) would have been impractical for use with a textile garment in the manner of a brooch, but they are appropriate for the holes provided in a thick strap. It is perhaps possible that such buckles might exceptionally have found a secondary use as brooches, but unless there is specific evidence to the contrary, it is safer to regard them as buckles for straps. A constriction on a single frame to limit the movement of the pin is generally an indication of a brooch rather than a buckle (nos. 39, 419, & 465, figs 37, 58 & 64, are the only exceptions in this present volume).

BUCKLE/BROOCH

Copper alloy

The following item has characteristics of both buckles and brooches as defined in this volume (see above). It could have served either function.

212 BWB83   acc. no. 5921   (context 298)
ceramic phase 11   fig 39
d 35mm; a crude animal head projects from a thicker

area of the frame, opposite a constriction for the sheet pin, which has been bent by use.

There are thus affinities with both brooches (the constriction for the pin and a projecting decorative element), and with buckles (the sheet pin); the animal head can be compared with a lip for the pin. The bending of the pin seems to be more characteristic of buckles than of brooches, though it is not an absolutely definitive trait.

A similar object was found at Princes Risborough (Pavry and Knocker 1957/8, 158–9 fig 11 no. 5 – Buckinghamshire County Museum acc. no. 244:58 (27)) has false-lettering decoration (cf brooches nos. 1309 & 1313); the pin here too is bent.

COMPOSITE CIRCULAR BUCKLE

(?)with broken spacer

Copper alloy

213 BWB83   acc. no. 205   (context 314)
ceramic phase 12   fig 39
Incomplete; d 23mm; engraved zigzag on frame; pin notch and lip; narrowed bar; two broken projections at the inside edge imply there was a forked spacer for a composite plate; the pin has a trace of a grip at the base.

Cf O'Brien 1988, 107 no. 255, and oval buckles with composite plates nos. 322 etc.

CIRCULAR FRAMES WITH CENTRAL BARS

Copper alloy

214 BWB83   acc. no. 2840   (context 292)
ceramic phase 11   fig 40
d 16mm; iron-wire pin; frame bent.
Buckles of this form were used for spurs in the late-medieval period (Blanche Ellis, pers. comm.).

Cf an example with a plate (Palmer 1980, 183 fig 23 no. 9), excavated in Oxford and dated to the mid 16th century. There are also several similar buckles in the Boymans-van Beuningen Museum in Rotterdam (nos. F7123–8). The lack of larger copper-alloy buckles of this form among the recent London finds is surprising – see fig 34 and cf Ward-Perkins 1940, 279 & pl LXXVII no. 4 & pl LXXIX no. 9.

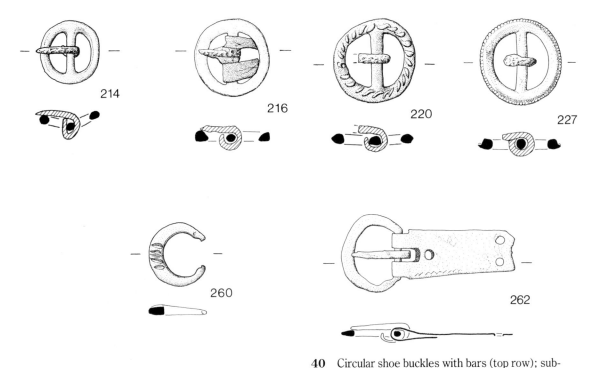

40   Circular shoe buckles with bars (top row); sub-circular buckles (bottom row); (1:1)

Lead-tin (shoe buckles)

All are from early 15th-century (ceramic-phase 12) deposits. Pins are of iron wire. Although the large numbers listed below suggest that these were a standard form in London, they are not readily paralleled elsewhere (there is a cruder example in the Boymans-van Beuningen Museum in Rotterdam – acc. no. F6859). The absence of this type of buckle from the latest deposits at the Billingsgate watching brief is a further hint that the large groups from the Trig Lane and particularly Swan Lane sites are not typical of all ceramic-phase 12 assemblages – possibly these buckles were introduced somewhat after the start of the 15th century.

plain frames

215   SWA81   1446   (2105)
d 20mm; pin incomplete; frame worn by pin; on leather strap.

216   SWA81   2881   (2106)   fig 40
d 21mm; lead-tin (MLC); on leather strap.

217   SWA81   3031   (2103)
Battered and distorted; d 21mm; bar broken from strain on strap; pin incomplete.

218   SWA81   652   (2084)   fig 19B
d 21mm+; lead-tin (MLC); pin missing; frame and bar as preceding item.

219   SWA81   980   (2112)
Incomplete; d 22mm; pin incomplete.

Decorated frames
(the bars are slightly offcentred)

raised cable decoration on frame:
220   TL74   2056   (368)   fig 40
d 22mm; lead-tin (MLC); pin incomplete; on a quarter from a low boot (cf Grew and de Neergaard 1988, 73 fig 107).

raised, bevelled band along centre of frame and beading along edge:
(the number and size of the beads varies – see fig 40 for no. 227 and fig 19C for no. 243)

	site	acc. no.	context	diameter (mm)	pin (+ present, – missing)	wear on frame	remarks
221	SWA81	994	2103	21	incomplete	+	leather attached
222	SWA81	2023	2106/7	21	–	+	
223	SWA81	3302	2112	21	–	possible	frame distorted; on leather strap
224	SWA81	3359	2112	21	incomplete	possible	
225	TL74	2152	1388	21+	–	possible	frame incomplete
226	SWA81	889	2100	22	+	+	frame distorted; on leather strap
227	SWA81	977	2112	22	incomplete	+	
228	SWA81	1093	2100	22	incomplete	+	frame distorted
229	SWA81	1488	2113	22	+	possible	slightly distorted; leather attached
230	SWA81	2051	2106	22	–	+	
231	SWA81	2211	2106	22	incomplete	–	leather attached
232	SWA81	3292	2112	22	–	+	worn from strap
233	SWA81	3300	2112	22	–	+	frame distorted; on leather strap
234	SWA81	4547	2103	22	–	+	on leather strap
235	SWA81	4692	2103	22	incomplete	+	on leather strap
236	TL74	1432	368	22	–	+	on leather strap
237	TL74	3587	275	22	+	possible	on leather strap
238	SWA81	998	2106	c.22	+	+	frame distorted leather attached
239	SWA81	999	2103	c.22	incomplete	+	frame distorted
240	SWA81	849	2101	22.5	incomplete	+	leather attached
241	SWA81	899	2106	22.5	incomplete	–	frame slightly distorted
242	SWA81	1077	2100	22.5	–	possible	frame distorted
243	SWA81	2037	2101	22.5	–	possible	frame distorted; bar bent
244	SWA81	749	2097	23	–	+	frame distorted; bar broken off
245	SWA81	844B	2113	23	–	+	bar broken off
246	SWA81	972	2082	23	incomplete	+	leather attached
247	SWA81	978	2112	23	incomplete	+	leather attached
248	SWA81	982	2112	23	–	+	frame distorted
249	SWA81	996	2103	23	+	possible	leather attached; pin bent
250	SWA81	1213	2100	23	incomplete	possible	frame corroded; on leather strap
251	SWA81	1999	2108	23	–	+	frame distorted; bar broken off
252	SWA81	2023	2106/7	23	–	possible	corroded; bar slightly bent
253	SWA81	2024	2106/7	23	incomplete	+	
254	SWA81	2979	2084	23	–	possible	corroded; leather attached
255	SWA81	3291	2112	23	–	+	
256	SWA81	3303	2112	23	incomplete	+	frame distorted; on leather strap
257	SWA81	5017	2082	23	incomplete	+	bar broken off
258	TL74	3247	368	23	incomplete	+	leather attached
259	TL74	3578	368	24	incomplete	+	frame distorted; on leather strap

These distinctive lead-tin buckles (no. 236 analysed, MLC), apparently of standard forms (five plain and 40 decorated examples), were for shoes (Grew and de Neergaard 1988, 75–76). Just how this new fashion related to the longer established, smaller plain-circular form of shoe buckle of a similar alloy (see above) is not clear. Numbers 140 and 245, one of each form, appear together on one piece of leather.

SUB-CIRCULAR (THREE-QUARTER CIRCLE) FRAMES

Frames categorised here as sub-circular are annular apart from a short, straight part long enough only for the strap or plate to be attached (similar frames that are elongated are listed as D-shaped).

Copper alloy

260 BIG82   acc. no.2483   (context 2196)
ceramic phase 8   fig 40
Incomplete; 14×16mm; grooves in outside edge; stubs are probably from narrowed bar.
Cf Fingerlin 1971, 49 fig 30.

Iron

261 TL74   3418   (368)   12
Corroded; 22×24mm; tin coating; pin incomplete; on leather strap *c.*160×16mm (torn off at other end, and with holes presumably for lost mounts).

SUB-CIRCULAR FRAME WITH PLATE

Copper alloy

262 BWB83   acc. no. 5811   (context 306)
ceramic phase 11   fig 40
17×20mm (33×13mm); slightly tapered plate is shorter at the back; recessed for frame; slot for sheet pin and holes for three rivets (only one of which went through the sheet at the back); engraved zigzag survives along one side.

SIMPLE OVAL FRAMES

Copper alloy

(these have a slight angle at the corners of the inside edge)

263 BWB83   acc. no. 2689   (context 330)
ceramic phase 11   fig 41
Incomplete; 32 × estd 65mm; wide outside edge has notch for pin, and punched circles forming patterns of lines and fields; pin missing.

264 BWB83   3980   (317)   11   fig 41
Incomplete; 50x*c.*70mm; outside edge is at an angle.

Iron

265 BWB83   568   (108)   10   fig 41
19×27mm

266 BC72   1858   (79)   11 fig 41
sub-oval; 28×26mm; frame irregular and rectangular in section; pin bent by strain on strap.

267 BWB83   3393   (314)   12   fig 41
24×36mm; tin coating; pin incomplete.

Lead/tin

268 BWB83   5818   (298)   11   fig 41
28×24mm; pin missing.

269 BWB83   5890   (unstratified)   fig 41
31×29mm; lead-tin (MLC); very worn by strap; notch for missing pin could also be a result of wear.

OVAL FRAMES WITH OFFSET, NARROWED BARS

Copper alloy

Cf Fingerlin 1971, 75 figs 94–5, 98–9 & 101.

270 BIG82   acc. no. 3077   (context 5364)
ceramic phase 6   fig 42 & colour pl 1A
Incomplete; 13×16mm; copper frame and roller, with traces of gilding on former (AML/MLC); frame tapers towards missing bar; outside edge is recessed for sheet roller, which has a central groove and double lines of punched, opposed triangles to each side; pin missing.

271 BIG82   2451   (2879)   7   fig 42
15×28mm; bar protrudes at sides; pin missing.

(no. 272 is reclassified as an iron frame, listed after no. 277)

273 SWA81   2693   (2052)   8
Incomplete and distorted; 14×*c.*20mm; as following item; bar and pin missing.

274 SWA81   1156   (2145)   9   fig 42
15×16mm; bar protrudes at sides; tin coating (MLC); pin missing.

275 BWB83   716   (306)   11
13×12mm; notched lip; bar offset and narrowed; sheet pin.

276 BWB83   1494   (136)   11
12.5×15mm; notched lip; knop at each side of outside edge; bar protrudes at sides; sheet pin.

277 BWB83   5439   (301)   11   fig 42
14.5×26mm; bronze frame (AML); notch for pin, which is missing; bar has thicker rectangular area in middle; tin coating; frame slightly worn by pin.

The thickening on the bar may have been intended to suggest a stronger support for the pin.

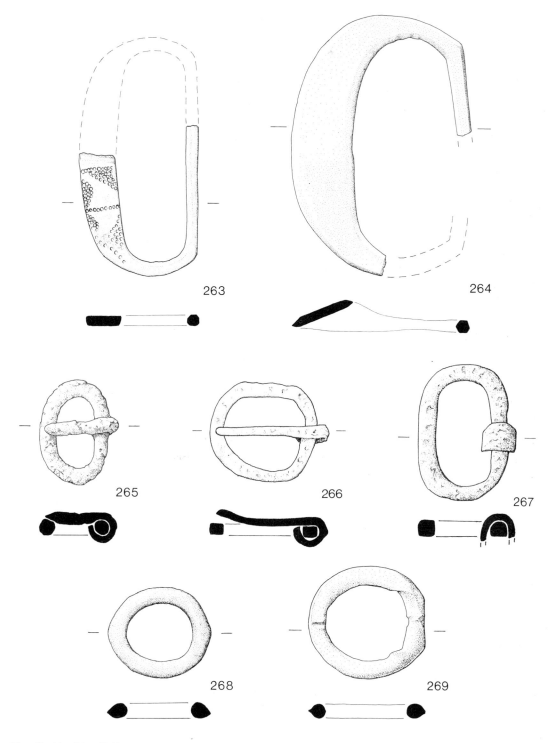

263

264

265

266

267

268

269

41 Oval buckles (1:1)

Iron

272 (numbered out of sequence) BIG82 2873
(5222) 7
18×28mm; the narrowed bar protrudes at sides;
notch; pin 26mm long; tin coating (MLC).

The longevity of this simple form may have
ended by the turn of the 15th century. The
buckles listed here seem to suggest a change
from gilding to tin coating during the 13th century
in this category.

278 SWA81 468 (2017) 9 fig 42
15×16.5mm; wire pin; tin coating (MLC).

OVAL, LIPPED FRAMES WITH NARROWED, OFFSET BARS

Copper alloy

279 BWB83 acc. no. 4487 (context 285)
ceramic phase 11 fig 42
18×21mm; leaded gunmetal (AML); lip notched for
missing pin.

280 BWB83 5919 (287) 11
Fragment of frame *c.*25mm wide; lip notched for
missing pin. From a buckle at least 30mm wide, unless
the surviving part is distorted.
Cf preceding item for probable similar form.

281 BC72 1024 (25) 11
Corroded; *c.*17×*c.*26mm; bar protrudes at one side;
incomplete sheet pin.

282 TL74 2144 (2608) 11 fig 42
22×27mm; notch flanked by two grooves; wire pin.

283 SWA81 1959 (2117) 12 fig 42
26×33mm; notch for pin; bar has a ridge marking the
offset; the sheet pin is bent by strain from the strap.

The frame is very similar in shape to those of the
series of oval buckles with composite plates (nos.
322–30).

(cf nos. 306–11 with plates)

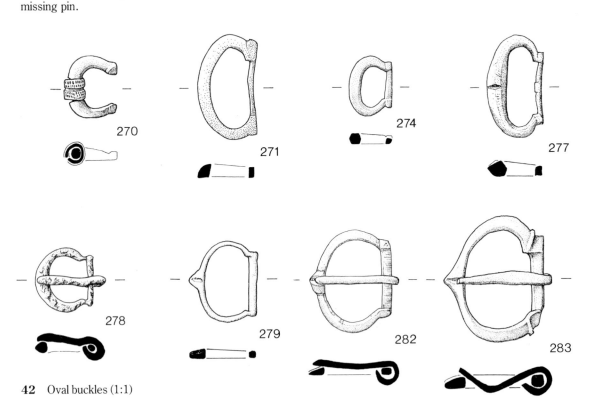

42   Oval buckles (1:1)

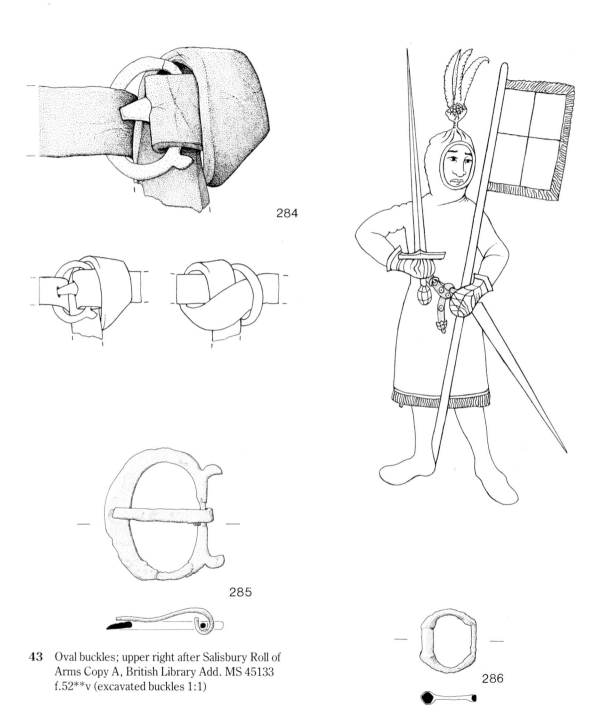

43 Oval buckles; upper right after Salisbury Roll of
Arms Copy A, British Library Add. MS 45133
f.52**v (excavated buckles 1:1)

284

285

286

OVAL FRAMES WITH CURVED PROJECTIONS ON INSIDE EDGE

Copper alloy

284 BWB83 acc. no. 43 (context 156) ceramic phase 11 fig 43

Distorted; 30×32mm; recurving projection at each side of bar; pin incomplete; attached to two lengths of leather strap 16.5mm wide (both torn off at both ends). One end of one strap is knotted around the buckle, passing in front of the frame and then behind the bar, to be looped up over the front of the other strap (where this is attached to the bar), and down between the frame and the part already in front.

Knotting a strap so that it hangs vertically at the front is shown in contemporary representations of military dress (eg Hartshorne 1891, nos. 52, 54, 61 & 64 – late 14th to mid 15th century; Clayton 1979, pl 5 no. 3 – dated to 1354; representations of knights in the 1463 Salisbury Roll of Arms and a later copy – Payne 1987, pls 14 & 13; cf Fingerlin 1971, 365 figs 413 & 414, which are both representations of St George from the 1430s. In all these depictions a sword belt worn with armour has a knot which, unlike the excavated example, initially passes *behind* the buckle frame – see fig 43.

285 TL74 270 (306) 11 fig 43

Corroded; 33×34mm; frame as preceding item, with pin notch; the sheet pin is bent from strain on the strap.

Cf Ward-Perkins 1940, 277, pl LXXVI no. 6, Fingerlin 1971, 392, fig 450 no. 257, & 399 fig 455 no. 293 – both writers note the similarity of frames of this shape to a Lombardic-letter C or D (probably a coincidental trait), and Hume 1863, pl VIII no. 2.

OVAL FRAME (?)WITH ROLLER

Copper alloy

286 TL74 acc. no. 1555 (context 1956) ceramic phase 11 fig 43

15×17mm; outside edge is constricted, probably for a missing roller; bar narrowed; pin missing. The expanded sides on the inside edge suggest that this is a buckle frame, rather than from a folding clasp. The gradation in the thickness of the frame is analogous to the shape of some of the buckles in the following category.

OVAL FRAMES WITH ORNATE OUTSIDE EDGES

Copper alloy

These all have the bar offset and narrowed. The description immediately following the dimensions for each frame refers to the outside edge; in several cases the decorative features here furnish a notch for the pin.

Comparable examples with plates suggest that many of those listed here could originally have had them too, though no. 293 retains part of the leather strap attached directly to the frame: this is irreconcilable with the use of a plate, unless the buckle was reused as found. For a general discussion of buckles of this style, see below on those with plates (nos. 312 etc).

287 BIG82 acc. no. 3085 (context 5364) ceramic phase 6

16×17mm; two knops flank pin notch; D-section wire pin incomplete.

As no. 312 with trace of plate.

288 BIG82 2439 (2898) 7 fig 44

17×18; two knops flank a constriction for the corroded sheet roller; wire pin.

289 BIG82 2523 (2853) 8 fig 44

16×19mm; two knops flank five grooves; slight lip; pin missing.

290 BIG82 2401 (2853) 8

17×20.5mm; six grooves; pin missing.

291 BIG82 2321 (2591) 8 – contaminated deposit

15.5×21.5mm; brass (AML); four knops flank a central notch; pin missing

Cf nos. 296 & 318 for very similar frames.

292 BIG82 2302 (2171) 8 fig 44

18×25mm; gunmetal (AML); four knops; pin missing.

Cf nos. 302 and 318 for similar frames; the latter has a plate.

293 BIG82 2336 (2591) 8 – contaminated deposit fig 44

21×36.5mm; brass frame, roller and pin (AML); two grooved knops flank a constriction for the sheet roller, which is unevenly grooved both parallel with the pin and at a right angle to it; cast pin has transverse ridge; leather from folded strap 13mm wide survives (torn off at both ends).

The outside edge is heavier than in the other frames listed here.

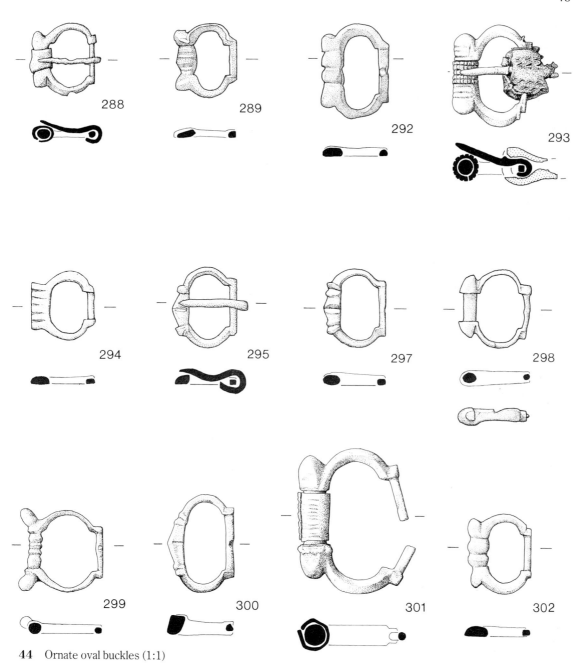

44 Ornate oval buckles (1:1)

294 SWA81 1318 (2018) 9 fig 44
17×18mm; brass (AML); five grooves; pin missing.

295 SWA81 2200 (2061) 9 fig 44
18×22mm; gunmetal frame, bronze pin (AML); notched lip between two knops; wire pin is worn and bent.

296 BWB83 2673 (334) 11
15×19.5mm; four knops; wire pin.

297 BWB83 1934 (308) 11 fig 44
16×20mm; gunmetal frame (AML); three grooves, the outer two emphasised by flanges; slight lip; pin missing.

298 BWB83 4543 (285) 11 fig 44
19×20.5mm; brass frame (AML); two knops flank a constriction, presumably for a missing roller; pin missing.

299 TL74 2140 (1956) 11 fig 44
22×22mm; gunmetal frame (AML); narrowed outside edge has three grooves, flanked by two prominent knops; pin missing.

300 BWB83 5922 (298) 11 fig 44
18×25mm; the notched lip is flanked by paired ridges; the outside edge is set at a slight angle; bar worn from missing pin.

301 BWB83 4023 (352) 11 fig 44
Distorted, *c.*25×*c.*35mm; bronze frame and roller (AML); two knops, and central constriction for the crudely grooved sheet roller; pin missing. The roller seems to have worn the frame at one side over a period to produce marked lipping here; the bar is broken, presumably by strain on the strap.
Cf no. 317 with plate.

302 BWB83 5863 (314) 12 fig 44
17.5×21mm; similar to no. 292.
(?residual in later context).

OVAL FRAMES WITH OFFSET, NARROWED BARS, AND RECESSED PLATES

Copper alloy

303 BIG82 acc. no. 2827 (context 5113)
ceramic phase 6 fig 45 & colour pl 1D
13×18mm (17×15.5mm); copper frame, plate and pin (AML); offcentred pin notch; cast pin has transverse ridge; trapezoidal plate has slot for pin and holes for two rivets – one of iron survives; double curving lines of opposed punched triangles along sides and outside edge, and following perimeter of inside edge; trace of gilding (MLC).

304 BIG82 3045 (2560) 8 fig 45
16×21mm (43×15mm); sheet pin is incomplete; tapering plate (incomplete at back) has slot for pin, three rivets, and engraved line around edges and sides; remains of gilding.

Iron

305 SWA81 4796 (2030) 9 fig 45
14×18mm (32×13mm); pin has transverse ridge;

tapering plate has round end, slot for pin and one iron and two copper-alloy rivets (MLC); tin coating; on leather strap 77×16mm (cut transversely at other end; stitching holes suggest this was sewn onto a longer piece).

OVAL, LIPPED FRAMES WITH PLATES

All have offset bars; in all but nos. 308 and 311 they are narrowed (cf nos. 279–83, which lack plates).

Copper alloy

306 BWB83 acc. no. 4545 (context 274)
ceramic phase 9 fig 45
13×11mm (17×10mm); brass frame (AML); notch for missing pin; the tapering plate is recessed for the frame, and has a slot for pin and holes for the single rivet; leather from strap survives.

307 BWB83 17 (108) 10 fig 45
12×16mm (14×6mm); gunmetal frame, bronze plate (AML); plate has holes for missing pin and the single rivet; leather from strap 9mm wide survives, cut off close to the plate.
The cut strap suggests intended reuse.

308 BWB83 2679 (330) 11 fig 45
12.5×13mm (21×8mm); notch for pin; plate is recessed for the frame, with a slot for missing pin, and holes for the single rivet.

309 BWB83 2726 (329) 11 fig 45
13×15mm (18×11mm); notch for pin; cast pin has flanges at sides; plate has irregular (?broken) end, slot for pin, holes for single missing rivet, and tin coating; textile survives from strap.

310 BWB83 2355 (154) 11 fig 45
18×21mm (18×11mm); bronze frame, gunmetal plate (AML); notch for missing pin; crude plate has holes for pin and the single iron rivet.

311 BWB83 6397 (283) 11 fig 45
19×62mm (24×55mm); notched lip for sheet pin; plate is recessed for frame, and has slot for pin, and four dome-headed rivets; tin coating; leather from strap survives.
This wide buckle may be from a sword belt.

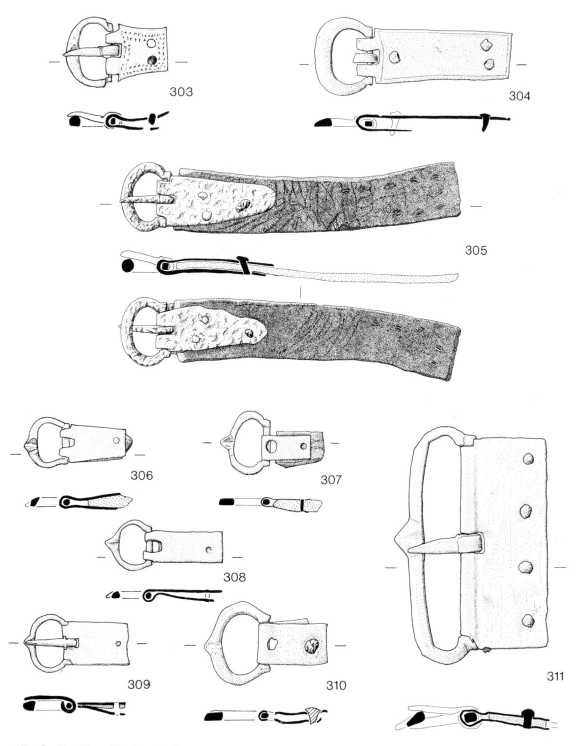

45 Oval buckles with plates (1:1)

OVAL FRAMES WITH ORNATE OUTSIDE EDGES, AND PLATES

The London finds suggest that this basic form, with all its variety, was a long-lasting fashion, in use from the late 12th to the late 14th centuries (Fingerlin dates most of those she publishes around the middle of the 13th century, though the evidence for this narrow time span is not made clear). For production of such buckles at the Guildhall Art Gallery site and from the Thames Exchange site in London, see Manufacturing Evidence, p 123. Similar evidence dated to the 13th century has also been found in Lund in Sweden (Bergman and Billberg 1976, 206 fig 149). For a range of similar buckles both in England and on the continent, cf Fingerlin 1971, 66–67 & 69 figs 51–59, 62 & 66–72, Meyer 1979, section 3.4.5, Meyer and Wyss 1985, fig 67, Capelle nd, 2, figs 16 & 17 nos. 288, 294 & 298 (these unstratified frames are published together with earlier material, but they may well be of comparable date to the London examples), Groeneweg 1987, 69 & 70 nos. 502, 503 & 529, Mårtensson and Wahlöo 1970, 64 no. 89, and unpublished examples in the Boymans-van Beuningen Museum in Rotterdam. The tomb effigy of Berengaria (queen of Richard I, died 1230 or later) shows her wearing a buckle of the present category – see fig 10.

These buckles all have the bar offset and narrowed. The description immediately following the dimensions for each frame refers to the outside edge. In several cases the decorative features here also furnish a notch for the pin. The main decorative motifs on the outside edge – grooves and knops (sometimes together), and in fewer instances ridges – show no clear chronological trends on the limited evidence of the examples listed here, though the two examples attributed to the late 12th century (ceramic phase 6) have knops. Limited analysis has indicated that brass, bronze and gunmetal were all used for frames of this series – again no chronological trend is apparent.

Copper alloy

312 BIG82 acc. no. 2851 (context 5020)
ceramic phase 6 fig 46
14×16mm (plate very fragmentary); two knops flank pin notch; the wire pin has two transverse grooves near loop; tin coating (MLC); a tiny scrap of corroded sheeting survives, presumably from the plate.

313 BIG82 2431 (3511) 7 fig 46
14×18mm (40×13.5mm); paired large and small raised bands to each side of notch; cast pin has transverse ridge; plate is recessed for frame and has two engraved conjoined crosses reserved within a field of zigzags, slot for pin, and holes for four rivets, the three surviving ones in redder metal (including one that is bent over) are probably replacements.

For similar engraved decoration cf no. 325

314 SWA81 530 (2040) 9 figs 16B & 46
14×16.5mm (32×11mm); three knops with raised bands between; the incomplete cast pin has a transverse ridge; the plate has holes for the pin, engraved sinuous line defined by straight lines along sides and inside edge, and five prominent rivets with subspherical heads – one of which has a rove (this one at least is a repair); leather from strap survives.

315 TL74 2136 (2422) 9 fig 46
17×22mm (24×17mm); outside edge protrudes slightly at the sides; sheet roller; the incomplete, corroded plate is recessed for the frame and has holes for two missing rivets and a slot for the wire pin.

316 SWA81 2113 (2063) 9 fig 46
23×22mm (30×13mm); copper frame and plate (AML); bar worn by the missing pin; outside edge protrudes at each side and has a notch; the plate is recessed for the frame, has a transverse ridge next to the slot for the pin, an integral rivet, and traces of tin coating (MLC).

A notably robust buckle for its size; the plate was presumably cast and then folded. This is the only buckle among the recent finds with an integral rivet in the plate.

317 SWA81 2091 (2031) 9 fig 46
18.5×25mm (24×17mm); brass frame and roller, gunmetal plate (AML); outside edge protrudes at the sides and has a sheet roller with parallel grooves; the damaged plate is recessed for the frame, and has holes for the missing pin and four rivets – the two surviving ones are domed, have tin solder (MLC) and are bent (not hammered) at the back; there is an additional hole on the fold of the plate, suggesting the sheeting was reused.

Cf no. 301, a similar frame which lacks a plate.

318 BWB83 1179 (361) 11 fig 46
16×23mm (*c*.36×16mm); gunmetal frame, brass plate (AML); four knops; incomplete plate is recessed for

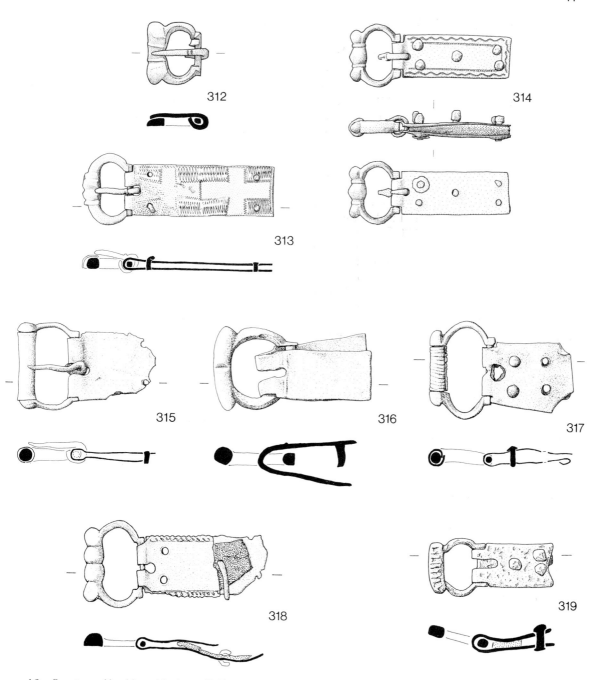

46 Ornate oval buckles with plates (1:1)

frame, and has engraved zigzags defined by straight lines along the sides; slot for missing pin; surviving holes for three rivets – a bent piece of wire *c*.15mm long remains, suggesting the plate was repaired; leather from strap survives.

Iron

319 SWA81 3921 (2018) 9 fig 46
15×15mm (22×11mm); two knops flank grooves; pin missing; plate is recessed for frame, with three dome-headed rivets and slot for pin; tin coating; leather from strap survives.

OVAL FRAMES WITH INTEGRAL PLATES

Copper alloy

(The reddish colour of both buckles suggests a relatively pure copper)

320 BIG82 acc. no. 2453 (context 2914)
ceramic phase 8 fig 48
Corroded; 44×16mm; crude; hole for missing pin is broken or corroded through; holes for two rivets; plate tapers in middle, where there are traces of engraved zigzags along one side; curving profile.

321 BWB83 2214 (128) residual in recently redeposited material fig 48
Incomplete; 34×13mm; copper frame (AML); frame broken on one side; tapering plate has hole for pin, two projections on one side and is broken at a possible rivet hole; wire pin possibly bent by strain from strap; a mark next to the pin may have been intended to be a second rivet hole. A very crude item.

A similar buckle in the Ashmolean Museum (acc. no. 410.1981) has a curved profile, the end terminates in a scroll or hook and there are traces of gilding (fig 48). The curved profile is probably an original feature, suggesting a highly specialised function. Another example, of iron, is from Hadleigh Castle (Drewett 1975, 143–44 no. 361 fig 29). Further, somewhat similar, though much more decorative and robust buckles, which also terminate in hooked ends, survive on mid 13th- to mid 14th-century spurs (B Ellis in Alexander and Binski 1987, 259–60 nos. 166 & 167).

The above two London buckles may be from spurs (Blanche Ellis, pers. comm.), though their relative weakness seems difficult for this interpretation.

OVAL FRAMES WITH COMPOSITE RIGID PLATES

These are all of copper alloy. They have a forked spacer for separate sheets soldered on at the back and front to form a hollow plate. The frames are lipped and bevelled, the plates too are sometimes bevelled, and the bars are offset and constricted for the pins. The buckles in this series are notably well finished. See p 395 for analysis of the parts of these buckles.

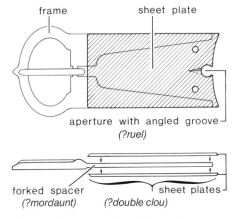

47 Terminology for buckles with oval frames and forked spacers for composite plates

322 BWB83 acc. no. 1263 (context 108)
ceramic phase 10 fig 48
16×19mm (28×14mm); gunmetal frame, brass plates (AML); notch for the sheet pin, which is in an apparently illogical position on the opposite side of the frame from the two preceding features; plate has two rivets, and concave end, with a round, grooved aperture on the front, and an additional central hole in the back. Frame and plate perhaps turned back to front relative to the pin when reused.

323 SWA81 3886 (2054) 11 fig 48
16.5×17mm (23×12mm); gunmetal spacer and back plate, brass front plate (AML); triangular lip; frame worn by (?)cast pin, which is incomplete; plate has two rivets and concave end with round apertures (grooved only on front); fibres from textile strap survive.

324 BWB83 3629 (395) 11 fig 48
22×23mm (24×17mm); gunmetal frame, brass plates (AML); notch for missing pin; frame protrudes on each side at junction of narrowed bar and frame; pin missing;

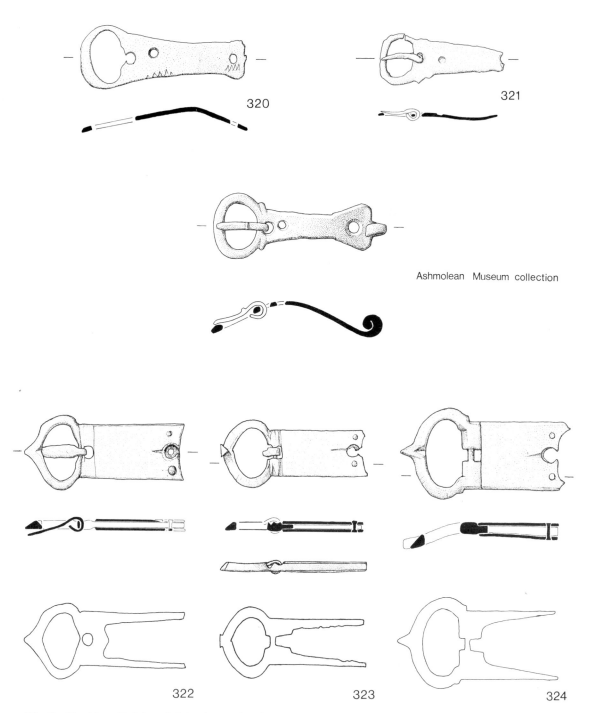

Ashmolean Museum collection

320

321

322   323   324

48 Oval buckles with integral plates (upper three),
and composite plates (lower three); (1:1)

plate has two rivets, bevelled sides and concave end with round apertures (grooved only on front).

325 BC72 2859 (150) 11 figs 30 & 49
23×27mm (14×20mm); gunmetal frame, bronze plate (AML); notched for (missing) pin; corroded plate has three rivets, and engraved transverse zigzags and other motifs; concave end has round apertures (grooved only on front); fragment of tablet-woven worsted strap survives.

For similar engraved decoration cf no. 313.

326 BWB83 38 (149) 11 fig 49
23×30mm (34×21mm); bronze frame, gunmetal plate (AML); the notch is worn by the wire pin, which is itself worn by the strap; plate has ogival inside edge, with a round, grooved aperture at front; the sheets are held by three rivets (one with a rove) of an original four; leather survives from strap. The pin and rivets are probably replacements.

327 BWB83 4452 (275) 12
17×18mm (22+×11.5mm); notch and triangular lip; pin missing; back sheet of plate is broken off at the surviving rivet hole, front sheet missing.

328 BWB83 5812 (310) 12
15×18mm (26×12mm); slight notch for missing pin; plate has concave end and single rivet.

329 BWB83 5905 (314) 12 fig 49
19×25mm (27×18mm); notch for bevelled, cast pin, which has transverse ridge with side flanges; plate has concave end and two rivets; leather from strap survives.

330 SWA81 751 (2097) 12 figs 49 & 17B
Worn; 26×32mm (40×26mm); gunmetal frame and plate (AML); pin missing; plate has engraved zigzags along sides, obliquely, and in centre; holes for two rivets.

For a different frame and plate of this category see nos. 213 and 515.

These buckles with their distinctive composite plates seem to have been a widespread mid 14th- to early 15th-century form in this country. A buckle of this form (dated to the early or mid 14th century) was excavated at the waist of a male body at Leicester (Clay 1981, 133 & 135 no. 25). Buckles of this style may have come gradually to supersede those with ornate outside edges and folded plates (nos. 312 etc) as the top of the range of mass-produced buckles, following a period in the late 14th century when both forms appear to have been in use (manufacturing evidence from

the Thames Exchange site suggests that both were produced together in at least one London workshop). The rarity of comparable examples on the continent led Fingerlin (who cites only two from abroad – 1971, 116 & 114 nos. 180–87) to identify them as a specifically English form. Those ascribed above to the late 14th century all have grooved apertures in at least the top sheet of the plate, while those from 15th-century contexts lack apertures and grooves. The variety in shape evident among the spacers presumably reflects the practices of different manufacturers over the period of production (cf the different alloys used in the series, p 395). The hollow plates correspond in form and in method of assembly with some strap-ends, including some earlier ones which could have inspired the transfer of the design to the buckles themselves. The grooved aperture first appears on strap-ends attributed to ceramic-phase 9 deposits, see nos. 664 etc (late 13th- or early 14th-century). Ward-Perkins described the buckles as 'pronged' and the strap-ends as 'forked' (1940, 272 nos. A3150 etc, and 267–69 nos. C979 etc) and attributed them to the 14th century. For further, similar items, see under folding clasps (fig 78, bottom left) and hinged strap-connecting plate no. 1217.

The forked spacer of the above examples could be what is referred to as the 'double point' in regulations of the London Girdlers' Guild which were recorded in 1344: '. . . no master of the trade will make girdles or garters (*ceyntures* or *garreters* – ie buckled straps) unless there is *ruel* under the bar; no tissue of silk or wool or thread [ie linen?] or leather of six times, five times, three times or double width will be garnished [furnished with metal accessories], unless it has a double point (*double clou*) in the buckle and in the tongue (*mordaunt*), and the bars are to have a double point as far as the *ruel* below – this applies to 'closeharness'[?] as well as to other items – there is to be a ruel below the bar, whether it [ie the strap] is wide or narrow (cf Riley 1868, 216). The references to the varieties of belt and the different sizes of straps remain obscure, but some of the contemporary terms for the parts of a buckle etc can tentatively be interpreted by reference to the present type as in fig 47. (It is possible that the regulations refer to some other kind of buckle, but there are great difficulties in interpretation if this is so). The 'double point'

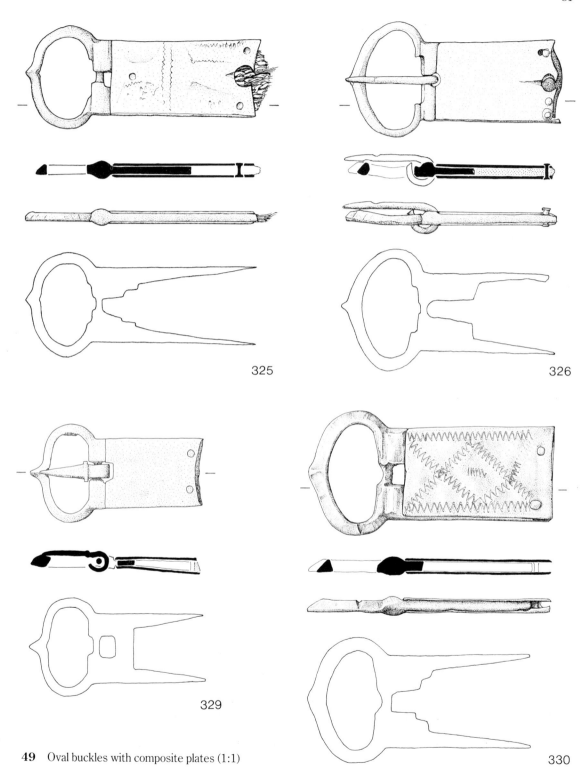

325

326

329

330

49 Oval buckles with composite plates (1:1)

probably refers to the forked spacer (the term cannot readily be applied to any other part of contemporary buckles among the recent finds; though it could perhaps be taken to mean 'rivet', there seems little reason for the regulations to insist on what was anyway a universal feature without which a plate could not have functioned at all); the bar (*barre*) is presumably what in this present volume is termed the plate, and the 'tongue' (*mordaunt*) – a word that has usually been taken refer to the pin – seems best interpreted as the metal sleeve which in this study is termed the strap-end (this latter interpretation of the word may also be more appropriate for contemporary references cited by Hume, the first of which has a late 13th-century gloss which seems to differentiate between the 'mordaunt' and the 'tongue', here apparently called a *hardiloun* – 1863, 126 & 133 – the language is obscure in the extreme). The 'ruel', perhaps the most difficult element to identify, is presumably the small hole at the end of the plate (called the (grooved) 'aperture' in this volume).

On this interpretation (which is not without its difficulties, though none of the other forms of buckle from the appropriate period seems to allow each of the parts mentioned to be readily identified) the 1344 regulations would appear to be trying to ensure that these particular buckles and the corresponding strap-ends (all the excavated examples of which are notably well made and neatly finished) would be provided with a strong armature – the spacer – to run the full length of the plate. The added aperture (otherwise a purely decorative feature) would thus provide a ready indication of the type and quality of these buckles, while the angled groove (probably made by a file) would serve to emphasise the thickness of the sheeting, and therefore the quality of the plate. It would have been very difficult to produce a long, angled groove in the much thinner sheeting used for most folded plates (a plate sheet with the grooved aperture, found separated from the rest of the buckle, is 1mm thick – SWA81 acc. no. 1785 from phase-12 context 2103). A buckle in which the prongs of the spacer fell short would not have had full internal support.

The present composite form with the cast forked spacer seems to represent the most labour-intensive products as well as the best quality available among mass-produced buckles in the middle and late 14th century. These buckles may be contrasted with contemporary forms with folded sheet plates, which lack internal support. The large numbers found of the latter clearly show that they were in widespread use – they were presumably cheaper buckles, and their plates often became bent.

DOUBLE OVAL FRAMES

Copper alloy

331 BWB83 acc. no. 4006 (context 292)
ceramic phase 11
16.5×11mm; tin coating (AML); edges are straight externally, with transverse grooves; pin missing.
Cf nos. 378–86 with plates.

332 BC72 4304 (150) 11 fig 50
33×25mm; gunmetal with tin coating (AML); pin notch; iron-wire pin.

333 BC72 4305 (150) 11 fig 50
34×25mm; as preceding item, but frame angled, and sheet copper-alloy pin.

334 TL74 442 (414) 11 fig 50
76×67mm; both edges are angled; bar has a recess only on one edge, for the sheet pin, which is broken off; engraved lines and (less emphasised) zigzags; slightly distorted.
   This wide buckle may have been for a sword belt. Cf MoL acc. no. A3138 for the decoration and size, and also strap-end MoL acc. no. 84.199/5 (fig 87).

335 TL74 1427 (368) 12
22×14mm; frame angled; pin missing.

336 SWA81 2990 (2101) 12
22×14.5mm; as preceding item.

337 TL74 1861 (368) 12 fig 50
22×15mm; frame slightly curved.

338 TL74 2175 (368) 12
as preceding item, but slightly angled frame.

339 TL74 3550 (368) 12 fig 50
as preceding item.

340 TL74 3649 (368) 12
23×16mm; as preceding item.

341 TL74 1110 (317) 12
21×18mm; as preceding item.

342 SWA81 1482 (2113) 12 fig 50
distorted; 40×43mm; oblique grooving; pin missing.

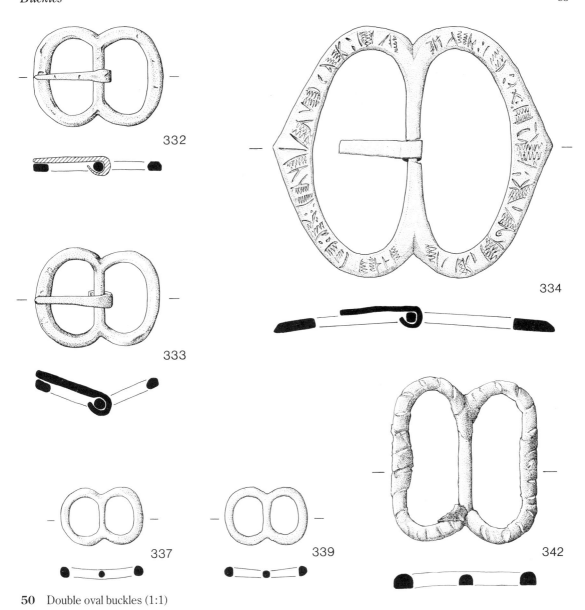

332

333

334

337   339   342

50   Double oval buckles (1:1)

343 SWA81 806 (2103) 12 figs 51 & 18A
47×49mm; frame slightly angled, with a series of
knops along the perimeter, each of which has been
drilled with a blind hole; decorated with crude, multiply
engraved oblique lines; bar narrowed; tin coating;
(?)sheet pin bent from use; an associated fragment of
leather strap 26mm wide has a rectangular mount (see
no. 1052).
Cf AR Goodall 1979, 137 & 140 fig 25 no. 137, from

Ospringe. A similar buckle with a flat profile (MoL acc.
no. 4305, fig 51) is of much neater workmanship; it
retains a folded plate, and the secondary decoration is
confined to a series of multiply engraved oblique lines
within an elongated lozenge on each edge. There was
presumably a basic design with several variants. A
simpler, somewhat later buckle of comparable form
was excavated on a male body in Leicester (Clay 1981,
133 & 135 no. 32).

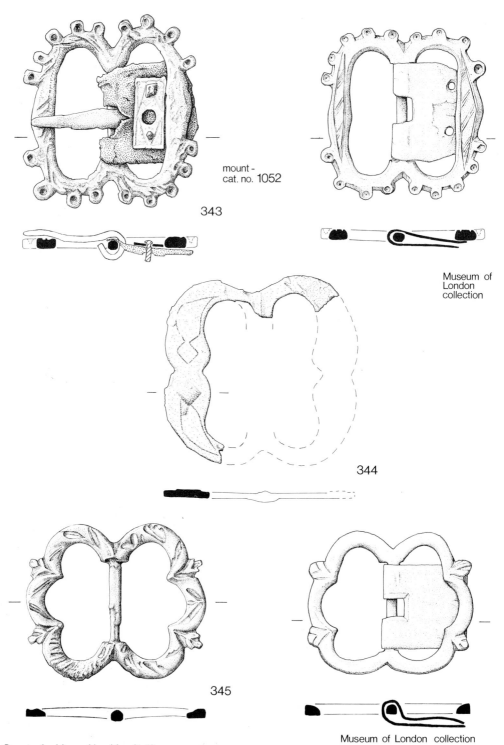

mount -
cat. no. 1052

343

Museum of
London
collection

344

345

51 Ornate double oval buckles (1:1)

Museum of London collection

Frame with bilobed edges

Copper alloy

344 TL74 2680 (368) 12 fig 51
Corroded fragment; *c*.48×47mm; surviving edge is
constricted at the centre and has engraved conjoined
tear-and-(?)lozenge motifs.
Cf tin frame no. 377 for similar decorative motifs.

Frame with trilobed edges

Copper alloy

345 SWA81 2039 (2101) 12 fig 51
50×42mm; tripartite plant-like motifs (cf trefoils) in the
angles of the lobes; multiply engraved oblique linear
decoration; bar narrowed; pin missing.

A similar buckle (MoL acc. no. 81.439) retains a
folded plate; the motifs in the angles of the lobes are
simpler and there is no secondary decoration.

52   Double oval iron buckles (1:1)

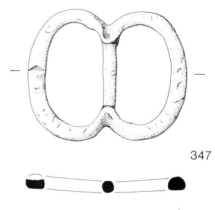

347

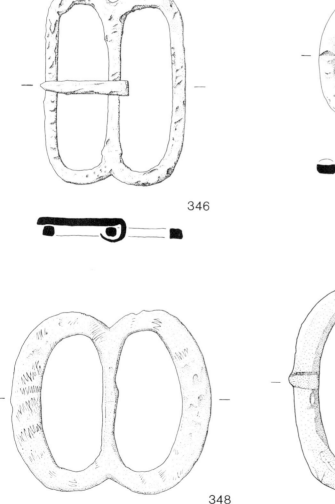

346

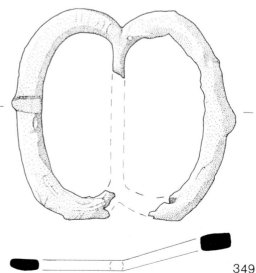

348

349

Double-oval frames continued, plain unless stated

Iron

346 BWB83 3110 (290) 8 fig 52
38×51.5mm; tin coated.

347 BC72 4141 (88) 11 fig 52
43×34mm; bar narrowed; notch for missing pin.

348 BC72 1906 (79) 11 fig 52
54×48mm; delicately engraved zigzags; pin missing.

349 BWB83 3100 (285) 11 fig 52
c.57×*c*.55mm; angled frame; bar incomplete; worn offcentral notch for missing pin.

Lead-tin

The following small buckles seem to have been for shoes; no. 353 survives on one (cf Grew and de Neergaard 1988, 75–76) and shoes from elsewhere also retain them (eg Goubitz 1987, 8 fig 11 & 25 fig 31, a shoe from the Netherlands with two

such buckles). They seem to have been used regularly for pattens (open-style footwear in which two leather side elements are joined by straps across the instep) – an example in the Museum of London's established collections retains one (see Waterer 1946, pl 1 no. 12), and several pattens found recently in Bruges have surviving buckles of this form (eg Goubitz 1988, 153–58 figs 109/5, 110, 110 bis, 111, 114 & 114 bis; none of those found recently in London has a double buckle – bent nails seem to have been used fairly commonly there as a makeshift alternative, and a buckle of plain-circular form survives on an example from the BOY86 site – acc. no. 422). Thanks to Olaf Goubitz for discussion of this point.

Analysis of nos. 350–51 and 362 indicates they are of pewter (AML, lead-tin MLC). Pins are of iron wire; wear is on frame, from the pin. Most of these buckles have symmetrical loops, but in nos. 354 and 357 they differ slightly.

53   Double oval lead/tin shoe buckles (1:1)

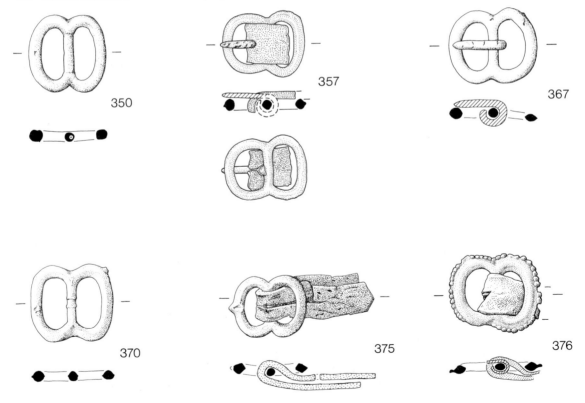

350

357

367

370

375

376

plain frames (for shoes)

(see fig 53 for nos. 350, 357, 367, 370, & 375, fig 19D for no. 354 and fig 19E for no. 356)

	site	acc. no.	context	dimensions (mm)	ceramic phase	pin	wear on frame	comments
350	BWB83	740	306	20×19mm	11	missing	+	bar narrowed
351	BWB83	5864	305	20×19.5mm	11	missing	on back at side	bar set back
352	SWA81	2990	2101	22×14mm	12	missing		
353	TL74	3432	368	12×15mm	12	+		lipped frame; on vamp of ankle shoe or low boot
			(cf Grew & de Neergaard 1988, 71 fig 105)					
354	SWA81	845	2113	19×16mm	12	missing	+	on leather strap; frame distorted
355	SWA81	2491	2269	c.19+×17mm	12	missing	+	frame distorted
356	SWA81	881	2112	22×17mm	12	(?)missing		frame distorted; parts of both leather straps survive
357	SWA81	2927	2108	22×17mm	12	+		frame obscured; on leather strap
358	SWA81	3533	2108	c.25×17.5mm	12	+	+	distorted; (?)outside loop is almost at a right angle to the other
359	SWA81	3301	2112	20×18mm	12	missing	+	frame distorted & broken; leather from strap survives
360	SWA81	1489	2113	21×18mm	12	+		slightly distorted
361	SWA81	2877	2106	21×18mm	12	missing	+	
362	SWA81	2930	2108	21×18mm	12	incomplete	(?)worn	
363	SWA81	2978	2084	21×18mm	12	incomplete	(?)unworn	on leather strap
364	TL74	2714	275	21×18mm	12	incomplete	(?)unworn	
365	SWA81	894	2102	21.5×18mm	12	missing	+	on leather strap
366	SWA81	1814	2081	21.5×18mm	12	incomplete	+	on leather strap
367	SWA81	3360	2112	22×18mm	12	+	(?)unworn	
368	SWA81	3299	2112	20.5×19mm	12	missing		frame distorted; on leather strap
369	SWA81	3293	2112	21×19mm	12	missing		leather from strap survives
370	SWA81	1475	2113	21.5×19mm	12	missing	+	bar constricted for pin
371	SWA81	981	2112	22×19mm	12	incomplete	(?)unworn	leather from strap survives
372	SWA81	1207	2100	22×19mm	12	missing		leather from strap survives
373	SWA81	835	2107	?×19mm	12	incomplete		frame incomplete
374	SWA81	976	2112	21×19.5mm	12	missing	+	
375	SWA81	850	2102	21×25mm	12	incomplete	+	notch and lip; on leather strap 9mm wide (cut off at both ends)

decorated frame (for shoe)

376 TL74 2013 (275) 12 fig 53
24×20mm; lead (MLC); beaded edge; one loop is narrower than the other; pin incomplete; on quarter from ankle shoe or low boot (cf Grew and de Neergaard 1988, 72–73 figs 106 & 107).

This is the only non-ferrous white-metal buckle which analysis has suggested is made from lead un-alloyed with tin.

larger, decorative strap buckle

377 SWA81 2038 (2101) 12 fig 54
Corroded; 51×39mm; tin frame, tin-coated (?iron) pin (AML); a quadrilobate motif at centre of both edges and flanking opposed tear-and-circle motifs are defined by a raised border; both edges are engrailed; iron pin.

The present appearance may not give an adequate indication of the original decoration.

See no. 344 for similar decorative motifs.

DOUBLE OVAL FRAMES WITH PLATES

Copper alloy

(the plates all have slots for pins, which are of iron wire where they survive)

378 SWA81 acc. no. 2129 (context 2030) ceramic phase 9
17×11.5mm (17×6.5mm); brass frame and plate, the

former tin-coated (AML); as preceding; corroded plate has hole for single rivet; pin missing.

379 BWB83 4557 (274) 9
17×12mm (16×6mm); tin-coated frame, bronze plate (AML); frame has straight edges, with transverse grooving; plate has single iron rivet.

380 SWA81 622 (2051) 9 fig 54
19×12mm (18×7mm); bar projects at sides; frame has tin coating; pin missing; the crude plate has a single iron rivet (MLC).

54 Double oval buckles, and oval buckle with bar lower right (1:1)

381 SWA81 2960 (2050) 9 fig 54
19.5×12mm (16×6mm); bent plate has single offcentred rivet; leather from strap survives.

382 BWB83 5837 (298) 11 fig 54
14×11mm (16.5×6mm); straight edges; plate has holes for single missing rivet; pin missing.

383 BWB83 5816 (305) 11
15.5×11mm (18×5mm); as preceding; leather from strap survives.

384 BWB83 3443 (298) 11 fig 54
17×11mm (21×10mm); gunmetal frame and plate, both with tin coating (AML); as preceding; angled frame has transversely grooved edges; tapering plate has hole for single missing rivet.

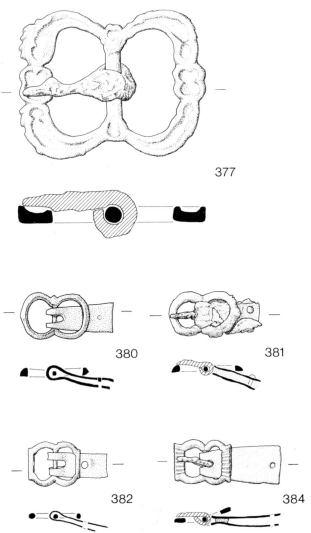

377

380   381

382   384

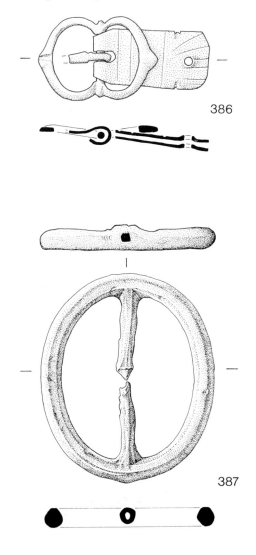

386

387

385 BWB83 5836 (291) 11

15.5×14mm (16×8mm); as preceding item, but no grooves, pin missing and no leather surviving; plate is looped around one of the edges (the buckle could have functioned with the frame in this illogical position, but it is more likely that it was put together in this way as a temporary expedient to avoid loss prior to use or re-use).

The above eight small buckles of distinctive form probably had a specialised purpose. None has been found on an identifiable object. Although they correspond in size with buckles found on shoes, no definite shoe buckle has a plate.

386 BWB83 5813 (298) 11 fig 54

32×21mm (31×16mm); both edges are angled; notch for incomplete (?cast) pin; bar projects at sides; the plate is angled for the frame, with crudely engraved transverse and radiating lines, and paired nicks on each side, with the metal between bent slightly back; tin

coating on frame and plate; hole for the single iron rivet.

OVAL LEAD-TIN FRAME WITH CENTRAL BAR

387 SWA81 acc. no. 2052 (context 2106) ceramic phase 12 fig 54

47×55mm; lead-tin (MLC); corroded bar is broken at (?)constriction for missing pin; a hollow lengthways through the bar suggests that it may have been strengthened internally by a thin, iron rod (as the handles of late-medieval lead-tin spoons sometimes were) – now corroded.

D-SHAPED FRAMES

(frames with similar outlines but with oval apertures are listed under oval frames)

55 D-shaped buckles (1:1)

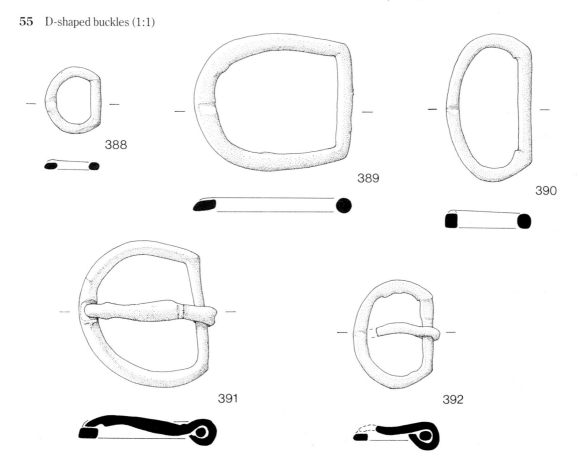

388

389

390

391

392

Copper alloy

388 BWB83 acc. no. 1607 (context 108)
ceramic phase 11 fig 55
15×17mm; notch for missing pin.

389 BWB83 1657 (286) 11 fig 55
42×35mm; notch for missing pin.

390 TL74 349 (414) 11 fig 55
22×38.5mm; notch for missing pin.

391 BWB83 4495 (285) 11 fig 55
Distorted; 33×39mm; notch has become raised at
sides from wear from the cast pin, which has a
transverse ridge and is itself worn from the frame and
strap.

392 BWB83 4423 (313) 12 fig 55
20×27mm; offcentred notch for wire pin, which is
incomplete.

393 SWA81 2942 (2109) 12
Incomplete; 23×36mm; pin missing.

Iron

394 BIG82 2922 (3529) 6
35×32mm; pin incomplete.
Cf BIG82 acc. no. 2800, which is on a stirrup (fig 58).

395 BIG82 2906 (3807) 7 fig 56
17×17mm; frame hollow at back; notch for pin; tin
coating.

396 SWA81 463 (2018) 9 fig 56
23.5×17.5mm; frame has oval aperture and one
straight side, the section varies considerably at different points; like the frame, the pin shows no sign of
finishing after initial shaping by the smith. Thicker parts
of the frame would preclude the pin (which seems to
survive intact) from moving along it to a point where it
could actually reach the opposite edge. The uneven
frame has much in common with that of unfinished

56 D-shaped buckles (1:1)

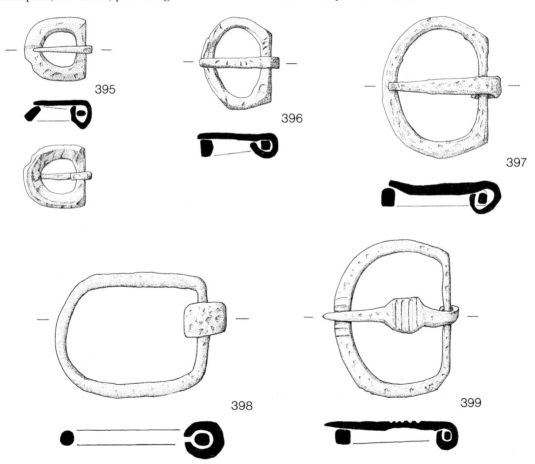

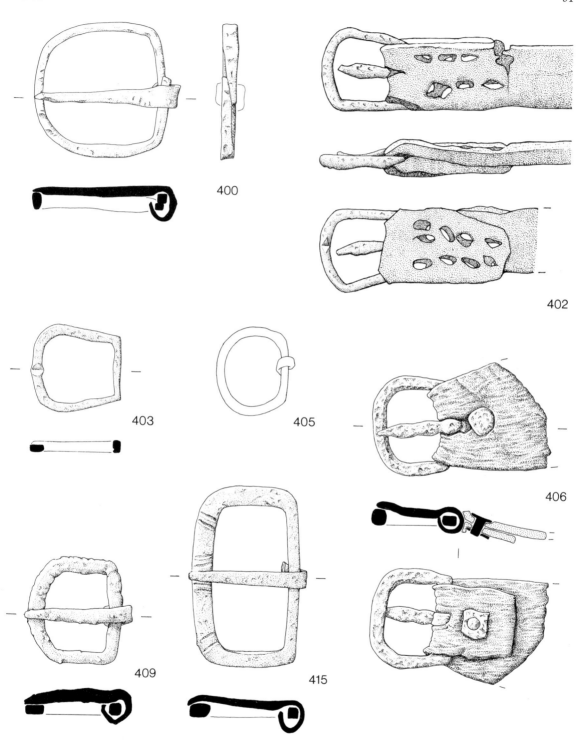

57 D-shaped buckles (1:1)

buckle no. 496. Although the crudeness and apparent impracticability of using it suggest that this present buckle may be unfinished, the attachment of the pin appears to argue against this.

397 SWA81   3943   (2040)   9   fig 56
36×28mm; tin coated; pin bent by strain from strap.

398 BWB83   3095   (274)   9   fig 56
43×33mm; tin coated; pin incomplete.

399 SWA81   3927   (2030)   9 fig 56
32×42mm; pin notch is flanked to each side by two grooves, which retain tin coating (MLC) that has presumably been lost from the rest of the surface; pin has transverse grooves.

400 BC72   4122   (250)   10   fig 57
36×34mm; pin notch is flanked by two grooves to each side; the two original ends of the strip from which the frame was made have not been joined by the smith; tin coating.

The presence of the pin and the coating indicate that this buckle was considered finished.

401 BC72   4116   (88)   11
24.5×22mm; slightly trapezoidal; tin coating; pin missing.

402 BC72   3043   (150)   11   fig 57
c.25×22mm; slightly trapezoidal; notch for (incomplete) pin; on folded leather strap 157×17mm (torn off at other end).

403 BC72   4212   (150)   11   fig 57
24×23mm; slightly trapezoidal; notch for missing pin; tin coating.

404 BC72   2444   (79)   11
Frame slightly irregular in shape; 24×23mm; tin coating; pin missing.

405 TL74   3418   (368)   11   fig 57
24×24mm; tin coating (MLC); pin incomplete; leather from strap survives (drawn from x-ray plate).

406 BWB83   233   (307)   11   fig 57
c.22×25mm; tin coating; attached by rivet with squarish rove to bunched leather up to 29mm wide (not necessarily a strap; torn off at other end).

Perhaps not a dress accessory.

407 BWB83   410   (359)   11
25×26.5mm; slightly trapezoidal; tin coating; pin missing.

408 BC72   722   (39)   11
c.25×26.5mm

409 BWB83   4379   (131)   11   fig 57
24.5×27mm; notch for pin; tin coating.

410 BC72   1774   (55)   11
25.5×29.5mm; frame broken; pin missing.

411 BWB83   3181   (256)   11
29×30mm; pin missing.

412 BWB83   3074   (369)   11
31×37.5mm; pin missing.

413 BWB83   4173   (300)   ?11
37×43mm; tin coating.

414 BWB83   1629   (17)   12
41×43mm; tin coating; pin missing.

415 BWB83   2921   (265)   12   fig 57
29×49mm; oblique grooves in outside edge retain tin coating that has presumably been lost elsewhere.

416 TL74   1143   (275)   12   fig 58
44×49mm; concave sides; notch for missing pin; on leather strap *c*.62×36mm (cut off at other end, with 24 holes, some with surviving iron rivets and copper-alloy roves from missing mounts along the centre; further holes with traces from rivets were to attach the strap to the buckle, and to double the thickness of the leather at the other end; additional decorative strip of leather near buckle).

A second, accompanying leather strap *c*.230×35mm may have been attached to this to make up the complete belt (one end is cut, the other is skived; nine holes along the centre were probably to accommodate the buckle pin).

417 SWA81   3863   (2008)   residual in recently deposited material   fig 58
33×35mm; lipped frame; tin coating (MLC).

418 SWA81   1739   (unstratified)   fig 58
40×41mm; outside edge has grooves flanking notch; pin has transverse ridge; tin coating.

An iron buckle with a D-shaped frame (24×34mm) survives on the strap of a stirrup from a ceramic-phase 7 deposit (BIG82 acc. no. 2800 from context 5221); the frame has a notably deep, rectangular section – see fig 58.

Tin

419 BWB83   2678   (330)   11   fig 58 & colour pl 1E
Distorted, *c*.40×*c*.41mm; tin (AML), with small amount of lead (MLC); beading along sides and outside edge; notch for missing pin; bar is constricted for pin, and is broken at this point.

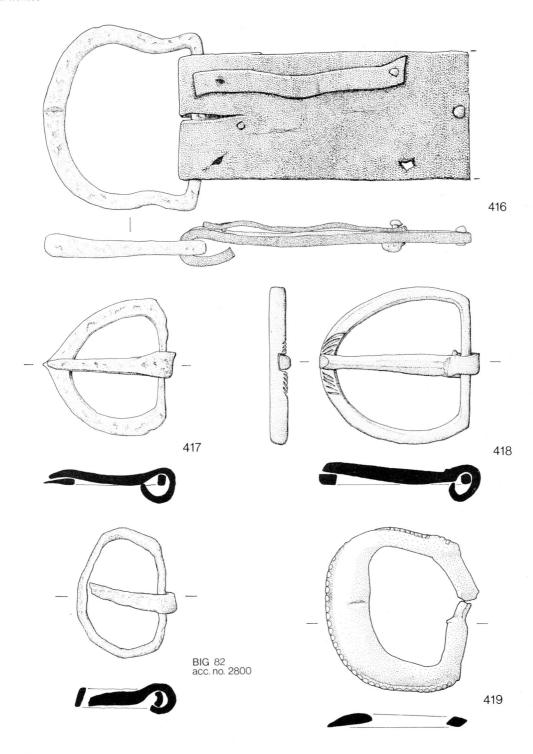

BIG 82
acc. no. 2800

58   D-shaped buckles; stirrup buckle lower left (1:1)

D-SHAPED FRAMES WITH PLATES

Copper alloy

420 SWA81 acc. no. 554 (context 2016) ceramic phase 10 fig 59
13×15mm (plate very fragmentary); wire pin.

421 BWB83 1650 (317) 11 fig 59
21×15mm (28×10.5mm); gunmetal frame, brass plate (AML); collared knop on outside edge (cf lip); ridge at each side near plate; pin missing; plate is recessed for frame, and has slot for pin and holes for single missing rivet – the latter flanked by transverse engraved zigzags.

Cf Hume 1863, pl X no. 6 (nos. 11 & 14 in the same plate are strap-loops of similar design, possibly ensuite fittings or all deriving from the same workshop).

Iron

422 SWA81 2239 (2050) 9 fig 59
30×42mm (29×28mm); pin has transverse ridges, and tip is tapered in the vertical plane; copper-alloy plate is recessed for frame, and has slot for the pin, and holes

for two iron rivets; leather from strap 33mm wide survives.

Lead-tin

423 BWB83 3764 (338) 11 fig 59
12.5×15mm (23×17mm+); lead-tin (MLC); incomplete and corroded copper-alloy plate has holes for missing pin, and for the one surviving rivet.

D-SHAPED FRAME WITH CENTRAL BAR AND PLATE

Copper alloy

424 BWB83 acc. no. 339 context (309) ceramic phase 12 fig 59
15×12mm (10×15mm); frame has curved profile; bar and outside edge are separate rods, the latter having a sheet roller; plate has slot for pin (which is missing) and single rivet; tin coating on all parts; leather from strap survives.

This is the only D-shaped frame among the recent finds in which the inside edge is the curved one.

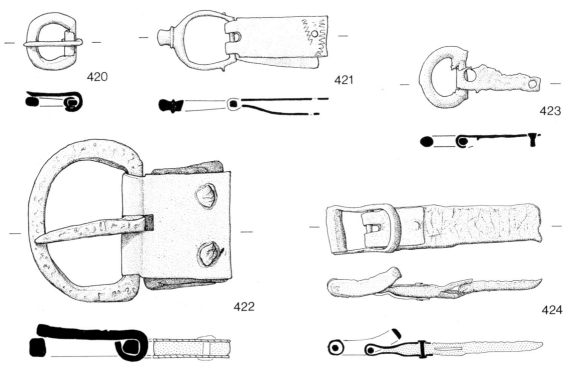

59 D-shaped buckles with plates (1:1)

RECTANGULAR AND SUBRECTANGULAR FRAMES

Copper alloy

425 TL74 acc. no. 2138 (context 416)
ceramic phase 11 fig 60
17×30mm; pin notch (filing for this has left a slight notch at a corresponding point on the bar); sheet pin.

426 BWB83 5866 (298) 11 fig 60
20×19.5mm; frame is bevelled; outside edge is narrowed for sheet roller; file marks on frame and sheet pin.

427 BWB83 5868 (298) 11
Slightly trapezoidal; 16×26mm; (?engraved) grooves in thick outside edge; notch is worn by wire pin; bar narrowed.

This buckle probably originally had a plate – cf nos. 435 & 436.

Iron

428 BWB83 3142 (269) 9 fig 60
42×41mm; tin coating; sides are looped at the ends for the solid roller.

Cf Ward-Perkins 1940, 277 & pl LXXIX nos. 1 & 2, identified as harness buckles.

This heavy-duty form, which would have required a high level of skill to manufacture, seems to have lasted unaltered into the post-medieval period. A more detailed consideration of similar buckles will appear in a volume on horse equipment (Clark forthcoming).

429 BWB83 353 (147) 11
27×21mm; tin coating.

430 BC72 2409 (83) 11 fig 60
15×24.5mm; tin coating.

431 BC72 1825 (67) 11
30×40mm; pin missing.

432 BWB83 3941 (310) 12 fig 60
15×20mm; tin coating; sheet roller; pin missing.

433 SWA81 923 (2102) 12
19×28mm; tin coating.

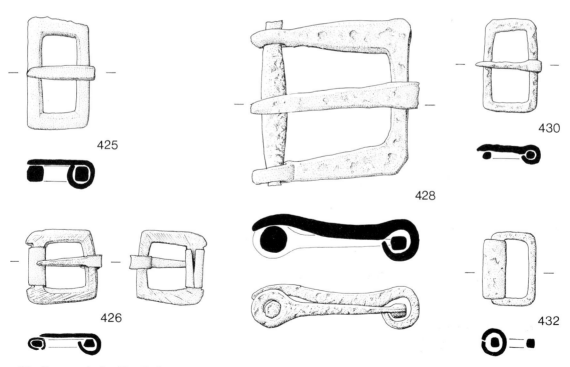

60 Rectangular buckles (1:1)

RECTANGULAR AND SQUARE FRAMES WITH PLATES

Copper alloy

434 BWB83 acc. no. 4425 (context 317 area) ceramic phase 11 fig 61
14×12mm (25×9.5mm); brass plate and frame (AML); thick outside edge has three (?)filed grooves on back and front; bar narrowed; plate is recessed for frame and has slot for missing pin, and holes for the single rivet.

435 BWB83 4589 (285) ?11 fig 61
14×13mm (26+×9mm); bronze frame, gunmetal plate (AML); frame is slightly trapezoidal; five filed grooves

on outside edge; pin missing; plate is recessed for frame, has holes for the pin, and is broken off at a probable rivet hole. Assembled with the decorated front of the frame placed so as to be on the same side as the narrower (unrecessed) back of the plate.

436 BWB83 1938 (308) 11 fig 61
14×14mm (23×11mm); brass frame and plate (AML); thick outside edge has notch for the wire pin, which is folded in a U (ie not fully looped) around the bar, and may be a replacement; tapering plate is recessed for frame and has holes for the pin and for a single missing rivet.

437 BWB83 1417 (279) 11 fig 61
14×13mm (24×17mm); frame has slightly convex sides, with a ridge near each corner; thick outside edge

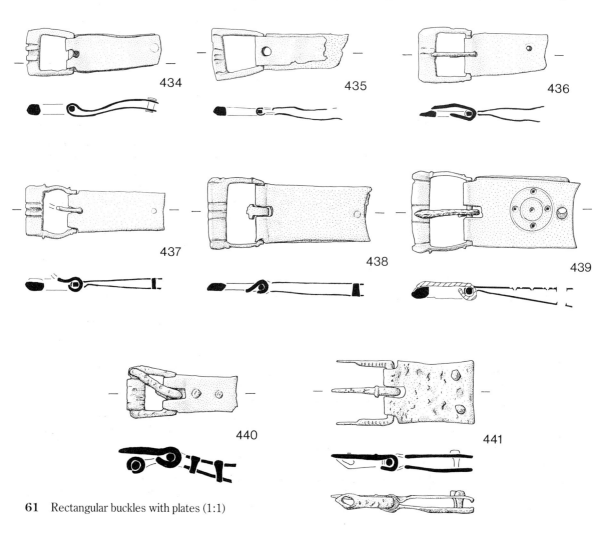

61 Rectangular buckles with plates (1:1)

has three filed grooves; bar offset and narrowed; plate is recessed for frame, and has slot for incomplete wire pin, and holes for single rivet.

438 BWB83 5904 (298) 11 fig 61
16×18mm (32×15mm); as preceding item, but frame has five filed grooves, incomplete cast pin has side flanges, and plate has concave inside edge; leather from strap survives.
Cf Palmer 1980, 183 fig 23 no. 12, excavated in Oxford.

439 BWB83 277 (204) 11 fig 61
17×21mm (31×18mm); frame as for preceding item, except bar not offset; iron-wire pin; plate as for preceding item, with two concentric compass-engraved circles and five drilled holes.

Cf folding clasps nos. 551–59 for the shape of the frames of the three preceding items.

Iron

440 SWA81 684 (2072) 9 fig 61
13×13mm (20×10mm); outside edge is narrowed for grooved sheet roller; plate has slot for wire pin, and two rivets; tin coating; leather from strap survives.

441 SWA81 506 (2018) 9 fig 61
Frame and pin distorted (shape restored in fig); 16×17mm (25×16mm); hole in each side for missing solid roller; transverse grooves on sides retain tin coating (present, though worn, on rest of surface); pin has flanged transverse ridge; plate is recessed for frame, with slot for pin, and two dome-headed rivets.

RECTANGULAR AND SQUARE FRAMES WITH CENTRAL BARS

Copper alloy

442 BWB83 acc. no. 1916 (context 209)
ceramic phase 9 fig 62
33×28.5mm; brass frame (AML); bar offcentred; bevelled sides and edges; bar and frame worn by missing pin.

443 SWA81 1809 (2081) 9 fig 62
Corroded; 26×34mm; edges each have four deep rabbets, with lengthways and transverse paired grooves (?filed) across the thicker areas; bar and pin missing; the frame is curved in profile and has broken.

Despite its relative heaviness, the narrowness at

some points means that the frame was not correspondingly robust.

There is a buckle of similar form but different size in the Boymans-van Beuningen Museum in Rotterdam (acc. no. F6996).

444 TL74 2137 (416) 11 fig 62
17×15mm; pin missing.

445 BWB83 2728 (329) 11 fig 62
20×16mm; bronze frame (AML); seven (?)filed grooves on outside edge; flanges for strength on sides next to holes in frame for separate, offcentred bar (missing); pin missing.

Similar buckles from London (fig 62, private collection), and Meols (Hume 1863, pl IX no. 7) retain a combined pin and bar. The frame is similar to those of the 'locking buckles' with a curved arm (absent from the recent finds assemblages), though it lacks the groove in the outside edge by which the arm was held closed (cf Ward-Perkins 1940, 279–80 & pl LXXVII nos. 11 & 12). The arm was presumably to hold a purse or knife.

446 BC72 1724 (55) 11
33×30mm; bevelled edges and sides – the latter are slightly concave; a rectangular tab on lower side has a central hole; iron pin; the tab's aperture is worn internally at the lower left corner; on leather strap of varied width (up to 21mm at one point – which is 4mm wider than the aperture of the buckle frame) and 153mm long (torn off at other end). An accompanying piece of strap (presumably the other end of the attached length) is *c*.265mm long (crudely cut at one end, torn off at the other).
Cf no. 457 (from the same deposit), which has a plate.

447 BC72 5323 (55) 11 fig 62
Frame slightly concave on all sides; 42×41mm; gunmetal frame (AML); crude, multiply engraved oblique lines within single-line borders engraved on sides and edges; pin missing.

448 TL74 3424 (368) 12 fig 62
21×18mm; incomplete iron pin (MLC); on vamp of shoe (of indeterminate style).
This seems to be the only rectangular-frame buckle, and the only one of copper alloy, known surviving on a medieval shoe (Olaf Goubitz, pers. comm.). It may have been transferred from another item.

449 TL74 2156 (368) 12 fig 62
Broken and distorted; 32×35mm; brass frame (AML); the corners and bevelled; notch for (?)wire pin.

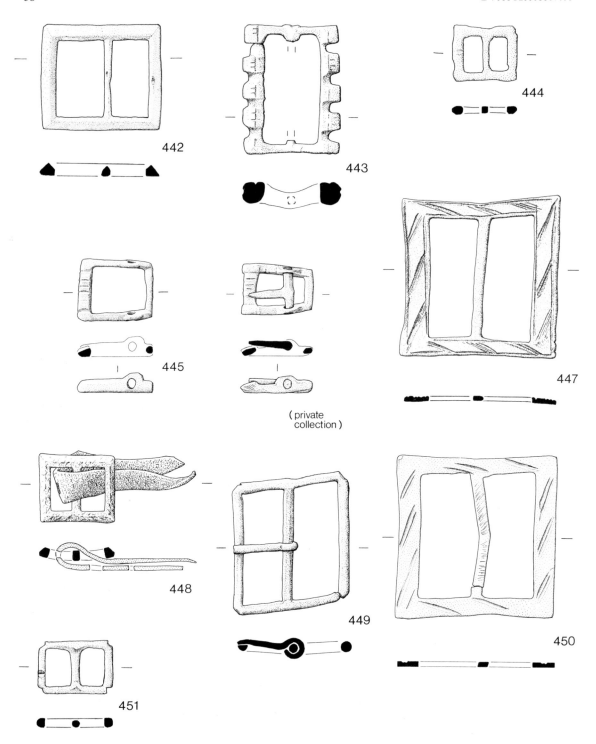

442

443

444

445

(private
collection)

447

448

449

450

451

62   Rectangular frames with central bars (1:1)

450 BWB83 5867 (310) 12 fig 62
43×43mm; paired oblique engraved lines along the slightly concave sides and edges; the bar is prominently filed, and has been bent and broken.

451 SWA81 851 (unstratified) fig 62
20×14mm; bronze frame (AML); bar set back; each corner has a right-angled rabbet; offcentred notch for missing pin.

See no. 459, and on no. 461, both of which have plates.

Lead/tin

452 SWA81 1837 (2117) 12 fig 63
19×19mm; lead-tin (MLC); frame bevelled towards centre; bar slightly bent by pressure on strap; iron pin.

453 SWA81 1995 (2108) 12 fig 63
22×22mm; as preceding; lead-tin (MLC); bar has constriction for missing pin.

454 TL74 2159 (274) 12 fig 63
As preceding item, bar broken; pewter (AML).

455 SWA81 3032 (2103) 12 fig 63
Slightly distorted; 26.5×22.5mm; lead-tin (MLC); trefoil motif at each corner; sides obliquely hatched; bar and frame worn by (missing) pin.

456 BWB83 5094 (unstratified) fig 63
Distorted and broken; *c*.17×14mm; lead-tin (MLC), tin (AML); bar offcentred; pin missing.

RECTANGULAR FRAMES WITH CENTRAL BARS AND PLATES

Copper alloy

457 BC72 acc. no. 1511 (context 55)
ceramic phase 11 fig 63 & colour pl 1G
37×38mm (25×20mm); gunmetal frame (AML); bevelled edges and sides, pin notch; a rectangular tab on the lower side has a central hole, which has not been fully trimmed of excess metal from the mould; the iron pin is incomplete; iron plate has slot for pin, and holes for two iron rivets; tin coating on all these parts; portion of leather strap 19mm wide survives, with two iron mounts (no. 907).

Cf no. 446 (from the same deposit), which has the same form of frame, and is attached directly to the strap without a plate. The tab was probably to hold a sword – in the present example it does not appear to have been used.

458 SWA81 1490 (2113) 12 fig 63
Slightly distorted; 27×21mm (18×14mm); frame has curved profile at centre; quarter-circle rabbet at each corner; bar set back from sides; incomplete sheet pin is bent and has transverse grooves; plate has slot for pin, and holes for two incomplete (?iron) rivets; tin coating on all parts (MLC); leather from strap survives.

459 SWA81 3338 (2106) 12 fig 63
27×30mm (17×*c*.24mm); rabbet at each corner of frame; notch for missing pin; bar notched at edge for pin loop; incomplete plate has slot for the pin, and holes for two missing rivets; leather from strap survives.

Iron

460 SWA81 4354 (2082) 12 fig 63
Very corroded – described and drawn from x-ray photograph; 26×26mm (*c*.17×*c*.17mm); plate with (?)two rivets; on leather strap *c*.285×15mm (other end torn off), (?)fastened on the buckle so that the strap makes a loop *c*.240mm in diameter.

461 TL74 3344 (368) 12 fig 63
Corroded; 31×31mm (18×18mm); concave sides, and quarter-circle rabbet at each corner; (?)filed transverse lines on sides; bar slightly narrowed; curved profile at centre; slightly trapezoidal plate has tin coating (MLC), with slot for pin, and two rivets; on leather strap 56×19mm (torn off at other end – an accompanying piece of leather is *c*.240mm+ in length).

See Stothard 1876 (pl opposite p 164) showing the effigy of the Earl of Warwick (died 1439), whose breastplate is attached by a simple rectangular buckle with rabbets at the corners. Buckles with a curved-profile frame sometimes survive on armour, eg to attach the tasset (the protection for the thighs and lower trunk).

TRAPEZOIDAL FRAMES

(several frames that are marginally trapezoidal are listed with rectangular examples)

Copper alloy

462 BWB83 acc. no. 2746 (context 351)
ceramic phase 11 fig 64
19×17.5mm; bevelled outside edge; pin missing; unworn, possibly unused.

463 BWB83 5868 (298) 11
16×26mm; outside edge grooved and worn at pin notch; bar narrowed; wire pin.

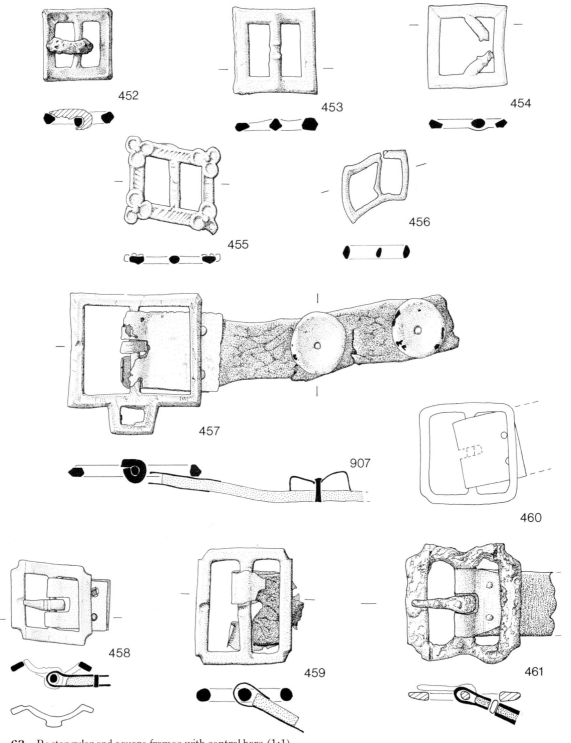

63   Rectangular and square frames with central bars (1:1)

464 BWB83 1906 (79) 11
54×48mm; pin missing.

465 BWB83 1926 (313) 12 fig 64
28×19mm; brass (AML); pin notch; bar has constriction for (missing) pin.

TRAPEZOIDAL FRAMES WITH CENTRAL BARS

Copper alloy

466 BC72 acc. no. 1822 (context 81) ceramic phases 10–11 fig 64
58×42mm; pin notch; bar has constriction for (?)cast pin, which has been bent by pressure on the strap.

467 BWB83 4431 (317 area) ?11 fig 64
21×19mm; gunmetal frame and roller (AML); narrowed outside edge with sheet roller; bar has constriction for missing pin.

468 TL74 2139 (1956) 11
As preceding item; roller missing.

469 SWA81 3208 (2103) 12 fig 64
21×20.5mm; incomplete iron pin.

The pin appears to have been added the wrong way round relative to the wider of the two apertures (cf no. 467).

470 TL74 1283 (1457) 12 fig 64
Distorted; 72.5×44.5mm; three lobed projections on engrailed outside edge; notch for pin; offcentred bar has constriction for missing pin.

The pin would have been *c*.60mm long.

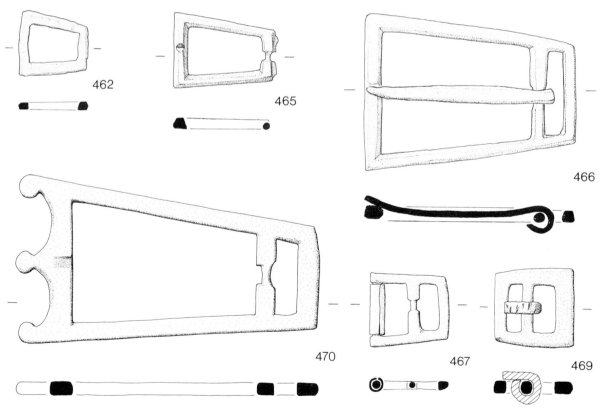

64 Trapezoidal buckles (1:1)

FRAMES WITH CENTRAL BARS – OTHER SHAPES

Copper alloy

471 TL74 acc. no. 636   (context 453)
ceramic phase 12   fig 65
Incomplete; 58×70mm; concave sides and edges, engraved with opposed, oblique lines (herringbone pattern); raised quatrefoil-like motif at each corner; bar broken off; pin missing.

A complete example 52×64mm in the Salisbury and South Wiltshire Museum retains its sheet pin, and has a notch for this in the frame (Saunders 1986, 8 top line right; acc. no. SD537).

472 TL74 2650   (368)   12   fig 65
28.5×30mm; inside loop is rectangular, larger outside one is oval, with pin notch; bar narrowed in centre for missing pin.

Cf Geddes 1985 (197–98 nos. 15–19), Oakley 1979 (251 & 253 fig 108 no. 24), M Henig in Sherlock and Woods 1988 (181 no. 14 & 183 fig 55), and Henig and Woods ibid (211 no. 24 & 212 fig 68), and for iron Continental examples Fingerlin 1971 (191, 334 & 343 figs 321 & 323 nos. 65 & 74).

Another buckle of this form found in London (fig 65, MoL acc. no. 85.378/1) retains the leather strap, which is attached by being folded around the rectangular part of the frame and secured by two rivets through the two thicknesses to a rectangular bar-mount – the frame would thus appear as worn to be of simple oval form unless examined closely. The recent discovery of a similar buckle in situ on a leather girdle in a late-medieval burial at Merton Priory in Surrey may, when the bones have been analysed, provide an indication of the sex of the wearer (Greater London Archaeology Dept, Museum of London MPY86 acc. no. 344; the belt also has three iron sexfoil mounts).

DECORATIVE LEAD/TIN FRAMES WITH CENTRAL BARS OF IRON

(none of the bars or pins survives)

473 BWB83 acc. no. 2111   (context 290)
ceramic phase 9 (?intrusive item in earlier deposit) fig 65
29.5×26mm; lead-tin (MLC); opposed pairs of raised tear shapes with triangular recesses between form the frame edges; a hollow cylindrical housing for the bar protrudes on each side.

Cf Ward-Perkins 1940 (pl LXXVIII no. 6), Fingerlin 1971 (185 & 397, fig 306 no. 286), and for the decorative motif, eyelet no. 1219.

In view of the date of the following two buckles, and the early 15th-century eyelets and strap-ends with similar designs (see on possible ensuite fittings p 246), this is probably an intrusive early 15th-century buckle.

474 SWA81 1212   (2100)   12 fig 65
Incomplete; 14×27mm; lead-tin (MLC); right-angled rabbet at each corner; frame curved in profile at centre; broken at holes for bar.

See on no. 461.

475 SWA81 1094   (2100)   12   fig 65
Somewhat worn; 29.5×30mm; tin (AML/MLC); frame curved in profile at centre; raised sinuous lines define plain and cross-hatched areas on the edges; a cylindrical housing for the bar projects on each side; the decorative modelling, which emphasises the division between the frame and the bar, continues on the back.

Marshall and de Reuck illustrate a similar buckle with a decorated plate (1989, 6 – fourth row, right).

LEAD/TIN BUCKLES WITH INTEGRAL HOLLOW PLATES

This early 15th-century group is defined by the hollow plate, which is cast together with the frame. The frames are highly decorative, and of various shapes. Only one pin (also of lead/tin, on no. 480) survives, though parallels have them of iron wire (possibly replacements). Some of the frames are of lead-tin alloys, while others gave no reaction when tested for lead.

476 SWA81 acc. no. 846   (context 2113)
ceramic phase 12   fig 66
17×18mm; lead-tin (MLC); rectangular frame; concave bevelling on the sides is interrupted by a ridge; two projecting loops to hold the (missing) separate bar are broken; two rivets; leather from strap survives.

477 SWA81 3297   (2112)   12   fig 66
Frame fragmentary; 17×32mm; tin (AML); plate has concave end, two rivets, and hole for missing pin; cylindrical housing for the separate iron bar protrudes at the sides; leather from strap survives.

478 SWA81 1072   (2100)   12   fig 66
Frame fragmentary; 21×20mm; tin (AML); plate has concave end; outside edge is recessed and has cylindrical housing for separate iron bar; the frame has broken off

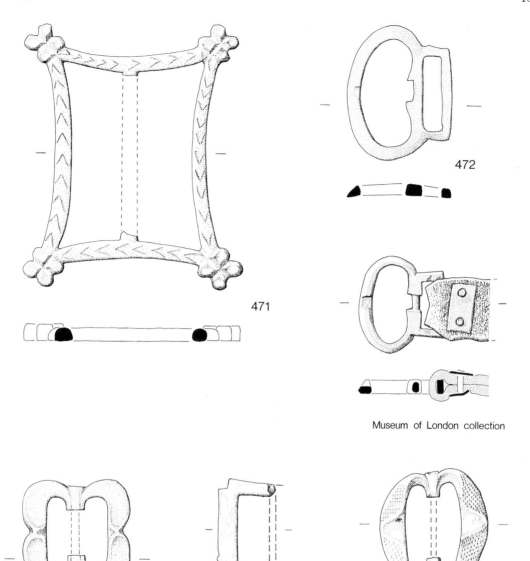

471

472

Museum of London collection

473 474 475

65 Ornate frames with central bars – various shapes,
including frames with iron bars (1:1)

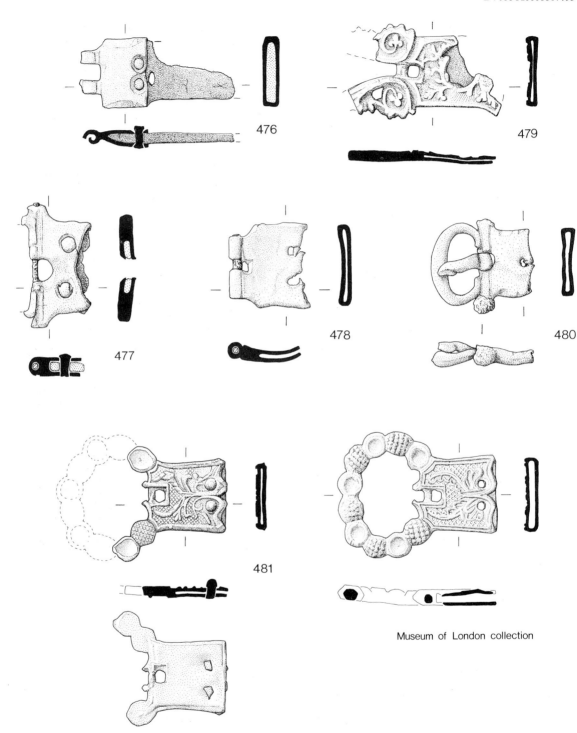

66   Ornate lead/tin buckles with integral hollow plates
      (1:1)

Museum of London collection

and the holes for the two missing rivets have been torn open.

479 SWA81 1960 (2117) 12 fig 66
Fragment; 41×24mm; tin (MLC); surviving part of frame has voluted trefoils and irregular ridged sides; plate has concave surviving side, and foliate motif on hatched field, all within a raised border line.

480 SWA81 3612 (unstratified) fig 66 &
colour pl 1F
27×24mm; high-tin alloy with some lead (MLC), tin (AML); loop of ovoid frame is discontinuous; plate has bevels at the sides and holes for a single rivet – the hole at the front has been torn open; a cylindrical housing for the iron bar protrudes at the sides. This is the only buckle from the recent excavations which retains a pin of lead/tin alloy.

481 TL74 1394 (2184) unphased fig 66
Incomplete; 33×21mm; pewter (AML); similar to other more complete London finds (Ward-Perkins 1940, 270 fig 85 no. 5, 273 & pl LXXVI no. 3; Fingerlin 1971, 381 fig 441 no. 187, also Roach Smith 1857, fig 26, 5; another in a private collection retains an iron-wire pin). Minor variations indicate that each frame is from a different mould. The parallels show that the frame would have been circular, originally *c*.45×*c*.33mm, consisting of alternate cross-hatched convex and plain concave roundels; the elaborately shaped plate has a plant motif on a cross-hatched field; two dome-headed rivets survive on the present example; the conceit that the one-piece plate has been assembled from separate pieces of sheeting (as in copper-alloy buckles with composite rigid plates) has been carried onto the back, where a raised area suggests a separate piece of sheeting.

All six buckles in this early 15th-century series from the recent excavations are in some way broken, though other examples which are complete are known from London (see parallels for no. 481). The continuing attempts of the Girdlers' Guild to outlaw fittings of what they saw as inferior metals (see p 18f) could well have been intended, in part at least, to try to keep non-robust items of just this kind off the market. The hollow plate may have derived from those on the series of copper-alloy buckles with composite plates from the mid 14th and early 15th centuries (nos. 322 etc). The imitation of composite elements in some of these buckles (nos. 480 & 481) may have been intended to suggest to the customer at the time of purchase that they were actually higher-quality composite versions (in this respect the former item misled

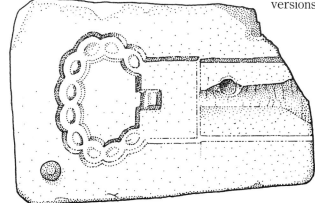

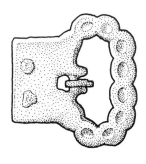

private collection

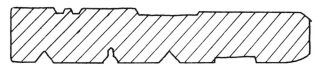

67 Stone mould and possible product, both found in Salisbury (private collection – 1:1)

finds staff making an initial assessment of the method of construction).

A few buckles of this series have been found outside London. Some have been recovered in Salisbury (private collection, fig 67) and one was discovered in Bruges in Belgium (Vandenberghe 1988, 169 top line left). Similar, highly decorative forms are known in copper alloy and silver (eg AR Goodall 1981, 67–68 fig 66 no. 11; Fingerlin 1971, 169 no. 385, 318 no. 36, and also 167 no. 1 – on a baldrick with a horn in Aachen, Germany). The series probably continued in fashion beyond the period covered by this present volume.

Part of a stone mould for making buckles of this category has been found in Salisbury (private collection – fig 67). It has a shallow slot at the base for an insertion (presumably a block of metal) which would have projected into the area of the plate to make it hollow. (The other side of the mould was for producing circular buckles of d 19 to 40mm – the latter with a central bar – none of the buckles it would have produced is precisely paralleled among the recent London finds).

BUCKLES OF VARIOUS FORMS, WITH INTEGRAL, BEVELLED PLATES

In all these buckles the dimensions are for the complete object (frame and plate together). The plate has a single hole for the pin – all those that survive are of iron wire. Riveting arrangements are varied, and often markedly crude – a possible pointer to reuse or a need for repair in the majority of these distinctive buckles.

Copper alloy

482 SWA81 acc. no. 2261 (context 2279) ceramic phase 7 fig 68

25×13mm; gunmetal (AML); oval frame; notched lip; bilobed plate has integral rivet with irregular polygonal sheet rove; pin missing; leather from strap 8mm wide survives.

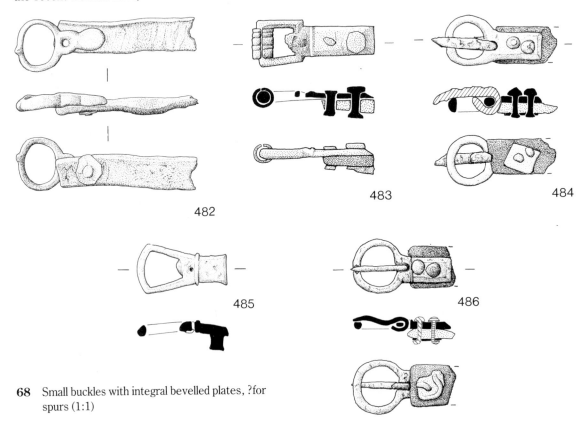

482   483   484

485   486

68 Small buckles with integral bevelled plates, ?for spurs (1:1)

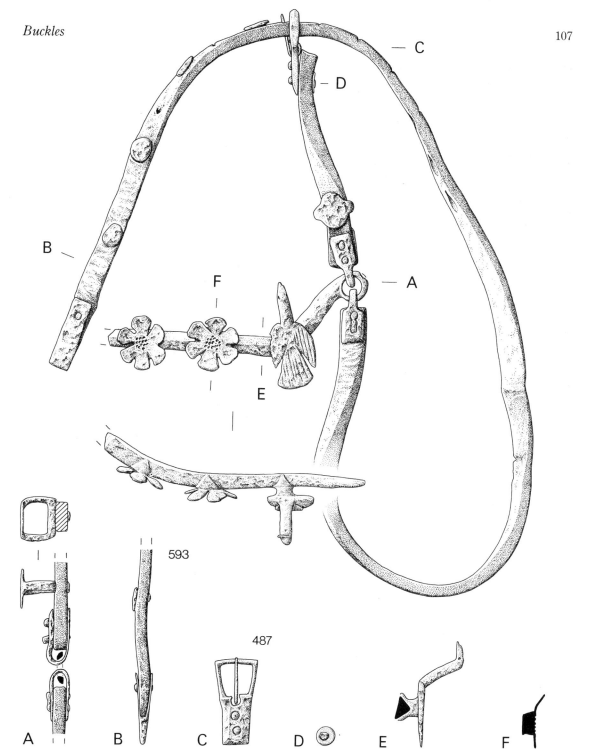

69 Spur and strap: (A) connectors and strap loop,
(B) strap-end, (C) & (D) buckle and rove,
(E) & (F) decoration on spur (1:1)

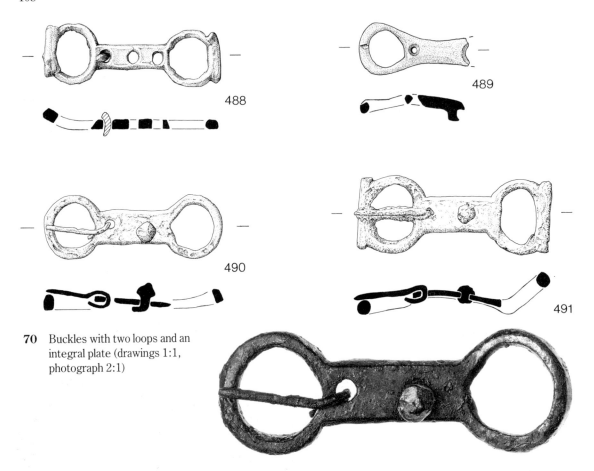

488

489

490

491

70 Buckles with two loops and an integral plate (drawings 1:1, photograph 2:1)

Iron

483 SWA81 3393 (2141) 9 fig 68
32×12.5mm; slightly trapezoidal frame; grooved sheet roller; plate has a transverse ridge and two rivets – one with a very large head and an (?)iron rove; tin coating on all these parts; pin incomplete; leather from strap survives.

484 SWA81 626 (2051) 9 fig 68
25×13mm; circular frame; plate has two dome-headed copper-alloy rivets, which share a rectangular copper-alloy rove; tin coating on frame, plate and rivet heads (MLC); leather from strap 9.5mm wide survives.

485 SWA81 780 (2051) 9 fig 68
24×13mm; trapezoidal frame; plate has transverse ridge and single rivet; pin is corroded and incomplete; tin-coating.

486 SWA81 2874 (2070) 9 fig 68
26×13mm; circular frame; pin notch; plate has transverse ridge and two dome-headed, bent tacks, one of

which is of copper alloy and the other of lead/tin – these share an irregular-shaped rove; tin coating on plate and pin; on leather strap 36×10mm (torn off at other end).

487 BC72 3664 (250) 10 fig 69C
On a spur strap: 22×12mm; frame is slightly trapezoidal, and the sides are continuous with the plate (offset at the bevel); two dome-headed rivets with roves; tin coating; the pin has apparently broken or worn through the hole in the plate; on a short, thick strap *c*.57×8mm and 4mm thick (for accompanying strap-end, see no. 593).

The small buckles of this 13th/14th-century grouping probably had a special function. The last example, in situ on a spur, is from a deposit possibly later than the other four, but it provides a possible interpretation (favoured by Blanche Ellis – pers. comm.) for the category as a whole. It remains to be seen whether this piece of evidence holds true for future finds of buckles of the series. The strength of the integral plates and frames, relative

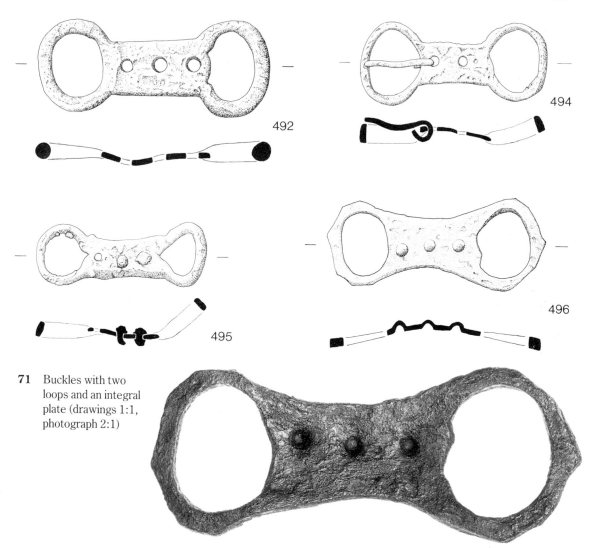

71 Buckles with two loops and an integral plate (drawings 1:1, photograph 2:1)

to their size, suggests that they were designed to stand up to fairly rough use, though the pins are not notably robust.

BUCKLES WITH TWO LOOPS AND AN INTEGRAL PLATE BETWEEN

These distinctive late 13th- to 14th-century buckles must have had a specialised function, which has so far not been identified. The rivets were presumably for attachment to a strap on the reverse. Only one loop was furnished with a pin; the other was either capable of sliding, or it served to hold a strap down

but not immobile. The pin hole is always closer to the buckle loop than the rivet hole is to the other loop. The slightly S-shaped profile of some of these buckles may suggest that they were intended to connect two straps which lay parallel but a little offset from each other. The tinning might point to use outdoors – perhaps on armour or horse equipment (cf AR Goodall 1984, 339). The wire pins are not very robust, so perhaps relatively little strain was anticipated.

The slightly arched section widthways across several of the plates, and the loop lacking a pin are features that can both be compared with the upper parts of some medieval horse curb-bits (eg Ward-

Perkins 1940, 78 fig 18 no. 2), though the conventional buckle loop at the other end of these present items has no obvious function in such an object. The points of similarity may be completely coincidental.

Copper alloy

488 SWA81 acc. no. 514 (context 2020)
ceramic phase 9 fig 70
49×16.5mm; circular loops with straight outer edges which protrude at each side; plate has three holes; tin coating (MLC); an incomplete iron pin or rivet survives.

Cf AR Goodall 1984, 339–40 fig 190 no. 79 for an incomplete copper-alloy example found in Exeter, and reference to another from Scotland.

Iron

489 SWA81 601 (2065) 9 fig 70
Incomplete, one sub-circular loop survives; 30+×14mm; pin notch; plate has two holes (one retaining a rivet) and part of another hole; tin coating (MLC).

490 SWA81 470 (2017) 9 fig 70
49×16.5mm; slightly tear-shaped loops; plate has two holes, one with a faceted, dome-headed rivet, the other with a wire pin; tin coating (MLC).

491 SWA81 2205 (2065) 9 fig 70
51×19mm; oval loops with straight outside edges, which protrude at the sides; plate has two holes, one with a dome-headed rivet, the other with a pin; tin coating (MLC).

492 SWA81 600 (2065) 9 fig 71
64×25mm; oval loops; plate has three holes, with a rivet in the central one; tin coating.

493 SWA81 2090 (2031) 9
Incomplete, one oval loop survives; 33+×17.5mm; plate has one complete hole and part of another; there is a grooved shoulder at the junction of the loop and plate on each side; tin coating (MLC).

494 SWA81 3079 (2025) probably 9 fig 71
51×20mm; oval loops; plate has two holes, one with a wire pin, which is bent by pressure from the strap; tin coating (MLC).

495 BWB83 5239 (343) 11 fig 71
47×17mm; slightly tear-shaped loops; plate has three holes, two with rivets; there is a projection at the junction of the plate and frame on each side; one frame has a notch for the missing pin.

496 BWB83 3413 (308) 11 fig 71
Unfinished; 59×23mm; the oval loops are irregular in

thickness; the plate has three punched depressions, marking where holes were intended to be.
Presumably discarded during manufacture.

PARTS OF BUCKLES

Frame fragment

Tin

497 BWB83 acc. no. 2683 (context 330)
ceramic phase 11 fig 72
Tin (AML), lead-tin (MLC); ornate curved edge of a frame; 41mm+ wide; opposed tendrils, each with two volutes towards the sides; abraded decoration in centre.

This fragment is also published in a study of earlier medieval finds (Pritchard forthcoming, no. 121 fig 3.36). The decoration can be paralleled in both periods, but the position in the chronological sequence and the proliferation of ornate lead/tin buckles towards the end of the medieval era on the waterfront sites may mean that the later dating is more likely.

Buckle plates

Only examples with distinctive features are included – a number of undiagnostic plates and fragments from the usual sites have been omitted.

All the plates are folded, complete, rectangular, recessed for the buckle frame, and with a slot for the pin, unless otherwise stated. They are listed in order of increasing width (ie approximate strap width – second dimension) within ceramic phases. 'Single rivet' here indicates that there was only one originally; 'one rivet' indicates that there is surviving evidence for one, though there may have been others on a missing portion of the plate.

Copper alloy

498 BIG82 acc. no. 3159 (context 4201)
ceramic phase 7
Broken off at fold; 34×12mm; holes for five rivets; engraved zigzags within double lines along sides and outside edge.

499 BIG82 2840 (4105) 7 fig 72 & colour pl 4A
35×12mm; slightly tapering; engraved zigzags along sides and inside edge; holes for five rivets, of which four (of a redder alloy) survive. The rivets are roughly attached, their ends being left ragged by the hammering. They represent reuse/repair of the buckle.

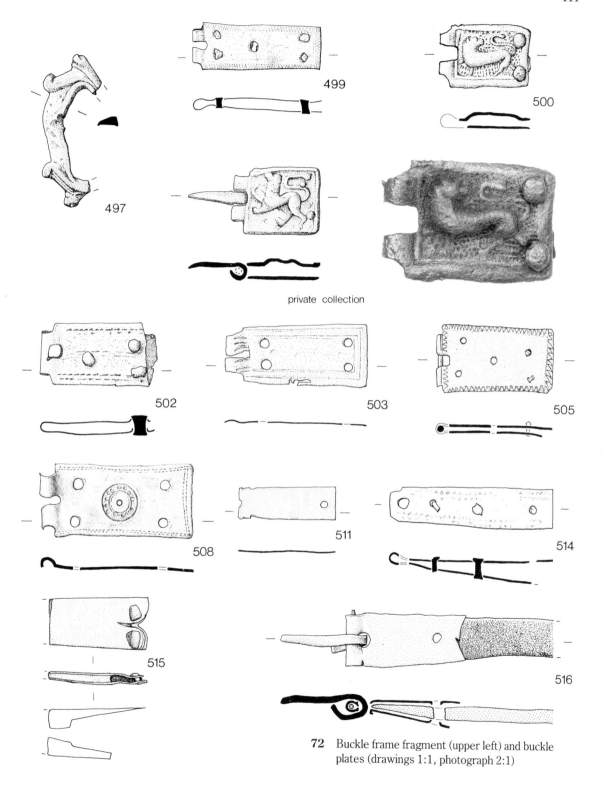

private collection

497

499

500

502

503

505

508

511

514

515

516

72 Buckle frame fragment (upper left) and buckle plates (drawings 1:1, photograph 2:1)

500 BIG82 2719 (4086) 7 fig 72
24×17mm; copper (AML); the design of a lion passant regardant in a raised rectangular linear frame was die-stamped – the stippled field was added by multiple punching; trace of gilding; two dome-headed rivets.

A similar buckle plate from Suffolk, but with the lion guardant, has been erroneously published as a clasp 'probably of 8th-century date' (Hinton 1974, 25–6 & pl VIII no. 20, presumably following Wilson 1964, 109), and another with the lion passant guardant came from a 13th-century context in Norwich (Margeson 1985, 204–05 no. 8). Further examples in private collections from London and elsewhere, and Hume 1863, fig XII no. 25, show that there was a widespread series of these plates with lions in various heraldic stances.

Cf Ramsay in Alexander and Binski 1987 (374 no. 434) for a die stamp of the kind perhaps used for similar plates, but which is slightly larger than the present one.

501 BIG82 2433 (2514) 8
Broken off at fold and then folded again; c.45×13mm; holes for four missing rivets, and central hole which is square; tin coating (MLC).

502 BIG82 2252 (2243) 8 fig 72
31×16mm; end possibly broken off; holes for pin; three double lines of roughly punched, opposed triangles; three roughly hammered and unevenly placed rivets.
A crude item.

503 BIG82 2494 (2596) 8 fig 72
Broken off at fold, and folded in half and at corners of inside edge (shape restored in drawing); c.40×16mm; slightly tapering; recessed for frame; four missing rivets; engraved double lines along sides, inside edge and beside slot for pin.

504 BWB83 1204 (367) 9
Broken off at fold; 28×10mm; slightly tapering; one iron rivet of an original two survives; holes for fragmentary iron (?)pin.

505 BWB83 3206 (260) 9 fig 72
32×17mm; engraved zigzags along perimeter; holes for five rivets; two of which survive; thin bar from frame survives.

506 BWB83 4050 (362) 9
Broken off at fold; c.39×17mm; slightly tapering; trace of double engraved lines along sides; holes for five missing rivets.

507 BWB83 4982 (366) 9
Fragment, 38+×19mm; engraved zigzags around sides and surviving edge; holes for three rivets – the two surviving ones were crudely applied.

508 SWA81 3265 (2141) 9 fig 72
Broken off at fold; 41×20mm; sides and end slightly concave; holes for five missing rivets, the smaller central one being in the middle of concentric double and single compass-engraved circles, with an uneven ring of small punched circles superimposed; double line of opposed, punched triangles along sides and end.

509 SWA81 1240 (2146) 9
39×27mm; brass (AML); worn; front has slightly concave sides; fold torn off on one side; holes for five rivets – two of which survive (one having a domed head) with square roves; double lines of punched rectangles along sides and inside edge.

510 BWB83 2049 (367) 9
Incomplete and broken off at fold; c.30+×28mm; hole for pin; four (?originally five) missing rivets.

511 BWB83 4118 (361) 11 fig 72
26×8mm; broken off at probable hole for pin; slightly tapering, with an expansion at that point; sides slightly bevelled; hole for single missing rivet.

512 BWB83 4231 (359) 11
Fragment of front, 22+×10mm; surviving holes for three missing rivets; engraved zigzags along sides.

513 BWB83 3771 (338) 11
34×10mm; broken off at fold; corners on inside edge cut to an angle; holes for five rivets, one of which survives.

514 BWB83 3741 (338) 11 fig 72
44×10.5mm; holes for pin and three crude rivets; double line of punched, opposed triangles along sides.
The rivets are possibly replacements.

515 BWB83 3718 (348) 11 fig 72
Part of composite buckle with forked spacer (cf nos. 322–30) 27+×13mm; broken off through plate and spacer; biconvex end, with central groove at front; two crudely applied rivets.

516 BC72 3101 (150) 11 fig 72
31×14mm; crude; concave end; two roughly pierced holes for surviving sheet pin; retains bar separated from frame; holes for single missing rivet; leather strap 95×12mm (torn off at other end) survives.

517 BWB83 4114 (361) 11 fig 73
Fragment, 25+×15mm; broken off at fold; surviving holes for two missing rivets; one larger central hole and part of another survive; crudely engraved zigzags along sides and outside edge; the holes are pierced from the reverse, presumably through from the other face that is now missing.

518 BWB83 5280 (341) 11
*c.*28.5×15mm; corroded; broken off at fold; double line of opposed, punched triangles along sides; holes for three rivets – a crude one survives.

519 BWB83 1647 (318) 11 fig 73
24×16mm; 'slot' for pin has irregularly shaped sides, which indicate that it has probably been worn from two original holes; single missing rivet.

520 BWB83 2718 (329) 11 fig 73
Worn; 33×16mm; brass frame (AML); end broken off at front; recessed for frame; holes for pin, and others for five rivets, four of which survive – one with a pointed end (ie a tack) is crudely bent, and the central one holds a sexfoil mount (d 14mm) with concave lobes, roughly engraved, double discontinuous lines along sides.

521 BWB83 5368 (343) 11
22×17mm; in addition to the holes for the two rivets (one of which survives incomplete) there are two larger holes and part of a third.

522 BWB83 2674 (334) 11 fig 73
35×17mm; incomplete; holes for five rivets – the four surviving ones are crudely applied; the zigzag-cut sides and outside edge are defined by straight engraved lines; leather from strap 18mm+ wide survives.

523 BWB83 1971 (318) 11
Broken off at fold; 34×18mm; ?slot for pin; holes for five missing rivets; double line of punched, opposed triangles along sides and end.

524 BWB83 2758 (373) 11
Broken off at fold; 34+×22mm; holes for five missing rivets, and larger central hole.

525 BWB83 2759 (373) 11
*c.*34×21mm; similar to preceding item, but lacks rivet hole at one corner (perhaps not from same original object, despite being from same deposit).

526 SWA81 389 (1031) 11
Corroded; 29×24mm; double line of opposed, punched triangles along slightly concave sides and inside edge; holes for five rivets, the two surviving ones being dome-headed.

527 BWB83 3843 (257) 11
Corroded; 37×24mm; broken off at fold; holes for four rivets (two of which survive) and two further holes near outside edge; engraved zigzags around perimeter.

528 SWA81 1785 (2103) 12
30.5×17mm; concave end has round, grooved aperture; two rivets.
Cf buckles with composite rigid plates (nos. 322–30) and other items referred to there for the grooved aperture.

529 BWB83 5912 (310) 12
Broken off at fold; 39×17mm; discontinuous engraved lines along sides; holes for five missing rivets.

530 SWA81 941 (2102) 12 (? residual in later context) figs 73 & 18B
Broken off at fold; 26×21mm; holes for two missing rivets; decorated, by paring away the metal, with a

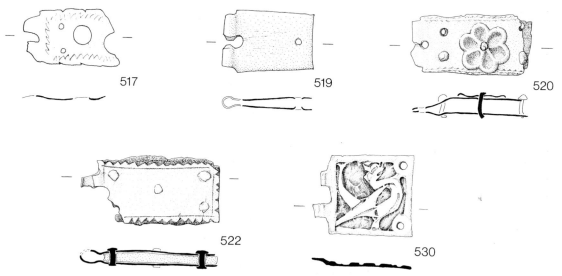

517 519 520

522 530

73 Buckle plates (1:1)

winged, two-legged beast having a dragon-like head
and fish-like tail, with multiple stamping to indicate
feathers or scales. This plate is thicker (over 1mm)
than the others described here, as is appropriate for
the decorative technique. The rough surface of the
areas made lower was presumably for keying enamel
(ie champlevé), though none survives.

Cf Geddes and Carter 1977, 287–88 fig 130 no. 7 – a
13th-century plate decorated with a centaur, excavated
at Kings Lynn. Fingerlin published several buckles with
enamelled frames and plates, as well as some un-
attached plates decorated in this way (1971, 37 & 39
figs 8–21); of these only an openwork plate with a bird
(fig 19) has an English provenance; number 136 (fig
13), a plate with a fantastic bird, dated to the first half
of the 13th century, is closest stylistically to the
London example (though, like all these enamelled
plates illustrated by Fingerlin, it lacks a hole for the pin,
and therefore presumably came from a double-loop
buckle; this form is not represented among the recent
London finds).

Since the Kings Lynn parallel is from a 13th-century
context and the enamelled buckles published by
Fingerlin are regarded as an early group, the present
plate, with decoration that would have been archaic in
the early 15th century, was probably residual in the
context in which it was found.

Iron

531 BWB83 3394 (309) 12
Corroded; 36×24mm; (?)two rivets; tin coating has
some lead present (MLC).

Fragments of plates cut for secondary use

Copper alloy

532 SWA81 acc. no. 3070 (context 2039)
ceramic phase 9 fig 74
28+×24.5mm; one edge cut off and one side apparently broken off; triple engraved irregular lines around
surviving sides and edge; holes for three rivets survive.

533 SWA81 3959 (2030) 9 fig 74
28×8mm; one side cut off, one edge broken off; hole
for one rivet survives; double line of punched, opposed
triangles along edges and surviving side.

Comparanda for plates
(probably not from buckles)

Copper alloy

534 BWB83 acc. no. 1882 (context 317)
ceramic phase 11 fig 74
Fragment; 20+×13.5mm; broken off at possible slot
for pin and at grooved round aperture or hole; roughly
engraved parallel lines divide the sheet into one
rectangular and three triangular fields, the former
having apparently randomly placed, roughly engraved
lines, and two of the latter having engraved zigzags; no
obvious provision for rivets survives.

535 BWB83 5064 (391) 11 fig 74
Incomplete; 23+×15mm; faint double lines of

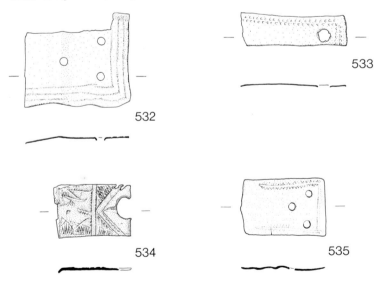

74 Buckle plates cut for re-use
(top row), comparanda for
buckle plates (bottom row);
(1:1)

532

533

534   535

opposed, punched triangles along sides and end; holes for three rivets.

Buckle pins

Only separate cast or cut sheet pins with distinctive features are included here (plain examples less than 35mm in length are omitted, since they are well represented on buckles described above). Tips are pointed, unless otherwise stated. Those with the loop missing or damaged probably broke during use. All are of copper alloy.

sheeting

536 SWA81   acc. no. 1756   (context 2032) ceramic phase 9   fig 75
l 45mm; flat tip.

537 BWB83   4106   (269)   9   fig 75
l 45mm; rounded tip.

538 BWB83   2289   (110)   11   fig 75
l 37mm; flat tip.

539 BWB83   3691   (300)   ?11   fig 75
l 40mm; blunt tip.

cast

540 BIG82   2309   (2498)   9
l 48mm; ridged tip.

541 BWB83   4397   (274)   9   fig 75
Loop incomplete; l 57mm; ridged grip.

542 BWB83   4120   (361)   11
Loop missing; l 36mm; ridged grip.

543 BWB83   4904   (287)   11
Loop missing; l 41mm; ridged grip.

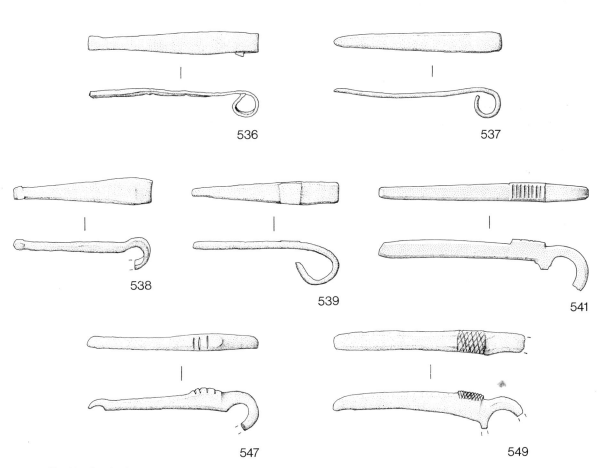

75   Buckle pins (1:1)

544 BWB83 4131 (293) 11
l 41.5mm; loop incomplete; worn by frame near blunt tip.

545 BWB83 2220 (151) 11
Loop missing; l 45mm; ridged grip; blunt tip.

546 TL74 787 (431) 11
Loop incomplete; l 46mm; ridged grip; blunt tip.

547 BWB83 2180 (146) 11 fig 75
l 46.5mm; loop incomplete; ridged, rounded grip, worn by frame near tip.

548 BWB83 2057 (131) 11
l 50mm; ridged grip; worn by frame near tip.

549 BWB83 1446 (389) 11 fig 75
l 52mm; loop incomplete; curving shaft; cross-hatched grip; worn by frame near blunt tip.

550 BWB83 5370 (296) 11
Distorted, l 54.5mm; ridged grip; loop pulled apart; worn against frame near tip.

FOLDING STRAP CLASPS

All the known examples are of copper alloy, with a folded sheet plate, and most have a folding end (both are rectangular unless otherwise stated). The folding ends are recessed for the frame, and often have a separate bar-mount (solid, and secured with a single rivet unless otherwise stated).

The plates are generally more robust than those for buckles, are recessed for the frame, with rivets (single unless otherwise stated) only at the ends and are usually undecorated (the last two points contrast with many plates for buckles). The width range (8–16mm) is markedly narrower than that of buckle plates. Clasp plates do not seem to have been designed to withstand any great strain on the straps, though very few are distorted.

These items are known from contexts from the late 13th/early 14th to early 15th century (ceramic phases 9 to 12). Some, if not all, of them probably functioned together with the shield-shaped strap ends (nos. 732–42, all from ceramic-phase 11 contexts), which also have a bar-mount. For the possible manner of use see fig 76B; cf no. 559 and strap-end no. 738, which respectively have a projection and a corresponding recess at the suggested point of joining. These features are quite unusual among examples of these two categories of fitting listed in this volume, so there may well have been other ways of fixing the clasps.

Simple frames (one piece)

In the following items, unless otherwise stated, the sides of the frame are slightly convex, with a ridge near each corner – traits very similar to

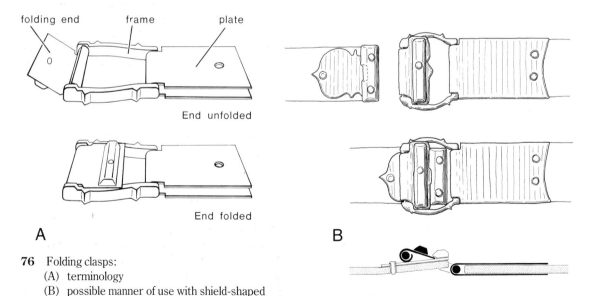

76 Folding clasps:
    (A) terminology
    (B) possible manner of use with shield-shaped strap-end

those on the frames of some of contemporary buckles (cf no. 437 etc).

551 BWB83 acc. no. 1292 (context 124)
ceramic phase 9 fig 77
14×11mm (22×8.5mm); folding end has bevelled bar-mount (cut from a longer piece); plate has bevelled sides and its rivet is cut by a compass-engraved circle that surrounds five drilled holes, four being blind, and the central one is wider and deeper than the others; leather from strap survives.

The cutting of the rivet by the secondary decoration shows that the latter was added after the strap had been attached.

552 BWB83 4531 (276) 9 fig 77
14×14mm (36×10mm); brass frame, plate and bar (AML); frame lacks ridges; folding end is missing; the plate has five drilled holes in an area made slightly convex by filing, and which was originally flanked by a solid bar-mount at each end (each mount being held by a single rivet – one mount survives); a separate internal sheet plate (between the bar-mounts) was presumably to give strength at the points weakened by filing.

553 BC72 4174 (250) 10 fig 77
15×13mm (22×10mm); all parts brass (AML); the incomplete folding end has a central recess, and curved, protruding sides, and a crudely filed ovoid mount; leather from strap survives.

554 BWB83 5197 (298) 11 fig 77
13×8mm (32×6mm); bar-mount has two rivets; plate has bevelled sides.

555 BWB83 3723 (353) 11 fig 77
14×11.5mm (19×9.5mm); plate is of relatively thin sheeting (not bevelled).

556 BWB83 1652 (286) 11 fig 77
14×12mm (8.5×22mm); gunmetal frame, brass plate (AML); folding end has an arch-section bar-mount; plate has concave end.

557 BWB83 2732 (329) 11
31×13mm; as preceding item, but one dome-headed rivet survives, and decoration on plate is discontinuous engraved lines.

558 SWA81 3972 (2006) 12
15×12mm (19×10mm); folding end has a plain bar-mount; plate has slightly concave end; leather from strap survives.

559 BWB83 5815 (310) 12 fig 77
15×20.5mm (28×11.5mm); folding end has a bar-mount and a central angled protrusion on the outside

edge; plate has a concave end at the front and holes for two missing rivets.

Frame, probably from folding clasp

560 BWB83 5869 (298) 11
14×16mm; as basic form for preceding items.

Plates, probably from folding clasps

These lack provision for a pin, but are recessed at the corners of the outside edge, presumably to accommodate frames.

561 SWA81 2744 (2065) 9
Folded; *c*.21×13mm; holes for (?)three rivets, two of which survive.

562 BWB83 2274 (147) 11 fig 77 & colour pl 4B
32×17mm; brass plate, with bronze repair (AML); consists of an original worn plate, with a second piece of folded sheeting added as a repair to the outside edge; the former has holes for a missing rivet; the latter has engraved zigzags and a single surviving rivet, as well as a hole for another on the back only; leather from the strap survives.

The hole lacking a rivet and the decoration on the second sheet may both be from an earlier use.

563 BWB83 5144 (unstratified – from area of the site where phase-11 deposits predominated) fig 77
Slightly corroded; 36×18mm; hint of engraved lines around perimeter; holes for six rivets, of which the two central ones with domed heads survive; leather from strap survives.

The two surviving rivets may be replacements.

Clasps with composite frames

(these have no mount on the folding ends, unless stated otherwise)

564 BWB83 1424 (355) 11 fig 78
Fragment – sheet frame sides and folding end; 4+×11mm; edge of folding end has two V-shaped nicks and oblique, roughly engraved lines which follow this profile within a field defined by a transverse line.

565 BWB83 528 (333) 11 fig 78
14×17mm (22×14mm); brass frame and plate (AML); frame consists of three sides of sheeting and separate

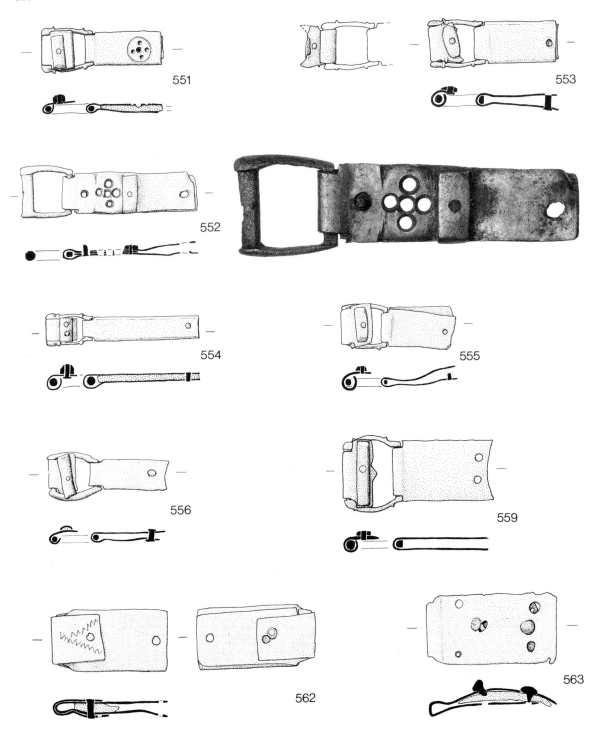

77 Folding clasps (above) and plates from folding
clasps (bottom row) (drawings 1:1, photograph 2:1)

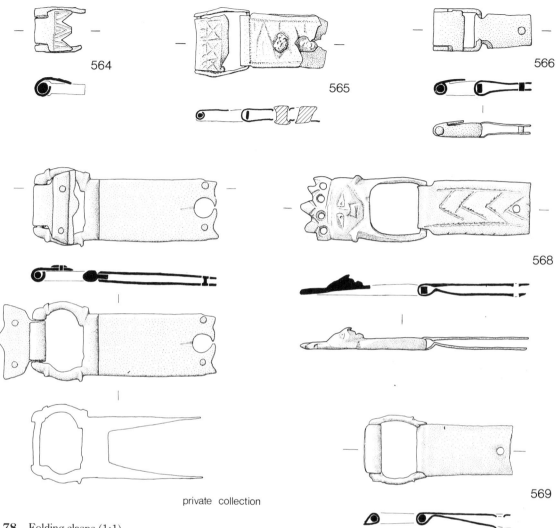

564

565

566

568

569

private collection

78 Folding clasps (1:1)

but fixed roller; the folding end has a crude, engraved cross motif repeated three times within a grid of straight lines with hatching along the outside edge; the incomplete plate has two clumsy iron rivets, and an engraved motif of angled lines and strokes, all in a field defined by discontinuous straight lines along the edges.

The rivets are presumably replacements.

Cf Geddes and Carter 1977 (288–89 fig 130 no. 15) – a frame and plain folding end of the same form.

566 BWB83 5814 (310) 12 fig 78
12.5×11.5mm (16×10mm); the frame is recessed for the plate, and consists of three sides and a separate but fixed roller; the corroded plate tapers, and is recessed

for the frame; folding end has extended recess at each side for the frame.

Cf Fairclough 1979, 126–27 fig 153 no. 8.

Unrepresented among the clasps listed above, but known from three examples found in London (fig 78, private collection) is a form consisting of two sheets attached to a forked spacer, that is comparable to buckles with composite rigid plates nos. 322–30). The shape of the spacer, which is integral with the frame, is in each case simpler than those for the buckles. Two of the plates have round, grooved apertures, which a third example lacks (implying that they date respectively to the late 14th and early 15th centuries – again by analogy with the buckles). The only undamaged example (see fig 78) provides a potential clue to the angle at which the frame might have lain relative to the plate during use. This may be applicable to all the clasps listed above, though the hinged joints could have catered for a variety of different positions.

Folding end

567 BWB83 5907 (303) 11
10×15mm; with bar-mount.

Clasps lacking folding ends

Copper alloy

568 BWB83 5817 (308) 11 figs 16C & 78
34.5×17mm (30×14.5mm); the frame is recessed for the plate; outside edge has an integrally cast crowned head with protrusions at the sides (perhaps for hair), and four holes in the crown; the folded plate is recessed for the frame, has three roughly engraved chevrons in a field defined by a line to each side; the single rivet, possible of iron, is missing.

Further examples of these distinctive, well-made two-part clasps with crowned heads have been found on the site of a medieval village in Lincolnshire believed to have been deserted around the middle of the 14th century (A de Reuck, pers. comm. – see Marshall and de Reuck 1989, 7 IVD), and another found at Dover has raised hands to the sides of the head (all in private collections).

A similar item with a fleur taking the place of the crowned head was found at the SUN86 site (acc. no. 409).

569 BWB83 4434 (unstratified) fig 78
16×18mm (26×13mm); frame and plate brass (AML); ridges on sides near each corner; bar narrowed and outside edge recessed; the plate has a concave end, and a hole for a single missing rivet; sheet roller.

This is similar to the basic form of the most common kind of folding clasps listed above, but instead of the folding end it apparently has a roller.

The precise way in which the two preceding clasps would have functioned is obscure.

OTHER CLASPS

Copper alloy

570 SWA81 acc. no. 1259 (context 2128)
ceramic phase 9 fig 79
Brass (AML); plate 45×17mm, with four dome-headed rivets, one with a rove of irregular shape; double line of opposed, punched triangles around perimeter; a swivelling tab with a D-shaped terminal and bar passes through a hole in the plate, and is held in place by the other end having been hammered like a rivet; leather from strap survives.

571 SWA81 2108 (2065) 9 fig 79
Crude bar-mount 44×17mm, with tab similar to that of preceding item; one of the two rivets has an irregular rove.

The roves on each item presumably indicate repair.

These fittings are probably one element from a form of clasp, the corresponding part of which is not represented among the assemblages from the main sites included here. A strap found in London (fig 79, second from bottom, private collection) has two kinds of mounts and a plate (now broken) at the surviving end, with a central aperture and a swivelling panel which in shape resembles a modern keyhole cover; although this fitting is stylistically distinct from nos. 570 and 571, it provides an indication of the likely corresponding part of this form of clasp. The tab would be inserted through the aperture when the swivelling panel is moved aside, and the D-shaped terminal would keep the two parts together when the panel is returned to a position blocking all the aperture except for the part that accommodates the shaft of the tab (see fig 79, top right). It is not known whether such clasps were for dress or for another purpose.

Iron

572 BC72 3593 (150) 11 fig 79
Possible clasp; 31×10mm; two conjoined, voided circles with T-shaped projection having cable-like decoration (the metal in this area appears to have been abraded subsequent to retrieval); tin coating; fixed by rivet with rove through both arms of a circular notched end tab to skived leather strap (c.51×10mm, with two crude holes, torn off at a possible third).

Presumably a clasp rather than a non-functional strap-end. For accompanying mount of similar form on a second piece of strap, see no. 1102.

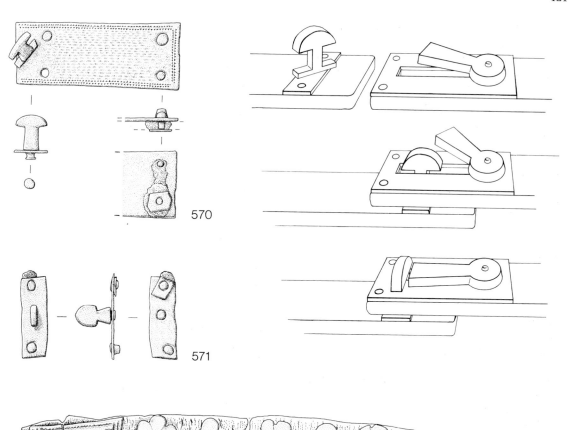

570

571

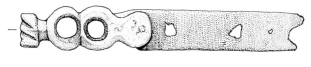

572

79 Clasps: above – locking clasps (left), and suggested manner of joining (right); below – possible clasp (excavated items 1:1, reconstruction not to scale)

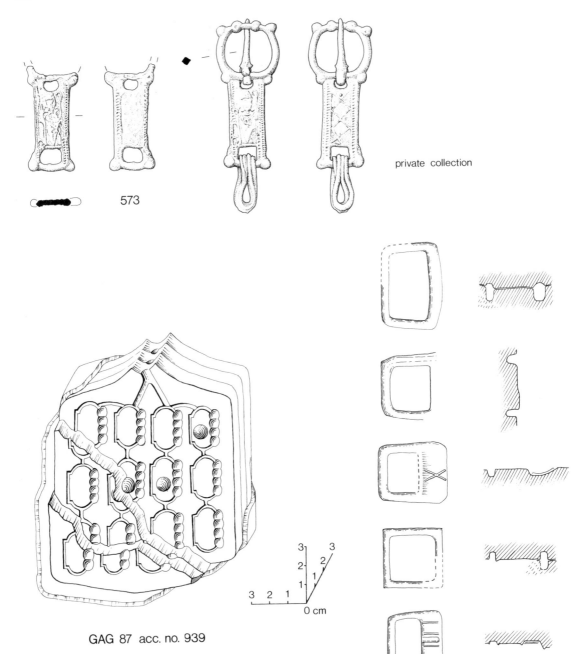

private collection

573

GAG 87 acc. no. 939

OPT 81 acc. no. 87

80 Top row: non functional buckle pendant (left), and
parallel (right); below: reconstruction of ceramic
mould for mass production of one form of buckle
(left), moulds for different forms of buckles cast
together (all 1:1, except mould at left 1:2)

NON-FUNCTIONAL BUCKLE

Pewter buckle souvenir

573 BWB83 acc. no. 3690 (context 300)
ceramic phase ?11 fig 80
Frame (incomplete) and plate cast in one piece,
27×13mm; pewter (AML), lead-tin (MLC); plate has
crude figure of an archbishop facing, holding crozier and
with hand raised in blessing, standing between rows of
hatching; hole for missing pin and larger hole at other
end; knop at each corner; stub of frame survives.

More-complete examples (eg Thames Exchange site
acc. no. 1227, MoL acc. no. 80.70/3, and Mitchener
1986, 32 no. 23) show that the frame would have had
four knops on the outside edge, and the lead/tin alloy
pin would have had side flanges. The backs of the
plates on the parallels have a lozenge design between
hatching similar to that on the front (this is faintly
discernible, though it has not registered well on no.
573). Links of lead/tin chain attached to the hole at the
inside edge of the plates of the unpublished examples
show that these objects were decorative pendants.
They are probably pilgrims' souvenirs from Canterbury
relating to the cult of Thomas Becket. (Together with
other pilgrim souvenirs these will be discussed in detail
in a forthcoming volume).

MANUFACTURING EVIDENCE

This aspect is not discussed in detail here, since
evidence of production in the assemblages found
on the main sites included in this volume is
relatively scanty. Only one iron buckle among
those listed above, no. 496, seems to have been
discarded unfinished and in a state in which it
could not be used. Others appear unfinished in
minor ways, but probably were used, as the
presence of pins implies – nos. 396 and 400.
There are extensive finds relating to the production of copper-alloy buckles in London from some
of the more recently excavated sites (Boys'
School, Guildhall Art Gallery and Thames
Exchange), as well as a ceramic mould (acc. no.
87) for buckle frames and perhaps strap loops,
and also some strap loops still joined together
(no. 1235), all from the Copthall Avenue site. The
most complete ceramic mould so far recovered,
from the GAG87 site (acc. no. 939, see fig 80)
clearly demonstrates the mass production of standard forms in the 14th century or earlier. The
mould unit used in one operation consisted of at
least half a dozen layers, each for casting a dozen
buckle frames. This suggests that it is appropriate to think in terms of hundreds of these objects
being manufactured at any one time. For a stone
mould found in Salisbury, probably for casting
lead/tin buckles with integral plates, see fig 67.
Comparable finds from the Muchpark Street site
in Coventry include ceramic moulds for casting
copper-alloy buckles, some copper-alloy frames
that are still joined together, and stone moulds
probably for similar items in lead/tin (Bayley and
Wright 1987, 84–88).

Strap-ends

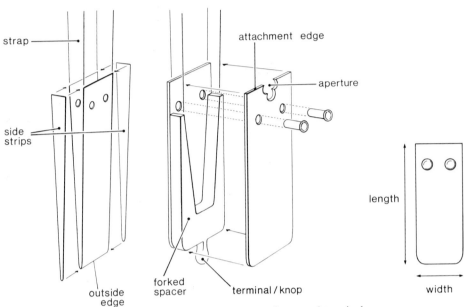

81 Strap-end terminology

The strap-ends included in this survey were made from the usual range of base metals; namely copper, copper alloys including bronze, brass and gunmetal, different alloys sometimes being used for components of the same strap-end (eg nos. 676 & 693), lead-tin, tin, and iron which was invariably tin-coated. Strap-ends made from lead-tin or tin do not occur in deposits before the late 14th century (ceramic phase 11) and are in forms exclusive to these metals, although it appears that they copied strap-ends made from costlier metals in their general design. There are none made from precious metal or ivory and none are set with gemstones, although these are known from written sources to have been worn by wealthy Londoners. Lead/tin solder is the only type of solder encountered here, not unexpectedly in view of the absence of precious metal. Rivets were usually made from a similar metal to that of the strap-end, although iron rivets were occasionally teamed with a strap-end of copper alloy (eg nos. 576 & 765), and brass rivets with copper (no. 728), and vice versa, most of which are probably repairs. Roves, which are either circular

or lozenge-shaped, often accompany rivets where the strap-end consists of a single plate (nos. 728, 731, 732–38 & 768) and possibly where an end has been refitted with a new strap (nos. 618–19). An unusual hinged copper-alloy fitting from a late 13th-century deposit preserves possible traces of enamel (no. 727) and may have been inspired by Limoges-type champlevé enamelwork. A narrow strap-end with a hook made from copper (no. 728) and a brass two-piece strap-end (no. 619) were mercury-gilded.

There is at least one unfinished strap-end from the assemblage, a relatively ornate piece made from tin and decorated in international gothic style with a female saint, who stands within a trefoil arch (no. 717, figs 99 & 100). This is, however, an isolated example, unlike a group of strap-ends in various stages of manufacture from a late 15th-century London workshop, which was recovered from the site of Blossom's Inn, close to Cheapside (AR Goodall 1981, 63), but which lies outside the chronological scope of this study. Despite the absence of workshop waste, an insight into working techniques can be gained

CATALOGUE SCHEME

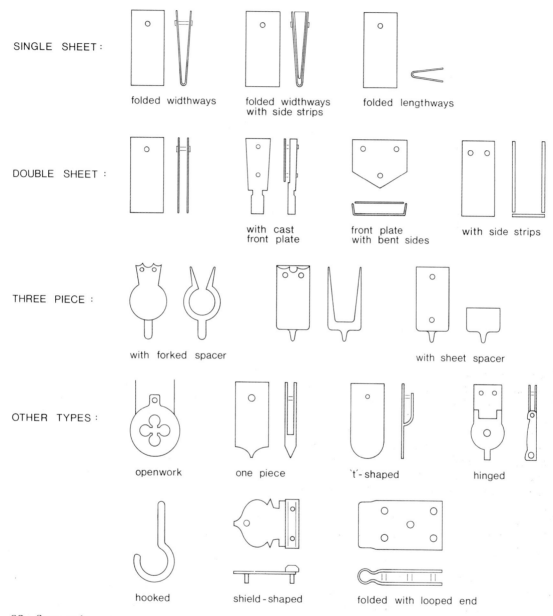

SINGLE SHEET:

folded widthways   folded widthways   folded lengthways
                    with side strips

DOUBLE SHEET:

with cast   front plate   with side strips
front plate   with bent sides

THREE PIECE:

with forked spacer   with sheet spacer

OTHER TYPES:

openwork   one piece   `t´- shaped   hinged

hooked   shield - shaped   folded with looped end

82 Strap-ends

from a close examination of the strap-ends that have been preserved and it is apparent that although two strap-ends may look very similar they were not always made in the same way (eg nos. 659–60 and 696–98; nos. 694 and 714).

Strap-ends dating from the middle of the 12th century to the late 13th century are not common from the city: there are two from the early 13th century (ceramic phase 7) – nos. 612 and 767, and two from the middle of the 13th century (ceramic phase 8) – nos. 623 and 630. Nevertheless, this evidence is not persuasive in arguing that strap-ends were unfashionable at the time, since there is much less 12th– and early 13th-century metalwork among the excavated material from London than there is from the 14th and early 15th centuries. Indeed it is apparent from effigies of the 13th century that strap-ends were usually fitted to girdles worn by those of high status (see figs 10 & 139).

Whether most of the strap-ends were attached to girdles or some other type of strap or belt is not always easy to determine. A strap-end made from a folded strip of sheet iron occurs on a spur leather (no. 593, fig 69). As a consequence another iron strap-end riveted to a leather strap of very similar dimensions, and with a second (broken) strap-end terminating in a loop can also be identified as forming part of a spur leather (no. 646). The strap-end on the latter spur leather has a different construction since it was made from four pieces of iron instead of only one. Hence no uniformity of manufacture can be anticipated among strap-ends, even when they are attached to straps serving a similar use, and this complicates identification.

Strap-ends made from rectangular strips of tin-coated iron folded double were also used on a small proportion of shoe straps during the first half of the 15th century (Grew and de Neergaard 1988, 76 fig 110). Shoe buckles, by contrast, are more often lead/tin (see nos. 115–210) and, unlike girdle accessories, appear not to have been made in matching sets. Thus, although it appears that most iron strap-ends were not part of everyday dress, it is not possible to exclude them entirely. There is, indeed, an elaborate iron strap-end with an acorn knop which resembles a number of those made from copper alloy in its style of decoration (no. 607, fig 85). Nevertheless, strap-ends of iron are only represented in a few categories, and this contrasts with the wide variety of strap-ends made from copper alloy, which it can be argued more convincingly were worn with everyday dress.

Occasionally fittings similar to strap-ends were not attached to straps. A honestone from the village of Lyveden, Northamptonshire, for example, has a looped attachment plate of copper alloy riveted to it (Bryant and Steane 1971, 53 fig 12 r).

SHEET METAL FOLDED WIDTHWAYS

(Rectangular unless stated)

Copper alloy

574 SWA81 acc. no. 629 (context 2051) ceramic phase 9
Brass (AML); single rivet; 18.5×7.5mm.

575 SWA81 3263 (2141) 9 fig 83
Gunmetal (AML); V-shaped, with straight end; two rivets, one through each arm; engraved zig-zags within diagonal lines; on leather strap, which is folded double; 27×28mm.

576 BC72 4284 (150) 11 fig 83
Brass (AML); as no. 574, but with holes for two rivets, one of which, of iron, survives; discontinuous engraved lines down the centre flanked by lines at sides; on leather strap; 74×8mm.

577 BWB83 2270 (286) 11
Gunmetal (AML); single rivet; 14×11mm.

578 BWB83 28 (138) 11 fig 83
Brass (AML); single rivet; bevelled sides; 15×11mm; on leather strap 9mm wide.

579 BWB83 1293 (112) 11
Single rivet; 16×11mm.

580 BWB83 3719 (341) 11
Single rivet; 27×10–12mm.

581 BC72 4471 (150) 11
Brass (AML); single rivet; *c*.21×15mm.

582 BWB83 4001 (292) 11 fig 83
Brass (AML); straight end, with corners cut diagonally; attachment edge has a grooved trefoil aperture flanked by notches; two rivet holes; the back is shorter than the front and lacks rivet holes; probably a re-used plate of a composite strap-end with a forked spacer, 22.5×16mm.

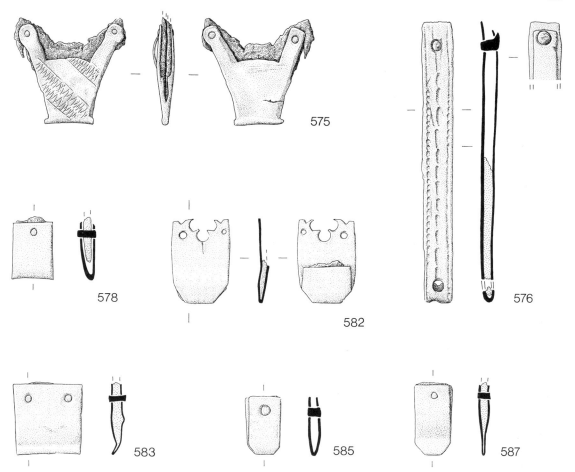

575

578

582

576

583

585

587

83 Strap-ends made from sheeting folded widthways (1:1)

583 BWB83 3760 (338) 11 fig 83
Two rivets; on leather strap 17mm w; 19×18–19mm.

584 BC72 2728 (79) 11
Broken off along fold; holes for two rivets; 37+ ×max 27mm.

585 BWB83 5898 (309) 12 fig 83
Copper (AML); straight end, with corners cut diagonally; single rivet; 15×9mm.

586 TL74 2691 (275) 12
Two rivets; 18×16mm.

587 SWA81 2510 (2102) 12 fig 83
Straight end with corners cut diagonally; single rivet; 19×19.5mm; on skived leather strap 9.5mm w.

588 TL74 2398 (368) 12 fig 136 & colour pl 5B
Brass (AML); trapezoidal; single rivet; the end has a

ridge engraved with Vs and crosses; 21×22mm; on leather strap 13mm w. For accompanying mounts, see no. 1187.

Iron

(Tin-coated unless otherwise stated)

589 SWA81 5029 (2018) 9
(?) Two rivets; 17×7.5mm; on leather strap 7mm w.

590 SWA81 4854 (2072) 9
Back attachment edge more rounded than front with two small notches; single rivet; 14×13mm; on leather strap 19mm w.

591 SWA81 4872 (2079) 9 fig 84
End engraved with a series of grooves; single rivet; 29×23mm; on leather strap 29–32mm w.

592 SWA81 1746 (2000) 9 fig 84
Corroded; damaged attachment edge notched on front; 30×19mm; probably tin-coated.

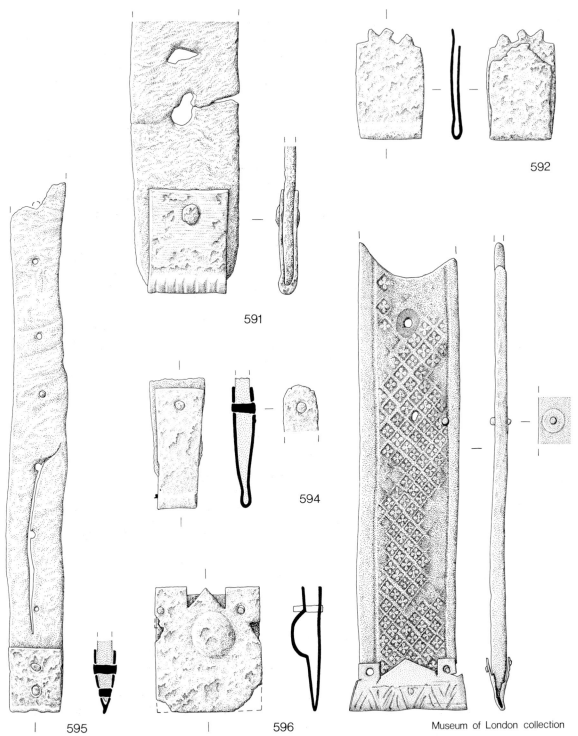

592

591

594

595

596

Museum of London collection

84 Strap-ends made from sheeting folded widthways;
lower right MoL acc. no. 86.106/1 (1:1)

593 BC72 3664 (250) 10 fig 69B
Single rivet; 19×6mm; on leather spur strap 430mm long.

594 BC72 4615 (250) 10 fig 84
Tapering; single rivet, inserted from back; 32×max 14mm; probably tin-coated; on leather strap 16mm w.

595 BC72 2298 (79) 11 fig 84
Two rivets; 17×15mm; on leather strap 13–15mm w.

596 BWB83 5625 (204) 11 fig 84
Central boss; attachment edge has two notches, two more notches at the sides; two rivets; 33×30mm.

597 SWA81 4855 (2084) 12
Damaged; single rivet; 14×15mm; on leather strap 14mm w.

The simplest form of strap-end from medieval London consists of a strip of sheet metal folded in two along the outside edge, with the strap riveted in place between the metal. None of the strap-ends described here comes from a deposit dated earlier than the late 13th century (ceramic phase 9). Among 24 examples, nine are of tin-coated iron, one is copper, and 14 are copper alloy, of which at least six are brass and two are gunmetal (fig 271); there are none made from tin or lead-tin. Most are rectangular or square but one made from copper alloy is trapezoidal (no. 588, fig 136 & colour pl 5B), another is V-shaped (no. 575, fig 83), and others made from iron gently taper and sometimes have a slight constriction above the outside edge (nos. 592 & 594, fig 84). The thickness of the sheeting varies but widths are more consistent with one group clustering around 11mm (nos. 577–9 & 585), and a second group at 16mm (nos. 581–83 & 586). The narrower strap-ends have only one rivet close to the attachment edge. An exception is a strap-end 75mm long, which had two rivets to hold the strap in position, since the leather extends the full length between the metal of the end rather than stopping a short distance below the attachment edge (no. 576, fig 83); unusually, the one rivet preserved is iron; this may indicate that it was repaired. Strap-ends exceeding a width of 15mm have two rivets at the attachment edge.

The simplicity of these strap-ends marks a change from those made of folded metal in the Anglo-Saxon period. These were often cast in moulds before being folded, and are frequently decorated with animal ornament. During the 14th century, by contrast, folded sheet metal strap-ends generally had very little decoration, and they would have been among the cheapest strap-ends that could be purchased. Exceptions are a long, narrow strap-end engraved on the front with a series of discontinuous lines, and a V-shaped strap-end, which was more intricately cut in outline and is engraved with diagonal lines and zigzags (no. 575, fig 83). The latter example is also unusual in having a strap composed of two thicknesses of leather; it could be, perhaps, a chape rather than a strap-end.

Occasionally the attachment edge was decoratively cut, and this includes strap-ends made from iron. Four of the iron strap-ends have notched edges including one with notches like an inverted M cut in the front (no. 596, fig 84). The attachment edge of a brass strap-end is cut with a trefoil aperture and groove similar to that of a composite strap-end (no. 582, fig 83), and it is probable that the piece was originally intended as a front plate of a composite strap-end and was later folded into its present form. This latter strap-end also had two of its corners trimmed off, and this feature recurs on two others of similar date (nos. 585 & 587). Decoration was sometimes focussed close to the outside edge although the use of folded sheeting precluded knops or pointed terminals, which are associated with composite forms of strap-end. An iron strap-end, for example, has a series of grooves (no. 591, fig 84). By the 15th century decoration along the outside edge appears to have become more popular on folded strap-ends of copper alloy. This is illustrated here by a trapezoidal strap-end, which is engraved with Vs and crosses (no. 588, fig 136). Among further examples in the collection of the Museum of London, one, which probably dates to the early 15th century, has a pattern stamped along its outside edge and its attachment edge is cut in the form of an inverted M (MoL acc. no. 86.106/1, fig 84). This strap-end is riveted onto a leather strap, which is itself patterned all over with a stamped device of four pellets (forming a quatrefoil) within a lozenge frame. Thus, while such strap-ends would have been easy and cheap to produce it should not be assumed that the girdles to which they were fitted were necessarily plain.

SHEET METAL, FOLDED WIDTHWAYS, WITH TRIANGULAR SIDE STRIPS

Copper alloy

598 SWA81 acc. no. 3266 (context 2141) ceramic phase 9 fig 85
Brass (AML); tapering; single rivet; 27×max 9mm.

599 BWB83 4197 (401) 11 fig 85
Brass (AML); single rivet; 21×7mm.

600 BWB83 4186 (401) 11
Brass (AML); tapering; single rivet; 26×max 14mm; on leather strap 12mm w.

601 BWB83 5281 (341) 11 fig 85
Brass (AML); single rivet; 23×14mm.

602 BWB83 5282 (341) 11
Bronze (AML); single rivet; 18×15mm; on leather strap 13mm w.

A refinement on the form of strap-end previously described has narrow side strips soldered into place, which usually extend the full length of each side so that the strap was completely enclosed within a casing of metal. It is possible that some of the strap-ends included in the previous group could have lost their side strips, but none retains traces of solder which would have indicated their former presence.

There are five of these strap-ends from dated London deposits: no. 598 from a layer dating to the late 13th or early 14th century (ceramic phase 9), and nos. 599–602 from layers of the late 14th century (ceramic phase 11). All these strap-ends were made from copper alloy, and two retain traces of their leather straps (nos. 600 & 602). They are relatively short and narrow, having only a single rivet at the attachment edge, which is consistent with their narrow width. Each has a straight attachment edge and is undecorated.

SHEET METAL, FOLDED LENGTHWAYS

Copper alloy

603 BWB83 acc. no. 2133 (context 290) ceramic phase 9
Brass (AML); tongue-shaped; attachment edge damaged; single rivet; 31+×15mm.

604 BWB83 2210 (146) 11 fig 85
Brass (AML); tongue-shaped; single rivet; 40 ×max 7mm.

605 BWB83 5853 (298) 11 fig 85
Brass (AML); tongue-shaped; V-shaped notch at attachment edge on front; single rivet; flat, tapering knop with notches; front engraved with three lines marking the position of the end of the strap; 69 ×max 11mm; on leather strap 10mm w.

606 BWB83 4719 (309) 12 fig 85
Brass (AML); tapering; concave attachment edge; knop has two extra metal plates, one on each face – the front one with filed grooves; two rivets, one at attachment edge securing strap, and one through knop; engraved lattice panel in linear border defined by a lower line on front; 78×max 11mm; on skived leather strap 10mm w.

Strap-ends were also produced in the 14th century by folding copper alloy sheeting along one side (nos. 604–06, fig 85), a method that was similarly used for some cosmetic tools, including tweezers (see nos. 1778–79). The four strap-ends of this form from recent excavations in London are long and narrow. Despite their length, only one rivet was used to secure the girdle because the strap only extended a short distance between the metal. Thus on the two examples where the leather is preserved, the girdle extends for less than a quarter of the actual length of the strap-end, and this is reflected in the decoration on the front plate, which is limited to the upper section, and may have acted as a guide to the girdler who fitted the end to the strap. The short piece of the leather inside these strap-ends contrasts with the length of that present in a strap-end folded widthways which required a second rivet to hold the girdle in position (no. 576).

A further feature of the two decorated strap-ends is that a knop has been cut in outline in the metal sheeting. One of these has then had two small pieces of sheeting riveted to the front and back to emphasise the ornament.

85 Strap-ends: top row made from sheeting folded widthways with side strips, middle row made from sheeting folded lengthways, bottom left wrought iron, bottom right cast leaded bronze (1:1)

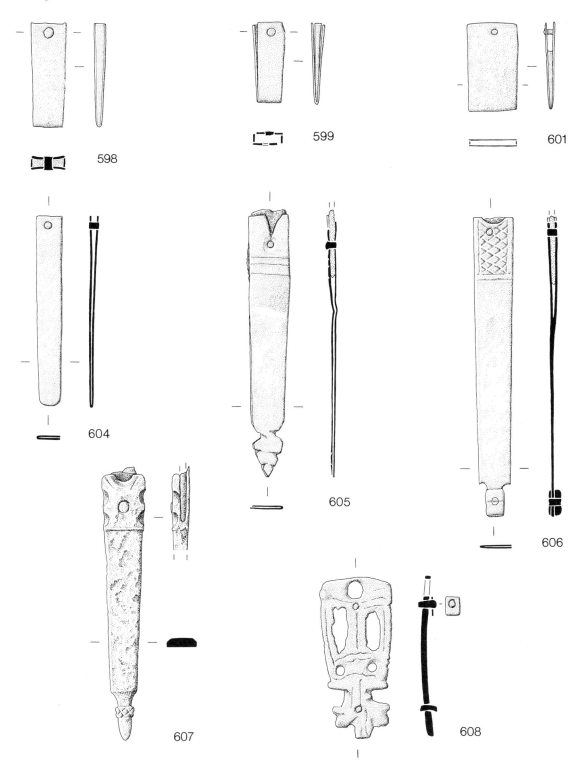

598

599

601

604

605

606

607

608

WROUGHT IRON STRAP-END

607 BC72 acc. no. 2628 (context 79) ceramic phase 11 fig 85
Wrought, leaving upper part bifurcated; tin-coated; tapering; concave attachment edge on front with notches to each side, and also along sides in an upper area defined by a transverse groove which marks the position of the end of the strap; acorn knop; single rivet; 71×max 12mm; on leather strap.

A one-piece iron strap-end from a late 14th-century deposit (ceramic phase 11) resembles two strap-ends in the previous group in its dimensions, decoration, and method of attachment. It was probably made by folding a strip of iron double during smithing; no seamline is visible. A fork at the attachment edge enabled the skived end of the leather girdle, which is 11mm wide, to be fitted between the metal. The leather extends inside the strap-end to the limit of the decoration 15mm from the attachment edge, and is held in place by a single iron rivet. An acorn knop completes the decoration. The back of the strap-end is plain.

CAST IN ONE PIECE

Copper alloy

608 SWA81 acc. no. 9 (context 161) ceramic phase 9 fig 85
Leaded bronze (AML); slightly concave; convex attachment edge; trefoil terminal; two rivets; decorated with roughly engraved lines and openwork; 42×max 19mm. A crude item.

A one-piece strap-end recovered from a late 13th- or early 14th-century deposit (ceramic phase 9) in London is distinctive in its form and style of decoration, which includes openwork circles and a trefoil knop (no. 608, fig 85). In addition, it is made from leaded bronze, which is rare among dress accessories at this period, although strap loops among production waste dated to the 14th century found at Copthall Avenue (OPT81) are leaded gunmetal (no. 1235, fig 147). Strap-ends cast in one piece with openwork decoration were common in late Anglo-Saxon England and, while this strap-end is unlikely to date so early, it may belong to this tradition.

TWO-PIECE STRAP-ENDS

Sheet metal

Copper alloy

609 SWA81 acc. no. 3373 (context 2134) ceramic phase 9 fig 86
Brass (AML); tongue-shaped; two dome-headed rivets; 19×11mm; on silk strap.

610 BWB83 3716 (341) 11 fig 86
Corroded; copper (AML); tapering; roughly engraved with curved lines in rectangular and triangular fields; single dome-headed rivet; 33×max 13mm.

611 BWB83 2288 (286) 11 fig 86 & colour pl 4C
Bronze (AML); tongue-shaped; pointed end; damaged attachment edge has trefoil aperture; two rivets; engraved zigzags with flanking lines along sides; marking-out guidelines engraved on back; 95×15mm.

Iron

612 BIG82 3183 (5224) 7
Tongue-shaped; tapering; slightly concave attachment edge; single rivet; (?)tin-coated; 37×max 12mm.

613 BWB83 4407 (108) 10
Single rivet; two engraved transverse lines and angled grooves at notched attachment edge; tin-coated; 30×max 18mm; on leather strap 17mm w.

Cast front plate and sheet back plate

Copper alloy

614 BWB83 2733 (328) 11 fig 86
Brass (AML); front plate has series of engraved diagonal lines along sides and terminates in a human head, with cabling for hair on front and back, and at neck on back only; attachment edge of back plate broken off; two rivets; 40×max 11.5mm; on leather strap.

Circular form

Copper alloy

615 BWB83 3997 (292) 11 fig 86
Incomplete; back plate, knop from front plate and knop reinforcement; brass (AML); wavy edge; bridge at attachment edge; one rivet through knop; l 65 ×d 52mm.

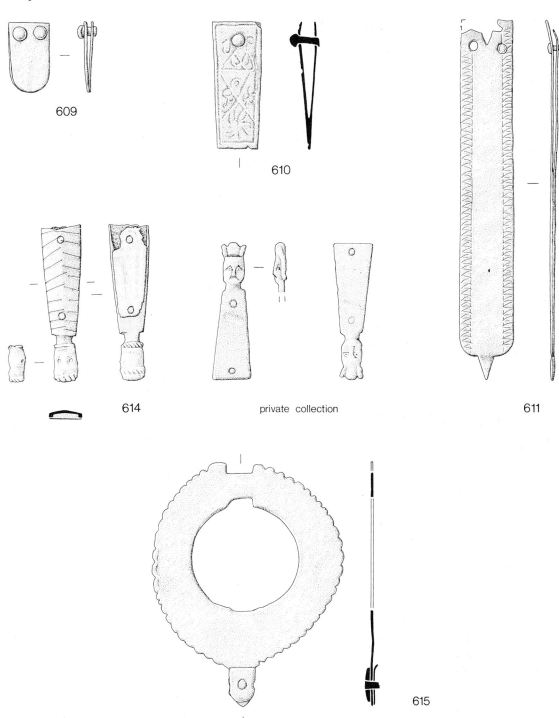

609

610

614

private collection

611

615

86 Two-piece strap-ends;
centre, P Shaffery Collection

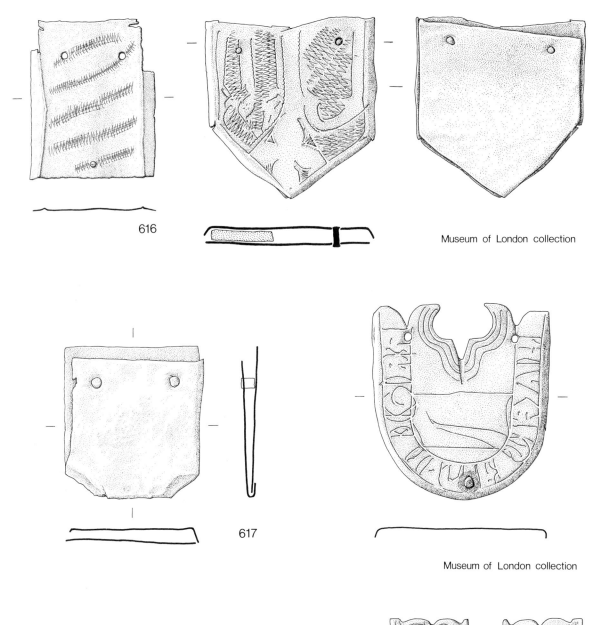

616

Museum of London collection

617

Museum of London collection

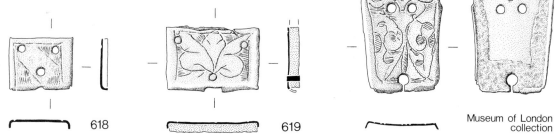

618   619   Museum of London
                                                                              collection

87 Two-piece strap-ends with bent sides; top right MoL acc. no. 80.73/9. centre right MoL acc. no. 84.199/5, lower right MoL acc. no. 82.144/12 (1:1)

Front plate with bent sides

Copper alloy

616 BWB83 2110 (290) 9 fig 87
Gunmetal (AML); front plate only; flattened; engraved diagonal lines and zigzags; holes for three rivets; 38×28mm.

617 BC72 2878 (119) 10–11 fig 87
Brass (AML); corners diagonally cut; two rivets; 40×37mm.

618 SWA81 2971 (2084) 12 figs 31 & 87
Brass (AML); front plate only; holes for three rivets which were fitted with circular roves; notch cut in outside edge; engraved rectangle encloses two diagonal lines and areas of zigzags; 9×18mm; on silk tablet-woven strap 15.5mm w which has left an impression in corrosion products on the reverse of the plate.

619 SWA81 3023 (2103) 12 fig 87
Brass with mercury gilding (AML); as preceding, but engraved foliate pattern in the rectangular frame against a field of zigzags; three iron rivets including one with its circular rove; 16×25mm; on leather strap 25mm w with flesh face on the outside.

Iron

620 BWB83 2266 (108) 10 fig 88
Tongue-shaped; tin-coated; six rivets; 50×35mm.

621 BWB83 3434 (293) 11
Tongue-shaped; four rivets; tin-coated; 56×28mm; on leather strap.

622 BWB83 139 (256) 11 fig 88
Circular; (?)tin-coated; four rivets; d 45mm; on leather strap 36mm w.

Another simple form of strap-end consists of two opposed pieces of metal, namely a front and a back plate. Most were soldered together at the outside edge. The end of the strap, which was skived to fit between the plates, was secured at the attachment edge with one or more rivets, depending upon the dimensions of the strap-end. An iron strap-end of this type (no. 612) dates from no later than the early decades of the 13th century (ceramic phase 7) but it is similar to later examples.

This form of strap-end is marked by a considerable variety of shape and decoration. A brass strap-end from a late 14th-century deposit has the unusual combination of a cast front and a back plate of thin sheeting (no. 614, fig 86). A hollow in the reverse of the front plate enabled the leather strap to fit in place, and the strap-end was assembled with two rivets and also soldered. The decoration represents a man's bust, his hair picked out by cabling and his body by a series of grooves added after the plate was cast. Few anthropomorphic strap-ends are known from this period although a slightly smaller strap-end in a private collection, which was made for a girdle of similar width (ie 10mm), is in the form of the bust of a man with a crown (fig 86).

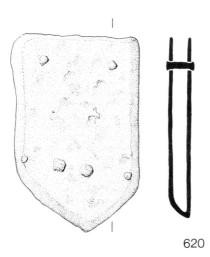

620

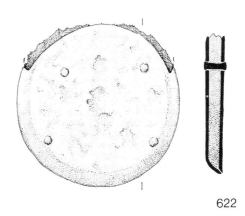

622

88 Two-piece strap-ends with bent sides (1:1)

A few two-piece strap-ends appear not to have been soldered (eg nos. 616–22). As a consequence they tend to have more rivets than was customary for other forms; one, for example, had six rivets (no. 620, fig 88). A general characteristic of this group is that the front plate was cut slightly larger than the back so that the edges could be bent over to encase the strap. The leather of the strap, therefore, did not need to be skived. The group includes most of the widest strap-ends from 14th-century deposits; there are three, for example, which measure 35mm, 36mm and 37mm (nos. 617, 620 & 622, figs 87 & 88). Even wider strap-ends of this form (up to 46mm wide) are represented from the city in the collections of the Museum of London (eg Ward-Perkins 1940, 270 fig 85 no. 8; Fingerlin 1971, 393 no. 262 fig 298; MoL acc. nos. 84.199/5 & 80.73/9, fig 87). There are also small strap-ends of this form. Two from early 15th-century deposits are wider than they are long and have straps held by three rivets (nos. 618 & 619, figs 31 & 87); the former has a strap tablet-woven from crimson silk thread, and the latter, which is mercury-gilded, has a leather strap that is riveted to the end with the flesh face on the outside.

The front plates of these strap-ends with bent sides are often decorated (MoL acc. no. 82.144/ 12, fig 87), and an example in the collection of the Museum of London shows that the back was also sometimes patterned (Ward-Perkins 1940, 270 fig 85 no. 7; Fingerlin 1971, 398 no. 289 fig 453–54). A back plate does not always appear to have been present, or it may have been removed when a strap-end was repaired or a strap was replaced. Thus, the small gilded strap-end is attached to its leather strap by iron rivets with roves, which probably indicate that it was repaired and the impression of circular roves are visible on the back of the silk strap. The two small strap-ends (nos. 618 & 619) also have a distinctive notch or recess in the outside edge which was presumably designed to hold another fitting; they can be compared with the recesses in mounts fitted to shield-shaped plates (nos. 733 & 738, fig 103) and folding strap clasps (no. 553, figs 76 & 77).

TWO-PIECE SHEET-METAL STRAP-ENDS WITH SIDE STRIPS

(Some have marks in solder from missing strips)

Copper alloy

Straight ends

623 BIG82 acc. no. 2305 (context 2514) ceramic phase 8 fig 89
Brass (AML); tapering; lead/tin solder (MLC) secures three separate side strips; two rivets; 70×max 16mm; on leather strap 15mm w.

624 SWA81 3308 (2134) 9
One plate only; gunmetal (AML); tapering; single rivet; mark from side strip in solder; 63×max 11mm.

625 SWA81 423 (2018) 9
One plate and side strip only; attachment edge broken off; tapering; surviving l 38mm.

626 BWB83 4574 (285) 9 fig 89
Brass (AML); tapering; single dome-headed rivet; 20×max 14mm.

627 BWB83 1646 (318) 11 fig 89
Front plate only; gunmetal (AML); concave attachment edge; vertical row of punched ring-and-dot motifs, flanked along each side by an engraved line; hole for single missing rivet; 90×max 11mm.

628 BWB83 5893 (318) 11
Lower part of one plate and side strip only; tapering; part of one rivet hole; 19+ max 14mm.

629 BIG82 2315 (2278) 12 fig 89
Brass (AML); tapering; attachment edge broken off; double lines of punched opposed triangles along sides; 33+×max 10.5mm.

Tongue shaped

630 BIG82 2324 (1668) 8 fig 89
Front plate only; mark from side strip; holes for two rivets; engraved discontinuous double lines along sides; 115×max 17mm.

631 SWA81 2127 (2030) 9 fig 89
Single rivet; 31×max 6mm.

632 SWA81 782 (2051) 9
Attachment edge broken off; surviving l 16mm.

633 BWB83 5900 (298) 11
One plate only; hole for single rivet at attachment edge; 25×max 6mm.

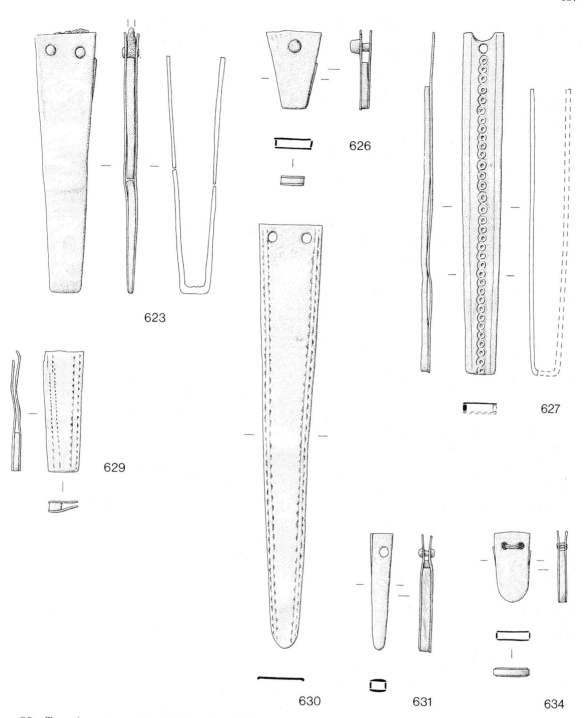

89 Two-piece strap-ends with side strips (1:1)

634 BWB83 5899 (303) 11 fig 89
Two rivet holes, through which a strand of wire has been inserted, presumably as a repair; 18×9mm.

635 BWB83 4612 (286) 11
As no. 633; 19×max 9mm.

636 BWB83 2670 (330) 11
Hole for single rivet; *c*.25 e 9mm.

637 BWB83 5892 (298) 11
One plate only; single rivet; 23×max 10mm.

638 BWB83 5896 (298) 11
One plate only, as preceding item (they probably formed a pair), but lacks rivet; 23×max 10mm.

639 BWB83 5124 (346) 11
Front plate only; brass (AML); as no. 630, but end broken off, and triangles engraved along attachment edge; 37+×max 17mm.

Angled end

640 BWB83 3992 (292) 11 fig 90
Single rivet; 32.5×15.5mm.

Semi-circular

641 BWB83 1324 (108) 10 fig 90
One plate and part of square-sectioned side strip only; holes for four rivets.

Trapezoidal

642 BWB83 5901 (303) 11 fig 90
Brass (AML); trapezoidal; concave attachment edge; front roughly engraved with curving and straight lines to sides of a pair of central vertical lines and within a border line; one rivet; 30×max 19mm.

Form of terminal uncertain

643 BWB83 3213 (264) 9
Attachment edge of (?)back plate only; tapering; holes for two rivets, one of which survives; 30+ ×max 16mm.

644 BWB83 1325 (108) 10
One plate only; end broken off; mark from side strip in solder; holes for two rivets; 20+×max 12mm.

645 BWB83 5903 (310) 12 fig 90
Incomplete; tapering end is broken off and side strip missing (a mark from the latter remains in the solder); tapering; roughly engraved curving lines within border lines at sides; one dome-headed rivet, and hole for another; 39+×max 14mm.

Iron

646 SWA81 4986 (2051) 9
Tapering; tin-coated; single rivet of tin-coated copper alloy (MLC); 24×max8.5mm; on leather strap 8–9mm w and 400mm l. Probably from a spur – cf no. 593.

647 TL74 701 (370) 11
Tin-coated; two rivets; 34×38mm; on leather strap.

A form of strap-end which had emerged by the middle of the 13th century comprises separate front and back plates with narrow side strips approximately 2mm wide in between. The strips were usually made from sheeting but more robust square-sectioned strips were also used (no. 627, fig 89, & no. 641, fig 90). The use of side strips meant that rivets were only needed at the attachment edge to hold the strap in place, and this distinguishes them from certain other forms. Narrower strap-ends generally have one rivet but a few strap-ends with a width of less than 15mm have two (no. 634, fig 89, no. 644, & no. 645, fig 90), including one which was repaired with wire. A semi-circular strap-end, which at 47mm is the widest of those included here, has four rivets (no. 641, fig 90). Trapezoidal strap-ends, which are wider at their outside edge than their attachment edge, are another form which occurs in strap-ends of this kind (fig 90, no. 642 & MoL acc. no. 4549).

These strap-ends range in length from 18mm to 115mm. Some of the longer examples required more than one side strip (eg no. 623, fig 89). It could be significant that the two earliest strap-ends catalogued here (nos. 623 & 630, fig 89) are both long ones reflecting a particular fashion of the 13th century which is apparent from contemporary tomb effigies (fig 139). Number 630 is punched with double lines of opposed triangles. Similar decoration is present on a broken strap-end recovered from an early 15th-century deposit (no. 629, fig 89) and it is probable that this later example is residual. Other decorated strap-ends of this form are limited to one with punched ring-and-dot ornament (no. 627, fig 89), which is an unusual motif on a strap-end at this period, a trapezoidal strap-end which is divided on the front into two panels engraved with linear ornament (no. 642, fig 90), and a further example with linear engraving (no. 645, fig 90). However, most of these strap-ends from London are undecorated.

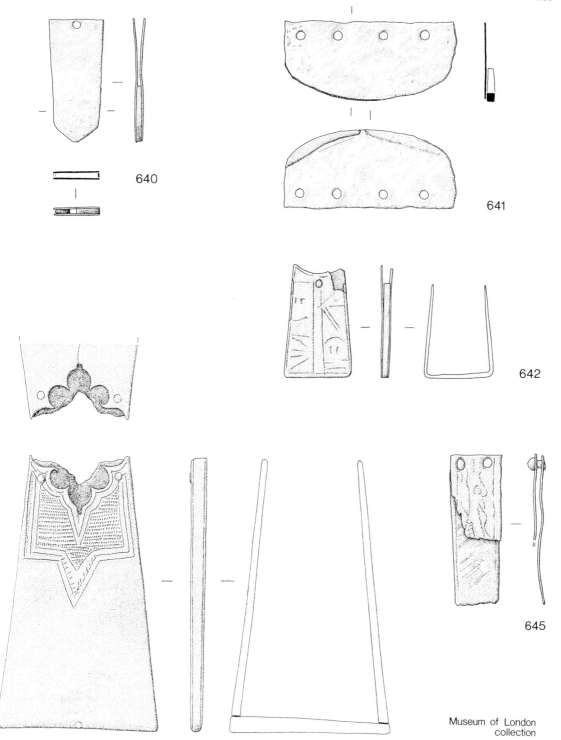

640

641

642

645

Museum of London
collection

90 Two-piece strap-ends with side strips; lower left MoL acc. no. 4549 (1:1)

The attachment edges are also marked by a large degree of uniformity, being either straight or concave. However, a large trapezoidal strap-end with side strips in the collections of the Museum of London is cut at its attachment edge with a trefoil aperture and groove imitating strap-ends with forked spacers (MoL acc. no. 4549, fig 90).

COMPOSITE STRAP-ENDS WITH FORKED SPACERS

Circular forms

Copper alloy

648   SWA81   acc. no. 1445   (context 2105) ceramic phase 9   fig 92

91   Composite strap-end with a forked spacer, no. 650 (2:1)

Incomplete; back plate, and spacer with acorn knop; brass, with lead/tin solder (AML); two rivet holes, that near the side is possibly from a repair; l 45×d 30mm.

649   BC72   2729   (79)   11   fig 92
(?)Front plate only; spade-shaped grooved aperture; two rivets; d 37mm.

650   BWB83   196   (291)   11   figs 91 & 92
Circular, with flaring upper part, scalloped attachment edge with central groove; brass (AML); knop broken off; front plate has grooved rounded aperture; engraved with an octofoil within an eight-armed star of interlocking square bands, framed by broken and complete circles, and with a foliate pattern above; the back has two intersecting lines engraved in the centre; the spacer forms a complete circle; two rivets; l 53+ ×d 32mm; on leather strap 20mm w.

651   BIG82   622   (75)   ?residual in post-medieval context   fig 92
Circular, with flaring upper part, bronze (AML); spacer only; acorn knop; d 15.5mm.

652   BWB83   5321   (unstratified)   fig 92
Circular, with flaring upper part; concave attachment edge; hole for single rivet; collared knop; l 34× d 13mm.

Tongue-shaped forms

Copper alloy

Grooved aperture and pointed ends

653   BWB83   303   (290)   9   fig 93
Scalloped attachment edge; round grooved aperture; two rivets; tapering sides; 35×max 14mm; on leather strap.

654   BWB83   6   (110)   11   fig 93
Brass (AML); scalloped attachment edge; round aperture, grooved on front; two rivets; 26×12.5mm; on leather strap 11mm w.

655   BWB83   5854   (298)   11
Scalloped attachment edge; round grooved aperture on front; back plate broken off at attachment edge; holes for two rivets; 36×13mm.

656   BWB83   4422   (313)   12
As no. 655; 36×max 14mm; trace of leather strap.

Pointed ends

657   BWB83   4516   (274)   9
Concave attachment edge; single rivet; 40×14mm; on leather strap 11mm w.

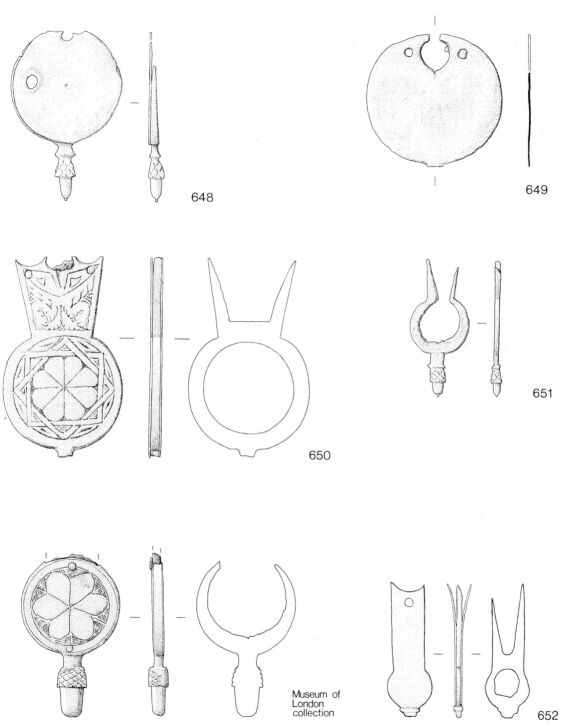

648

649

650

651

652

Museum of
London
collection

92 Composite strap-ends with forked spacers;
lower left MoL acc. no. 80.283/11 (1:1)

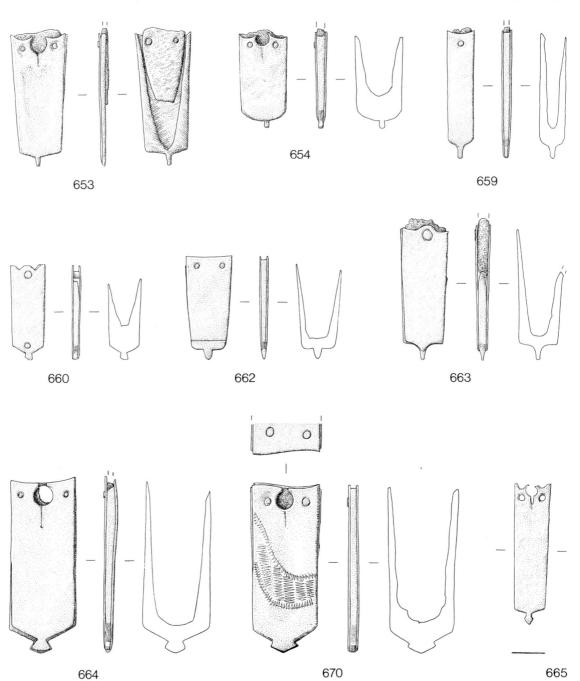

653

654

659

660

662

663

664

670

665

93 Composite strap-ends with forked spacers (1:1)

658 BWB83 5855 (282) 11
Brass (AML); single rivet; 44×max 6mm; on leather strap.

659 BWB83 4565 (279) 11 fig 93
Concave attachment edge; single rivet; 32×7mm; on leather strap.

660 BWB83 654 (256) 11 fig 93
Gunmetal (AML); two notches in attachment edge; two rivets; 25×9.5mm.

661 BWB83 112 (265) 12
As no. 660; 37×max 10mm.

662 BWB83 4726 (309) 12 fig 93
Brass front and back plates (AML); slightly concave attachment edge on front, straight edge on back; two rivets; 27×max 12.5mm; on leather strap.

663 BWB83 5857 (309) 12 fig 93
Brass (AML); biconcave attachment edge; single rivet; 35×max 12.5 mm; on leather strap 12mm w.

Grooved aperture and flat lozenge knops

664 BWB83 1141 (367) 9 fig 93
Concave attachment edge; round aperture, grooved on front plate; two rivets; 46×18mm.

665 BWB83 3767 (338) 11 fig 93
Front plate only; scalloped attachment edge; holes for two rivets; 38×max 10mm.

666 BWB83 3525 (387) 11
Gunmetal (AML); slightly concave attachment edge; flat knop; round aperture, grooved on front; two rivets; 37×13mm.

667 BWB83 3725 (348) 11
Front plate and spacer only; similar to no. 664; 39×15mm.

668 TL74 248 (306) 11
Similar to no. 664, but back plate incomplete; brass (AML); 45×max 16mm.

669 BC72 2391 (83) 11
Bronze plate and spacer (AML); similar to no. 664, but knop broken off; *c*.50×21mm.

670 SWA81 1912 (2112) 12 fig 93
Brass (AML); round aperture with groove at front; flat knop; asymmetrical band of engraved zigzags; two rivets; 45×max 19 mm.

Grooved aperture and trefoil knop

671 BWB83 4399 (274) 9 fig 94
Brass (AML); front plate and spacer only; part of concave attachment edge; round grooved aperture; two holes for rivets at attachment edge; three rivets above knop are presumably a repair; 44×12mm.

Grooved aperture and acorn-type knops

672 BWB83 2116 (290) 9 fig 94
Brass (AML); concave attachment edge; round aperture with groove on front and back plates; two rivets; 55×max w 16mm.

673 BWB83 377 (377) 11 fig 94
Gunmetal (AML); round aperture with groove at front; two rivets; 50×max 15mm.

(no. 674 has been reclassified and is listed after no. 682)

675 BWB83 5856 (309) 12 fig 94
Brass (AML); concave attachment edge; round aperture, grooved at front; two rivets; 52×15mm.

Acorn-type and collared knops

676 BC72 4172 (250) 10 fig 94
Brass front and back plates, gunmetal spacer (AML); knop has single collar; front plate engraved with faint zigzags near attachment edge; two rivets – the upper secures the strap 7mm w, and the lower, of redder metal, the spacer; 36×7.5mm.

677 BWB83 3737 (338) 11 fig 94
Brass (AML); collared knop; single rivet; 30×9mm; on tablet-woven strap.

678 BWB83 2722 (329) 11
Slightly concave attachment edge; acorn-type knop; single rivet; 35×max 9mm.

679 BWB83 2768 (361) 11
Brass (AML); acorn knop; single rivet; 28×9.5mm.

680 BWB83 3745 (338) 11 fig 94
Spacer only; with collared knop; 26+×10mm.

681 BC72 4280 (150) 11 fig 94
Spacer and fragments of plates only; all bronze (AML); knop has two collars; 66+×13mm.

682 BWB83 2353 (137) 11 fig 94
Spacer only; 26+×max 13.5mm.

674 (numbered out of sequence) BWB83 4731 (309) 12
Brass front and back plates (AML); knop with single collar; single rivet; 25×6mm.

683 SWA81 3971 (2006) 12
Brass (AML); acorn knop; one plate slightly longer than the other; two rivets, one at each edge (in a redder metal, like the spacer); 32×8mm.

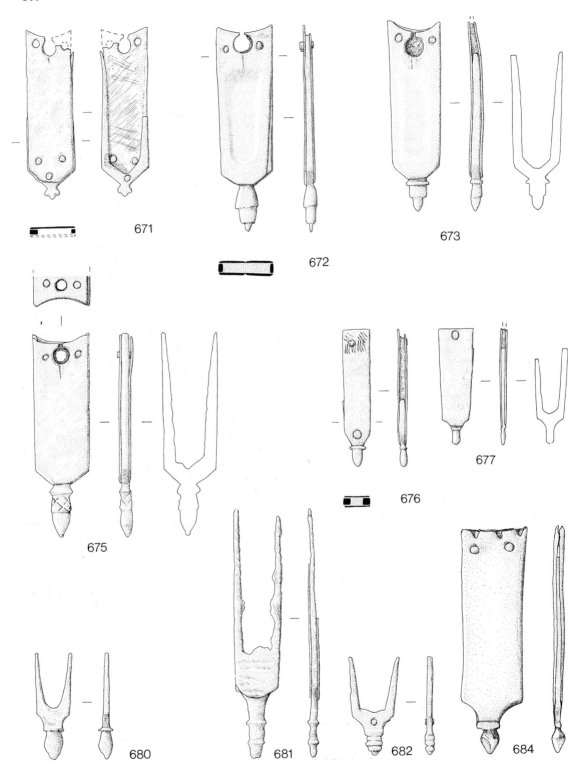

671   672   673

675   677   676

680   681   682   684

94   Composite strap-ends with forked spacers (1:1)

684 SWA81 941 (2102) 12 fig 94
Copper (AML); concave attachment edge with three notches cut in front plate, knop with single collar; 58×max 18.

Angled end

685 BWB83 4191 (401) 11 fig 95
One plate and spacer only; hole for single rivet; 29×12.5mm.

Trapezoidal end

686 BWB83 1203 (367) 9 fig 95
Gunmetal (AML); concave attachment edge; hole for single rivet; side strip is of a redder metal; 39×max 20mm.

Form of terminal uncertain

687 BWB83 4544 (274) 9
Front plate only; concave attachment edge; round grooved aperture; blunt terminal; holes for two rivets; mark from spacer on reverse; 43×16mm.

688 BWB83 1593 (108) 10
One plate only; attachment edge broken off, but (?)remains of aperture; one rivet hole immediately below; mark from spacer on reverse; 22+×max 9mm.

689 BWB83 5897 (318) 11 fig 95
Front plate only; concave attachment edge; round grooved aperture; top engraved with foliate motif; mark from spacer on reverse; holes for two rivets, one of which survives; 35×max 10mm.

690 BWB83 4187 (401) 11
Terminal broken off; two rivets, one at each end; *c.*38×max 10.5mm; on leather strap 8mm w.

691 BWB83 4727 (309) 12
One plate only; concave attachment edge with groove; mark from spacer on reverse; three rivets of redder metal; 22×13mm.

A form of strap-end that does not appear to have been introduced until the late 13th or, more probably, early 14th century (ceramic phase 9) has a forked spacer. All the examples studied here were made from copper alloy – brass, gunmetal, bronze – but the metal content of the different components is not always the same, even in a single item (eg no. 676), and this tends to result in a slight colour contrast between the components.

Most of these strap-ends are tongue-shaped, but circular examples were also made, including some with a flared attachment edge. Ilse Fingerlin suggested that this variant was the prototype for buckle frames with forked spacers (Fingerlin 1971, 116), but the dating evidence from London is too slight to advance this argument. However, there are more strap-ends of this composite form from recent excavations than buckles of this kind, and it is probable that some of the smaller strap-ends were paired with different forms of buckle. These composite strap-ends continue to occur in deposits dating to the early 15th century (ceramic phase 12) but the numbers diminish, and the form can generally be considered to belong to the 14th century. Artistic representations confirm this dating (Ward-Perkins 1940, 266 fig 84 no. 20).

The use of a cast spacer enabled these strap-ends to have elaborate knops, and as result strap-ends of this form can be sub-divided into several groups according to the pattern of the

95 Composite strap-ends with forked spacers (1:1)

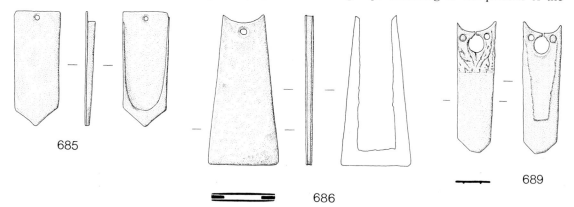

685

686

689

outside edge; from these groupings different sizes of strap-ends can be identified. The simplest form of outside edge takes the form of a V (no. 685, fig 95). It was more common to have a small protruding point, which is usually reflected in the outline of the front and back plates as well the spacer (nos. 653–61, fig 93). An exception is no. 662 where only the spacer has such a protuberance. Both these styles were copied by strap-ends with flat sheet-metal spacers (see nos. 692–701), but the outline of the attachment edge is much more varied on strap-ends with a forked spacer. These include scalloped and curvilinear edges (nos. 660 & 663, fig 93) and, significantly, four have a round aperture with a groove (nos. 653–56, fig 93), a pattern which required two rivets, one on either side of the aperture, even when the strap-end was narrow. This form of attachment edge, which is common on strap-ends with forked spacers, may be referred to in the 1344 regulations of the London Girdlers' Guild (see pp 80 & 82).

Another type of knop is in the form of a flat lozenge (nos. 664–70, fig 93) and this is particularly characteristic of some wider strap-ends (up to 21mm wide). There are six examples from 14th-century deposits in London (ceramic phases 9 and 11) and only one from a deposit of the early 15th century (ceramic phase 12). The front plate invariably has a round aperture with a groove, and two rivets at the attachment edge. The back plate is similar, except that the groove is usually absent (eg nos. 664 and 666), and sometimes there is no aperture (eg nos. 670, 673 and 675). A strap-end, which has a knop in the form of a trefoil rather than a lozenge, appears to have been repaired with three rivets close to the outside edge (no. 671, fig 94).

More pronounced knops resembling acorns or collared with grooves were also popular among this form of strap-end, and for these the front and back plates stopped short of the knop. Hence a front plate engraved with a foliate pattern (no. 689, fig 95) can be identified as belonging to this group. The smallest knops are poorly modelled and the length of the fork did not always extend as far as the attachment edge, which in its turn was sometimes straight rather than having a round aperture and groove. By contrast, the larger strap-ends (15mm to 18mm wide) have well-modelled knops and long forks (nos. 672–73, 675 & 684 fig 94).

The front plate of these strap-ends was sometimes decorated. This could be an abstract pattern of engraved zigzags (no. 670, fig 93 & no. 676, fig 94). Similar engraved patterns can be observed on other composite strap-ends of this form recorded in earlier publications, for example from Covehithe, Suffolk (Fingerlin 1971, 384 no. 209 fig 191), Oxford (Goodall & Goodall 1977, 148 fig 30 nos. 20 and 26), and London (Faussett 1856, XXXI figs 1 and 2), and on the matching form of composite buckle (see nos. 325 & 330, figs 30 & 49); they are also a common decoration on different forms of strap-end and other accessories. Foliate patterns positioned immediately below the attachment edge also occur (no. 689, fig 95). A high-quality circular strap-end with this type of pattern (no. 650, figs 91 & 92) is further embellished with an octofoil inside an eight-pointed star and a circle, for which a pair of compasses was used to mark out the pattern. The reverse of this strap-end was also preliminarily marked-out to be engraved, as if it was initially undecided whether the plate was going to be used for the front or the back. A circular strap-end with an acorn knop from London is patterned in a similar way with a sexfoil (MoL acc. no. 80.283/11, fig 92).

The popularity of strap-ends of this form is apparent from their imitation in pewter, in which miniature copies were produced (eg MoL acc. no. 84.267/2, fig 99).

COMPOSITE STRAP-ENDS WITH SHEET SPACERS OCCUPYING THE WHOLE WIDTH

Copper alloy

Angled ends

692 BWB83 acc. no. 4515 (context 285) ceramic phase 9 fig 96
Corroded; angled end; single rivet; 25×7mm.

693 BWB83 1139 (366) 9 fig 96
Brass with gunmetal spacer (AML); two rivets, one for strap and one for spacer; engraved with two quatrefoils

96 Composite strap-ends with flat spacers; lower right MoL acc. no. 80.65/4 (1:1)

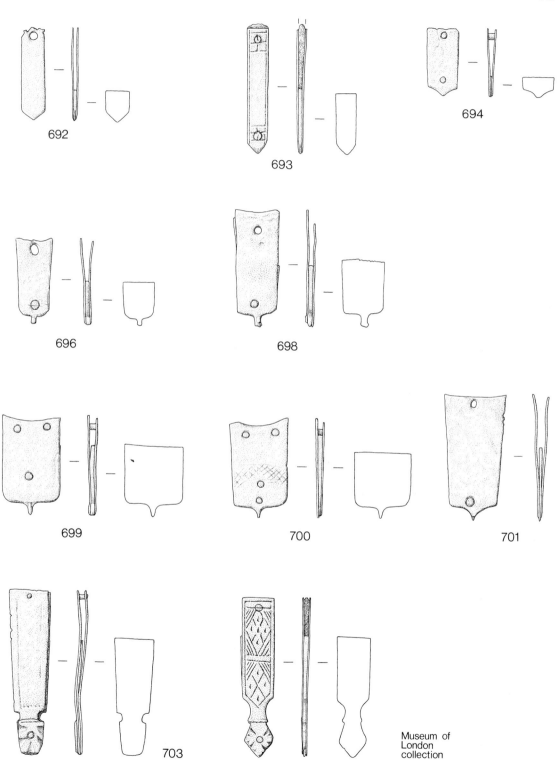

692

693

694

696

698

699

700

701

703

Museum of
London
collection

in linear frames (the tooling cuts the rivets); 33×7mm; on leather strap 6.5mm w.

694 BWB83 5291 (341) 11 fig 96
Biconcave end; two rivets, one for strap and one for spacer; 17×max 10mm.

Pointed ends

695 BWB83 2370 (290) 9
Gunmetal (AML); one plate and spacer only; two rivets, one for strap and one for spacer; 25×12mm.

696 BWB83 2720 (328) 11 fig 96
Concave attachment edge on front and straight edge on back; two rivets, one for strap and one for spacer; cutting line on back plate; 22×max 10mm.

697 BWB83 2124 (307) 11
One plate only; slightly concave attachment edge; two rivets, one for strap and one for spacer; 31×max13mm.

698 BWB83 1163 (361) 11 fig 96
Brass (AML); concave attachment edge; two rivets, one for strap and one for spacer; 32×max 13mm.

699 BWB83 399 (256) 11 fig 96
Gunmetal (AML); concave attachment edge; three rivets, two for strap and one for spacer; 26×16mm.

700 BWB83 1597 (292) 11 fig 96
Gunmetal (AML); concave attachment edge; four rivets, two for securing strap and two for spacer; band of engraved cross-hatching; 26×16mm.

701 BWB83 320 (204) 11 fig 96
Gunmetal (AML); biconcave end; two rivets, one for strap and one for spacer; 34×max 17mm.

Other terminals

702 SWA81 3769 (2023) 11
Incomplete; bronze front or back plate, gunmetal spacer (AML); attachment edge and rivet broken off; single rivet for spacer; lozenge knop; 26+×10mm.

703 BWB83 3987 (207) 11 fig 96
Brass (AML); two rivets, one for strap and one for spacer; knop with additional sheet having radiating grooves; 43×max 11mm.

A slightly less-robust form of composite copper-alloy strap-end has a spacer of sheeting sandwiched between the front and back plates. All twelve examples catalogued here come from 14th-century deposits and it appears that this form was relatively shortlived. They range in

width from 6.5mm to 17mm, and, except for one small strap-end (no. 692, fig 96), they have at least two rivets, one to secure the strap and the other to secure the spacer. Two of the wider strap-ends have two rivets at the attachment edge (nos. 700 & 699, fig 96), and one of these has a second rivet through the spacer. The narrower strap-ends have a V-shaped terminal, while the wider examples have a small protuberance. An exception is no. 703, the longest of these strap-ends, which has a terminal decorated with radiating grooves made by riveting an extra piece of sheeting to the front. The only other decoration present on any of these ends is a band of cross hatching engraved on the front of one of the wider strap-ends (no. 700, fig 96), and two engraved quatrefoils, each centring around the rivets of a narrow strap-end (no. 693, fig 96). This strap-end was riveted to a skived leather strap. The other strap-ends of this form do not preserve any trace of a strap, but an example which is decorated with lozenges and an elaborate quatrefoil knop has a silk tablet-woven strap (MoL acc. no. 80.65/4, fig 96).

COMPOSITE STRAP-ENDS WITH OPENWORK DECORATION, AND SHEET SPACERS OCCUPYING THE WHOLE WIDTH

Copper alloy

704 TL74 acc. no. 273 (context 306) ceramic phase 11 fig 97
Brass (AML); attachment edge and upper portion broken off; knop only of back plate; front engraved with a leaf on a field of horizontal lines within a frame; openwork panel with trefoil arch and part of a stem; the spacer also has an openwork panel; two rivets passing through spacer; 44+×13mm.

705 TL74 726 (415) 12 fig 97
Back plate, spacer, and part of front plate; acorn knop; scalloped attachment edge with round aperture, grooved on front; engraved with a band of three saltires in a grid, below which is a stem bearing an acorn within an openwork panel; 57×15mm; two rivets secure the leather strap; another rivet below the openwork goes through the spacer, and a fourth through the knop.

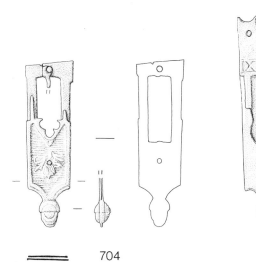

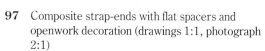
704 705

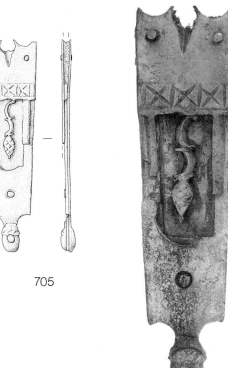

97 Composite strap-ends with flat spacers and openwork decoration (drawings 1:1, photograph 2:1)

There are two copper alloy composite strap-ends with openwork decoration, one from a deposit of the late 14th-century (ceramic phase 11) and the other from a deposit of the early 15th-century (ceramic phase 12) (nos. 704 & 705, fig 97). Only the latter preserves its attachment edge, which has a round, grooved aperture in the front plate and two rivets holding a leather strap, comparable to many of the composite strap-ends with forked spacers. The top edge of the internal spacer corresponds to the line engraved above the three saltire crosses which decorate the front plate, and this is also where the leather of the girdle terminates. The spacer of the other strap-end is slightly narrower, and would have been appropriate for a girdle approximately 14mm wide.

The decoration on the strap-ends emphasises the popularity of acorn motifs at this period. In addition to acorn knops, they have an openwork motif of an acorn on a sinuous stem reserved against the back plate (the girdle did not extend this far between the plates). This was not a robust design, and on one of them the acorn is broken off. The surface of the back plate may have been coloured to enhance the acorn but no difference is apparent now. The latter strap-end also has a leaf embellished on its front plate

beneath a trefoil arch, while this portion of the other strap-end is missing. These strap-ends are paralleled by others from London, Wales and the continent (Fingerlin 1971, 101 figs 145, 146 & 147; Lewis 1987, 271, 273 & 276 fig 3 no. 7), although they are not common and no two are precisely alike. A buckle plate with similar decoration from Liège, Belgium, suggests that they were made in sets (Fingerlin 1971, 101 fig 144).

LEAD/TIN STRAP-ENDS CAST IN ONE-PIECE

Various shapes with openwork decoration

(Dimensions are given for diameter or length×width, with width of strap opening in brackets)

706 BWB83 acc. no. 4436 (context 256) ceramic phase 11 fig 98
Incomplete; pewter (AML); circular; openwork quatrefoil at front and back; attachment edge broken off; d 21mm (15mm).

706

707

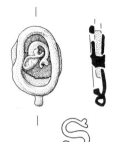

708

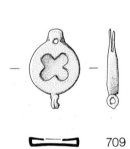

709

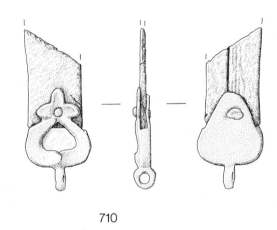

710

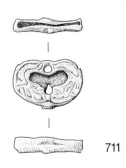

711

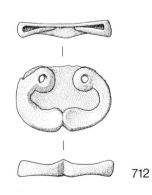

712

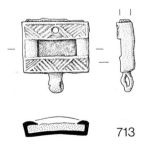

713

98 Cast lead-tin strap-ends (1:1)

707 SWA81 653 (2084) 12 fig 98
Incomplete; tin (AML); pyramidal, with circular attachment edge; end broken off; openwork square on front; single rivet; 15+×10mm (9mm); on leather strap.

708 SWA81 3405 (2082) 12 fig 98
Distorted; pewter (AML); oval, with loop; oval aperture in front, with a S-shaped mount riveted through the centre onto leather strap; loop in terminal; 19×14mm (10mm).

709 SWA81 3404 (2082) 12 fig 98
Tin (AML); circular; loop in terminal; narrow attachment edge; hole for single rivet; openwork quatrefoil on front; 21×14mm (11mm).

710 SWA81 1167 (2100) 12 fig 98
Tin (AML); openwork triangle (cf two opposed tear shapes); loop in terminal; trefoil-shaped attachment edge; single rivet; openwork triangle fitted with a thin sheet of white metal between the leather of the strap and the strap-end; 27×18mm (14mm). Cf mount on a similar folded strap – no. 1223.

711 SWA81 1954 (2108) 12 fig 98
Incomplete and distorted; oval, with terminal broken off; trefoil opening in front; stylised engraved foliate decoration; two rivet holes, the upper one through both front and back and the lower one through the back; 13×18mm (15mm).

712 SWA81 3403 (2082) 12 fig 98
Oval; opposed tear-shapes with terminal lobes, giving angled trefoil opening in front; two rivet holes; V-shaped nick cut in end (perhaps to make it neat following damage to an original terminal); holes for two rivets; 17×25 mm (22mm).

713 SWA81 3815 (unstratified) fig 98
Rectangular, with loop in terminal; openwork rectangle on front; diagonally hatched opposed triangles; single rivet; 18×18mm (16mm); on leather strap.

Plain

714 BWB83 99 (204) 11 fig 99 & colour pl 5C
Tin (MLC); tapering; pointed terminal; open at sides; single tin rivet (MLC); 19×9.5mm; on leather strap up to 12mm w. For accompanying sexfoil mounts see no. 1022.

715 BWB83 5313 (unstratified)
Incomplete; hollow sleeve form; pointed terminal; attachment edge broken off; 31+×9mm.

Decorated

716 BWB83 4042 (293) 11 fig 99
Incomplete; tin (AML); end slightly angled; slightly concave attachment edge; conjoined double-circle aperture at front, with five smaller openwork circles; one of original two dome-headed rivets survives; 43×41mm.

717 TL74 610 (453) 12 figs 99 & 100
Incomplete; tin (AML); rectangular; attachment edge broken off; misshapen acorn-type knop; decorated with two full-length figures of a female saint standing within a trefoil arch (the second figure is broken off); 66+×13mm.

One-piece strap-ends cast in moulds were common in Anglo-Saxon England but they appear to have undergone a temporary decline by the late 13th century when composite forms gained in popularity. A revival in the production of one-piece strap-ends in the late 14th century coincided with the introduction of new forms, and the use of pewter and tin which helped to satisfy the mass demand for these accessories.

Twelve of these one-piece strap-ends, which were recovered from deposits dating to the last quarter of the 14th century (ceramic phase 11) and the early 15th century (ceramic phase 12), are catalogued here. Such strap-ends were, like the corresponding buckles of tin and lead-tin, cast in three-part moulds which resulted in the finished piece being hollow (see fig 67). The strap was slotted into the hollow, where it was usually riveted with one or two rivets. Where part of the strap is preserved (on five out of the 12 examples), it is made of leather, and on one of these where the leather is unusually thin the sides of the strap were folded inwards so that a double thickness of leather resulted, with the grain side on the exterior (no. 710, fig 98). These strap-ends often have openwork decoration on the front and sometimes also on the back. This, which would have left the strap visible, was not always the intention however, for on one strap-end of this type a piece of thin sheeting was inserted between the strap and the end, thereby concealing the leather (no. 710); on another a separate S-shaped mount was riveted through the leather strap and the back of the strap-end (no. 708, fig 98). A rivet hole through the back of another strap-end (no. 711, fig 98) suggests that this

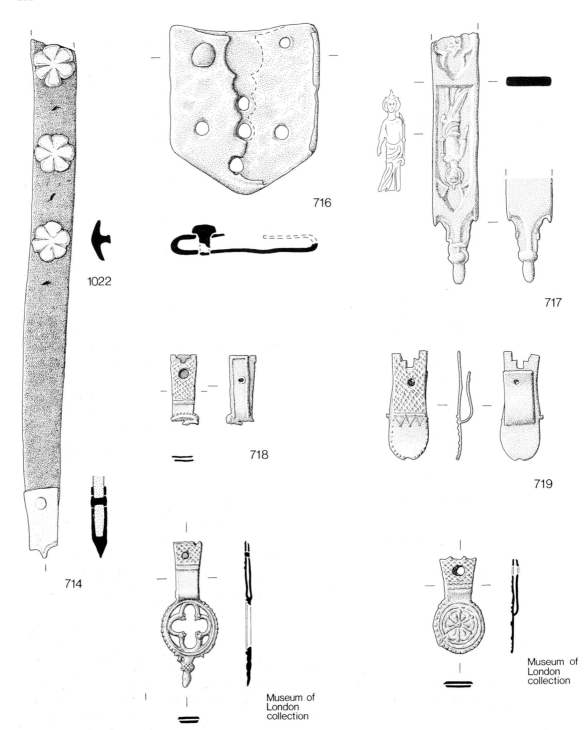

99 Cast lead-tin strap-ends; lower left MoL acc. no.
84.267/2, lower right MoL acc. no. 4513 (1:1)

100 Unfinished lead-tin strap-end, no. 717 (2:1)

strap likewise had a mount covering much of the leather, while a strap-end of the same design (but from a different mould) has a piece of sheeting inserted instead of a mount (MoL acc. no. 80.102 /1).

A loop is another feature of many of these strap-ends, and as on the contemporary strap-ends in copper alloy consisting of a hinged plate and loop, the internal diameter of the loop is only 1.5mm. The mount in the form of a S suggests that this strap-end was worn with the loop horizontal.

The most ornate of the strap-ends made from tin appears never to have been finished and it is probably safe to assume it was a London product (no. 717, figs 99 & 100). Its attachment edge is now broken so that its original form can only be conjectured. The front is decorated with two female saints each of whom stands within a trefoil arch; they were probably identical although only one remains intact. The outside edge was finished with a knop, but the metal along the casting seam has not been filed away round it and the strap-end was apparently abandoned in a semi-finished state. The strap-end was intended for a narrow girdle no more than 13mm wide.

PEWTER STRAP-ENDS, CAST IN A T-SHAPE AND FOLDED

718 BIG82 acc. no. 4210 (context 401) ceramic phase 11 fig 99
Incomplete; pewter (AML); broken off below the strap divide; attachment edge of front has trefoil aperture; back tab is shorter, narrower and plain, with a straight attachment edge; cross-hatching on upper part of front; hole for one rivet; 18+×7mm wide at strap divide.

719 BWB83 2351 (unstratified) fig 99
Pewter (AML); front has stepped aperture at attachment edge and hole for single rivet; plain rectangular back plate; cross-hatching on upper part of front, with a band of zigzags beaded on the lower angles, and beading around the edge; 29×11mm wide at strap divide.

A form of lead-tin strap-end which was presumably cast in a T-shape has a central tab on the reverse that was folded to accommodate a strap. The strap was secured by a single rivet apparently made from a similar metal to the end (see MoL acc. no. 84.267/2, fig 99). Two strap-ends of this type have been recovered from DUA excavations (nos. 718 & 719, fig 99), but only one is from a dated deposit, namely the late 14th century (ceramic phase 11). However, as other lead-tin strap-ends from London do not come from deposits earlier than this, it seems probable that their output began around the second half of the 14th century. These strap-ends are all decorated with cross-hatching at the front attachment edge. Below this the decoration varies. Number 719 has a band of zigzags and a beaded edge, it may also have had a small knop originally, but the edge is damaged at this point. An incomplete strap-end probably had openwork decoration below a beaded border, and this type of decoration is common on other strap-ends of this form which were evidently mass-produced (eg Mitchiner 1986, 68 no. 122; MoL acc. no. 84.267/2, fig 99). In view of the flimsy character of these small items it is questionable whether any of them were actually worn as strap-ends, and it has been suggested for a group of smaller replica belt-ends from Norwich that they had devotional connotations and were purchased at pilgrim shrines (Spencer 1980, 19).

TWO-PIECE STRAP-ENDS WITH A HINGED PLATE AND LOOP

Length and width are for both parts together, with internal diameter of loop hole at end given in brackets; all are cast:

Copper alloy

720 BWB83   acc. no. 4606   (context 279) ceramic phase 11   fig 101
Brass (AML); tapering; concave attachment edge; two rivets; loop with a flat back and central hole; 32×max8mm (2.5mm).

721 BC72   4859   (25)   11   fig 101
Incomplete and corroded; gunmetal (AML); engraved cabling defined by linear border along sides; hinged part ends in a stylised animal head, which is broken off at the loop; two rivets; 39+×9mm; on leather strap.

722 SWA81   2027   (2106/2107)   12   fig 101
Gunmetal (AML); engraved linear border on plate; single rivet; 29×10mm (2mm).

723 BWB83   113   (265)   12   fig 101
Brass (AML); concave attachment edge; two rivets; loop has two notches on terminal; 33×10mm (2mm); on silk tablet-woven strap.

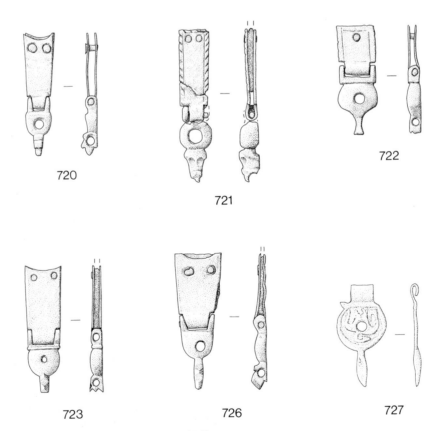

720   721   722   723   726   727

101   Strap-ends with a hinged plate and a loop (1:1)

724 SWA81 1202 (2100) 12
Bronze (AML); concave attachment edge; single rivet;
loop similar to that on no. 720; 34×10mm (2mm).

725 BC72 731 (15) unphased
Corroded; similar to preceding item; 33×max10mm
(2mm).

726 BWB83 41 (12) unphased fig 101
Gunmetal (AML); similar to no. 720;
36×max13mm (2.5mm); on leather strap.

A small group of copper-alloy strap-ends from late
14th-century (ceramic phase 11) and early 15th-
century (ceramic phase 12) deposits in London
are composed of two pieces – a hinged, double-
sided plate to which a strap was riveted, and a
cast loop. The loop has a central hole and the
reverse is flat; it terminates in a small loop, 2mm
or 2.5mm diameter, which is sometimes styled in
the form of an animal head. This second loop is at
right angles to the rest of the strap-end. These
strap-ends range in width from 8mm to 13mm and
have straight or concave attachment edges with
one or two rivets.

Comparative examples described by Ilse Fingerlin suggest that these ends form pairs, which
were connected by a hook and possibly a chain
(Fingerlin 1971, 441 no. 443 fig 241). Any connecting link would have to have been very fine for
the London fittings since the internal diameter of
each loop is tiny, but the end of the loop was
clearly subject to strain since one loop has broken
at this point (no. 721, fig 101). These strap-ends
may not necessarily have been worn with dress,
one interpretation is that they were a form of
book fastener (Henig 1988, 181 nos. 9–11 fig 54)
and in view of the prevalence of these items in
ecclesiastical contexts this is an attractive
hypothesis.

Comparable strap-ends found in northern
France (Fingerlin 1971, 464 no. 521 fig 240) and
in the Netherlands (Boymans-van Beuningen
Museum, Rotterdam, acc. nos. F6554–62) indicate that they had a continental, as well as English,
distribution.

HINGED FITTING

Copper alloy

727 SWA81   acc. no. 3380   (context 2139)
ceramic phase 9 fig 101
Possible strap-end; copper (AML); cast; circular, with
central hole; folded hinge at attachment edge; damaged
terminal; decorated with a stylised long-necked beast
in relief; traces of a greenish material could be corroded enamel (AML); l 27mm×d 14mm.

A fitting of uncertain purpose, although classified
here as a strap-end, has a hinge at one end and a
damaged terminal at the other, which may originally have been in the form of an animal head; in
between is a flat, round disc with a central hole
(no. 727, fig 101). The disc is decorated with a
long-necked, humped-back beast, probably of
mythical origin, shown in profile. It is made from
copper and has traces of what may be enamel. It
is the only item of this form represented here
and, although it was recovered from a late 13th-
or early 14th-century deposit (ceramic phase 9),
it probably dates to the early part of the 13th
century.

SINGLE PLATES WITH A HOOK

Copper alloy

728 SWA81   acc. no. 2106   (context 2025)
ceramic phase 9 fig 102
Mercury-gilded copper plate, brass rivets (AML);
inward-curving hook; two rivets with roves; 33×6mm;
on leather strap consisting of two thicknesses of
leather 8mm w.

729 SWA81 1904 (2137) 9 fig 102
Gunmetal (AML); plate has bevelled edges; outward-
curving hook; three rivets; on leather strap; 57×7mm.

Iron

730 BWB83 8 (110) 11 fig 102
Tin-coated; outward-curving hook; single rivet;
corners at end cut diagonally; 32×22mm; on leather
strap consisting of two thicknesses of leather with grain
side outermost 27mm w. For accompanying bar-mount
see no. 1146.

731 BWB83 3970 (307) 11 fig 102
Tin-coated; outward-curving hook; slightly serrated
attachment edge; two flat-headed rivets with roves;
54×21mm.

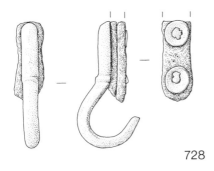

728

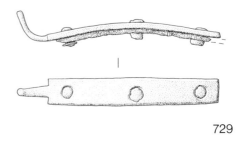

729

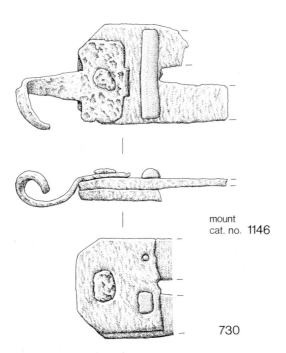

mount
cat. no. 1146

730

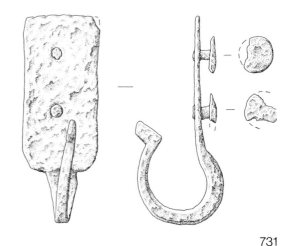

731

102   Strap-ends with hooks (1:1)

SHIELD SHAPED SHEET PLATES WITH BAR-MOUNTS ETC AT ATTACHMENT EDGE (GE)

All the bar-mounts are cut from longer rods (of D-shaped section unless otherwise stated); unless otherwise stated, rivets have roves. NB in each case the length is that of the plate and the width that of the mount where this survives. See fig 76B for the possible function of the notch on no. 738.

(dimensions given are for the plate, with those for the bar-mounts in brackets)

Copper alloy

732   BWB83   acc. no. 5906   (context 318) ceramic phase 11   fig 103
Slight notch in each side of plate; point at inside edge; rectangular bar-mount; two rivets, the one through the mount retains a rove; 13×9mm (3×9mm).

733   BWB83   5823   (303)   11   fig 103
Brass (AML); round inside edge; two notches and

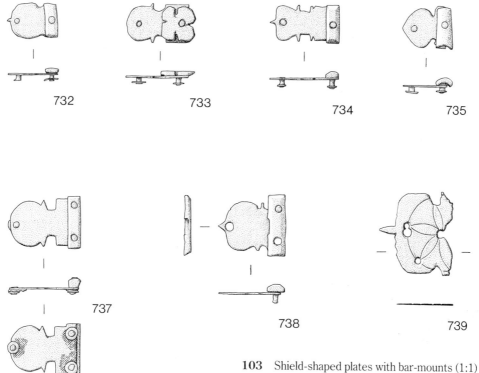

103 Shield-shaped plates with bar-mounts (1:1)

point on each side; crude quatrefoil mount has recess on the underside; two rivets with roves; 19×9mm (9×9mm).

734 BWB83 3773 (338) 11 fig 103
As no. 732, but three notches on each side of plate, and both rivets have roves; 9×10mm (3.5×10mm).

735 BWB83 5918 (298) 11 fig 103
Gunmetal (AML); notch on each side of plate; angled inside edge; both rivets have roves; bar-mount has arched section 14×11mm (4.5×11mm).

736 BWB83 1241 (110) 11
As no. 732, except inside edge is straight; mount and one rivet not preserved; 20×12mm.

737 BWB83 5197 (306) 11 fig 103
Brass (AML); inside edge is rounded; notch and point on each side; three rivets; 19×14mm (3.5×15mm); on silk tablet-woven strap.

738 BWB83 5169 (157) 11 fig 103
Brass (AML); as preceding item, except the mount has a recess on its underside; one rivet preserved; 18×16mm (5×16mm).
See fig 76B for the way this kind of fitting may have been used with a folding clasp.

739 BWB83 2102 (307) 11 fig 103
Incomplete; part of plate only; notch at each side; point on inside edge; part of compass-engraved sexfoil within a circle – the edges and the centre of the sexfoil are pierced (this decoration presumably relates to an earlier use of the sheeting); a hole near the inside edge was pierced a second time for a rivet.

740 BWB83 5091 (unstratified)
Two notches on each side of plate; round inside edge; three rivet holes; mount missing; 24×19mm.

741 BWB83 5090 (unstratified)
As preceding item, except one rivet hole may have been pierced a second time; 24×20mm.

742 BWB83 5134 (unstratified)
As no. 732, except for two notches on each side of plate and round inside edge; two rivets at end and possible one at inside edge; c.26×c.21mm (3×21mm).

Although none of these distinctive fittings from the recent excavations retains more than traces of its associated strap, a roughly cut, straight edge (at the straight end of the plate) on the leather attached to another example recovered more recently (MoL acc. no. 88.87/2) suggests that they were indeed put at the ends of straps. A more specialised function than for other strap-ends is suggested by the shape of the sheeting and by the mount on the outside edge. This may in part be clarified by considering the purpose of the recess facing towards the inside edge in the mounts on nos. 733 and 738. The latter strap-end can neatly be joined to folding clasp no. 559, with the projection on the folding end fitting into the mount's recess, to make a firmly closed two-part clasp (see p 116 and fig 76B). The shield shape and side notches of the plates may have been to give more flexibility than straight edges in fitting the two elements together in the manner suggested.

There was clearly considerable variety in detail on both the shield-shaped strap-ends and the folding clasps. While the former are so far restricted to deposits dating to the late 14th century (ceramic phase 11) on just one site, the latter occur in contexts attributed to ceramic phases 9 to 12 on several sites (late 13th- or early 14th- to early 15th centuries). The range of these fittings available, even during the period of over-lap with folding clasps in the late 14th century, is probably not represented in its entirety by the examples listed here. There is no satisfactory pairing among the fittings recovered during the recent excavations other than that illustrated in fig 76B. A wider range of examples is required before any more of the very precise pairings can be demonstrated, or perhaps other ways of using these fittings might be considered instead.

FOLDED SHEETING, WITH WIDE GAPS AT THE FOLDS

Possible strap-ends (GE)

The following items are tentatively identified as strap-ends. They have no hole for a buckle pin and cannot therefore be buckle plates, and they lack recesses at the sides, the presence of which (without a pin hole) would have suggested that they were plates for folding clasps. They are comparable in form to iron strap-ends surviving on the series of short straps with two groups of mounts thought to be from spurs (see eg no. 1182 under Mounts – fig 136). Several of those strap-ends have a gap that has been deliberately ex-

panded within the fold, so that it is of an appropriate size to accommodate a buckle frame, though there is no evidence that any of them ever did so. This all suggests that sheeting was cut into rectangles, which were folded as part of the process of mass-production, and the resulting items could then be used either for strap-ends, or be further adapted with a slot or holes to accommodate pins, for use as buckle plates.

Six of the following items are decorated on both the back and the front – nos. 745, 749, 750, 752 & 756, and no. 754 seems to have different decoration on each face (the more ornate tooling being on the opposite face from the decorative rivet heads). The implication is that both faces would have been visible, though there is no ready explanation of how that might be the case. There is limited decoration on the back of definite strap-end no. 614, but this does not in itself constitute a clear enough parallel by which the dual decoration of the present group of items can be explained away. Those examples in which the corners at the end are slightly angled could have been used for folding clasps, though they too are decorated on both faces. There may also be an overlap between the present category and the strap-ends folded widthways. Number 758, listed under the present category, has the prominent gap at the fold on one face only, and really lies between these two types.

Surviving ends of leather straps are skived.

Copper alloy

743   BIG82   acc. no. 3159   (context 4201)
ceramic phase 7
Incomplete; 31×12mm; broken off at fold; engraved zigzags, defined by double lines, along sides and attachment edge; holes for five rivets.

744   BWB83   5115   (325)   9   fig 104
15×5mm; single missing rivet. A very narrow item if from a strap.

745   BWB83   5004   (325)   9   or residual in later deposit
24×10mm; double line of punched, opposed triangles along sides, end and attachment edge on both faces; five dome-headed rivets; on leather strap.

104   Sheet fittings with looped ends; lower right, front plate of strap-end (1:1)

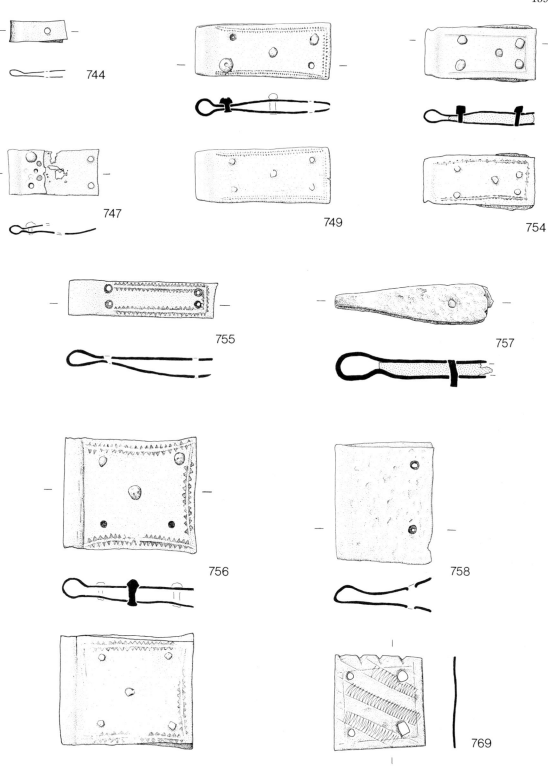

744

747

749

754

755

757

756

758

769

746 BWB83 2374 (290) 9
Fragment, 12+×12mm; holes for two rivets survive; lines of opposed, punched triangles along each side.

747 SWA81 3264 (2141) 9 fig 104
Incomplete and corroded; 25×12mm; incomplete front is punched with circles (two of which have formed holes); holes for four rivets, one of which survives and is dome-headed.

748 SWA81 4824 (2061) 9
19×13mm; single rivet; on leather strap.

749 SWA81 1100 (2126) 9 figs 15B & 104
38×14mm; worn; four of an original five rivets survive, two of yellow alloy (similar to the sheeting) and with domed heads, and two of redder alloy, one of which has a larger and cruder domed head; double line of punched, opposed triangles along sides and end on both faces; on leather strap.

750 SWA81 3958 (2030) 9
Incomplete; 33×21mm; corners at end slightly angled; double line of punched, opposed triangles along sides and attachment edge on both faces; two of five rivets survive; on leather strap.

751 BWB83 1654 (286) 11
Broken off at fold; 36×10.5mm; double engraved lines along sides and end; holes for five missing rivets.

752 BWB83 1235 (110) 11
30×11mm; plate is slightly trapezoidal, with five dome-headed rivets; double line of punched, opposed triangles around edges on both faces.

753 BWB83 2732 (329) 11
31×13mm; lines of opposed, punched triangles at sides and attachment edge; holes for three rivets, a dome-headed one survives.

754 BWB83 2473 (351) 11 fig 104
30×14mm; slightly angled corners at end; five rivets with large heads – the central one is broken; engraved lines around sides and attachment edge on that face, (?) double lines of opposed, punched triangles on the other; on leather strap.

755 BWB83 4712 (300) ?11 fig 104
40×9mm; double line of punched, opposed triangles along sides and slightly concave attachment edge; holes for four missing rivets.

756 SWA81 510 (unstratified, from 2026 area) ?9 fig 104
36×30mm; slightly concave sides; double lines of opposed, punched triangles along sides and attachment edge on both faces; holes for five rivets, three of which survive and are dome-headed.

Iron

757 BC72 4419 (150) 11. fig 104
Tapering; single rivet; notched attachment edge; tin-coated; 41×max10mm; on leather strap.

758 BWB83 3044 (110) 11 fig 104
26×30mm; tin-coated; holes for two rivets.

See also the plates on short straps with two groups of mounts, nos. 1169 – 1186.

PAIRED SHEET PLATES

Copper alloy

759 BWB83 acc. no. 5902 (context 298) ceramic phase 11
Tongue-shaped; two rivets; 19×9mm.

760 BWB83 715 (306) 11
End broken off; tapering with concave sides; single rivet; 36+×10mm.

761 BWB83 2164 (142) 11
Incomplete; as preceding item, but only one plate; 40+×12mm.

762 TL74 1124 (10) 12
Incomplete; one corner at attachment edge cut diagonally; one rivet preserved; 18×22+mm.

Separated metal plates

(from either front or back unless otherwise stated)

Copper alloy

Tongue shaped

763 SWA81 1031 (2127) 9
Two rivet holes at attachment end; 24×17mm.

764 BWB83 5891 (309) 12
Lacks any rivet hole; 30×10mm. Probably unfinished.

Straight end

765 BWB83 3101 (285) 9
Tapering; concave attachment edge with two iron rivets; 29×max19mm.

Pointed end

766 BWB83 4624 (279) 11
Attachment edge broken off; 20+×max11mm.

Uncertain end forms

767 BIG82 2844 (5222) 7
Incomplete plate; tapering; two rivet holes; 25+×max21mm.

768 BWB83 4113 (361) 11
Incomplete plate; brass (AML); ornately shaped, broken attachment end (?scalloped), with round aperture; end broken off; two rivets, one with a rove; 30+×22mm.

769 BWB83 5372 (303) 11 fig 104
Front plate; notched attachment edge; holes for four rivets – round holes on one side, larger and squarer ones on the other; engraved zigzags between diagonal lines within linear frame; 25×max25mm.

Mounts

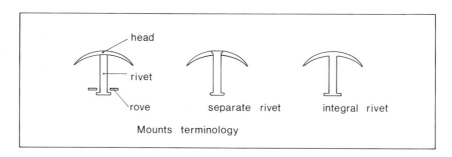

Mounts terminology

105

This category includes various fittings, studs etc, which are in the main purely decorative, though arched pendent mounts, strap plates, eyelets, strap loops, and perhaps some other items included here had a specific function. Mounts usually have rivets for attachment to leather or textile (see nos. 921 & 919 for examples of the same form for both materials), but a few other items, which may have been attached in different ways, are also included.

Probably the great majority of the mounts described here would have gone on girdles and other straps, though they are also known occasionally on other items – on a purse (no. 1701 fig 232) and probably on an early 15th-century shoe (Grew and de Neergaard 1988, 38 fig 60 – SWA81 acc. no. 4620), and see Rorimer (1972, 68–69 figs 87 & 88) for a Spanish tomb effigy from the 13th century which appears to show a proliferation of mounts all over a surcoat worn with armour.

Surviving examples still in place and contemporary depictions suggest that mounts like those described below were rarely if ever used singly; rather their overall decorative effect depended largely on repetition on the strap or other object. Combinations of more than one form, apparently always of the same metal, sometimes occur together (see on combinations and possible en-suite fittings pp 244–46). Mounts were, however, not invariably of the same metal as the buckles they accompanied (eg nos. 907 & 457). There is a distinct possibility, since survival of the material to which mounts were originally fixed is quite limited, that some of those included here were not dress accessories at all, but were attached to items of furniture, book covers, caskets, etc (see nos. 1061–62, 1143 & 1284–87). This may especially be the case with some of the more robust items. There is also a large potential overlap with various horse trappings. The survival of attached leather does not always mean that the mount went on a strap (where it definitely is from one this is indicated).

Different effects could be produced by altering the pattern or orientation of mounts of the same form (eg no. 802 fig 108, no. 1068 & parallel, fig 125, & the bar-mounts in fig 138 at bottom), and even by using slightly different ways of mounting on the leather (see nos. 858 & 895 fig 112).

The wrought-iron mounts are of relatively simple forms (plain circular etc) because of the difficulty of making elaborate forms in this metal. The stamped sheeting mounts of copper alloys (sometimes very thin, eg nos. 1049 & 1051, fig 123, & 1098, fig 128) and iron (invariably tin-coated) are remarkable survivals – these objects are among the most vulnerable to corrosion of all the metal categories considered in this volume. Sheet copper-alloy mounts first appear in early 13th-century deposits (ceramic phase 7 – no. 1098), and they proliferate in the late 14th and early 15th centuries. Sheet-iron mounts, which first appear in late 14th-century deposits and continue into the next century, also include some quite elaborate forms (eg no. 1085, fig 126). The three largest and most visually impressive of all the mounts (no. 933, fig 116) are composite, with armorial decoration, and are of a type used on several other items in addition to dress.

CATALOGUE SCHEME :

Arranged by the shape of head , flat mounts are described before domed etc examples in each category, and those with separate rivets precede those with integral ones. Where two dimensions are given they are in order of length then width↑ .

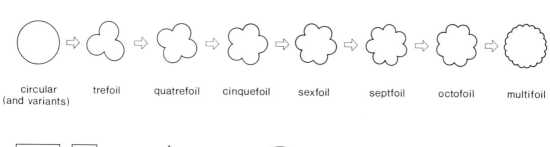

circular (and variants)   trefoil   quatrefoil   cinquefoil   sexfoil   septfoil   octofoil   multifoil

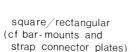

other non-figurative mounts, including polygons .

square/rectangular (cf bar-mounts and strap connector plates)   lozenge   figurative shapes shell, stars etc.

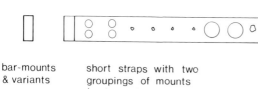

bar-mounts & variants   short straps with two groupings of mounts (various shapes)   circular mounts with pendent motifs   bar-mounts with pendent loops   arched pendent mounts

asymmetrical mounts with ridge & aperture   strap connector plates   eyelets   strap loops

openwork and foil mounts lacking rivets   manufacturing evidence   comparanda

spangles

The *order* in which the mounts are listed is as follows: The headings under which they are described are primarily according to shape; within this they are divided according to metals, grouped into those with *separate* rivets and those with *integral* ones (usually cast); mounts with a single rivet are followed by those with two, and then those with more; in the categories comprising large numbers of items flat-headed mounts are followed by domed ones, and then those with more complex profiles or ornate decoration. (The order varies slightly in some categories, depending on the particular emphasis of different traits among the listed mounts.) In each of these sub-groupings items are then listed according to the date (ie ceramic phase) of the deposit in which they were found, in order of increasing object size within each phase. A few categories are defined by criteria other than shape alone; thus functional eyelets are a separate series, and mounts lacking obvious means of attachment are also listed together.

Unless otherwise stated, copper-alloy and iron mounts are of sheet metal, with separate rivets (stamped into shape if they are other than flat), and lead/tin ones are cast. Where rivets are of a different metal from the mount head, the former are shown in section drawings in outline; rivets of the same metal are shown solid. Almost all the lead/tin mounts have integral rivets – it would have been quite difficult to attach a separate rivet to a head of these materials (though see no. 1064 fig 125 for lead-tin heads on copper-alloy rivets). The pressure necessary to effect the fixture of the rivet has in no case involved obvious damage to the head, which is sometimes delicately decorated; fixture was presumably effected by striking the rivet while the head rested against padding such as leather.

Rivets are present unless otherwise stated. Those 8mm or more in length are specified, since the mounts on which they are found may not have been for leather of the usual thickness for straps (there seems to be no criterion based on form that differentiates the mounts with long rivets). Although it is possible to attach mounts by bending a long rivet round (this was often how nails were attached to wood), it seems from the evidence available from the recent finds to have been relatively rare in dress accessories (eg mounts 802 & 1079, which are mounted together

on one strap, fig 108). Unused mounts with long or tapering rivets might have been intended to have these cut down prior to use. In copper-alloy mounts separate rivets are relatively uncommon for cast heads (eg nos. 791–92, fig 107), while nos. 1064, 1097 and 1104 (figs 125, 127 & 128) are the only mounts with heads of lead-tin and separate rivets among the finds. Riveting might seem more appropriate for attaching mounts to leather than to textile – nevertheless mounts nos. 915 and 919 (cf no. 913 fig 114), both with relatively thin, wire-like rivets, have surviving scraps of textile at the back, as does no. 855, which has a thicker, bent rivet or shank (fig 111). Unless otherwise stated, *roves* are circular, *c*.3mm in diameter, and of copper-alloy sheeting (whatever the metal of the mount itself). Only two of the items listed below have rivets with roves of lead/tin (nos. 830 & 1064), but these seem to be more common among London finds of late-medieval date in private collections. Numbers 869 and 871 have decorative roves at the front as well as functional ones at the back (fig 112).

Mount-like items with tapering shanks that end in points (cf nails and tacks), and which sometimes have decorative heads (see no. 1300), are not fully listed here, since they are more likely to have been attached to wooden furnishings or upholstery than to girdles, but see no. 1129 for tacks on a strap (fig 130). There may have been no rigid division as far as contemporaries were concerned, and improvised repairs are likely to have extended the usage of what was to hand in ways initially surprising to the present-day analytical mind. This is occasionally true of regular practice (ordinary iron nails were apparently a normal means of holding together the straps on late 14th-century pattens in London – Grew and de Neergard 1988, 93–96 figs 128–31).

Mounts still on leather are set with the heads on the grain side where this can be determined, unless otherwise indicated. Solder seems to have been used, as well as hammering, on the rivets of several of the mounts described below (including some still attached to leather straps – eg no. 1194). Reuse of elements of these mounts from items attached to rigid objects of metal (buckle plates etc) does not seem to be a satisfactory explanation for every instance of this, and it is likely that separate rivets were regularly attached to the mounts by both methods together. The presence of solder on a rivet certainly does not mean that an item was not a dress accessory.

Some types of mount, such as copper-alloy sexfoils, occur in two basic forms – plain with one or two rivets, and also with a central hole and two rivets to the sides (eg nos. 952 & 990, fig 119). Those with larger central holes were sometimes used when a series of mounts was used on the part of a strap where there were holes for the buckle pin (fig 143). The mounts here doubled as strengthening surrounds for the pin holes. Eyelets can be seen as a more rigid kind of hole surround than the centrally holed mounts with rivets. Not all centrally holed mounts were actually used with buckles; a few are still attached to leather straps which lack corresponding holes (eg no. 1132 fig 133) – here the holes in these fittings are purely decorative.

CIRCULAR MOUNTS

Plain, flat heads, with holes for single, separate rivets

Copper alloy

(only nos. 776 & 787 have rivets surviving)

770 SWA81 acc. no. 1101 (context 2126) ceramic phase 9 fig 107
d 9mm

771 SWA81 434 (2018) 9
d 18mm; one face has parallel marks.

772 SWA81 3250 (2141) 9
Corroded; d 18.5mm+.

773 SWA81 587 (2055) 9
As preceding item; d 19mm.

774 SWA81 1496 (2046) 9
As preceding item.

775 SWA81 1925 (2135) 9
As preceding item.

776 BWB83 18 (108) 10 fig 107
Six of at least eight original mounts, each d 6mm and with a rove, on a leather strap (58×6mm, torn off at one end, possibly at both; the mounts' heads are on the flesh side of the leather.

This tiny strip is presumably a purely decorative element from a larger object.

777 BC72 4628 (250) 10 figs 18C & 107
d 23.5mm; irregular central hole; parallel marks in two directions at right angles on both sides.

778 BWB83 2188 (157) 11 fig 107
d 14mm; edges bent down at a right angle from the stamping.

779 BWB83 4185 (401) 11 fig 107
d 20.5mm; oval hole to one side of central rivet hole.

780 BWB83 1351 (108) 11 fig 107
d 24mm; central rivet hole and six other irregular ones.

781 BWB83 3749 (338) 11
d 24mm

782 BWB83 2351 (147) 11
d 26mm; irregularly cut from sheeting; folded in half; parallel marks on visible face.

783 BWB83 4564 (279) 11
d 31mm

784 BWB83 4183 (401) 11
d 34mm; parallel marks on one face.

785 BWB83 5840 (282) 11
d 35mm; additional hole near edge.

786 BWB83 1409 (146) 11 fig 107
d 35.5mm; irregularly cut from sheeting; crudely-pierced hole.

787 BWB83 5872 (309) 12
d 12mm; rivet has rove.

788 BWB83 5404 (310) 12
d 15mm

789 BWB83 4740 (309) 12
d 15.5mm

790 BWB83 5843 (310) 12
d 36mm; segment missing from the circle.

Four of the mounts in the above series have parallel striations on the surface (fig 18C). Although these marks look rather similar to those on sheeting that has been rolled flat in a mill, on no. 777 the marks do not run in the same direction on both faces. The earliest stratified example here must be from the early 14th century at the latest – some 150 years prior to the accepted date for the invention of the rolling mill (traditionally by Leonardo da Vinci – see Usher 1957, 340). Anthony North (pers. comm.) suggests that these marks are from the polishing of the sheeting prior to cutting out the mounts.

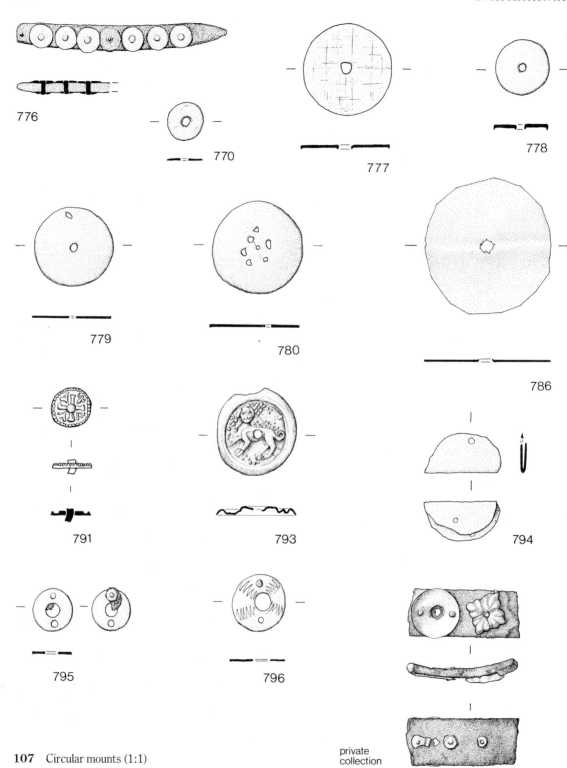

776

770

777

778

779

780

786

791

793

794

795

796

private
collection

107 Circular mounts (1:1)

Circular – flat, with single, separate rivets

decorated heads

Copper alloy

791 SWA81 619 (2065) 9 fig 107
d 10mm; cast head, with cross moline having alternate fleur-de-lis and Lombardic V motifs in the angles, beaded border.

792 SWA81 2155 (2030) 9
As preceding item; rivet missing.

793 BC72 4135 (88) 11 fig 107
d 23mm; brass (AML); design stamped from a die – hound passant guardant on a field of lozenges, in plain raised border; rivet missing.
 Cf nail/tack no. 1300 for a similar item. Further stamped discs of this kind found in London (private collections) depict a lion, and a bird of prey.

Circular – flat, with two separate rivets

Copper alloy

794 SWA81 519 (2040) 9 fig 107
d 19mm; folded in half; crudely cut from sheeting; rivets missing.

795 BWB83 7 (110) 11 fig 107
d 10.5mm; one rivet survives, with rove; large central hole; leather survives.

796 SWA81 852 (unstratified) fig 107
Corroded; d 14mm; large, slightly offcentred hole; at least four engraved radiating zigzags; two iron rivets.

The two preceding mounts could have acted as surrounds for holes for buckle pins in straps. A similar mount on a leather strap found in London is accompanied by another of elaborate quatrefoil form (fig 107 – private collection); here the leather is not pierced at the point corresponding with the hole in the mount.

Circular – flat, with single, integral rivet

Copper alloy

all probably cast

797 BWB83 1239 (110) 11 fig 108
d 10mm; rove d 9mm; organic material, probably leather, survives.

798 TL74 559 (415) 11 fig 108
d 10mm; copper (AML); five circles punched unevenly around the edge.

799 BWB83 4900 (317) 11
d 15.5mm

800 BWB83 1572 (108) 11
Head folded; d 24mm; rivet 8mm long.

Lead/tin

801 BC72 3524 (250) 10 fig 108
Eight surviving mounts of tin (RAK, two analysed), each d *c.*6.5mm, in two groups on a leather strap 132×9.5mm (torn off at both ends; crude holes between the groups).
 Probably an incomplete short strap originally with two groups of mounts – see nos. 1168 – 1186.

802 TL74 2031 (414) 11 fig 108
Nine mounts, each d 9mm, on folded leather strap with lozenge-shaped mount no. 1079; several of the rivets are bent over rather than hammered; tin (B Gilmour, Royal Armouries, HM Tower of London); the surviving mounts are in four pairs along the centre and also at the side, with another single mount at the side; there are holes for further missing mounts.

803 BWB83 3619 (386) 11 fig 109
Lead-tin (MLC); d 12mm; quatrefoil motif with dots in external angles and in centre of each lobe, all within a raised border.

804 BWB83 5884 (287) 11
Tin (MLC, RAK); d 12mm; rivet 9mm long.

805 BWB83 1278 (110) 11 fig 109
Ovoid, max d 12mm; four concentric rings of dots.
 The ovoid outline is probably attributable to a deficiency of metal in a circular mould, as the outermost ring is incomplete.

806 BWB83 4981 (376) 11
d 12mm; bevelled edge.

807 BWB83 2280 (128) 11
Tin (RAK); damaged; d 12.5mm; rivet broken off; head possibly domed originally.

808 BWB83 4044 (293) 11 fig 109
d 13mm; tin (AML; lead-tin, MLC); bevelled edge.

809 BWB83 5160 (157) 11 fig 109
d 13mm; bevelled edge; four radius lines on the back probably include guidelines put on the mould by the cutter (cf no. 850).

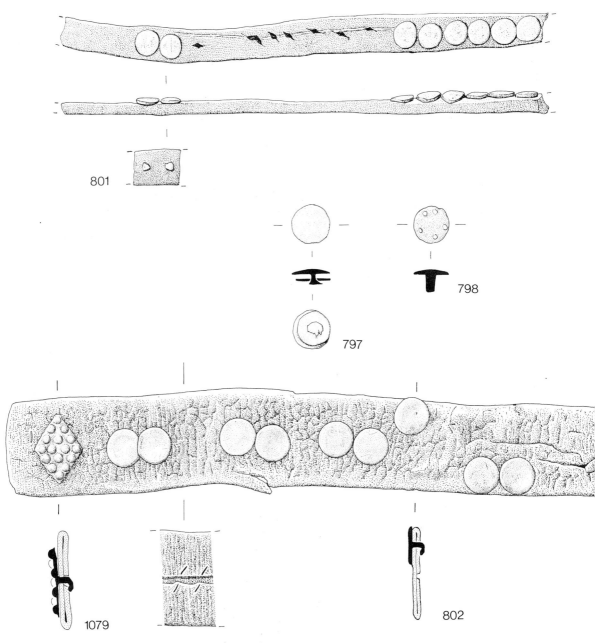

108 Circular mounts: lozenge mount on lower strap is no. 1079 (1:1)

810 BWB83 4985 (376) 11
Crumpled and abraded; d 18mm; trace of ?dots in field; rivet 10mm long.

811 SWA81 884 (2112) 12 fig 109
Eight surviving mounts and holes from others now lost,

each an openwork six-pointed star in a beaded border, d 10mm, on leather strap 355×14mm (torn off at both ends, engraved line along each edge).

812 SWA81 1962 (2103) 12
Mount as those of preceding item.

Since both contexts are from the same dump, these may originally have been part of the same object.

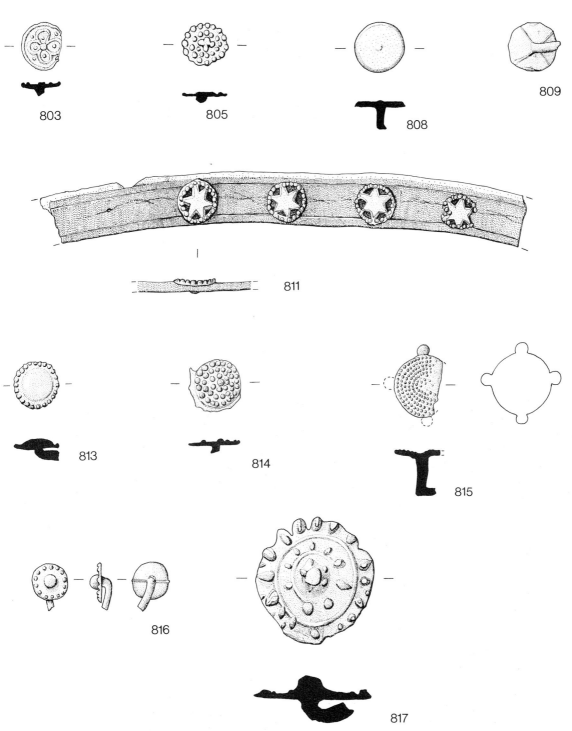

109 Circular mounts; shape of no. 815 restored from
a parallel (1:1)

813 BWB83 5068 (319) 12 fig 109
d 12.5mm; slightly domed centre; beaded border.

814 BWB83 3237 (265) 12 fig 109
d 13mm (+ excess metal from the casting); three concentric rings of dots.

815 SWA81 2977 (2084) 12 fig 109
Incomplete, d 15.5mm; tin (AML, RAK); eight concentric rings of dots and knop at edge; rivet 10mm long.

Parallels from London (private collections) indicate that there would originally have been four knops around the edge. One of the parallels retains a lead/tin rove. Cf fig 157A.

816 BWB83 5099 (unstratified) fig 109
Tin (MLC); d 9mm; central boss and beaded edge.

817 BWB83 4435 (unstratified) fig 109
d 32mm; lead-tin (RAK); crude decoration of three concentric rings of thick, radiating strokes, with plain ring between the two outer ones; shank *c*.12mm long; the metal did not fill one end of the mould in casting, resulting in an irregular profile, especially where the relief decoration has determined the edge.

Circular – flat, with two integral rivets

Lead/tin

818 SWA81 3289 (2112) 12 fig 110
d 10mm; central hole.

Possibly a buckle-pin hole surround.

Circular – plain domed, with single, integral rivets

Copper alloy
probably cast

819 SWA81 1581 (2209) 6 fig 110
d 14mm; gunmetal (AML); rove appears integral.

820 BIG82 2516 (3135) 7 colour pl 1C
Corroded; d 14mm+; brass (AML), (?)gilded (MLC).

821 SWA81 1256 (2149) 9
d 17mm

822 BWB83 5789 (295) 11
d 10mm

823 SWA81 2969 (2031) 12 fig 110
d 9.5mm

See no. 1293 for a similar mount attached to wood.

Lead/tin

824 SWA81 636 (2078) 9 fig 110
d 7mm; rivet 11mm long is bent over.

Cf no. 1302, which has a tapering, pointed shank.

825 SWA81 1505 (2046) 9
Lead-tin (MLC); d 8mm; rivet broken off.

826 SWA81 2741B (2065) 9
d 8mm

827 BWB83 1290 (124) 9
Distorted; d 11mm.

828 BWB83 2134 (290) 9
d 14mm

829 BC72 1885 (83) 11 fig 110
Five surviving mounts of lead-tin (MLC, two tested), each d 8mm, on a leather strap 95×12mm (torn off at both ends; holes for two other mounts now missing); further holes suggest the strap may earlier have had other mounts set in a different configuration.

Cf short straps with two groups of mounts nos. 1168–86.

830 TL74 513 (414) 11 fig 110
Seventeen surviving domed mounts, each d 8.5mm (extra metal at the edge where the mould did not meet precisely has produced minor differences) and with lead/tin roves, on leather strap 290×25mm (cut rounded at one end, crudely cut off at the other), and a hole for at least one missing mount presumed to be of the same form (for the accompanying mount of a different shape, see no. 1107).

831 BWB83 2248 (131) 11
High-tin lead alloy (RAK); d 9mm; rivet broken off.

832 BWB83 1401 (150) 11 fig 110
d 10mm

833 BWB83 1404 (150) 11 fig 110
d 11mm; rivet *c*.15mm long.

834 BWB83 1252 (138) 11
d 11mm; lead/tin (RAK).

835 BWB83 5161 (157) 11 fig 110
d 12mm

836 BWB83 2161 (142) 11
Folded; d 13mm; tin (MLC); head multiply knocked around centre; rivet 9mm long.

837 BWB83 5027 (380) 11
d 13mm; tin (AML, RAK).

110   Circular mounts (1:1, except no. 830 1:2)

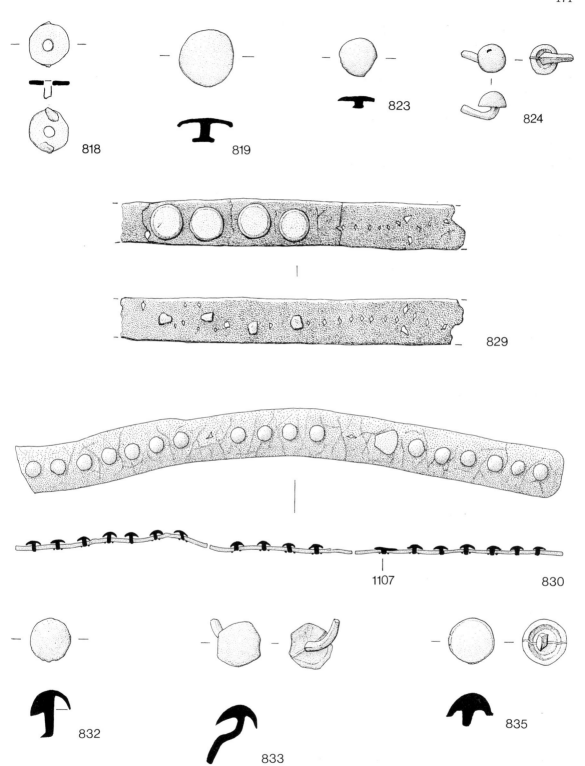

818

819

823

824

829

1107 830

832

833

835

838 BWB83 1474 (136) 11
d 14mm; tin (AML, RAK).

839 BWB83 4021 (352) 11
d 21mm; tin (AML); rivet *c*.15mm long.

840 BWB83 3602 (391) 11 fig 111
d 22mm; tin (AML, RAK).

841 BWB83 1394 (110) 11
Lead-tin (RAK); d 24mm; rivet missing.

842 BWB83 5037 (359) 11
Lead-tin (MLC); d 24mm.

843 BWB83 4511 (285) 11
Tin (RAK); d 25mm

844 BWB83 1391 (110) 11 fig 111
d 25mm; apex abraded; eight small grooves at the edge
are slightly suggestive of an octofoil design.

845 BWB83 4699 (291 area) ?11
Lead-tin (MLC); d 26mm; rivet missing.

846 BWB83 1397 (110) 11
Tin (AML); incomplete, or possibly cast with insufficient metal (cf no. 817); d 29mm; rivet *c*.15mm long.

847 SWA81 883 (2112) 12
Two surviving tin mounts (RAK); each d 13mm, on
leather strap 84×16mm (both ends torn off); heads on
flesh side of the leather.

848 SWA81 2787 (2108) 12 fig 111
Lead-tin (MLC); incomplete; d 19mm; surface of head
uneven.

849 SWA81 2999 (2101) 12 fig 111
d 19mm+; edges folded back to make the head an
irregular rectangle.
    Perhaps folded when no longer used as a mount.

Further mounts of this form are on short strap no. 1186
(fig 126).

Circular – domed, with ornate heads and single, integral rivets

Lead/tin

850 TL74 611 (370) 11 fig 111
d 36mm; tin (MLC); there are several voids where the
metal did not flow in the mould; six-armed wavy star in
raised border; the radiating lines on the back which are
not from a casting seam are probably cutting guidelines
from the mould.
    Cf no. 855.

851 SWA81 1949 (2101) 12

d 14.5mm; central round recess and beaded edge; on
leather strap 37×16mm (torn off at both ends).

852 SWA81 847 (2100) 12 fig 111
As preceding item, d 15mm, with ?prong at one side;
strap 110mm long.

853 SWA81 890 (2100) 12
As no. 851, d 15mm; tin (MLC); strap 75mm long.

854 TL74 2118 (368) 12 fig 111
As preceding three mounts, but with two small prongs
on perimeter; on one of two pieces of leather strap
totalling *c*.223×13mm (not necessarily originally
joined, torn off at both ends).
    A similar mount found in London (fig 111, private
collection) has a loop at one side, suggesting that the
prongs on no. 854 are where one of these has broken
off; on the parallel the inside of the loop is worn,
implying that some pendent item may have been
suspended here (cf bar-mounts with loops nos. 1189–
93).

Presumably nos. 852 and 853 (from the same
dump deposit, and perhaps no. 851 too, which is
assigned to the foreshore below) were originally
part of the same object. The central recess would
be suitable for mounting a stone (see also button
no. 1379 of similar design, which has a glass stone
in place). There is no definite evidence that nos.
851–54 were ever actually furnished with stones.
In the first three, the shanks have been slightly
bent over, and possibly hammered, though neither operation was firm enough to produce the
expected clear signs of permanent fixture. On no.
854 the rivet has definitely been hammered.

855 SWA81 1078 (2100) 12 fig 111 &
colour pl 4H
d 19mm; tin (AML); six-armed wavy star, in raised
border, rivet *c*.11mm long; the radiating lines on the
back which are not casting seams are probably cutting
guidelines from the mould; fibres, possibly from textile
(MLC), were found under the bent rivet.
    Cf no. 850 (from a phase-11 deposit), and button no.
1380 for a similar design.

111   Circular mounts (1:1)

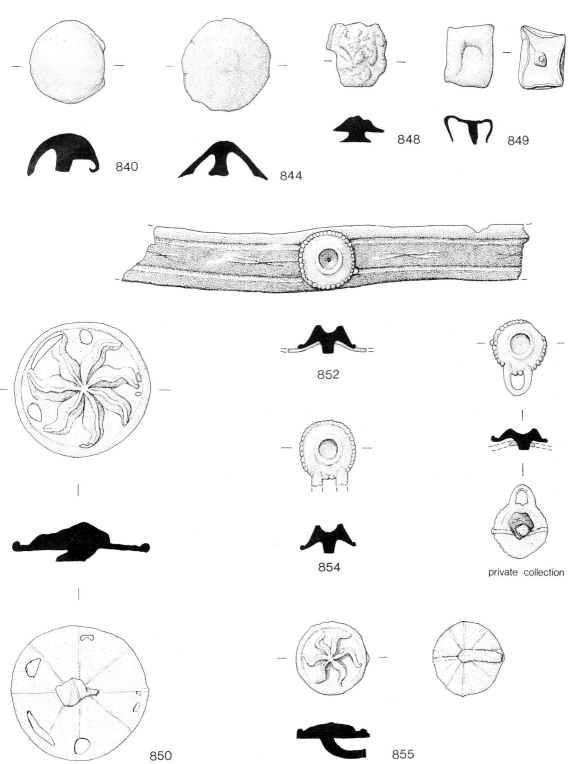

840

844

848

849

852

854

private collection

850

855

Circular – plain domed, with single, separate rivets

Copper alloy

(these have a central hole for the rivet)

856 SWA81 2741A (2065) 9 fig 112
d 8mm; cast; rivet missing.

857 BWB83 4995 (366) 9 fig 112
d 15mm; edge beaded at some points; rivet missing.

858 SWA81 4386 (2032) 11 fig 112
Two surviving mounts, each d 10mm and with a rove, on leather strap 39×10mm (both ends torn off); the mounts, which have dug into the leather, apparently did not continue at one end.

859 BWB83 2400 (290) 11
d 11mm

860 BWB83 3726 (348) 11
Distorted, d *c*.12mm; rivet missing.

861 BWB83 1365 (149) 11
d 13mm; rivet missing.

862 BWB83 5878 (298) 11
d 13mm; rivet missing.

863 BWB83 1349 (156) 11 fig 112
d 18mm; irregularly trimmed.

864 BC72 1763 (55) 11
d 20mm; rivet incomplete.

865 SWA81 757A–K (2097) 12 fig 112
Eleven mounts, each d 11.5mm; brass (AML); the rivets have roves; scraps of leather survive.
   See no. 871.

866 SWA81 2219 (2114) 12
Single mount as preceding items (no leather).

867 BWB83 5874 (314) 12
d 16mm; irregularly trimmed; three concentric rings of raised dots; rivet missing.

868 BWB83 5413 (310) 12
Distorted, d *c*.18mm; no rivet.

869 SWA81 1088 (2100) 12
d 18mm, six engraved radiating lines at edge; rivet has domed rove at front and flat rove at back.

870 SWA81 1089 (2100) 12
As preceding item, but lacks rove at front.

871 SWA81 758A-C (2097) 12 fig 112
Two mounts as preceding items, and one that is flattened, d 19mm; brass (AML); some radiating lines are paired.

These mounts may have come from the same leather object as mounts no. 865.

872 SWA81 3820 (unstratified)
d 15mm; rivet missing.

The following copper-alloy items have single, separate shanks of various metals and lack a central hole:

873 SWA81 1610 (2176) 6
d 10mm; corroded iron shank is bent over 12mm from the head.

874 SWA81 1596 (2182) ?6
d 14mm; back partly filled with lead; shank missing.

875 BWB83 2393 (290) 9
d 10mm

876 TL74 725 (415) 10
d 10mm; back partly filled with lead; lead shank.

877 TL74 562 (414) 11 fig 112
d 10mm; brass head, back partly filled with lead-tin (AML); lead shank 12mm long.

878 BWB83 1399 (150) 11
d 10mm; soldered lead shank (MLC) *c*.10mm long.

879 BWB83 2247 (151) 11
d 10mm; back partly filled with lead; shank missing.

880 BWB83 1412 (146) 11
d 10mm; back partly filled with lead; copper-alloy wire shank *c*.10mm long.

881 BWB83 4387 (358) 11
d 10mm; no shank or solder.

882 BWB83 2249 (151) 11
d 11mm; solder for missing shank.

883 BWB83 2191 (157) 11
Damaged; d 11.5mm; back partly filled with lead; shank missing.

884 BWB83 4200 (401) 11
d 14mm; solder for missing shank.

885 BWB83 2731 (328) 11
d 17; back filled with lead; incomplete iron shank.

886 BWB83 3839 (257) 11 fig 112
d 17mm, back partly filled with lead; iron shank.

887 BWB83 2730 (328) 11
d 18mm; back filled with lead; trace of iron shank.

888 BWB83 4599 (318) 11
Distorted, d *c*.18mm; no shank or solder.

The long, thin shanks on the preceding items, together with the copious lead in the backs of

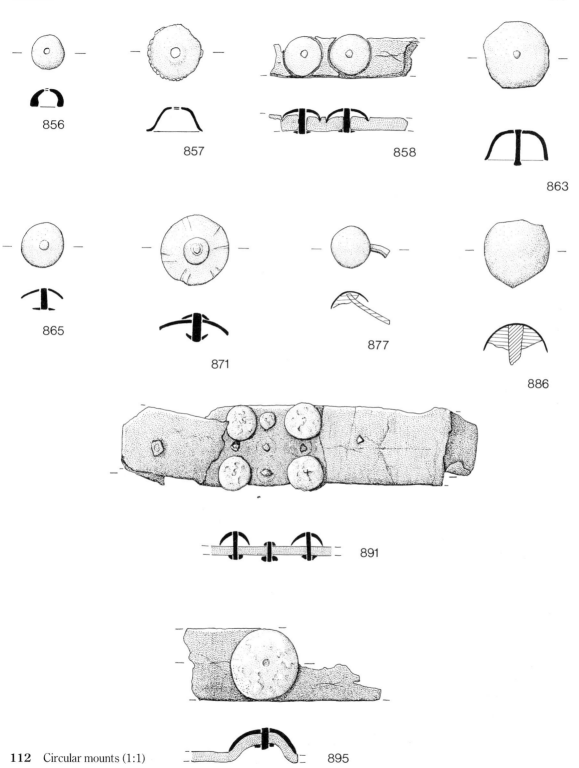

856

857

858

863

865

871

877

886

891

112 Circular mounts (1:1)

895

many of them, define them as a separate group from the other mounts described here. Presumably fixture was effected by bending the shanks; those of lead could not have been very secure. These items, apparently covering a period from the late 12th to the late 14th century, may have been mounts for more robust articles than items of dress. See also no. 1045.

Circular – plain domed

(single, separate rivets unless otherwise stated, continued)

Iron

nos. 891, 895 & 898 may be wrought

889 SWA81 acc. no. 1105 (context 2132) ceramic phase 9
Irregular head; d 11mm; tin coating; leather survives.

890 SWA81 472 (2018) 9
d 18mm; tin coating.

891 BC72 2909 (123) 10–11 fig 112
Nine mounts in three rows of three, the surviving ones at each corner being d 10mm (the lost heads may have been smaller), on leather strap 98×22mm (cut with angled corners at one end, torn off at the other); holes for two further flanking mounts in the middle of the strap.
Cf short straps nos. 1168–1186.

892 BC72 2946 (118) 10–11
One slightly damaged mount, d 11mm, with a possible rove, survives from an original four on a leather strap 81×10mm (both ends torn off; another hole in the middle of the strap may have been for a buckle pin).

893 BWB83 4331 (157) 11
Flattened; irregular outline, d 18mm; tin coating; rivet missing; edge split at three points.

894 BC72 3879A & B (150) 11 fig 232
Two mounts, each d 15mm; head divided into 12 raised, radiating bands, each alternate one is slightly more pronounced than the others, giving an almost hexagonal outline; tin coating; the rivets have roves; on a decorative purse no. 1701, which probably had five such mounts originally, together with rectangular mounts no. 1058.

895 BWB83 301 (4) 11 fig 112
d 19mm; tin coating; a rectangular iron rove holds the mount to a leather strap 19×57mm (torn off at both

ends). The short rivet draws the strap forward out of the flat plane.

896 BC72 2736 (79) 11 fig 113
Incomplete; holed (?damage) near centre; d 37mm; tin coating on both sides; two rivets survive.
Presumably domed rather than concave – cf no. 908 for a similar but concave mount.

897 TL74 3239 (275) 12
Five surviving mounts, each d 12mm and with tin coating, on leather strap 310×14mm (torn off at one end, ?cut at the other), with the marks of perhaps ten more mounts now lost, including one at the end that an imprint suggests was square.

898 SWA81 2673 (unstratified)
d 18mm; (?integral rivet); iron rove.

Circular – domed, with two separate rivets

Copper alloy

899 BWB83 2410 (290) 9 fig 113
d 13mm: additional central hole; rivets have roves. Possibly a buckle pin-hole surround.

900 SWA81 1783 (2103) 12 fig 113
d 15mm; cable-decorated ring between two raised circles; torn metal in centre may be damage rather than wear from a buckle pin; rivets missing.

Circular – ornate, domed heads
Single, separate rivets unless stated

Copper alloy

901 BIG82 acc. no. 2307 (context 2514) ceramic phase 8 fig 113
d 14mm; flat; beaded border; quatrefoil in centre; rivet missing.

902 BWB83 5877 (298) 11 fig 113
d 16mm; raised, five-pointed star in raised cable border; offcentred hole may be damaged; rivet missing.

903 BWB83 3746 (338) 11 fig 113
d 23mm; faceted centre; flat border of squarish bosses; rivet missing.

904 BWB83 3856 (unstratified)
Incomplete, torn at edge; d 22mm+; brass (AML); domed around large central hole; flat edge with two concentric rings; no rivet.

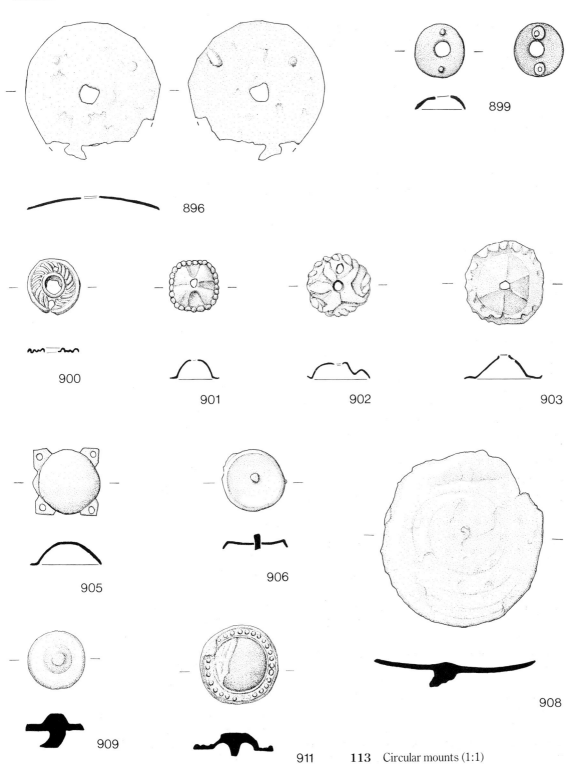

896

899

900

901

902

903

905

906

908

909

911   **113**   Circular mounts (1:1)

Circular – domed, with holes for four separate rivets

Copper alloy

905 BWB83 2725 (328) 11 fig 113
17×18mm; brass (AML); four flat, angled tabs at edge, each with a hole for a missing rivet.
    Possibly from a book cover – see on no. 1062.

Circular – concave heads

Copper alloy

906 BC72 acc. no. 4181 (88)
ceramic phase 11   fig 113
d 16mm; vertical edge; single rivet.

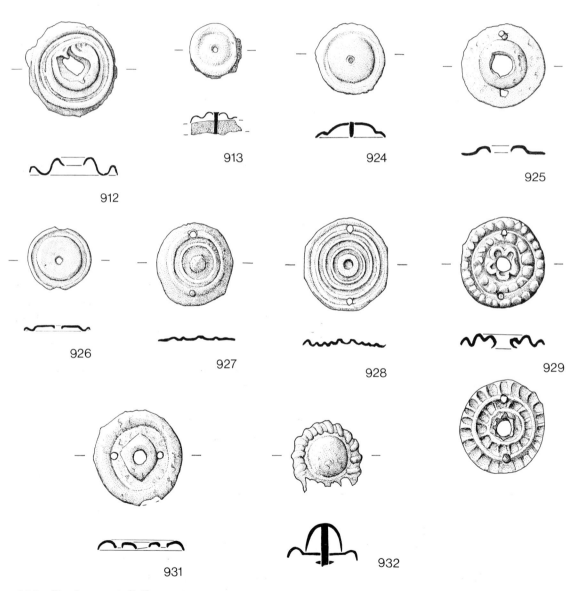

114 Circular mounts (1:1)

Iron

907 BC72 1511 (55) 11 fig 63 & colour pl 1G
Two mounts, each d 15mm, with vertical edges, tin coating and a copper-alloy rivet, on a leather strap 16mm wide, to which rectangular buckle no. 457 is attached.

908 BC72 2735 (79) 11 fig 113
Incomplete; d 45mm; tin coating on both sides; trace of concentric (?lathe-turning) marks on front.

Cf no. 896 for a somewhat similar mount that is probably convex.

Circular – ornate forms

Domed centre and flat perimeter, with single integral rivets

Lead/tin

909 BWB83 acc. no. 5885 (context 291)
ceramic phase 11 fig 113
d 14mm

910 BC72 1793 (55) 11
d 17mm; no rivet.

911 BWB83 5888 (314) 12 fig 113
d 20mm; ring of beading within raised border.

Circular – domed centre with concentric ring, with single, separate rivets

Copper alloy

912 BWB83 4155 (219) 9 fig 114
Edge torn, centre distorted (originally domed?); d 25mm; rivet missing.

The following items are among the commonest forms of mount from the late-medieval period. Organic survivals indicate they were attached to both leather and textile.

913 BC72 4398 (89) 11 fig 114
d 13mm; leather survives.

914 BWB83 5020 (389) 11
d 14mm; rivet has rove.

915 BWB83 5882 (330) 11
d 14mm; ring stamped offcentrally; scraps of textile survive.

916 BWB83 5889 (330) 11
d 14mm

917 BWB83 1441 (119) 11
d 14.5mm; rivet missing.

918 BWB83 1244 (138) 11
d 15mm; as preceding item.

919 BWB83 3772 (338) 11
d 15mm; brass (AML); rivet has rove; scrap of woollen textile survives (identification by FP).

920 BC72 2716 (79) 11
d 16mm; brass (AML); rivet missing.

921 BC72 5319 (88) 11 fig 115
Four mounts d 16mm, as preceding item, on large piece of leather (for description of this and accompanying larger mounts, see no. 930).

922 BWB83 4456 (275) 12
d 18mm; rivet missing.

923 BWB83 1953 (unstratified)
d 14mm; rivet has rove.

Iron

924 BC72 4182 (88) 11 fig 114 & colour pl 4G
d 19mm, tin coating.

with two separate rivets

Iron

925 BWB83 4416 (109) 11 fig 114
d 23mm; flat edge, raised ring around large central hole; tin coating; one rivet with rove survives. Possibly a surround for a buckle-pin hole.

Circular – flat centre, rabbeted ring around

Copper alloy

926 BC72 1793 (55) 11 fig 114
d 17mm; single, separate rivet is missing.

Circular – concentric rings, with holes for two separate rivets

Copper alloy

927 BWB83 5492 (396) 11 fig 114
d 22mm; three rings; rivets missing.

928 BWB83 1289 (112) 11 fig 114
d 24mm; five rings; rivets missing.

115 Circular mounts on leather (1:2; separate mount
1:1)

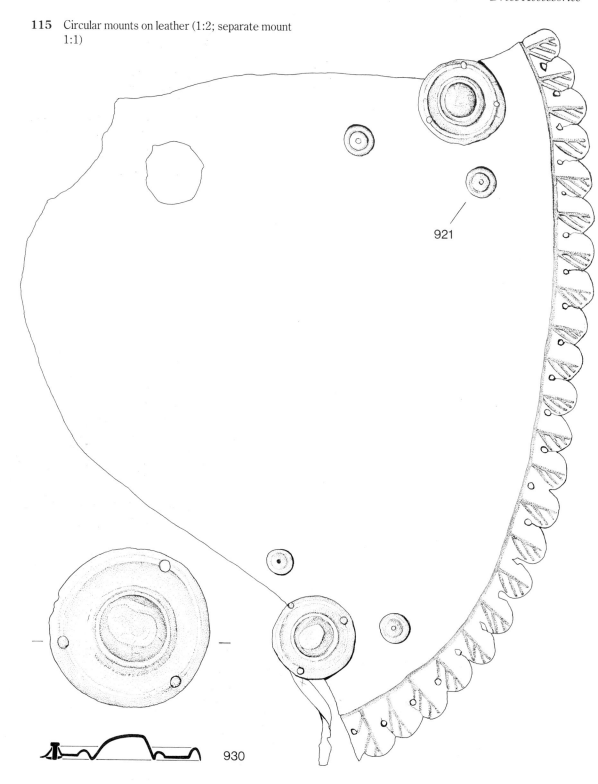

921

930

**NB: All scales for the colour plates are approximate —
for accurate dimensions, see catalogue entries**

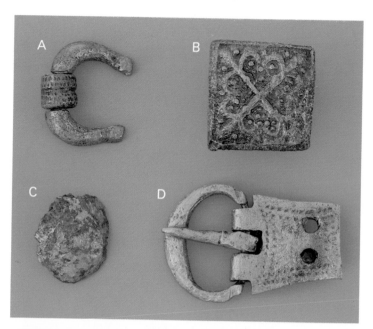

Plate 1
A–D gilded copper items:
A buckle no. 270
B mount no. 1063
C mount no. 820
D buckle no. 303
E & F lead/tin buckles nos. 419 & 480
G copper alloy buckle with iron plate
no. 457, and iron mounts no. 907
– all tin coated
(2:1, except G 1:1)

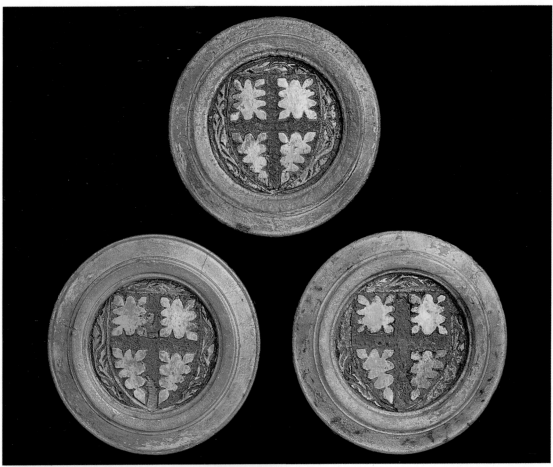

Plate 2
Top: armorial mounts no. 933 – copper alloy with silver coating and enamel or niello
(diameters *c.* 60mm)
Bottom: gold finger rings nos. 1613, 1612 & 1610
(2:1)

Plate 3
Pendent tin-coated sheet-iron leaves
no. 1188 (row of three 1:1)

Plate 4
A buckle plate with replacement
  rivets no. 499
B Brass (?)clasp plate with bronze repair no.
  562
C copper-alloy strap-end no. 611,
  showing differential corrosion and
  corrosion products

Plate 4 *continued*

D & E copper-alloy and iron composite
mounts:
reddish centre and yellow border,
Museum of London acc. no. 85.13
/ 7; iron centre with tin-coated
border, no. 932

F pewter hexagram mount with blue
glass stone, no. 1094

G tin-coated iron mount no. 924

H tin mount no. 855

(A, B & H 2:1, D–G 1.5:1, C 1:1)

Plate 5

Leather straps with fittings:

A strap no. 1182 with tin-coated iron
mounts

B strap end no. 588 and circular mounts
with loops for pendants no. 1187

C strap end no. 714 and sexfoil mounts
no. 1022 (all of tin)

D bar-mounts no. 1132

E & F strap with various mounts –
Museum of London acc. no. 89.65

(all 1:2, except E approx 1:10, & F 1:1)

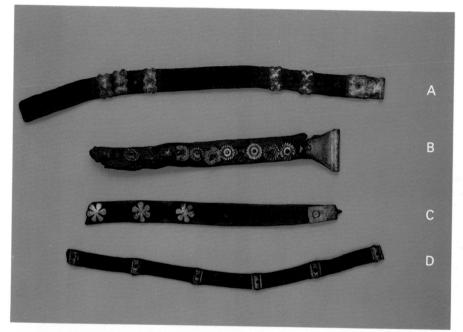

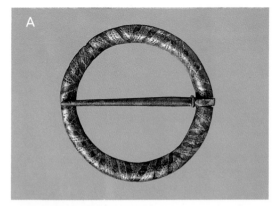

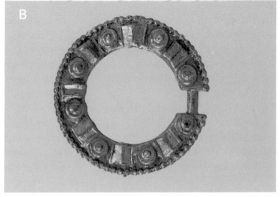

Plate 6
Brooches (2:1, except A 1:1)
A gunmetal with lead inlay, no. 1314
B pewter, no. 1323
C silver, no. 1337
D copper alloy, no. 1343
E pewter with decayed glass stones, no. 1344

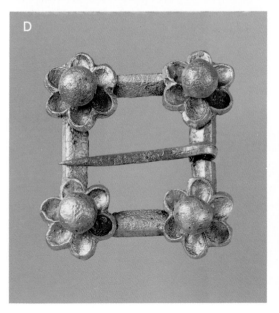

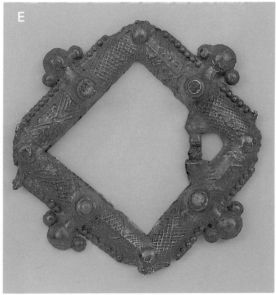

Plate 7

A tin button with glass stone, no. 1379
B high-tin bronze button, no. 1384
C pins with glass heads, nos. 1468 & 1469

D pins with red-coral heads, nos. 1471 & 1472
E pin with pewter head of Christ, no. 1470
(buttons 4:1, C, D & E 2:1

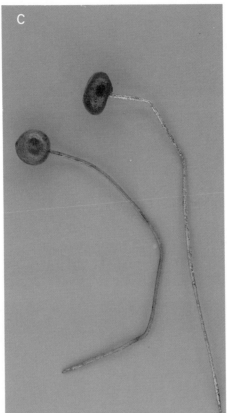

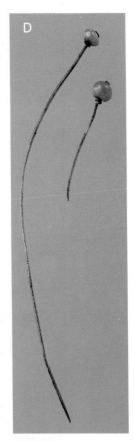

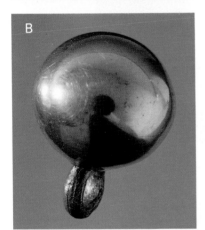

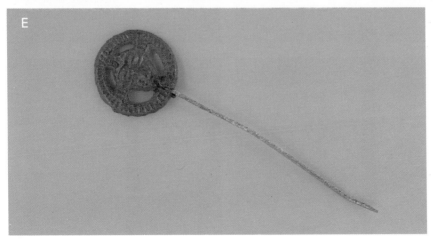

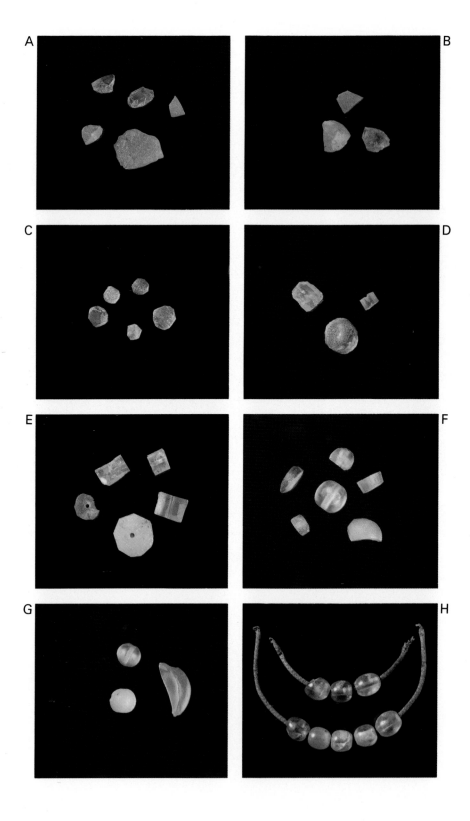

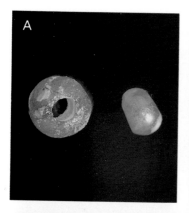

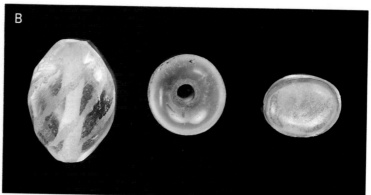

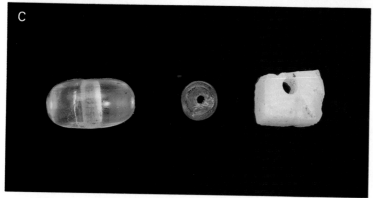

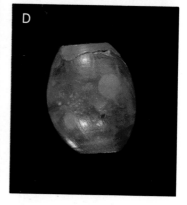

Plate 8

Top: Stages of manufacture of amber beads:
A untrimmed blocks
B initial trimming (stage A in text)
C faceted – for round beads (stage A)
D broken during drilling of the hole (stage B)
E hole drilled, turning not started (stage C)
F discarded during initial turning (stage D)
G discarded during final polishing (stage E)
(A–G all BC72 acc. no. 4790, approx 1.25:1)
H beads on silk string, no. 1489 (slightly reduced)

Plate 9
A glass beads nos. 1586 & 1587
B rock-crystal beads nos. 1583 & 1582, and soudé gem no. 1589
C amber beads showing principal colours – left yellow (no. 1501); centre orange (no. 1502); right offwhite (no. 1534)
D amber bead with stress lines, no. 1508
(A 3:1, B & C 2:1, D 4:1)

er xxxj bruder der do stach, hieß leupolt
vnd was ein paternoster

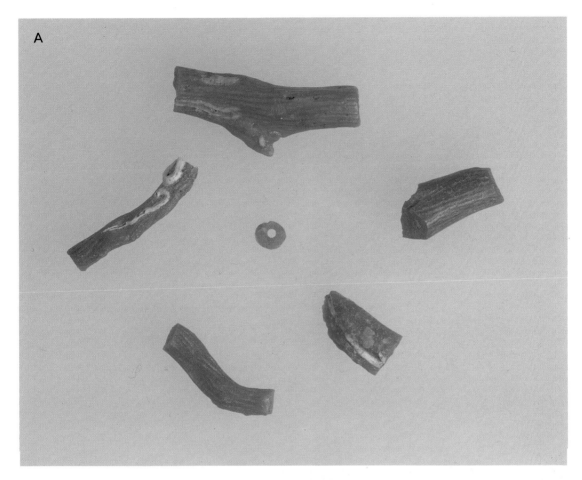

A

Plate 11
A red-coral waste, including tiny piece
   with drilled hole no. 1551 (centre)
B pearl no. 1588
C tin bead (private collection, see no.
   1584)
(A approx 3.5:1, B approx 2.5:1,
C approx 3:1)

B

C

Plate 10
Turning beads for paternosters – German, c.1425
(from Treue et al. 1965, pl 24)

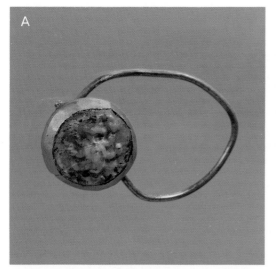

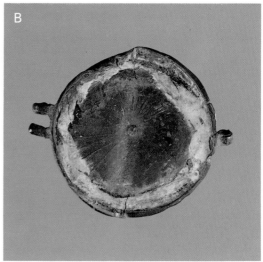

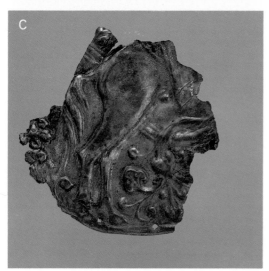

Plate 12
A finger ring with multicoloured glass cameo, no. 1618
B lead-tin mirror case with cement and traces of glass, no. 1710
C silver-gilt mirror case fragment, no. 1718
(A 2:1, B 1.5:1, C slightly enlarged)

Circular – ornate decoration of rings etc

Copper alloy

929 BC72 4325 (150) 11 fig 114
d 22mm; central hole pierces a reserved cinquefoil, cable-decorated ring around, surrounded by beading; one iron rivet of original two survives. The central hole has ragged edges. Piercing was perhaps not for a buckle pin.

930 BC72 5319 (88) 11 fig 115
Two mounts, each d 43mm, with tall central boss and two concentric rings, and three rivets with roves, on irregularly cut piece of leather (c. 338×339mm; one edge has fringe of tabs defined by an engraved line and with engraved central and oblique lines – cf leaf-pattern); for accompanying smaller circular mounts see no. 921.

Iron

931 BWB83 580 (108) 10 fig 114
d 24mm; raised central lozenge, with concentric ring; tin coating; single rivet is missing.

932 SWA81 946 (2102) 12 fig 114 & colour pl 4E
Incomplete composite mount; d 18mm; central dome, and separate disc with tin-coated corded border; rivet has rove. The apparent restriction of the tinning to the decorated border was probably to vary the colours.

Cf. four similar mounts (d 20mm) of copper alloys (colour pl 4D, MoL acc. no. 85.13/7) and the series of central mounts on the strap in colour pl 5E & F. In all these the border is a yellowish-gold colour and the central dome is redder.

Circular – composite armorial mounts

Copper alloy, with silver coating

933 SWA81 acc. no. 893A-C (context 2112) ceramic phase 12 fig 116 & colour pl 2
Three similar circular armorial mounts; each d 60mm, consisting of a frame, with turning marks and radial cracking on the back; smoothed on the front, which retains traces of silver coating that overlaps onto the back; each has three square-section rivets of varying thicknesses soldered to the back; a flange around the inner rim of the frame has been bent over at certain points to retain a disc d 39mm, with champlevé decoration – the design is a shield with a cross engrailed in a bordure engrailed, all in dark material (probably enamel or niello), against a reserved, silver-coated field; the shield is surrounded by silver-coated foliage reserved against a dark enamel or niello background; engraved zigzag keying can be seen in one example where the dark material in the arms of the cross has been lost.

The mounts vary between c.43.5 and 57.5gms in weight, the main difference apparently being in the frames – though differential preservation may have played a minor role – showing a lack of close standardisation despite the similar overall appearance. The central roundel of A has on the back the incomplete incuse outline of a five-petalled double rose-like flower (or a single flower with a waved border); this was presumably stamped on the thick sheet of metal from which the roundel was cut and has nothing to do with the mount itself. Corrosion products on B included an unexplained squarish outline on the back, while those on C bore the mark of a coarse, open-textured cloth in tabby weave (fig 116, top right); surviving fibres have been identified as wool (F Pritchard).

Analysis (AML/MLC) by J Bayley, S Keene and P Wilthew) has shown that the frame and central roundel of B are of low-zinc brass, and that the silver has been applied by the technique of mercury silvering (cf the more familiar mercury gilding). Since niello can have a composition similar to the sulphide corrosion products found on these mounts, it is not possible to distinguish between them chemically so as to be certain whether the dark material is niello, or degraded enamel together with corrosion from the metal of the roundels.

Papworth (1961, 606) lists nothing under this blazon, but gives over a dozen alternatives for the nearest one mentioned – *argent, a cross engrailed sable* (this differs in the absence of the engrailed border); since the correspondence is not precise, none of these is likely to be relevant to the excavated mounts.

Several parallels for this form of mount are known. There is an outer ring in the Museum of London collection (acc. no. 85.13/1). A mount of similar form and construction, but with four rivets, and the gilt frame pierced probably for re-attachment, and with different arms, was found at Rievaulx Abbey. The arms have been tentatively identified as those of Abbot John III (in office in 1449). It has been suggested that this mount was appropriate for a case containing the Abbot's travelling chalice and paten (Dunning 1965, 53–55 fig 2 and pl XXI). Another example, with the centre still apparently uncleaned, was excavated at the village site of Goltho (Beresford 1975, 94–95 fig 44 no.

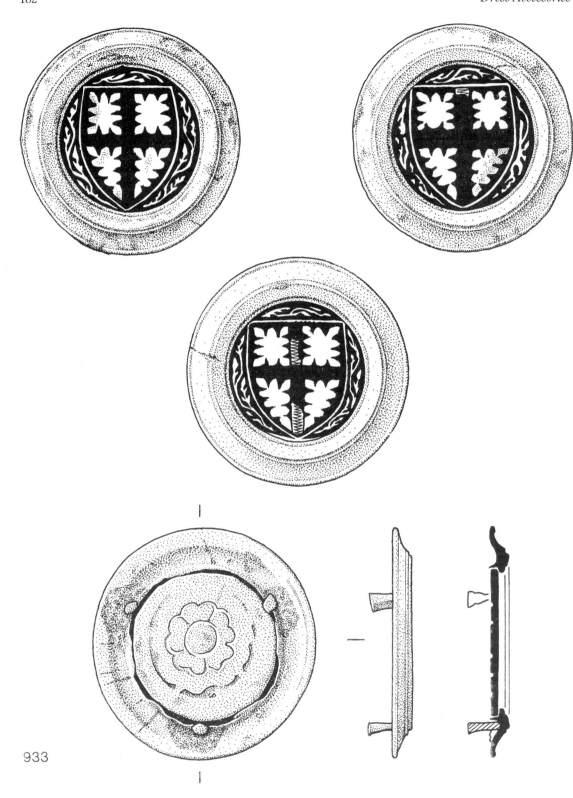

933

933

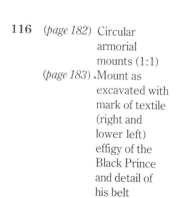

116 (*page 182*) Circular
armorial
mounts (1:1)
(*page 183*) Mount as
excavated with
mark of textile
(right and
lower left)
effigy of the
Black Prince
and detail of
his belt

38). A well-documented mount of this form, of *c.*1440, with the arms of Thomas Ballard, is set as the print in the base of a maplewood mazer (Ashmolean collection – see Glanville 1987, 17 fig 3, and St John Hope 1913, 381).

At least eight mounts apparently also of this kind, with leopards' heads (a motif that figures on the accompanying sword pommel) are set to the sides of a larger, quadrilobate mount on the sword belt on the effigy of the Black Prince (died 1376) at Canterbury Cathedral – see fig 116, right. Several other tomb effigies of knights have sword belts with a series of large round mounts, often with flower motifs delineated in relief rather than with arms.

Three further enamelled mounts, with additional decorative outer frames, found in Bedfordshire (Chamot 1930, 39 no. 21 pl 15A–C), have religious motifs, and have been interpreted as morses (clasps for ecclesiastical copes). Another mount of this kind, also with an additional border, has the badge of Richard II (Campbell 1987B, 524 no. 725), and two roundels found without any frames appear to have further family arms (Hemp 1936, 293–94 nos. 5 & 6). A slightly later example without enamel has a foliate motif in relief (Margeson 1985, 58 & 62, fig 42 no. 49).

The parallels provide several possible alternative uses for such mounts. They firmly place them in an upper-class context – which is consistent with the individual workmanship, as well as the (?)personal heraldry, of the London examples. These are easily the heaviest and the most immediately impressive of all the mounts found recently in London. The discovery of the three mounts together in a foreshore deposit, one bearing the mark of a coarse cloth which might have been wrapped around all of them (fig 116 right), could perhaps suggest that they were abandoned covertly rather than lost or discarded deliberately by their original owner. They would presumably have been readily traceable by means of the arms at the time.

RING MOUNTS

With two separate rivets

These mounts are presumably purely decorative. The shape has determined the need for two rivets rather than one.

Copper alloy

934 BWB83 acc. no. 5057 (context 297)
ceramic phase 11 fig 117

d 27mm; cast; the solid ring consists of a series of bosses; one rivet survives.

935 SWA81 2068 (2109) 12 fig 117
d 17mm; brass with silver coating (AML); cable decoration; trace of iron rivets.

See p 21 for the use of silver on base metal.

Iron
(both have tin coating and are U-shaped in section)

936 BC72 2767 (83) 11 fig 117
d 23mm; rivets have roves.

937 BWB83 2927 (113) unphased
d 27mm; rivets missing.

See also girdle no. 20 for further possible iron mounts of this kind. Nine surviving ring mounts, apparently of lead-tin, on a late 13th-century leather belt excavated in Southampton, are superficially similar to the two preceding mounts. Those at one end of the belt surround the buckle-pin holes (though they serve no obvious strengthening purpose). The accompanying trapezoidal buckle frame is sufficiently large to fit around them (Harvey 1975, 296 & 299, no. 2156, fig 262).

TREFOIL

Holes for three separate rivets

Copper alloy

938 BWB83 acc. no. 2207 (context 151)
ceramic phase 11 fig 117
Damaged, estd d 29mm; domed centre; knop at the end of each lobe; cusps in external angles; rivets missing.

QUATREFOILS

With separate rivets

Copper alloy

939 SWA81 acc. no. 2242 (context 2075)
ceramic phase 9 fig 117

117 Top line – ring mounts; below, trefoil, quatrefoil and cinquefoil mounts (1:1)

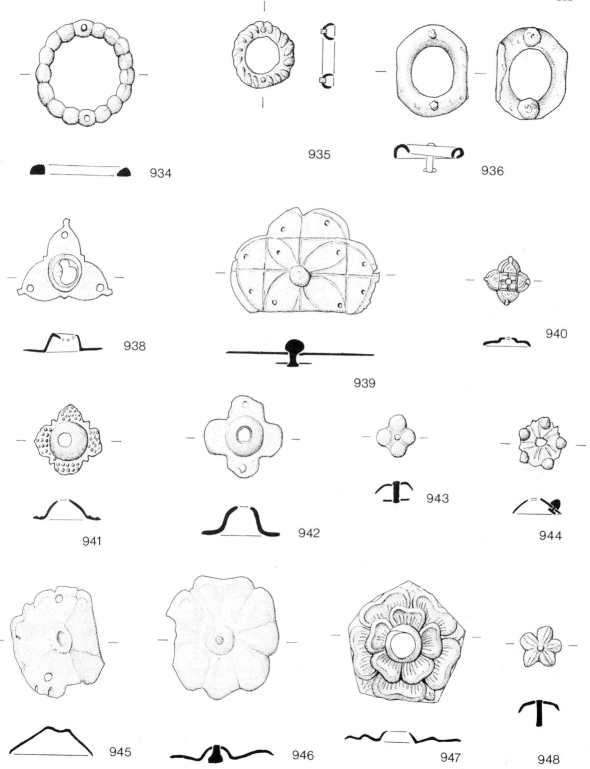

934

935

936

938

939

940

941

942

943

944

945

946

947

948

Incomplete; d 40mm; engraved edge, quatrefoil and grid, each square having a punched circle in the centre, all within a border line; the single dome-headed rivet has a rove, d 9mm; a scrap of leather with one cut edge survives.

940 BWB83 1262 (108) 11 fig 117
d 12mm; bevelled edges; knop at end of each lobe; reserved central square with line border and obliquely hatched cross; lobes have line borders and obliquely hatched fields; single missing rivet.

Cf Fairclough (1979, 126–27 no. 10 fig 53) for a rather similar mount with two rivets and leather surviving.

941 BWB83 1906 (401) 11 fig 117
d 18mm; domed centre; cusps in external angles; field of dots on the lobes; single missing rivet.

942 BWB83 1287 (112) 11 fig 117
d 21mm; domed in centre; holes at centre and for two missing rivets.

Iron

943 BC72 2549 (88/1) 11 fig 117
Five mounts, each d 11mm, with domed lobes and tin coating; on leather short strap no. 1179.

CINQUEFOILS

Domed, with separate rivets

Copper alloy

944 BWB83 acc. no. 2084 (context 307)
ceramic phase 11 fig 117
d 13mm; cusps and pairs of radiating engraved lines between lobes, each of which has a purely decorative dome-headed rivet; central hole for missing functional rivet.

Cf a complete belt with gold and enamelled fittings including similar (though far more expensive) mounts, each with eight decorative knops; on these the central hole houses the attaching rivet (Fingerlin 1971, 425–27, no. 364 fig 502 – Musée de Cluny collection, Paris).

945 BWB83 1575 (108) 11 fig 117
Incomplete; d 29mm; faceted; each lobe apparently has a bifid edge; cusps between; holes for two missing rivets. A crude heraldic rose design.

Five-petalled flowers in relief, with single, separate rivets
(conventional heraldic roses)

Copper alloy

946 SWA81 1672 (2112) 12 fig 117
Incomplete; d 32mm; domed centre; bifid petals; solder for missing rivet.

947 TL74 1874 (368) 12 fig 117
Pentagonal sheet 32×31mm; five-petalled double rose; brass (AML); large central hole with domed edge; no rivet. Possibly unfinished.

Iron

948 BC72 2594 (79) 11 fig 117
Four mounts, each d 12mm; domed, with raised central dot and ridged lobes; tin coating; on short strap no. 1177.

SEXFOILS

Flat, with separate rivets

Copper alloy

949 SWA81 acc. no. 429 (context 2018)
ceramic phase 9 fig 119
d 14mm; recessed outline in each lobe; single rivet missing.

950 BWB83 1237 (110) 11 fig 119
d 13mm; two rivets with roves.

Sexfoils – domed

Copper alloy

Flower-like sexfoil mounts in copper-alloy sheeting are the most numerous of all those recovered. The faceted ones were clearly in common use by the middle of the 14th century, and they continued to be a popular line late into the next century. Waste offcuts, presumably from similar mounts, are present among an assemblage of manufacturing material found at the Blossom's Inn site in London (provisionally dated from associated pottery to the last quarter of the 15th century – MoL acc. no. 21111). Mounts of this kind have been found widely outside London (eg

Harvey 1975, 258–59 & fig 241 no. 1757; Oakley 1979, 252–53 & fig 109 nos. 38 & 39).

951 SWA81 425 (2018) 9 fig 119
Corroded; d 13mm; a thin strip of sheeting is looped through the hole and around a wire ring.

Cf circular mounts with pendent motifs nos. 1187–88.

The following sexfoils show something of the varying degree of attention paid to cutting out the flower shapes. They are presumably the products of several workers over a period of a century or more. The same variations (A-D, fig 118) are evident in mounts attributed to each ceramic phase represented, suggesting a number of different manufacturers at any one time.
(diameters for flattened mounts are given in brackets as the distortion makes them wider than they were originally)

Sexfoils – domed, with separate, single rivets
(all are faceted)

Copper alloy

952 BWB83 acc. no. 4504 (context 285) ceramic phase 11 fig 119
d 14mm; variation B; rivet missing.

953 BWB83 5876 (303) 11
d 14mm; B; rivet missing.

954 BWB83 5164 (157) 11
Damaged, d *c*.16mm; C; rivet missing.

955 BWB83 5881 (298) 11
d 17mm; A; rivet missing.

956 BWB83 5880 (292) 11
d 18mm; B; rivet missing.

957 BWB83 4508 (285) 11
d 19mm; C; rivet missing.

Sexfoils – domed, with two separate rivets
(faceted unless stated)

Copper alloy

958 BWB83 acc. no. 2405 (context 290) ceramic phase 9
d 16mm; variation D; two parallel sides are probably from the strip from which it was cut; one rivet with rove survives.

959 BWB83 2112 (290) 9 fig 119
d 21mm; A; one rivet survives.

960 BWB83 2412 (290) 9
Incomplete; d 21mm; B; hole for one missing rivet survives.

961 BWB83 4950 (383) 11 fig 119
d 14mm; C; edges of lobes removed; rivets have roves.

962 BWB83 1473 (157) 11
15mm; D; one rivet with rove survives.

963 BWB83 5883 (295) 11
As preceding item.

964 BWB83 4041 (293) 11
d 15mm; A; rivets have roves.

965 BWB83 4682 (291 area) 11
d 15mm; B; rivets missing.

966 BWB83 3603 (391) 11
d 15mm; B; one rivet missing.

stamped out to   trimmed to shape   irregularly   trimmed
shape of lobes   of lobes   trimmed   polygonally

A   B   C   D

118   Details of finishing of sheet sexfoil mounts

967 BWB83 5871 (304) 11
d 15mm; D; rivets missing.

968 BWB83 4443 (256) 11
16mm; C; one rivet survives.

969 BWB83 2684 (330) 11
d 17mm; A; rivets missing.

970 BWB83 1300 (129) 11
d 17mm; (?)A; one rivet with rove survives.

971 BWB83 650 (256) 11
d 17mm; C; rivets missing.

972 TL74 2182 (1956) 11
d 17mm; C; rivets missing.

973 BWB83 4116 (361) 11
d 17mm; C; one rivet survives.

974 BWB83 1403 (110) 11 fig 119
d 17mm; D; rivets have roves.

975 BWB83 1543 (256) 11
d 18mm; C; rivets missing.

976 BWB83 2171 (150 area) ?11
Flattened (d 19mm); C; rivets missing.

977 BWB83 5236 (306) 11
Incomplete, flattened (d 20mm); D; rivets missing.

978 BC72 4862 (25) 11
Corroded; d 21mm; D; rivets possibly survive.

979 BWB83 3589 (378) 11
Flattened (d 23mm); B; rivets missing.

980 BWB83 5829 (303) 11
Flattened (d 23mm); B; rivets missing.

981 BWB83 341 (309) 12
d 14mm; A; rivets have roves; on leather (?)strap.

982 BWB83 5875 (314) 12
d 15mm; D; rivets missing.

983 SWA81 1950A–C (2102) 12 fig 119
Three similar items from at least two different stamps:
each *c*.18×14mm, D, with rivets having roves (one
rove in each is missing).

The oval shape seems in at least one case (illustrated) to result from the sheet strip from which these
were cut being narrower than the diameter of the
stamp.

984 SWA81 3363 (2112) 12
d 20mm; C; rivets have roves.

985 BWB83 4479 (unstratified)
d 15mm; C; rivets missing.

Sexfoils – domed, with two separate rivets and central hole
(not faceted unless stated)

These were probably used as surrounds for buckle-pin
holes (see archer's wrist guard, fig 143).

Copper alloy

986 BWB83 2150 (290) 9
d 15mm; faceted; variation C; one rivet survives.

987 BWB83 2407 (290) 9 fig 119
d 17mm; B (trimmed apart from two sides which are
parallel, probably from the original sheet strip); one
rivet survives.

988 BWB83 738 (306) 11 fig 119
d 11mm; A, the lobes are defined by radiating lines;
rivets have roves.

Thicker sheeting than the other mounts here.

989 BWB83 2258 (154) 11 fig 119
d 13mm; A; rivets missing.

990 BWB83 3526 (387) 11 fig 119
d 13mm; C; rivets missing.

991 BWB83 2236 (151) 11
d 13mm; faceted; C; rivets missing.

992 BWB83 2122 (307) 11
Incomplete; d 13mm; faceted; D; central hole has
untrimmed edges folded back; rivets missing.

993 BWB83 4008 (292) 11
d 13mm; faceted; D, trimming has removed edges of
lobes; rivets missing.

994 BWB83 2338 (147) 11
Incomplete; d 14mm; D; faceted; rivets missing.

995 BWB83 1574 (108) 11
Incomplete; d 15mm; B; one rivet with rove survives.

996 BWB83 1307 (129) 11 fig 119
d 17mm; A; rivets missing.

997 BWB83 2232 (151) 11
Incomplete, d 17mm; A; rivets missing.

998 BWB83 2208 (146) 11
Incomplete; d 17mm; faceted; C; one rivet survives
with rove.

999 BWB83 5873 (310) 12
d 15mm; A; one rivet survives, with rove.

1000 BWB83 4736 (309) 12
d 16mm; A; rivets missing.

1001 SWA81 2100 (2102) 12 fig 119
d 18mm; D; central hole is worn; one rivet has a rove.

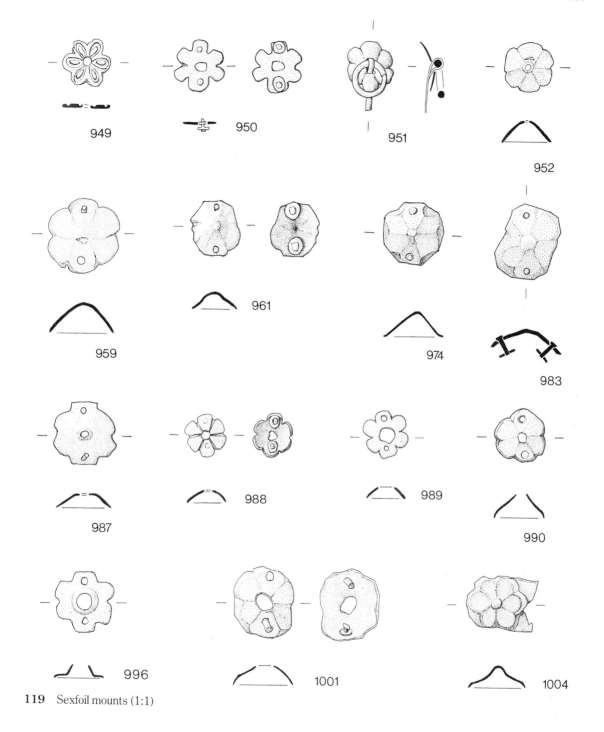

949 950 951 952 959 961 974 983 987 988 989 990 996 1001 1004

119 Sexfoil mounts (1:1)

1002 SWA81 2509A (2102) 12
d 18mm; D.

1003 BWB83 1954 (unstratified)
d 15mm; D; rivets have roves.

Sexfoils – unfinished

(all are domed and faceted, but lack a hole)

Copper alloy

1004 BWB83 4012 (292) 11   fig 119
d 15mm; torn off at two sides; retains additional part of
original sheet strip 14mm wide.

1005 BWB83 1573 (108) 11
d 16mm; irregularly torn from sheeting.

1006 BWB83 5121 (unstratified)
d 19mm; A; retains piece of untrimmed metal at edge.

Sexfoils – domed centre and domed lobes

(single, separate rivets are missing)

Copper alloy

1007 BWB83 1189 (113) 11   fig 120
d 16mm
    Cf octofoil no. 1039.

1008 BWB83 1451 (119) 11   fig 120
d 18mm; three pairs of contiguous wide and narrow
lobes.

Sexfoils – domed centre and domed lobes, with holes for two separate rivets

Copper alloy

1009 BWB83 5825 (303) 11
Flattened (d 17mm); rivets missing.

1010 BWB83 1672 (282) 11   fig 120
d 33m; raised boss on each lobe.

Sexfoils – domed centre and flat lobes, with holes for two separate rivets

Copper alloy

1011 BWB83 3766 (338) 11   fig 120
d 14mm; lobes defined by radiating lines; additional

offcentred hole; stamped out to shape of lobes; traces
of solder on back and front.

1012 BWB83 2341 (147) 11
d 15mm; brass (AML); crudely cut out; one rivet
survives.

Sexfoils – other ornate variants

Copper alloy

1013 BWB83 1655 (286) 11   fig 120
Incomplete; d 29mm; flat centre; bifid lobes, with two
concentric rings of raised bosses set in pairs within
raised dividing lines on each lobe; no surviving hole or
rivet.
    Cf a heraldic rose.

1014 BWB83 1909 (292) 11   fig 120
Unfinished; rectangular sheet 23×25mm; stamped
with sexfoil motif of three concentric rings, each with
raised bosses, those in the outer two rings being in
pairs.
    Discarded without being trimmed or pierced.
    See also the mount on buckle plate no. 520, fig 73.

Sexfoil – flat, with integral rivet

Copper alloy

1015 BWB83 4002 (292) 11   fig 120
d 17mm; ? cast; lobes defined by a radiating lines; a
central raised circle corresponds with the position of
the single rivet.

Sexfoils – domed centre with domed lobes, single separate rivets

Iron

1016 BC72 2596 (79) 11   fig 120
Four mounts, each d 11mm and with tin coating; on
leather short strap no. 1181.

Sexfoils – flat, with integral rivets

Lead/tin

1017 BWB83 5887 (310) 11
High-tin lead alloy (MLC); d 13mm; central hole; two
rivets (?)cut off.

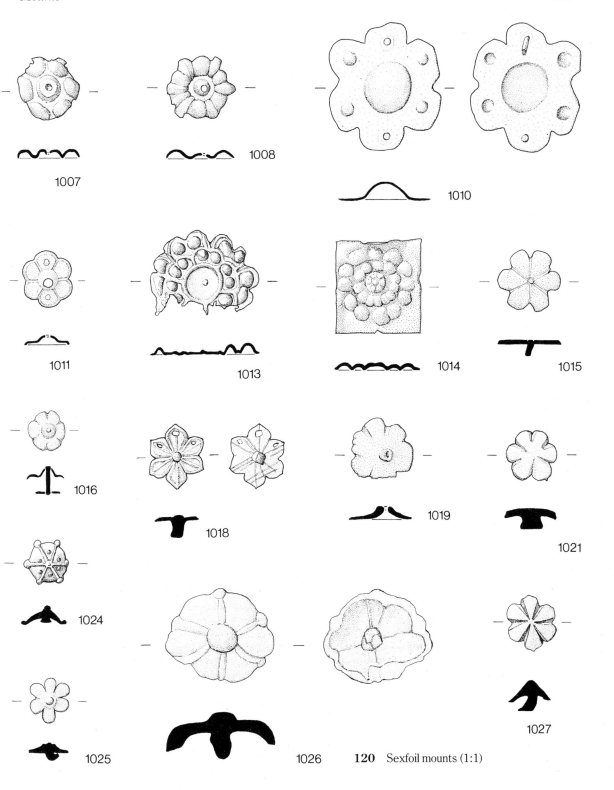

1007

1008

1010

1011

1013

1014

1015

1016

1018

1019

1021

1024

1025

1026

1027

120 Sexfoil mounts (1:1)

1018 BWB83 1936 (308) 11 fig 120
d 15mm; lead-tin (RAK); relatively naturalistically modelled flower, each petal having a central vein; single rivet; irregular hatching on back from scratches on mould.

Three holes are presumably from bubbles in the casting.

Sexfoil – domed centre, with single, separate rivet

Iron

1019 BWB83 2123 (307) 11 fig 120
Incomplete, d 17mm; irregular lobes, divided by recessed lines; rivet missing; tin coating (MLC).

Sexfoils – domed, with single, integral rivets

Lead tin

1020 BWB83 1570 (108) 10
Lead-tin (RAK); d 13mm.

1021 BWB83 1571 (108) 10 fig 120
Lead-tin (MLC); d 14mm.

Probably from same object as preceding item.

1022 BWB83 99 (204) 11 fig 99 & colour pl 5C
Three surviving mounts; tin (AML, one tested); each d 11mm, on leather strap 139×11mm (torn off at one end) with holes for six more lost mounts, and a surviving strap-end (no. 714).

1023 BWB83 5886 (291) 11
d 12mm; lead-tin (RAK).

1024 SWA81 2125 (2110) 12 fig 120
d 11mm; tin (AML); central boss; radiating lines between the lobes terminating in knops; each lobe has a dot near the centre; rivet incomplete. Presumably a mount rather than a button.

1025 SWA81 2026A & B (2106/2107) 12 fig 120
Two similar items, both tin (AML, MLC); each d 11.5mm and with circular groove around centre.

1026 BWB83 5058 (319) 12 fig 120
Lead-tin (MLC); distorted; d 28mm; central boss; raised lines between lobes, each terminating in a boss.

A conventional heraldic rose.

1027 BWB83 4461 (unstratified) fig 120
Tin (RAK); d 15mm.

Sexfoils – domed centre and lobes etc, with integral rivets

Lead/tin

1028 BC72 1510 (55) 11 fig 121
Twelve lead-tin mounts (MLC, two tested), each d 11mm, with single rivets, on round perimeter tabs on a fragment of leather 176×75mm (torn off along one side; one tab lacks a hole for a mount); the mount heads are on the flesh side.

1029 SWA81 2041 (2101) 12 fig 121
d 18mm; tin (AML, MLC); lobes alternately dished and domed; hint of cross hatching on domes; central hole; two rivets. Possibly a buckle pin-hole surround. For the motif, cf eyelet no. 1227 from the same deposit, and see fig 157B.

1030 BWB83 92 (unstratified) fig 121
Seven surviving tin mounts (AML, lead/tin MLC); each d 12mm, with a central boss surrounded by beading, and a single rivet, on leather strap 200×11mm (torn off at both ends, with holes for two more lost mounts). The decorative detail puts these among the most naturalistically flower-like of the lead/tin mounts.

SEPTFOILS

Copper alloy

1031 BWB83 acc. no. 3999 (context 292) ceramic phase 11 fig 122
d 21mm; flat, with separate rivet; lobes of irregular sizes, with engraved lines between; trimmed to shape of lobes; offcentred dome-headed rivet.

Lead/tin

1032 BWB83 2199 (146) 11 fig 122
d 13mm; lead-tin (RAK); domed centre and lobes; single, separate rivet.

1033 BWB83 5884 (287) 12 fig 122
Incomplete and distorted, d *c.*26mm; domed and faceted; one rivet of original two survives.

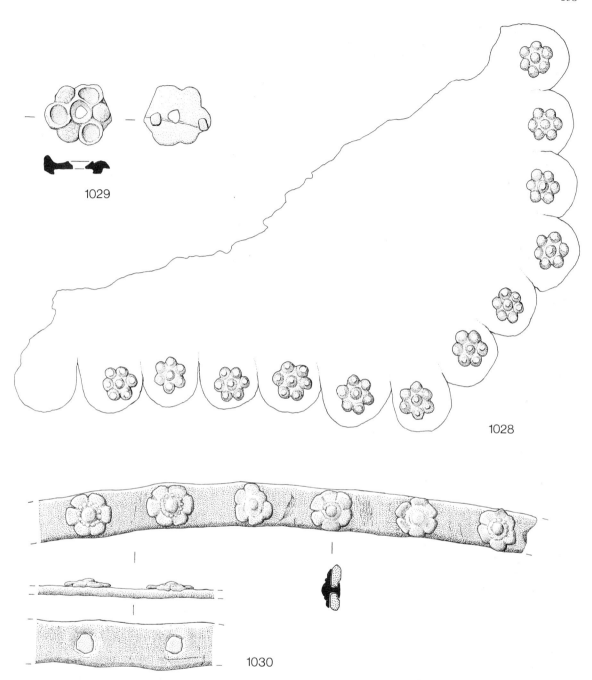

1029

1028

1030

121 Sexfoil mounts (1:1)

OCTOFOILS

Domed, with holes for separate, single rivets

Copper alloy

1034 SWA81   acc. no. 2134   (context 2030)
ceramic phase 9   fig 122
d 15mm; stamped out to shape of lobes; rivet missing.

1035 SWA81   3045   (2061)   9
As preceding item; incomplete.

1036 SWA81   420   (2018)   9
Possibly flattened; d 23mm; stamped out to shape of lobes.

1037 BWB83   2685   (330)   11   fig 122
d 19mm; brass (AML); stamped out to shape of lobes.

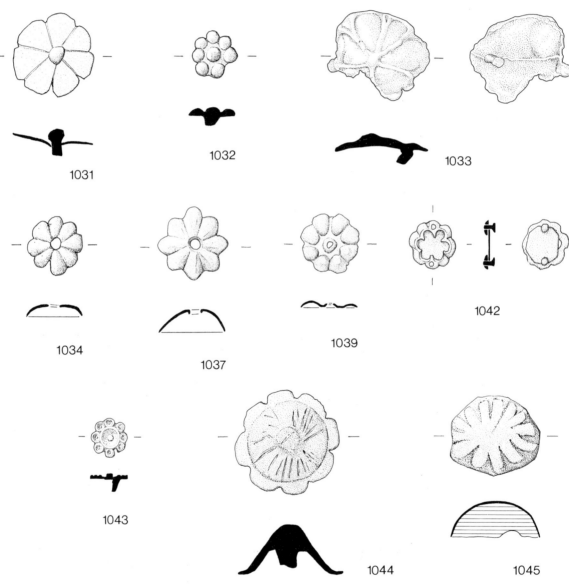

1031

1032

1033

1034

1037

1039

1042

1043

1044

1045

122   Septfoil, octofoil and multifoil mounts (1:1)

Octofoils – domed centre and domed lobes, with holes for separate, single rivets
(all rivets are missing)

Copper alloy

1038 BWB83 5835C (207) 11
d 15mm

1039 BWB83 3238 (265) 12 fig 122
d 16mm; stamped out to shape of lobes.
 Cf sexfoil no. 1007.

Octofoils – composite, with separate frame and backing sheet

Copper alloy

1040–42 SWA81 947, 948 & 1789 (2102) 12
fig 122
Three similar mounts from the same deposit – each
d 12.5mm; brass (AML); cast frame in each is eight-
lobed externally, and six-lobed internally about a central hole; two rivets hold the frame to an irregularly cut
polygonal backing sheet and would also have fixed the
mounts in place.

Octofoils – with single, integral rivets

Lead/tin

1043 BWB83 3211 (264) 9 fig 122
d 10mm; dished centre with raised dot in middle; eight
irregularly spaced lobes, each with a raised circle and
dot.

1044 BWB83 4430 (unstratified) fig 122
d 28mm; lead-tin (MLC); domed centre; edges of lobes
flat; crude, radiating scratches give a slightly more
naturalistic flower-like appearance.

MULTIFOIL

Copper alloy

1045 BWB83 acc. no. 5827 (context 310)
ceramic phase 12 fig 122
d 24mm; domed, 13-lobed mount; back filled with lead;
(?)separate rivet missing.
 Cf nos. 873–88 for other items with lead in the
hollow backs.

RECTANGULAR/SQUARE MOUNTS

Including square mounts orientated as lozenges on
surviving straps – alternative orientation may sometimes be found for mounts of identical form (see no.
1068 and parallel, fig 125). For rectangular mounts
10mm or less wide, see bar-mounts nos. 1132–46; for
other rectangular mounts (generally plainer examples)
see strap plates nos. 1202–16.
 NB within ceramic phases the following mounts are
listed in order of increasing size of second dimension –
ie approximate strap width.

Flat, with separate rivets

Copper alloy

1046 BIG82 acc. no. 2424 (context 3394)
ceramic phase 7 fig 123
Cast; 30×25mm; gunmetal, with copper rivet (AML);
openwork lattice of four rectangles, each of a slightly
different size; central boss; holes for four rivets, one of
which survives; more robust than most mounts described here, so possibly from an item other than
dress.

1047 SWA81 2965 (2031) 9 fig 123
11×15mm, divided by grooves into three fields, the
central one with holes for two missing rivets and the
outer two having a series of transverse grooves.

1048 BWB83 4695 (307) 11 fig 123
16×21mm; degenerate version of a double-headed bird
(?rather than a scallop shell); beaded border; holes for
two missing rivets.

1049 BWB83 5935 (295) 11 fig 123
Orientation uncertain; 15×29mm; central hole flanked
by holes for two missing rivets; stamped beading
around perimeter. Possibly a strap-plate, though the
sheeting is rather thin (cf no. 1051).

1050 BC72 1869 (55) 11 fig 123
15×36mm; one corner cut at an angle; engraved
black-letter d or p on a field of engraved zigzags, all
within border lines; holes for two missing rivets.

1051 BWB83 5936 (310) 12 fig 123
48×15mm; two stamped floral motifs of seven and
eight dots, each with the central dot stamped from the
other side; stamped beading around the perimeter;
holes for four missing rivets; coating, probably tin
(MLC).

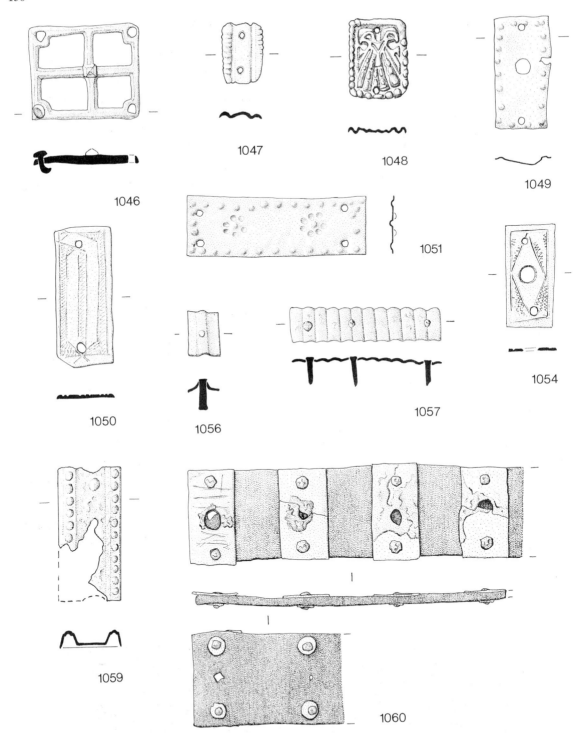

1047

1048

1049

1046

1051

1050

1056

1057

1054

1059

1060

123 Rectangular mounts (1:1)

Possibly a strap-plate, though the sheeting is rather thin (cf no. 1049).

1052 SWA81 806 (2103) 12 fig 51
9×19mm; engraved line border around central lozenge; engraved zigzags in surrounding triangular fields; tin coating; holes in centre and for two iron rivets, which attach it to a leather strap 28×23mm (torn off at one end, possibly at both).

For associated buckle, see no. 343.

There is a similar mount on the strap in colour pl 5E.

1053 BWB83 5833 (310) 12
Mount as preceding, but 13×23mm; no obvious coating; one iron rivet survives.

1054 SWA81 1792 (2102) 12 fig 123
As preceding item, but 13×29mm.

1055 SWA81 2069 (2169) 12
As preceding item, but 13×29mm.

Iron

1056 BC72 2554 (83) 11 fig 123
Three mounts, *c*.11×9mm, with central ridge widthways, tin coating, and single rivet, on short strap no. 1175.

1057 BC72 2622 (89) 11 fig 123
40×9mm; corrugated profile; tin coating; on short strap no. 1170.

1058 BC72 3879 (150) 11 fig 232
Four mounts, varying between 30×11 and 32×8mm, with corrugated profile, and two rivets with roves; tin coating; on purse no. 1701 together with circular mounts no. 894.

1059 BC72 4287 (150) 11 fig 123
Incomplete; 17×34mm; raised bar at each edge with row of bosses; sides apparently concave; tin coating; one of two rivets survives.

1060 BC72 2555 (2109) 12 figs 123 & 124
Five mounts, each 12×25mm (two are broken in two) with a central hole and two rivets with copper-alloy roves; tin coating; on leather strap 168×26mm (cut at one end, torn off at the other); further rivets indicate that two other mounts have been lost; the strap has been crudely pierced at each of the holes in the mounts, which are scratched on the front, particularly those near the cut end of the strap.

The one at the point where the strap is cut could have acted as a strap-end, while the holes in the leather (not present where the missing mounts were fixed) and lengthways scratches may suggest use with a buckle.

Rectangular – domed centres, with separate rivets

Copper alloy

1061 BWB83 3667 (359) 12 fig 125
Probably cast; brass (AML); 15×14mm; bevelled at edges; hole for single missing rivet.

1062 BWB83 3996 (292) 12 fig 125
17×18mm; engraved double perimeter line; holes for four missing rivets.

A similar item was found at Castle Acre Castle (AR Goodall 1982, 238–39 no. 41 fig 44).

Squarish mounts with a domed centre could be for book covers (cf Baart et al. 1977, 403 nos. 759 and 760 – these are both of post-medieval date). The bevelled edges of no. 1061, which would make it flush with the surface to which it was attached (an unusual feature among mounts), might be particularly suitable for this purpose, but its single, central rivet is perhaps less appropriate for this. See also nos. 905 & 1099 for further possible book mounts.

124 Strap with rectangular mounts (2:1)

Square – with single integral rivet

Copper alloy

1063 BIG82 153 (2888) 8 fig 125 & colour pl 1B
Cast; copper (AML); 16×16mm; field of dots inside raised border; central saltire cross with arms terminating in fleurs de lis; trace of gilding (MLC).

A relatively robust mount.

Rectangular/square
– pyramidal, with single, separate rivets

Lead/tin

1064 BIG82 5958 (6220) 6 fig 125
Three lead-tin mounts (MLC), each *c*.7×6mm, with radiating angled grooves, and copper-alloy rivets with lead/tin roves; on two lengths of leather strap up to 42×8mm (both with further crude holes, and cut at one end, torn off at the other – one length has a hole probably for another missing mount) – these are attached to opposite ends of a thinner strap 302×15mm (cut at both ends) that passes through a D-section oval lead/tin loop 6×30mm, which has a trace of banding and a concavity at one end; the mounts are also each riveted through further pieces of thicker leather which are cut at one end and torn off at a point where they widen at the other.

The function of this complicated object is unknown. No obvious parallel for the loop, which may be a distorted slide of some kind, has been traced.

These are the earliest lead/tin strap mounts by over a century among the assemblages discussed here (spangles nos. 1269 etc have no obvious connection with straps); there is only one other instance of mounts with lead/tin roves, and only one other lead/tin mount with a separate rivet. The decoration is paralleled on later mounts nos. 1072–73 and 1075. Cf leather girdle no. 17 (fig 24) for stamps of somewhat similar design.

Rectangular/square
– pyramidal, with single, integral rivets

Lead/tin

1065 SWA81 596 (2055) 9
Lead-tin (MLC); incomplete; 15×11.5+mm; beaded border; rivet 9mm long.

1066 SWA81 458 (2018) 9 fig 125
Tin (MLC); possibly flattened, 15×15mm; low-relief pyramidal head; beaded border with larger bead at each corner; rivet 10mm long.

1067–71 BWB83 16 (108) 10 fig 125
Tin (MLC); 10×10mm; pyramidal head with raised central boss and beaded border; set lozenge-fashion on fragment of leather strap 17mm wide.

BWB83 acc. nos. 21 (illustrated), 22, 23 & 24 from the same deposit are all similar and all tin (AML, MLC). All five items are presumably from the same strap.

Five further identical mounts are set orientated parallel to a leather strap 12mm wide (private collection, fig 125); these show how a different effect could be obtained using the same basic items.

1072 BWB83 19 (108) 10 fig 125
Tin (MLC); 19×21mm; central boss, radiating angled grooves around; on fragment of leather strap 16mm wide.

1073 BWB83 25 (108) 10
As preceding item; tin (MLC); leather survives.

The two preceding items, from the same deposit, are probably from the same strap.

1074 SWA81 2779 (2032) 11 fig 125
High-tin lead alloy (MLC); incomplete; crude; 9×9mm; pyramidal centre; a surrounding groove is subdivided into squares by transverse lines.

1075 BWB83 5417 (286) 11 fig 125
Tin (AML, MLC); 13×12mm; radiating angled grooves; leather survives.

1076 BWB83 2660 (330) 11 fig 125
Tin (MLC); 15.5×16mm; similar to nos. 1067–71, with additional raised central square having cross-and-four-pellets motif.

LOZENGE (DIAMOND) SHAPED

Copper alloy – with two separate rivets

1077 SWA81 acc. no. 2136 (context 2081) ceramic phase 9 fig 125
Cast; 13×11mm, fleur de lis in beaded border; rivets have tin on the shanks (MLC).

125 Square, and (bottom row) lozenge-shaped mount (1:1)

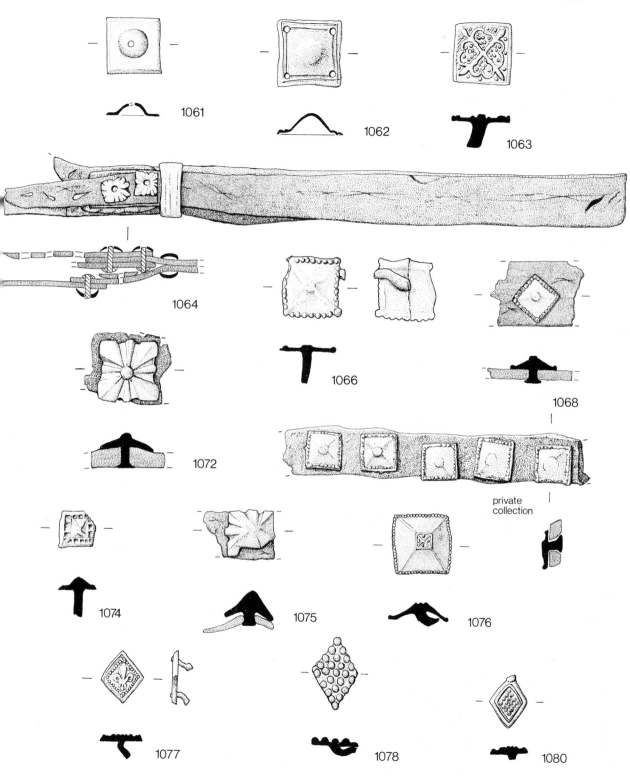

1061

1062

1063

1064

1066

1068

1072

private
collection

1074

1075

1076

1077

1078

1080

Two rivets for such a small item, together with its relative robustness, may suggest that this mount was attached to a rigid object (the tin could be from solder, which is known on several strap mounts).

Tin – with single, integral rivets

1078 BWB83 5157 (157) 11 fig 125
11×17mm; tin (AML); field of dots.

1079 TL74 2031 (414) 11 fig 108
As preceding item; 13×18mm; tin (B Gilmour, Royal Armouries, Tower of London); on leather strap with circular mounts (no. 802); the rivet is bent over rather than hammered.

There is a similar mount in the Boymans-van Beuningen Museum in Rotterdam (acc. no. F7228, found at Oud Krabbendijke).

1080 SWA81 2751 (2114) 12 fig 125
Tin (MLC); 11×13mm; field of dots within double-line border; rivet broken off.

FIGURATIVE MOUNTS

Copper alloy

Crown

1081 SWA81 acc. no. 1095 (context 2100)
ceramic phase 12 fig 126
22×20mm; openwork crown with five voided circles above beading; central hole for missing separate rivet.

Shells

cast, with single, separate rivets having roves

1082 SWA81 2220 (2114) 12
12×11mm

1083 SWA81 1790 (2102) 12 fig 126
11×12mm

Fleur de lis

cast, with two separate rivets

1084 BWB83 4711 (247) unphased fig 126
12×18mm; brass (AML); one rivet survives.

Iron

Letters

1085 BC72 3415 (150) 11 fig 126
Four complete and fragments of some twelve further

Lombardic-letter H mounts, each *c.*21×17mm, and with tin coating and three rivets having roves, on leather strap 325+×17mm (torn off at both ends).

The dating assigned to the context (*c.*1350–*c.*1400) makes it unlikely, but not impossible, that the H is a royal initial – Henry IV's reign having begun in 1399 (see p 3). Crowned Hs would be more appropriate for a royal association.

Lead/tin

(with single, integral rivets unless otherwise stated)

Fleur de lis

1086 SWA81 1970 (2065) 9 fig 126
Lead-tin (MLC); incomplete; 14×16mm; openwork fleur in beaded circular border.

Shield-shaped

1087 BC72 3620 (250) 10 fig 126
Two mounts of tin (AML, MLC), each 10×11mm, on leather strap 92×10mm (torn off at both ends); their uneven surfaces may be the result of corrosion, but this is not certain. The orientation of the shields suggests that the strap may have been worn vertically. Cf two similar mounts (with smooth surfaces) on a leather strap also having lead/tin sexfoil mounts, found at the SUN86 site (acc. no. 711), and another London strap with shield-shaped and pyramidal mounts (MoL acc. no. A26321, Fingerlin 1971, 87 fig 124).

Leaves/plants

1088 SWA81 1480A & B (2113) 12 fig 126
Two tin mounts (RAK): each 15×13mm; tripartite leaf on stem, each leaflet having three points; the rivet survives only on one mount. Minor differences show that the two mounts are from different moulds.

1089 TL74 1960 (275) 12 fig 126
Two tin mounts (MLC), each 17×20mm, with three pinnate, serrated leaves with two curled leaflets at base; one mount is partly worn flat; together with four domed, circular tin mounts, on short strap no. 1186. The mounts are set on the flesh side of the leather.

1090 SWA81 2885 (2106) 12 fig 127
Tin (MLC); 16×15mm; trefoil with stem; raised central dot.
Another similar trefoil mount (21×23mm) found in London has a central hole and two rivets, and was probably a surround for a buckle-pin hole (private collection).

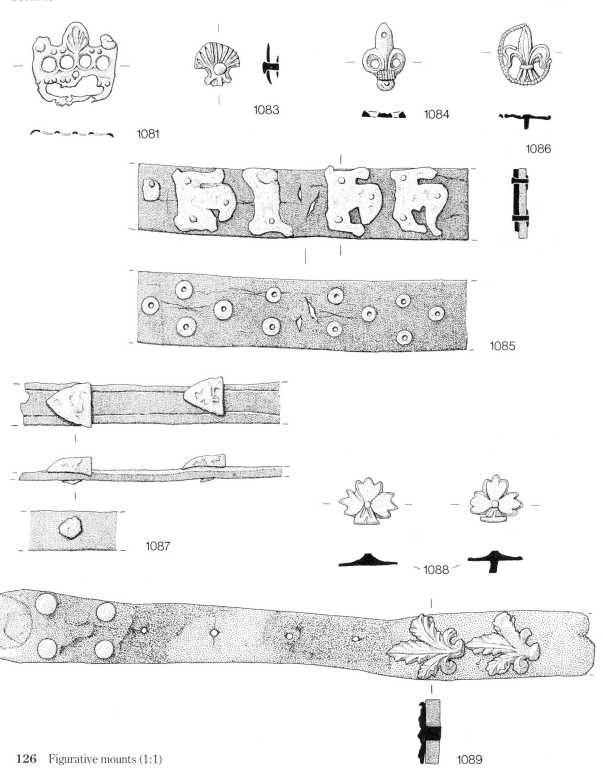

1081

1083

1084

1086

1085

1087

1088

126 Figurative mounts (1:1)

1089

1091 SWA81 2101 (2107) 12 fig 127
Highly stylised motif; tin (MLC); 21×16mm; pair of
opposed trefoils with recurving, bifurcated stems,
which rejoin at the edges to frame them; each branch of
the stems has a lateral shoot; central vein on each
leaflet; two rivets.

Woman's head

1092 SWA81 1668 (2112) 12 fig 127
Tin (MLC); 13×20mm; facing female bust; the right-
angled headdress (which completely obscures the hair)
has a row of raised bosses, each with a surrounding
ring; the gown has an angled, cross-hatched collar,
below which is a raised boss in a circle in the centre,
perhaps intended for a button.

A similar mount from London in a private collection
retains a lead/tin rove.

The headdress is characteristic of the late 14th
century. Mounts in the form of both female and male
heads are known of stamped copper-alloy sheeting
(MoL acc. nos. 80.13, 81.200/1, 81.266/2, & 85.241/5
– two similar mounts, are all female heads with similar
head-dresses, while acc. no. 87.188/1, a bearded man's
head, could be slightly later in date).

Stars

1093 SWA81 1138 (2144) 9 fig 127
d *c*.15mm; six-pointed star; lead/tin (MLC); apparently
cut from a larger object with a rivet or shank (now
missing).

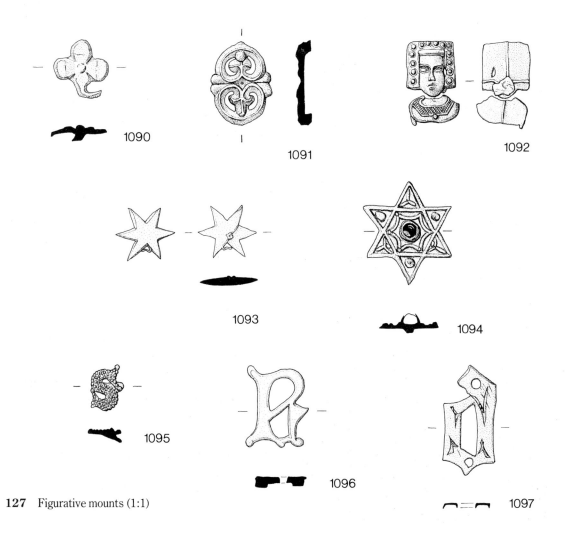

127 Figurative mounts (1:1)

Presumably a mount, though the lentoid section is easier to parallel among later buttons.

1094 BWB83 288 (367) 9 fig 127 & colour pl 4F
d 27.5mm; six-pointed star; pewter (AML); raised linear hexagram, with alternate trefoils and bosses in the points; six-arched motif in the middle surrounds a central collet holding an incomplete blue-glass stone; shank broken or cut off; reuse is indicated by two pierced holes by which the mount could have been sewn in place.

On the supposed magical apotropaic properties of the Solomon's seal motif, see Spencer's discussion of a late-medieval hexagram brooch found in Christchurch (1983, 81–83).

Letters

1095 SWA81 1667 (2112) 12 fig 127
Broken off at one end; 8×12mm; tin (AML); Lombardic-letter S with field of raised dots.

Cf the plainer S-mount with strap-end no. 708 (fig 98). Two leather straps in the British Museum collection (acc. nos. 83.4–26, 14 and 15, both found in London) retain series of plainer S mounts of lead/tin.

These cheap mounts echo the motif of the upper-class collars of SS in precious metals (Spencer 1985, 449–51).

1096 SWA81 3811 (unstratified) fig 127
16×21mm; tin (AML; lead-tin, MLC); variation of a Lombardic-letter R, with triangular projection at the right; two rivets.

1097 SWA81 814 (2097) 12 fig 127
29×14mm; tin (AML); hollow-backed black-letter d or p; multiply engraved decoration; holes for two missing separate rivets.

NON FIGURATIVE MOUNTS

Copper alloy – with separate rivets

1098 BIG82 acc. no. 2445 (context 2636) ceramic phase 7 fig 128
10×19mm; bronze (AML); grid with trilobate sides, two voided slots and incuse beading; two missing rivets; very thin sheeting.

1099 BIG82 3569 (3232) 7 fig 128
Cast; slightly corroded; three-armed mount; 32×33mm; central boss with radiating lines and engraved zigzags around the centre and each of the three rivets.

Possibly from a book cover – see on no. 1062.

A similar mount was excavated at St Augustine's Abbey, Canterbury (Henig and Woods, in Sherlock and Woods 1988, 212 & 215 no. 46 fig 68, described as 'almost certainly a belt fitting').

1100 SWA81 623 (2051) 9 fig 128
Incomplete; 11×16mm; rounded central element with raised band to each side; one hole of original two for missing rivets survives; a tripartite end survives on one side.

Presumably originally symmetrical. Cf MoL acc. no. 81.176/50 for a complete mount of this form, 22.5mm long (from a very similar die) with the design less crisply registered.

1101 BWB83 4588 (286) 11 fig 128
d 21mm; trilobed outline, with cusps in the external angles; brass (AML); three rabbeted roundels, each with a reserved six-pointed star; single missing rivet.

Iron

1102 BC72 3593 (150) 11 fig 128
Wrought; two conjoined circles; 11×9mm; single, separate rivet; tin-coated; on leather strap (68×10mm, torn off at both ends, and with crude holes along centre).

For the (?)clasp on an accompanying piece of leather, see no. 572.

1103 BC72 2517 (89) 11 fig 128
Two mounts of uncertain design: conjoined letters (?SI) *or* crowned device (?M or conjoined rings); each 14×11mm; tin coating; on short strap no. 1169.

Pewter – (?)with separate rivet(s)

1104 SWA81 549 (2016) 12 fig 128
Pewter (AML; lead-tin, MLC); possibly an incomplete mount; 19×estd originally *c*.35mm; lozenge with central vertical slot, beading along perimeter; three crude fleurs de lis in both main fields; loop survives at one side; scratching on front.

Perhaps intended as a letter O. If this was a mount rather than a pendant, it is one of very few of lead/tin to have had separate rivets.

Non-figurative lead/tin mounts continued – with single integral rivets

1105 SWA81 3223 (2274) 9 fig 128
Tin (RAK); lentoid; 8.5×11mm; beaded border.

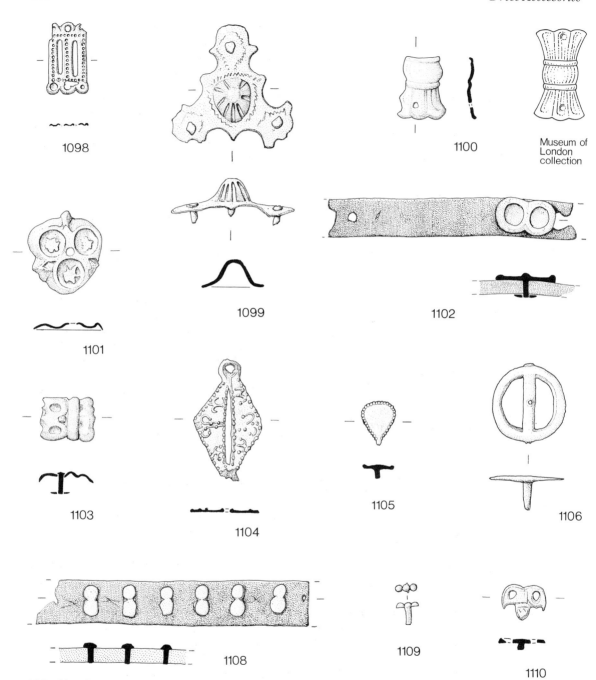

Museum of
London
collection

1098

1099

1100

1101

1102

1103

1104

1105

1106

1108

1109

1110

128 Non-figurative mounts (1:1)

1106 SWA81 459 (2018) 9 fig 128
Lead-tin (MLC); ring with central bar; d 19mm; raised central boss.

(Despite the superficial similarity to lead-tin buckles of a similar size with a central bar, there is no connection, since the buckles are all from early 15th-century deposits.)

1107 TL74 513 (414) 11 fig 110
Sub-triangular mount (somewhat similar to a rose petal), 13×14mm (for strap and accompanying domed circular mounts, see no. 830).

The spacing of the holes in the strap suggests that another mount of this form, rather than another of the smaller, circular ones, may have been lost from the adjacent position.

For copper-alloy mounts, which could also have gone in pairs, see nos. 1199–1201.

1108 BC72 2060 (79) 11 fig 128
Fifteen mounts; tin (MLC, two tested); each a conjoined pair of slightly domed circles, 4×8.5mm, rather abraded, on leather strap 209×11mm (torn off at both ends); holes for six other mounts now lost.

Cf no. 1111 for mounts of similar design.

1109 SWA81 3286A–C (2112) 12 fig 128
Three tin (RAK) mounts, each 5.5×1.5mm and consisting of a row of three joined dots.

The rivets are, if anything, more substantial than the beading which forms the decorative head of these, the tiniest of all the mounts recovered.

1110 SWA81 1963 (2103) 12 fig 128
High-tin lead alloy (MLC); 9×12mm; two opposed, pierced lentoid elements, with a central protrusion, which has a groove and three triangles at the point of junction.

1111 TL74 1184 (275) 12 fig 129
Series of pewter (AML, lead-tin (MLC) mounts on damaged, but substantially complete piece of quite thick (3mm) leather, 193×266mm, with no two sides parallel, and one slightly incurved. The two shorter sides have a row of mainly fragmentary mounts (some lost), the head of each, set on the flesh side of the leather, being a conjoined pair of discs, both with a raised border ring, 7×14mm. The row of mounts ends *c.*20–40mm away from one end of the shorter side of the leather, and continues a similar distance on the longest side. There are three crude slashes near each side of the leather almost parallel with the row of mounts, close to where these end. (This object was found folded approximately in half.)

The crude mounts were presumably to provide extra protection along part of the edge of what was already a robust piece of leather. The triple slashes could have been for the insertion of laces, but there is no wear consistent with this. The points at which the slashes occur lack the concentration of mounts at other points. This object may be an archer's forearm protector, rather than a leg covering (cf Roach-Smith 1854, 132 no. 656). The placing of the mount heads on the softer flesh side of the leather may have been because a suede-like surface was wanted. Cf no. 1108 for mounts of similar design.

Non figurative lead/tin mounts continued – with two integral rivets

1112 SWA81 1486 (2113) 12 fig 129
Tin (MLC); incomplete, 13×17.5mm; circle offcentrally pierced, with beaded trefoil, conjoined to pierced lozenge, both elements with intermittent beading externally; one rivet survives.

Presumably originally symmetrical. Cf a mount with a central pierced lozenge flanked by paired, pierced circles from the SUN86 site (acc. no. 1051).

1113 SWA81 3295 (2112) 12 fig 129
Lead-tin (MLC); incomplete openwork mount; d 24mm; six of original seven trefoils radiating from a central ring; one rivet survives. Wear suggests that this was probably set around a hole for a buckle pin.

POLYGONAL MOUNTS

Domed octagons

Copper alloy

All with single holes; numbers 1114–19 and 1124–27 are presumably mounts, though none has a surviving rivet in the central hole (nos. 1120–23 are definitely mounts).

1114 BWB83 acc. no. 2153 (context 290)
ceramic phase 9 fig 130
d 17mm; with dished centre.

1115 BWB83 1402 (110) 11
d 11mm

1116 BWB83 4003 (292) 11
As preceding item

1117 BWB83 2745 (329) 11
d 12mm

129 Non-figurative mounts; top left, (?) archer's
wrist guard (1:2) and centre right restored (1:8)
(individual mounts 1:1)

1118 BWB83 1578 (108) 11 fig 130
d 20mm

1119 BWB83 4593 (286) 12
d 13mm; engraved radiating lines.

Various octagons – domed unless stated

Copper alloy

1120 BWB83 5196 (306) 11 fig 130
d 15mm; holes in centre and for two missing rivets.
This may be a surround for a buckle-pin hole in a strap.

1121 BWB83 2238 (131) 11 fig 130
d 17mm; brass (AML); two concentric rings of bosses;
single rivet.

1122 SWA81 2509B (2102) 12
Irregularly cut out; 15×19mm; the two rivets have
roves.

1123 SWA81 1082 (2100) 12
d 25mm; flat; single missing rivet.

Irregularly cut polygons

Copper alloy

(flat unless stated; all have a single central hole)

1124 BWB83 2350 (147) 11 fig 130
d 13mm; hole slightly distorted.

1125 BWB83 1592 (108) 11
Sub-square; d 13mm; hole offcentred.

1126 BWB83 3768 (338) 11 fig 130
d 16mm; hole in middle, and larger offcentred one.

1127 BWB83 4737 (309) 12
d 22mm; domed.

Similar, larger items (d over 25mm) probably had
nothing to do with dress, and are omitted – no parallel
of a similar size has been traced that is still attached to
anything, or that retains a rivet. A polygonal rove,
d 8mm, set on the back of buckle no. 482 (fig 68), is the
closest parallel noted for the group so far, but the
difference in size may mean that these items are
unrelated. The crudeness of most of these quite
common objects suggests that they may not have been
intended to be seen. They could have acted as relatively heavy-duty roves. Several seem to have received
rough treatment.

Composite polygonal mount

Copper alloy and iron

1128 BWB83 5209 (308) 11 fig 130
Elongated octagonal copper-alloy sheet, 18×23mm,
with domed circular iron mount, d 15mm, having a
single iron rivet.

The rivet could have been attached to leather etc,
since it has not been hammered over flush at the back
of the sheeting just to hold the iron mount in place.

LOST MOUNTS

*(attested by marks on straps – of uncertain forms and
metals)*

1129 SWA81 acc. no. 4954 (context 2062)
ceramic phase 9 fig 130
Irregular, cut fragment of copper-alloy sheeting
(?offcut), and another lost mount (evidenced by a
dome-headed copper-alloy rivet with solder on the
shank), on leather strap 87×13mm (cut at one end,
torn off at the other) with impressed line along each
side, and series of V-shaped cuts along centre; terminating at two dome-headed copper-alloy tacks (ie with
pointed ends), which are bent over at the back to hold
the irregular mount, which curves back, away from the
leather; the strap has been crudely slashed with a sharp
instrument lengthways.

The enigmatic piece of sheeting, which has not been
paralleled on any other strap, is presumably some kind
of first-aid repair; the intended function is obscure.

This is the only leather item in this catalogue from
the recent excavations having a mount of any kind held
by a tack (though the girdle in colour pl 5E has several
mounts secured by bent, pointed shanks – see nos.
1300–02 and discussion).

1130 TL74 3251 (368) 12 fig 130
Leather strap 370×30mm (torn off at both ends) with
roves, iron rivets and rust marks on the leather from a
group of six mounts (possibly circular, ?d c.8mm).

1131 TL74 618 (368) 12
Two pieces of leather strap, together c.260+×42mm
(probably originally joined, cut with angled corners at
one end, torn off at the other), with corroded traces
and marks indicating 19 former mounts, all possibly
circular, ?d c.9mm, set in a row centrally, with pairs
after every fourth one (the pattern perhaps differed
slightly at some points).

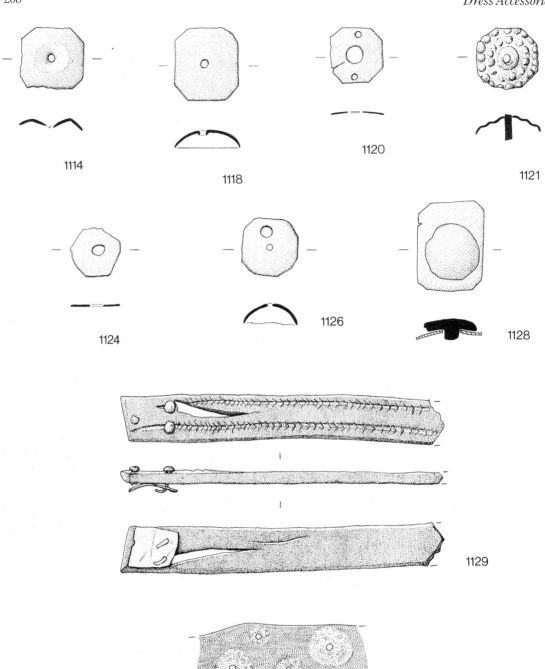

1114

1118

1120

1121

1124

1126

1128

1129

1130

130 Top two rows, polygonal mounts; below, straps
with missing mounts   (1:1)

Further lost mounts are evidenced by:

a leather strap in two separate parts accompanying iron buckle no. 416 – the leather of this apparently complete girdle has holes and some roves surviving from about thirty missing mounts set in a single row along the centre;

leather girdle no. 19 with paired rivets from at least three mounts (possibly circular, ?d *c*.15mm – see fig 26);

leather girdle no. 20 with two sets of paired rivet holes for (?)ring mounts d 14mm, and with six surviving dome-headed iron rivets in a central row at the other surviving end (possibly used as mounts in their own right – see fig 27).

See also girdle no. 26 for iron pins (cf rivets) set in patterns to give a similar effect to mounts – fig 29.

BAR-MOUNTS

and variants

'Bar' is a contemporary term used of girdle mounts of a particular form (Hume 1863, 131–33, citing three occurrences in Chaucer – eg the sergeant-at-law in the Canterbury Tales is wearing clothes described as 'rood but hoomly in a medlee cote, girt with a ceint [girdle] of silk with barres smale' – Prologue, lines 328–29, and also a 13th-century reference to girdles 'barred with silver', *stipata argento*, and mid 14th-century orders for 30 buckles together with 60 bars, and for 60 buckles together with 6 bars). Although it is not certain precisely which mounts would have been referred to as 'bars', bar-mounts are for the present purpose defined as those in which the width (discounting the central lobe in some examples) is 10mm or less, and equals no more than half the length (ie the dimension transverse to the strap). This rather arbitrary definition serves to isolate a group of quite simple mounts of a distinctive narrow form – though they can be seen as continuous with larger mounts listed as rectangular (thus no. 1047 appears under rectangular mounts, but no. 1132, which falls just outside the above definition, is listed under the present heading because of the similarity to no. 1164; its distinctive form and method of manufacture is paralleled among these mounts and not elsewhere). Although some bar mounts are very plain when seen singly in isolation, they make an effective decoration when several are set together or in combination with mounts of other forms.

Bar-mounts were normally attached transversely in a row on straps, usually evenly spaced, and generally spanning the full width of the leather (though see on no. 1140 and fig 138, bottom for exceptions, and cf Hume 1863, fig on p133). They may be set very close together, or more widely spaced. Contemporary depictions show them on men's waist belts and sword belts, as well as on horse-harness straps etc – eg the sword belts on four of the 13th-century sculptured effigies of knights in the Temple Church of St Mary in London (see fig 132, and cf RCHM 1929, 140–41, pls 182–83 nos. 3, 4, 7 & 8); the horse in the St Martin group sculpture at Bassenheim in Germany has them on the straps of the head harness and on the girth strap which

Bar mounts and variants: these have a length of 10mm or less, and which is no more than half their width.

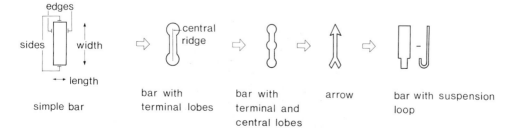

simple bar

bar with terminal lobes

bar with terminal and central lobes

arrow

bar with suspension loop

holds the saddle in place (Pinder 1952, pl 72), and the horse of the Rider in Bamberg Cathedral in Germany has them here and also on the reins (see fig 132); a dragon is symbolically restrained by a leash with similar mounts in an Italian painting of the Virgin Saints (Pradella of the *Ognissanti Polyptych*, of *c*.1360–65 by Giovanni da Milano).

The mounts occur in both solid (cast or wrought) and stamped sheet-metal forms. They have a hole for a rivet at each end unless otherwise stated. Those with a single central rivet are known in situ on leather and silk straps, and also on the ends of folding clasps and on the shield-shaped plates thought to be the corresponding parts of these clasps (see fig 76).

A specialised version of the bar-mount (with two rivets) is hooked at one end; these were used with pendent loops (see nos. 1189–93), or in pairs to hold arched pendent mounts on girdles (see nos. 1196 & 1198).

There is a possibility that some bindings for caskets, particularly incomplete examples, might be wrongly identified as bar-mounts for straps (cf

examples in situ on caskets: Beckwith 1972, 137 no. 90 pl 199 from the early 12th century; Cherry 1982, pls XXXa, XXXIVa, & XXXVIIIb – lower mount in centre; Longhurst 1926, 165 pl 51 nos. LXXIV & LXXV – both dated to the 15th century). Numbers 1166–67 are thought to be from caskets; they are published below for comparison.

While all these mounts, and in particular the solid ones (over two thirds of those listed below, counting multiple finds still on a strap as one), would to some extent have strengthened the straps and protected them from damage, the decorative appearance was probably the most important consideration. Bar-mounts cover the whole period considered in this volume.

The order in which the following items are listed under shape categories is according to increasing strap width (second dimension) within each ceramic phase.

All except one of the mounts listed below are of copper alloy; see nos. 1182–83 for further similar iron examples.

132   Effigies of knights in Temple Church of St. Mary, London, showing bar– and other mounts: top left, both mid 13th century; bottom left, late and mid 13th century; top right, mid 13th century. Bottom right, horse of the Rider of Bamberg Cathedral, Germany, showing bar-mounts on various parts of the harness

Simple bars

1132 CUS73 acc. no. 300. (context IV, 55) ceramic phase 9 fig 133 & colour pl 5D
Six surviving solid mounts; fronts brass (backs 'gunmetal' – this probably includes solder – all tested, (AML); each between 5×7.5 and 6.5×8mm; central hole, and a groove having hatching, possibly punched, along each edge; on leather girdle no. 2; some roves survive. Minor variations between individual mounts are readily apparent.
Published by Henig (1974, 199–200 fig 42 no. 238).

1133 LUD82 307 (1046) 9 fig 133
Two solid mounts, each 4×8mm, with a single rivet, on one of two lengths of leather girdle no. 3.

1134 CUS73 225 (I,12) 9 fig 30
Three solid, D-section mounts, brass (AML, one tested), varying between 4.5×9 and 5×8.5mm, each with a single rivet; set on a silk strap – see p 48 (fig 30, top). The absence of further holes in the piece with the three mounts shows that the mounts did not continue on the surviving portion.

1135 CUS73 859 (I, 12) 9
Twelve surviving solid mounts, each between 4×9 and 5.5×10.5mm, brass and gunmetal (AML, five tested), with a groove having (?)punched triangles along each edge, on two lengths of leather strap, totalling 220×11mm (both torn off at the ends, possibly originally joined together), and holes indicating the loss of

perhaps five more mounts. Minor variations between individual mounts are readily apparent.
Published by Henig (1974, 199–200, fig 42 no. 239).

The mounts on the four preceding straps appear, from the varied angles of the sides and from a broken lip at that point (particularly evident in no. 1132), to have been cut from longer bars.

1136 SWA81 3428 (2141) 9 fig 133
3×14mm; sheeting; rivets missing.

1137 SWA81 5095 (2051) 9 fig 133
5.5×16mm; sheeting; central ridge; edges and one end curve towards the back; one rivet survives.

1138 SWA81 603 (2065) 9 fig 133
4×17mm; solid; D-section; one rivet survives, with lead/tin solder; cut from a longer bar.

1139 SWA81 925 (2050) 9 fig 133
Ten surviving sheet-brass (AML) mounts (holes indicate the loss of six more), each 5×17mm, the rivets having roves, on three lengths of leather strap, totalling *c.*410×16mm (torn off at ends – two definitely join, the third probably did).

1140 SWA81 416 (2018) 9
Imprints from at least six lost (?sheeting) mounts, each 5×18+mm on leather strap 125×22mm (cut at one end, torn off at the other); two rivets survive; four mounts seem to have been set in pairs, the other two singly.

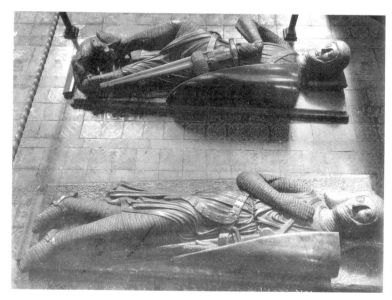

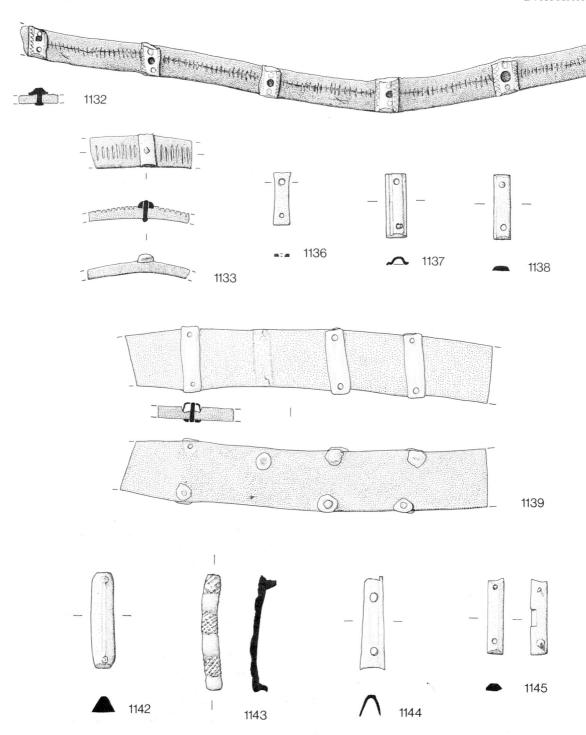

133 Bar-mounts (1:1)

This is an unusual instance of bar-mounts being set with other than regular spacing.

1141 SWA81 430 (2018) 9
5.5×25mm; sheeting; one rivet survives.

1142 SWA81 2128 (2030) 9 fig 133
6×26mm; solid; central ridge; rivets missing.

1143 BWB83 4466 (256) 11 fig 133
4×30mm; solid; alternate plain and cross-hatched fields along bar; integral rivets.

This is the only bar mount with integral rivets; it may perhaps have been for a casket or other rigid object, rather than for a strap.

1144 BWB83 3253 (265) 12 fig 133
6×24mm; folded sheeting; central ridge; rivets missing.

1145 BWB83 5133 (unstratified) fig 133
4×20mm; solid; D-section; angled recess in middle of one edge; rivets survive; corrosion products on the back suggest that this was fixed to a smoother surface than leather.

Probably from a shield-shaped strap-end like no. 738 (fig 103).

A simple bar-mount with two rivets is used as a form of rove on the strap with the parallel for buckle no. 472 (fig 65).

Iron

1146 BWB83 8 (110) 11 fig 102
5×24mm; solid; two rivets; on leather strap with strap-end no. 730.

Bars with terminal lobes

Copper alloy

1147 BIG82 2511 (2853) 8 fig 134
4×25mm; sheeting; two iron rivets.

1148 SWA81 3429 (2141) 9 fig 134
7.5×13mm; sheeting; lozenge-shaped bar.

1149 SWA81 426 (2018) 9 fig 134
7×20mm; sheeting; central ridge; on fragment of leather strap 23mm wide and with impressed lines lengthways defining where the rivets are set.

1150 SWA81 3427 (2141) 9 fig 134
5×22.5mm; solid; central ridge; rivets missing.

1151 SWA81 1881 (2133) 9 fig 134
6×29.5mm; sheeting; central ridge; rivets missing.

1152 SWA81 431 (2018) 9
8×33mm; sheeting; central ridge; rivets missing.

1153 SWA81 3076 (2030) 9
Mount as no. 1149, but 7×33.5mm.

Bars with terminal and central lobes

Copper alloy

A leather strap with mounts of this form (alternating with circular ones having a beaded border) has been published as a harness strap (Guildhall Museum Catalogue 1908, 144 no. 4613 & pl LXXIV nos. 2 & 11) – there seems to be no specific reason to connect it with horse equipment.

1154 BIG82 3267 (3561) 6 fig 134
6.5×32mm; solid; central hole; rivets missing.

1155 SWA81 597 (2055) 9 fig 134
6×10mm; sheeting; central hole; rivets have roves and traces of lead-tin solder (MLC); leather survives from strap.

1156 SWA81 422 (2018) 9
6×18mm; solid; central hole; bar is hatched horizontally; rivets missing.

1157 SWA81 424 (2018) 9 fig 134
7×22mm; as preceding item; one rivet with solder survives.

1158 SWA81 1942 (2063) 9 fig 134
8×31.5mm; solid; bar tapers from centre; central hole with raised, bevelled surround; raised terminal lobes; one rivet with traces of solder survives.

1159 BWB83 4553 (274) 9 fig 134
13×39mm; rectangular sheeting; squarish hole in raised central squarish area (both orientated as lozenges); raised bar and trilobed terminals; probably unfinished, since it has not been trimmed; no rivets.

1160 BWB83 1508 (108) 11 fig 134
10×16mm; solid; central lobe is crudely cross-hatched; part of one rivet survives.

1161 BWB83 3605 (368) 11 fig 134
9×19mm; solid; gunmetal (AML); central lobe is cross-hatched; part of one rivet survives.

1162 BWB83 5832 (291) 11
12×22mm; solid; (leaded) bronze, with tin coating (AML); central lobe is cross-hatched; one rivet survives.

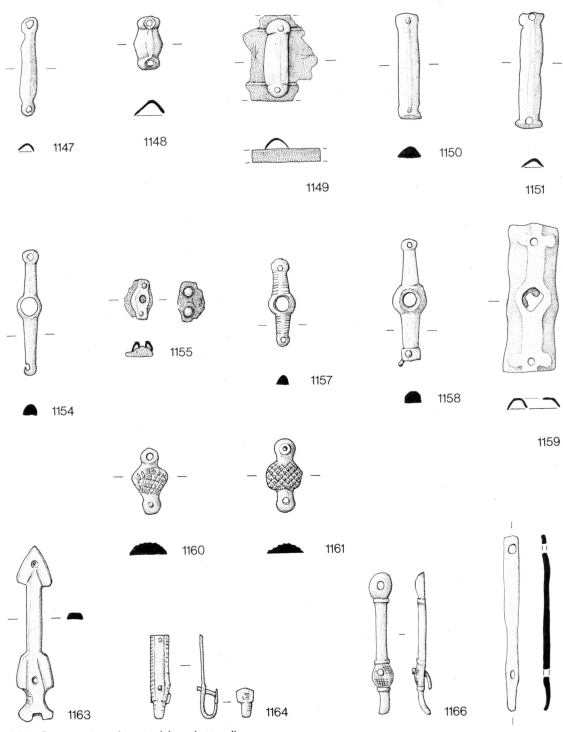

134 Bar-mounts, and two at right on bottom line,
probable casket mounts   (1:1)

Arrow shaped

Copper alloy

1163 BWB83 2714 (329) 11 fig 134
9×45mm; solid; rivets missing.

Bars with a suspension loop

Copper alloy

These are all solid, with a loop at one end that has an expanded terminal at the back; (for mounts of this kind retaining pendent loops or arched pendants, see nos. 1189–93 and 1194–98).

1164 BWB83 2492 (351) 11 fig 134
5×22mm; groove with transverse hatching along each edge; one rivet survives.

1165 BWB83 5846 (298) 11
5.5×32mm; plain groove along each edge.

The two preceding items are definitely belt fittings, but the decoration on no. 1164 is almost identical to that on the binding mounts on a late-medieval casket (Cherry 1982, pl XXXVIII). The following two objects (which predate most of the bar-mounts listed above) are probably casket bindings – though no. 1166 in particular looks like a variation on the preceding strap mounts with a suspension loop. Here the broken loops are probably for lid hinges.

1166 BIG82 2842 (4064) 6 fig 134
Incomplete, slightly corroded; cast; copper, with one brass and one copper rivet (AML); 6×37mm; (?)loop broken off; two lobes, with trace of decoration on one, and ridges to each side.

1167 BIG82 2926 (4103) 7 fig 134
Incomplete; 4.5×47mm; plain bar, (?)loop broken off; rivets missing. The bar has been distorted by knocking from each side.

SHORT STRAPS WITH TWO GROUPS OF MOUNTS
(various shapes)

These seventeen distinctive leather straps have several common features: the mounts are set in two distinct groups towards each end, the strap between has a series of clumsily pierced holes along the centre, and is often very abraded in this area; one end usually has a folded fitting like a strap-end, and the other has either a large, crudely cut hole (sometimes with the leather from its centre left attached at one point, so as to form a crude tab), or another folded plate. The variety of the mounts on the sixteen straps from a single late 14th-century dump at the BC72 site is extraordinary.

The length of the complete straps, the disposition of the mounts, and the wear on some parts (eg on the plant mounts of no. 1186, fig 126, mount at right) seem to be consistent with the function of the spur straps which pass over the instep of the foot (David Horne, pers. comm.). The two groups of mounts would thus be set on each side of the foot; where there were more-decorative ones at one end (as on no. 1186), these would probably be worn on the outer side, where they would be more visible. No matching pairs of straps were recovered at the BC72 site (although nos. 1173 and 1174 have similar mounts, there are differences in the sizes of the strap and other details).

The degree of decoration on some of these items exceeds that on other identified spur straps from excavations. The present straps also include some wider than any others from the excavated assemblages which have so far been identified with spurs. While these points do not invalidate the suggested identification, they do reinforce the impression that these particular straps were out of the ordinary.

The sixteen straps from BC72 are from a group of dump deposits which is notable because of indications that the assemblage of finds it produced is an unusually high-class one (see p 3). The assemblage could represent items discarded from a store, perhaps from a well-endowed organisation such as the nearby Great Wardrobe (Grew and de Neergard 1988, 29). Probably very few institutions would have owned such showy equipment for so many riders. It is possible to speculate, therefore, that this group of material may include parade items, bearing in mind the proximity of the storehouse of the extended royal household. Although not as spectacular, the assemblage from the TL74 site from which no. 1186 came perhaps also suggests a military milieu.

These items are included here because the forms of mounts they include may well also figure on girdles etc (compare mount no. 1057 from strap no. 1170, with mounts no. 1058 on purse no. 1701 figs 123 & 232), and also because a number of loose mounts were recovered from the same deposits as nos. 1168–85 (nos. 801 and 829 may be further incomplete items of this present category). The details given here are to allow researchers to assess together all the mounts and straps from these deposits, whether at present they can be identified accurately or not.

The summary descriptions that follow are set out according to the arrangement on a typical example of a strap of this kind (see fig 135 and cf nos. 1182 & 1186 in figs 136 & 126). The straps are all of leather, and the folded plates (presumably strap-ends like nos. 589 etc) are all of tin-coated iron and have a single rivet. The straps are listed in order of increasing length of the surviving portion. These items will be fully considered in another volume (Clark forthcoming).

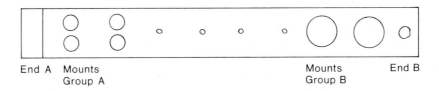

End A   Mounts   Mounts   End B
         Group A   Group B

135   Schematic diagram of short strap with two groups of mounts

end A	**mounts (shape)**	**group A** (no. & configuration)	**group B**	**end B**	**total no. of mounts**
Stamped sheet-iron tin-coated mounts (all ceramic phase 11):					
1168 BC72	acc. no. 2372 (context 89) strap 64+×10mm				
plate	uncertain motifs; 14×10mm; rivets have roves	2 (?+1 lost)	(torn off)	(torn off)	**7**
(probably the other half of the following item)					
1169 BC72	2517 (89) strap 110+×11mm (see no. 1103, fig 128)				
(torn off)	(see preceding item)	1+	1	two holes	**2+**
1170 BC72	2622 (89) strap 115+×10mm (see no. 1057, fig 123)				
plate	rectangular; corrugated in section; 11×40mm; 3 rivets	1	(missing)	(torn off)	**1+**
1171 BC72	1605 (55) strap 120+×15mm				
plate	circular, with central hole; 2 rivets d 13mm	4	(missing)	(torn off)	**4+**
1172 BC72	2310 (79) strap 122+×11mm				
rivet	circular, domed; d 11mm	3 (+1 lost)	– (hint of rivet hole)	(torn off)	**4+**
1173 BC72	2595 (79) strap 158+×10mm				
rivet	circular, domed; d 9mm	2 (+1 lost)	(4 lost)	(? torn off)	**7**
1174 BC72	2593 (79) strap 161+×25mm				
plate with 2 circular mounts, d 9mm	circular, domed; d 9mm	(lost; ?3 rows of 4)	1 rivet survives (? 3 rows of 3 mounts)	(?torn off)	**21 +2 on plate**
1175 BC72	2554 (83) strap 165×13mm (see no. 1056, fig 123)				
(plate lost)	rectangular with transverse central ridge, varied in size – up to 11×10mm	3 (+1 lost)	(1 rivet)	hole	**5**

end A	mounts (shape)	group A (no. & configuration)		group B	end B	total no. of mounts
1176 BC72 plate	1676 (55) strap 175×12mm circular, domed; d 6.5mm	4(+1 lost) single row	4 single row		tab	**9**
1177 BC72 plate	2594 (79) strap *c*.180×13mm (see no. 948, fig 117) domed cinquefoils with ridged lobes d 12mm	3(+1 lost)		1(+2 lost)	hole	**7**
1178 BC72 plate	2412 (89) strap 182+×13mm (lost; rivets survive)	(3 lost)		(4 lost)	(torn off)	**7**
1179 BC72 plate missing	2549 (88/1) strap 186×13mm (see no. 943, fig 117) quatrefoils with domed lobes; rivets have roves	4		1(+3 lost)	hole	**8**
1180 BC72 plate	1715 (55) strap 192×12mm bar-mounts with central lobe & trilobate sides; 8×12mm	3(+1 lost)		(3 lost)	crude hole	**7**
1181 BC72 plate	2596 (79) strap *c*.195×11mm (see no. 1016, fig 120) sexfoils with domed centre & lobes; d 11mm	4		1(+1 lost)	rivet	**6**
1182 BC72 plate	2478 (79) strap 197×11mm (fig 136 & colour pl 5A) bars with raised centre & bilobate sides; 7×11mm	2(+3 lost)		3(+1 lost)	hole	**9**
1183 BC72	2759, an identical mount from the same context, was almost certainly also from this strap (fig 136).					

Lead/tin mounts (ceramic phase 11):

1184 BC72 (torn off)	2551 (83) strap 139×36mm pairs of conjoined, domed roundels; 5×11mm	10(+5 lost) (3 rows of 5)		2(+8 lost) (2 rows of 4 + central row of 2)	?tab among group of mounts	**25**
1185 BC72 plate	3591 (150) strap 186×11mm circular, domed; d 4.5mm	9(+3 lost) some abraded (2 rows)		14 (2 rows)	crude hole	**26**
1186 TL74 plate	1960 (275) strap 166×19mm (see no. 1089, fig 126) A: domed, circular d 5mm. B: plants	2 (single row)		4 (2 rows)	(torn off)	**6**

These items clearly demonstrate the interchangeability of forms of mount on one category of strap.

CIRCULAR MOUNTS WITH PENDENT MOTIFS

Copper alloy

1187 TL74 acc. no. 2398 (context 368) ceramic phase 12 fig 136 & colour pl 5B

Thirteen composite loops, in varying states of completeness, along centre of leather strap, 127×12mm (torn off at one end, strap-end no. 588 on the other); the surviving parts of the mounts suggest that each consisted of a stamped circular sheet with an engrailed edge, d 8.5mm, with oblique, lines (cable pattern)

around a domed centre; the single rivet has a rove, and a looped end at the front with a freely moving U-section sheet ring.

The following iron items (from the same deposit) suggest that the rings here are loops from incomplete sheet pendants. Cf also sexfoil no. 951/fig 119.

Iron

1188 TL74 1096 (368) 12 fig 136 & colour pl 3

28 whole or fragmentary stamped-sheet pinnate leaves, each 21×59mm, with veining; a loop at the top of each is attached to the looped end of a rivet, which passes through a U-section sheet ring, and has a

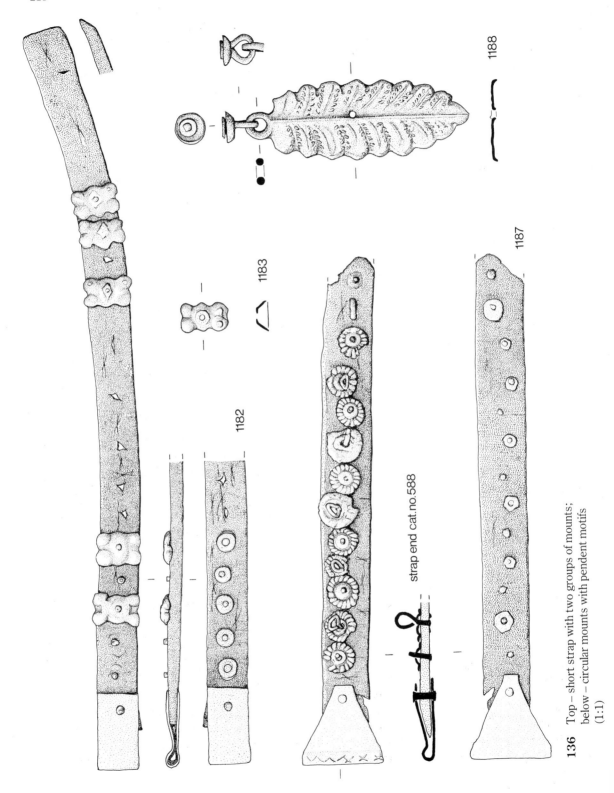

1188

1183

1182

1187

strap end cat.no.588

136 Top – short strap with two groups of mounts;
below – circular mounts with pendent motifs
(1:1)

copper-alloy rove. Each leaf is tin-coated, and has been pierced near the middle from the front by a pin hole; all but five mounts are substantially complete. TL74 acc. nos. 1088A–C from the same deposit are three similar loops (rivets and attachments), presumably from pendants similar to or included among acc. no. 1096.

When found, the mounts were in contact with woollen cloth of dress weight in tabby weave (Pritchard 1982, 205 fig 1), though the association may be entirely fortuitous (cf Rhodes 1982B, 90). This remarkable group illustrates the different degree of detail registered on stamped objects according to the amount of pressure used in the stamping process.

The leaves somewhat resemble the rusty-back fern (*ceterach officinarum* – D Vaughan, pers. comm.), though probably no specific plant was intended.

A slightly smaller leaf mount of different form is known in copper-alloy sheeting (MoL acc. no. 80.82/ 33).

Leaf pendants are shown hanging in large numbers from the sleeves of the armour of St George in a late 15th-century painting (fig 137), though metal leaves were apparently out of general fashion by that time (Scott 1980, 36), and they also figure in horse trappings; cf the 15th-century painting *The Conversion of St Hubert* – reproduced in Chenevix-Trench (1970, 63).

BAR-MOUNTS WITH PENDENT LOOPS

The width (second dimension) given for these mounts omits the hook on the lower side – ie the stated dimension reflects the width of the strap. All the pendent loops except that on no. 1191 have a constriction at the point of suspension. All are cast.

Copper alloy

1189 BWB83 acc. no. 5937 (context 298) ceramic phase 11 fig 138
4×8.5mm, d of quadrilobate pendant 11mm; D-section bar has single rivet.

1190 BWB83 4991 (399) 11 fig 138
6×11mm, d of circular pendant 13.5mm; brass (AML); bar recessed at edges, with punched triangles here; two rivets.

1191 BWB83 2738 (329) 11 fig 138
4.5×14mm, d of circular pendant, 12mm; D-section bar has two rivets.

1192 BWB83 3668 (359) 11 fig 138
Pendent loop only; circular with collared knop; l 18mm.

1193 SWA81 3382 (2139) 9 fig 138
Pendent loop only; approximately D-shaped, having offset for suspension and knops with radiating grooves at angles; l 13mm; tin coating.

Two copper-alloy bar-mounts with circular pendent loops survive as a pair flanking a strap loop, on a leather strap with other mounts, found in spoil removed by contractors from the TEX88 site; see fig 138 (MoL acc. no. 88.461/2). A purse or knife could have been suspended between the pair of loops which would thus be analogous in use to arched pendent mounts (see below).

Two further copper-alloy bar-mounts with quadrilobate pendent loops are known from London (MoL acc. nos. 80.69/13 and 80.549/1). Other mounts with loops include one from Oxford (AR Goodall 1977, 152 no. 80 fig 31) and another from Goltho, Lincolnshire (AR Goodall in Beresford 1975, 93 fig 44 no. 28). A silk tablet-woven girdle in the National Museum of Denmark is garnished with silver mounts, including a bar-mount with a trapezoidal pendant, patterned with dotted knops (Fingerlin 1971, 362–63 no. 126, fig 409), and a suite of girdle fittings from a grave in Yugoslavia dating to the late 14th century includes a matching mount and loop with elaborate foliate decoration (ibid, 445–46 no. 465). On the Danish girdle, the mount and loop are positioned on the left of the buckle as worn.

ARCHED PENDENT MOUNTS

(Purse hangers)

These consist of a freely swinging, singly or multiply arched element, held at each end, usually by a bar mount, to a girdle. Some if not all of these items were used to attach purses or knives to the belt.

The following items were identified by analogy with examples represented in mid 13th-century French sculpture. The parallels include mounts similar to no. 1198, carved on a mid 13th-century statue of King Clovis from Moutiers-Saint-Jean

137 Detail of St George's parade armour with pendent leaves, laces with chapes at elbow and sexfoil mounts – from the Trinity Altarpiece by Van der Goes, 1470s (the fashion for leaves was rather outmoded by the time the picture was painted)

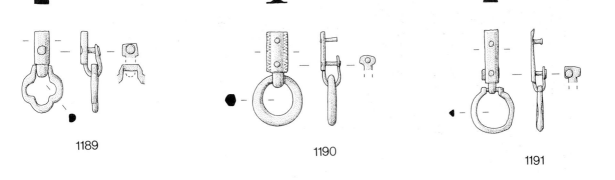

1189   1190   1191

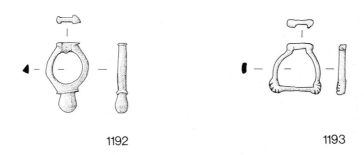

1192   1193

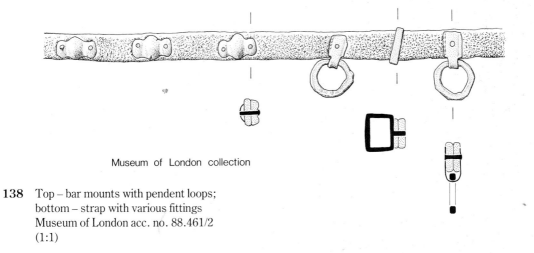

Museum of London collection

138   Top – bar mounts with pendent loops;
bottom – strap with various fittings
Museum of London acc. no. 88.461/2
(1:1)

and also one worn on the right on a lady's effigy from Normandy (fig 139). Both of the fittings are depicted with a suspended purse and the latter also has a knife suspended from it (the sculptures are now in the Cloisters Museum, New York – Rorimer 1972, 31 fig 30, and Wixom 1988/89, 59 right; see also fig 10 this volume).

An ornate example still on a belt was found around the body in the tomb of the Castilian Infanta Fernando de la Cerda (died 1275) in the royal mausoleum at the Convent of Las Huelgas near Burgos in Spain. This richly jewelled appendage, worn on the left side of the body, may, from the positions of the precious stones, not have been functional (see fig 140, and Fingerlin 1971, 331–33 no. 61 & pls 368 left & 369). The Spanish mount could be a purely decorative, aristocratic version of the functional item.

A similar fitting with three arches is depicted on the girdle worn by Mary Magdalen in the *Altarpiece of the Seven Sacraments* (attributed to Rogier van der Weyden, *c.*1445). This one is worn to the left of the girdle fastening, which here takes the form of a roundel. Nothing is shown suspended from this example, perhaps because any accessory was removed indoors. The large, trapezoidal pendent mount referred to in the previous section, fixed by a single bar-mount to a continental European belt (Fingerlin 1971, 362–63 no. 126 fig 409, attributed to the early 15th century) has a straight horizontal rod instead of arches; this example could have been used with a vertical strap passed through the centre (thanks to N-K Liebgott at Nationalmuseet in Copenhagen for allowing this object to be examined). A mid 13th-century effigy of a lady at St Thibault-

139   Purse hangers – details of mid 13th century
         French sculptures:
         (left)   ? King Clovis, from Moutiers-Saint-Jean
         (right)   ? Margaret of Gloucester, from
                   Normandy

en-Auxois in France appears to show a purse suspended from a U-shaped fitting of another type not identified among the recent finds (Neil Stratford, pers. comm.).

Excavated mounts of the present type have in the past often been published as handles (eg Hume 1863, 197 and pl XX nos. 2–4 & 6–10; Jackson 1986, 276–77 no. 5 fig 7).

Number 1194, one of the earliest of these items, is of a slightly different character from the others (which are all cast), but the basic similarity is clear. The cast examples are notably well-made and neatly finished.

All of the excavated examples are of copper alloy. They are listed in order of length, within ceramic phases.

1194 SWA81   acc. no. 4086   (context 2137)
ceramic phase 9   fig 140
Single drawn-wire arch, l 35mm, looped at each end through a sheet-metal mount, which at the front has a subrectangular terminal with an engraved saltire cross, and at the back a wedge-shaped end; the mounts are secured by rivets with roves and traces of solder (MLC) to a plain leather strap 7mm wide and c.305mm long (torn off at both ends).

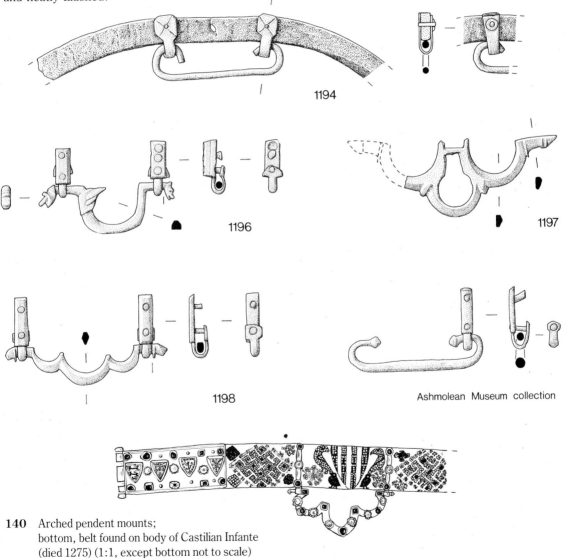

140   Arched pendent mounts;
bottom, belt found on body of Castilian Infante (died 1275) (1:1, except bottom not to scale)

1195 CUS73 39 (I,12) 9
Incomplete; l 45mm; two (?of original three) arches, the surviving ones being of different sizes; expanded end with collar. The original length would have been just over 60mm.
    Published by Henig (1974, 194 & 196 no. 133).

1196 BWB83 2347 (137) 11 fig 140
Single arch, l 37mm; there is an animal's head at each end of the pendent element – the larger head is complemented by an integrally cast wing on the curve, so that together these give the appearance of a dragon-like beast; the two suspension loops have D-shaped terminals at the back, and are separate from the bar-mounts at the front (each 9×4mm), which were originally connected to them by two rivets – two of these and part of a third survive; a replacement rivet in a different position has been added.

1197 BWB83 1905 (401) 11 fig 140
Incomplete; two (?of original three) arches, l 42mm+; central inverted keyhole-shaped opening, flanked by an open semicircle; two prongs at the top echo the cusps in the external angles between the arches; the surviving end has a collared expanded terminal; the back is flat, in contrast with the three-dimensional modelling of the front. The original length would have been just under 60mm.
    A virtually identical item (broken at almost the same point), was excavated at Winchester (Biddle forthcoming, no. 2394 – Nick Griffiths, pers. comm.).

1198 BWB83 5838 (324) 12 fig 140
Three arches, l 43mm; the central arch is larger than the two flanking ones; there is a collar on each expanded end; the bar-mounts, each 13×4mm have subrectangular terminals at the back and each retains two rivets.

The size of the bar-mounts in each case indicates the approximate width of the strap to which the mount was attached – on the Burgos example (see above) the two mounts on the front of the belt presumably served the same function as the bar-mounts in the London examples. On this assumption, the straps for nos. 1196 and 1198 would, like that for no. 1194, have been considerably narrower than the 43mm-wide Burgos belt, which was apparently for a sword on the other side of the body (Collin nd, 6). Bar-mounts nos. 1164 and 1165 may be from similar appendages. A form intermediate between that of no. 1194 and the other mounts of this category listed above consists of a cast single arch of similar shape to

no. 1194, but with expanded terminals. This type is so far represented in London by two examples (TEX88 acc. no. 285, and MoL acc. no. A11140 found at Tabard Street); there are two examples in the Ashmolean Museum (acc. no. 1927.6439, and no. 1873.38 – found at Woodperry, Oxon – which retains a bar-mount for a strap *c*.12mm wide – JW 1846, 120 fig 8, and 122 – fig 140 in this volume; another example, excavated at Chertsey Abbey, was apparently held by two metal slides, of a type not identified among the recent London finds, instead of bar-mounts – Poulton 1988, 67 fig 44 no. 10).

    None of the above mounts has wear marks on the arches to indicate that something was definitely suspended from them, though a holder for a purse or other item seems the most probable explanation of their function.

ASYMMETRICAL MOUNTS WITH A RIDGE AND APERTURE

Copper alloy

The following items would probably have had some specialised purpose; this has not yet been identified. Number 1201 indicates that they were strap mounts. The apertures are all crudely cut rectangles.

1199 SWA81 acc. no. 1810 (context 2081)
ceramic phase 9 fig 141
Rectangular; 14×32mm; aperture at middle of off-centred transverse ridge; roughly engraved oblique lines, some making V motifs; two missing rivets.

1200 SWA81 1845 (2106) 12 fig 141
15×17mm; one edge has two angled sides, the other has four slightly angled projections; aperture in middle of transverse ridge; engraved oblique lines and border; parts of two iron rivets survive.
    (A small penannular copper-alloy sheet ring found attached by corrosion products to the mount is unlikely to have had any significant association with it.)

1201 SWA81 888 (2100) 12 fig 141
Mount 16×17mm, with one trilobed edge and the other having two angled sides, on leather strap 55×18mm (torn off at both ends); the ridge of the mount runs transversely across the strap; two iron rivets; oblique, multiple engraved hatching in fields defined by

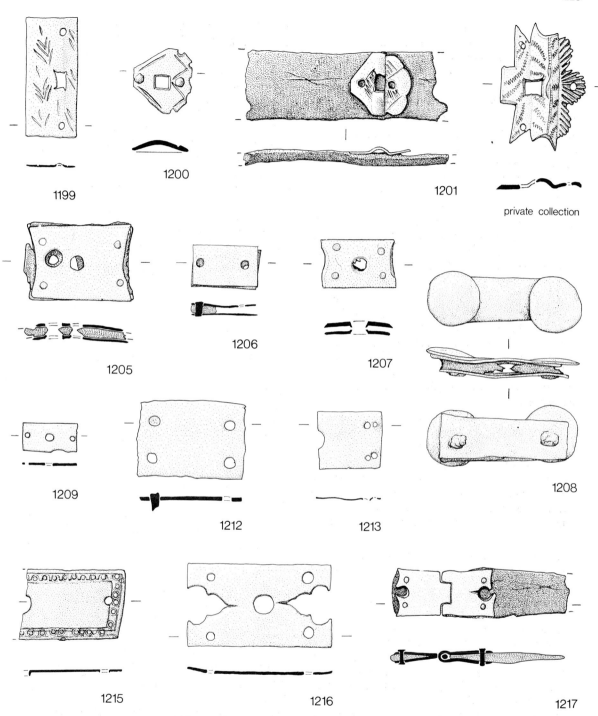

1199

1200

1201

private collection

1205

1206

1207

1208

1209

1212

1213

1215

1216

1217

141 Top row, asymmetrical mounts with a ridge and aperture;
below, rectangular strap plates   (1:1)

opposed, oblique engraved lines, outside which the surface has tin coating (MLC).

These three mounts contrast with virtually all the other non-figurative ones described in this volume, in that they lack symmetry about a line transversely through the strap. Although the shape of the last two is broadly comparable to that of eyelets nos. 1223 and 1224 (also of early 15th-century date, fig 142), they cannot be either for buckle pins or for lace holes, as no. 1201 has no hole in the leather. None of them has obvious wear around the aperture or on the back of the ridge. Those having the form of nos. 1201 and 1202 could have been set in pairs, perhaps to flank some central item symmetrically – cf flat mount no. 1107 of lead/tin, which lacks an aperture, and could be one of an original pair (fig 110). The period of use of these mounts could be quite brief – perhaps little more than 50 years between the mid 14th and the early 15th century. A larger, more elaborate example of copper alloy has been found in the River Thames in London (private collection – fig 141).

RECTANGULAR STRAP-PLATES

These items usually consist of two rectangular or subrectangular sheets riveted together. They are listed in order of increasing width (second dimension) within ceramic phases. Some are quite crude. The straps do not often survive, but those that do suggest that there was probably more than one function – see discussion below.

(all are of copper alloy)

Complete examples
(both sheets surviving)

1202   BWB83   acc. no. 2219   (context 146)
ceramic phase 11
15×11mm; one edge at front slightly concave; two rivets; leather from strap survives.

1203   BWB83   1425   (355)   11
Subrectangular; brass (AML); 23×14.5mm; four rivets.

1204   BWB83   2736   (329)   11
24×19mm; holes for four rivets, two of which survive; orientation of strap (from which leather survives) uncertain.

1205   BWB83   1535   (256)   11   fig 141
27×20mm; brass (AML)   concave edges; four rivets, and two larger holes at the centre and towards one end; retains leather from two straps with contiguous cut ends in the middle of the rectangle (both torn off at the ends of the plates); the metal is worn around the offcentred hole and the leather is pierced here, while the other hole is partly blocked by the leather.

1206   SWA81   2349   (2102)   12   fig 141
17×10mm; one of two rivets survives; leather from strap survives at one edge, possibly cut transversely near the centre.

1207   SWA81   917   (2102)   12   fig 141
19×13mm; brass plate, copper rivets (AML); crudely filed concave edges (except for one at the back which is straight); large central hole, which is worn, and others for the four rivets.

Composite, decorated plate

1208   BWB83   3994   (292)   11   fig 141
Crudely cut rectangular sheeting 33×14mm, and corresponding back plate, held together by two circular, slightly dome-headed rivets, d 14mm; degraded leather survives.

Single plates
(perhaps from incomplete strap-plates)

1209   BWB83   6040   (338)   11   fig 141
15×8mm; crudely cut out; holes for two rivets, one of which survives; larger central hole.

1210   BWB83   1242   (110)   11
Slightly corroded; 18×11mm; crudely cut out; holes for two rivets, one of which survives.

Possibly part of a buckle plate or strap-end, though the present shape appears to be the result of deliberate cutting.

1211   BWB83   4474   (256)   11
14×13mm; holes for two missing rivets.

1212   BWB83   1577   (108)   11   fig 141
20×14mm; holes for four rivets, one of which survives.

1213   BWB83   5911   (305)   11   fig 141
Fragment, 17+×15mm; broken off about large central hole; two pairs of holes near each edge; in both pairs each hole is pierced from a different side.
Presumably reused.

1214   BWB83   5935   (295)   11
19×15mm; holes for two rivets, and larger, offcentred

hole; row of raised dots stamped around edges and sides.

1215 BWB83 5910 (303) 11 figs 15A & 141
Fragment, 27+×19mm; broken off at large central hole; hole for one rivet; row of stamped circles between parallel engraved lines along sides and surviving edge.

1216 BC72 4143 (88) 11 fig 141
39×22mm; trefoil aperture with angled groove at each edge; large central hole, and others for four missing rivets.

The grooved apertures are more elaborate versions of those on several buckle plates (cf nos. 322 etc).

The surviving leather in no. 1205 provides evidence that a possible function of these late 14th/ early 15th-century items was to connect two lengths of strap, but among finds from Ospringe and Battle Abbey are mounts of this kind in which the leather, although decayed, appears to be continuous through the plate (AR Goodall 1979, 139 & 141 fig 26 no. 145; Geddes 1985, 158–59 no. 33 – ibid no. 46 is too decayed to be certain about this; thanks to Barry Knight for making it possible to examine the last two objects). The significance of the large holes (in some cases with traces of considerable wear around the edges) in the middle of several of the plates is unknown. The wear does not seem to be at an angle, as on eyelets thought to be worn from buckle pins (see nos. 1218–1228). When the leather beneath survives at this point, it is not always pierced; this seems to argue against these plates having some kind of swivelling latch like those on clasps nos. 570 and 571.

Only no. 1208 of the complete plates listed here is decorative, though some of the incomplete examples and others elsewhere are quite ornate (see the parallels cited above, and Henig and Woods in Sherlock and Woods 1988, 211–12 no. 32 fig 68). As with many narrow strap fittings, little strain would have been anticipated for the plates where a strap or straps were held only by a single rivet at each end.

Hinged plate

1217 BWB83 5 (110) 11 fig 141
Two interconnecting, folded sheet plates; together 26×13mm; the hinge pivots on a bar; biconcave ends, each with a grooved, round aperture; leather 13mm wide survives from straps (torn off at ends).

The hinged connection gave scope for over 180-degree swivelling, perhaps suggesting a function unconnected with everyday dress, eg armour or horse equipment. The grooved apertures are comparable with, but slightly cruder than those on contemporary composite buckles and strap-ends with forked spacers. Cf MoL acc. no. 107/7, and Henig and Sherlock in Sherlock and Woods 1988, 191 no. 22 and 193 fig 59.

EYELETS
(hole reinforcements)

These were used mainly as surrounds for buckle-pin holes in straps or for lace holes in other items, though some may have been purely decorative. They were presumably attached while the leather was temporarily softened, perhaps with steam or by boiling.

All are of lead/tin

1218 SWA81 acc. no. 901 (context 2079) ceramic phase 9 fig 142
Tin (MLC); plain circular; d 11mm; back and front identical; worn around edge of hole.

1219 BWB83 5570 (308) 11 fig 142
Incomplete, d 13mm+; two of (?)four tear-shaped lobes survive.

1220 SWA81 4769 (2112) 12 fig 142
Tin (MLC); d 11mm, having a crudely engraved quatrefoil motif on the front with an outer stroke framing each side; on one of two associated fragments of leather strap (together totalling 116×14mm; apparently not originally joined; torn off at each end); there are two further smaller holes along the middle of the piece with the eyelet.

1221 SWA81 880 (2112) 12
Tin (MLC); d 12mm; similar to preceding item and on similar strap.

The preceding two items from the same deposit have the edge of the hole worn on one side, presumably by a buckle pin. They are probably both from the same strap.

1222 SWA81 801A-D (2106) 12 fig 142
Four high-tin lead alloy (AML) eyelets similar to no. 1218, each d 12–13mm, and each with a scrap of leather attached; two have the edge of the hole worn at one side.

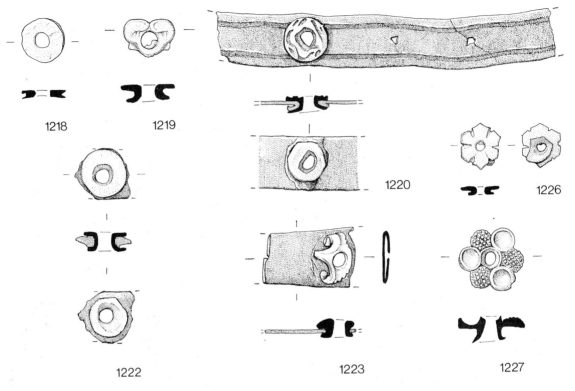

142 Eyelets (1:1)

In same finds bag was acc. no. 801E – part of a leather strap 13mm wide and cut transversely at one end.

1223 SWA81 807 (2103) 12 fig 142
Tin (AML, lead-tin MLC); 11×15mm; consists at one edge of a pair of opposed, bevelled volutes sprouting from a single stem, and the other edge is flat and engrailed; edge of hole is worn on one side; on leather strap 23×15mm (folded over at both sides to meet along centre of back, and torn off at both ends).

1224 SWA81 991 (2103) 12
Lead-tin (MLC); as preceding item; leather survives from strap.
The above two items from the same deposit were presumably from the same strap.

1225 SWA81 992 (2103) 12
Lead-tin (MLC); d 11mm; grooves define six bicuspid lobes; leather survives.

1226 SWA81 3290 (2112) 12 fig 142
As preceding item; lead/tin (MLC); (no surviving leather).

1227 SWA81 3645 (2101) 12 fig 142
Lead-tin (MLC); d 17mm; sexfoil; lobes alternately domed and dished, the former with fields of cross hatching.
Cf sexfoil mount no. 1029 from the same deposit for a similar design, and see fig 157B.

1228 SWA81 2117 (2103) 12
Lead-tin (MLC); incomplete; one disc, d 8.5mm, is in its original state, the other side (possibly also a disc) is folded. It is uncertain which side was the front.
Cf nos. 1218 etc for the probable original form.

The wear at the edges of the holes in several of the above items is presumably from buckle pins, or possibly laces. The holes in nos. 1225–26 seem too small for use with buckle pins. Although the majority of these eyelets are from early 15th-century deposits, no. 1218 appears to be from earlier than the middle of the 14th century.

See rectangular mounts no. 1060 (fig 124) for a possible different solution to the prevention of wear around buckle-pin holes, using sheet mounts.

STRAP LOOPS

(loops to hold down loose parts of straps)

Those listed are of cast copper alloy, though iron versions are also known.

There are two basic categories – those with rivets (integral when external, and separate when internal to the frame), and those with a pair of opposed projections. Examples of the first variety are known still in situ on straps – on an archer's wrist guard (fig 143), and flanked by a pair of bar-mounts with pendent loops (fig 138, bottom). There are also iron examples – on a decorated spur (BC72 acc. no. 3664 – see fig 69), and a notably heavy example survives as part of an iron buckle (fig 150 – Ashmolean Museum acc. no. 1873.85). On spurs the form goes back to the Viking period (Ottaway 1985, 26). It is assumed that those with projections also went on straps, where they too would presumably have been set at a right angle to the leather or textile. This category could have been moved back and forth along the strap. The two basic forms thus appear to be fixed and adjustable versions of the same item, intended to hold down the otherwise loose end of a strap which overlapped beyond the buckle. Many latter-day waist belts have a small loop of the same material as the strap itself, set close to the buckle to serve the same function. In the excavated examples the apertures are all

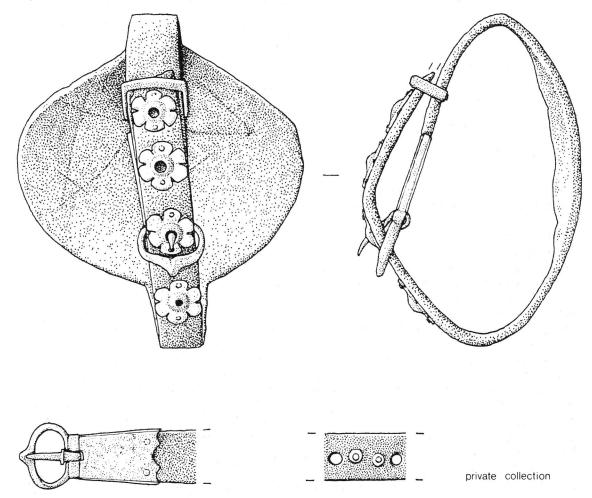

private collection

143 Archer's wrist guard (1:1)

large enough, and some seem to be specifically shaped to cater for a strap furnished with mounts (see fig 143). Included here, but not certainly for the same purpose, are some composite objects (nos. 1266–68) with discontinuous frames and separate bars (items somewhat similar to the latter and with a separate bar forming one edge of the frame are from a form of folding clasp – see nos. 565–66, fig 78).

Similar loops of the main forms have been found widely in England, eg in Exeter, Kings Lynn, York and Southampton (AR Goodall 1984, 342 fig 191 nos 98, 99 & 137; Geddes and Carter 1977, 288–89 fig 130 no. 13; Tweddle 1986, 206 and references). They have sometimes been misinterpreted as incomplete buckles. Those discovered at Meols in Merseyside were published as 'hasps' on the mistaken assumption they were a form of clasp (Hume 1863, 106–11 and pl X).

Objects in the three categories are described in chronological (ceramic phase) sequence, and in order of increasing strap size (third dimension, given in brackets) within each phase.

Frames with rivets

All are copper-alloy; rivets are present unless otherwise stated. Measurements are given in the order a, b, (with c in brackets indicating the maximum width for the strap); see figs 144 & 146.

Oval/ovoid frames with external rivets

1229 SWA81 acc. no. 2743 (context 2065) ceramic phase 9
12×12.5mm (6mm).

1230 SWA81 3262 (2141) 9 fig 145
12×13mm (7mm); base projects at both sides; silk fibres (MLC) are apparently wound around the rivet – these may not be from the strap.

1231 SWA81 2114 (2063) 9 fig 145
14×13mm (9mm)

1232 BWB83 2362 (290) 9 fig 145
17×12mm (12mm); gunmetal (AML); rectangular rove on rivet.

1233 BWB83 5238 (306) 11
17×13.5mm (12mm)

1234 SWA81 3071 (unstratified)
12×13mm (7mm)

Rectangular/subrectangular frames with integral external rivets

1235 OPT81 94 (42) 9 fig 147
Five mounts still joined from the mould, each approximately 15×19mm (10mm); leaded gunmetal (AML). The rivets are longer than those on the other examples listed here, and would probably have been cut shorter before use.

A ceramic mould from the same site (acc. no. 87 from deposit 49, probably of about the same date) was for producing several different types of fittings, includ-

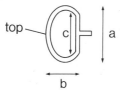

144 Oval strap loops, order of dimensions

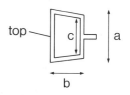

146 Rectangular strap loops, order of dimensions

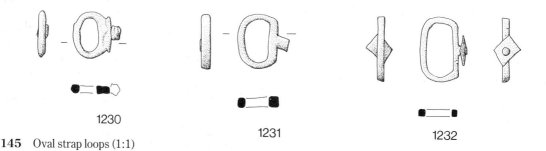

145 Oval strap loops (1:1)

1230   1231   1232

ing buckle frames and some loops apparently similar to the present ones. Ceramic moulds of this kind might perhaps only be used once, and it is unlikely that the present mounts would have been the product of that particular one. See manufacturing evidence under Buckles, p 123 & fig 80.

1236 SWA81 1255 (2149) 9 fig 147
17×13mm (13mm)

1237 BWB83 2155 (290) 9 fig 147
23×14mm (19mm) rivet has rove d 10mm.

1238 BWB83 2753 (345) 11
12×13mm (8mm); trapezoidal frame.

1239 BWB83 2754 (345) 11 fig 147
As preceding; possibly from same original object.

1240 BWB83 1481 (354) 11
12×13mm (8mm); trapezoidal frame.

1241 BWB83 4128 (361) 11
12×12mm (9mm)

1242 BWB83 2754 (345) 11
12×13mm (9mm)

1243 BWB83 5862 (292) 11
13.5×11mm (9mm)

1244 BWB83 2139 (307) 11
14×13mm (11mm)

1245 BWB83 4121 (361) 11 fig 147
16×14mm (12mm); broad top; rectangular rove on rivet.

1246 BWB83 5860 (298) 11
17×11.5mm (13mm); trapezoidal frame; rectangular rove on rivet.

1247 BWB83 3594 (357) 11 fig 147
19.5×16mm (15mm); rivet missing.

The three examples with rectangular roves (nos. 1232, 1245 & 1246) have these set lozenge-fashion relative to the frame, perhaps marginally increasing the rigidity of the attachment.

Rectangular/subrectangular frames with separate internal rivets

1248 BWB83 5861 (303) 11 fig 147
11×12mm (8mm)

1249 BWB83 5858 (282) 11 fig 147
20×16mm (15mm)
    A notably robust example.

Five-sided, arched frames with internal rivets

Angled arches are only known on frames where the rivet is internal – ie where part of the aperture would be occupied by the fixed lower strap.

1250 BWB83 2359 (290) 9 fig 147
15×11mm (12mm)

1251 TL74 275 (306) 11 fig 147
14×13mm (8mm)

1252 BWB83 1415 (146) 11 fig 147
20×14mm (14mm)

1253 BWB83 5859 (291) 11
19×12mm (15mm)

An archer's leather wrist guard (fig 143) with copper-alloy fittings (private collection, found in spoil from the Billingsgate site) has a similar loop in situ holding down the loose end of the strap (which has broken off at this point). The arched top of the frame is clearly intended to provide room for the sexfoil mounts (reinforcements for the buckle pin holes) to pass through. Cf AR Goodall 1984, 341–42 fig 191 no. 137 (interpreted as a swivel for a harness or a dog's lead).

A loop with a decorative shield on top is illustrated by Griffiths (1989, 2 & 4 fig 11).

Frames with pairs of internal projections

These seem to be the earliest form. They are characterised by two opposed internal projections about a third of the way along the shorter sides of the frame. They are often trapezoidal, the projections being closer to the narrower end, but rectangular ones and examples with curved tops also appear. Some have decoration on the top (usually the longest edge), and this is occasionally closely comparable with bar-mounts for straps. Wear seems to be concentrated internally at the corners, and is consistent with abrasion from straps. There is no evidence to suggest that there was ever a sheet roller lying between the projections, and it is thought that each of these objects is complete as found. Attachment was presumably effected by passing one end of a strap through the narrower end of the aperture below the projections, leaving the wider top part for the other end of the strap. The omission of a central part to the bar may have been a way of catering for a strap with mounts at the centre. Cf Hume 1863, pl X, nos. 18–22 & 24; Steane and Bryant

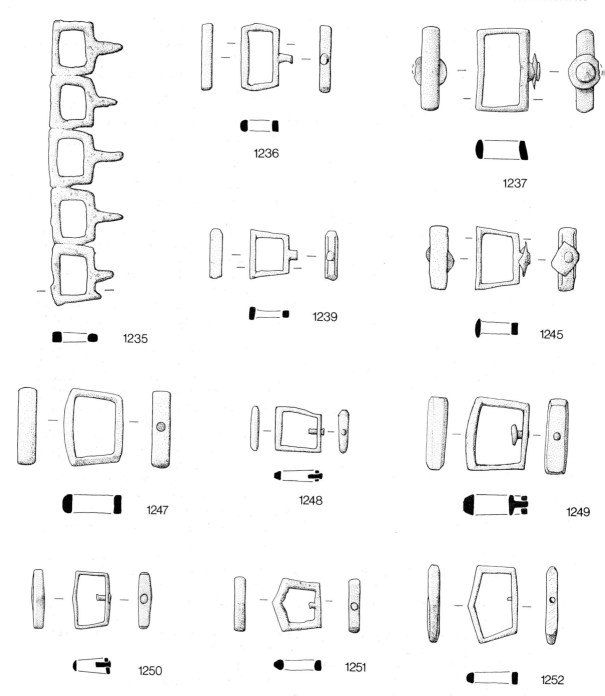

147 Rectangular and five-sided strap loops (1:1)

1975, 108 figs 24, 28 & 29; Tweddle 1986, 206–7
fig 97 no. 729, with references.

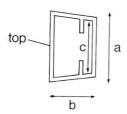

148   Strap loops with internal projections, order of
dimensions

Dimensions are given in the order a, b (with c
in brackets indicating the maximum width for a
strap through at the base).

1254 BIG82 acc. no. 2859 (context 5066)
ceramic phase 6   fig 149
19.5×14mm (15mm); at the top there are grooves at
the corners and a hole in the middle – these features
were probably decorative.

Cf bar-mounts with lobes at the ends and middle, and
a central hole, eg nos. 1154 & 1158, the former also
being from a deposit attributed to ceramic phase 6.

1255 BIG82 2703 (3367) 6 fig 149
27×18mm (21.5mm); brass (AML).

1256 BIG82 2522 (3071) 7 fig 149
15×11.5mm (9mm); knop in middle of top.

1257 BIG82 3168 (2636) 7 fig 149
16×12mm (11mm); subrectangular knop in middle of
top.

1258 BIG82 2313 (2516) 8 fig 149
21×15.5mm (14mm)

1259 BIG82 2355 (2831) 8 fig 149
21×18mm (11mm); knop in middle of top.

1260 BWB83 3505 (175) 6–9 fig 149
29×18mm (21mm); paired knops in middle and single
ones at corners of top; prominent file marks.

1261 BWB83 1608 (108) 10 fig 149
17.5×17mm (12mm); knops in middle and at corners of
top, the former with a ridge to each side.

See on no. 1263, and cf a similar loop from the
SUN86 site (acc. no. 1321).

1262 BWB83 4614 (279) 11 fig 149
Curved top; 22×17mm (15mm).

1263 BWB83 5923 (318) 11 fig 149
29×22mm (21mm); knops in middle and at corners of
top.

Compare the top with bar-mounts having lobes at the
ends and the middle, though those closest in shape
have a central hole.

1264 BIG82 2399 (2560) unassigned context,
possibly phase 7
18.5×13.5mm (12.5mm); knop in middle of top.

1265 BWB83 4707 (247) unphased fig 149
Curved top; 28.5×18mm (19mm).

Composite, probably related items,
discontinuous at base, with separate internal bars

As in the preceding category with opposed projections, the bar lies about a third of the way along
the shorter side of the frame. The sides and top
of the frame are of sheet metal – these are liable
to distortion, particularly at the ends. Attachment
was presumably effected by passing a strap between the two free ends of the frame and the bar,
leaving the top aperture for the other, loose end
of the strap. The angled top may have been to
cater for mounts on the strap.

If interpreted correctly, attachment at the base
would have been neither robust nor resilient. The
shape of the ends here is not suitable for sliding.
Fixture to a strap might be effected by bending
the ends against it, but regular repetition of this
operation would be impractical. It seems unlikely
that both of the following examples and a parallel
from outside London (Hume 1863, pl X no. 2) are
all incomplete at the base.

Dimensions are given as for frames with pairs
of internal projections (above).

1266 BWB83 1682 (317) 11 fig 150
Distorted; *c.*17×12mm (*c.*10mm); top is angled at
centre; rectangular-section bar.

This is the only frame from the present categories in
which the height exceeds the width.

1267 BWB83 2308 (286) 11 fig 150
Slightly distorted; 19×*c.*15mm (14mm); top is similar
in form to a solid bar-mount (see eg no. 1142) – it may
here have been turned to a different angle from that
originally intended.

1268 BWB83 5908 (308) 11
Distorted; 22×*c.*17mm (20mm); as no. 1266.

The earliest form of the strap loops described
above seems to be that with internal projections
(nos. 1254–65), apparently current from the late
12th to the late 14th centuries. The oval, rectangular and five-sided forms all seem to last from

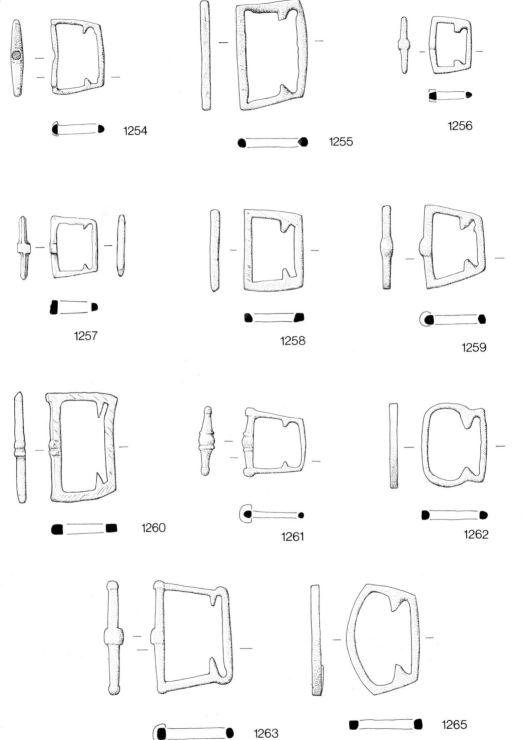

1254

1255

1256

1257

1258

1259

1260

1261

1262

1263

1265

149 Strap loops with internal projections (1:1)

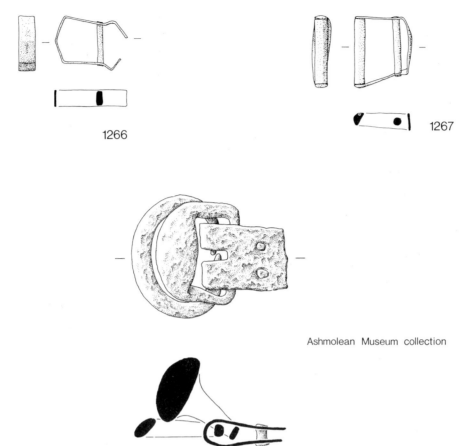

1266

1267

Ashmolean Museum collection

150 Top, composite loops;
bottom, buckle with strap loop (1:1)

the late 13th century to the end of the 14th century; the first of these types (nos. 1229–34) may predominate in the early part of this period, and the second seems to become more popular towards the end, but the number of examples from which these inferences are drawn is very small.

The similarity of the tops of the more decorative examples (eg no. 1263, fig 149) to some bar-mounts may suggest that matching items from the two categories were used together ensuite, though the only object on which they appear together has very diverse forms (fig 138, bottom).

The enigmatic composite objects (nos. 1266–68) seem so far to be confined to the late 14th century. No strap loop among the recently excavated groups is known from a context assigned to

the 15th century. The manufacturing evidence from the Copthall Avenue site, which includes both strap loops and buckle frames, underlines the close connection between these items.

SPANGLES

(Peter Stott)

Spangles were manufactured in moulds from a tin-lead alloy often of approximately 60% tin and 40% lead, a mixture meriting the term pewter (nos. 1270 & 1280 analysed, AML; cf Mitchiner and Skinner 1983, 46). Although no moulds have been discovered, it is clear from their finish and from reference to contemporary items in lead-tin that this was their method of manufacture. They are flat (no more than 0.5mm thick) and are in the form of a disc with an extension incorporating two holes which are normally circular, although they may also be rectangular. They are decorated in relief on one face only, the other face being blank. The disc part carries the main design element, which is usually geometric or zoomorphic and is often contained within a beaded border. The extension is sometimes hatched.

The present catalogue of spangles from excavations represents only a fraction of those found in London during the last decade. Of finds not included below, the Museum of London has to date recorded two from the Thames at the Vintry, eight from Bull Wharf (Mills 1983, 6; Mitchiner and Skinner 1983, 46), 69 found in spoil removed from contractor's excavations at the Billingsgate Lorry Park site, and large numbers are at the time of writing being recovered at the Thames Exchange site (Museum of London and private collections). Collectively, this body of material, and indeed the Billingsgate and Thames Exchange finds alone, represent the largest concentration of spangles found so far. Other finds known to the writer are three from the High Street excavations in Perth (Scottish Urban Archaeological Trust), two from Eastgate, Beverley (pers. comm. D Evans), a single example found in a field in Norfolk (pers. comm. Sue Margeson), at least five from excavations at Dundas Wharf, Bristol (pers. comm., Les Goode), those from the Seine in Paris (Forgeais 1866, 242–219) a single example from St Denis near Paris (Meyer et al. 1983, 119 no. 69), and a few from the Netherlands (van Beuningen collection). Judging by this volume of finds, it is clear that they would have been more familiar to contemporaries than may have been thought.

Discussing the finds from the Seine, Forgeais proposed that the design of these objects was reminiscent of a purse, presumably of a kind gathered at the neck by a drawstring, and thus that they were intended as a miniature imitation and were worn to mimic the affectations of the rich, who wore purses conspicuously as a demonstration of wealth and prestige. He also suggests that they may have had an additional religious character as imitations of the bags carried by pilgrims (Forgeais 1866, 215). Thus he applied the name *aumonières* (alms purses) to these objects, a name which has continued in use in France (Meyer et al. 1982, 119). He dated them to the 13th and 14th centuries.

Further discussion of spangles (Mitchiner and Skinner 1983; Mills 1983) took the view that spangles (also called sewn tokens, ampulliform tokens, 'jangles' (sic) and alms-purse tokens in the former article) had a monetary function, and that they were forerunners of the kind of 13th-century bifacial leaden tokens found in Dublin (Dolley and Seaby 1971, 446–48), Paris (Forgeais 1866), London (Roach-Smith 1854, 156–57; Mitchiner and Skinner 1983, 47–54) and elsewhere.

Spangles account for all but one of the earliest lead/tin items from the recent excavations to be listed here as mounts. Unlike virtually all the other objects in this category, spangles have no undoubted connection with straps. The two holes strongly imply that they were intended to be stitched, and the fact that they are designed on one side only indicates that they lay flat against some kind of surface, hence the adoption of the term 'spangle', denoting a small metallic ornament. There is, however, no obvious evidence of wear around the holes which might have been expected if they had been sewn in place. On the other hand, there is a tendency for bending and breakage to occur immediately adjacent to the holes, perhaps as a result of suspension, or because the metal is here at its thinnest and most vulnerable. But there is no evidence so far to suggest in what situations spangles were used.

The archaeological evidence suggests that the production and use of spangles began as early as the late 12th century. Two examples (nos. 1269–70) were found in deposits dated to this period, and this is supported by the results of excavations in Perth and Beverley. The context of one of the spangles from High Street, Perth has been dated to the later 12th century by pottery and dendrochronology, while those from Eastgate, Beverley, appear to have been deposited between the 1180s and the early 13th century, as they were found with a pottery assemblage interpreted as being contemporary with a documented fire in 1188. To be consistent with their supposition that spangles were an early form of token coinage, Mitchiner and Mills suggested that they ceased to circulate after the introduction of pewter tokens, which the former places in the early 13th century (Mitchiner and Skinner 1983, 46) and the latter *c*.1260 (Mills 1983, 6). By contrast, two examples catalogued here suggest that spangles were still in use, if not necessarily manufactured, in the late 13th century, and perhaps up to the early 14th-century (nos. 1280 and 1281). Although the large number of spangles from Billingsgate came from material removed from the site and dumped, there was a great quantity of coins up to 1351 from the same source, with a particular emphasis on the Edwardian sterling phase of 1279–1351. Many of the spangles may have been contemporaneous with this group of coinage. The possibility should be considered that spangles may have continued in use up to the middle of the 14th century. No development in the style of the designs is detectable over this late 12th-century to early 14th-century period, and the differences in the quality of execution, choice of design, decoration and size appear to have been concurrent.

It is difficult to accept that these tiny objects would have been very effective as badges of authorisation (Mitchiner and Skinner 1983, 38). They would hardly have been very conspicuous when worn and the ranges of symbols with which they are decorated, far from having any official character, appear to be a random selection of popular and attractive images. It is also fanciful to suggest, as Forgeais has, that they bear specific heraldic significance. Their similarity to leaden tokens of the 13th and 14th centuries, is, however, obvious and it is understandable that discussions about their function should have proceeded along numismatic lines. But this interpretation is over-specific and the comparison should be broadened to take account of lead-tin items with a wider range of functions (for example, pilgrim badges, spoons, finger rings and brooches), with all of which spangles share similarities in style of decoration. In particular, the medium was in demand for the production of cheap jewellery and, in the absence of firm indications of any further significance, it is best to regard them as no more than a widely available adornment of a particular shape. The origin of their form is mysterious and no improvement on Forgeais' conjecture will be made here.

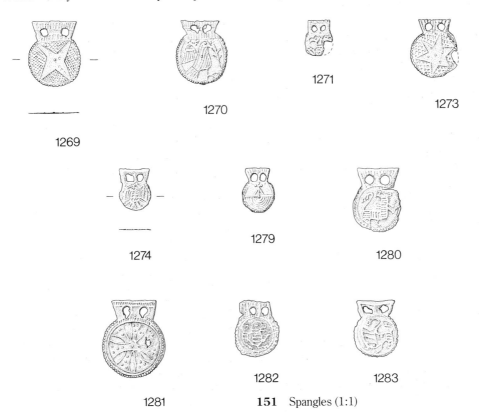

151 Spangles (1:1)

1269 BIG82 acc. no. 2838 (context 3562) ceramic phase 6 fig 151
d 14mm; four-pointed star on cross-hatched field; beaded border; hatched extension with plain section between holes; casting tang at top of extension.

1270 BIG82 2841 (4064) 6 fig 151
d 13.5mm; lead-tin (AML); bird right with branch; beaded border; extension hatched at upper edge.

1271 BIG82 2442 (2972) 7 fig 151
d 7.5mm; double headed bird displayed; hatching on upper edge; incompletely cast.

1272 BIG82 2444 (2506) 7
d 7mm; as preceding item (different mould).

1273 BIG82 2727 (4012) 7 fig 151
d 13mm; six-pointed star, incorporating five pellets, on cross-hatched field.

1274 BIG82 2242 (2284) 8 fig 151
d 9mm; bird displayed, looking towards the left; beaded border.

1275 BIG82 2470 (2591) 8
d 7mm; as preceding item (different mould); extension broken off.

1276 BIG82 2464 (2591) 8
d 8mm; (?)ship design (cross over concentric semi-circles); beaded border; hatching on extension.

1277 BIG82 2353 (2831) 8
d 8.5mm; as no. 1271 (different mould).

1278 BIG82 2673 (2591) 8
d 9.5mm; rearing quadruped left, looking right.

1279 BIG82 2682 (2591) 8 fig 151
d 9mm; as no. 1276 (different mould).

1280 SWA81 3378 (2139) 11 fig 151
d 17mm; pewter (AML); rearing quadruped right; beaded border; hatching at upper edge of extension.

1281 BWB83 393 (264) 11 fig 151
d 17mm; geometric design consisting of overlapping curved lines and groups of pellets; beaded border; hatching on upper part of extension.

1282 SWA81 2293 (unstratified) fig 151
d 12mm; as no. 1280 (different mould) beaded border; hatching on extension; excess metal around edge.

1283 BIG82 2531 (unstratified) fig 151
d 12mm; quadruped left, looking back towards the right; beaded border; hatching on extension; excess metal on extension.

LEAD/TIN MOUNTS
LACKING RIVETS

These may have been sewn onto items of dress, or they could have been attached to caskets etc by other means. The first is cut from sheeting, the others are cast.

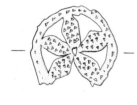

1284

1285

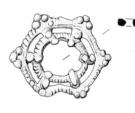

1286

1287

152 Mounts lacking rivets (drawings 1:1, photograph 2:1)

1284 SWA81 acc. no. 2107 (context 2065) ceramic phase 9 fig 152

High-tin lead alloy (MLC); incomplete; crudely cut openwork sheeting roundel; d 23mm; ring around central cinquefoil, with hole in middle; stamping all over one face has produced corresponding raised dots on the other.

The central hole in this flimsy item may once have held a rivet.

1285 SWA81 3066 (2107) 12 fig 152

Lead-tin (MLC); folded (shape restored in drawing); 15×*c*.15mm; central cross with two arms terminating in trilobes, which are joined at both sides by extensions from opposed trefoils stemming from the other two arms.

Cf four similar mounts found at Oude Krabbendijke, now in the Boymans-van Beuningen Museum in Rotterdam (acc. nos. F7234–6 & –8).

1286 BIG82 2753 (3919) unphased fig 152

Lead-tin (MLC); d 27mm; two concentric transversely hatched rings, joined by six arms, each consisting of two dots and terminating in trilobes on the outside of the larger ring.

1287 SWA81 3309 (unstratified) fig 152

Thin lead sheet (AML); cast (Anthony North, pers. comm.); rectangular, 26×12mm; lion passant, plant motif to side and possibly another below; beaded border.

Presumably glued in place rather than set behind a frame. Perhaps not an item of dress, but from a more rigid object.

MANUFACTURING EVIDENCE

Copper alloy

Several sites have produced manufacturing evidence, though none of this dumped material pinpoints the certain location of a workshop. It is hoped that this aspect will be more fully discussed elsewhere.

1288 BWB83 acc. no. 5177 (context 308) ceramic phase 11 fig 153

Irregularly cut octagon; d 17mm; pierced at edge; crudely stamped with four circles, as if for multifoil motif.

Presumably discarded unfinished.

See also bar-mount no. 1159 fig 134, which appears to have been stamped into shape but not trimmed, and unfinished sexfoils nos. 1004–06 & 1014, & also no. 947.

Iron sheeting

1289 BWB83 2969 (131 area) 11

Domed circle, d 12mm; tin coating; no sign of rivet. Presumably the head for a mount stamped into shape, but discarded without having had a rivet attached.

1290 BC72 4472 (150) 11 fig 153

As preceding item; d 17mm; tin coating; no rivet or hole. The overlap caused by the shaping of the dome shows up clearly.

Offcuts from the manufacture of discs:

1291 BWB83 625 (151) 11 fig 153

Irregular shape; tin coating.

1292 BWB83 3349 (309) 12 fig 153

Strip with line of eight discs removed.

The last two items represent several fragments of iron sheeting waste found at the BWB83 site, which are tin coated on both sides, and from which circles of various diameters have been cut (cf nos. 1289–90).

The above pieces of sheeting are complemented by large numbers of other pieces of offcut sheet waste from several waterfront sites, though little of this can be associated directly with dress fittings. At the BOY86 site a few 15th- or possibly 16th-century pieces of sheeting were found stamped out into shapes which correspond with mounts found on the site, but lack the relief detail that was presumably added by a second stamping.

Stone mould

One part of a limestone mould for casting various lead/tin domed circular and other mounts was found at TEX88 (acc. no. 1030, from a context probably of late 14th-century date) – fig 154. (A chalk mould from TL74, acc. no. 1649 – Rhodes 1982B, 89 – is probably not for dress accessories.)

A casting of five lead/tin domed circular mounts retains the complete sprue – fig 153, bottom (found in Canterbury with other late-medieval items, private collection); the mounts constitute only a fifth by weight of the metal cast, so it would have been necessary to recycle four fifths of the total (Dana Goodburn-Brown, pers. comm.). It is not known at present how representative this item is of production practice of the time.

See Ramsay (in Alexander & Binski 1987, 395–96 no. 450) for a copper-alloy mould of a kind that may have been used to produce some of the thinner ornate sheet mounts.

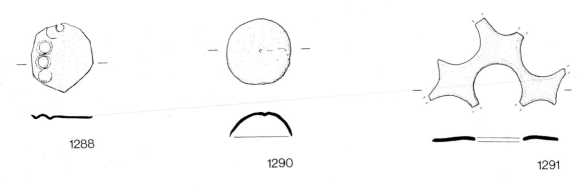

1288

1290

1291

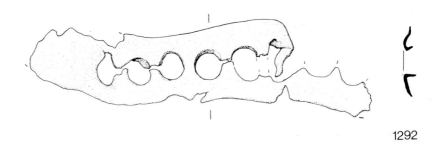

1292

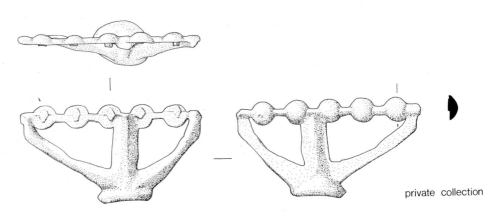

private collection

153 Top, waste from manufacture of mounts;
bottom, five mounts with sprue still attached
(1:1)

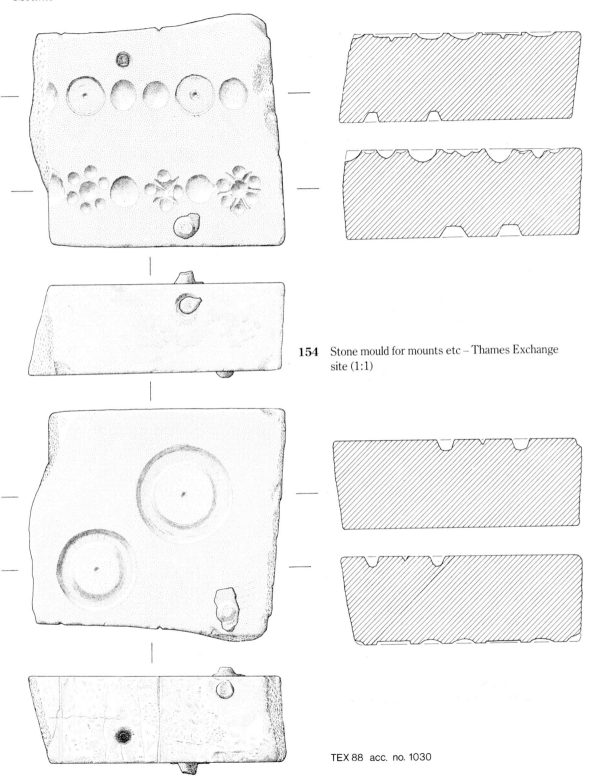

154 Stone mould for mounts etc – Thames Exchange site (1:1)

TEX 88 acc. no. 1030

COMPARANDA

(mounts attached to items other than leather or textile)

Circular, domed mounts

Copper alloy

1293 SWA81   acc. no. 438   (context 2018) ceramic phase 9   fig 155
d 9mm; attached by an iron rivet or nail through a central hole to a sliver of wood (now 9×24mm).
Identical in form to mounts nos. 819 etc.

1294 BWB83   2127   (307)   11
d 16mm; copper (AML); attached to fragment of iron sheeting.

Sexfoil and octofoil mounts

Copper alloy

1295 BIG82   2804   (4100)   7   fig 155
Four sheet mounts, set on two joined strips of copper alloy sheeting, which together measure 108×10mm and are tin-coated on both sides: two sexfoils, each d 10mm, with raised edges and three dots along the centre of each lobe, and two incomplete mounts from which trilobed ends survive (possibly fleurs de lis). A hinge loop at one end of the strips and a hole at the other suggest this may be binding from a casket.

1296 BWB83   5834   (318)   11
Sexfoil, d 9mm, with domed centre, trimmed to shape of lobes and with engraved lines between the lobes, attached by single rivet to rectangular strip of similar sheeting 10×30mm (broken off at one end); the two additional holes near the edge of the mount, which would usually be taken to be for rivets, are useless here.
Cf sexfoils nos. 958 etc.

1297 BWB83   2737   329   11   fig 155
Dished sheet sexfoil; d 17mm; cut out to shape of lobes; attached by dome-headed rivet, and probably soldered, to broken sheeting strip (apparently of the same alloy) 6×20+mm.
Cf also nos. 520 and 1343 – (a sheet copper-alloy buckle plate and a copper-alloy brooch) both with sexfoil mounts with concave lobes, and also BC72 acc. no. 3664 (fig 69) – an iron spur with two wrought-iron sexfoils soldered onto the band.

Lead/tin

1298 BWB83   4663   (108)   10   fig 155
Incomplete octofoil; d 17mm; single integral rivet; domed centre; lobes each have a raised dot in the middle; set on rectangular iron sheet 8×12mm.

1299 BWB83   5826   (314)   12   fig 155
Cast lead (MLC) filling from back of domed sexfoil mount (cf nos. 952 etc.).
Perhaps comparable to the lead filling the back of some of the domed, circular mounts nos. 873 etc., though the present item has no trace of a rivet.

TACK/NAIL-LIKE OBJECTS

With tapering, pointed shanks

(cf also the copper-alloy tacks securing a kind of mount in no. 1129 and the mounts secured by pointed shanks on the strap in colour pl 5E)

Copper alloy

1300 BWB83   acc. no. 4717   (context 300) ceramic phase ?11   fig 155
Stamped-sheet head, d 17mm, on pointed shank; copper (AML); the design is a squatting beast with a bearded human face, and the neck is contorted so that it looks backwards; it has a central tuft of dorsal hairs and a brush-like tail; beaded border. This is presumably a tack for soft upholstery, since hammering would have damaged the decoration. If the head had been found alone, it would probably have been interpreted as a dress mount (cf no. 793).
The highly fanciful beast is broadly comparable with those in marginal drawings in many manuscripts from around the middle of the 14th century (eg Luttrell Psalter, passim).

Iron

1301 BWB83   4636A & B   (108)   10   fig 155
Two octofoils; d 20mm; lobes defined by rabetted lines. Rather robust compared with other dress mounts, these may be nails with decorated heads and the points broken off.

Lead/tin

1302 SWA81   2968   (2031)   9   fig 155
d 7mm; the shank, l 11mm, is bent over. The metal seems too soft for a tack, but the point is not appropriate for most dress fittings.

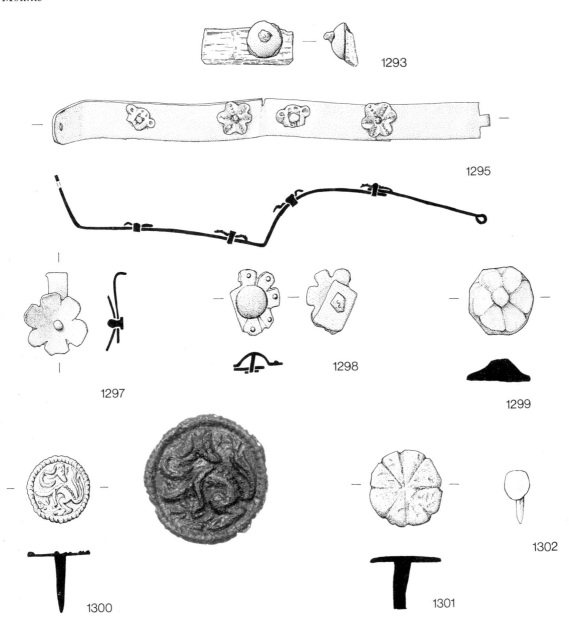

1293

1295

1297

1298

1299

1300

1301

1302

Cf no. 824, which has a non-tapering rivet (fig 110).

It is probable that all these items are mounts, and that the tapered shank in the present example did not have a distinct purpose – ie some tack-like items may simply be mounts with slightly different forms of rivet. Buckle plate no. 520 has a copper-alloy tack used instead of a rivet. Cf also tin mounts nos. 802 and 1079, which have bent shanks (fig 108).

155 Mounts – comparable items (drawings 1:1, photograph 2:1)

Combinations of diverse strap fittings, and possible ensuite items

Mounts of different forms, and combinations of mounts with buckles, strap-ends etc survive in place on some leather straps from the recent excavations. The various fittings on each strap are usually of one principal metal or alloy, though individual items with different metals in major constituent parts are known, eg buckles in which the frames are iron and lead-tin, and the plates are copper-alloy (nos. 422 & 423). One strap combines a copper-alloy buckle with iron mounts (nos. 457 & 907), but here tin coating on all the metal fittings gave them a similar outward appearance.

Surviving combinations are as follows:

Ceramic phase 11 (late 14th century)

BC72   acc. no. 5319:
two types of circular mount on a large piece of leather (nos. 921 & 930 in this volume, fig 115).

BC72   acc. no. 3879:
corrugated rectangular + ornate circular mounts on purse no. 1701; iron with tin coating (nos. 1058 & 894 in this volume, fig 232).

A similar corrugated rectangular mount (no. 1057, fig 123) on short strap no. 1170, found in the same dumps as acc. no. 3879, could be from a suite of accessories decorated with the same motifs, and intended to be worn together.

BWB83   acc. no. 8:
a hooked strap-end and bar-mount; both iron; (nos. 730 & 1146 in this volume, fig 102).

TL74   acc. no. 2031:
circular mounts + lozenge-shaped mount; all tin (nos. 802 and 1079 in this volume, fig 108).

TL74   acc. no. 513:
domed circular mounts + petal-like mount; all lead/tin) (nos. 830 and 1107 in this volume, fig 110).

Ceramic phase 12 (early 15th century)

SWA81   acc. no. 3405:
strap-end, with S-shaped mount on strap in its centre; both lead/tin; (no. 708 in this volume, fig 98).

TL74   acc. no. 2398:
strap-end with incomplete composite mounts with missing pendent motifs; all copper alloy (nos. 588 and 1187 in this volume, fig 136).

BC72   acc. no. 1151:
rectangular copper-alloy buckle and two convex circular iron mounts; all with tin coating; possibly a sword belt (nos. 457 and 907 in this volume, fig 63).

Girdle TL74   acc. no. 1291B:
uncertain forms – (?)ring mounts + six dome-headed (?)rivets (possibly mounts), (no. 20 in this volume, fig 27 see p 000).

BWB83   acc. no. 99:
sexfoil mounts and strap-end; all tin (nos. 1022 & 714 in this volume fig 99 & colour pl 5C).

Further examples are:

The series of late-14th/early-15th century short straps (nos. 1168–1186 in this volume) which have various mounts of iron and lead/tin, together with strap-ends of iron (see fig 136 for no. 1182, and fig 126 for no. 1186, which has two kinds of mount).

SWA81   acc. no. 806 (probable association), 15th-century: double-oval buckle + rectangular mount (similar to that accompanied by various other mounts on the strap in colour pl 5E, see below); both copper-alloy, mount partly tin-coated (nos. 343 and 1052 in this volume, fig 51).

An elaborate mid 14th-century spur BC72 acc. no. 3664 (fig 69) includes a buckle (no. 487 in this volume), a strap-end (no. 593), circular mounts and a strap loop, all of iron.

Parallel for unstratified mount no. 796:
pierced circular disc + elaborate quatrefoil; both copper-alloy, fig 107 (?late-medieval).

The archer's wrist bracer (fig 143) includes sexfoil mounts, a strap-loop, a composite buckle and a strap-end (the last two having forked spacers); all of copper alloy (cf Fingerlin 1971, 114 fig 187 for a similar combination on another London strap).

Further London finds include a locking clasp combined on a strap with sexfoil and stemmed trefoil

mounts, all of copper alloy (see fig 79 in this volume, cf Mitchiner 1986, 133 nos. 359a–c, and 218–19 no. 798), and another strap (in two pieces – fig 156 this volume) has four different kinds of lead/tin mounts – circular with a beaded edge, stemmed trefoil, sexfoil, and shell-shaped (there are traces of red colouring on one of the lengths of leather strap), cf Mitchiner ibid, 132 no. 357. These items were found in spoil removed by contractors from the Billingsgate site – the former is in a private collection, and the latter two pieces are MoL acc. no. 87.51/11. A leather strap (fig 138) with a strap loop flanked by a pair of bar-mounts, each with a pendent ring, and accompanied by bar-mounts of a different form, all of copper alloy, were found in spoil removed from the TEX88 site (MoL acc. no. 88.461/2; an oval buckle with a plate may be from the same strap).

A spectacular London find of a nearly complete leather waist belt 770×34mm retains most of an original 154 or more copper-alloy mounts of three different forms (colour pl 5E & F – MoL acc. no. 89.65). A row of composite circular mounts (like the parallels for no. 932, colour pl 4D) down the middle is flanked on each side by a row of mounts with a central dome having traces of silver coating (XRF, B Gilmour), surrounded by four smaller lobes (a form not represented among the assemblages from the main sites included in this volume) and at one end is a rectangular mount like nos. 1052–55. The circular mounts are notable for having pointed shanks that have been bent over for fixture, rather than the usual rivets (those for the other mounts on the strap have roves). The leather retains traces of a textile covering on both the back and front; only the buckle appears to be missing. This highly decorated belt, perhaps for a sword, is probably of the kind depicted on the earlier effigies of knights in St Mary's Church at the Temple in London – on these sculptures the sword belts have bar-mounts together with other forms (see fig 132). They are the most local survivals among a large number of upper-class tomb effigies and brasses which depict such combinations (see eg Clayton 1979, passim).

The evidence for *ensuite items* is far more conjectural. A limited number of different fittings can be grouped together on the grounds that their decoration is so similar as to suggest that they may have been worn together; the available dating evidence certainly allows them to have been in use at the same period. However, none of these items have come down in the suggested combinations – indeed, one of them survives on a

156 Four types of mount on two lengths of a strap – Museum of London collection (d of circular mounts 18mm)

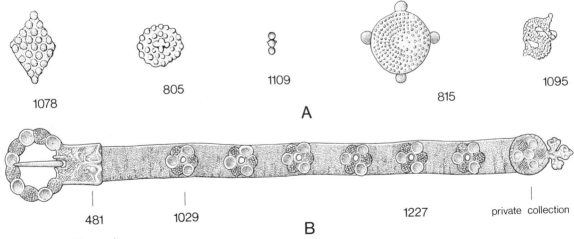

157 Possible ensuites:
    (A) mounts with fields of dots (1:1)
    (B) fittings with motifs of alternate dished and
          cross-hatched lobes (cf nos. 481, 1029 &
          1227 – not to scale)

strap together with mounts of completely different forms (lozenge mount no. 1079 – see below – appears together with plain circular mounts no. 802, see fig 108). It is possible that common design traits are indicative of production from a particular workshop (eg the composite buckle and strap-end on the archer's wrist bracer in fig 143, both with forked spacers; cf also Hume 1863, pl X buckle no. 6 together with strap-loops of similar design nos. 11 & 14). Diversity of decoration in various fittings may have been sought by the wearer quite as much as the repetition of motifs. The following suggested groupings therefore require further evidence before any of them can be confirmed as actual usage:

lead/tin mounts with fields of dots forming the decoration – circular mounts nos. 805, 814 & 815, lozenge mounts nos. 1078 & 1079, letter-S mount no. 1095, and no. 1109 (three mounts, each of which consists of three joined dots); see fig 157A (cf Mitchiner 1986, 133 nos. 366a–c).

lead/tin strap fittings with alternate cross-hatched bosses and dished roundels – eyelet no. 1227, buckle no. 481, a strap-end with a corded border and a foliate terminal (also found in London, private collection), and probably also mount no. 1029; see fig 157B.

lead/tin strap fittings with motifs based on opposed tear shapes – buckle no. 473, eyelet no. 1219, and strap-end no. 712 (figs 65, 142 & 98).

The acorn terminals on several strap-ends (eg nos. 672–84, fig 94) may perhaps be compared with acorn-headed pins (nos. 1485–87, fig 199); brooch no. 1327 and finger ring no. 1631, both of lead-tin, have similar quatrefoil motifs (though the former object has been attributed to ceramic phase 9 and the latter to phase 11; figs 163 & 218). A similar motif also appears on a brooch from Oud Krabbendijke (Netherlands) in the van Beuningen collection. Simple designs probably had a very wide currency.

Probable clasp no. 572 of double-ring form on a leather strap is accompanied by another length of strap with mount no. 1102 of similar basic form; both fittings are of iron (figs 79 & 128) – these two items, though not conclusive proof, are the closest the excavated accessories come to providing clear evidence for the use of suites of fittings with common motifs in London at this period.

Brooches

These were pinned at the neck to fasten two parts of the clothing together (fig 158, cf Ward-Perkins 1940, 273–75), or used purely decoratively, by both men and women. Suitably shaped brooches might extend the means of fastening garments in more elaborate ways than the most obvious means of using the pin (fig 159).

158 Figure representing the Synagogue, Bamberg Cathedral, Germany (from Sauerlandt nd)

Two basic types of brooch may be distinguished: those with open frames and having a separate, swivelling pin, and those with an integral, rigid pin, which often lack a definable frame. The latter form are all of lead/tin. In those with a frame, the pin could be passed through the textile on both sides of a collar, or through a single fold in the garment, to be held in place against the opposite side of the frame by the drape of the fabric. In the others the pin was pushed vertically or horizontally into the fabric of the garment and, in the case of those examples lacking a catch, the brooch was held in place by little more than its weight. Brooches of the second main category are analogous in terms of manufacture to the more common pilgrims' and retainers' badges

159 Woman with brooch securing loops on a cloak. Percy tomb, Beverley Minster, *c*.1340

(which are to be described in a different volume). The items in this category which are described below are designated brooches and included here because no indication has been recognized on them of the wearer's adherance to a specific cause or group, or devotion to a particular saint or shrine. This distinction between decorative *brooches*, and *badges* showing political or religious allegiance, may not always have been considered important by the makers or wearers. The prevalence of religious motifs and references in everyday life in the medieval period makes brooches with such ubiquitous phrases as 'Ave Maria . . .' difficult to categorise rigidly in this way. Items with this and other universally popular legends are also included below as brooches because, in the present state of knowledge, there is no definite indication of origin at any particular shrine.

A 13th-century gold brooch found at Writtle in Essex has a legend which may be rendered 'I am a brooch to guard the breast, so that no ruffian may put his hand there' (J Cherry in Tait 1986 38 no. 319); this woman's brooch is a rare instance of one that can with confidence be identified as being specifically for a member of one sex. It has not proved possible to make any such attribution for the brooches listed below.

Note: the large B-shaped iron and copper-alloy fittings with pins which have recently been published as brooches or pendants (Wilmott 1982) are considered by the present writer to be too large and robust to be a form of dress fitting. These and similar unpublished objects are therefore not included in this study. Their scale and solidity may be more consistent with items of horse furniture. No iron brooch has been identified among the recent finds.

OPEN FRAME
AND OTHER BROOCHES
WITH SEPARATE PINS

(pins are present, and of the same metal as the frame, unless stated)

The distinction between plain annular brooches and plain circular-frame buckles is not immediately clear-cut to present-day observers. Plain annular and other open frames in which the pins are attached to a constriction at one point (or otherwise confined to a limited area as in no. 1330, and other instances where the pin is looped through a hole in the frame, as in no. 1344) are described in this study as brooches, while those with the pin free to move around the entire circumference of

the frame are described as buckles (see more detailed discussion of the distinction, p 64f). Number 212 shares characteristics of both categories, and is described as a buckle/brooch; a small silver annular item (no. 211) lacks a constriction for the pin, though the precious metal and size might suggest it was primarily decorative, and therefore used as a brooch; number 39 has a constriction for the pin, but is still attached to a strap, and therefore must have functioned as a buckle; these three objects are listed under Buckles.

Plain annular frames

Copper alloy

1303 BIG82 acc. no. 2443 (context 3506) ceramic phase 7
d 14mm; tin coating (MLC).

1304 BIG82 2053 (1928) 8
Corroded; d *c*.21mm; copper (AML); frame appears from x-ray to have constriction for pin.

1305 SWA81 3935 (2270) 9 fig 160
d 18mm; crude; angled, unevenly-cut sheeting with constriction for pin made by cuts from the external edge; traces of gilding (MLC) on front; trace of tin coating on pin.
   Cf no. 1338.

1306 SWA81 1685 (1280) 9
d 20mm; gunmetal (AML); tip of pin bent; pin loop not joined.

1307 BWB83 335 (259) 11 fig 160
d 23mm; gunmetal (AML); frame and pin worn at points of contact, the latter bent by strain from use; pin loop not joined.

Decorated annular frames

Copper alloy

1308 BIG82 acc. no. 2812 (context 5363) ceramic phase 6 fig 160
d 23.5mm; copper (AML); bevelled, robust frame, giving two visible surfaces when worn; these are decorated with engraved zigzags and punched dots, those on the wider outside band being bordered by an engraved line on each side; the pin has a transverse ridge.

The decoration on this brooch may, like that on nos. 1309 and 1313, have hinted at lettering to the illiterate,

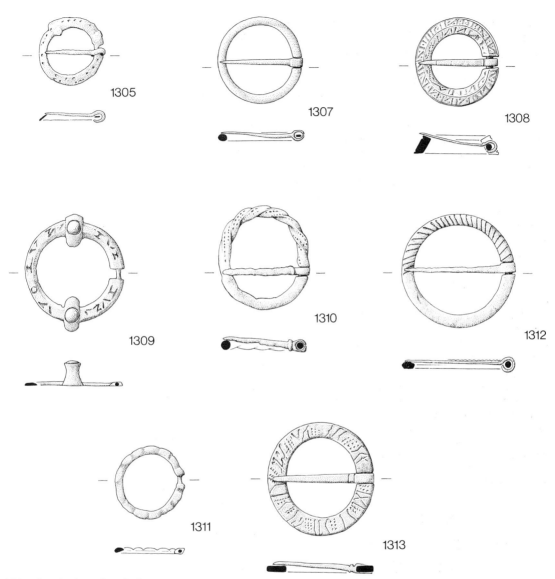

160   Annular brooches (1:1)

but in the present instance the lines are much further removed from true letters than on the other two examples.

1309   BIG82 2317 (2591) 8 fig 160
Broken at constriction for missing pin; d 28mm; gunmetal (AML); bevelled frame with engraved false lettering and two collets, which taper from oval bases to round tops – both retain broken fragments of glass stones, which appear yellowish-green, and are set with calcium carbonate (AML).

1310   BIG82 2429 (3216) 8 fig 160
d 30mm; copper (AML); cable pattern on frame to one side of the pin; transverse lines divide the other half into fields alternatively plain and with double lines of opposed, punched triangles.

   Cf MoL acc. nos. 4081 & 4091, Anon. 1979, 279–80 no. 1372 fig 174, and Hassall and Rhodes 1974, 66–67, for copper-alloy brooches with a similar division of the decorative scheme on the two halves of the frames.

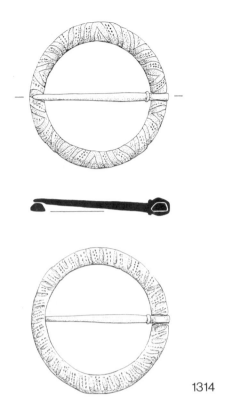

161 Reversible annular brooch:
top – front and back as worn (1:1)
bottom – back as worn (2:1)

1314

1311 SWA81 2186 (2055) 9 fig 160
Corroded; d 20mm; gunmetal (AML); series of constrictions along frame, dividing it into (? faceted) fields, pin missing.

1312 SWA81 682 (2072) 9 fig 160
Corroded and broken; d 31mm; brass frame and pin (AML); the frame is plain on one side of the pin, on the other it has cable decoration; series of arc-like engraved lines (possibly keying for enamel, though no trace survives).

1313 SH74 17 (234) 9 fig 160
d 30mm; gunmetal (AML); engraved false lettering; the pin has a transverse ridge.

1314 SWA81 2141 (2050) 9 fig 161 & colour pl 6A
d 37mm; gunmetal frame and pin (AML) with inlaid lead strips (MLC); the frame is decorated with oblique bands, alternatively the metal of the frame and an inlaid strip, the former having paired lines of opposed, punched triangles; on one face the direction of the bands is reversed in each of eight approximately equal sectors of the frame, these changes being slightly offset from the constriction for the pin; on the other face the bands all run in one direction; the pin has a

collar; the frame and pin are worn at the points of contact.

The offsetting of the pin relative to the decoration implies that the frame was completed before the pin was added. This notably elegant brooch could be worn with either face to the front – the only difference in appearance apart from the decoration being the very insignificant one of a flatter or a rounder section; the intention was clearly that there should be a choice, since the collar goes right round the shaft of the pin (this is a rare instance among the brooches or buckles of such a pin, decoration on almost all other surviving pins being restricted to one side, though cf brooch no. 1318, which has lost all but a trace of the pin).

1315 TL74 2150 (2455) 9 fig 162
d 28mm; gunmetal frame (AML); the frame has two plain sectors (one with a constriction for the pin) and two with cable decoration; the pin has a transverse ridge.

1316 BWB83 398 (264) 9 fig 162
d 18mm; somewhat corroded; bronze frame (AML); sinuous engraved zigzags on front; irregular, engraved arc-lines on back.

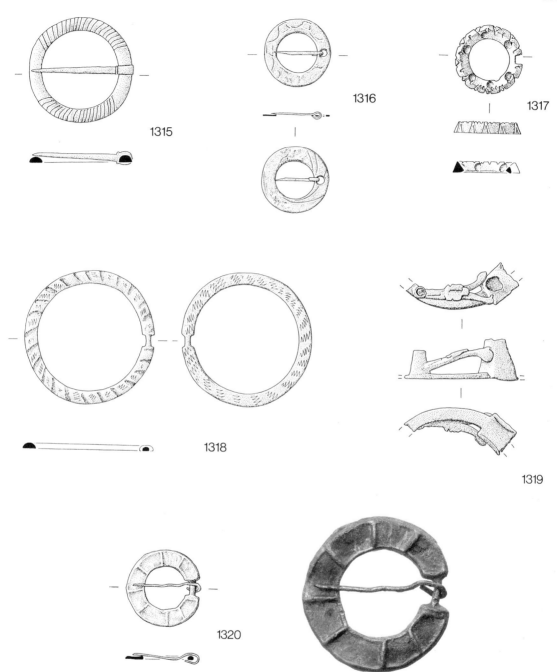

1315

1316

1317

1318

1319

1320

162 Annular brooches (no. 1318 is reversible)
(1:1, except photograph 2:1)

1317 BWB83 4401 (274) 9 fig 162
d 18.5mm; gunmetal (AML); triangular-section frame, giving two visible surfaces as worn; the inner is decorated with unevenly spaced (?)drilled, blind holes, and the outer and the apex with filed grooves, which make a series of V shapes; pin missing.

A similarly decorated, but more elaborate brooch recovered from spoil dumped from the Billingsgate site (private collection) retains the pin. Neither example provides any evidence that the voids functioned as collets for stones, or that they once held enamel. The decoration seems intended simply to give variety to the surfaces.

Cf also Musty 1969, 147–49 fig 28, 2 for similar decorative blind holes on an annular copper-alloy brooch (dated tentatively to the 13th century), several more-elaborate copper-alloy brooches in the British Museum collection have both blind holes and collets (the latter formerly containing stones, eg acc. no. 67.3–20.24; see Hattatt 1987, 334 & fig 108 no. 1345, for a published example); acc. no. AF 2723, also in the national collection, with both blind holes and grooves, is a closer parallel to no. 1317.

1318 BWB83 4240 (307) 11 fig 162
d 45.5mm; gunmetal frame (AML); spiral decoration on one face – alternate bands are of inlaid tin (MLC), with engraved oblique zigzags on the other bands; the other face has only engraved oblique zigzags; trace of iron pin (possibly tin-coated) survives.

A reversible brooch, as no. 1314, though in the present instance there is a more readily discernible difference between the decoration on the two faces.

1319 BWB83 2734 (328) 11 fig 162
Fragment; estd d *c*.35mm; bronze with trace of gilding (AML); part of frame with one small, parallel-sided collet containing cement, and a larger, tapering one; a piece of sheeting with foliate decoration applied above the frame rises to surround the top of the tapering collet.

This fragment of an elaborate brooch is the sole multiple-collet example among the present excavated groups (no. 1309 has only two collets). The arrangement with a secondary foliate plate in addition to the frame and collets is closely paralleled on several brooches, including a small silver-gilt one with amethysts found in dumped spoil removed from the Billingsgate site (MoL acc. no. 84.354). Cf also Bury 1982 (58 & 65, case 12 board B no. 3) – a gold brooch set with rubies and sapphires, for which a French origin and 13th-century date are suggested; Cherry 1983

(77–78); idem 1987 (485–86 no. 651) – a gold brooch set with garnets and sapphires.

Lead/tin

1320 BIG82 2746 (4178) 6 fig 162
d 21mm; pewter (AML); frame has a series of raised transverse lines; the tin-coated (MLC) copper-alloy wire pin is looped round a very narrow constriction in the frame.

1321 SWA81 2354 (2266) 7 fig 163
d 19.5mm; pewter (AML); series of transverse lines between those along the borders; pin and the outer bar of the hole are missing; there are voids where the metal failed to fill the mould; traces of wear from pin.

1322 BIG82 2328 (2580) 7 fig 163
d 17mm; pewter (AML); series of transverse ridges along the frame; the pin has a ridge and is distorted and bent.

1323 BIG82 3053 (5277) 7 fig 163 & colour pl 6B
d 19.5mm; pewter (AML); circles with raised central bosses alternate with bifacially bevelled rectangles; beaded border; the missing pin would have rested in a groove in one of the rectangles. The decorative motifs imitate stones.

Cf MoL acc. no. 79.327/3 for a brooch with rather similar decoration.

1324 BIG82 2718 (2939) 8
Distorted; estd d *c*.20mm+; pewter (AML); cable decoration on front and back of frame, with hatching transversely to the spirals; worn from the pin, which is missing.

1325 BWB83 1517 (222) 9 fig 163
d 16mm; tin (AML); slightly bent; frame has cable decoration with secondary cabling along alternate spirals (cf Maryon 1971, 137 & fig 240 no. 34 – though the design on the present brooch is cast); slight constriction for the copper-alloy pin, which has tin coating (MLC).

1326 SWA81 1876 (2142) 9 fig 163
Slightly oval frame; max l 17mm; pewter (AML); the sides of the frame have a series of dots in the centre, flanked by fields of cross hatching; four roundels with cross hatching in their sunken centres divide the frame; cross hatching continues onto the edges of the frame, where it is interrupted by an undecorated, reserved field and the constriction for the pin. The finely detailed decoration is unusual in the present corpus (see no. 1344 for the only comparable example here).

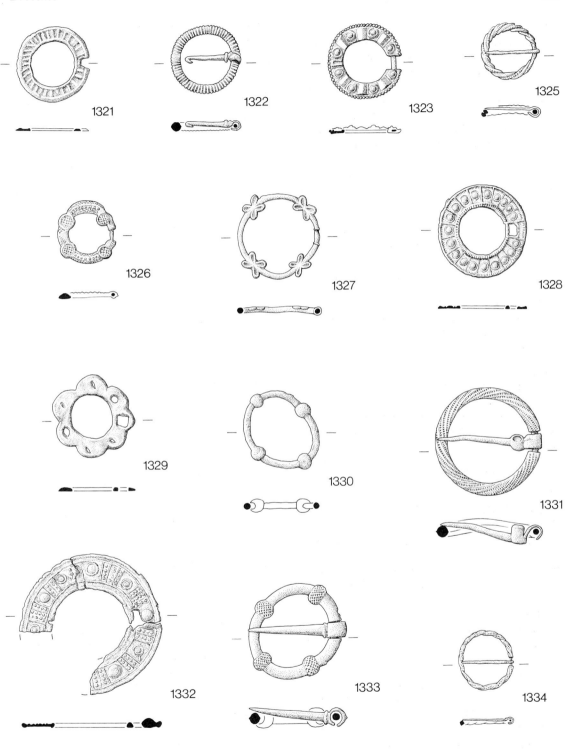

163 Annular brooches (1:1)

1327 SWA81 582 (2055) 9 fig 163
d 22.5mm; max l 25mm; pewter (AML); four quatre-foils on frame; a slight constriction for the missing pin is defined by collars. A similarly decorated, but slightly more robust brooch (found in the Thames in London, private collection) retains a lead/tin alloy pin.

Cf quatrefoil decoration on finger-ring no. 1631 (ceramic phase 11).

1328 SWA81 551 (2018) 9 fig 163
d 24mm; pewter (AML); a series of circles with raised central bosses (false stones) alternate with transverse lines; hatched inner and outer borders; pin missing.

1329 BWB83 1611 (108) 10 fig 163
d 23mm; pewter (AML); crude; seven-lobed outline, with irregular holes (intended to be round) in six of the lobes (all but two of which are blocked to a greater or lesser extent by surplus metal), and a squarish hole for the missing pin. This frame may, from the metal still blocking the holes and from the absence of visible wear from a pin, have been discarded without having been finished or used.

1330 BWB83 3593 (357) 11 fig 163
Slightly distorted; estd d *c.*21mm; pewter (AML); four plain knops on frame (there is no constriction); pin missing.

Similar brooches retaining their pins are known from London (private collections). Cf also British Museum collection no. AF 2713 – a similar, but larger brooch in silver.

1331 BWB83 4417 (256) 11 fig 163
Slightly distorted; pewter (AML); d 28.5mm; decoration as on preceding item; the pin has a collet at the base, from which the stone is missing.

1332 BWB83 2148 (126) 11 fig 163
Incomplete and distorted, found folded; d *c.*37mm; lead (AML), lead-tin (MLC); circle-and-dot motifs within radiating lines (false stones) alternate with transverse bands with dots; pin missing.

1333 SWA81 2273 (unstratified) fig 163
Slightly distorted; d *c.*26mm; pewter (AML); four cross-hatched knops on frame; transverse ridge on pin.

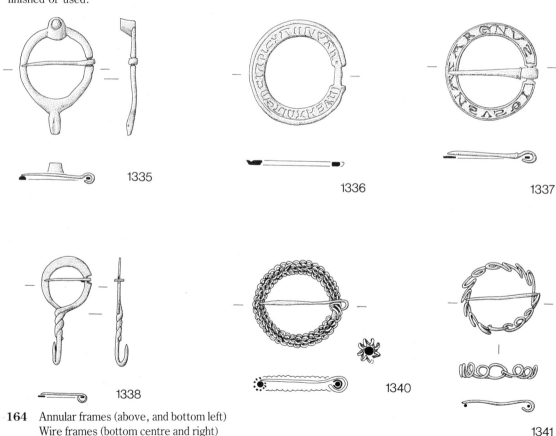

1335

1336

1337

1338

1340

1341

164 Annular frames (above, and bottom left)
Wire frames (bottom centre and right)
(1:1)

Silver

1334 BIG82 2705 (3512) 7 fig 163
d 16mm; silver (AML); weight 0.75 grammes; cable-decorated frame, with beading running along the spirals; the pin has a transverse ridge.

Annular frame
with decorative elements to each side

Copper alloy

1335 SWA81 acc. no. 2139 (context 2030) ceramic phase 9 fig 164
d 20mm, max l 31mm; gunmetal (AML); the tapering collet is angled outwards and contains the remains of a broken glass (MLC) stone – corrosion products mean the original colour is uncertain; a protrusion on the other side of the frame has a central groove; there are prominent file marks on the back.

This is the only example in the present corpus of what was a quite common type of brooch, several of which are among chance finds from London. Some of the finer examples have the equivalent of the grooved projection in the form of two hands clasping a jewel (eg Bury 1982, 58 & 65, case 12 board B nos. 7 & 8; Hinton 1982, 30 pl 12; Cherry 1988, 143–61, gives a list of known brooches of this form; see also Hattatt 1987, 330–31 no. 1334 fig 107). A London example in a private collection has an animal's head here. The present example, a cheap, simple version, presumably imitates the basic form of more expensive brooches.

Annular frames – with legends

Pewter

1336 BIG82 1938 (1806) 8 fig 164
d 27.5mm; pewter (AML); AVEMARIAG/RCIAPLCNA:[INVAN] (Lombardic letters), linear border – the legend and border are engraved; pin missing.

The blundered *gracia* and the omission of the central bar of the E of *plena*, together with the unusual form of M and the use of two apparently distinct forms of N, point to the mould having been made by an illiterate or sub-literate worker.

Many similar lead/tin alloy brooches with versions of *Ave Maria . . .* legends are known among chance finds in London (for the legend, see Evans 1921, 58),

including several in which (as in the present example) the end of the legend cannot be interpreted fully. (Cf Mitchiner 1986, 129 no. 332.) A mould, described as being of 'hardened clay', for two broadly similar *Ave Maria* brooches was found at Astill, Norfolk (Anon 1803, 275 & pl XLVIII fig 4).

Silver

1337 BWB83 714 (306) 11 fig 164 & colour pl 6C
d 25.5mm; silver frame and pin (AML); weight 2.35 grammes (36.25 grains); IESVS NAƺARENVS in line border (Lombardic letter) the pin has a transverse ridge; the pin and frame show signs of wear at the points of contact, and the pin has become bifurcated at the tip (possibly at a point of weakness deriving from the smithing process) so that in its present state the brooch is unusable. The weight (after cleaning but without removing all patination) is marginally greater than that of two pennies of the period 1351–1412, which were required to weigh 18 grains each (North 1975, 273). The possible relationship to the specification for contemporary coins may have been deliberate (see below).

Cf Cuming 1862, 229 for a similar silver brooch with the same legend. Fifteen of the sixteen silver and gold annular brooches from North Britain listed by Callander (1924, 169–71) have variants of this legend, and it is also very frequently represented on annular brooches of precious metal in the British Museum and Victoria and Albert Museum collections.

For the apotropaic powers attributed to the commonly used title *Jesus Nazarenus Rex Judaeorum*, see Evans 1922, 128–9, cf eadem 1921, 58. Brooches including 'Jesus Nazarenus' in the legend were made for magical purposes from five pennies in the 14th century – ibid 127 (two pennies would have lacked the power of the five specified in this context). Mr R Lightbown suggests that precious-metal brooches might be made from melting down coins simply because these were a ready source of bullion (pers. comm. and cf Lightbown 1978, 98, referring to the practice in medieval France). The frame and pin in no. 1337 appear to be of different alloys (see p 391, where analysis indicates that the frame is far more debased than the relatively pure pin); this makes any possible connection with specie more complicated. Number 1334, the only other certain silver brooch in the present corpus, has no obvious relation to the weight of contemporary coins (see also item no. 211, listed under buckles, for a further possible silver brooch).

Hooked annular brooch

Copper alloy

1338   SWA81   acc. no. 1493   (context 2113)
ceramic phase 12   fig 164
1 29.5mm; annular frame d 14mm, with a nick in the side where the wire pin is attached; the ends of the frame extend, tightly twisted together, at a right angle to the pin; one end is cut off and the other curves round in a hook, which is filed to a point.

The frame and hook are apparently made from a length of drawn wire, which is somewhat thicker than that of the pin; the frame has been hammered flat, and the twisted part has also been slightly hammered.

The function of this small item is obscure – it was presumably used in the manner of a brooch, with the hook for attachment to something else. The slight angle at which the hook lies is similar to that on 16th-century hook-ended belt tags which were probably joined together in pairs. It is possible that the present item is a forerunner of these, though the brooch-like method of fixture here seems to be at the wrong angle for joining to have been effected in precisely the same way; for this reason it would probably not have been as satisfactory for joining the ends of a strap as it would for holding parts of a textile garment together. The hook could perhaps have held a chain or pendant vertically. Cf no. 1305.

Annular/oval frames with twisted wire decoration

Copper alloy

1339   BIG82   acc. no. 3068   (context 5400)
ceramic phase 6
d 26mm; gunmetal frame and silver pin (AML); the decorative spirals are slightly damaged; the basis of the frame is a wire ring with the ends joined by opposed loops; around this armature, thinner wire, which had already been densely spiralled, was then wound in larger spirals (the thinner wire may originally have been one length – it is now broken); the D-section pin was added without a special gap being made in the spirals.

1340   SWA81   363   (720)   6 or later   fig 164
A less-damaged example, similar to the preceding one; the spirals are very neat and regular; frame 24×22.5mm; bronze (AML); the pin has been added at the point where the ends of the outer spirals join; the outer spirals consist of about 35 major loops, each

having about seven or eight smaller spirals – ie some 200 minor loops in all.

The overall effect of the spirals in the two preceding brooches – an apparently complicated, dense decoration – is achieved by the repetition of a very simple process.

1341   BWB83   1442   (389)   11   fig 164
d 21mm; brass frame and pin (AML); frame is a wire ring of widely spaced spirals (simpler than in the two preceding brooches), with a larger gap for the wire pin; the frame is joined by inserting one end with a loop in the opposite direction from the others into the first loop at the other end. There is a fragment of a similar brooch in the National Museum of Denmark (acc. no. D 596/1971, found at Slagelse).

A small gold brooch found in York having quite similar spiralled–wire decoration, also round a plain annular armature (Daniells 1979, 27), shows that this style was current in high-quality brooches too. Cf Margeson 1985, 56–57 fig 38 no. 4 for a more elaborate wire frame for a religious badge, probably of post-medieval date.

Quatrefoil frame

Copper alloy

1342   BWB83   acc. no. 5804   (context 298)
ceramic phase 11   fig 165
22×23mm; bronze (AML); frame has series of transverse bands; pin missing.

Rectangular frame

Copper alloy

1343   BIG82   2287   (2278)   8   fig 165 & colour pl 6D
22×23mm, frame has separately cast sexfoils attached at each corner by spherical-headed (d *c*.5mm), cast rivets; D-section wire pin. An unusually three-dimensional brooch.

Lozenge-shaped frame

Pewter

1344   SWA81   3377   (2139)   9   fig 165 & colour pl 6E
max 36×36mm; pewter (AML); the frame is divided

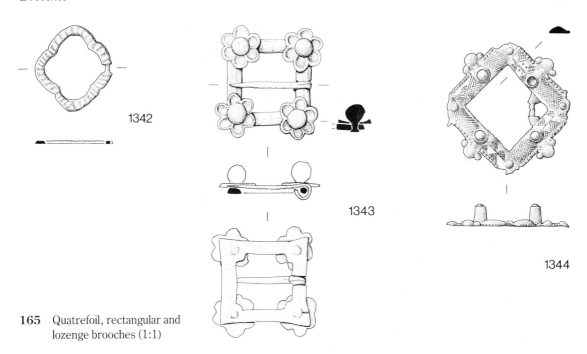

165   Quatrefoil, rectangular and lozenge brooches (1:1)

into areas alternately with cross hatching, and opposed, hatched and plain or dotted triangles, within a beaded border; three of the four collets in the middle of the sides retain green glass stones, and there is a raised boss at each corner; a larger boss, flanked by two smaller ones, adjoins the frame beside each collet; the missing pin would have been attached to the internal bar. The back is pitted with bubbles from the casting process. There is some evidence of wear from the pin on the frame. Damage on the outer edge at each corner may indicate that further decoration has been broken off; the symmetry of the design as recovered would probably have made the brooch acceptable for wearing, even if some original elements were missing.

Probable pentagonal frame

Pewter

1345   BIG82   3141   (2591)   8   fig 166
Fragment of frame; estd original d *c.*38mm; pewter (AML); an inner ring and an outer (?)pentagon are transversely ridged and there are traces of an outer, thinner plain ring; there are solid, false collets with shallowly hollowed tops at the points of juncture of the elements of the frame.

A similar brooch, found in dumped spoil from the Billingsgate site and retaining its copper-alloy wire pin (private collection), gives the probable original appearance of the present example.

Hexagonal frames

Pewter

1346   BWB83   5806   (298)   11   fig 166
Incomplete; 27×25mm; pewter (AML); frame decorated with a row of dots within line borders, and with larger dots at each corner; pin missing.

1347   BWB83   5098   (unstratified)
Smaller fragment of a brooch similar to the preceding; pewter (AML); Although the design is identical, minor differences in the size and positions of the dots indicate that these brooches are from different moulds.

A third, somewhat more complete example (also lacking the pin) was found in spoil dumped from the Billingsgate site (private collection). A larger lead/tin alloy brooch of similar outline has an illiterate legend (MoL acc. no. 84.122).

Six-lobed frames

Pewter

1348   BWB83   4555   (274)   9   fig 166
Incomplete; max d *c.*34mm; pewter (AML); solid, false collets internally and externally at the points and

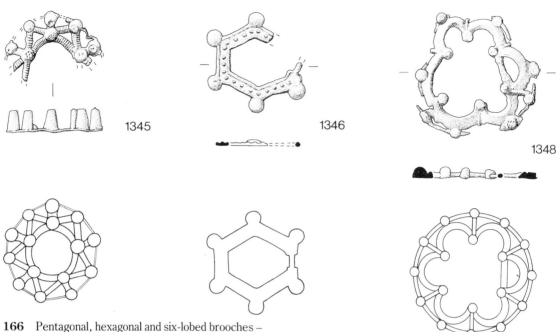

166 Pentagonal, hexagonal and six-lobed brooches –
original shapes restored below (1:1)

externally at the apexes of the arcs, with traces of a
thinner band around the edge; bar for missing pin spans
one arc.

1349 BWB83 5803 (298) 11
A less-complete example identical in design to the
preceding brooch (possibly from the same mould);
pewter (AML); pin missing.

A somewhat more complete example (also lacking
the pin) was found in spoil dumped from the Billingsgate site (private collection). The possibility that the
false collets in the preceding five brooches were
painted to simulate stones has not found any support
from the results of analysis.

Large, highly decorative brooch

Pewter

1350 SWA81 acc. no. 442 (context 2018)
ceramic phase 9 fig 167
Fragment from an ornate circular brooch; pewter
(AML); cross-hatched boss with part of cable-
decorated curving band attached.
The complete frame of what appears to be a similar,
circular brooch, 85mm in diameter, was found in spoil
dumped from the Billingsgate site (private collection –

the brooch was stolen in 1987, and has not been
recovered at the time of writing); it has a cross-hatched
inner ring with alternate square and circular motifs and
a cabled inner border, surrounded by a ring of eight
sexfoils alternating with rayed bosses, surrounded by
eight dotted bosses alternating with fleurs de lis, and
with a cabled band running outside the bosses and
inside the fleurs. Though the decoration on the bosses
differs in detail, the broad similarity in design suggests
that the fragment is an outer element from a brooch of
closely comparable design.
The large size of this brooch is comparable with that
of one depicted on the tomb effigy of a 14th-century
Danish Queen (fig 167) and on a 12th-century statue of
the Queen of Sheba at Chartres in France (Evans 1952,
pl 7a), but there is seemingly no ready secular parallel
in this country. Cf the morses (clasps) on medieval
ecclesiastical copes (eg Clayton 1979, pl 56 no. 6). The
size is impressive, and the existence in base metal of at
least two variants implies a popular market. See also
no. 1374.
Large brooches remarkably similar in overall form
and in the combination of diverse decorative motifs
were worn by peasant women in parts of Norway up to
the last century (Noss 1985A, 26–29, 36–39, 55, 71 &
80, and idem 1985B, 3–5 & 7; cf Gerlach 1971, 36–37
pl 18. The designs were very regionalised in the rural

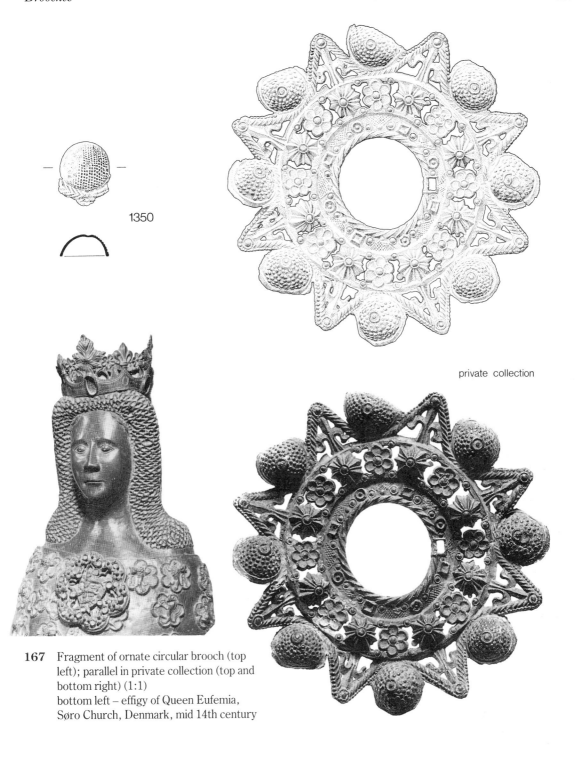

1350

private collection

167 Fragment of ornate circular brooch (top
left); parallel in private collection (top and
bottom right) (1:1)
bottom left – effigy of Queen Eufemia,
Søro Church, Denmark, mid 14th century

society of the Norwegian valleys, but this probably has no bearing on medieval English urban fashions in brooches).

Open frame brooches with highly stylised figurative motifs

Lead-tin

1351 BIG82 acc. no. 2475 (context 2909) ceramic phase 8 fig 168
Fragment of a bird brooch; l 20mm; pewter (AML); wing with areas of linear and cross hatching, and a hole for the missing pin, and part of the circular frame.
A complete brooch with similar decoration, and retaining the pin, was found in dumped spoil from the Billingsgate site (private collection, fig 168); the complete crudely executed design consists of two opposed, outward-facing birds' heads, two wings, and a single tail on the annular frame; these brooches are possibly from the same mould. Cf also Mitchiner 1986 (130 no. 337) for a similar, incomplete brooch from a different mould.

The bird motif seems to have been quite popular for cheap brooches in London. Another two-headed version is known, as is an example with a single head. Further comparably crude lead/tin alloy brooches of the same general character from London have two men holding a fleur de lis aloft, and two animals apparently attempting to devour a man (all private collections). A stone mould for producing somewhat similar brooches with opposed, facing bird-like creatures has been excavated in a (?)14th-century deposit in Bristol (Dundas Wharf site 21/82 AQB no. 107).

1352 SWA81 1265 (2150) 9 fig 168
Fragment; max l 37.5mm; pewter (AML); the decoration is linear, on a stippled field: two opposed, outward-facing animals, each with an eye and the mouth depicted by lines that continue into a key pattern running

down the centre of the neck; strips connecting the mouths to the necks may be seen as tongues, though they serve the practical function of strengthening the brooch; a (?)foot with parallel curved lines is raised as in the heraldic rampant position. Although the last elements might at first sight appear to be wings, the complete design (see fig 168) supports the presumption that they are forelegs.

A complete brooch of the same design, retaining the pin and measuring *c*.35×*c*.35mm, was excavated at Bryggen in Bergen, Norway, from a deposit thought to be associated with the fire of 1332 (Ågotnes nd, 8; Bryggen Museum acc. no. 40082); it shows that the design is symmetrical – the key pattern continues along the animals' bodies, and there are curving lines at the base, suggesting that they are squatting on their hind legs. The distinctive style of decoration is quite unlike that on any other item in this corpus of dress accessories, and no obvious parallel has been traced. At present the place of manufacture of these brooches cannot be pinpointed.

BROOCHES WITH INTEGRAL PINS

(all are of lead/tin alloys and from three-part moulds, unless otherwise stated)

Although there are broadly similar disc brooches to nos. 1353 etc from about the time of the Norman Conquest, eg in the 11th-century Cheapside hoard (Guildhall Museum Catalogue 1908, 119 & pl 54 nos. 1–26; VCH London 1909, 160 fig 17), and from recent excavations (eg TEX88 acc. no. 1039), there seems to be no definite continuity through the 12th and 13th centuries. The

1351

private collection

1352

168 Figurative open-frame brooches; no. 1352 restored after brooch excavated in Norway (1:1)

reappearance of secular lead/tin alloy brooches of this one-piece form in the 14th century comes rather later than the introduction of religious souvenirs of the same basic form. The similarity to pilgrim badges of the earliest (?late 13th- or early 14th-century) disc brooches listed below could mean that the latter are non-explicit versions of religious souvenirs. If so, the delayed emergence of a market for the secular one-piece brooches is even more marked (the earliest figurative examples listed below are from the late 14th century). The definite secular brooches described below are all from the late 14th and early 15th centuries.

The wide range of subject matter among those brooches with figurative designs may broadly be compared with the more naturalistic marginal drawings of late-medieval manuscripts. Notable among the brooches listed below for their unusual degree of accurate detail in representing a natural form are those with a three-dimensional violet growing out of a grassy tuft (nos. 1364 etc.).

These cheap, figurative brooches are a remarkable manifestation of mass-produced popular art. Some motifs appear in several different ver-

sions, and were clearly very fashionable. A few are known both in England and the continent. Completely absent among the recent finds, and apparently unknown in England so far, are the highly explicit pornographic brooches of the kind found in some numbers both in France and the Netherlands (Forgeais 1866, 257–69; Hopstaken 1987, 49–56).

Presumably many, if not all, of these lead alloy brooches would once have been painted, though only traces of red colouring survive on a few of the comparable pieces not included here.

Non figurative designs
Disc brooches

1353 BWB83 acc. no. 440 (context 284)
ceramic phase 9 fig 169
Incomplete; d *c.*21mm; four fleurs de lis around a central boss, all within a four-lobed tressure, with a dot at each point and in the interstices, surrounded by a band with dots and a running scroll with trefoils; beaded border.

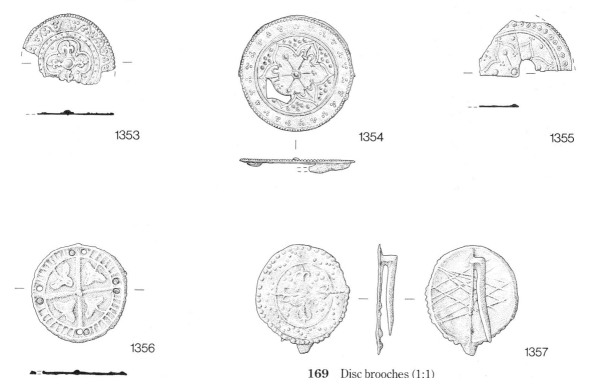

1353   1354   1355

1356   1357

169 Disc brooches (1:1)

1354 SWA81 542 (2012) 11 fig 169
d 30mm; fleur de lis at the end of each of three bars (cf sceptres) which cross at the centre, within a double tressure of six pointed arches, with trefoils at the points and dots in the outer interstices, all surrounded by a band with a running scroll with trefoils, within a beaded border; pin incomplete; pewter (AML); a bubble formed during the casting has resulted in a sizeable void.

1355 BWB83 5013 (293) 11 fig 169
Incomplete; apparently pierced centrally, trimmed at the edge with a sharp instrument, folded in two (this has resulted in breakage, and the loss of one half) and then in two again – now unfolded; d 27mm+; central boss with radiating lines, originally within a double tressure of six ogival pointed arches, with trefoils at the points and dots in the outer interstices, surrounded by a band with circle-and-dot motifs, all within a beaded border.

The three above brooches have designs very similar to a number of devotional ones with legends referring variously to Christ, the Virgin, St Thomas Becket, and the Three Kings (cf

Mitchiner 1986, 79 no. 155a; 78 nos. 149–50; 71–2 nos. 129–33; Spencer 1982, 309 no. 3 pl 5).

1356 BWB83 1454 (292) 11 fig 169
d 25.5mm; crude; plain cross with four trefoils; hatched border; a small stub on the back is presumed to be from a pin that has been cut off; the disc has been pierced by four pairs of holes near the edge, by which it could be sewn onto a garment.

1357 TL74 1094 (368) 12 fig 169
d 25mm; crude; four fleurs de lis radiating from a (?)circle in the centre, with three dots in each space between, all in a band with a running zigzag of dots between line borders, with a beaded edge. The design is poorly registered; non-alignment of the part of the mould for the front with the two parts for the back and the pin has resulted in the edge beading extending beyond the flan on one side, so that the dots give the disc an irregular outline. The back is cross-hatched, from scratches presumably for alignment of the two mould parts.

This brooch has been published (Spencer 1982, 320 no. 17 pl 16), and attention was drawn to the degeneracy of the design. The suggestion that this poorly

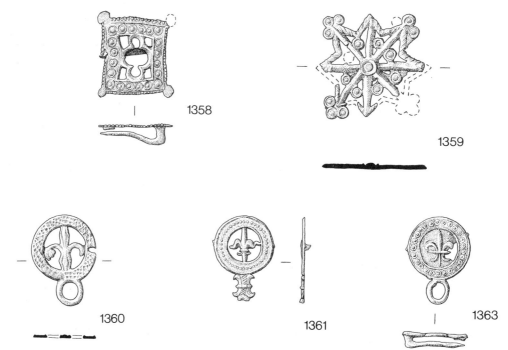

1358

1359

1360

1361

1363

170 Top left, rectangular brooch
top right, symmetrical brooch
bottom fleur de lis brooches (1:1)

produced brooch is the latest of the series still holds good for this now extended corpus.

Rectangular brooch

1358 SWA81 753 (2097) 12 fig 170
Slightly distorted and damaged; 28×22mm; central four-arched openwork motif, within band of circles and dots with beaded border; three (?of an original four) bosses survive at the corners; catch for pin on reverse.

Symmetrical openwork brooch

1359 SWA81 2075 (2109) 12 fig 170
Incomplete (described as if complete); 28×27+mm; pewter (AML); eight lines radiating from a central circle and dot, with a ring of circle-and-dot motifs in the angles; a cross-hatched border gives an eight-pointed star outline, which has clusters of three circles and dots at alternate points. A fragment of a pin or a catch loop was found broken off in the same storage box.
Probably non-figurative, though the eight radiating elements can be taken as arrows (cf Spencer 1980, 26 no. 119 for a badge in which arrows may refer to the martyrdom of St Edmund).

Figurative designs

Fleurs de lis

1360 SWA81 acc. no. 1998 (context 2107)
ceramic phase 12 fig 170
18×25mm; crude; fleur in cross-hatched circular border; loop below; pin missing.

1361 SWA81 1477 (2113) 12 fig 170
Incomplete; 16×23mm; fleur in circular border with ring of beading; below is part of a three-part motif with a band at the narrowed centre; trace of pin survives.

1362 SWA81 2146 (2108) 12
Incomplete; 13.5×16mm; similar to the preceding, but broken off below the circular border.

1363 TL74 2251 (368) 12 fig 170
16.5×23mm; fleur in similar border, but with circle-and-dot decoration.

The last example has been published (Spencer 1982, 316 no. 14 & pl 14; thirty similar brooches, practically all from different moulds, are mentioned. Cf also Spencer 1980, 19 nos. 66–69, and Mitchiner 1986, 167–68 nos. 508 & 512–17). The fleur de lis, may, as a symbol of the Virgin, refer to any of a number of shrines, or it may be non-specific. Some of these pinned fleurs retain various items suspended from chains from loops at the base; some pendent items – a mitred head of Thomas Becket and others with a letter T – perhaps suggest the shrine of Our Lady Undercroft at Canterbury (ibid), and MoL acc. no. 82.8/5 has a two-sided medallion with annunciation scenes.

Subsequent finds respectively have a miniature lead-tin purse, a miniature set of bagpipes, and a conjoined pair of leaves (cf Spencer ibid, 322 note 48) hanging here, for all of which, especially when considered together, it is difficult to find a specific religious context.

The above four fleurs are included here because the extended range of accompanying trinkets may mean that they were from the medieval equivalent of the modern charm bracelet, on which a crucifix can appear alongside anything from a rabbit to a motor car.

Violets

1364 SWA81 830 (2107) 12 fig 171
Incomplete; 34×30mm; grassy bank, with flower on a sinuous stem, flanked on the left by a damaged broad leaf on a stem, and on the right by another damaged stem; part of the pin and catch survive. The flower is in the round, necessitating a four-part rather than the usual three-part mould.

For the flower, cf Mitchiner 1986 (166, no. 497 – wrongly described as a Canterbury bell).

1365 SWA81 1494 (2113) 12 fig 171
Incomplete; grassy bank similar to the preceding, but with the tussocks more individually emphasised, and with two outer stems surviving, the central one having broken completely off; a scroll at the base, with beading along the bottom, has the black-letter legend 'veolit.in.ma.ye. . . .' (last part illegible) the pin and catch are intact; pewter (AML).

1366 SWA81 1671 (2112) 12
& 1367 SWA81 2235 (2115) 12
Two round broad-leaves, probably from brooches of the same category as the preceding items (though the foliage on the trees on some badges showing the martyrdom of St Alban is quite similar – Spencer 1969, 35 nos. 1 & 2). Other badges and brooches could have similar leaves.

Further incomplete brooches with this design (again from a different mould) have an additional

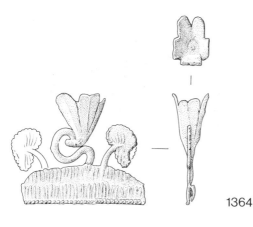

1364

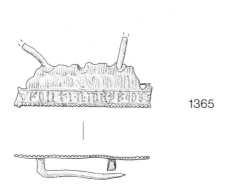

1365

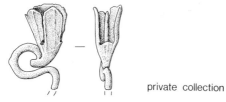

private collection

171 Violet brooches (drawings 1:1, photograph 2:1)

(?)flower bud or lanceolate leaf to the left of the flower (eg Spencer 1980, 32 no. 157), and a detached flower retains the style in the centre – this is somewhat more prominent than in nature (private collection, fig 171).

The significance of the 'violet in May . . .' (?Mayday or Maytime) legend is uncertain. There was almost certainly no legend on no. 1364. The flower and the leaves are accurately portrayed parts of the violet (*viola odorata*), a long-established favourite flower of the hedgerow and horticulture (Harvey 1981, 23, 29, 132, 164 & 179). Many pilgrim souvenirs and retainers' badges include legends (eg Spencer 1980, 29 no. 134), and there are also a few apparently non-specific brooches of late-medieval date which have them as well (eg a plough with 'God speed the plough' – private collection, and see on no. 1370). The violet brooches could have had a general or a specific allusion. It is possible that they were associated with the celebration of May

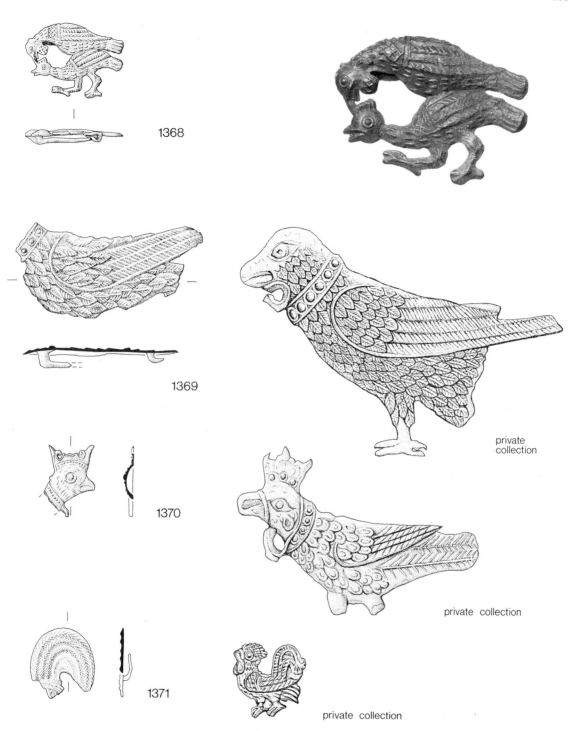

1368

1369

1370

1371

private
collection

private collection

private collection

172   Bird brooches (drawings 1:1, photograph 2:1)

Day (see Hornsby et al. 1989, 55 no. 21 for a different kind of May-Day brooch).

Birds

1368 BWB83 14 (136) 11 fig 172
27×21mm; cock and hen mating; the male bird's comb is missing; the pin and catch on the back are intact; pewter (AML).

Several versions of brooches with this design are known (Mitchiner 1986, 216–17 nos. 787–92, wrongly described as fighting cocks), representing at least three different moulds in addition to the one for the present example; others (again from more than one mould) have been found in the south Netherlands (Hopstaken 1987, 57 no. 308, and two further examples from Dordrecht and Reimerswaal in the van Beuningen collection).

If this internationally popular sexual motif had any particular significance, it is now unknown.

1369 BWB83 13 (125) 11 fig 172
Fragment; 51×31mm; bird's body, with wing addorsed and a collar with bosses around the neck; stylistically less accomplished than the following example (in which the bird faces in the opposite direction).
Cf Spencer 1980, 30 no. 141.

1370 SWA81 1666 (2112) 12 fig 172
Fragment 14×20mm; crowned head of a bird of prey, which also wears a beaded collar around the neck; part of a loop is attached to the edge of the collar.

This fragment is modelled in higher relief than was usual for lead-tin brooches; the back is hollowed from the mould so that less metal would be used.
Cf Mitchiner 1986, 197–98 nos. 682–87 and 214 nos. 769–772 for similar, more complete examples from at least seven moulds (three of which produced a bird facing left and four facing right); Mitchiner's no. 770 was found in Salisbury; that one and no. 769 retain a scroll with the uncertain black-letter legend 'be ..ape.. iollye mery' (?'be happy, jolly, merry'); cf also ibid 127, nos. 322–24 – birds with the legend 'cockney look on me'. None of the published examples includes a chain, which is known on other versions (at least ten similar crowned-bird brooches, some on chains, have been found in the Netherlands and are now in the van Beuningen collection – seven from Oud Krabbendijke, and one each from Reimerswaal, Amsterdam and Dordrecht).
Mitchiner's division into early 15th-century 'eagle' badges and later 15th-century 'hawking' badges is not supported by any significant differences in the anatomy

of the birds, and both of the suggested categories are represented in late 14th-century to early 15th-century contexts at the Billingsgate and Swan Lane sites. Mitchiner's claimed 'stratigraphic evidence' has not been presented.

1371 SWA81 939 (2102) 12 fig 172
Fragment; 18×17mm; tail of a cock; a stub on the back may be part of a pin catch.

Cf Mitchiner 1986 (212 nos. 759–60) for similar brooches (the suggestion that the bird is a reference to Cockney Londoners cannot be substantiated). A complete example was found on the Bull Wharf Thames-side site in London; further examples found in London and Salisbury retain traces of red paint (all in private collections).

The large number of different badges depicting various birds of prey is striking, but the understanding of their significance has advanced very little.

Griffin

1372 SWA81 1665 (2112) 12 fig 173
Incomplete; 25×27mm; griffin with wings open; the hind quarters and part of the front foot are missing; part of the pin survives.

A more complete brooch (fig 173), apparently the mirror-image of the present one, suggests that the griffin was probably passant (Mitchiner 1986, 119 no. 300. There is no strong reason for connecting this common heraldic animal with Edward III, as claimed).

Wild man with pestle

1373 SWA81 2078 (2109) 12 fig 173
Incomplete, 29×33mm; (?)wild man, wearing baggy, cross-hatched hood, grimacing, holding a pestle in both hands, and urinating; only one leg survives; hair on the naked body is depicted by rows of strokes in relief; the pin (which, unusually for brooches in the present category, is aligned horizontally) and its catch survive; relief lines on the back imply a four-part mould if they are all seams, but it is more likely that they include setting-out guidelines from the cutting of the mould.

Cf a less-complete example from the SUN86 site (acc. no. 939). A complete brooch has been found in Salisbury (fig 173, Salisbury and South Wiltshire Museum collection – see Spencer forthcoming, where the figure is taken to be an ape); this one and another example illustrated in Mitchiner (1986, 282 & 288 no. X325), shows that the figure is standing with legs

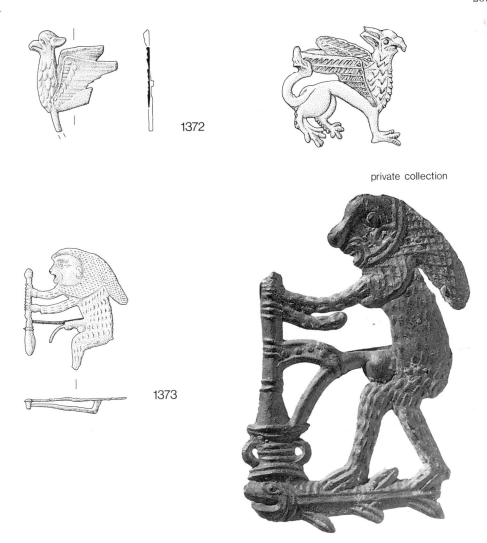

private collection

1372

1373

173 Griffin and wild man brooches; (drawings 1:1, photograph 2:1)

Salisbury and South Wiltshire Museum collection

apart, on a fish, which has a mortar on its head; the pestle is being used to pound the contents of the mortar, which include the urine being added at the same time. The wild man's forcefully opened mouth may be intended simply as a grimace, or to indicate howling, chanting etc. A figure in a similar pose but from a cruder mould is part of another brooch of this kind (Ward-Perkins 1940, 264 & pl LXXIV no. 60). Three further examples, have been found in the south Netherlands. Two, from Reimerswaal and Nieuwlande are in the van Beuningen collection (nos. I 0143 & I 1406), and one in which only the main figure, with a

canine head, survives, has been published (Hopstaken 1987, 52, no. 277 – dated to the early 15th century and interpreted as a badge from a *carnaval en erotiek*). The thought underlying this obviously secular design is obscure. A pun on 'pestle/piss' could explain the allusion, but none has been traced, and such an explanation would have to account for the continental parallels as well.

Brooches with circular frames

Leaf

1374 BC72 2037 (83) 11 fig 174
Possible brooch; two separate parts: slightly oval, hollow-backed frame (maximum d 88mm – probably distorted from an original circle), with bevelled inner and outer edges; the main motif on the raised band along the frame is a series of raised bosses, each in a circle and flanked by pairs of dots; a beaded border is surrounded on the inner bevel by two concentric raised, stepped rings; the outer bevel has opposed plain and cross-hatched triangles, and a beaded border; on the reverse, a broken stub diametrically opposite a retaining clip is presumably the remains of a pin or hook; in the centre, a separate, solid, broad-leaf with a flat back and deeply divided lobes has veining, and an undulating surface at the front to suggest natural curling; the stem is beaded along both sides, and broadens out at the base, where it is attached to the frame by a blob of solder; the reverse of the leaf retains patches of a dark coating that is visually similar to the

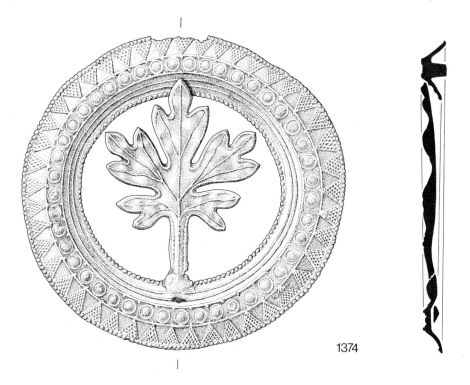

1374

174 Top, leaf brooch with circular frame bottom, woman's head in circular frame (1:1)

1375

blackening on some mirror cases (see on no. 1718). The stylisation means that the leaf cannot be identified with any particular tree or plant. Although the leaf was found soldered to the frame, the two parts, may not have been associated in this way originally. While the beading on the leaf's stem could be a continuation of that around the edge of the frame, the mould seam-line on the back of the frame has no counterpart on the leaf, even though that is on the same alignment. The leaf seems to be too long by some 5mm to fit within the frame (the solder obscures what would be the actual point of attachment, but there is no obvious break on the opposite side of the frame or at the top of the leaf, where these two elements would have been joined if they originally went together). The combination of the almost naturalistic leaf with the simple linear decoration of the frame is not readily paralleled among other lead-alloy dress accessories known from medieval London. It is difficult to imagine such a large frame being used without a central element, despite the difficulties in the way of regarding the leaf as an original component. Were it not for the clip and hint of a pin, the frame might have been suitable for a mirror, though no clear parallel can be cited. Until a more complete object of this type is found it is best to regard this as a secondary combination, the original central part having been discarded and replaced with the leaf. For the large size, cf no. 1350.

The following brooch lacks a pin:

Woman's head:

1375 TL74 acc. no. 2520 (context 416) ceramic phase 11 fig 174

Some elements missing; no pin; d 29mm; consists of two parts, both lead/tin (MLC) – an openwork component soldered at four points to a backing disc; the disc has two pairs of stubs on each side; the openwork part depicts a woman's head with a hatched headdress extending down beside the neck on each side, and, on the bust, a series of lobes which may be the top of the clothing, all within an eight-arched tressure with (?)trefoils at the points on each side, all within a circular band with a beaded border. The stubs on the backing disc probably represent loops originally on each side.

This item has been published (Spencer 1982, 315 no. 12) and the headdress identified as belonging to the period 1370–1420; Spencer remarks that the backing plate's original loops (by which the roundel could be sewn onto clothing) are characteristic of continental manufacture, probably French. The attribution is the more striking now that this object is seen as the sole representative of the type among the items considered in this volume under the category of dress accessories. It may be a pilgrim souvenir from an unrecognised shrine (ibid), but it is included here because there is no unequivocal religious connection.

The above 73 brooches from recent excavations allow some important trends to be identified. The non-selective retrieval of all brooches in the field, including fragments, gives a more reliable idea than was previously available of the relative popularity of different categories in medieval London (see table 5). These trends may well be applicable elsewhere.

The very high proportion of lead/tin brooches comprises exactly half of those in which the pin is separate from the frame, and all 24 of those where the means of attachment is integrally cast (this includes no. 1375, probably of foreign origin, originally with loops for sewing it in place). These base metals thus account for two thirds of the brooches listed here – a sharp contrast to other published series of comparable date in major collections. The emphasis on these cheap metals becomes more pronounced towards the end of the three-hundred year period considered here. It is quite likely that some of the brooches among the quarter of the total which have integral pins (and which are all from the later contexts) will in due course be identified as specifically religious trinkets – the stylistic links with pilgrim souvenirs are clearly very strong, and some may well have been produced by the same manufacturers (Brian Spencer, pers. comm.). It is nevertheless possible to see within the series with integral pins the development of purely secular brooches out of a religious mainstream, just as cathedral shops today stock a range of secular items.

Of the brooches with separate pins, the half of the total that are made of lead/tin is almost exactly matched by the number of copper-alloy examples. While the majority of white-metal brooches can be designated pewter, no. 1325 (fig 163) is of relatively unalloyed tin. There are only two brooches of silver, and gold is not represented among the recently excavated groups apart from coating on copper-alloy brooches nos. 1305 and 1319 (figs 160 & 162) – the former a

Table 5 Brooches – metals used

	Phase 6	Phase 7	Phase 8	Phase 9	Phase 10	Phase 11	Phase 12	Total
Copper	2	1	4	10	-	5	1	23
Lead/tin with separate pin	1	3	4	8	1	5	-	22
Lead/tin with integral pin	-	-	-	1	-	7	14	22
Silver	2	1	-	-	-	1	-	2
Years (AD)	1150	1200	1250	1300	1350 ←10→	1400	1450	Total 69

very crude object, which the present-day commentator may find surprising in association with the precious metal. The silver (or silver-coated) pin on copper-alloy brooch no. 1339 appears similarly anomalous. Tin coating was applied to several of the other copper-alloy brooches. The absence of iron (apart from a few of the wire pins) emphasises the importance of the decorative aspect of these accessories (by contrast the functional plain, circular buckles include many iron examples).

Little direct comparison is possible between these recent finds and the brooches, mainly of silver and gold, but including a few of copper alloy, from North Britain published by Callander (1924, 160–84). The assertion (Ward-Perkins 1940, 274) that these specific types were restricted to the north no longer holds true in all cases (cf Cherry 1985, 21 & 23–24 figs 17, 2 & 18). There is no octagonal brooch among the recent finds to compare with those from Scotland. This may be a reflection of the limits of the sample recovered in London.

The annular London brooches, among which there is a great diversity of decoration, make up almost a third of the total listed above. Spiralling ornament around the frame was popular, and took several different forms, with further variety achieved, for instance, by restricting the spirals to different areas of the frame and leaving the remainder plain. Annular brooches were apparently used up to the 18th century in rural Gloucestershire (Evans 1921, 40). Multiple lobed and geometric forms are also prominent, with crude figurative motifs present from the mid 13th century, but naturalistic representations became much more popular in the early 15th century.

The remarkable crudeness of the least accomplished lead/tin alloy brooches among the recent finds (nos. 1320 & 1321, figs 162 & 163) is the more striking when contrasted with the elegance of some of the others (eg no. 1314, fig 161 & colour pl 6A). Although it is made of base metal, no. 1319 (fig 162) is as elaborately manufactured as comparable examples in gold, and a lot of work on a small scale went into putting the rather crude decoration in the mould for evenly for lozenge-shaped brooch no. 1344 (fig 165 & colour pl 6E), and on twisting the wire evenly for nos. 1339–41 (fig 164).

The collets on some copper and lead/tin examples contain separate glass or paste stones (none is of a natural mineral), while others of lead/tin (nos. 1323, 1328, 1332 and 1345–49 – colour pl

6B & figs 163 & 166) have integrally cast false stones, which could perhaps originally have been painted.

Although the brooches listed above give a general indication of the range of forms and motifs available at the cheaper end of the market, several traits known widely elsewhere, such as blind holes with grooves (no. 1317), collets and raised foliage (no. 1319) and opposed decorative side elements (no. 1335) are each represented by only a single example here (figs 162 & 164). There is no known parallel for the hooked brooch (no. 1338 – fig 164) or the composite rectangular one (no. 1343, colour pl 6D). Other motifs, such as the violet brooches – represented by four

examples from the same site (nos. 1364–67, fig 171) – may have enjoyed a brief, but relatively spectacular vogue that the excavated groups happen to have highlighted. This extensive sample of recently excavated brooches is still too small for reliable inferences about changing fashions at a more detailed level.

The talismanic aspect of the two brooches with legends referring to Mary and to Jesus is clear (nos. 1336 & 1337), and similar associations were perhaps intended for those with false-lettering too. Some of the coloured-glass stones might also have carried overtones of protection against disease and other misfortunes (cf hexagram mount no. 1094, colour pl 4F).

Buttons

Most were for fastening garments; a few may be purely decorative.

Research into medieval buttons has until recently had to concentrate almost entirely on depictions in contemporary art, notably monumental sculptures and illuminated manuscripts, and on evidence from documentary sources. This was because virtually no surviving examples were known. Scattered references to the few excavated buttons do not seem previously to have been collated with the other evidence, and those which have been considered in detail by a dress historian (Nevinson 1977) date from almost the end of the medieval period (see cloth buttons below).

The new close-fitting fashions for outer garments from the 13th century onwards (Nevinson 1977, 38), meant a widespread need for simple fasteners at the collar (a brooch might serve the same purpose here, see figs 158 & 176) and on the sleeves (cf Pinder 1952, nos. 43, 45 & 79), and by the middle of the 14th century a row of buttons down the length of the front of the outer tunic had become fashionable (fig 175). The next century's more complicated styles for clothing for the rich could use quite plain buttons to a very elaborate overall effect (as on the sleeve in Filedt-Kok 1985, 205 no. 106), though the simple functional use continued for all classes (ibid, 208 no. 108, 210 no. 110a, 214 no. 113), just as it does today. It has been claimed that the introduction of buttons into England may be dated to about the 1330s (Newton 1980, 15–18). Buttons are depicted on sculptures in Germany which have been dated to the 1230s and have been described as the earliest evidence for buttons in Europe (White 1978, 238 & 273). The recent finds from London and elsewhere, together with other evidence, considerably expand and significantly alter this picture. Buttons for closing garments are known on an exotic Far-Eastern costume introduced into Sweden as early as the 9th century (Arbman 1940, pl 93 no. 1, cf Blindheim et al. 1981, 280 & pl 35, 10d-C4312 for another metal example of similar date from Kaupang in Norway). No continuity of usage in north-west Europe has been established from these isolated late first-millenium finds. From the information now available, it seems likely that buttons were first introduced into Europe via trade routes from the East, but that they probably came into the repertoire of everyday dress in England and continental Europe in the early 13th century.

A particular difficulty with the documentary evidence is the lack of precision in terminology. The main meaning of the contemporary term *bouton*, a lump, and its more specific application to the bud of a plant, were extended to a range of decorative dress fittings of similar shape, not only buttons in the modern sense (Nevinson 1977, 38). By the middle of the 14th century it was apparently possible to use the derivative verb in the generalised sense of "to fasten'. Two garments are described in the Great Wardrobe accounts of 1343–44 as *boutonata cum laqueis serici et punctibus*, 'fastened with silken laces and points' (Newton 1980, 25).

Although the knotted leather toggles in common use from the late 11th century onwards to fasten medieval shoes and boots in much the same way as the buttons described under this present heading (eg Grew and de Neergaard 1988, 20–23), are sometimes referred to by modern commentators as 'buttons', no contemporary use of this term for shoe fastenings has been traced until the late 15th century, and no metal buttons are known on shoes datable to the period considered in this volume (June Swann, pers. comm.).

The excavated buttons described below can be divided into three major categories:
Cast buttons of medieval date (nos. 1376–96, figs 178–79) are usually solid, either of lead/tin with integral shanks, or of bronze with separate, embedded wire shanks and a tin coating. They were produced in moulds (cf Bergman and Billberg 1976, 207 fig 151 top, for one element of a two-part 13th-century stone mould for 11 small

175 Wooden figure of Walter de Helyon showing buttons on front of tunic and sleeves, from Much Marcle, Hereford and Worcester, *c*.1360

176 Head of Dietrich, showing buttons and holes at collar (after sculpture at Naumberg Cathedral, Germany)

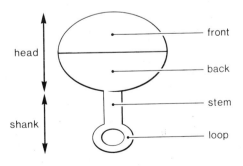

177 Terminology for buttons

buttons of the former kind, found in Lund in Sweden).

Composite sheeting buttons   (nos. 1397–1404, fig 179) were usually made from two stamped hemispherical pieces of copper-alloy sheeting soldered together, and with a wire shank soldered in place.

Cloth buttons   consist of a bunched scrap of cloth sewn into a ball (these are briefly mentioned below – see fig 180, but are considered in greater detail in a companion volume on textile finds – Crowfoot et al. forthcoming).

CAST BUTTONS

(solid buttons with integral shanks, from three-part moulds: all are of lead/tin)

1376   BIG82   acc. no. 3403   (context 3204) ceramic phase 7   fig 178
Biconvex; d 8.5mm; tin (AML), lead/tin (MLC); front plain except for beading around edge (bubble near centre is accidental); back is plain; shank is now bent over.

1377   BIG82   2649   (2591)   8   fig 178
Biconvex; d 11mm; tin (AML); front and back plain; shank has loop on a stem.

1378   BIG82   2508   (2853)   8   fig 178
Biconvex; d 12.5mm; pewter (AML); front (abraded) apparently plain except for a series of dots or zigzags around the edge; back plain; shank now bent over.

1379   BIG82   2338   (2745)   8   fig 178 & colour pl 7A
Biconvex; d 12mm; tin (AML); the front has a yellow-glass stone in a plain collet, with beading around the edge; back plain; shank has loop at a right angle to the stem. The stone was fixed by stamping the surrounding collet.

A similar example with a green-glass stone (private collection) was found in spoil from the Billingsgate site.

1380   BWB83   4924   (373)   11   fig 178
Abraded; biconvex; d 13mm; high-tin pewter (MLC); beaded edge; central hole, presumably for a missing stone of a different material.

Cf lead/tin mounts nos. 851–54 (from phase-12 contexts) which are very similar in design.

1381   SWA81   1782   (2103)   12   fig 178
Flattish disc; d 12mm; tin (AML); the front has a six-pointed wavy star with a central dot, and a raised border with a series of dots; plain back; shank has loop on a stem (now bent over).

Cf mounts nos. 855 etc, and Ward-Perkins 1940, 122 & pl XX no. 5 (a copper-alloy stud with a similar decorative motif, attributed to the 15th century).

1382   SWA81   1090   (2100)   12   fig 178
Possible button – no surviving shank; d 15.5mm; tin (MLC); slightly convex front (with void from bubble in casting) and diametrical rabbeted band, which terminates short of the edges in a circle at each end.

The bevelled back with its concave centre is not a usual feature of mounts. The decoration may have been intended to recall the aperture on a rumbler bell.

A similar item (d 14mm) comes from the recent SUN86 site (acc. no. 932, unstratified).

1383   BIG82   2482   (2560)   unstratified context (possibly with phase-7 pottery)   fig 178
Biconvex; raised rim at edge; d 13mm; high-tin bronze (MLC); front damaged; front and back plain; stem of shank survives.

Solid, plain buttons with separate shanks from two-part moulds

(all are of copper alloy; the wire of the shanks is not obviously drawn)

1384   BIG82   2322   (2591)   8   fig 178 & colour pl 7B
Spherical; d 9mm; high-tin bronze (AML); fragment broken from the body; embedded copper-alloy shank; the surface of the sphere is highly reflective; probably highly polished.

1385   BIG82   2359   (2544)   8
Biconvex; d 8mm; bronze with tin coating (AML); stubs of embedded copper-alloy shank remain.

1386   BIG82   5734   (2591)   8   fig 178
As preceding; d 11mm; bronze with tin coating (AML); embedded copper-alloy shank.

1387   SWA81   3432   (2141)   9
As preceding; d 8mm; back incomplete; embedded shank missing; no visible coating.

1388   SWA81   1831   (2004)   9   fig 178
As preceding; bronze with tin coating (AML); stubs of copper-alloy shank remain.

1389   SWA81   1225   (2146)   9
As preceding; d 9mm.

1390   SWA81   1311   (2018)   9
As preceding; d 10mm.

1391   SWA81   2167B   (2030)   9
As preceding; bronze with tin coating (AML); front

Buttons

275

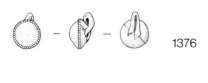

1376

1377

178 Buttons (drawings 1:1, photograph 4:1)

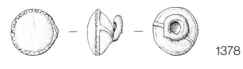

1378

1379

1380

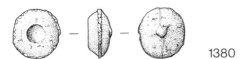

1381

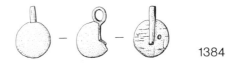

1384

1382

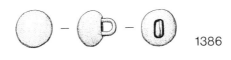

1386

1383

1388

slightly damaged (an impressed dot here may not be an original feature).

1392 BWB83 4124 (361) 11
Biconvex; d 9.5mm; embedded shank missing.

1393 BWB83 3707 (309) 12
Biconvex; d 10mm; bronze with tin coating (AML); embedded copper-alloy shank.

1394 BWB83 5140 (unstratified)
Biconvex; d 9mm; embedded shank missing, but traces of iron here may indicate that it was not of the more usual copper alloy.

1395 SWA81 4826 (unstratified)
Biconvex; d 11mm; stubs of embedded iron shank survive; tin (MLC).

The surface would probably have been highly polished, though it is now slightly dulled. Cf no. 1384.

Hollow tin button from a three-part mould

1396 BWB83 2121 (290) 9 fig 179
Originally (?)spherical, now flattened; d 18mm; tin (AML); the front has four interconnecting fields of raised parallel lines around a central ring; the back has two possible blow-holes along the casting seam; shank missing; slush-cast.

Cf Lindahl and Jensen 1983, 138 fig 16, 2 for a somewhat similar design on a silver-gilt roundel attached to a dress hook from a late 13th-century Danish hoard.

Hollow buttons in white metals seem otherwise to be known so far only from the post-medieval period. This object could be intrusive, but the other finds from the deposit all appear to be medieval.

COMPOSITE BUTTONS OF SHEETING

(unless otherwise stated, all are of copper alloy, made of two pieces of stamped sheet metal soldered together, with a separate shank that passes through a central hole in the back)

1397 SWA81 2167A (2030) 9
Biconvex; d 10mm; brass (AML); front and back plain, the copper-alloy shank is at a right angle to the body.

1398 SWA81 2740 (2065) 9 fig 179
As preceding; d 11mm; brass (AML); front incomplete; blob of solder on inside of back; front and back now separated.

1399 SWA81 1312 (2018) 9
As preceding; front missing; d 12mm; brass, with lead/tin solder (AML).

1400 SWA81 3073 (2030) 9
As preceding; d 13.5mm; shank missing; front and back brass (AML).

1401 SWA81 581 (2055) 9
As preceding; d 14.5mm; gunmetal front and back (AML); shank missing.

1402 SWA81 685 (2072) 9 fig 179
Plano-convex; d 8mm; front and back plain; brass shank (AML).

1403 SWA81 1808 (2081) 9 fig 179
Made of four pieces of copper-alloy sheeting; d 22mm; front damaged – this part is set in an irregular band with a raised outer edge (the latter was stamped to produce the shape); plain convex back; the front circular band curves over to cover the edge of the back, and the flat inner field surrounding the central hole has a series of motifs apparently stamped 17 times (rather than a design based on a single stamp), each consisting of a quatrefoil in a rectangular field; one end of the stamp has consistently not registered because of the angle at which the punch was held; the sheeting in the centre has an overlying applied piece of copper-alloy sheeting, apparently with concave edges, and reminiscent in style of Lombardic lettering; wire shank.

1404 TL74 2121 (unstratified – found with spoil attributable to ceramic phases 9–10) fig 179
Biconvex; d 13mm; the copper-alloy drawn-wire shank is at a right angle to the body.

Cf Palmer 1980, 184 fig 24, and fiche 2 CO1 nos. 45–48 for similar examples ascribed to the late 13th- to the late 15th centuries.

CLOTH BUTTONS

Two fragments of woollen textiles recovered from mid 14th-century deposits (BC72 context 250, acc. nos. 3573/1 (see fig 180) and 3424/1C, attributed to ceramic phase 10 – mid 14th century) retain respectively 12 buttons and the corresponding worked button holes on part of a sleeve, and five buttons. Each button consists of a piece of cloth gathered together and sewn into a ball *c*.9mm in diameter (cf Nevinson 1977, 41 figs 4 & 5). Round cloth buttons between 4 and 6mm in diameter, and loose, flatter ones between 14 and 35mm in diameter, come from late 14th-

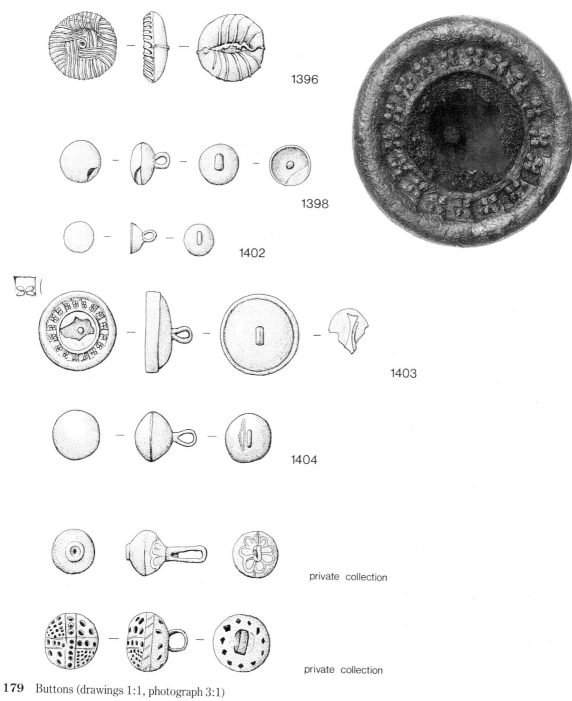

1396

1398

1402

1403

1404

private collection

private collection

179 Buttons (drawings 1:1, photograph 3:1)

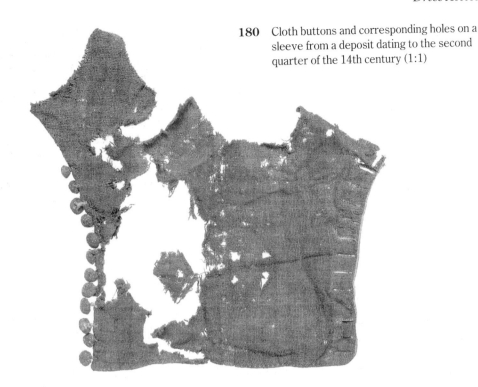

180 Cloth buttons and corresponding holes on a sleeve from a deposit dating to the second quarter of the 14th century (1:1)

century deposits at the same site. The largest of these may originally have had a separate disc inside as a stiffener, and may have been purely decorative. These items and other textile fragments with button holes from the same deposits will be more fully discussed in a companion volume on the textile finds from medieval London (Staniland in Crowfoot et al. forthcoming).

See Evans (1952, 47–48 fig VI) for a surviving late-medieval French pourpoint (man's upper garment) with cloth buttons.

The significance of the excavated medieval buttons

Few buttons from medieval deposits in England have been published: Goodall & Goodall 1977, 148 nos. 32–34 and 150 no. 34, found in Oxford, are dated to 1250–1325; Frere 1954, 140–41 fig 23, Tebbutt 1966, 53–4 fig 5h – the same type as in Frere above, though described as a hanging ornament; later examples are Palmer 1980, 184 fig 24, & fiche 2 CO1 nos. 45–48; Rigold 1971, 147–8 fig 11 (this may be a mount); Platt and Coleman-Smith 1975, 258 & 261 fig 242, no. 1772 (possibly a button); Geddes & Carter 1977,

288–9 fig 130 no. 22, dated to 1250–1350, is of a form which can only be paralleled in the post-medieval period; further medieval buttons have been found in Winchester – Biddle 1990. Roach-Smith (1854, 153 no. 757) mentions excavated buttons apparently of 14th-century date from London, but gives no details.

A stone mould probably of late 13th- or early 14th-century date from Coventry is published as evidence for manufacturing buttons, but the highly decorative motifs are more consistent with other items among the London finds, and so it would be safer, in the absence of the products themselves, to regard them as brooches, or as mounts accompanying the strap loops and perhaps buckles that were apparently being produced on the site (Bayley & Wright 1987, 86–87 no. 11).

References to 'buttons' occur in documentary sources in England from *c*.1300 onwards (Whiting 1968, 65 nos. B630, B634 & B635). Evidence for functional buttons, that is, ones used to close garments, is provided by monumental representations from at least the 14th century. The first reliable archaeological evidence for such buttons – ie with corresponding holes along the other side of the garment – was recognised in the pieces of 14th-century clothing described above (Nevinson 1977), see fig 180. In the absence of evidence for corresponding holes for any of the metal buttons described above, it is unknown in each case whether they were functional or purely decorative. A rather similarly shaped object of lead/tin (private collection, recovered along with 14th-century items from spoil derived from the Billingsgate site) may have been a form of pendant rather than a functional button (fig 179, second from bottom). It has a long shank, a collet for a stone (now missing) on the front, and a series of decorative lobes in relief on the back. The decoration on the back would not have been visible if the object were in use as a button; it might perhaps have served, like some buttons at the collar (see fig 176, and Pinder 1952, figs 43, 45 & 79) to be seen as an ornament most of the time, while it was always available for use to fasten the garment against the cold or rain. Neither possibility can be eliminated for any of the metal items described above, though the plainer examples are perhaps unlikely to have been purely decorative (cf Nevinson 1977, 38).

Most of the excavated London buttons are very plain. The cast ones include what seems to be the earliest known example in Britain so far of these now universal items (no. 1376, dated to *c*.1200–1230, fig 178), and they span the whole of the subsequent period considered in this study. Although Newton (1980, 4, 15–18) has argued from the Great Wardrobe accounts of royal purchases that buttons – including silk-covered

silver and silver-gilt ones – were introduced for the sleeves and at the front of the tunic with a change to tighter fitting fashions around 1340, at least four of the solid buttons listed above predate this by 80 years or more (nos. 1376–1379; the first was lost over a century earlier). Numbers 1376, 1378 and 1380 have beading around the edge, no. 1379 has beading around a glass stone, and no. 1381 has a central star motif (fig 178).

Among the metals used (see table 6), tin figures prominently. In at least two examples, no. 1381 and the hollow decorated button no. 1396 (figs 178 & 179), analysis shows that it is very pure. Number 1384 retains its mirror-like, highly reflective surface, which must have been produced by special polishing (its appearance in colour pl 7B is the result of only gentle manual cleaning by conservation staff); it is also very hard, a fragment having splintered off when it was knocked (a softer alloy or pure tin would probably have sustained a dent, but remained unbroken). Numbers 1385–86, 1388, 1391 and 1393 have an added coating of tin to make them shiny. Despite the plain shape of these buttons, a row of the very shiny ones would have been very striking on a garment.

The prominence of relatively pure tin in the buttons from prior to the late 14th century (nos. 1376–79, fig 178) contrasts with its near absence from girdle fittings (buckles, mounts etc – see table 4 p 25) of comparably early date. This suggests that the manufacturing traditions may have been separate, at least until copper-alloy sheeting was used for buttons, probably from the

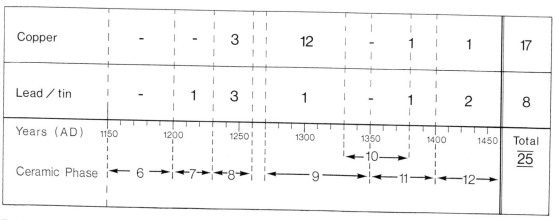

	1150	1200	1250	1300	1350	1400	1450	Total
Copper	–	–	3	12	–	1	1	17
Lead / tin	–	1	3	1	–	1	2	8
Years (AD)	1150	1200	1250	1300	1350	1400	1450	Total $\underline{25}$
Ceramic Phase	←— 6 —→ ←7→ ←8→			←——— 9 ———→	←—10—→ ←11—→	←12—→		

Table 6 Buttons – metals used

late 13th century onwards. The alloys used in buttons prior to that could suggest that the metalworkers who made basemetal finger-rings and brooches may also have produced buttons. The connection with brooches may be a strong one in view also of the similar function of closing two parts of a garment together.

All of the datable composite buttons of copper-alloy sheeting are attributable to ceramic phase 9 (*c*.1270–*c*.1350); most are plain and biconvex, but no. 1402 has a flat front (fig 179). Number 1403, made from at least five pieces, of a variety of copper alloys, is the most complicated of these buttons in terms of manufacture and of decoration, and is also the biggest one (fig 179). Its quatrefoil motifs were probably stamped repeatedly rather than once for the whole design – a very common technique in the decoration of metal and leather. This is one of the smallest objects recovered from the recent excavations to have been treated in this way. The damaged central device, possibly a letter, could mean that this was a forerunner of the livery buttons of later centuries.

Both the solid and the hollow forms of button continued well into the post-medieval period with little change, though there was a far wider variety of designs available then (cf Noël-Hume 1970, 91) than is suggested for the 13th to 15th centuries by these recent finds. Number 1404 (fig 179) in particular is not visually distinguishable from some 16th- and 17th-century buttons.

Although the existence of bone buttons has been inferred for the medieval period on the basis of waste offcuts from which circular objects have been cut, it seems strange that so far no corresponding bone button of has been reliably identified. Until an unequivocal medieval button of bone is found (cf MacGregor 1985, 101–02) it is better to regard the waste-bone panels as evidence of the manufacture of other items (see nos. 1557–81 under Beads).

None of the above medieval buttons from London excavations is of precious metal. A very tiny gold filigree button-like object (MoL acc. no. 87.51/10, d 5mm) was found in medieval spoil from the Billingsgate site – it is presumably too small to have been functional. In 1376, a Richard Bor was imprisoned in London for silvering 240 buttons of *latone* in order to try to sell them as pure silver (Riley 1868, 397–98). Silver-gilt buttons from the late 14th century have been found in Denmark (Lindahl and Jensen 1983, 140–141).

The buttons from the recent excavations do not include examples of all the medieval types now attested in London. Figure 179 (bottom) shows one of a handful of known composite sheet copper-alloy buttons with holes roughly gouged to make pierced decoration. These came from 14th-century spoil removed by contractors from the Billingsgate site (private collections) and they have also been recovered from the Thames Exchange site. At present these few examples provide the sole evidence for what was quite probably a popular line.

The recent London finds of buttons from securely dated medieval deposits provide first-hand evidence for the use of base metals for these items from the early 13th century onwards. The variety now recorded, despite the plainness of most examples, suggests that functional buttons were probably used widely in the lower levels of urban society at that time. The documentary and monumental evidence, which primarily relates to upper-class usage, has thus been put into perspective as only part of the picture. A number of phrases with a proverbial ring, current from the beginning of the 14th century onwards and each amounting to 'not worth a button' (Whiting 1968, 65 nos. B630–635), can now be related to actual examples produced for the popular market.

Lace chapes

Chapes or tags of the type listed below (nos. 1405–1436) were put on the ends of laces of leather or of textile (principally plaited silk to judge from slightly later survivals – see fig 181). The contemporary name *points*, which was apparently used by transference of the laces themselves as well as of the metal tags on the ends (cf *pourpoint*, a man's laced, or sometimes buttoned, upper garment of the late-medieval period) presumably originated by reference to these tapering tubes. Other contemporary terms are *aglets, anlettes* and *aiguillettes*. The chapes protected the ends of laces, and facilitated threading them through corresponding eyelets in a garment (for eyelets excavated at the recent sites, mainly from early 15th-century contexts, but including some of earlier date, see nos. 1218–28 under Mounts). The chapes that are of mid 14th-century date or later, can, in view of the traces of leather and other fibres found in some of them, be regarded with some confidence as being for laces. Assuming the two similar items found in

mid 13th-century (ceramic phase 8) deposits are to be positively identified as chapes, they are the earliest examples known (nos. 1405 and 1406). Other complete plain chapes of between 25 and 40mm in length are from contexts attributable to *c*.1330 or later. These chapes exhibit so little variation that the form can be regarded as standardised (stamped decoration, as for example on a post-medieval chape found in Norwich – Margeson 1985, 57–58 no. 8 fig 38 – appears to be a refinement of a later period than that covered by the present study).

All the excavated chapes are of copper-alloy sheeting, bent into tubes, with a straight seam along the side. Unless stated otherwise they are complete, tapering, and with an edge-to-edge seam. Several ends have been finished – that is, they seem to have been neatly bent inwards,

181 Silk braid with chapes – Museum of London collection (1:1, no acc. no.)
centre: detail (2:1)

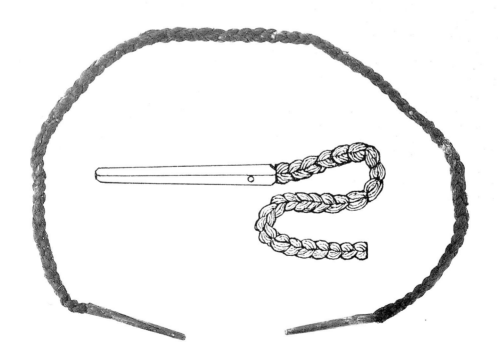

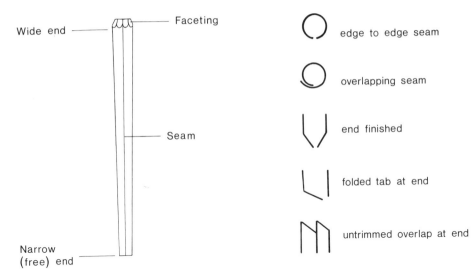

Wide end — Faceting

Seam

Narrow
(free) end

edge to edge seam

overlapping seam

end finished

folded tab at end

untrimmed overlap at end

182 Lace chapes: terminology

perhaps by being rotated under pressure while held at an angle against a flat surface (fig 183), and several others show faceting at one or both ends. Although filing (as opposed to chamfered cutting, as claimed by Oakley – 1979, 263) is a possible explanation for the faceting at the free end, this seems impractical for the other end into which the lace would already have been fed before finishing could be carried out. The sharper facets may be the result at the free end of filing, or at both ends of crimping with a pincer-like tool, or perhaps they were produced by hammering or rubbing the ends at an angle (figs 189 & 183). A few of the late 14th- and early 15th-century chapes have small rivet holes near the wider end. Although the rivets are missing in most instances, they are shown by x-ray photographs to be present in three examples. Traces of rust on several chapes suggest that the rivets were of iron.

Only nos. 1405–1436 listed below (all 40mm or less in length) are certainly lace chapes. The function of nos. 1437–1449 all from contexts earlier than the middle of the 14th century (ceramic phase 9 or earlier), and which are generally longer and more diverse in form than the later ones, is uncertain.

The contents of all the tubes were examined by Glynis Edwards (Ancient Monuments Laboratory, HBMC), who has identified the material where survival and condition permit as leather

(two certain examples and another possible one) or textile fibres (three possible examples) presumably representing original laces.

Ceramic phase 8 (*c.*1230–*c.*1260)

1405 TL74 acc. no. 574 (context 415)
l 40mm, d varies 3.5 – 1.5mm; brass (AML).

1406 TL74 637 (416) probably phase 8
fig 184
l 40mm, d 3 – 2mm, ends filed, overlapping seam; brass (AML).

Ceramic phases 10–11 (*c.*1330–*c.*1400)

1407 BC72 3743 (118)
l 29.5mm, d 2.5 – 1.5mm; brass (AML); wide end with untrimmed overlap.

Ceramic phase 11 (*c.*1350–*c.*1400)

1408 BWB83 2701 (328)
l 23mm, d 2 – 1.5mm; brass (AML); wide end possibly broken off.

1409 BC72 4154 (88)
l 26mm, d 2 – 1mm; brass (AML); possible rivet hole.

1410 BC72 4465 (150)
l 29mm, d 2.5 – 1mm; brass (AML); narrow end faceted; rivet present; contents degraded leather.

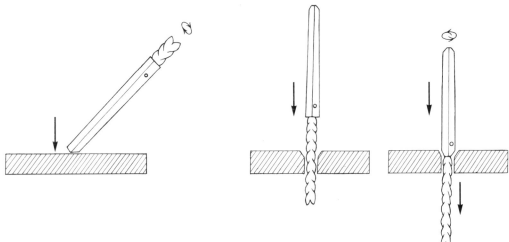

183 Possible ways of finishing the ends of chapes;
left – free end; right – wide end

1411　BWB83　2339　(109)
l 29.5mm, d *c*.2.5 – *c*.1.5mm; brass (AML); wide end
has untrimmed overlap.

1412　BC72　1812　(55)
l 30mm, d 2.5 – 1mm, wide end has untrimmed overlap; rivet hole; brass (AML).

1413　BC72　4153　(88)
l 30mm, d 2 – 1.5mm; brass (AML); ends faceted;
rivet hole; contents degraded leather.

1414　BC72　4152　(88)　fig 184
l 30mm, d 2.5 – 1.5mm; brass (AML); wide end
faceted, narrow end folded inwards; rivet hole.

1415　BWB83　2253　(151)
l 31mm, d *c*.3 – *c*.2mm; brass (AML); narrow end
faceted; contents fibres, possibly silk.

1416　BWB83　4997　(359)
l 32mm, d 2.5 – 1.5mm; brass (AML); narrow end and
possibly wide end faceted.

1417　BC72　3816　(89)
l 32.5mm, d 2.5 – 1.5; brass (AML); narrow end
possibly broken off, wide end faceted, rivet hole;
contents parallel fibres (ie not spun), possibly textile.

1418　BC72　4151　(88)
l 34mm, d 2.5 – 1.5mm; brass (AML); narrow end
faceted; rivet hole.

1419　BC72　4200　(88)
l 34mm, d 2.5 – 1.5mm; brass (AML); wide end
broken off, narrow end faceted.

1420　TL74　2245　(416)
l 35mm, d 2 – 1mm; brass (AML).

1421　BC72　2532A–F　(79)
All brass (AML).
A–E all have both ends faceted and rivet holes:
A)　l 31mm, d 2–1mm.
B)　l 33.5mm, d 3.5–1.5mm; contents possibly silk
fibres.
C)　l 34mm, d 3–1mm.
D)　l 35mm, d 2–1mm.
E)　l 35mm, d 2.5–1mm; rivet present.
F)　l 35mm, d 1.5mm (not tapering), seam spirals
around shaft, no rivet hole (? unfinished, or not a
chape).

1422　BWB83　2680　(330)
l 38.5mm, d 2.5 – 2mm; brass (AML); narrow end
faceted.

1423　BWB83　1410　(146)
l 39mm, d 3 – 1.5mm; brass (AML).

1424　BWB83　4700　(291 area)
l 40mm, d 3 – 2.5mm; brass (AML).

Ceramic phase 12 (*c*.1400–*c*.1450)

1425　BWB83　4454　(275)
l 26mm, d 1.5 – 1mm; brass (AML); narrow end
faceted.

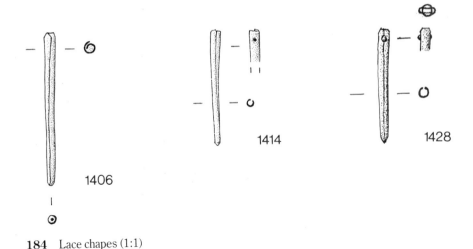

184   Lace chapes (1:1)

1426   TL74   1281   (368)
l 26mm, d 2 – 1.5mm; brass (AML); both ends faceted; rivet hole.

1427   TL74   1279   (368)
l 28mm, d 2 – 1mm; brass (AML); both ends faceted; rivet hole.

1428   SWA81   2236   (2115)   fig 184
l 30mm, d 2 – 1.5mm; brass (AML); both ends faceted; rivet present.

1429   SWA81   1098   (2100)
l 30mm, d 2.5 – 1.5mm; gunmetal (AML); both ends faceted; rivet hole.

1430   SWA81   2035   (2106/2107)
l 30.5mm, d 2.5 – 1.5mm; brass (AML); both ends faceted; rivet present.

1431   TL74   2209   (368)
l 31.5, d 2.5 – 1.5mm; brass (AML); both ends faceted; contents ?degraded leather.

1432   TL74   119   (364)
l 32mm, d *c*.2 – 1mm; gunmetal (AML); wide end faceted.

1433   TL74   1280   (368)
l 33mm, d *c*.2 – 1.5mm; brass (AML); wide end possibly broken off, narrow end faceted; rivet hole.

1434   BWB83   1924   (313)
l 35mm, d 2.5 – 1.5mm; brass (AML); narrow end faceted; rivet hole.

1435   SWA81   4989   (2082)
l37mm, d 2.5 – 1mm; brass (AML); wide end faceted.

Unphased

1436   BWB83   2269   (128)
l 27mm, d 2 – 1.5mm; brass (AML); narrow end faceted; rivet hole.

In contrast to the above items, some mainly earlier objects of a broadly similar character, which are all more than 40mm in length and have no evidence of rivets, cannot be identified with certainty. None of them contains identifiable material that can be interpreted as the remains of a lace. The same is true of later examples of comparably large size. These bigger items are listed below as possible chapes (nos. 1437–1449). Traces of wood in a brass (AML) tube 39mm long, *c*.5mm in diameter and broken off at both ends (BIG82 acc. no. 4058, from a ceramic-phase 7 deposit) hints at other functions for some of these items.

Discussion

The tighter, figure-hugging fashions from the 14th century onwards (Newton 1980, 3 & 8) would have produced a great demand for laces. Cf AR Goodall (1983, 232) for a similar chronological pattern in the chapes found at Sandal Castle in Yorkshire. The London assemblage adds to the pre-1400 finds of chapes in Northampton (Oakley 1979, 263) and at Sandal Castle (Goodall no. 40).

Two forms of chape were defined at Northampton (Oakley 1979, 262–63): Oakley's type 1
corresponds with those having edge-to-edge
seams, (the second category there, with a fold
along each seam, appears to be of post-medieval
date, and is unrepresented among the medieval
London finds); no chapes with overlapping seams
like no. 1445 are mentioned in the Northampton
report. There is apparently a greater variation in
length among the late-medieval chapes in Northampton than among the London finds.

Some excavated chapes in the Museum of
London (Costume Dept. collection) are still
attached to silken thread, which is plaited into
both tubular and flat laces. In several instances
the complete lace survives, with a chape at each
end (fig 181). The available indications suggest
that these particular items may be somewhat
later than the chapes in this present study, but
they are the only complete excavated laces with
typologically identical chapes so far traced in this
country. While a slightly later date (?16th
century) may mean that they have no direct

185 Devil with laced gown, 12th century
(after Winchester Psalter)

bearing on the chapes described above, one of
these previously unpublished examples is illustrated here, because of the fixed reference point
they provide. The items in the Museum's collection include:– a group of ten laces, all approx.
30.5mm in length, and another incomplete example (no acc. nos.): examples found at Moorfields,
attributed to the 16th century (former Guildhall
Museum collection) – acc. no. 22491, (not
plaited, but a tabby-woven ribbon) incomplete;
acc. nos. 22493–4, two incomplete laces, each
with a single chape, one being knotted at the free
end (perhaps these originally went together as
one lace): further unnumbered, complete laces
vary in length between 260 and 370mm: a lace
390mm long retains a chape at one end and the
other is frayed.

A gross of '*poynts* of red leather' listed in a
London haberdasher's inventory of 1378 has been
cited as the earliest traced reference to these
items (Cunnington and Cunnington 1973, 108),
but twelve dozen silk cords for tying on *aillettes*
appear in a record of purchases of horse trappings
for a tournament at Windsor in 1278 (Lysons
1814, 299), and a 1343–44 Great Wardrobe
account mentions two corsets fastened with
silken laces and points (*cum . . . punctibus* –
Newton 1980, 25 – here the chapes seem to have
been noted specifically). See also on a London
agletmakere involved in a dispute in 1365 (Veale
1969, 143), a mention by Chaucer (cited in
Nevinson 1977, 38), the inventory of the stock of
a London glove and purse maker from 1396
(Veale 1969, 144–45), and the *poyntes* noted in a
Wardrobe account of Richard II (Baildon 1911,
514), for other 14th-century references. A devil
illustrated in the 12th-century Winchester Psalter
is wearing a long gown laced at the front (fig 185)
– one end of the lace, with a possible chape,
seems to be shown in this highly stylised illumination (Wormald 1973, pl 21 folio 18; the garment is
discussed by Staniland – 1969, 10–13). Fifteenth-
century continental-European illustrations depict
laces, in some instances with chapes clearly
visible, in women's dress at the front of the
bodice (and on sleeves?), and in men's dress
attaching sleeves and hose to the body garment,
and also on the cod-piece. The Marienaltar painting of 1460–65 by the Master of the Marienleben
(National Gallery inventory no. 706) seems to
show a belt with two narrow pendent thongs at

one side ending in chapes, worn by a woman. Pourpoints and aketons (both jacket/tunic-like garments, the latter worn with armour) apparently had fastening laces with metal chapes in the mid fourteenth century (Newton 1980, 55 and 136, citing another Great Wardrobe account of 1343–44, where 216 aiguillettes for nine aketons are noted – ie 24 for each aketon).

The reference to an *agletmakere* in London in 1365 shows that lace chapes were made in the City a century after the form seems to have been introduced (Veale 1969, 145). Nevertheless, one gross 'agulet' (sic) were among the goods imported by ship to London in 1384 (Public Record Office, Customs Accounts E122/71/8 – reference kindly provided by Vanessa Harding). By 1466 the range of items in different metals made by London 'chapemakers' (ie makers of chapes for swords and daggers) included *anlettes* (chapes for laces) of two types – tailed and round (Sharpe 1912, 64). The difference between these two kinds remains enigmatic in view of the uniformity of the chapes identified from early 15th-century deposits.

Although drawstrings are known on excavated shoes from London from at least as early as the 11th century, and lacing to fasten footwear seems from excavated specimens to have continued in use over the whole period considered in this present volume (Grew and de Neergaard 1987, 2–3), the only metal shoe-lace ends among the recent finds are flat tabs, made from folded iron sheeting (cf strap-ends nos. 589 & 593). There is no indication among the excavated chapes which items of clothing (or other articles, such as bags or cushions laced at the side) the laces would have been used to fasten.

It has been suggested that chape-like objects were used as holders for pins (Groves 1966, 49 and pl 58, cf Nöel-Hume 1970, 255). As has been pointed out (IH Goodall 1975, 145) this is unlikely to have been the function originally intended for these objects, though it may have been an occasional secondary use.

Some pens made of copper-alloy sheeting are known from 15th-century contexts, with the same edge-to-edge seams on the tubes as for the chapes (eg Woods 1982, 256–57 no. 4 fig 25 – this

186   Undressing for the bath (a servant bores a spy hole from the next room); 15th century (after Wavrin Master, *Histoire de Girat de Nevers*, Bibliothéque Royale, Brussels MS 9631 f.11)

187   Virgin and Child (by Jean Fouquet) early 15th century

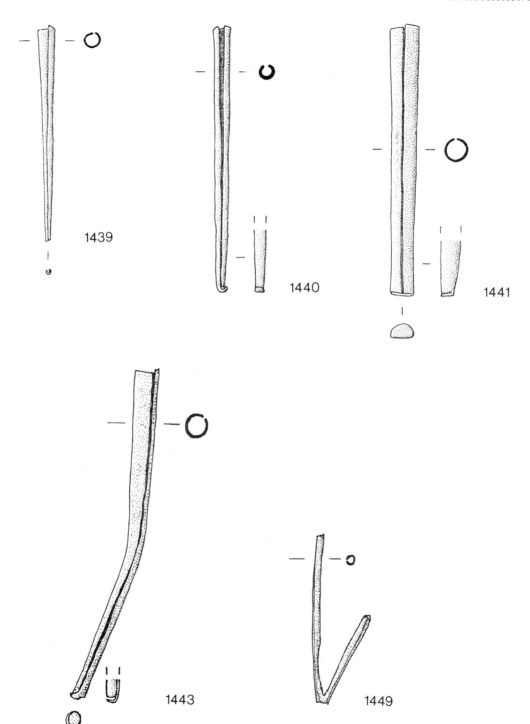

188   Possible lace chapes (1:1)

Der lxxxvj bruder der do starb, hyeß Dyetz Gürtner Nestler

189 Lace-chape maker, German, *c.*1425 (from Treue et al. 1965, pl 73)

one has a tiny spoon at the opposite end from the nib, though MoL acc. nos. A2405 and 1574 are plain here, like the free ends of chapes). The similar size of these pens provides an alternative interpretation of the larger, more robust but incomplete items of this general type (for example no. 1437; the other items of comparable size here seem either too flimsy to have been pens, or they differ in having the wider ends neatly cut off transversely).

If all the items listed below are also regarded as chapes, it is possible to see a gradual standardisation in size and in the finishing of the ends, with the longer, larger-diameter ones becoming less common after the middle of the 14th century. Since late-medieval depictions indicate a greater elaboration in some arrangements involving laces, with a stronger emphasis on their decorative possibilities than previously, it might have been expected that variation in chapes themselves would have increased.

POSSIBLE LACE CHAPES

Ceramic phase 8 (*c.*1230–*c.*1260)

1437 TL74   acc. no. 2203   (context 1347)
l 43mm, d 4.5mm (not obviously tapering), broken off at both ends, the sheeting is thicker at one end; gunmetal (AML).

Ceramic phase 9 (*c.*1270–*c.*1350)

1438 SWA81   3371   (2134)
l 57mm, d 5 – 6mm; gunmetal (AML); narrow end broken off.

1439 SWA81   1893   (2137)   fig 188
l 58mm, d 4.5 – 6mm; gunmetal (AML); wide end faceted and has untrimmed end overlap.

1440 SWA81   625   (2051)   fig 188
l 70.5mm, d 5 – 3mm; bronze (AML); wide end faceted, narrow end has folded tab; the sheeting is relatively thick.

1441 SWA81   1187   (2149 area)   fig 188
l 72.5mm; d 8 – 6mm; gunmetal (AML); narrow end has folded tab, wider end has untrimmed overlap.

1442 SWA81   1684   (1280)   probably phase 9
l 85mm, d 10 – 4mm; bronze (AML); narrow end has folded tab.

1443 SWA81   1967   (2065)   fig 188
l 90mm, d 6 – 3mm; bronze (AML); narrow end has folded tab.

1444 BWB83   3587   (163)
l 100mm, d 4.5 – 3.5mm, both ends broken off; bronze (AML).

Ceramic phase 11 (*c.*1350–*c.*1400)

1445 BWB83   3732   (338)
l 59mm, d 6 – 4mm; brass (AML); overlapping seam.

1446 BWB83   1680   (317)
l 61mm, d *c.*5 – *c.*4mm; brass (AML); narrow end has a folded tab (the corners of which have not, as on the other examples, been rounded off); relatively thick sheeting.

1447 BWB83   2721   (329)
l 63mm, d *c.*4.5 – *c.*2.5mm; gunmetal (AML); narrow end has tab folded over.

1448 BWB83   4633   (299)
l 67mm, d *c.*5 – *c.*3mm; bronze (AML).

1449 BC72   4156   (88)   fig 188
l 70mm (bent), d 1.5mm (not tapering); gunmetal (AML); contents degraded fibre – uncertain whether textile, leather, or roots.

Hair accessories

Changes in hairstyles and headdress are very noticeable from the figurative art of the 12th to 15th centuries, but until recently little of this was reflected in the archaeological record. Excavated material from London is now beginning to redress this lack and detailed evidence is becoming available for the first time. Accessories discussed here include four silk mesh hairnets, a hair-piece stitched to a silk filet (hairband), wire frames to which veils were attached originally and fragments of silk-covered wire and purl (coiled wire). Pins are described in a separate chapter, although many of them would have held hair and veils in place.

Knotted mesh hairnets became part of the usual headdress for women in 13th-century England. They were often worn with two white linen bands: one, a *barbette*, passed under the chin and the other, a *filet*, went round the forehead (frontispiece & fig 139; Cunnington and Beard 1960, 10 and 79). Silk thread was used for four hairnets of this type recovered from the city, one from a late 13th-century deposit (ceramic phase 8), two from a deposit of the second quarter of the 14th century (ceramic phase 10), and a tiny fragment from a deposit of the late 14th century (ceramic phase 11). The nets were made in the round with a netting needle; a cord was subsequently threaded through the long loops at the crown and a fingerloop braid was stitched to the short loops at the lower edge. A more detailed account of them is given in a companion volume in this series (Crowfoot et al. forthcoming). Seven silk hairnets of knotted mesh were recovered from deposits in Dublin which are provisionally dated to the 11th or 12th centuries (Pritchard 1988, 156), but the London examples appear to be the earliest preserved from England.

The filet and barbette had declined in popularity by the early decades of the 14th century and women's hair became more visible. The old style was superseded in fashionable circles by plaits worn on each side of the face (figs 9 & 190), a fashion which had begun to evolve in France before the end of the 13th century (Evans 1952, 214). An illumination in the margin of the Luttrell

190   Plaited hairstyles *c.*1340 (after *The Romance of Alexander*, MS Bodl.264 f.173v)

191   Maid dressing her lady's hair *c.*1325–35 (after the *Luttrell Psalter*, BL Add. MS 42130 f.63)

Psalter shows a lady's long hair being prepared for pinning up in this style by her maid (fig 191), but only women who had long, thick hair could wear this style without the addition of a false hair-piece.

The recovery of a hair-piece from a deposit in London dating to the second quarter of the 14th century offers new information on how this style was achieved (no. 1450, fig 192). The piece is made from human hair which appears to have been blond originally. One plait 382mm in length is preserved complete and it is bound along its length with strands of similar hair, Z-twisted into fine cords, to help the plait hold its shape. There

is also part of a second hair-piece, or the piece may have been added to the full-length plait to give it extra body. The plait bends in the middle and from this it can be inferred that it was worn folded in two with the bend falling just below the ear. The plait was stitched with a strong two-ply thread of silk used double to a narrow silk braid which was woven using 26 tablets. This braid, which would have been worn across the forehead as a headband, was decorated along its length with a series of at least 18 mounts and, from the impression that the mounts have left outlined on the surface of the braid, it appears that they were of octofoil-form. The mounts seem to have been

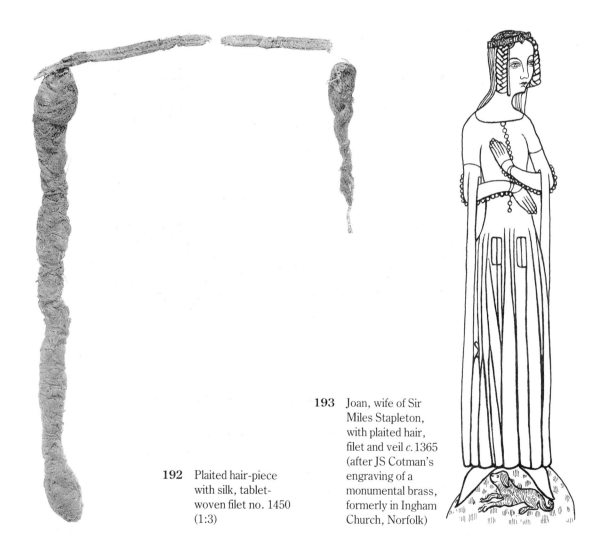

192   Plaited hair-piece
       with silk, tablet-
       woven filet no. 1450
       (1:3)

193   Joan, wife of Sir
       Miles Stapleton,
       with plaited hair,
       filet and veil *c.*1365
       (after JS Cotman's
       engraving of a
       monumental brass,
       formerly in Ingham
       Church, Norfolk)

stitched, rather than riveted, to the braid and then removed before it was discarded. This removal implies that the mounts were probably made from precious metal, perhaps with gemstones, since mounts of cheaper metals seem to have been thrown away with no desire to recycle them. A veil may have been placed under the filet at the back of the head in order to cover the neck as can be seen in contemporary depictions (fig 193).

The use of false hair was not a new departure in 14th-century England. Long plaits worn down the back, sometimes almost to the ground in the 12th century, often required the artful addition of extra hair, and from regulations issued by the church in Florence in the early 14th century it appears that plaits of flax, wool, cotton or silk were sometimes substituted for hair (Newton 1980, 131).

Examples of wire frames that were presumably used for headdress have also been recovered from deposits of the 14th and early 15th centuries in London (ceramic phases 9–12). These are made from drawn wire, usually copper-alloy but occasionally iron. The ends of the frame were sometimes hammered flat and pierced with a small hole (no. 1451); others appear to have been clenched or shaped into a point (nos. 1453–54).

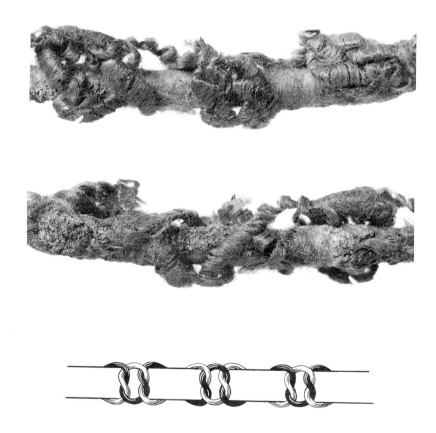

194 Silk-covered iron wire frame with figure-of-eight knots made
from two silk-covered copper alloy wires no. 1465:
(A) front, (B) back (5:1), (C) diagram of knots

Unthrown silk was bound round the wire in at least 11 examples (nos. 1455–65), all from a late 14th-century deposit where conditions of preservation were exceptionally good compared with elsewhere in the city. Onto this wire foundation finer and more flexible silk-covered wires were applied. One iron frame covered with silk has two interlinking silk-covered wires twisted round it in the form of tiny figure-of-eight knots (no. 1465, fig 194). These knots are in turn bound in place by silk thread. Another silk-covered wire frame, which is made from copper-alloy rather than iron, preserves traces of a silk veil stitched to the frame (no. 1461, fig 195). This veil is tabby-woven from Z-twisted thread and its open texture means that it would have been semi-transparent. There are fragments of seven other silk veils of this type from late 14th-century London but none of these are associated with a wire frame (Crowfoot et al. forthcoming).

The use in the 14th and 15th centuries of silk-covered wire has received scant attention. Similar wire is today sometimes called 'millinery wire' and its association with headdress is, therefore, longlived. It is possible that the output of female workers known in 13th-century Paris as *chapeliers de fleurs*, who are listed in the *Livre des Métiers* (Depping 1837, 246; Evans 1952, 24), involved the creation of wire headdresses. A bequest in 1328 by Roger Sterre to his daughter Matilda of a garland of pearls with silk streamers (Cal Wills 1889, 335) may refer to a product of this type but until documentary research on this topic has been undertaken much must remain speculative. Silk-covered wire could be twisted into a myriad of forms to decorate items of either secular or sacred use and it is generally artefacts of the latter type that have been preserved. These include a number of 14th and 15th-century reliquaries embellished with multi-coloured silk-wire flowers, often with seed pearls and beads threaded onto them, for example a 15th-century reliquary crown of St Kunigunde in Bamberg cathedral, West Germany, and ritual cushions known as 'paradise gardens' for nuns taking their vows (Meckseper 1985, 476–8, no. 392). By the 16th century similar wire decoration was sometimes used on bookcovers. Some motifs are made from wire which was coiled into a spiral form, a type of wire known as *purl* in the 16th century (Digby 1963, 10), and this helps to explain the lengths of small coiled wire among the pieces from London (nos. 1455–57, 1459 & 1460).

Another type of wire hair ornament from London is a double ended, U-shaped pin decorated with twisted wire which was found at Finsbury Circus (MoL acc. no. A1384; fig 196). The style of the twisted wire decoration, which is also associated with brooches (nos. 1339–41, fig 164), a finger ring (no. 1622, fig 217) and cosmetic tools (fig 251), suggests that it dates to the 14th century. It was probably used to hold in place a woman's linen headdress, the decoration imitating the effect of a frilled headdress edge such as that portrayed on the effigy of queen Eufemia of Denmark (fig 167; Newton and Giza 1983, 142–50).

Further examples of coiled wire from late 14th and early 15th-century deposits may have come from headdresses but this is uncertain since the pieces are fragmentary and, as pointed out above, wire of different gauges was used to decorate many types of artefact. One item merits attention here, although it does not appear to have been a hair accessory. This is a strip of delicate wire twisted into cinquefoils (no. 1467, fig 197). The cinquefoils are arranged in pairs which were formed by twisting two lengths of very flexible narrow gauge wire. Sometimes a pair of cinquefoils was worked from the same length of wire and sometimes alternate wires were used. The finished piece probably would have been stitched onto a cloth for decoration rather in the manner of a braid.

Hair-piece

1450 BC72 acc. no. 3695 (context 250) ceramic phase 10 fig 192
Plait of human hair, probably blond European (identified by Harry M. Appleyard), l 382mm; bound with Z-twisted cords of similar hair and stitched to a tablet-woven braid with a two-ply thread of silk which is used double. A second piece of hair, l 120mm, is twisted rather than plaited, attached to it at each end are threads of two-ply silk. The braid was woven with 26 tablets; the outer two tablets on each side had four holes and were given quarter turns in one direction, the remaining 22 tablets were threaded through two holes and were turned alternately backwards and forwards; surviving l 240mm, w 10mm. Groups of holes recur at intervals of *c*.10mm along the braid indicating where mounts were positioned.

195 Silk-covered, copper alloy wire headdress frame with traces of a silk veil no. 1461 (1:1)

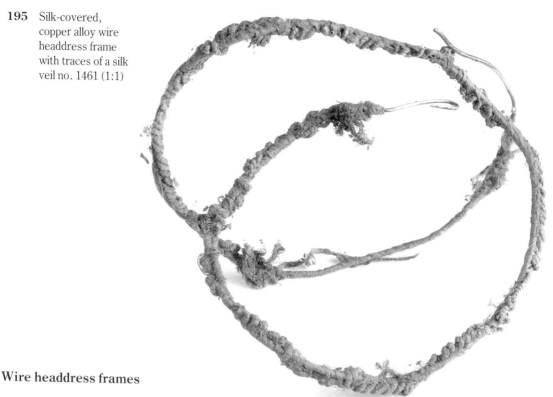

Wire headdress frames

Uncovered wire

1451 SWA81 acc. no. 1696 (context 2081) ceramic phase 9
Brass (AML); one end hammered flat and pierced and the other broken off; d 1mm; surviving l 400mm; d of hole 1.5mm.

1452 BC72 3989 (88) 11
Brass (AML); three conjoining fragments bent double and partly twisted; d 1mm; surviving l 475mm.

1453 SWA81 4998 (2069) 11
Brass (AML); one end clenched and the other broken off; bent out of shape; d 1.5mm; surviving l 300mm.

1454 SWA81 2166 (2102) 12
Brass (AML); one end clenched into a triangle and the other broken off; d 2mm; surviving l 350mm; w of frame 193mm.

Wire covered with silk

1455 BC72 3851 (89) 11
Brass wire including one piece with silver coating (AML) covered with silk thread and coiled into spirals; three fragments; d 0.2mm; longest piece 83mm.

196 U-shaped hairpin with twisted wire decoration, MoL acc. no. A1384 (1:1)

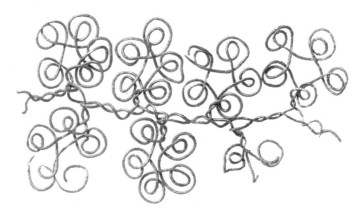

197 Brass wires twisted into pairs of cinquefoils no. 1467 (2:1)

1456 BC72 1860 (55) 11
Copper-alloy wire; three out of the four fragments appear to have been covered with silk, but it has generally decayed. The finer wire is coiled into spirals; d of wires (a) c.0.3mm, (b) 0.8mm; surviving l (a) 350mm, (b) c.800mm, 170mm and 105mm.

1457 BC72 2691 (79) 11
Brass wire (AML) covered with silk thread and partly coiled into spirals; two fragments; d 0.2mm; total surviving l c.800mm.

1458 BC72 3990 (88) 11
Copper-alloy wire covered with silk thread; d 1.5mm; surviving l 90mm.

1459 BC72 3992 (88) 11
Brass wire (AML) covered with silk and coiled into spirals; broken into at least eight fragments; d c.0.2mm; longest piece 220mm.

1460 BC72 3995 (88) 11
Copper-alloy wire covered with silk thread and coiled into spirals; four fragments; d 0.8mm; total surviving l 360mm.

1461 BC72 3624 (150) 11 fig 195
Copper-alloy wire bent into the form of a double circle and hooked at one end, terminating in a point. Covered with unthrown silk thread onto which foundation a series of coiled spiral loops made from twisted silk-covered wire are bound with silk. Silk veil stitched to wire with thread of two-ply silk; d of wire 1mm; surviving l 570mm.

1462 BC72 4499 (150) 11
Copper-alloy wire with traces of silk thread; 3 fragments; d c.0.6mm; total surviving l 565mm.

1463 BC72 4500 (150) 11
Brass wire (AML) covered with unthrown silk thread, much of which has decayed leaving the metal exposed; four fragments; d of wire c.0.3mm; total surviving l 400mm.

1464 BC72 4822 (150) 11
Brass wire (AML) covered with silk thread and coiled into spirals; three fragments; d of wire 0.8mm; surviving l 125mm.

1465 BC72 2062 (88) 11 fig 194
Iron wire covered with silk thread. Superimposed over this foundation are small knots made by interlacing two lengths of finer silk-covered wire (the metal core of which has disintegrated); these wires were then bound to the foundation with a silk thread; d of iron wire 2mm; nine fragments; total surviving l c.430mm.

1466 BC72 2613 (79) 11
Brass wire (AML) covered with silk thread and coiled into spirals S-twisted round a piece of silk-covered iron wire in a regular pattern; two fragments; (a) brass wire c.0.2mm, total surviving l c.465mm; (b) iron wire d 1mm; total surviving l 176mm.

Wire accessory of uncertain use

1467 TL74 2929 (275) 11 fig 197
Brass wire (AML) twisted into cinquefoils arranged in pairs. These were worked alternately from one side to the other using two wires. Seven pieces and numerous small fragments; d of wire c.0.4mm; total surviving l c.330mm.

Pins

More than 800 pins from six sites were examined for this survey. This does not represent the total extent of the collections as the quantity of pins from 14th and early 15th-century deposits is particularly extensive, but an exhaustive study was ruled out through lack of time. This abundance is not surprising especially when one considers that the trousseau of Princess Joan, who was contracted to be married in 1348, included 12,000 pins for her veils (Nicolas 1846, 75 & 145–6), while the cargoes of two Venetian galleys calling at Southampton in April 1440 on their way back from Flanders included 83,000 pins, which was the merchandise of seven merchants (Cobb 1961, 77–80). What is surprising is how few pins have apparently been excavated for this period from other towns in England.

The pins excavated recently in London not only demonstrate the vast increase in the use of pins by the 14th century, but also reveal changes in manufacturing methods that lead to a transformation in their size during the 12th century. The pin shank became finer due to a greater availability of drawn wire and in keeping with this the head, which was made separately from the shank, became smaller. This decrease in size affected how pins were used, since they would no longer have been worn instead of brooches to fasten thick outer garments. It is apparent from wardrobe accounts of the 14th century that pins were used to fasten veils (Staniland 1978, 228) and many examples are depicted in 15th-century art, where they are shown pinning the folds of linen headdresses or securing transparent veils to the hair or round the shoulders to the front of a gown (fig 198). It may be supposed that pins were put to a similar use in the late 12th and 13th centuries but evidence to confirm this is needed.

Pins with decorative heads continued to be produced, but they are far less common than in previous centuries and their diminutive size meant that the decoration would not have been immediately obvious to an onlooker. Indeed only 21 of the pins included in this survey proved to be decorated. Three of these were recovered from deposits dating from the late 12th century (ceramic phase 6) and they are particularly interesting

as the head of each was made from a different material to that of the shank. Fifteen of the other pins with decorated heads came from deposits dating to the 14th century (ceramic phases 9, 10 and 11). Three of these have coral heads, while on the other 12 the decoration draws on a limited repertoire of geometric patterns and lacks the virtuosity displayed by many of the larger pins of the Anglo-Saxon and Viking epochs which would have been worn more conspicuously. Three pins with acorn heads complete the range of decoration represented. Two of these are from deposits of the early 15th century and they would therefore have matched the ornament on some contemporary dress accessories, particularly strapends on girdles (see nos. 648 & 651, fig 92, no. 675, fig 94, and nos. 704 & 705, fig 97), and tassels on drawstring pouches, which were sometimes made to resemble acorns (Ceulemans et al. 1988, 208–9 no. 41).

Pins were also made from bone in medieval England (MacGregor 1985, 112) but there are none from deposits dated later than the early 12th century in recent excavations in the City (Pritchard forthcoming). Certain forms of pins with hipped shanks (ie shanks with a swelling towards the tip to help prevent the pin from slipping out of position) and, less often, looped heads, which were made from copper alloy as well as from bone up to the middle of the 12th century and possibly a little later, have been recorded from the City in the past (Roach-Smith 1859, pl XXXIV, nos. 26, 28 & 29; and pl XXXIV, nos. 20 & 21), and very recently from a site at Cannon Street. These are interpreted by some scholars as dress-pins and by others as hair-pins (Margeson 1982, 249), but whether all of them were indeed worn as dress accessories remains arguable. The virtual absence of bone pins after the early 13th century appears to have been because they could not compete in fineness with metal pins which were essential for use with fine veiling.

Three pins from late 12th-century London illustrate the introduction of new forms at this period. Their shanks are made from fine brass wire with a gauge of *c*.0.5mm; these are among the finest preserved from London for the whole

medieval period. Two have small round heads made from a blob of glass (colour pl 7C), which was placed on the shank in a semi-molten state without the use of solder. Analyses have shown that the glass has a high lead content. The head on no. 1469 is green, coloured by adding copper to the lead oxide and silica, and it is similar, for example, to that used in a setting of a contemporary brass finger ring (see no. 1620) and also to a pinhead from Coppergate, York (Radley 1971, 49). The other glass pinhead is near black (no. 1468), and this colour was also used for beads, annular finger rings, and inlays in stone and ivory carvings, although this is the first example apparently excavated from London. The third pin has a highly stylised circular head, cast in pewter, depicting the face of Christ framed by a nimbus with a billeted edge. The pinhead is partly carried out in openwork so that the head also takes on the form of a cross (no. 1470, fig 199 & colour pl 7E). A tiny hollow tube behind the decoration accommodates the top of the pin shank, the two parts being soldered together. The making of this pin presumably coincided with the start of the mass output of pilgrim badges commemorating the martyrdom of Thomas Becket, and the religious symbolism of the pinhead suggests that this may have influenced the way that it was worn.

From the character of these three pinheads there can be little doubt that they could have been made in England. Evidence from various towns, particularly York, shows that glass with a high lead content continued to be made in urban workshops to at least the late 12th century (Hendersen in Tweddle 1986, 226), while the high-medieval mass production of pewter jewellery, which had its beginnings in Anglo-Saxon England, is noted elsewhere in this volume (see p viii).

Most of the remainder of the pins came from deposits of the 14th and early 15th centuries, but there is a small number from 13th-century deposits, so that there is a continuous sequence for the period covered by the survey. Nine of the pins with decorative heads were selected for XRF analysis by the AML supplemented by two with plain spherical heads, which were picked out not

198 Stefan Lochner, triptych *c.* 1440, Cologne cathedral. Detail showing ladies wearing pins in their hair and dress

at random but because they looked different from the rest. One of these from a late 14th-century deposit (ceramic phase 11) proved to be silver (fig 199, no. 1488 – BWB83 acc. no. 2755), and the head and upper 5mm of the shank of the other pin (which is the longest pin in the collections) is tin coated, causing it to appear whiter presumably in simulation of silver (fig 204 SWA81 acc. no. 444). No other examples of pinheads coated with tin were identified in the collections and, although a coating may have been very thin so that it quickly wore off, it seems unlikely that the practice was widespread before the 16th century, with the exception of some larger cloak-size pins which are earlier than the period of this survey (Armstrong 1922, 77).

Examination by eye and with a binocular microscope enabled most of the pins lacking in decoration to be divided into two basic types: those with solid heads and those with wound-wire heads (fig 200). A few could not be so easily classified and it is uncertain to which category they belong, or whether they can be considered to form a further group. In addition a large number of pins had lost their heads. Traces of solder and bent shanks indicated that these pins had been used and could not, therefore, lay claim to represent the unfinished stock of pinners. No differences were discernible with regard to the pin shanks, and fine grooves along the length of most shanks indicate that the wire was pulled through metal drawplates (Caple 1983, 277).

The solid heads of pins are spherical or hemispherical, with a range of variations in between since they appear to have been hammered into shape rather than being cast in moulds (fig 201). The hemispherical heads can be either flat on top or flat on the underside and this is also illustrated by the two most common types of decorated pinheads, the pentagonal heads generally having a flat underside and those with quadrants and dots that are flat-topped (fig 201). It is, however, unusual for the plain pinheads to be as flat as the decorated heads, which were smoothed with a file.

Pins with wound-wire heads appear to have been introduced into London at a similar period to those with solid heads (described above) and to have abounded in similarly large numbers. They also can be sub-divided into two types, those with spherical heads and those with heads that have

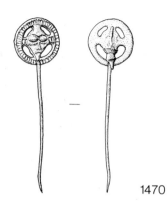

1470

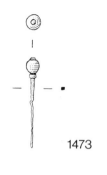

1473

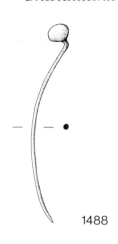

1488

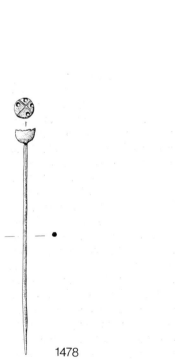

1475

1478

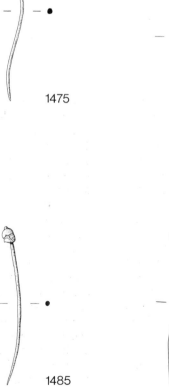

1476

1485

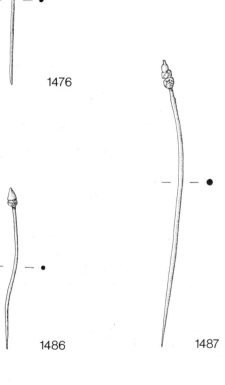

1487

1486

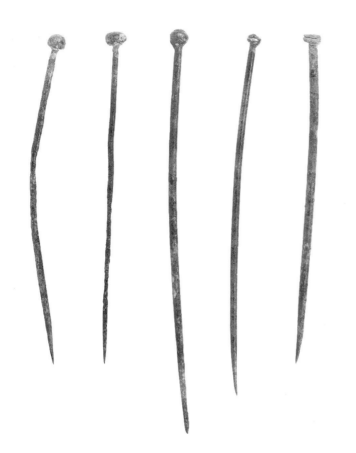

200 Pins from a late
14th-century
deposit in London.
The two on the left
have solid heads and
the three on the
right have wound-
wire heads (2:1)

been stamped flat (fig 200). The wire was twisted round the shank in either a Z or a S-direction; two twists were usual which corresponds to Christopher Caple's findings and indicates that there was a uniformity of head wire length throughout the industry (Caple 1986, 140–3). Generally wound-wire pinheads are smaller than those which were wrought.

Pins with decorative heads from the 14th and early 15th centuries fall into five groups. A red coral head distinguishes one type, of which three, all from 14th-century deposits, are represented here (colour pl 7D, nos. 1471–72, fig 199, no. 1473). Two of these have been summarily published before, when the head was tentatively identified as red jasper (Henig 1974, 196, nos.

199 Pins with decorated heads, except no. 1488 which is silver (1:1)

137–8 fig 40). The third example is a more recent find and was identified as coral at the Ancient Monuments Laboratory by Marjorie Hutchinson. The coral heads, unlike those made from glass, are pierced through the centre with a hole. This was probably accomplished with a fine steel drill similar to that described by Theophilus for piercing pearls (Hawthorne and Smith 1979, 191–2). To fix the head on the shank, a small length of wire was twisted round the shank and soldered in place to form a collar. Next the head was placed onto the shank coming to rest on top of the wire collar. The protruding shank was then cut off just above the coral head and hammered flat so that the metal splayed outwards securing the coral in place. Coral beads were attached to wire in a similar manner for use on other ornaments of dress and display, such as brooches, pendants, crowns and reliquaries, and their use as pinheads may have developed from this. (See pp 309–11 for the work-

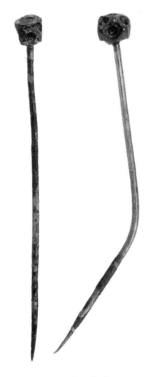

201 Pins with different forms of solid heads from a late 14th-century deposit in London (2:1)

202 Polygonal-headed pins with dot ornament: on the right no. 1483 and on the left no. 1484 (2:1)

ing of red coral in 14th-century London).

The other four types of decorated pins have solid metal heads which differ only in their form or manner of decoration. Pins with pentagonal heads appear to have been worn in the first half of the 14th century (nos. 1474–77, figs 199 & 201). These were followed by pins with hemispherical heads decorated with a pattern of quadrants with dots, made by stamping the flattened head with a die (nos. 1478–82, figs 199 & 200), and also by polygonal-headed pins with dot ornament (fig 202, nos. 1483–84). The latter recall similar patterned pinheads of earlier epochs, although these were always larger (eg Addyman and Hill 1969, 68, fig 26, nos. 6–8; Waterman 1959, 78, fig 11, nos. 5–7 & 10–12). A pin with a cubic head patterned with dots in the manner of dice was also reco-

vered from a 14th-century deposit. By the early 15th century pins with heads shaped in the form of acorns were being worn (figs 199 and 203, nos. 1485–87) and analysis reveals that two of these have heads made from gunmetal rather than brass, which was used for the shank. The fact that pins with similar decoration have been reco-vered from several sites in the City suggests that they must have been mass-produced. That none of these patterns appears as yet to have been recorded elsewhere in Europe begs the question whether all pins were imported, as is frequently asserted. There is also evidence that a certain type of pin was particularly associated with Eng-land, since among several thousand pins purch-ased in 1400 from Jehan de Bréconnier, a Parisian pinner, for the Duchess of Orleans were 500 *de la façon d'Angleterre* (Longman and Loch 1911, 16).

Although it appears that the repertoire of decoration employed on pins of the 14th and early 15th centuries was extremely limited, without these examples from London even this conclusion would not have been possible, since depictions of pins in contemporary art do not show decoration.

Pins with decorative heads have a restricted range of shank length compared with those from the rest of the collections, where a much greater diversity in length is apparent. Thus the pins with decorative heads range in length from 37mm to 84mm whereas other pins with solid heads range in length from 29mm to 199mm and those with wound-wire heads range from 24mm to 113mm (fig 204). It may, therefore, be surmised that the former had a more limited use.

203 (left) Pins with acorn heads, nos. 1485–87 (2:1)

204 Pins with long shanks from 14th-century deposits in London. The three on the left have solid heads and the one on the right has a wound-wire head. The head of the pin with a fine-gauge shank on the centre right is tin coated. (1:1)

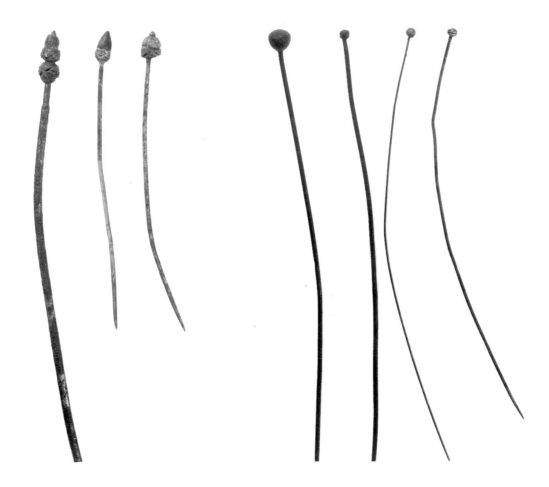

Pins with decorated heads from late 12th, 14th and early 15th-century London.

	site, acc. no. & context	ceramic phase	fig	head type	head size (mm)	length (mm)	gauge of shank (mm)	metal of head /shank
1468	BIG82 2867 (4761)	6	pl 7C	'black' glass	6	52	0.5	brass
1469	BIG82 3405 (6974)	6	pl 7C	green glass	5	50	0.5	brass
1470	BIG82 3259 (6219)	6	199 pl 7E	head of Christ	12	45	0.5	pewter/brass
1471	CUS73 48 (I, 12)	9	pl 7D	red coral	4	84	0.8	–
1472	CUS73 95 (V, 8)	9	pl 7D	red coral	4	broken	0.8	–
1473	BWB83 4568 (279)	11	199	red coral	4	broken	0.9	bronze
1474	BWB83 2185 (108)	10		pentagonal	3	42	0.8	–
1475	BC72 4581 (123)	10–11	199	pentagonal	4	37	1	–
1476	TL74 123 (306)	11	199	pentagonal	3	41	0.9	–
1477	BWB83 5156 (157)	11		pentagonal	3	45	1	–
1478	BC72 2539 (79)	11	199 & 201	quadrants with dots	5	59	1	–
1479	BC72 3930A (88)	11		quadrants with dots	4.5	54	1	–
	BC72 3930B (88)	11		quadrants with dots	4.5	61	1	–
1480	BC72 3769 (89)	11		quadrants with dots	5	64	1	brass
1481	BWB83 1660 (137)	11		quadrants with dots	5	62	1.2	–
1482	TL74 2327 (416)	11		quadrants with dots	4.5	59	1	–
1483	BWB83 5156 (157)	11	202	14 facets with dots	4	41	1	–
1484	BWB83 3073 (283)	11	202	10 facets with dots	3	39	1	–
1485	TL74 120A (364)	12	199 & 203	acorn	3	42	0.9	brass/brass
1486	TL74 120B (364)	12	199 & 203	acorn	2	42	0.9	gunmetal/brass
1487	BC72 2930 (113)	?	199 & 203	acorn	3.5	77	1.2	gunmetal/brass

Precious metal

1488	BWB83 2755 (341)	11	199	spherical	5	47	0.8	tin coating, silver

Beads

The 217 beads and related items discussed below are made from materials more diverse than those for any other category of object in this volume. Semi-precious minerals – especially amber (which comprises more than three quarters of the objects in this section) and also jet and rock crystal are represented, but there are no precious materials. Manufacturing waste and associated finished beads (interpreted as accidental losses in the workshop) comprise amber, jet and red-coral items. Some of the evidence for amber-bead making from the BC72 site has already been published (Mead 1977, 211–14); it can now be dated more closely, and is here presented in a different format, together with similar material found on other sites. Only two glass beads are included, and there are also only two of metal. No wooden bead or definite example of bone from the sites included here comes from the period with which this present study is concerned (both of the latter materials are represented among beads of 16th-century date from waterfront sites). Waste pieces of bone from which beads were cut are included below, since they are clear evidence for the use of bone beads which have not been recovered. Beads, including pearls, were used in large numbers as elaborate trimmings for dress in the late-medieval period (eg St John Hope 1907, 474 pls XLVIII & XLIX and D King in Alexander and Binski 1987, 471 no. 606 for seed pearls set in trails on a mitre).

It is likely that many of the larger beads described below were for rosaries. Rosaries should properly consist of three *chaplets*, each of 15 *dizaines* of Ave Marias (each of 10 smaller beads) and 15 Paternosters (each being a single larger bead), but the number of beads varied in tne medieval period (Evans 1970, 50). The medieval paternosterers of London do not have a high profile in published records (Veale 1969, 141) though they had given their name to Paternoster Row to the north of St. Pauls Cathedral by the early 14th century (Harben 1918, 459). A London jeweller's stock in 1381 included beads of wood, white and yellow amber, coral, jet and silver gilt, Ave beads of jet and blue glass, and cheaper sets of bone for children (Riley 1868,

455). Most of these materials are represented below, apart from silver (instead there are cheaper tin versions) and wood, and the glass beads that have been recovered are green. The recent finds also include beads of crystal. The coral beads below are probably too small to be from rosaries. The tiniest of them all (no. 1551) would have had to accompany a number of similar beads of the same material even to exploit its striking colour. Recovery of items as small as beads is somewhat haphazard. Sieving is probably the ideal means of recovery, but it was not carried out on the sites represented below.

A relatively simple descriptive classification has been adopted for the shapes of the beads described below, in preference to very complex alternatives used elsewhere, since the value of presenting this evidence at a greater level of detail is not clear (cf Guido 1978, 4 & 5).

AMBER

For a recent assessment of Baltic amber and its use (principally in a prehistoric context) see CW Beck in Todd 1985; for a wider summary of the material and its occurrence, see Webster (1975, 510–12). The large number of well preserved amber items recovered includes three groups of material representing bead-manufacturing waste: items from TL74 layers 2515, 2525, 2529 and 2532 – all from the same ceramic-phase 9 dump (late 13th/early 14th century), from BC72 context 250 of ceramic phase 10 (mid 14th-century, cf Mead 1977), and from TL74 context 306 of ceramic phase 11 (late 14th-century). The great majority of all these items are unfinished. Apparently finished beads are listed first; those from the same contexts as the manufacturing waste are marked *. See under Jet, Red Coral and Bone below for further items from BC72 context 250.

A basic threefold colour division has been used below: orange, yellow and offwhite (translucent pale yellow) see colour pl 9C; the beads are complete and translucent unless stated.

Four pieces of amber from the following items, selected to cover the period and the different colours represented (nos. 1493, 1498, 1514 and 1524), were analysed by Mike Heyworth by infra-red spectroscopy (details in Heyworth 1988). Comparison of the absorption spectra obtained with data on amber from known sources indicates an absorption band between 8 and 9 microns for all the London samples, which is characteristic of amber from Baltic deposits. This does not, however, indicate whether the amber was imported from the Baltic Sea area, or was collected on the beaches of eastern England.

Medieval amber beads have been excavated in Canterbury and Southampton (Henig and Woods in Sherlock and Woods 1988, 228 no. 147; Platt and Coleman-Smith 1975, 275–76 no. 1956 fig 249).

Finished beads

Spherical/spheroid

Paternoster with amber beads

1489 BC72 acc. no. 1836 (context 79)
ceramic phase 11   colour pl 8H
Incomplete; two lengths of tubular tablet-woven silken braid (identification by F Pritchard – an earlier description as cotton in Mead 1977, 212, is erroneous), respectively 116 and 66mm, and presumed to be originally from a single piece of string; the former has five and the latter has three surviving rounded beads. The sizes and colours do not match precisely and the shaping is uneven – beads on the shorter piece of string vary between diameter 7mm, length 7.5mm and d 8, l 9mm (ie spheroid and oval), four of the beads are translucent orange, the other is slightly opaque; one bead has a fragment of twig as an inclusion, and they all have faults – stress marks, chips, areas of discolouration, etc. The variations and imperfections of the beads mean that this would not be considered a high-quality item by modern standards.

1490 TL74 2406 (*2529) 9
Spherical; d 3mm; yellow.

1491 TL74 2443 (*2525) 9
Incomplete; spheroid; d 4, l 5mm; yellow.

1492 TL74 2432 (*2525) 9 fig 205
Biconvex; d 5,l 3mm; yellow.

1493 TL74 2437 (*2525) 9
Incomplete; biconvex; d 6.5, l 4mm; yellow.

1494 BC72 2886 (*250) 10
Incomplete; spheroid; d estd c.8, l 7.5mm; yellow.

1495 BC72 4790A–G (*250) 10
Seven items, all spheroid:
d 3.5, l 3mm; yellow.
d 3.5, l 3mm; orange.
Incomplete; d 5, l 4mm; orange.
Spherical, d 6mm; yellow.
Incomplete; d 7, l 6mm; yellow.
Incomplete; d 8, l 6.5mm; opaque yellow.
Incomplete; d 12, l 15mm; orange.

1496 TL74 344D (*306) 11
Incomplete; spheroid, d 5+, l 6.5mm, yellow.

1497 TL74 344C (as preceding)
As preceding; d 6, l 5mm; yellow.

1498 TL74 344B (as no. 1496)
As preceding; d 6+, l 6.5mm; yellow.

1499 TL74 344A (*306) 11
Incomplete; spheroid; d 8, l 6.5mm; yellow with stress lines.

1500 TL74 982 (414) 11
As preceding; d 8.5, l 6mm; yellow.

1501 TL74 981 (414) 11 colour pl 9C.
As preceding; d 12, l 6.5mm; yellow.

Oblate spheroid/flat-ended

1502 TL74 1439 (47) 9 fig 205 & colour pl 9C
Flat ended; d 5, l 3.5mm; orange.

1503 BC72 4790H & I (*250) 10
Two items:
Oblate spheroid; d 5.5, l 2.5mm; yellow.
Oblate spheroid; d 7.5, l 3mm; yellow.

1504 BC72 1794 (55) 11
Flat ended; d 8.5, l 4mm; yellow, with opaque areas.

1505 TL74 343 (291) 11
Incomplete; flat-ended; d 8.5, l 5mm; yellow.

1506 TL74 560 (*306) 11
Incomplete; flat-ended; d 9,l 6mm; yellow.

Oval

1507 SWA81 1310 (2028) 9 fig 205
d 5.5, l 9mm; orange.

1508 BC72 4790J (250) 10 colour pl 9D
d 6, l 7mm; orange with stress lines.
Possibly discarded as a reject.

Other round shapes

1509 TL74 2438 (*2525) 9
Incomplete; one end convex, the other flat; d 8,
l 4mm; turning possibly not finished.

Squared

1510 TL74 2226 (2417) 9 fig 205
Corners faceted; 7×7mm, l 3mm; opaque yellow.

1511 TL74 2433 (*2525) 9 fig 205
Sides bevelled; 5.5×5.5mm, l 2.5mm; yellow.
Possibly discarded because chipped.

Polyhedral

Both appear to be from cuboids with facets at the
corners (ie 14-sided beads); one face (?the end) on
each fragment still has the marks from trimming
visible, the other surviving faces are polished.

1512 TL74 2407 (*2529) 9 fig 205
Fragment; estd *c*.14+×14+mm; yellow.

1513 CUS73 285 (III,10) 9
Fragment; estd *c*.16+×16+mm; yellow.

Unfinished beads

The pieces of amber recovered illustrate all the
stages of manufacture, from the block in its
natural state through to the finished bead. Each
stage is characterised by specific tool marks,
alone or in combination (see colour pl 8). The
block was first trimmed by a knife – into a roughly
cylindrical shape when a round bead was intended. Knife-trimming leaves a characteristic
combination of ovoid or bean-shaped pits together
with parallel lines (marking the direction of the
cuts, which are always at a right angle to the pits'
long axes). The pitting occurs where tiny lumps
of amber were dislodged by the cutting. The
central hole for the string was then drilled
through the trimmed block, starting from both
ends and meeting near the middle. The bead was
then mounted on a lathe and smoothed by turning
against a sharp tool to achieve the desired shape.
The initial turning left grooves on the surface,
which were removed in the final polishing. This
final stage was probably carried out by holding a
broad-ended tool against the lathe-turned bead.
The groups of waste material listed below are
categorised according to the stage of manufacture
reached, and whether the final shape was to be
rounded or squared etc. Some incomplete items
may have had evidence of a subsequent stage of
manufacture on the missing portion. Untrimmed
blocks, offcuts and fragments too small to be
categorised are omitted. Unworked pieces and
uncompleted items of amber have also been found
in York, though dating is uncertain (Tweddle
1986, 186).

Stages of manufacture (see colour pl 8 B–F)

		number of beads defined, all contexts
A	knife trimmed	22
B	broken during hole drilling	6
C	hole fully drilled, but no obvious sign of turning etc on exterior (?broken at first stage of turning or faceting)	61
D	broken, turning etc for shaping incomplete	40
E	broken, turning etc for shaping complete, but polishing incomplete	8
	total defined from all stages:	<u>137</u>

The above figures suggest that turning was the most
hazardous stage of manufacture (6 out of every 7
defined breakages) with initial knife-trimming next, and
relatively few breakages seeming to result from hole-
drilling (the figures may only be statistically valid for
rounded beads).

BC72 4790 (250) 10 colour pl 8 (cf Mead 1977,
211–2):

1514 & 1515

Rounded:

stage A	19
stage B	3
stage C	41
stage D	36
stage E	6

Squared:

stage B	1
stage C (also acc. no. 2885 from same context, cat no. 1515)	2
stage E	2

1516

Miscellaneous:

Incomplete fragment – quarter of a disc (fig 205); radius 11mm, 3mm deep; drilled hole in centre; one side turned for shaping and not polished, other (?)partly polished, but with straight (?)abrasion lines; edge turned for shaping, but not polished. Apparently from stage E, this item may be a bead of unfamiliar shape, though it may have been intended for some entirely different purpose.

total from context: 110

205   Top – amber beads, with reconstruction of no. 1512; bottom – jet bead waste fragment (drawings 1:1, photograph 6:1)

1517–21   TL74   (context 2515)   ceramic phase 9:
Rounded:

stage A	no. 2436	1
stage B	no. 2424	1
stage C	nos. 2400, 2421, 2422	3
total		5

1522–29   TL74   (2525)   9:
Rounded:

stage A	no. 2448	1
stage C	nos. 2430, 2431	
	also a disc-like bead – no. 2444	3
stage D	nos. 2436, 2442, 2446, 2447	4
total		8

1492

1507

1510

1511

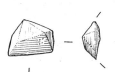

1512

1516

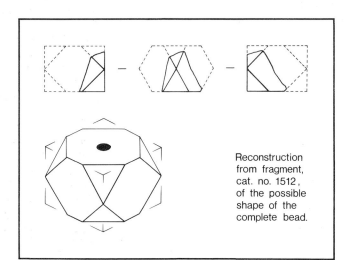

Reconstruction from fragment, cat. no. 1512, of the possible shape of the complete bead.

1546

TL74 (2529) 9:
1530–33
Rounded:
stage C nos. 2403, 2404, 2405; also a disc-like bead, possibly an offcut from a longer bead to remove a damaged end – no. 2402 4

1534
Squared:
stage A no. 2394 (colour pl 9C) 1

1535
Miscellaneous:
no. 2401 – spheroid bead; d 11, l 6mm; knife trimmed and with drilled hole; segment cut off at side with a knife; the hole (d 3mm) is wider than those in the other amber beads recovered. It seems most likely that this was intended to be a bead of larger diameter than the others here, but that it was damaged prior to turning, and the segment removed so that the undamaged part could be used. It is not clear from the part recovered whether this, the missing segment, or both pieces, would have been considered usable.
total from context 6

TL74 (2532) 9:
1536–38
Rounded;
stage C nos. 2413, 2414, 2415 3

1539
Squared;
stage B no. 2412 1
total from context 4

1540–42 TL (306) 11:
Rounded;
stage A no. 344 1
stage C nos. 242, 307 2
total from context 3

The following two single finds of unfinished beads (both of stage C as defined above) could be from other dumps of manufacturing waste or they may be stray losses:

1543 TL74 2217 (1877) 9
squared bead

1544 TL74 159 (291) 11
rounded bead

1545 An unused natural block of amber from SWA81 (context 2028) acc. no. 1309, ceramic phase 9, was the only waste piece recovered from the site, but a finished bead (no. 1507) was also found in the same deposit.

The above material clearly demonstrates the continuing import of what is, by today's standards, relatively poor-quality raw amber into London for manufacture in the late 13th and 14th centuries. 'German' amber was thought to be of poor quality relative to that from the East in the 15th century (Evans 1922, 224).

JET

1546 BC72 acc. no. 4792 (context 250)
ceramic phase 10 fig 205
Incomplete and unfinished bead; d 8, l 8+mm; knife trimmed, apparently broken during the drilling of the hole (the lines and pits on the surface are similar to those on the unfinished pieces of amber, including those from the same deposit (see above). See bone and red coral (below) for further associated items. This jet bead, presumably intended to be rounded, has reached stage C as defined in the preceding section on amber.

This mid 14th-century bead is the sole fragment of jet from the period included in this study among recent London finds, though jet beads from the late 15th or early 16th century have been recovered. Since jet beads were, judging from this one piece, almost certainly being manufactured along with amber and red coral (see above and below), it is surprising that more jet fragments were not recovered.

The source of the jet was probably Whitby in Yorkshire (cf Dunning 1965, 61). Jet- and amber-working waste has been found on the same site in York, though dating is uncertain (Tweddle 1986, 186). Finished jet beads have been excavated in Oxford (Henig in Lambrick and Woods 1976, 218–19 no. 44 fig 13).

Jet was believed, according to a 12th century source, to have anaesthetising powers (Evans 1922, 55). For its uses in general, see Webster (1975, 516–18).

RED CORAL

This material is well-known archaeologically from Iron-Age prestige goods, and also in medieval reliquaries and upper-class objects which have never been buried. Very little seems to have been recognised hitherto among excavated material of similar date to the London finds discussed here. Coral is mentioned in French and possible

English lapidaries from the 12th century onwards (Evans 1922, 198–99 & 221). It was thought to be effective against thunder and lightning, imprisonment, and defeat in battle, and in the medical realm against gout, sore eyes, and other diseases. A necklace of coral and lodestone was thought in *c*.1300 to assist in childbirth (ibid, 31–36, 55 & 112). None of this is necessarily of specific relevance to the excavated items.

Red coral (*Corallium rubrum*) grows in the Mediterranean Sea (see Webster 1975, 499–501). For contemporary awareness in north-west Europe of the marine origin of exotic red coral, see Evans (op cit, 227). The long-distance trade which brought this material to England was primarily based on other goods, such as spices and Italian textiles.

Five unworked pieces of coral (up to d 3, l 13mm, see colour pl 11A) found washed out of a section at the Trig Lane site may have come from the same dump as nos. 1547–51. One retains pieces of marine serpulid worm tubing on the surface. (Dr P Cornelius and Dr JD George of the British Museum, Natural History, kindly identified the coral and the casts.)

All three deposits in which coral items nos. 1547–51 were found also produced amber bead-manufacturing waste (see above), corresponding with unfinished item no. 1551 here.

The worked coral seems to have been cut with a knife into lengths, leaving a mark on one side close to the edge. This relatively hard material appears to have broken under the initial pressure from the blade. Since each item has such a mark only at one end, the pieces could have been produced by manually snapping the coral down to a double length, and using a knife to cut this into two pieces of the present size. It would be virtually impossible to snap this substance manually below a certain size.

It is difficult to see how the two small beads (nos. 1550 & 1551) and some of the unfinished items described below would have been used. The two largest pieces (no. 1548) could have been cut into shorter lengths to make beads, or they might have been intended for mounting without further adaptation as charms to help in childbirth or for babies (John Cherry, pers. comm., cf Evans 1922, as above). The relatively small size of most of the pieces recovered could imply that the quality of the products of the

industries represented was not particularly high (cf the amber above). Pins nos. 1471–73 have coral heads that are larger than any of the pieces described in this present section. The head of the last resembles a spheroid bead, d 4mm, while the other two are of less regular shape.

1547 TL74 acc. nos. 2381A–E (context 2532) ceramic phase 9
Five pieces, including two bifurcated ones, up to 24mm long; apparently untrimmed.
Cf stage A for amber above.

1548 TL74 2380A & B (2529) 9 fig 206
Two pieces up to 38mm long; apparently untrimmed.
Cf stage A for amber.

1549 TL74 2393A–H (2525) 9
Eight pieces up to 12mm long, including a thick basal piece attached to a fragment of white cup coral of a different family; two pieces are trimmed at one end.
Cf stages A and B for amber.

1550 TL74 2410 (2529) 9
Incomplete; d 3, l 4mm; sides mainly not trimmed, though there is at least one cut longitudinal face; drilled from both ends; possibly broken during the drilling of the hole.
Cf stage B for amber.

1551 TL74 2411 (2529) 9 fig 206 & colour pl 11A
d 1.5, l 1mm; sides knife-trimmed, ends possibly as intended, though this tiny bead might have been shortened by breakage; if a drill was used to make the minuscule hole (?not a natural feature), it would have been at about the limit of contemporary technology (see Hawthorne and Smith 1979, 191–92, for Theophilus' reference to fine steel drills for putting the holes in pearls).
Cf stage B or C for amber.

1552 BC72 4790 (250) 10 fig 206
d 3, l 2.5mm; ends cut and snapped; hole not drilled; sides not trimmed.
Cf stage A for amber.

These 18 items came from deposits at both sites which also produced amber working waste – they are therefore probably from the same two workshops.

BONE

No definite bead of bone was recovered from contexts of the period covered by this volume, but items which appear to be bead-manufacturing waste come from several different deposits. Con-

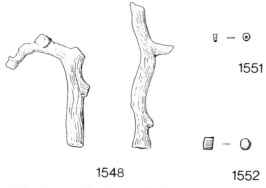

1551

1548   1552

206   Red-coral bead waste (1:1)

centrations of waste were found at the BC72 site and in the City Ditch at Ludgate (LUD82).

Identification of the bone is by James Rackham (Greater London Environmental Archaeology Unit), apart from no. 565, which was identified by P Armitage. While specific identification of the waste pieces and beads has not been possible, it appears probable that the distal shaft of cattle femurs, the shaft of cattle metapodials and possibly the ascending ramus of cattle jaws were being utilised to manufacture the beads. All three of these bones would give sufficient area of flat, thick material suitable for the manufacture of beads, but other bones could also be suitable.

Possible unfinished beads

1553   BC72   acc. no. 2256   (context 83) ceramic phase 11
Oblate spheroid bead(?); l 10, d 3.3mm; rounded sides; flat ends; incised line on one end, possibly from marking out for drilling the holes or cutting the beads from the block.

1554   BC72   4240   (88)   11   fig 207
Oblate spheroid bead(?); l 10, d varies from 4 to 7mm; uneven turning marks remain.

Cf the three waste panels from the same context (nos. 1574–75 & 1578).

1555 A finished, but unstratified oblate-spheroid bead (TL74 acc. no. 2230, d 7mm, l 7mm bone, possibly from an ox metapodial shaft, fig 207) can be identified with confidence, though it could be from a later period than that considered here (cf a similar example from an early 16th-century context, BC72 acc. no. 3, of bone – see fig 207). The holes drilled in both these beads – like those in nos. 1553 and 1554 – are of comparably large

diameter (both *c*.2.5mm) with that in no. 1582 of rock crystal. They are larger than the holes in the other excavated beads described here.

1556   BC72   4791A–C   (250)   10
Three unfinished pieces – all are knife trimmed at the sides and ends. In contrast with the preceding bone items and all the recovered panels from which bone beads were cut, the holes in these are drilled along the grain.

A)   d 6, l 11mm; both ends cut almost through, then broken; no evidence of turning (fig 207).
B)   incomplete; d 7+, l 10mm; one end cut and broken, turning has been started at the other end.
C)   as preceding; d 6+, l 9mm (fig 207).

Presumably A was accidentally lost prior to turning, while B and C broke at an early stage of that process.

(Amber, jet and coral beads were recovered from the same context.)

Turning-waste panels

Trimmed, flat panels of bone, from which beads have been cut by turning (cf colour pl 10). MacGregor (1985, 101–02, cf idem 1989, 115) discusses in detail similar items, which have been found widely in late-medieval and later contexts. Although MacGregor suggests that it may not be possible to decide whether the objects being made in each case were buttons or beads, the small diameter holes (up to d *c*.10mm) left in relatively thick panels (4.5mm+) by removal of the products seem consistent with the diameters of the two (?)later beads noted above. No convincing bone button seems to have been identified from the medieval period so far. Waste comprising panels and unfinished beads, as well as complete beads, have been recovered from late 15th/16th-century deposits at St Denis in France (Meyer 1979, 2.2.1, illustration reproduced by MacGregor 1989, 118 fig 3).

The following stratified panels are secondary evidence for bone beads in medieval London in the late 13th and 14th centuries (ceramic phases 9 and 11). Those marked with a star are especially convincing as bead-manufacturing waste in that in each case they retain an almost completed bead. The ones with holes in excess of 10mm in diameter would have produced disc-like rather than spherical objects.

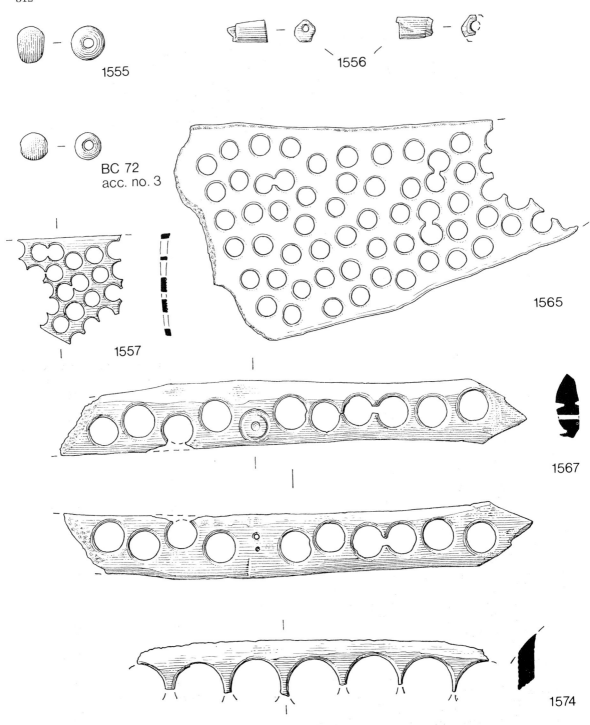

207 Bone beads – top left; waste – top right; waste panels – below
(1:1)

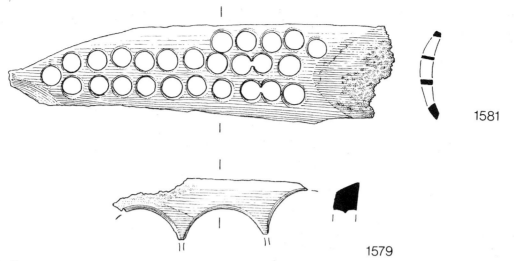

1581

1579

208   Bone-bead etc waste panels (1:1)

	site	acc. no.	context	ceramic phase	hole diameter (mm)	number of beads
1557	LUD82	203	1076	9	4.5	25+

Indeterminate; large, flat piece of bone, possibly fragment of scapula blade (fig 207).

1558	LUD82	202	1076	9	5.5	17+

Long-bone shaft, probably ox femur, distal shaft fragment.

1559	LUD82	276A	1041	9	6	20+ *

Long-bone shaft, ox-sized.

1560	LUD82	276B	1041	9	6	10+

Long-bone shaft, ox-sized.

1561	LUD82	263A	1060	9	6	14+ *

Long-bone shaft, probably ox distal femur.

1562	LUD82	263B	1060	9	6	9+ *

Long-bone shaft, ox-sized.

1563	LUD82	263C	1060	9	6	11+ *

Possibly fragment of ascending ramus of ox.

1564	LUD82	143	1077	9	6	24

Long-bone shaft, ox-sized animal, possibly portion of femur shaft.

1565	LUD82	172	1077	9	6	61+

Probably ox scapula (fig 207).

1566	LUD82	155	1042	9	7	11+

Long-bone shaft, ox-sized

1567	LUD82	171	1042	9	8	11*

Long-bone shaft, ox-sized animal, probably lateral side of ox metatarsus (fig 207)

1568	LUD82	145A	1077	9	8	7+

Long-bone shaft, probably ox femur distal shaft fragment.

* = single unfinished bead still in place

site	acc. no.	context	ceramic phase	hole diameter (mm)	number of beads
1569 LUD82	145B	1077	9	8	5+
Long-bone shaft fragment, probably ox-sized.					
1570 LUD82	264	1060	9	8.5	6+
Long-bone shaft, possibly ox metapodial.					
1571 LUD82	275	1078	9	8.5	16+
Long-bone shaft, ox-sized.					
1572 BC72	2658	79	11	5	6+
Long-bone shaft, possibly distal end of ox metapodial.					
1573 BC72	4371	150	11	8	12+
Long-bone shaft, ox-sized.					
1574 BC72	4013	88	11	13.5	7+
Indeterminate; ox-sized (fig 207).					
1575 BC72	4014	88	11	13.5	6+
Long-bone shaft, ox-sized.					
1576 BC72	4370	150	11	13.5	3+
Long-bone shaft, ox-sized.					
1577 BC72	4271	150	11	estd. 13–14	6+
Long-bone shaft, ox-sized.					
1578 BC72	4012	88	11	14	6+
Long-bone shaft, ox-sized; long bone shaft, probably distal posterior shaft fragment of ox metapodial.					
1579 BC72	2657	79	11	estd. 21+	3+
Indeterminate; ox-sized. (?too wide for beads) (fig 208)					
1580 TL74	1198	375	12 or earlier	10	5+
Long-bone shaft; ox-sized.					
1581 BWB83	6070	310	12	6	26
Long-bone shaft, ox-sized (fig 208).					

The LUD82 finds listed above are from the late 13th/early 14th-century fills of the city's defensive ditch, with the exception of the two from context 1042, which is interpreted as the fill of a pit dug into the material that had built up in the ditch (the pit fills could have reincorporated material dug out when the pit was cut). These items form the largest group of bone bead-making waste from London. BC72 contexts 79, 88 and 150, all from the same late 14th-century dump, together yielded eight panels (only the first two of which may have produced beads), complemented by what appears to be an unfinished bead (no. 1554 from context 88, see above), which has come from a quite different kind of bone. Apparent evidence for bone bead making (the possible unfinished beads) was found in only one deposit with evidence for bead making in other materials (amber, jet and coral) – BC72 250, of the mid 14th century. None of the above waste panels has such associations. It seems probable that the exotic materials, the purchase of which would have required a certain level of capital, were worked by specialists, whereas bones from butchery or the kitchen would have been almost universally available. Comparison with the results of detailed work on the far more extensive bone and antler manufacturing evidence (notably of combs) from *c*.1000 to *c*.1350 excavated at Lund in Sweden would probably suggest that the London bone waste, with a maximum of 15 pieces from any single site (Ludgate), corresponds with 'home-craft production' (the earliest stage defined at Lund, where it has been dated to *c*.1000 to 1020), which is taken to have catered for a limited, undeveloped market (Christophersen 1980, English summary 221–31). The discrepancy depends on a number of factors, not least the interpretation of how representative the dumped material found in London is of the industry it stands for. Because of this, the transfer of that analytical approach to the London bone waste seems inappropriate. Subsequent finds of far greater numbers of turning-waste panels, of slightly later date, from the BOY86 site may be more appropriate material for Christophersen's method.

For a late-medieval illustration of bead turning, see colour pl 10.

ROCK CRYSTAL

1582 SWA81 acc. no. 2506 (unstratified, found with spoil containing objects attributable to ceramic phases 8 & 9) fig 209 & colour pl 9B
Oblate spheroid; d 11.5, l 7mm; two incised lines define a central band; this band (the widest part of the bead) and the areas around the ends of the hole are considerably chipped from use.

1583 TL74 1119 (291) 11 fig 209 & colour pl 9B
Oval bead with seven facets, each spiralling approx-imately three quarters of the way around the surface over the full length; d 13, l 18mm; the cutting and polishing is even, apart from slight over cutting of one facet at each end; the hole may have been drilled right through from one end, though the same appearance could be the result of drilling a channel from each end to meet in the middle, and then drilling right through again to remove any unevenness at the point of joining (the slight magnification of the hole given by the cut of this bead could have induced the workman to carry out the extra operation); considerably chipped around each end of the hole, and at the high points along the edges of the facets.

Rock crystal was believed at the end of the middle ages to have been formed from ice over a long period of time (Evans 1922, 228). It is found in many locations, notably in the Swiss and French Alps (Webster 1975, 178). Its untinted clarity led to widespread use in prestige items. (see also soudé gem below)

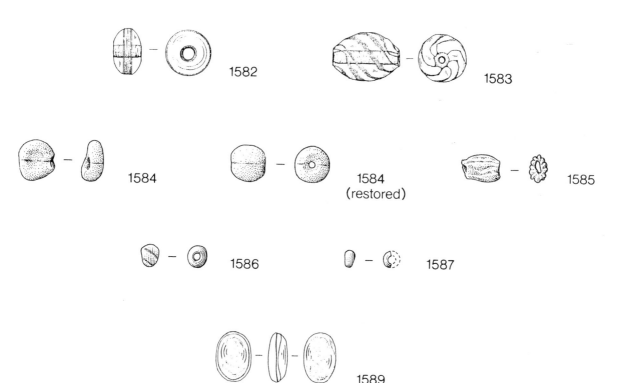

209 Top – rock-crystal beads; second row – tin beads; third row – glass beads; bottom – rock-crystal soudé gem (1:1)

TIN

1584 SWA81 acc. no. 2788 (context 2108)
ceramic phase 12   fig 209
Flattened; 1 9mm; tin (AML).
Presumably originally spherical – a spherical bead also found in London (private collection, colour pl 11C) is the same length and probably provides an indication of the original appearance.

1585 SWA81 3294 (2112) 12 fig 209
Distorted; 1 10mm; longitudinally ribbed; tin (AML); presumably originally oval.

No other excavated base-metal bead of early 15th-century date has been traced in this country. Pewter beads are known in the Saxo-Norman Cheapside Hoard (Guildhall Museum Catalogue 1908, 119 nos. 39–43 & pl LIV no. 13; VCH London 1909, 160 fig 17). One part of a 13th-century stone mould for metal beads has been excavated in Lund in Sweden (Bergman and Billberg 1976, 207 fig 151).

GLASS

Very few glass beads have been recovered from deposits of the period covered by this volume. (BIG82 acc. no. 3282 is thought to be residual from the Roman period – Margaret Guido, pers. comm. – and is therefore omitted here.) The difficulty of seeing these small objects in the ground is somewhat lessened (as with those of red coral) by their bright colouring. Their present sparsity may therefore suggest that glass was not very popular for beads among medieval Londoners. Sieving on future sites could throw further light on this question.

The cargoes of ships bringing goods to London in 1384 included 13 paternosters of *glasse*, 14 gross *bedes de glas* and three gross paternosters *de vitro* (Public Record Office, Customs Accounts E122/71/8 – reference kindly provided by V Harding).

Comments on the methods of manufacture of the two following beads were provided by J Bayley.

The diverse indications of date do not permit any useful inference.

1586 BIG82 acc. no. 3282 (context 4533)
ceramic phase 7   fig 209 & colour pl 9A

Spheroid; d 5.5mm; translucent green; surface decayed. Trace flanges at the ends suggest that this was produced by extrusion followed by cutting down to the size of the individual bead (ie a cane bead); the roughly parallel sides to the channel internally contrast to the concavity of beads produced by this method in earlier periods.

1587 TL74 1274 (368) 12 fig 209 & colour pl 9A
Incomplete; spheroid; d 4mm; translucent green; undecayed.
The channel flares more markedly at one end than at the other, a feature of beads produced by piercing a hot blob of glass set on a flattish surface with a sharp instrument.

UNMOUNTED ITEMS

Pearl

1588 TL74 acc. no. 3267 (context 2416)
ceramic phase 9   colour pl 11B
Spherical; d 4.5mm; pale pinkish-buff; no evidence for use. This, the only pearl recovered from the recent sites, is a perfect sphere – an unusual feature in the period prior to commercial culture – and its pink hue is uncommonly pronounced. By modern standards this pearl is of quite poor quality (staff of Cartier Ltd, pers. comm.). It is difficult to gauge how valuable it might have been considered by the medieval jewellery trade.

S Morris (British Museum, Natural History) comments that this object could not have passed into the dumps at the Trig Lane site as kitchen waste (despite the vast numbers of oyster shells found there) since the native edible oyster (*Ostrea edulis*) does not produce gem-quality pearls. It is probably significant that the same group of dumps produced some of the amber- and coral-working waste described above. A pearl of this quality was almost certainly an exotic import, intended for decoration, though Evans (1921, 63) notes a reference to English pearls in abundance. It is unlikely to be from a freshwater mussel (*Anodonta anodonta, A. cygnea,* or *A. margaritifera margaritifera*). A plausible source is the tropical marine pearl oyster (*Pinctada margaritifera*). The pearl trade of the Persian Gulf was at its height in the 13th–14th centuries, and this item, found in a deposit from the middle of this period, may have been imported from the Near East or India (cf Webster 1975, 447). Pearls were used in a range of different items of jewellery in the medieval period (Evans 1921, 36). Among goods imported to

London by Hugelin Gerard, a foreign (?Venetian) merchant, probably in *c*.1380, were two parcels of pearls valued at £124.6.6d and £211.4.2d (Public Record Office E101/128/13, reference kindly provided by V Harding).

Rock-crystal soudé gem

1589 TL74 acc. no. 2396 (context 2455) ceramic phase 9 fig 209 & colour pl 9B

12×9mm, two plano-convex pieces of rock crystal, one slightly larger than the other, each polished *en cabochon*, with the flat faces then stuck together – apparently by means of a thin layer of opaque pinkish-red material (deeper red at some points, especially on the surface) – to make a biconvex oval stone. Subsequent to being joined together, the twinned cabochon (*soudé*) has been wheel-polished from both sides (not as highly as the main faces) giving a smooth but slightly uneven girth, which does not coincide exactly with the join between the two parts. This gem could have been used in a ring or a brooch, or for a pendant with a metal band around the girth for attachment – and also concealing the join. We are grateful to Marjorie Hutchinson for discussion about this object.

It has not proved possible to analyse the material in the centre. Although x-ray diffraction might identify the reddish material, it is not feasible to obtain an adequate sample for the technique without damaging the object.

The original colour of this material was perhaps a more even, deep crimson-red than is apparent now. It may have been intended to give the impression that this was a natural red stone, such as a ruby (though it is unlikely to have deceived anyone familiar with genuine gemstones), or the substance itself may have carried some virtue. Compare the use of wax Paschal candles in amulets (stamped with the Lamb and flag and known as *Agnus Dei*) worn as a protection from evil (Evans 1922, 168). Some kind of protective container would have been necessary for wax, and it is possible that the two pieces of rock crystal in the present object were to protect the material between, at the same time keeping it clearly visible (a stamped design would not have been possible here). Similarly, at the end of the medieval period a pyx made with a crystal body allowed the host to be seen in the way that a monstrance would (Oman 1957, 80).

For 'doublet' stones (perhaps soudés) set in stars on the purple-velvet canopy of the carriage used by Princess Eleanor (the daughter of Edward II) at the time of her marriage to the Count of Guelders in 1332, see Safford (1928, 114). For composite stones in general see Webster (1975, 398–99).

This object is from the group of dumps which produced the pearl and evidence of amber and coral working (see above).

Chains

None of the small chains among the recent finds can unequivocally be identified as a dress accessory, though the first one described here probably was, and all of those listed below could have been. Necklaces are not common in medieval art until the end of the period considered here, and bracelets at this date are so rare that any example would be an exceptional object.

To judge from late-14th and 15th-century representations, elaborate collars for the neck were fashionable among the upper classes, often serving to indicate political allegiance. The use of precious metal and highly decorative linking might suggest that a chain was intended to be worn, but there seem to be no definite criteria. Most of the excavated chains are of relatively simple manufacture, with plain, round or S-links. Most are of copper alloy or iron, but one is of silver. It is assumed that none of the plainer base-metal chains would have been worn around the neck as a piece of jewellery in its own right. Some of them could have been used to hold groups of keys (like a modern key ring – a 16th-century group of seven keys on just such a copper-alloy chain was found at Queenhithe in London – private collection) or other valued possessions – see fig 210. Equally, this kind of chain may have been used for hanging scale pans from a balance arm, for censers, or for other purposes.

SILVER CHAIN

(probably a dress accessory)

1590 SWA81 acc. no. 2397 (context 2115) ceramic phase 12 fig 210
Two thin, plain rings, linked together, each d 22mm; combined weight 1.80 grammes; one link is broken and distorted.

Perhaps part of a collar or other item of jewellery, despite the thinness of the links.

Cf AR Goodall 1983, 231 & 233 fig 1 no. 4 for a remarkably precise parallel (including the break in one link) dated to c.1270–c.1400. See Scott 1986, 83 pl 83, for a chain collar from the 1440s possibly of an appropriate type, worn by an officer of the royal household, though here the links are both heavier, and

decorated. A precious-metal chain might be used to secure an elaborate badge, as with the Dunstable Swan jewel (Cherry 1987, 487–88 no. 659; see also idem 1973, 312, for discussion of chains of gold in the Fishpool Hoard), but the thinness of the two present links seems as incompatible with this as with the other functions suggested above.

OTHER CHAINS

(possibly dress accessories)

Round links

Copper alloy

1591 SM75 20 (146) 6–7 fig 210
l 107mm; each link, which consists of a ring of triply-spiralled drawn wire, interconnects only with the two adjoining ones; the wire has been obliquely cut at each end, and there are minor differences in the degree of overlap at the ends of the spirals; in most links the stack of spirals is slightly inclined, perhaps distorted from a straight stack arrangement.

Cf Mitchiner (1986, 251 no. 983) for an apparently complete chain 260mm long, joined to make a circle (found at Greenwich). This seems too long to be a bracelet as claimed by Mitchiner, but too short for a collar or to be worn doubled on the wrist. The sealed deposit in which the chain from the St Magnus site was found provides a dated context within an excavated sequence, but the early 16th-century date attributed by Mitchiner to this item is broadly consistent with other finds from Greenwich. Cf also Baart et al. 1977, 206, 208 & 210, nos. 379 & 385 for chains of this kind attributed to the early 17th century. This simple form of link seems to have continued to be made for at least four centuries.

S-links

Copper alloy

1592 TL74 2255 (1590) 9 fig 210
Four lengths (not continuous); total length 140mm+; copper (AML); chain consists of eight S-links of D-

1590

1591

1592

1594

1595

1599

210 Chains;
right, chain holding seal matrix – Museum of
London acc. no. 84.266/2 (1:1)

Museum of
London
collection

section wire, each *c*.20mm long, and with a separate loop of similar wire around the central point; simple joins; a loop with an expanding lug, which terminates in a rabetted rod, is connected to what appears to be a fragmentary link like the others.

The loop and lug were probably cast as one, but a break in the loop's circumference may suggest that it was made from the same wire as the links, with the projection added subsequently. A similar chain (MoL acc. no. 16,047) has a loop on one of the links in the middle of the chain, though there are some replacement links, and the present arrangements may not be the original ones. The lug in the present chain would presumably have been fixed into a housing to secure the chain for use, and possibly to act as a swivel.

Cf Heslop in Alexander and Binski 1987 (398 no. 458) for an iron chain with a swivel, attached to a seal matrix dated to the second quarter of the 14th century, fig 210, right (MoL acc. no. 84. 266/2).

1593 TL74 2188 (2924) 9
In four pieces; total l *c*.190mm+; copper (AML); relatively thin wire; two methods of joining are used: one loop into the adjoining loop of the next link, the other loop around the centre of the next link (ie through both its loops) – this gives a pair of doubly interconnecting, overlapping links with little flexibility between them, while the simple joins, which connect every two such pairs, allow for considerable flexibility at these points.

1594 TL74 2206 (1956) 11 fig 210
l 110mm; relatively thick wire; joining as for no. 1593.

1595 BWB83 3692 (300) ?11 fig 210
Total l 135mm; links and joining as for no. 1593.

1596 SWA81 2157 (2111) 12
Three links; total length *c*.13mm; brass (AML); links apparently as no. 1593; simple joining.

Iron

1597 BIG82 3731 (3204) 7
l 78mm; relatively thin wire; joining as for no. 1593.

1598 SWA81 3350 (2161) 9
In two pieces; total l *c*.250mm+; joining as for no. 1593.

1599 BWB83 5633 (204) 11 fig 210
l *c*.200mm; relatively thick wire; S-like links with loops at right angles, and each end meeting the next loop beyond the central point; simple joining; the resultant chain is roughly triangular in section and is tightly interconnected.

Only the first of the above chains can with any confidence be categorised as a dress accesssory. The recent discovery in London of a virtually complete 15th-century silver collar of SS 610mm long, probably worn by a minor official (ie below the rank of knight – Spencer 1985, 449–51), with parallels in art of the 1440s, has not been matched by site finds. Several different forms of chains for wearing have been identified among finds in Amsterdam (Baart et al. 1977, 204–11), but all these post-date the period under consideration in this study.

Some of the pewter items furnished with loops that are included in this volume in other categories were probably (on the evidence of more-complete parallels found in London) attached to crude chains with elongated ring-links (sometimes double) of the same alloy, though there is no hint of these among the objects recovered from the main excavations that have provided the material for this volume. See buckle souvenir no. 573 (cf MoL acc. no. 80.70/3 – fig 80) pendent leaves nos. 1602–04, fleur-de-lis brooches nos. 1360–63, and also MoL acc. nos. 86.362 & 86.406/1 – (fig 211; these last two items together are thought to have been a necklace, which also has pendent lead/tin bells). The fleur-de-lis brooches are part of a further wide range of related items, including pilgrim souvenirs, all of which were worn attached to or suspended from lead/tin chains. The excavated objects are all from the early 15th century, or possibly the late 14th century. Some, if not all, of this varied series of cheap trinkets may be souvenirs bought in Canterbury. The fragile chains which originally accompanied several of them may be seen as the late-medieval equivalent of the today's charm bracelet or necklace. Recycling of the metal following breakage because of their inherent weakness may be the reason for the underrepresentation of these chains in the excavated assemblages.

Pendants

This category covers a diverse range of items, some of which could have stood alone as personal ornaments, such as earrings, while others may have been elements of composite jewellery, such as bracelets and necklaces. Complete surviving examples definitely from the latter two categories are absent from the recently found assemblages (though see parallel for nos. 1602–04, fig 211, and no. 1591 under Chains). Earrings and necklaces are not common in contemporary artistic representations from the early part of this period, and this is reflected in the concentration of the majority of the items listed below in the early 15th century or just before.

Copper alloy

1600 BIG82 acc. no. 3047 (context 3347)
ceramic phase 7 fig 211
Nick Griffiths writes:
Triangular, 34×36mm; gilded copper (AML); the base has a scalloped edge with four indentations, from each of which a double line of opposed, stamped triangles rises to the apex, where they stop below a double horizontal line of smaller stamped marks; an angular projection at the top is pierced for suspension; the convex front has traces of gilding and a triple (originally quadruple) claw, held by an off-centred rivet. Copper-alloy pendants of this general character are normally identified as coming from horse harnesses, and it is difficult to isolate examples which were certainly or probably items of personal adornment. These latter tend to be small and to carry inscriptions of a romantic or talismanic nature (Griffiths 1986, 2). The present pendant is the only one of this kind from the recent excavations that can be identified as of probable personal use, since the lost stone which the claw originally held makes it very unlikely that it was used on a horse harness.

The only parallel known to the writer is a roughly triangular, gilded copper-alloy pendant with a blue cabochon (Tribbick 1974, 94 & fig 43 no. 30).

Lead-tin

1601 BWB83 5808 (298) 11 fig 211
Incomplete disc pendant; d 23mm; lead-tin (MLC); suspension loop at top; the device is a bird; very crude.

No other disc pendant with an apparently non-religious design has been traced from this period. Cf Mitchiner 1986, 168 no. 520, for an example with religious scenes.

Leaves

(See also sheet-iron examples no. 1189 listed under Mounts)

1602 SWA81 3400 (2082) 12 fig 211
l 20.5mm; asymmetrical tripartite leaf joined to a suspension loop; veining on both faces.

1603 SWA81 2033 (2106/2107) 12 fig 211
Incomplete; l 19mm+; lead-tin (MLC); similar to preceding, but more symmetrical and veined on the front only; oblique hatching flanks a central vertical rib on the back; coarser transverse ribbing appears on the front of each of the three parts.

The ribs on the back were produced by channels in the mould which may have served to help the metal flow evenly during casting; the ribbing on the front may have been intended to represent the natural curling of some leaves, such as oak.

1604 SWA81 760 (2097) 12
Incomplete, in two pieces; l c.22mm; similar to preceding but cruder, with radiating lines on back.

These leaves are highly stylised, and may not have been intended to represent any particular genus. Several parallels are known, eg Mitchiner 1986, 181 nos. 590–95, which are all similar to no. 1603 (the description of these as strawberry leaves is as erroneous as their attribution to the shrine of St Edward at Westminster); ibid 239 nos. 911–13 are pendent leaves of different types.

A lead/tin necklace or similar accessory (MoL acc. nos. 86.362 & 86.408/1 – acquired in two pieces) has seven surviving pendant leaves (?of an original eight) and two bells, see fig 211. The leaves in this case somewhat resemble field maple (acer campestre), though there was probably no intention to represent a particular species. Cf Mitchiner ibid, 215 no. 780 – a fragment, which has only a pendant bell surviving.

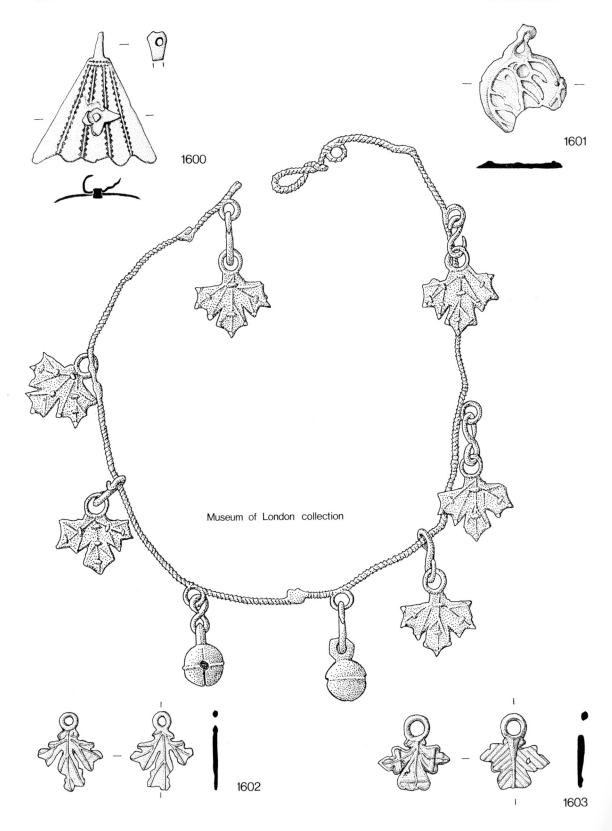

1600

1601

Museum of London collection

1602

1603

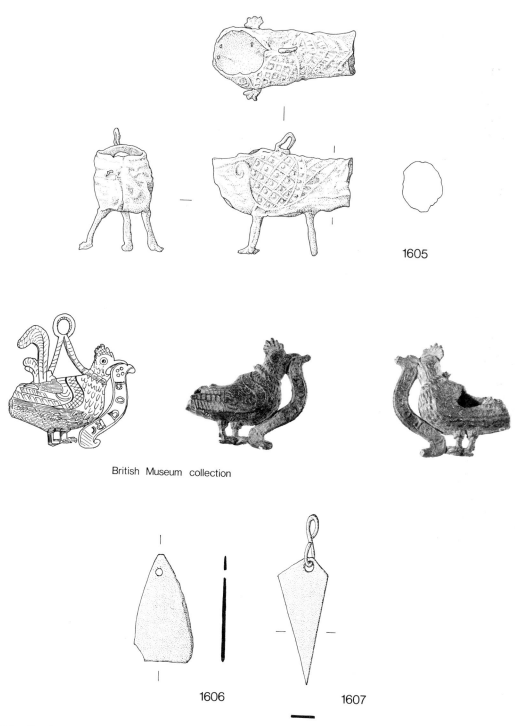

1605

British Museum collection

1606

1607

211 Pendants; centre, necklace – Museum of London acc. nos. 86.362 & 86.401/1 (1:1)

212 Top, bird pendants; bottom, simple pendants (1:1)

Cockerel

1605 SWA81 3285 (2112) 12 fig 212

Incomplete; modelled in the round; h 32mm+; tin (MLC); hollow bird's body with open rear end (head missing); cross hatching on the breast and wings to represent feathers, with the proximal ends of the wings defined by a beaded band and dots within the cross hatching here; the legs each have three toes (one leg has surplus metal to the sides); a third vertical projection in the centre at the rear lacks the modelling of the legs and appears to be a support for standing the object in the manner of a tripod; there is a suspension ring in the middle of the back; an oval area on the underside, between the feet and the projection, is cross hatched; this crude pendant was slush-cast in a three-part mould.

A similar, but smaller and more naturalistically detailed cockerel pendant, h 33mm, l 33mm (MoL acc. no. 86. 202/44) is complete, and includes a scroll held in the bird's beak, with a legend on both sides: VOΛOΙ*WW* E/:KOC·REL (mainly Lombardic letters) – ? 'look on me/cockerel'. Cf Roach–Smith 1854, 154 no. 709 (British Museum collection acc. no. 56, 7–1, 2170, fig 212 this volume), and Mitchiner 1986, 127 no. 322 (the legend here is taken to be 'look on me Cockney'). The latter example has an incomplete tripartite lead/tin chain link (cf ibid, 217 no. 794 for a complete link of this type) attached to the suspension loop. The legend's meaning may be the equivalent of today's 'wotcher cock', which has the same underlying image (Brian Spencer, pers. comm.).

The reason for the apparent provision for standing no. 1605 upright is not known. The open end might originally have been filled with some non-metallic substance (perhaps feathers, to give the bird a more strikingly realistic tail).

For another hollow pendant of this general character, see Ward-Perkins 1940, 264 & pl LXXIV no. 65. See also souvenir buckle pendant no. 573, listed under Buckles.

POSSIBLE PLAIN PENDANTS

non-figurative elements, perhaps from composite jewellery

Tin

1606 BWB83 2055 (367) 9 fig 212

16×28mm; tin (MLC); crude; an approximately isosceles triangle with rounded corners; flat in section; cast, and pierced near top; damaged at one of the lower corners.

Possibly not an item of dress, though tin would be an unusual metal to use for a weight or other purely functional item of this general character.

Copper alloy

1607 SWA81 1679 (2112) 12 fig 212

l 44mm; pendant and chain; brass (AML); irregular rhomboid of sheet metal, pierced and suspended from S-shaped wire link.

Finger rings

(Identification of gemstones by Marjorie Hutchinson and Roger Harding)

The thirty-seven finger rings from deposits of the late 12th (ceramic phase 6) to early 15th (ceramic phase 12) centuries manifest a variety of styles and offer a fresh perspective on those worn by ordinary townsfolk rather than by nobles or prelates. Five of the rings were made from precious metals and set with gemstones, but none are opulent pieces. The products of craftsmen working in base metals (copper, bronze, brass, gunmetal and pewter), on the other hand, are more fully represented and provide a useful corrective to the impression given by the magnificent medieval finger rings which occur in tombs, treasuries and hoards (see table 7, p 335). They also illustrate the manifold ways in which rings of precious metals were imitated in cheaper materials and often used coloured glass with a high lead content to simulate gemstones.

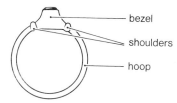

213   Finger ring terminology

Most finger rings can be classified under the general term of decorative rings (fig 213). One with a press-moulded glass cameo of a scorpion or crab (no. 1618) probably had amuletic significance for the wearer, and a gold ring with two tiny gemstones (no. 1611) could have been a form of love ring. There is also a possibility that some of the simple hoops may have been worn as guard rings to protect stone-set rings, but it is uncertain whether this practice was adopted during the period under survey. An early 15th-century tomb effigy made from alabaster of Lady Wykeham at St Mary's church, Broughton, Oxfordshire, for example, shows her wearing seven rings on her left hand, including four set with small cabochons on her fourth finger, two on her bottom joint and two on her upper joint (fig 214). The effigy probably represents the full extent of the lady's finery and it is unlikely that this number of finger rings would have been worn as part of everyday dress.

214   Alabaster effigy of Lady Wykeham, early 15th century, St Mary's church, Broughton, Oxfordshire (National Portrait Gallery)

Stirrup-shaped rings with imitation gemstone settings

1608 BIG82 acc. no. 2301 (context 2591) ceramic phase 8 fig 215
Pewter (AML); hoop rising to a pointed bezel set with a false cabochon; external d *c*.23mm; internal d 20mm.

1609 SWA81 2661 (unstratified) fig 215
Bronze (AML); slender hoop rising to a pointed bezel set with a glass cabochon; external d 21mm; internal d 17mm.

A form of finger ring popular in England from the middle of the 12th century for at least three hundred years was the 'stirrup-shaped' ring (Hinton 1982, 14), so-called in modern times on account of the shape of its hoop. The recovery of an example in pewter (no. 1608) from a deposit in London dating to the middle of the 13th century (ceramic phase 8) accords with the established chronology, while another made from bronze and set with a glass cabochon is unstratified (no. 1609). The pewter finger ring is set with a false stone, which was cast in one with the hoop. Its manufacture may be compared with other 13th- and 14th-century finger rings, which were mass-produced in pewter (see nos. 1630–43). The materials used for both these finger rings, show that they must have been among the cheapest produced. Other stirrup-shaped finger rings in base metal recorded from England have some-times proved, however, to be set with cabochons of semi-precious stones, such as garnets (eg Geddes and Carter 1977, 287, no. 2).

It is known that 'stirrup-shaped' rings were sometimes worn by women as well as by men.

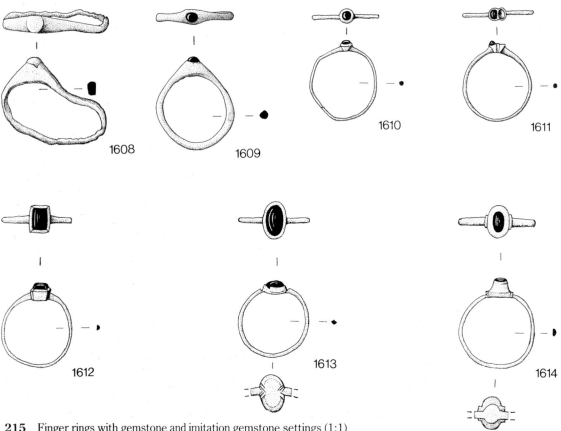

215 Finger rings with gemstone and imitation gemstone settings (1:1)

One of the jewels of St Alban's Abbey described and illustrated by the 13th-century chronicler, Matthew Paris, was a gold ring of this type set with a sapphire, which had reputedly belonged to Eleanor of Aquitaine. The same ring was apparently worn by Richard, nicknamed the 'Animal', a childhood friend of the Queen, who had his initials inscribed in niello on the bezel before he gave it to the Abbey (Oman 1930B, 81; Stratford 1984, 291–2, no. 318). Such finger rings are, however, more commonly associated with men and the large size of the pewter ring described here suggests that it was probably intended for a man. Although this form of finger ring appears to have been long-lived, it may be doubted whether it remained fashionable after the first half of the 13th century.

Decorative rings with rounded hoops set with gemstones or glass imitations

Other finger rings set with gemstones, both genuine and simulated, comprise five gold rings, three of brass, two of bronze, one of copper and one of gunmetal. An example in lead (fig 216, no. 1621) stands out from the rest of the group; its crude form and hollowed out bezel, which shows no trace of having held a stone, suggest that it could have served either as a jewellery-worker's trial-piece or a model from which a mould for casting a number of saleable finger rings was created.

Gold

1610 TL74 acc. no. 605 (context 429) ceramic phase 10–11 fig 215 & colour pl 2
Gold (AML); fine wire hoop with soldered lap joint; hoop soldered to bezel with a silver solder (AML); circular, cup-shaped bezel set with a pale almandine garnet cabochon (MH); external d 18mm; internal d 17mm; d of bezel 3mm.

1611 BC72 2035 (79) 11 fig 215
Gold (AML); fine wire hoop; bezel set with two cabochons, one a green emerald (MH) and the other missing leaving traces of a cement visible; external d 18.5mm; internal d 17; l of bezel 4mm.

1612 TL74 2263 (1717) 11 fig 215 & colour pl 2
Gold (AML); slender hoop soldered to bezel; transverse rectangular bezel, with pie-dish profile, set with a rectangular almandine garnet cabochon (MH); external d 18.5mm; internal d 17mm; l of bezel 7mm.

1613 TL74 2266 (2656) 11 fig 215 & colour pl 2
Gold (AML); slender hoop, lozenge-shaped in section; one shoulder repaired in antiquity with a lead/tin solder (MOL); transverse oval bezel, with pie-dish profile, set with an almandine garnet cabochon (MH); external d 18mm; internal d 17; l of bezel 9.5mm.

1614 BWB83 140 (292) 11 fig 215
Gold (AML); slender hoop with moulded shoulders; transverse oval bezel, with pie-dish profile, set with a sapphire cabochon (RRH); external d 20mm; internal d 18mm; l of bezel, 8mm.

The five gold finger rings were recovered from deposits dating to the second half of the 14th century (ceramic phases 10–11 and 11), which is perhaps an indication of increasing prosperity within London. These are the only accessories of gold among the assemblages considered in this volume; the great symbolic importance attributed to the incorruptible metal for ties of marriage, affection, and positions of trust, meant that if a person owned only one object of gold, it would probably have been a finger ring. Four of the rings are complete and were presumably accidentally lost by their owners; one of these underwent repair in antiquity and its hoop has (since excavation) again become detached from the bezel on one side. The fifth, which originally had two gemstones, is now missing a stone. The settings of four of these finger rings consist of a small cabochon gemstone but they differ slightly from one another. Quantitative analysis reveals that the rings also vary in their gold content, which range from 44%–45% at the lowest (nos. 1612 & 1611) to 75% (ie 18 carat gold) at the highest (no. 1610), and in the proportions of silver and copper used to debase the gold, see table 8 (p 390).

The smallest gold ring is composed of four elements; a fine, wire hoop, a small cup-shaped bezel consisting of a separate base and collet, and a tiny, pale almandine garnet cabochon (no. 1610, fig 215). The hoop has a higher gold content *c*.75% than the two-part bezel, which is *c*.55%–60% gold, debased with approximately equal amounts of copper and silver. To attach the hoop to each side of the bezel a silver solder was used. The hoop also has a join at one point on the

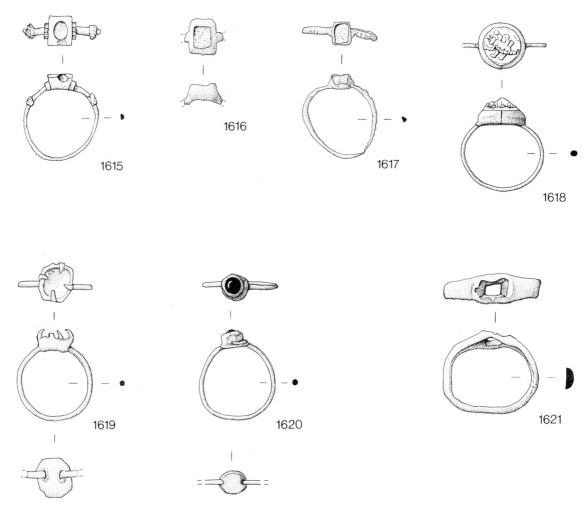

216 Finger rings with glass settings, except nos. 1616, 1617, 1619 &
1621 where the glass or stone are missing (1:1)

circumference, perhaps representing an adjust-
ment made to fit the finger of an individual
wearer, which was an important consideration,
especially as many gold finger rings set with gems
were bequeathed to persons of a different sex.
The unfussy style of the ring with its wire hoop,
cup-shaped bezel and gemstone cabochon was
evidently popular and comparable finger rings in
the Waterton collection in the Victoria and Albert
Museum include one set with a sapphire and
another with an emerald (Oman 1930A, 67 nos.
254–255, pl XI).

Another of the gold rings has a rectangular,
two-piece bezel (no. 1612, fig 215). The collet is

set with an almandine garnet. Both the hoop and
bezel are similar in composition, being $c.45\%$ gold
debased with roughly equal amounts of copper
and silver.

A third gold finger ring is also set with an
almandine garnet and the oval bezel matches the
oval outline of the cabochon (no. 1613, fig 215).
The hoop, which differs from the others described here in having a lozenge-shaped section,
was soldered to the bezel on each side; it evidently got broken subsequently and was mended with
a soft lead/tin solder, indicating that it was not
taken to a goldsmith for repair. Like the ring
previously described, the hoop and bezel were

made from metal of a similar composition, *c*.55% gold, debased with silver and copper, but here in the ratio of 2:1 rather than 1:1.

A gold ring with a slightly larger hoop also has a transverse oval bezel but it has the added refinement of moulded shoulders and is set with a sapphire rather than a semi-precious gem (no. 1614, fig 215). Qualitative XRF analysis indicated that the metal is 75% to 85% pure gold. A similar finger ring set with a sapphire in the Waterton collection (Oman 1930A, 67 no. 258, pl XI) has a larger cabochon and its shoulders are chased with leaves, and so it would have been more expensive.

A fifth gold ring has a tiny bezel, which was originally set with two stones (no. 1611, fig 215). A green emerald cabochon remains in position, while the missing stone, which would have been of a contrasting colour, probably red or purple, has left traces of the original cement at the base of the collet. The hoop and bezel were made from a metal of a similar composition, *c*.44% gold, debased with equal proportions of silver and copper.

That three of the gold finger rings are set with small cabochon garnets indicates their relative cheapness and popularity. Two further examples in the Waterton collection similarly have plain settings, one semi-circular and the other hexagonal, reflecting the natural outline of each cabochon (Oman 1930A, 67 nos. 256–257, pl XI). Such finger rings are rarely mentioned in the wills of 14th-century Londoners where bequests single out gold finger rings set with precious gemstones, for example a diamond, ruby, or sapphire and pearls (Cal Wills 1889, 506 & 653; Cal Wills 1890, 36 & 97). Consequently, it is only by considering all the available sources of information that a clearer understanding of what jewellery was worn in medieval London will emerge.

Copper and copper alloy

1615 BIG82 acc. no. 3284 (context 6507) ceramic phase 6 fig 216
Gunmetal (AML); hoop and bezel cast in one piece; slender hoop with moulded shoulders and a cable-patterned projection on each side; rectangular bezel originally set with an oval glass cabochon secured with a white lime-based cement (AML). (The glass cabochon is now separate from its setting). External d 20mm; internal d 18mm; l of bezel 7mm.

1616 SWA81 512 (2027) 9 fig 216
Bronze (AML); part of slender hoop, broken on either side of bezel; rectangular bezel with a rectangular setting containing a white cement, probably calcium carbonate (AML) with quartz inclusions, stone missing; l of bezel 9mm.

1617 SWA81 2500 (unstratified) fig 216
Copper (AML); slender hoop; shallow rectangular bezel with a rectangular setting containing a yellowish-white cement, probably calcium carbonate (AML), stone missing. External d 19mm; internal d 17mm; l of bezel 6mm.

1618 SWA81 2092 (2020) 9 fig 216 & colour pl 12A
Brass (AML); hollow round-sectioned hoop soldered to the edge of a collet set with an opaque, press-moulded glass cameo secured with a lead/tin solder (AML). The glass cameo is blue and white with localised streaks of red. It is decorated with a creature having a head, six legs and a tail, probably either a scorpion or crab. External d *c*.17mm; internal d 15mm; d of bezel 12mm.

1619 BWB83 2664 (330) 11 fig 216
Brass (AML); hollow round-sectioned hoop soldered to bezel with a lead/tin solder; octagonal bezel with four claws, stone missing but traces of the cement survive. External d 20mm; internal d 17mm; l of bezel 10mm.

1620 SWA81 383 (935 – recently redeposited) fig 216
Brass (AML); hollow round-sectioned hoop soldered to a flat plate; cabochon of green glass (MH) set within a collet. External d 21mm; internal d 18mm; d of bezel 6mm.

Lead

1621 BWB83 2769 (361) 11 fig 216
Lead (AML); flat hoop with an open-backed rectangular bezel cut into it, stone missing. External d 22mm; internal d 19mm; l of bezel 6mm.

It can be assumed that most finger rings made from base metal imitated those of precious metal. Indeed, some can be paralleled, including the earliest decorative finger ring with a bezel in this study which was recovered from a late 12th-century deposit (no. 1615, fig 216). It was cast in one piece and has two cable-patterned projections on the outside of the hoop in addition to moulded shoulders. The rectangular bezel was set with a glass cabochon cemented with calcium cabonate. A copper-alloy ring of similar form, but with a plain hoop, and set with a blue glass cabochon was excavated at Lyveden, Northamptonshire (Steane and Bryant 1975, 114, no. 51, fig 43). It has been dated stylistically to the 13th century. However, the date of the finger ring from London, and three examples in silver from the Lark Hill hoard, Worcester, which was concealed *c.*1173–74 or a few years later (Akerman 1855, 201, pl XVII, nos. 1–3; Thompson 1956, 148 no. 381; Stratford 1984, 293 no. 320a–c) indicate that these finger rings were already common in England by the last quarter of the 12th century. Further dating evidence in respect of finger rings of this general type comes from the tomb of Duke Albert de Cuyck, Prince-bishop of Liège (died 1200). He was buried with a silver finger ring, which has a cast hoop with moulded shoulders and an oval, rather than a rectangular, bezel (Musée Curtius, Liège).

A copper finger ring with a rectangular bezel which has lost its original setting, and is now in a very delicate state of preservation (no. 1617, fig 216), may also belong to the late 12th or 13th century, but it was not recovered from a stratified deposit. A bronze finger ring with a rectangular bezel which has lost most of its hoop as well as its stone or glass setting (no. 1616, fig 216) could have been produced at least fifty years before it was discarded in the late 13th century; it is possible, however, that rings of this style may have had a long period of production, just as stirrup-shaped rings did.

The settings of three decorative brass finger rings are individually distinct but the hoops resemble one another. These are round-sectioned and a seam-line visible round the circumferences of two of them (nos. 1618 & 1620) shows that they were made from a thin piece of sheet metal, rolled and hammered into its present form. The type of wire thus produced appears to have been used for the making of finger rings in London from at least the first half of the 12th century (Pritchard forthcoming), and was also used for other small accessories.

Among the settings of the three latter rings one with an octagonal bezel is claw-set (no. 1619, fig 216), but even though the four claws remain intact and a white cement was used as an adhesive, the stone is missing, perhaps because it got smashed or was re-used. It is the only finger ring catalogued here which has claws and although it

was recovered from a late 14th-century deposit (ceramic phase 11) its style suggests that it probably belongs to the 13th century. Comparable finger rings with claw-settings made from precious metal rather than brass include two which were given to St Albans Abbey in the 13th century. One had formerly belonged to Stephen Langton, Archbishop of Canterbury (died 1228) and the other to John, Bishop of Ardfert (died 1245) (Oman 1930B, 81–2; Stratford 1984, 291 no. 318).

The other two brass finger rings have separate collets, each made from a strip of sheeting, and both retain their stone settings. One is a small, green cabochon made from glass with a high lead content with copper added as a colorant (no. 1620, fig 216). No date could be assigned to the deposit from which it was recovered. The other, from a late 13th or early 14th-century deposit (ceramic phase 9), is a circular press-moulded glass 'cameo' with a device of a scorpion or crab (no. 1618, fig 216; colour pl 12A). The long tail and curved outline of the creature point to it being scorpion while its six legs are more typical of a crab (see, for example, the Chertsey floor tiles *c.*1250–70 showing the signs of the zodiac: Eames 1980, 149 and 164, nos. 525 & 573). There appears, however, to be little consistency in form between these two signs in different media. Moulded-glass pastes are otherwise unknown from 13th-century England and it is, therefore, unlikely that it was a canting device commissioned by a Londoner. It may have been worn as a talisman, illustrating the popular interest in the magical properties of engraved gems which sprang up in western Europe during the 12th century (Evans 1922, 96), and previously exemplified from England by a gold finger ring, set with a bloodstone intaglio, which was recovered from the coffin of a bishop in Chichester Cathedral, and is probably of late 12th-century date (Stratford 1984, 290–1, no. 314). The 13th-century scholastic, Albert Magnus, in his treatise *De Rebus Metallicis* extols the virtues of various astrological sigils including the signs of the zodiac (Evans 1922, 97). The choice of a crab or scorpion may, therefore, have been intended to protect the wearer against illness, particularly tertian fever, against which both these sigils were supposed to be especially efficacious (Evans 1922, 100). No other ring set with a press-moulded glass paste is known from this period; the method of assembly of the ring, however, does not differ significantly from that of the other brass rings in the present corpus and it cannot be assumed to be a piece of continental workmanship.

As one might expect, lead/tin solders were used on the brass finger rings to secure the hoops to the bezels. A similar solder was also used for the glass cameo, it being a method of fusing glass to metal that could be safely employed, whereas gemstones, which are prone to fracture when heated, were secured with a calcium carbonate cement similar to that used for fixing glass inside metal mirror-cases (see nos. 1708, 1710 & 1712).

Wire finger rings

1622 BWB83 acc. no. 2375 (context 290) ceramic phase 9 fig 217

Brass (AML); continuous length of thin wire wound round five times; external d 18mm; internal d 15mm.

Wire jewellery came back into vogue in England during the 14th century coinciding with the increased output of drawn wire (see brooches nos. 1339–41). Finger rings were made from wire with a narrow gauge in contrast to the chunky finger rings made from plaited and twisted wire that are common in the Viking period and which occur in England as late as the 1170s on the evidence of a ring in the Lark Hill hoard (Akerman 1855, 201, pl XVII, no. 6; Stratford, 1984, 293. no. 320d). A finger ring made from a short length of brass wire coiled round five times was recovered from a late 13th- or early 14th-century deposit (ceramic phase 9) in London (no. 1622, fig 217). Both ends were twisted under and over the previous coils to bind them together and to add a decorative finish. Although this was an extremely simple method by

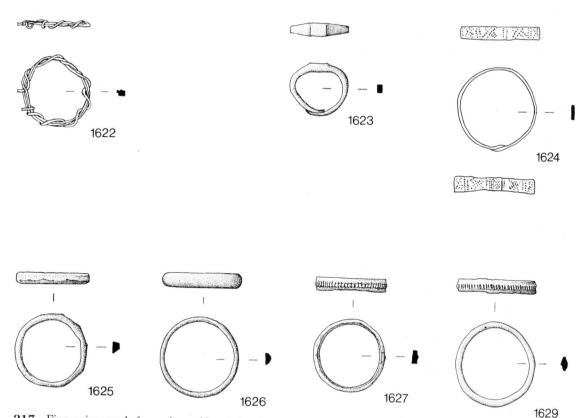

217 Finger rings made from wire, soldered sheeting or cast (1:1)

which to produce a finger ring, it is not a solitary example. Another in the collection of the Museum of London is made from two wires twisted together in opposing directions and finished with an imitation oval bezel (MoL acc. no. 81.266/11), and even a pin could be used, the head substituting for a stone (MoL acc. no. 86.109/8). These rings were yet another imitation of a form occurring in precious metal; one made from gold, for example, was recovered at Northolt manor (Hurst 1961, 293, fig 76 no. 30).

Simple hoops

Copper and copper alloy:

Soldered sheeting

1623 BIG82 acc. no. 2828 (context 4064)
ceramic phase 6 fig 217
Copper (AML); flat-sectioned, thickening towards a rectangular bezel; soldered lap joint on lower part of hoop; external d 15mm; internal d 11mm.

1624 BWB83 2713 (329) 11 fig 217
Brass (AML); flat-sectioned with soldered lap joint, decorated on the outside with a repeating pattern of a saltire cross divided by a bar; external d 21mm; internal d 19mm.

Cast

1625 BWB83 4732 (309) 12 fig 217
Brass (AML); plain D-shaped in section; external d 19mm; internal d 16mm.

1626 SWA81 1997 (2108) 12 fig 217
Brass (AML); plain, trapezoidal in section; external d 21mm; internal d 18mm.

1627 SWA81 2887 (2106) 12 fig 217
Gunmetal (AML); flanged hoop decorated on the outside with beading; external d 19mm; internal d 17mm.

1628 SWA81 2926 (2108) 12
Brass (AML); flanged hoop decorated on the outside with transverse grooves; external d 17mm; internal d 15mm.

1629 SWA81 2025 (2106/2107) 12 fig 217
Brass (AML); as preceding; external d 22mm; internal d 20mm.

Finger rings in the form of a simple hoop chiefly come from deposits of the early 15th century.

Two from earlier deposits are distinguishable technically as well as stylistically, since they were made from strips of sheeting rather than by casting.

The earliest hoop, which is also the only one made from copper, was recovered from a deposit of the late 12th century (ceramic phase 6) (no. 1623, fig 217). It has a finger span of only 12mm, and, therefore, was probably worn on an upper joint of the little finger or by a child. The strip of metal forming the ring has two narrow overlapping ends, which were soldered together. Opposite the soldered join, the upper part of the ring thickens into a poor imitation of a rectangular bezel. The other finger ring, made from brass sheeting, is patterned on the outside with a repeating sequence of bar-lines and saltires (no. 1624, fig 217). It is considerably larger in diameter and would have been worn by a man.

The five hoops cast in one piece range from 17mm to 22mm in diameter. Two plain examples made from brass are respectively D-shaped and trapezoidal in section (nos. 1625 & 1626, fig 217), whereas the other three hoops have a narrow flange round the outside. The flange on the hoop made from gunmetal is decorated with beading (no. 1627, fig 217), while the other two, which are brass and decorated with transverse grooves, form a pair (nos. 1628 & 1629, fig 217). The simple character of these patterns may mean that they were designed to be worn as guard rings, but the rough finish of the rings on the inside surface, especially on the three flanged hoops, suggests that they were not intended to be worn and that some other function for them should be sought.

Pewter finger rings

(All identifications as pewter AML)

Bezel soldered to hoop

1630 BWB83 acc. no. 77 (context 155)
ceramic phase 11 fig 218
Slender hoop, triangular in section; circular bezel set with a false flat stone edged with beading and four small false stones at the cardinal points. Remains of casting

218 Pewter finger rings

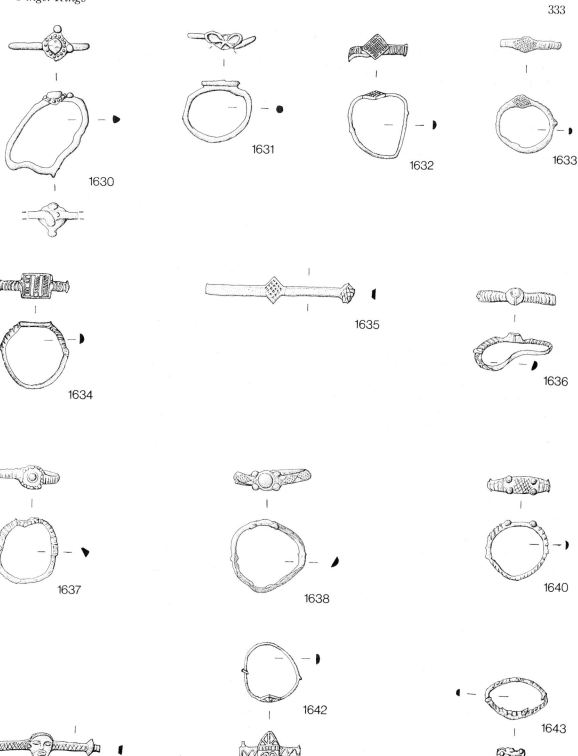

1630

1631

1632

1633

1634

1635

1636

1637

1638

1640

1641

1642

1643

seam on lower part of hoop opposite bezel. External d 25mm; internal d 21mm; d of bezel 10mm.

1631 BWB83 5849 (287) 11 fig 218
Slender hoop, round-sectioned; bezel in the form of a quatrefoil. External d 17mm; internal d 14mm.

Cast in one piece

geometrically shaped bezels

1632 BIG82 3037 (5277) 7 fig 218
Slender hoop, triangular in section, upper part decorated on the outside with transverse grooves; lozenge-shaped bezel with cross-hatching. External d 15mm; internal d 13mm; l of bezel 6.5mm.

1633 SWA81 522 (2040) 9 fig 218
Similar to preceding ring; external d 14m; internal d 12mm; l of bezel 7mm.

1634 BWB83 3678 (308) 11 fig 218
Slender hoop, triangular in section, upper part decorated on the outside with horizontal chevrons; rectangular bezel with three transverse bars. External d 18mm; internal d 16mm; l of bezel, 8mm.

1635 BWB83 4912 (309) 12 fig 218
Incomplete; slender hoop, flat-sectioned; lozenge-shaped bezel and projecting bezel decorated with cross-hatching on opposing lower part of hoop.

false-stone settings

1636 BWB83 4540 (285) 9 fig 218
Slender hoop, upper part decorated on the outside with transverse grooves and beading and the lower part with saltires; circular bezel set with a false cabochon. External d c.20mm; internal d 17mm; d of bezel 5mm.

1637 SWA81 457 (2018) 11 fig 218
Slender hoop decorated on the outside with transverse grooves; circular bezel with beaded edge set with a tiny false cabochon. External d 16mm; internal 14mm; d of bezel 6mm.

1638 SWA81 624 (2051) 11 fig 218
Slender hoop, upper part decorated on the outside with lozenges infilled with cross-hatching; circular bezel with four false stones at the corners of the shoulders. External d 19mm; internal d 17mm; d of bezel 5mm.

1639 BWB83 5243 (306) 11
Slender hoop, upper part decorated on the outside with a cable pattern; oval bezel with cabled edging surrounding a central hole. External d 18mm; internal d 16mm; d of bezel 7mm.

1640 BWB83 5093 (unstratified) fig 218
Slender hoop, triangular in section decorated on the outside with transverse grooves; rectangular bezel with cross-hatched decoration and a false stone in each corner. External d 16mm; internal d 14mm; l of bezel 8mm.

face masks

1641 BWB83 1248 (110) 11 fig 218
Incomplete; slender hoop, flat-sectioned, decorated on the outside with cross-hatching; bezel in the form of a face-mask.

1642 BWB83 5810 (310) 12 fig 218
Slender hoop, flat-sectioned, decorated on the outside with a chevron pattern; bezel in the form of a mitred head. External d 15mm; internal d 13mm.

1643 BWB83 5850 (313) 12 fig 218
Slender hoop, triangular in section, decorated on the outside with horizontal chevrons which reverse in each quadrant; bezel in the form of a crowned head. External d c.14mm; internal d 12mm.

The tradition of wearing finger rings made from lead alloy went back in London to the 10th century, when the metal was increasingly used to simulate silver. That many pieces were made locally can be inferred from the unfinished stock of finger rings, disc brooches and beads in the Cheapside hoard, which was hidden sometime during the 11th century (VCH 1909, 160).

By the early 13th century a new form of lead-alloy finger ring had emerged which has a bezel as well as a hoop. The earliest dates to c.1200 to 1230 (ceramic phase 7) (no. 1632), but the majority were found in deposits of the late 14th and early 15th centuries (ceramic phases 11 and 12). All were analysed for their metal content by XRF, which indicates that they were made from pewter and not tin.

Such rings were usually cast in three-piece moulds and no attempt was made to remove the remains of the casting seams, which are apparent on transversely opposite sides of each hoop. Two differ in having a separate hoop and bezel, which were required to be soldered together (nos. 1630 & 1631, fig 218). Both of these latter rings have plain hoops and only the former bears traces of its casting seam, which is on the lower edge of the hoop in contrast to those made in one piece. A similar two-piece finger ring with a bezel styled in the form of a sexfoil, and which is likewise from London, forms part of the Mitchiner collection (Mitchiner 1986, 89 no. 192). Finger rings cast in one piece, by contrast, are decorated on the outside with simple patterns such as transverse lines, lozenges, or chevrons either round the upper half of the hoop or all of it. From the size of the one-piece rings, which range from 14mm to 20mm, it is possible to suggest that they were usually worn on the upper joints of fingers and probably most frequently on the little finger, or by children. One of the composite rings with a diameter of 25mm would, however, have been too large for a child.

Despite the fact that very few rings of this character have previously received attention in print, they were obviously mass-produced. Two from deposits in London separated by some one hundred years are in a similar design, although of differing size (nos. 1632 & 1633, fig 218), and no. 1639 is paralleled by an example in the collection of the Museum of London (MoL acc. no. 80.70/20). A close stylistic affinity between these one-piece rings and many pilgrim badges, miniature strap-ends and other pewter jewellery is readily

apparent, cross-hatching, for example, is a common form of decoration on them all. A few of the rings may indeed have been pilgrim souvenirs, especially three with bezels in the form of face masks (nos. 1641–43, fig 218). One takes the form of a crowned head and another that of a mitred head, which could have commemorated visits to the shrines of St Edward the Confessor in Westminster Abbey and St Thomas at Canterbury. The sorrowful face portrayed on the third ring is similar, but not identical to another example from London in a private collection (Mitchiner 1986, 89, no. 191). A previous suggestion, however, that a pewter ring embellished with a cluster of false stones could have been a momento of Edward the Confessor's ring (Spencer 1980, 21, no. 81) is now considered unlikely (Brian Spencer pers. comm.). It is, indeed, apparent that many of the finger rings with false-stone settings imitated those set with gemstones or glass, thus the form and setting of no. 1636 is close to that of no. 1610, a gold finger ring set with a cabochon garnet, and also that of no. 1620, a brass finger ring set with green glass.

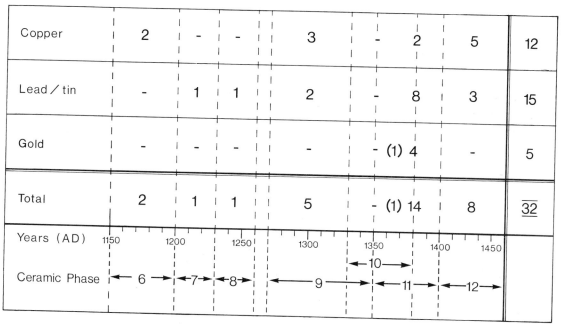

Copper	2	-	-			3		-	2	5		12
Lead / tin	-	1	1			2		-	8	3		15
Gold	-	-	-			-		-	(1) 4	-		5
Total	2	1	1			5		-	(1) 14	8		32
Years (AD)	1150	1200	1250			1300		1350	1400	1450		
Ceramic Phase	← 6 →	←7→	←8→			← 9 →	←10→	←11→	←12→			

Table 7   Finger rings – metals used   (1) = possibly silver gilt

Bells

Two types of bells were worn as accessories in medieval England: rumbler bells, which were a closed form containing a loose 'pea', and open bells, which had clappers fixed in position on the inside. The former first appear made from tin in London deposits of the early 13th century but these are a short-lived style which did not outlast the century. Spherical rumbler bells in both brass and tin become common from the late 13th century, but while brass bells were made to a standard design throughout the 14th and 15th centuries, tin bells reveal a variety of different forms.

The evidence for the use of bells as an ornament of fashionable dress in England before the late 14th century is negligible, although jesters and acrobats had adopted them earlier as a part of their everyday guise (fig 219) and so too had pilgrims and priests. In 1393–4 Richard II had two bells, which were bought for 16d from a goldsmith, fitted to a belt (*Item in ij campanellis ad magnam zonam domini, ponderans xvjd*, Baildon 1911, 507), and this fashion, which the king borrowed from courts on the continent, was aped by his courtiers. Although the manner in which the bells were fitted to the king's girdle is not specified, an English manuscript illumination dat-

ing to *c*.1400 depicts a man attired in a long, high-necked gown wearing a girdle round his waist from which a number of bells attached by cords, probably of coloured silk, dangle (Chaucer, *Troilus and Criseyde*, MS61, f.1v; Scott 1986, pl 45); a matching collar with a similar set of bells draws further attention to this whimsical fashion. Continental sources, which include tapestries woven in workshops in Arras and the Lower Rhineland, as well as paintings, add to the impression that this fashion was chiefly reserved for festive occasions or as an expression of courtly romance. Men invariably wore rumbler bells suspended on silken cords from girdles, or ostentatious collars – sometimes in the form of chains as portrayed by Konrad von Soest in a German altarpiece dated to the first quarter of the 15th century (*Kalvarienberg des sog. Wildunger Altares*, illustrated in Budde 1986, 62 fig 51) – or from wide sashes tied diagonally across the shoulder, which were worn in association with high-necked garments that came in all manner of lengths from the thigh down to below the ankle. Less frequently clapper bells were attached to girdles. These girdles were worn round the hip instead of being tightly fastened at the waist as was usual for girdles hung with rumbler bells, a

219   Jesters wearing hoods with rumbler bells *c*.1340 (after *The Romance of Alexander*, MS Bodl.264 f.85v)

220 Bells worn as dress accessories (after a Rhenish tapestry *c.*1385,
Germanisches Nationalmuseum, Nuremberg)

detail evident from a late 14th-century Rhenish tapestry, which shows ladies and gallants engaging in various games (fig 220; Hampe 1896, 111 no. 68 fig 7). Women were also accustomed to wearing bells on festive occasions in the late 14th and early 15th century, at least on the continent. The German tapestry already referred to shows a lady wearing bells attached to either side of a sash worn diagonally across the shoulder, while the betrothal portrait of Lysbeth van Duvenvoorde, painted *c.*1430, shows her wearing a high-waisted girdle to which rumbler bells were fitted by means of plied, bi-coloured cords so that they jangled on her hips (Fingerlin 1971, 361 fig 408). A similar girdle hung with bells can be seen in the alabaster effigy of Margareta, Queen of Sweden, Norway and Denmark (died 1412) which was erected in Roskilde cathedral, Denmark, in 1423 (Geijer, Franzén and Nockert 1985, fig 23).

There is little to distinguish the rumbler bells worn as an accessory of dress from those attached to the collars of pets or hunting dogs, or to horse harness, which were made in profusion; Richard Paternoster, for example, provided 800 little bells (*tintunabul'*) to be worn by horses in a jousting tournament at Windsor Park in 1278 at a cost of 3s per 100 (Lysons 1814, 302). Consequently, all the excavated rumbler bells from medieval London are included here, but among clapper bells only those which bear no indication that they were mementoes from the shrine of St Thomas at Canterbury are described, since these will be described in a volume in this series on pilgrim souvenirs (Spencer forthcoming).

Rumbler bells

Rumbler bells from medieval deposits in London are generally made from brass, gunmetal or tin. However, one early bell is copper, and another from an unstratified deposit is pewter.

Copper

The earliest of the rumbler bells is made from copper. It is otherwise similar to examples from deposits of the 13th and 14th centuries except that its loop is made from wire instead of from a narrow strip of sheeting.

1644   BWB83   acc. no. 3508   (context 175)
ceramic phases 6–9   fig 221
Top half + loop; d 17mm; d of loop 1.5mm.

Brass and gunmetal

These bells, from deposits of the late 13th to early 15th centuries (ceramic phases 9 to 12), were produced from four components: a suspension loop, cut from sheeting, a hollow body made in two halves by hammering a piece of sheet in a form, and a round, iron pea (fig 221). The loop was inserted upwards through a hole cut in the upper half of the body and the ends were bent outwards and then inwards, in the manner of a staple, so that it remained rigid rather than swivelling, and an aperture was cut in the lower half of the body. A lead/tin solder was used to join the two halves together, once the pea had been inserted, leaving a flanged seam line. This was a weakness in the design, since sixteen out of the twenty four examples have split apart at the seam. Brass rumbler-bells bearing geometric and heraldically-derived decoration have been recorded from London (eg Mitchiner 1986, 131 nos. 348–349), but none has been recovered from closely dated deposits.

	site	fig	accession number	context	ceramic phase	description
1645	SWA81	221	580	2055	9	Brass with iron pea (AML); complete; d 13mm; w of loop 1.5mm
1646	SWA81		1927	2135	9	Complete except for loop; d 18mm
1647	BWB83		2146	290	9	Top half + loop; flattened; w of loop 2mm
1648	BC72		4150	88	11	Brass (AML); top half + loop; flattened; w of loop, 3mm
1649	BC72		4310	150	11	Bottom half; d 24mm
1650	BWB83		1259	110	11	Top half + loop; flattened; w of loop 3mm
1651	BWB83		2066	142	11	Bottom half; d 22mm
1652	BWB83		1406	151	11	Gunmetal (AML); bottom half; d 23mm
1653	BWB83		1376	156	11	Complete except for pea; flattened; w of loop 1.5mm
1654	BWB83		2309	286	11	Complete except for pea; loop broken; flattened; w of loop 2.5mm
1655	BWB83		4640	299	11	Bottom half; d 17mm
1656	BWB83		1185	307	11	Top half + loop; flattened; w of loop 1.5mm
1657	BWB83		2069	308	11	Complete except for loop; d 16mm
1658	BWB83		2750	345	11	Bottom half; d 18mm
1659	BWB83		2751	345	11	Part of top half + loop; w of loop 2mm
1660	BWB83		5034	399	11	Top half + loop; flattened; w of loop 1.5mm
1661	SWA81		940	2102	12	Top half + loop; flattened; w of loop 2mm
1662	SWA81		955	2102	12	Top half + loop; d *c.*17mm; w of loop 1.5mm
1663	BWB83		3250	265	12	Top half + loop; flattened; w of loop 1.5mm
1664	BWB83		5305	326	12	Complete; flattened; w of loop 1.5mm
1665	BWB83		5306	326	12	Brass (AML); top + bottom halves; flattened
1666	TL74	221	2149	368	12	Brass; complete; d 34mm; w of loop 10mm
1667	BWB83		4885	(unstratified)		Top half + loop; d *c.*24mm; w of loop 2mm

Tin and pewter

Rumbler bells made from white metal, which, where analysed, has proved to be tin, with one exception which is pewter, show a great variety of style, and are generally more complete than those made from copper alloy. This is because they were made from fewer components and did not require soldering, except for one form, which copied those in brass. The earliest type, which is restricted to deposits of the 13th century (ceramic phase 7 and early phase 9), was cast in the form of an open bell, with the loop included. The outside was decorated with bands of opposed hatching, which radiate from four sides of the loop down to the tip of each tab or 'petal' (no. 1668, fig 221). Two of the four bells were also decorated with a circle (no. 1670, fig 221), or circle and dot (no. 1669) on the corners between the petals. To enclose the pea, which was also made of pure tin and cast in a mould, the four petals were pushed inwards to meet at a point below the loop.

221   Bells (1:1)

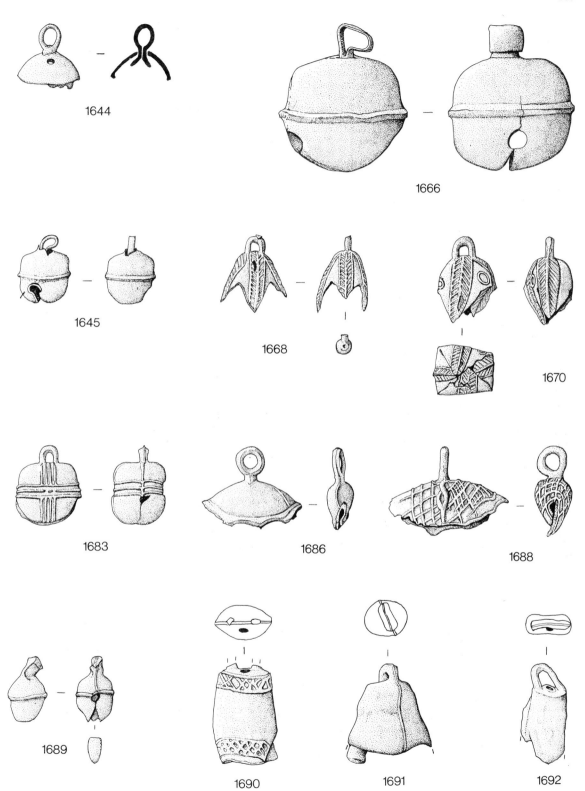

1644

1666

1645

1668

1670

1683

1686

1688

1689

1690

1691

1692

Tin rumbler bells with four petal-like tabs cast in one with loop:

	site	accession number	context	ceramic phase	description
1668	BIG82	3400	3232	7	Tin (AML); complete; decorated with bands of opposed hatching; (petals unfolded during conservation); h 18mm.
1669	BIG82	2702	3512	7	Tin (AML); complete but flattened; decoration as above, but with a circle and dot in each corner; h *c.*16mm.
1670	BIG82	3070	5277	7	Tin (AML); complete; decoration as above, but with no dot in circle; h 20mm.
1671	SWA81	2405	1594	9	Tin (AML); complete; decoration as no. 1668; h 17mm.

A more common type of tin rumbler bell, which first occurs in deposits of the late 13th century (ceramic phase 9) was cast in a spherical form. As with the previous type, the loop was included in the casting. A seam line runs round the bell from the loop, with the lower half of the seam left open so that the pea could be inserted. The sides of the bell were then pushed together to prevent the pea escaping. This method of assembly was appropriate in view of the softness of the metal. Such bells were decorated with simple ribs running vertically from the loop and horizontally round the girth.

White metal (tin) rumbler bells cast in one with loop, and decorated with a linear pattern:

	site	accession number	context	ceramic phase	description
1672	SWA81	396	2018	9	Tin with a small amount of copper and zinc added to the pea (AML); complete, decorated with 5 vertical and (?) 3 transverse ribs; d *c.*17mm, flattened
1673	SWA81	528	2040	9	Complete, decorated with 5 vertical and 4 transverse ribs; d *c.*16mm
1674	SWA81	2116	2065	9	Complete except for pea; decoration similar to preceding one; flattened
1675	BWB83	1516	222	9	As no. 1674; 4 vertical and 4 transverse ribs; flattened
1676	BWB83	2053	367	9	As no. 1674 but loop broken; (?)5 and 3 transverse ribs; flattened
1677	BWB83	2317	286	11	As no. 1674; 4 vertical and 3 transverse ribs; flattened
1678	BWB83	4627	287	11	As no. 1674; 3 vertical ribs; flattened
1679	BWB83	2723	328	11	As no. 1674; (?) 4 vertical and 3 transverse ribs; flattened
1680	BWB83	2717	329	11	Tin (AML); as no. 1674; 5 vertical and 4 transverse ribs; flattened
1681	BWB83	3661	359	11	As no. 1674; 3 vertical and 3 transverse ribs; flattened
1682	BWB83	5033	399	11	As no. 1674; 4 vertical and 5 transverse ribs; flattened
1683	BWB83	730	306	12	Tin (AML); complete; 4 vertical and 3 transverse ribs; d 17mm

A third type, which, on present evidence, appears not to have been introduced before the 14th century, copied brass rumbler bells in having a spherical body made in two halves, which required soldering together round the girth. As on the brass bells, the resulting seam formed an area of weakness. Casting the bell in two halves also enabled an aperture, which resembles those in brass bells, to be cut in the lower half. However, unlike brass rumbler bells, the loop was cast as part of the upper half of the bell, but it tended to break since it was joined to the body at one point rather than two, in contrast to the previous two types. One bell of this type is decorated with a chequered pattern (no. 1688, fig 221); it is the only example which has been identified as pewter. The others appear to have been left plain like contemporary ones made from copper alloy.

White-metal rumbler bells cast in two halves:

	site	accession number	context	ceramic phase	description
1684	BWB83	2373	126	11	Tin (AML); complete except for loop and pea; d *c.*21mm
1685	BWB83	2156	142	11	Top + bottom halves; flattened
1686	SWA81	1977	2108	12	Top half including loop; flattened. Fig 221
1687	SWA81	1015	(unstratified)		Top half; flattened
1688	SWA81	1016	(unstratified)		Pewter (AML); top half including loop; decorated on outside with a chequered pattern; flattened. Fig 221

A fourth type of tin rumbler bell from medieval London was cast in one with a pronounced horizontal seam round its girth, in addition to the usual, but less prominent seam running vertically of which the lower half remained open to insert the pea. It has a stem, instead of a loop, which was bent over to one side.

Tin rumbler bell cast in one with a stem:

	site	accession number	context	ceramic phase	description
1689	SWA81 fig 221	1682	2112	12	Tin (AML); complete; h 17mm; d 10mm.

These four varieties of white-metal rumbler bells do not exhaust the full range that was being produced in the late-medieval period.

See fig 211 for lead/tin bells on a necklace found in London.

Clapper bells

Three bells, all originally with clappers, possess no indication in the form of inscriptions that they were souvenirs from the shrine of St Thomas in Canterbury. The earliest one, which is decorated with two cross-hatched bands (no. 1690, fig 221), was recovered from a deposit dating to the late 13th century or first half of the 14th century (ceramic phase 9); the others are from deposits of the late 14th century (ceramic phase 11) and early 15th century (ceramic phase 12). This dating is significant since it has been claimed that it was not until the 15th century that inscriptions were replaced by simple decoration on small, ornamental clapper bells (Mitchiner 1986,163). The loops, which were included in the casting, are simple hoops in contrast with the trefoil and quatrefoil forms usually associated with Canterbury bells (eg Ward-Perkins 1940, pl LXVI no 7; Mitchiner 1986, 73 no. 135). XRF analyses indicate that these bells were made from tin without the addition of copper and bismuth that acted as a hardener, which has apparently been noted in some examples (Mitchiner 1986, 72 & 163–5).

	site	accession number	context	ceramic phase	description
1690	BWB83 fig 221	2118	290	9	Tin (AML); complete except for loop and clapper; decorated on the outside with cross-hatched bands round the top and rim; h 27+mm; d *c.*14mm, flattened
1691	BWB83 fig 221	5077	338	11	Tin (AML); lower edge damaged; simple loop; flattened, h 24mm
1692	BWB83 fig 221	3708	309	12	Tin (AML); complete except for clapper; simple loop; h 27mm; flattened

Purses

(Identification of leather by Glynis Edwards, AML)

Purses and pouches from medieval London include examples made from leather and from cloth. There is also a leather pouch which has a silk binding. Few are preserved probably because most were made from tawed leather (skin treated with alum and salt) which is unable to withstand most conditions of burial in the soil. Some, nevertheless, do survive, particularly in public record offices, enabling them to be compared with those recovered from excavations. Other pouches may have been made from linen or have had linen linings, and are therefore also likely to have decomposed where the soil is acidic. Traces of linen have, indeed, occasionally been observed when hoards of coins and jewellery have been found, for example the Lark Hill hoard dating to the late 12th century (Akerman 1855, 202).

Purses with metal frames appear not to have returned to widespread favour in England after the Anglo-Saxon period until the 15th century (Ward-Perkins 1940, 159), but part of a brass frame with a swivelling suspension loop was preserved in a 14th-century London deposit (ceramic phase 10–11), making it one of the earliest examples of its type surviving.

A survey of visual sources would add considerably to our knowledge of these accessories. Initial work shows that during the 13th and 14th centuries purses were worn by both men and women (figs 175 & 222–25). Usually a purse was worn on a girdle to the right of the buckle with some exceptions, for example, the effigies of Queen Berengaria at Espan in northern France (fig 10) and Clovis I at Sainte-Genevieve, Paris (now in the abbey church of Saint-Denis, Paris) (Erlande-Brandenburg 1984, no. 1), which were the work of continental craftsmen in the second quarter of the 13th century. Pouches that slotted onto a girdle appear, however, to have been worn on either side of the body and often at the centre front (fig 224). Their use was not restricted to carrying coins, although this was certainly one of their principal functions. A man depicted in the Luttrell Psalter can be seen checking his coins in a tasselled drawstring purse (fig 223), while in 1384 John Dugard, a Londoner, was accused of stealing a leather bag containing £70 13s 4d in nobles (ie 212 gold coins) (Sharpe 1904, 272). The latter bag was probably too heavy to have been worn; it may have resembled the tubular purses closed with drawstrings depicted in the wall paintings of the virtues, *Largesce* and *Debonereté*, in Henry III's painted chamber in the Palace of Westminster (Binski 1986, colour pls 5–6). Other bags were used for game and these were sometimes worn alongside a pouch on a girdle (fig 225).

The purses described here are classified according to the material from which they were made and their method of fastening. The terms purse and pouch are used interchangeably. More expensive purses, usually made from cloth such as velvet rather than leather, were sometimes called *hamondeys/hamodeys* in the 14th century (Riley 1868, 422) but the precise meaning of this term is uncertain.

Not only were different types of cloth used for purses but the type of leather also varied. An attempt was made to identify the species of animal skin in eight of the leather purses here by examining grain patterns using a binocular microscope up to a magnification of ×12.5 (Glynis Edwards, unpublished AML Report). This revealed that two examples, and possibly a further two, are made from deerskin (nos. 1693, 1695, 1696 & 1705); one is possibly either sheep or goatskin (no. 1694); and two are calfskin (nos. 1703 & 1706). It is not known whether any of the leather was dyed originally, although purses of red leather dyed with either madder or brazilwood are mentioned in written records (Riley 1868, 422) and an example is preserved in the library of Canterbury cathedral (Robinson and Urquhart 1934, 202 no. 26).

Drawstring leather pouches

There are three leather pouches that were closed with drawstrings from DUA excavations. One was recovered from a late 12th-century deposit

222 Countrywoman wearing a purse slung from her girdle *c.* 1325–35 (after the *Luttrell Psalter*, BL Add. MS 42130 f.163v)

223 Man wearing a tasselled purse containing coins *c.* 1325–35 (after the *Luttrell Psalter*, BL Add. MS 42130 f.186v)

224 Man wearing a leather pouch on his abdomen *c.* 1325–35 (after the *Luttrell Psalter*, BL Add. MS 42130 f.197b)

225 Gamekeeper wearing a gamebag, in addition to a pouch and a knife, from his girdle *c.* 1340 (after *The Romance of Alexander*, MS Bodl. 264 f.138)

(ceramic phase 6), another from a deposit of the late 13th or early 14th century (ceramic phase 9), and a third from a deposit of the late 14th century (ceramic phase 11). The style of these purses is very simple but the way that they were cut out and stitched together differs, presumably dictated by the size of skin available.

A small, 12th-century pouch was made from two pieces of leather, which were sewn together inside out and then turned so that the grain face was on the outside (no. 1693, fig 226). The purse was possibly made from deerskin; if so, its small size is surprising.

It was, however, apparently more common to make a pouch from a larger, rectangular piece of leather, which could be folded double along the bottom edge and stitched on each side (nos. 1694 & 1695). A leather pouch in the Museum of London's collection preserves its silk stitching, which was worked with tablets giving the edges a firm and decorative finish (MoL acc. no. 20732). This type of edging would have been unsuitable if the leather was subsequently to be turned inside out. Examples of drawstring pouches from Lubeck, north Germany, have two additional rows of stitch holes along each side and it appears that they were first of all stitched together with the grain face on the inside and then turned inside out and stitched again to provide a stronger edge (van Waateringe and Guiran 1978, 169 fig 71).

An example of a pouch made from a folded rectangular piece of leather comes from a late 13th- or early 14th-century deposit (ceramic phase 9) (no. 1694, fig 227). It is possibly sheep or goatskin and was pared down on the flesh side

to an even thickness before the sideseams were stitched with a fine thread. The top edge of the pouch was left plain apart from a series of slots through which a leather drawstring was inserted, and a slit at the centre of the back around which there is a number of stitch holes. This suggests that a strap or handle was sewn on at this point, which would have enabled the pouch to be slung from a girdle. The two ends of the drawstring were sewn together but its full length is not preserved.

A smaller pouch of a similar form from the late 14th century (ceramic phase 11) has stitch holes round its top opening, in addition to a seam on each side (no. 1695). A decorative edging, which was probably worked with tablets, must therefore have been added to the pouch originally. Two leather drawstrings pulled the bag closed, and a third strip of leather, through which the drawstrings slotted at the corners, was added to form a handle. Similar handles made from silk braids were often used in combination with drawstrings on silk bags (eg Schmedding 1978, nos. 14, 37, 91, 158, 160, 257, 258, 263 & 268–71), and a few are preserved in tawed white leather (Schmedding 1978, no. 255), but examples in tanned leather appear otherwise to be unrecorded.

The finishing of leather purses with silk is referred to by Chaucer in *The Miller's Tale* where he described the Carpenter's wife as wearing 'a purs of lether, Tasseled with silk, and perled with latoun' (Cawley 1975, lines 3250–1).

1693 SH74 acc. no. 641 (context 536) ceramic phase 6 fig 226
Possibly deerskin (AML). Part of a small drawstring pouch made from two pieces of leather cut to a similar pattern and sewn inside out. Grain/flesh stitch holes along sideseam. h 98mm; surviving w 65mm.

1694 SWA81 4908 (2063) 9 fig 227
Possibly sheep/goatskin (AML). Part of drawstring pouch made from a rectangular piece of leather folded double along its bottom edge and seamed on each side. There is a small vertical slit in the centre of the top edge which has stitch holes on each side. Drawstring composed of two strips of leather originally stitched together in the centre. Grain/flesh stitch holes along sideseams. Finished h 183mm; w 202mm.

1695 BC72 3285 (250) 10 fig 228
Probably deerskin (AML). Small drawstring pouch made from a rectangular piece of leather folded double

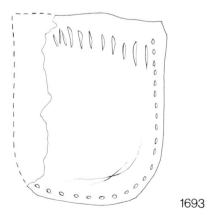

1693

226   Leather drawstring pouch (1:2)

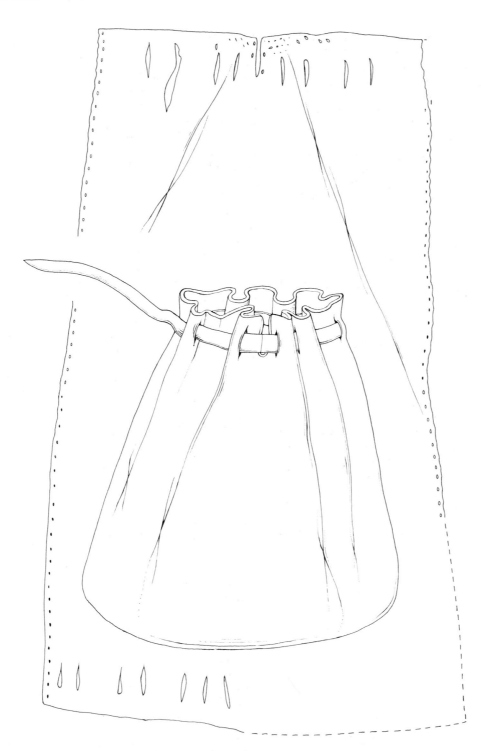

1694

227 Leather drawstring pouch, flat layout and reconstruction (1:2)

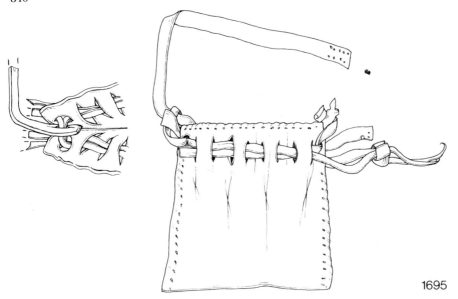

1695

228 Leather drawstring pouch (drawing 1:2,
detail 1:1, photograph 3:4)

along its bottom edge; seamed along each side and stitched round the top opening; grain/flesh stitch holes. There are two drawstrings, which were originally knotted at the sides, and a handle made from two strips of leather. These have a small slit at one end, which fitted into the top corners of the pouch and through which the drawstrings passed to secure the handle in position; stitch holes at the opposite ends show they were sewn together. Finished h 88mm; w 90mm.

Leather pouch with silk edging

A different type of silk edging from that worked with tablets is illustrated by an incomplete example where silk ribbon was used to bind the leather, which was recovered from a deposit dating to the late 14th century (ceramic phase 11) (no. 1696, fig 229). The leather used for the front is engraved with parallel lines. A similar technique was used to embellish some contemporary shoes with long piked toes (Grew and de Neergaard 1988, figs 119–121), which came from the same deposit. There is, however, a strong possibility that the pouch was made from recycled leather (not offcuts) since the decoration makes little attempt to reflect the shape of the pouch, and this is in contrast to the shoes where the decoration was designed to fit the shape of the uppers. As a further decorative touch the pouch was embroidered on the front and back with small knots

worked in cross-stitch using silk thread.

The upper section of this pouch is not preserved and its method of fastening is therefore uncertain. The lower edge was finished with silk ribbon. Two narrow ribbons were stitched together with a third concealed inside, which acted as a reinforcement. This type of edging appears to have superseded that worked with tablets, although it can be seen from the evidence presented here that the two methods were apparently both in use during the late 14th century. A small, red velvet reliquary pouch dating to the 15th century in the Abbey of St Maurice, Saint Maurice, Switzerland, has a similar silk binding stitched round its opening (Schmedding 1978, 191–2 no. 162). The impression gained from examining the London pouch is that, unlike the other examples, it was not professionally made.

1696 BC72 acc. no. 3617 (context 150)
ceramic phase 11 fig 229
Possibly deerskin (AML). Part of a small pouch made from two pieces of leather, of which neither the sides nor the top edge are preserved. The front is engraved with pairs of parallel lines and embellished with small crosses sewn in two-ply silk thread, which also appear originally to have adorned the back of the pouch. The edge is bound with two similar tabby-woven silk ribbons, which were sewn together by placing two of their selvedges side by side; the opposite selvedge of one

229 Leather pouch edged with silk ribbon no. 1696 (3:4). Detail showing engraved decoration and silk embroidery (5:1)

ribbon was then hemmed to the back of the pouch and the other oversewn to the edge of the front. Before the silk binding was sewn into position a third piece of ribbon, which had been folded double and sewn into a narrow cord by stitching both selvedges together, was placed inside the binding as a reinforcement cord. Further rows of stitch holes along the bottom of the pouch indicate that the present edging is not the original. Surviving h 92mm; surviving w 92mm.

Cloth pouches

Pouches made from cloth appear to have been popular in the 13th and 14th centuries, and although many are preserved as reliquary pouches, especially in cathedrals and abbeys on the continent, few have been excavated in England. There are four from the London excavations included in this survey, one from a deposit of *c*.1270 (ceramic phase 8) and three from deposits of the late 14th century (ceramic phase 11).

Only the top portion of the earliest pouch is preserved (no. 1697). It was made from at least five scraps of silk cloth of identical weave – a 1.3 weft-faced compound twill probably woven in Spain – and the top opening was finished with a tablet-woven edge worked with two, four-hole tablets (Pritchard 1985, 31 fig 6; Crowfoot et al. forthcoming). Part of a silk plait was found in association with the pouch and this was probably a drawstring from it. The pouch can be compared with one found in the medieval city ditch at Aldersgate earlier this century (Ward-Perkins 1940, 161 fig 49) which was made from a silk cloth patterned with heraldic devices; triple-towered castles on one side and fleurs de lis alternating with swans on the other. This cloth, which is a type of *pannus de aresta*, was also probably woven in Spain during the 13th century.

The cloth pouches from late 14th-century London are smaller than those of leather. They are made from a single rectangular strip of cloth which is folded double along the bottom edge. The side seams are tablet-woven with the weft being inserted through the cloth with a needle. The tablet weaving began along one side; round the opening at the top the pack of tablets was divided in half and first one side of the opening was worked and then the other; the two halves of the pack were reunited for seaming the opposite

side of the purse. The ends of the warp were tied into tassels. Further tassels were made separately and stitched into place.

All three 14th-century cloth pouches are made from fabrics which would not have been readily available a century earlier. Two examples are made from half-silk velvets with a long, solid, cut pile (nos. 1698 & 1699). One system of threads (the weft) has almost entirely decayed in the acidic soil conditions indicating it was a cellulose fibre, probably flax, and this has left the cloths in tatters. The silk tablet-woven edging, which was used to finish the pouches, has, however, enabled them to keep their original shape (fig 230). The third pouch does not have a drawstring fastening and instead a small handle made from a fingerloop braid was inserted through the hole in one corner (no. 1700, fig 231). This suggests that the pouch may have served a slightly different purpose and perhaps contained sweet-smelling herbs; lavender sachets are recorded in inventories at this period (Dillon and St John Hope 1897, 287 and 307). The silk cloth from which this pouch was made is a type of material that in the 14th century was often called *camoca* (King and King 1988, 69; Crowfoot et al. forthcoming); it is patterned with rows of hexagons containing beasts or birds intertwined with sprays of foliage, while heraldic devices form panels between the hexagons.

1697 TL74 acc. no. 2434 (context 2532)
ceramic phase 8
Part of pouch made from five pieces of silk cloth woven in an identical 1.3 weft-faced compound twill. The top edge was folded inwards once before it was finished in tablet-weave. Surviving h 40mm; w 90mm. (Crowfoot et al. forthcoming, no. 398).

1698 BC72 1849 (55) 11 fig 230
Drawstring pouch made from a rectangular strip of half-silk velvet folded double and finished along both the sides and top opening with a tablet-woven edge; the tassels in the corners are made from the warp ends of the tablet-woven edging with some extra threads looped in, and the tassel in the centre is sewn on to the velvet. h 80mm; w 75mm (Crowfoot et al. forthcoming, no. 349).

1699 BC72 3684 (150) 11
Pouch as preceding but in a more fragmentary state, lined with silk taffeta. h 80mm; w 70mm. (Crowfoot et al. forthcoming, no. 350).

230 Velvet drawstring pouch no. 1698 (3:4)

231 Cloth pouch no. 1700 (3:4)

1700 BC72 2822 (150) 11 fig 231
Pouch made from a rectangular strip of a pink and white lampas-woven silk cloth folded double and finished along both sides and round the opening with a tablet-woven edge, ending in a tassel in each bottom corner. A flat, five-loop finger braid is slotted through a hole in one corner below the opening to form a small handle. h 63mm; w 60mm. (Crowfoot et al. forthcoming, no. 339).

Leather purses with flaps

A very different style of leather purse was recovered from deposits of the late 14th century (ceramic phase 11) and early 15th century (ceramic phase 12), of which four were found together in a revetment dump at Trig Lane (nos. 1702–1705). These purses have a flap closing and were fitted directly onto girdles with the result that they were more secure than those with drawstrings which were a greater temptation to thieves. They appear to have been worn principally by men. The earliest of these purses from London is decorated with two different types of mount (no. 1701, fig 232; for the mounts, see nos. 894 & 1058). Part of a purse from a deposit dating to the first half of the 14th century (ceramic phase 9) may be an earlier example, but only one side of it remains and the top edge has been cut off (Jones 1975, 165–6 fig 31 no. 148). Three others from an early 15th-century deposit appear to have been undecorated (nos. 1702, 1703 & 1704), while a fourth was originally embroidered on the front (no. 1705). A similar purse, also originally embellished with embroidery (no. 1706), can, in addition, be considered to date to this period.

These pouches were often made from several pieces of leather. The smallest consists of six pieces (no. 1701, fig 232). The front section, which is backed with two smaller pieces of leather, does not appear to have been functional, except that it concealed the small container where coins would have been kept. The pouch would have been worn over a belt to which it appears to have been stitched.

A larger example of a somewhat similar pouch is less complete with four pieces only now remaining (no. 1702, fig 233). It appears to have been repaired with rivets and subsequently cut up for cobbling.

Part of the back of another purse is rather different as it has a series of vertical and horizontal slots where it must have been attached by thonging to a belt (no. 1703, fig 234). Meanwhile a piece from the front of a purse, bears an impression of a circular metal fastening, presumably a buckle (no. 1704, fig 234). It is possible that both fragments were originally part of the same purse and that one has shrunk more than the other in the ground.

The two purses from London with stitched decoration were made from at least two pieces of leather (nos. 1705 & 1706, figs 235 & 236). The front was cut to a semi-circular pattern and slit a little below its top edge to form a wide opening only slightly narrower than the finished width of a purse; below this opening pairs of slots were cut. This suggests that a flap with a wide tongue fitted into the opening and was secured by thongs or laces which passed through the smaller slots, although, admittedly, there is no sign of any wear or strain around these slots. The front was also pierced with awl holes marking out a pattern to be embroidered and the impression of the sewing thread is preserved. The pattern of the back extends to a greater height than the front, but as only part of one example is preserved, the purse cannot be fully reconstructed from the excavated portion. The front and back were subsequently sewn together with the grain face innermost and then turned inside out.

A similar purse to the latter decorated examples, from a 14th-century deposit in Stockholm, enables more details of construction to be ascertained (Dahlbäck 1982, 237 fig 208). The back piece is approximately three times the length of the front and a double-ovoid section was cut out from the centre of it. The leather was folded in half and stitched across the width of the purse to form a hollow tube at the top into which the girdle slotted. The part with embroidered decoration was stitched along its top edge to the back of the purse (no such stitch holes are present on the London pouches) so that the long horizontal slot formed an opening for the hand and not for a tongue. This meant that none of the decorative stitching on the front was exposed to view except when the purse was opened.

Sections of three rectangular purses of this type were recovered from a cistern at Dover castle where they were considered to date to the

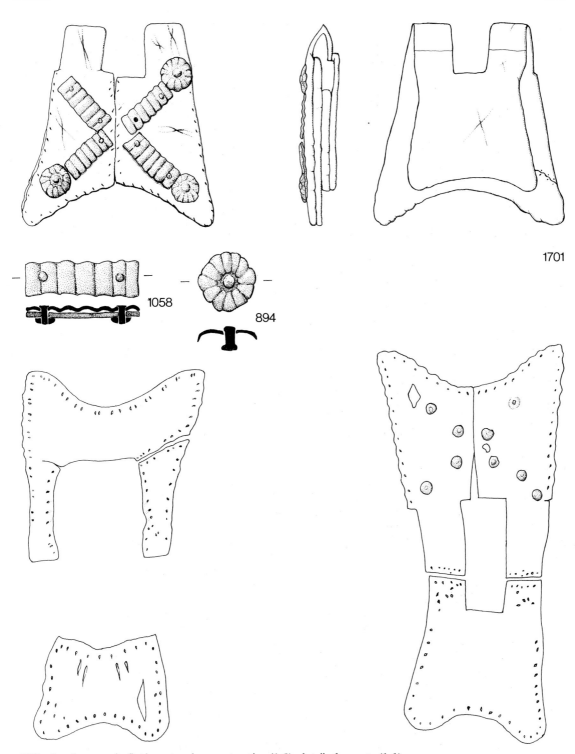

232 Leather pouch, flat layout and reconstruction (1:2), detail of mounts (1:1)

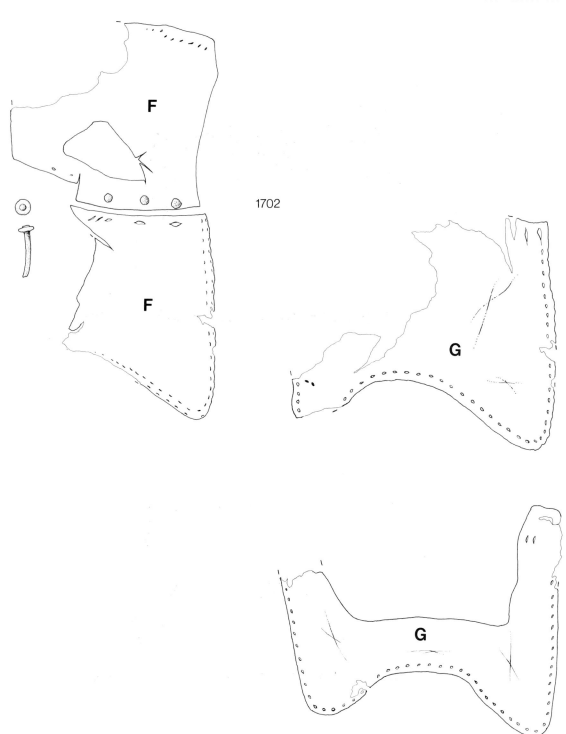

1702

233 Leather pouch. F = flesh face, G = grain face (1:2)

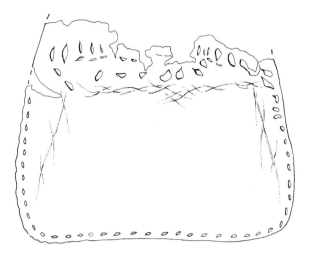

1703

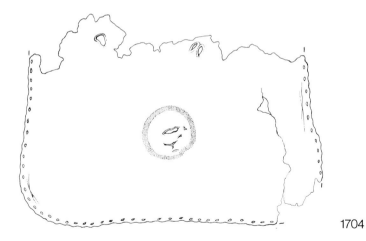

1704

234 Leather pouches (1:2)

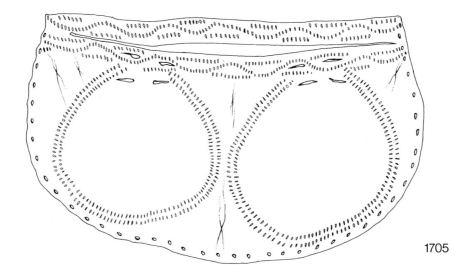

1705

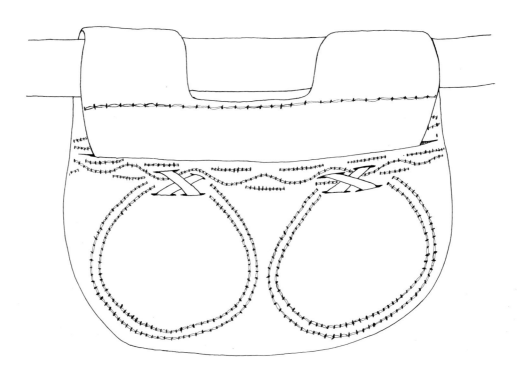

235 Leather pouch (1:2) and reconstruction showing how it might have looked originally

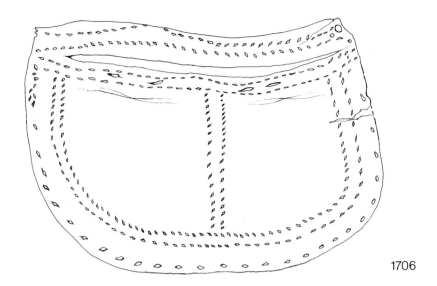

1706

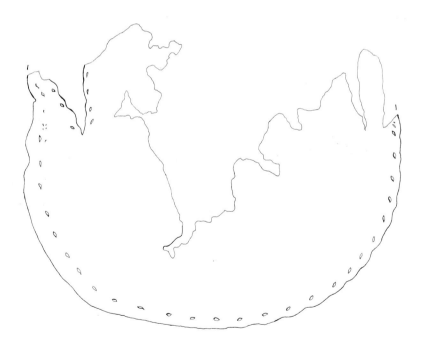

236 Leather pouch (1:2)

early 14th century (Cook et al. 1969, 104 nos. L15–17). A further English example was recovered from a site in Shrewsbury (Shropshire) (Mould forthcoming).

1701 BC72 3879 (150) 11 fig 232
Purse made from six pieces of leather. The front flap has a concave lower edge and is partly backed with two pieces of leather; stitch holes round the edge of the flap indicate that it was lined originally. The front of the flap is decorated with seven circular and rectangular tin-coated iron mounts (see nos. 894 & 1058 for further details). At some time the front was cut down the centre and stitched. The other two pieces of leather, which were originally stitched together, formed the actual container. The inside piece has two pairs of thong slots through which a drawstring would have passed. The two parts of the purse were stitched together with the seam worn behind the belt; and there are additional stitch holes for sewing the purse to the belt. Grain/flesh stitch holes. Max h 110mm; max w 100mm.

1702 TL74 451 and 650 (414) 11 fig 233
Incomplete; four pieces of leather. Two, which are from the front of the purse, are of a similar shape with a concave lower edge; there are two awl holes in the top corner of the inner piece; grain/flesh stitch holes along the sideseam of the latter piece and edge/flesh stitch holes in the outside piece. The top edge of the outside piece has been cut and riveted to a piece of leather which is now of an irregular shape since it was cut up for cobbling, grain/flesh stitch holes close to the bottom edge. A fourth piece of leather is from the back of the front flap and has two slots in the top corner corresponding to those on one of the other pieces, grain/flesh stitch holes round the edge of the seam. Max h 118mm; max w 139mm.

1703 TL74 629 (414) 11 fig 234
Calfskin (AML). Back of purse with inward-sloping sides; grain/flesh stitch holes along sideseam. Close to the foldline of the flap are three rows of slots, the upper row cut vertically and the others horizontally. Surviving h 118mm; w 142mm.

1704 TL74 306 (414) 11 fig 234
Leather too worn for species to be identified (AML). Front of purse with inward-sloping slides; grain/flesh stitch holes along sideseam; and an impression of a circular metal fastening. Surviving h 110mm; w 164mm.

1705 TL74 426 (415) 11 fig 235
Deerskin (AML). Front of purse cut to a semi-circular pattern. A horizontal slit was cut 12–13mm below the top edge and below this are four pairs of slots; it is decorated with stitching in the form of two circular panels with two undulating lines on each side of the slit. Grain/flesh stitch holes round sideseam, 5–9mm apart. h 116mm; w 201mm; w of slit 170mm.

1706 BWB83 311 (unstratified) fig 236
Calfskin (AML). Front and part of back of purse. Front as preceding except the slit was cut 15mm–17mm below the top edge and there are only two pairs of slots below the horizontal slit. The stitching on the front is in the form of two quadrants with paired lines on each side of the slit. The back piece is cut higher than the front and has a V-shaped slit cut to one side with stitching holes along each edge. h 110mm; w 185mm; w of slit 140mm.

Purse frame

A purse frame made from brass was recovered from a 14th-century deposit (ceramic phase 10–11, no. 1707, fig 237). It was probably originally semi-circular, although neither end is preserved. There is nothing to indicate how the container was attached, presumably it was oversewn to the frame in some manner, and a bag made from chamois leather with an elaborate semi-circular frame, which is preserved in Vienna, offers some guidance (Waterer 1968, pl 62). Another example of a purse frame from a 14th-century deposit has been excavated at Netherton, Hampshire (John Cherry pers. comm.). Manuscript illuminations show gamebags, which appear to have circular frames and were fastened with drawstrings, from the first half of the 14th century (fig 225) and it can be inferred that this was the purpose for which most purses with metal frames were used at this period.

1707 BC72 acc. no. 2960 (context 118)
ceramic phase 10–11 fig 237
Part of a brass (AML) purse frame, ? originally semi-circular, with a rotating suspension loop cast in two pieces and rove soldered on. The loop is decorated with three knops. Estimated internal d 100mm.

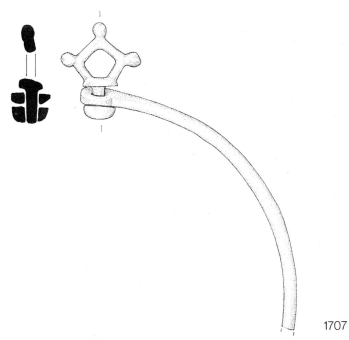

1707

237 Part of a brass purse-frame (1:1)

Cased mirrors

Small metal-cased mirrors have only recently been recognised among excavated medieval finds, having previously been attributed to the Roman period (Guildhall Museum Catalogue 1908, 61 no. 109 & pl XXIV no. 1). Over twenty examples with a distribution from Winchester to Perth are listed in a seminal article (Bayley et al. 1984, 399–402). Prompted by this publication, several further examples have been identified from all over the country. Two basic forms of round hinged case enclosing the actual glass (which rarely survives) were distinguished: a robust copper-alloy form, and a more varied category of lead-tin cases. The grozed glass was

held in place by a cement that occasionally survives as calcium carbonate.

To these two categories of cases may tentatively be added two discs of decorated sheet metal, which, by analogy with more expensive decorated cases of ivory, are probably from another category of larger mirrors, a complete example of which has yet to be found (cf figs 191 & 238).

(see frontispiece for a hinged mirror in use)

Lead-tin cases

These are basically similar to, but not as robust as, the copper-alloy cases described below. The cast decoration and the sizes vary. The sides of the cases (in contrast to those of copper alloy) are usually bevelled. Not all of the following listed objects are definitely mirror cases, but this seems the most probable identification.

1708 SWA81   acc. no. 3445   (context 2273)
ceramic phase 8   fig 239
Incomplete; pewter (AML); corroded; d 45mm; no surviving trace of lugs; decorated with a crude linear depiction of two opposed facing lion-like beasts in the rampant position, one of which is guardant, on a cross-hatched field; a plain vertical band lies between them, and there is a plain ring around the design; the lime cement and the lead backing for the glass survive extensively on the inside surface, but only traces of the glass remain (AML). (Published as pl LIIId in Bayley et al. 1984).

A similar incomplete case with two lugs found in spoil dumped from the Billingsgate site (MoL acc. no. 84.260/1) depicts a stag attacked by two hunting dogs (Bayley et al. 1984, 401), and another complete case with animal decoration is in the British Museum (acc. no. 1902, 5–29, 18).

1709 SH74   134   (386)   8   fig 239
Presumably a mirror case: pewter (AML); disc with no surviving trace of lugs, cement or glass; d 43mm; a central motif of four circles and dots lies within two concentric circles; this is surrounded by a cross-hatched field, with six semicircular arcs each defined by heavy lines, the centres of their circles being along the inside edge of another plain ring, again defined by

238   Using a mirror, after British Library MS Harl.6563

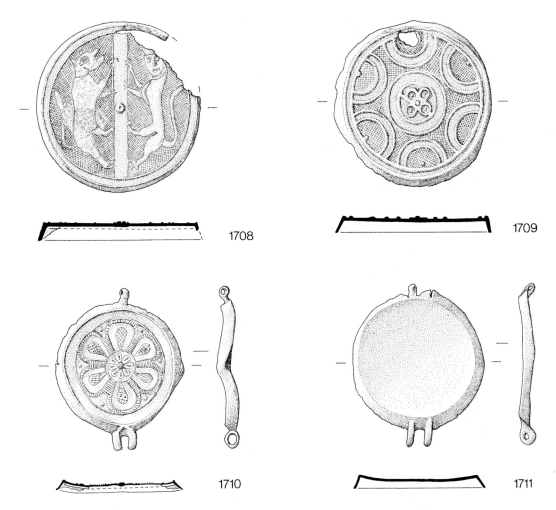

239 Lead-tin mirror cases (1:1)

heavy lines, which surround the entire design; there is a raised central dot at the point from which each circular element was scored in the mould with a compass; a hole near the edge may have been caused by a bubble in the mould during the casting.

Cf Bayley et al. 1984, 401 & pl LIIIe for a larger case with different decoration that also includes circles as a major component, found in spoil from the Billingsgate site. Another case with somewhat similar decoration was found in Lund in Sweden (Kulturen collection acc. no. KM 22069; Claes Wahlöo, pers. comm.).

1710 BIG82 2339 (2745) 8 fig 239 & colour pl 12B
Pewter (AML); disc with both single lug and pair pierced; distorted; d 30mm; central octofoil with six

multiply-outlined lobes radiating outwards (cf petals); the central fields of the lobes are variously obliquely or cross-hatched, in some cases with dots as well, and the outer fields are cross-hatched; there is a small boss between each pair of lobes, near the plain ring which surrounds the decoration; the cement (probably calcium carbonate – AML) and fragments of the glass, now brown in colour, survive internally; a black layer on top of the cement is probably the remains of the lead from the backing to the glass.

1711 SWA81 2123 (2057) 9 fig 239
Pewter (AML); disc with pair of pierced lugs and single unpierced lug; edge slightly distorted; d 32mm; the single lug has a slightly angular profile; undecorated; no trace of glass or cement.

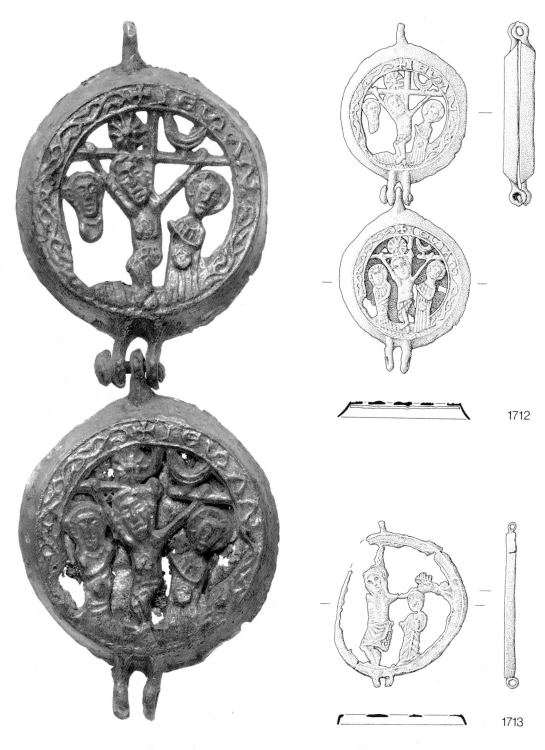

1712

1713

240 Openwork lead-tin mirror cases (photograph 2:1, drawings 1:1)

1712 BWB83 130 (257) 11 fig 240
Case complete; slightly distorted, so that the two parts do not close together as originally intended; d of both parts 34.5mm; lead-tin (AML); the openwork decoration on the two discs differs slightly in detail, in part at least because the metal did not flow evenly in casting, leaving voids and thin areas at different points; a crudely executed crucifixion scene features Christ on the cross in the centre, flanked by the haloed figures of Mary and St John, with the sun and moon above to the sides, and the surrounding legend ✚IƎ∿∧∾ (IESVS), which continues with a foliate scroll around; the disc which has the more completely registered scene retains a thin tin-foil backing (AML) that is missing from the other (in which the figure of Mary is disastrously disembodied by a bubble in the casting process). Even without the defect, the rendering of this conventional scene is not attractive. A cast rivet, apparently of the same alloy as the rest of the case, set through the lugs to act as the hinge, shows evidence of the non-alignment of the two parts of the mould at its head. Its other end is bent round to secure it in place. Traces of the cement, possibly calcium carbonate (AML), survive inside both parts of the case; fragments of glass were present at the time of discovery.

Despite their different appearance, the two major elements could have been cast in the same mould. The tin-foil backing of the glass would presumably have provided a more shiny background to the openwork design (which could perhaps have been painted). Published by Bayley et al. (1984, 401 & pl LIIIc).

1713 BWB83 346 (313) 12 fig 240
Incomplete and slightly corroded disc with single lug and pair all pierced; d c.40mm; lead-tin (AML), openwork scene similar to those on previous item, but somewhat more accomplished (Christ's ribs, St John's bible, and the drapery are more realistically depicted); the surrounding band is apparently plain; no trace of cement etc survives.

A case with a crucifixion scene similar to the two last examples, but from a different mould, was excavated in Bergen in Norway (Herteig 1969, fig 67 lower right – described as a pilgrim souvenir; these mirrors may well have been sold alongside other trinkets at shrines – Brian Spencer, pers. comm.).

Robust copper-alloy cases

These consist of two similar, slightly convex cast discs of c.30mm diameter, each with a single lug on one side and a pair on the other. One disc of each mirror has the single lug and the other has the pair drilled through (a separate, secondary process after casting) for a copper-alloy rivet which acted as the hinge of the case. The recessed inside surfaces of the discs in some instances retain a cement (calcium carbonate according to analyses – Bayley et al. 1984, 399) to hold the glass in place. Where it survives, the glass itself is convex, and coated on the back with a thin film of lead, which together provided the reflecting surface. The convexity gave a slightly magnified image, enhancing the small diameter (c.27–28mm) of the glasses. When the mirror was closed, the interconnection of the unpierced lugs provided an effective curb on lateral movement between the discs. These lugs could have had cord or wire bound around them to keep the case closed when not in use (or perhaps to secure it to the person if it was carried around – cf the chains on seal matrices discussed in the section on Chains – there is, however, no surviving evidence that the lugs were used in this way). Decoration seems invariably to consist of the outline of a crude, rounded, open cross in double lines of punched, opposed triangles, often with a pair of similar, straight, lines running diametrically between the lugs from side to side. Further details of manufacture are given by Bayley et al. In addition to the cases mentioned there, another possible damaged example has recently been excavated at Bristol (City Museum, acc. no. 21/1982 AHR 7E – Mike Ponsford pers. comm.).

1714 BIG82 acc. no. 2188 (context 2570)
ceramic phase 9 fig 241
Gunmetal (AML); case complete; slightly corroded; discs d 29.5 and 30mm; trace of decoration of double lines of opposed, punched triangles; this case has been opened and examined internally since recovery, but is now sealed in the closed position; no visible trace of glass or cement (AML); hinge rivet present.

1715 BWB83 121 (263) 9 figs 15C & 241
Disc originally with a pair of pierced lugs (only one of which survives); d 31mm; double lines of opposed, punched triangles in form of cross, and similar double lines diametrically.

1716 BWB83 4104 (269) 9 fig 241
Disc with single lug pierced; d 30mm; double lines of punched, opposed triangles in form of cross, and similar double lines diametrically; a trace of reddish

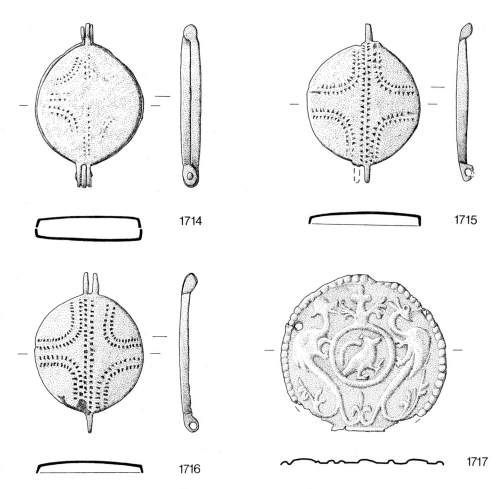

1714

1715

1716

1717

241 Top and bottom left, cast copper alloy mirror cases; bottom right,
possible mirror case of copper alloy sheeting (1:1)

material internally may be cement stained from the lead backing to the glass.

The economy of design which a present day observer might see in the use two similar components for each of these handy, mass produced mirrors, is to some extent belied by the more labour-intensive, secondary hole drilling and decorating processes. The two parts of no. 1714 appear from the discrepancy in the diameters to be from different moulds, hinting that a sizeable production enterprise probably lay behind these objects. This kind of ingenious use of identical components slightly adapted is not a common feature among medieval artefacts (but cf Fingerlin 1971, 442–43 pl 517 no. 449 – part of a late 14th

century belt). There are also parallels with the way the two components of the folding spectacle frames of bone found at the Trig Lane site were used (cf Rhodes 1982A, 57–73), quite aside from the common factor of optical glass. Both these objects use two identical main components, both could be folded to a compact disc which would protect the glass, and both have side lugs by which they could have been bound for secure closure (ibid, 62). It would be interesting to know whether these sometimes similarly named glass items (mirrors and spectacles could both be referred to as *spectacula* in late-medieval records – though there were other terms too) were also manufactured by the same craftsmen, despite the different materials of the respective holders.

Sheet discs with repoussé decoration

These are probably parts of composite mirrors, which would not necessarily have been hinged. An alternative possibility, that they are prints from mazer bowls, seems unlikely in view of similarity of design between no. 1718 and ivory mirrors, and the coating (similar to that on definite mirrors) on its back. The place of manufacture of the two objects described below is not known.

Copper alloy

1717 BWB83 197 (308) 11 fig 241
Disc not quite complete; d 44.5mm; brass (AML); decoration:– bird advancing to right, down-turned crescent above, all within a raised circle, (the remaining elements are symmetrical) central fleshy-leaved plant (cf acanthus) with tripartite motif at top, two opposed bipeds (?birds) with duck-like heads and long tails, which turn into a scrolled plant motif and shared central fleur de lis below, cling to the outside of the raised circle, as if contemplating devouring the plant which lies between them; the disc has a beaded border; two holes for rivets survive near the edge.

The decoration was probably hammered up against a die-block. The style would have been archaic in the 14th century and indicates that this object was probably made in the 13th; it may have been an heirloom, or residual in the context in which it was found.

The brass bowls, produced in great numbers in Nuremberg in Germany and in the area of Dinant in present-day Belgium in the late-medieval period, and used for display in the home (Haedeke 1970, 78–79), are probably the best-known items decorated by this technique; further research is needed before the origin of the present disc can be suggested.

Silver

1718 BWB83 4499 (unstratified – found in an area with a preponderance of late 14th century items) fig 242 & colour pl 12C
Fragment; silver gilt (AML/MLC); weight 3.08 grammes; decoration:– hind quarters of a stallion probably depicted at a walk, with part of the (?)long outer garment of the rider; above and below is stylised foliage with fleshy voluted trefoils and buds or berries growing from a sinuous stem, and a five-petalled flower; the back has a black, shiny coating that is visually similar to the galena (lead sulphide) identified on a mirror like nos. 1714 etc above, which was found in Essex (Bayley et al. 1984, 399). This coating may have been intended to provide a dark foil against which the image on the reflecting surface would have been enhanced. The fragment also has two pierced rectangular holes and a running groove close to the surviving part of the irregularly cut, rounded edge. Assuming that the complete object was originally circular, the diameter would have been *c*.80mm or just over.

By contrast with the preceding item, the crisper decoration here was probably raised by hand. Although too little survives to be certain of the complete design on this accomplished, very high quality piece, a broad comparison may be made with the hunting scenes on some mirror cases of ivory (eg Dalton 1909, 129 & pl LXXXVIII nos. 377–79: no. 378, acc. no. 1856, 6–23, 102 – see fig 242, this volume – is of a similar diameter to that suggested for the present fragment; see also Natanson 1951, nos. 43–45, dated to *c*.1320–40). A copper-alloy case decorated with a lizard (Metropolitan Museum, Cloisters collection, New York, acc. no. 47.101.47) is a rare survival of a complete, high-quality mirror from the medieval period.

The movement of the horse is more vividly depicted on the present fragment than on any of the comparable ivory cases. The style suggests an early 14th-century date, and though the ivory parallels have been credited with a continental origin, there is no reason why the present precious-metal one may not be from an English workshop (RW Lightbown, pers. comm.). The style is very similar to that on a smaller silver-gilt mazer print (d *c*.55mm) which depicts a lion attacking a bird-like creature against a background of foliate motifs (St John Hope 1887, 138 fig 1).

The holes near the edges of the above two objects were presumably for rivets. Until a more complete parallel for this suggested category of mirror case is found, the identification cannot be regarded as certain. The blacking on the back of no. 1718 is visually similar to that on the back of a lead-alloy leaf found attached to an annular frame (no. 1374, d 88mm, described under Brooches); the object has no definite connection with mirrors – the evidence suggesting that there was a pin is a strong argument that it was an unusual kind of brooch. The possibility that it is from some kind of standing mirror may, however, be strengthened by evidence from future finds.

1718

242 Top, silver-gilt mirror case – right, reverse showing black coating;
bottom, ivory mirror case with comparable scene (British
Museum collection) (top left and bottom, 1:1; top right, 1.5:1)

The mirrors in the first two categories above, which were mass-produced for a popular market, seem from the available indications of date to have been introduced in the middle of the 13th century. In the present small sample (11 items) all the cases attributable to the period before the middle of the 14th century are of lead-tin, while the robust copper-alloy ones were apparently current in the late 14th century – a time when those of lead-tin adopted a stereotyped religious motif for their decoration. The cast copper-alloy mirrors probably derive from a series of fine, (?)late 13th-century enamelled examples produced for an upper-class clientele in France (eg Swarzenski and Netzer 1986, 21 and 102–03 no.

33). Dating for the two sheet-metal examples is less certain. The high quality of no. 1718, an individually worked version in precious metal, contrasts markedly with almost all the other objects described in this volume.

One thousand mirrors were among the goods brought by ship, probably from the Low Countries, to London in 1384 (Bayley et al. 1984, 401–02). No details are given which would allow these imports to be identified with any of the types of mirrors discussed here. The craftsmen in London who called themselves 'mirrorers' could have manufactured at least some of the items described above during the 14th century (Veale 1969, 141 & 143).

Combs

Three out of the four basic comb forms as defined by Patricia Galloway (Galloway 1976, 154–6) are present in the assemblages which are the subject matter of this study. They are simple double-sided combs carved in one piece, which include all those of wood, horn and ivory, one single-sided composite comb and one double-sided composite comb, which are both made from antler (fig 243). The descriptive terms advocated by Galloway are followed, except that in accordance with a more recent study 'tooth-plate' and 'end-plate' are substituted for 'tooth segment' and 'end tooth segment' for composite combs (MacGregor 1985, fig 43). Furthermore, following Arthur MacGregor, the term 'side-plate' rather than 'connecting-plate' is used in the text to refer to bone-plates riveted to horn since they do not hold together a series of tooth-plates.

Considerable attention was paid to the styling of hair in the medieval period, causing combs and

Double-sided Simple Comb

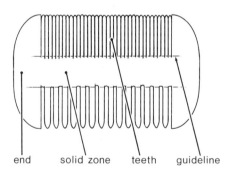

end   solid zone   teeth   guideline

Single-sided Composite Comb

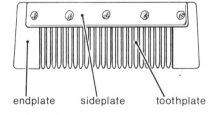

endplate   sideplate   toothplate

243   Comb terminology

mirrors to become associated in popular imagery with vanity (fig 244). It is, therefore, ironic that so few combs should be preserved from England for the years *c*.1150 to *c*.1450, whereas for the previous centuries they are among the commonest artefacts from urban sites. A study of the combs from London for this later period substantiates a long-held explanation of why the number is so low, for out of 36 combs recovered between 1972 and 1983 thirty-two were made from wood, one from horn and another from elephant ivory. Such materials are extremely sensitive to soil conditions and it is generally only in anaerobic deposits that they are preserved in the ground. The apparent preference for box-wood combs in late-medieval London is in marked contrast to the evidence of earlier centuries, where multi-piece combs of antler or horn and bone were common (Pritchard forthcoming), whereas none of wood has been recorded from the City for the period between the collapse of the Roman empire and the late 12th century. This change in the materials used for combs was part of a general decline in the working of antler throughout northern Europe, which in England has been attributed in part to an increased protection extended to deer as forests were set aside for the royal chase (MacGregor 1985, 32–4), whereas in Denmark it has been related to a change in land use as forests were cut down to make way for more extensive agriculture (Christophersen 1980, 226).

The switch from composite combs of antler to one-piece combs of boxwood that is so evident in London is not as noticeable on the continent, where one-piece combs made from metapodial bones tended to supplant antler, particularly in Scandinavian and German towns (Wiberg 1977, 202; Broberg and Hasselmo 1981, 72–84; Ulbricht 1984, fig 2, and pls 22–26, 61–63). Consequently, the absence of such bone combs from London is surprising but, since bone survives better than horn, ivory or wood in the prevailing soil conditions, this evidence probably accurately reflects their limited use in the city.

While the archaeological evidence indicates that wooden combs gradually replaced those of

244   Mermaid holding a mirror in one hand and a comb in the other *c*.1325–35 after the *Luttrell Psalter*, BL Add. MS 42130 f.70b)

antler in medieval London, it is impossible to estimate how commonplace horn combs were. There is only one preserved from the period under survey, no. 1721, whereas there are at least five from the period 900 to 1150. Four of these latter combs were, however, identified on the basis of their bone side-plates, which were a feature of horn combs in the 10th to early 12th centuries. Since the change to one-piece combs of horn coincided with the decline in output of antler composite combs and an upturn in the manufacture of combs of wood, the evidence points to a reorganisation of workshops specialising in the production of combs during the 12th century.

The extent to which ivory combs were in everyday use can also only be conjectured. They are more frequently mentioned in documents than other kinds of comb on account of their high prestige, but such source material is unrepresentative of medieval society as a whole. By the 15th century they appear to have been commonplace among the upper classes, and the value of 6d placed upon one in the papers of the Pastons in the early 1470s (Davis 1971, 362) suggests that they were becoming cheaper as elephant tusks from India and Africa grew more plentiful in western Europe. The pattern of long-distance

trade in ivory, however, remains far from clear and it has recently been asserted that supplies of ivory into western Europe could have been greatly reduced during the late-14th and 15th centuries causing other materials such as bone, specially treated to imitate ivory, to capture the market for a time (Stratford 1987, 108–09).

Antler

(Antler identified by James Rackham)

1719   BIG82   acc. no. 2729   (context 4449) ceramic phase 7   figs 245 & 246
Double-sided composite comb with tooth-plates and connecting-plates cut from antler, and two end-plates and a centre-plate of bronze (AML). The connecting-plates are decorated with a pattern of openwork crosses and the comb is held together with rivets of copper alloy. No fine teeth are preserved and they appear to have been filed smooth after breakage. l 77mm; 9 fine: 3 coarse teeth per 10mm.

1720   WAY83   128   (130)   9   (pre 1279) fig 245
End fragment of composite, single-sided comb with narrow connecting-plates held together with copper-alloy rivets, which pierce the tooth-plates. A hole was drilled through the end-plate. 10 teeth per 10mm.

Combs nos. 1719 and 1720 from 13th-century deposits (ceramic phases 7 and 9) are the only two made from antler which fall into the period of this survey. The latter comes from a deposit with a *terminus ante quem* of 1279 and sherds of associated pottery suggest that the comb could have been discarded up to a century earlier. Both follow the tradition of Roman, Saxon and Viking-Age antler combs in being made with separate tooth-plates and connecting-plates, as necessitated by the nature of the raw material, but they possess important stylistic differences. In addition, they are held together with rivets of copper alloy rather than of iron, which was usual for earlier composite combs (except for some combs in the 7th century and occasionally when copper-alloy rivets were used for repairs).

The single-sided antler comb has narrow connecting-plates, D-shaped in section, which extend the full length of the comb, and were apparently undecorated (no. 1720, fig 245). It was assembled with copper-alloy rivets, and while their exact sequence cannot be determined

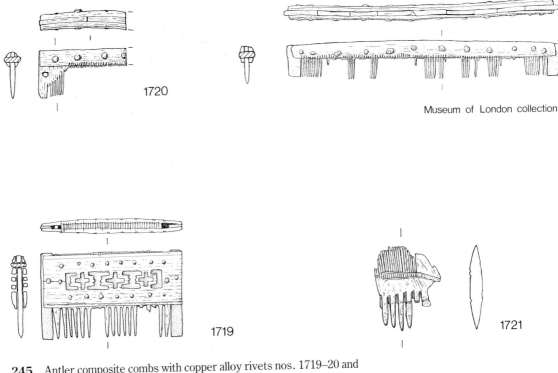

1720

Museum of London collection

1719

1721

245 Antler composite combs with copper alloy rivets nos. 1719–20 and
top right MoL acc. no. A14724, horn comb no. 1721 (1:2)

because of the comb's fragmentary condition, it appears that the rivets pierced the tooth-plates as well as sometimes passing between them. A hole in the end-plate would have enabled the comb to be suspended from a girdle or chain and is a feature that is absent from later-medieval combs which appear often to have been kept in pouches. The style of the comb, with its plain connecting-plates, extravagant use of rivets, finely spaced teeth and pierced end-plate conforms to a number of contemporary examples from Schleswig in north Germany, and Lund in south Sweden (Ulbricht 1984, pl 29 no. 6 and pl 70 nos. 2–3; Persson 1976, 324 and 326 figs 291 & 292 nos. 25 & 35–36). There is, at present, insufficient evidence from England to judge how common they were in this country; one has been recorded from Southampton (Ian Riddler, pers. comm.) and an unprovenanced example was given to the London Museum by its first director, Guy Laking (MoL acc. no. A14724, fig 245).

The other antler comb from a 13th-century London context was originally double-sided, but

the more closely spaced teeth were at some stage filed down to the level of the connecting-plates, perhaps because of breakage (no. 1719, figs 245 & 246). The comb is rectangular with two tooth-plates, 28mm and 35mm wide, in contrast to earlier composite combs which usually had narrower tooth-plates and more of them, numbering as many as fifteen on one 10th-century comb of exceptional length from London (Pritchard forthcoming, fig 3.76). Sandwiched between the connecting-plates are two strips of bronze sheeting rendered visible by a series of three openwork crosses cut in the antler connecting-plates. Two thicker strips of bronze were added as end-plates and the whole comb was assembled with nineteen rivets of copper alloy, of which only the outer two secured the bronze end-plates.

Composite combs incorporating metal sheeting became popular in northern Europe during the 12th century. Openwork patterns cut into connecting-plates of antler or bone frequently took the form of crosses, and single-sided as well as double-sided combs were decorated in this manner. These occur on the continent (Ulbricht 1984, pl 28, no. 1, pl 29, no. 1 and pl 72, nos. 1–3) and in England, where they have been recorded from Northampton and York (Baldwin Brown 1915, 391, pl LXXXVI, no. 2; Waterman 1959, pl XVIII, no. 2) as well as from London (VCH 1909, 165, fig 27, Baldwin Brown 1915, 391, pl LXXXVII, no. 1), the latter comb having fanciful animal head end-plates and an exaggerated humped back. This form of openwork decoration may ultimately have derived from that on liturgical furniture such as reliquary crosses, which sometimes had relics secured within similar cut-out shapes behind transparent panes of horn. Although the Billingsgate comb was originally double-sided, an unusual feature of it, namely the presence of bronze end-plates which extend only

to the top of the connecting-plates rather than to the complete height of the comb in its double-sided form, suggests that it could have been reassembled with short metal plates replacing taller ones of antler, perhaps after some of the finer spaced teeth were broken.

Examination of another double-sided composite comb incorporating strips of sheeting preserved from London shows that it too was made from antler (James Rackham, pers. comm.) and assembled with rivets of copper alloy, rather than of bone as stated in earlier literature (MoL acc. no. A1598; Ward-Perkins 1940, 291, pl LXXXVIII, no. 2). The end-plates and three tooth-plates range from 15mm to 17mm in width, and each is pierced with two rivets thereby ensuring that the strips of metal lying beneath each connecting-

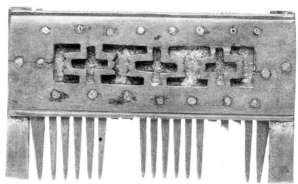

246 Antler double-sided composite comb, no. 1719 (1:1), with detail showing the remains of the row of fine teeth

plate were held securely in position (fig 247). A further feature of this composite comb is the pronounced concave outline of both grades of teeth, which is rare among double-sided combs of this period.

It can, therefore, be seen that composite combs of antler lingered on in use in London throughout the 12th and early 13th centuries, during which period fresh styles were introduced, probably from the continent.

Horn

1721 BC72 no. acc. 3410 (context 250)
ceramic phase 10 fig 245
Fragment of double-sided comb with guidelines scored in pairs for both sets of teeth on both faces; h 45mm; 9 fine: 2 coarse teeth per 10mm.

A horn comb from a deposit of the early 14th-century (ceramic phase 10) is double-sided (no. 1721, fig 245) but unlike those from London dating from the 10th to the middle of the 12th centuries no bone side-plates were added. Also unlike earlier combs, the end that is preserved, albeit only in part, appears to have been cut to a geometric pattern. This corresponds to the ornate ends that can be observed on a number of contemporary wooden combs (nos. 1729–32), and illustrates how stylistically similar combs made from different raw materials tended to be in

the 14th century. Indeed the practice of aping the appearance of combs made from more costly materials caused regulations to be issued in Paris in 1324 forbidding bone combs to be produced in imitation of ivory ones so that customers would not be defrauded (de Lespinasse 1892, 672).

Wood

(Wood identifications by Rowena Gale – RG, and Jane Squirrell – JPS)

Convex ends

1722 SWA81 acc. no. 1417 (context 2187)
ceramic phase 6 fig 248
Buxus sp. (RG). End fragment, two grooves along both faces of solid zone; h 56mm; 10 fine : 2 coarse teeth per 10mm.

1723 SWA81 1355 (2207) 6 fig 248
Buxus sp. (RG). End fragment, two grooves along both faces of solid zone; h 60mm; 10 fine : 3–4 coarse teeth per 10mm.

1724 BC72 4830 (250) 10
Buxus sp. (RG). End fragment, incised line along centre of solid zone on both faces; h 74mm; 9 fine : 3–4 coarse teeth per 10mm.

1725 BC72 4851 (250) 10 fig 248
Buxus sp. (RG). End fragment, incised line along centre of solid zone on both faces; h 92mm; 9 fine : 3 coarse teeth per 10mm.

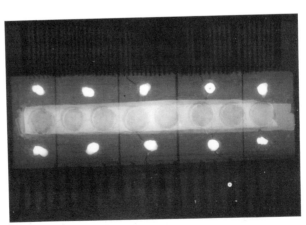

247 X-ray of antler double-sided comb, MoL acc. no. A1598 (1:1)

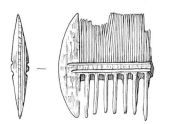

1722

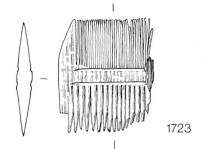

1723

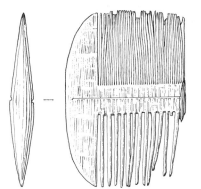

1725

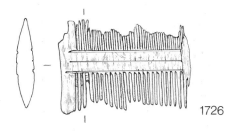

1726

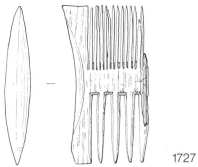

1727

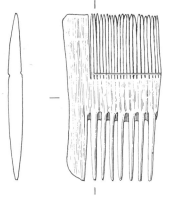

1728

248 Wooden double-sided combs (1:2)

Concave ends

1726 CUS73 acc. no. 148 (context I,12) ceramic phase 9   fig 248
Probably *Buxus* sp. (RG). Broken one end, median line and guidelines for both sets of teeth on both faces; h 51mm; 8–9 fine : 4 coarse teeth per 10mm. (Henig 1975, 153, no. 7, fig 25)

1727 BC72 3735 (250) 10 fig 248
Buxus sp. (RG). End fragment, faint guideline for fine teeth on one face; h 83mm; 5 fine : 1 coarse tooth per 10mm.

1728 BC72 3730 (150) 11   fig 248
Buxus sp. (RG). End fragment, guidelines for fine teeth on both faces; h 88mm; 6 fine : 2 coarse teeth per 10mm.

Ornate ends

1729 CUS73 acc. no. 162 (context III,10) ceramic phase 9   fig 249
Probably *Buxus* sp. (RG). End fragment, guidelines for both sets of teeth on both faces; h 50mm; 9 fine : 3–4 coarse teeth per 10mm. (Henig 1975, 153, no. 5, fig 25)

1730 CUS73 149, (I,12)   9   fig 249
End fragment, guidelines for both sets of teeth; end and solid zone decorated with openwork; h 64mm; 7–8 fine : *c*.4 coarse teeth per 10mm (Henig 1974, 199, no. 245, fig 42)

1731 BC72 1512 (55)   11   fig 249
Buxus sp. (RG). End fragment, guidelines for both sets of teeth on both faces; h 87mm; 7 fine : 2 coarse teeth per 10mm.

1732 BC72 4263 (150)   11   fig 249
Buxus sp. (RG). End fragment, guidelines for both sets of teeth on one face; h 85mm; *c*.6 fine : *c*.2 coarse teeth per 10mm.

Straight ends

1733 CUS73 acc. no. 113 (context V,13) ceramic phase 9
End fragment; h *c*.64mm; 4 coarse teeth per 10mm. (Henig 1975, 153 no. 6 fig 25)

1734 BC72 1719 (55)   11
Buxus sp. (RG). End fragment; h 81mm; 9 fine : 2 coarse teeth per 10mm.

1735 BC72 1876 (79)   11
Buxus sp. (RG). End fragment, no teeth preserved; h 99mm.

1736 BC72 2848 (88) 11
Buxus sp. (RG). End fragment, guideline for fine teeth on one face; h 73mm; 7 fine : 3 coarse teeth per 10mm.

1737 BC72 4108 (88) 11 fig 249
End fragment, solid zone decorated with openwork; h 85mm; 9 fine : 3 coarse teeth per 10mm.

1738 BC72 2634 (89) 11 fig 249
Buxus sp. (RG). End fragment; h 80mm; 7 fine : 2 coarse teeth per 10mm.

1739 BC72 4337 (150) 11
Buxus sp. (RG). End fragment, guidelines for both sets of teeth on both faces; h 85mm; 7 fine : 2 coarse teeth per 10mm.

1740 BC72 4259 (150) 11
Buxus sp. (RG). End fragment, guidelines for coarse teeth on both faces; 2–3 coarse teeth per 10mm.

1741 MIL72 73 (502/23A) 11
Buxus sp. (RG). Edge fragment with strands of cut human hair adhering to surface; 9 fine : 3 coarse teeth per 10mm.

1742 TL74 1089 (368) 12
Buxus sempervirens (JPS). End fragment, guidelines for fine teeth on one face; h 85mm; 8 fine : 3 coarse teeth per 10mm.

1743 TL74 1135 (368) 12 fig 249
Buxus sempervirens (JPS). End fragment, decorated along solid zone with an engraved ring-and-dot pattern alternating with openwork; h 82mm; *c*.8 fine : 3 coarse teeth per 10mm.

1744 SWA81 1713 (2102) 12
Buxus sp. (RG). End fragment, faint guideline for fine teeth on one face only; 6 fine : 2 coarse teeth per 10mm.

1745 SWA81 1780 (2103) 12 fig 250
Buxus sp. (RG). End fragment, solid zone decorated with an inscription carved in relief on a tooled ground, framed with double lines and painted yellow. The end of the comb is rilled. Inscription in black-letter, *vous* [. . .] / [. . .] *byen*; pigments, yellow ochre (MLC) and orpiment (AML, J Bayley). Faint guidelines for both sets of teeth on one face. h 133mm; 8 fine : 3 coarse teeth per 10mm.

Fragments lacking ends

1746 CUS73 acc. no. 151 (context I,12) ceramic phase 9
Fragment, line incised along centre of solid zone on both faces; h 73mm; 9 fine : 4 coarse teeth per 10mm. (Henig 1975, 153 no. 8 fig 125)

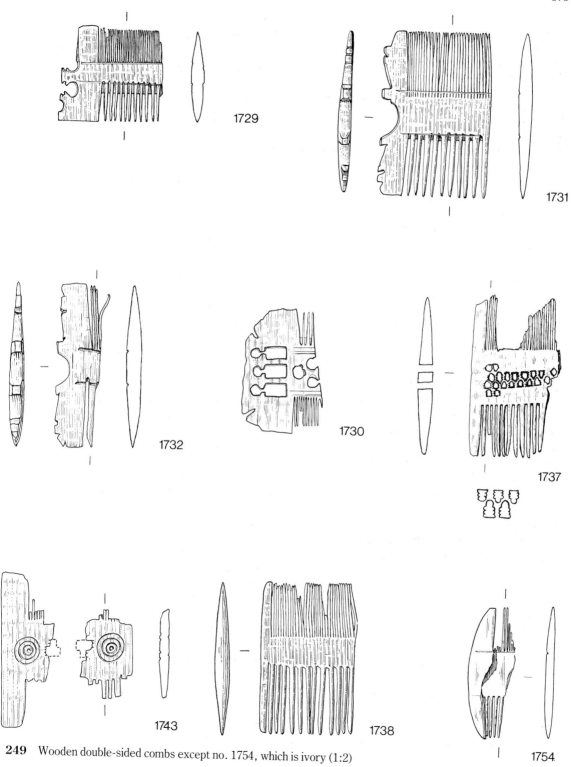

249 Wooden double-sided combs except no. 1754, which is ivory (1:2)

1747 BC72 1559 (55) 11
Buxus sp. (RG). Fragment; h 85mm; 8 fine : 2–3 coarse teeth per 10mm.

1748 BC72 1720 (55) 11
Buxus sp. (RG). Fragment; 8 fine : 4 coarse teeth per 10mm.

1749 BC72 2114 (79) 11
Buxus sp. (RG). Fragment; h 84mm; 8 fine : 2–3 coarse teeth per 10mm.

1750 BC72 2328 (79) 11
Buxus sp. (RG). Fragment, faint guidelines for fine teeth on both faces; h 91mm; 7 fine : 2–3 coarse teeth per 10mm.

1751 BC72 3430 (88) 11
Buxus sp. (RG). Fragment; 7 fine : 2 coarse teeth per 10mm.

1752 BC72 2847 (88/1) 11
Buxus sp. (RG). Fragment; 8–9 fine : 3 coarse teeth per 10mm.

1753 SWA81 1169 (2112) 12
Buxus sp. (RG). Fragment; h *c.*58mm; *c.*8 fine : 3 coarse teeth per 10mm.

Fragments of 32 wooden combs have been recorded from the excavations covered in this survey, two from deposits of the late 12th century (ceramic phase 6), eight from deposits of the late 13th to mid-14th centuries (ceramic phases 9 and 10); sixteen from the late 14th century (ceramic phase 11), and five from the early decades of the 15th century (ceramic phase 12). All appear to be boxwood, a fine-grained wood, which has the advantage of not warping once it has been seasoned, and which was obtained from mixed deciduous woodland. Re-examination of a 14th-century comb from London previously identified as 'probably hazel' (Rhodes 1980, 112 no. 133) shows that it too is box (Rowena Gale, pers. comm.).

Each comb was made from a rectangular block of wood and is double-sided, with the usual division of fine teeth on one side, and coarser, more widely-spaced teeth on the other. The position of the teeth was frequently marked out with guidelines, sometimes incised on both faces for both sets of teeth (nos. 1726, 1729, 1731 & 1739, figs 248 & 249), sometimes just for the finer set on either one face (no. 1727, fig 248 & nos. 1736, 1742 & 1744) or both faces (nos. 1750 & 1728, fig 248); exceptionally just for the coarse

teeth on both faces (no. 1740); and sometimes along the centre of the solid zone (nos. 1724, 1746 & 1725, fig 248). Such lines could be exploited decoratively by deepening them into grooves, which is a feature of two late 12th-century combs (nos. 1722 & 1723, fig 248). The teeth were cut with a two-bladed saw (Pinto 1952, 176), after which the comb was planed down on both sides so that in section it became lentoid. No comb is now complete so that the proportions of height to length remain speculative. All, however, were fairly small with only one, which is the most elaborate, exceeding a height of 100mm.

The shape of the ends can be classified as convex, concave, straight and ornate. Convex ends occur on two combs from the second half of the 12th century (ceramic phase 6) and on three from a deposit dated to *c.*1330–1340 (ceramic phase 10). Ornate ends are confined to four combs from 14th-century deposits (ceramic phases 9 to 11). Combs with concave ends are similarly limited to 14th-century deposits (ceramic phases 9, 10 and 11). Straight ends, by contrast, do not appear until the late 14th century (ceramic phase 11) when they quickly appear to have superseded previous styles. Such chronological trends as seem to emerge should, however, be treated warily since combs in other collections, show, for example, that straight ends were not unusual among ivory combs of the 12th century (Beckwith 1972, 132 nos. 65–66). Elongated H-profile combs with straight ends, nevertheless, appear to have gained widespread favour during the late 14th century and 15th centuries and continued to be popular throughout the 16th century (MacGregor 1983, 262).

The 'solid' zone offered additional scope for decoration and a few examples exquisitely carved with fretwork, which were principally made in Parisian workshops, having been preserved, including one bearing the monogram and coat of arms of Margaret of Flanders (died 1405) (Erlande-Brandenburg et al. 1987, 138 no. 8). Not surprisingly those excavated from rubbish dumps beside the Thames are of a lower quality but they are nonetheless of interest in revealing what cheaper combs looked like. One comb from a deposit dating to between 1270 and 1350 (ceramic phase 9) has an openwork pattern (no. 1730, fig 249; Henig 1974, fig 42 no. 245), and

250 Wooden double-sided comb with inscription (drawing 1:2, photograph 3:4)

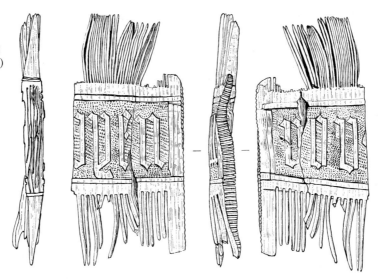

1745

another comb with this form of patterning was recovered from a deposit of the late 14th century (no. 1737, fig 249). The remainder from 14th-century deposits lack decoration apart from simple transverse grooves, which also served as guidelines.

Two out of the three wooden combs from 15th-century deposits are decorated. One has an incised ring-and-dot pattern alternating with openwork (no. 1743, fig 249). The other (the largest of the wooden combs) is more elaborately tooled with an inscription in black letter (no. 1745, fig 250). The inscription was carved against a ground enhanced with punching, which was a widely used ploy intended to conceal marks left on the surface of the wood by a gouge (Chris Green, pers. comm.). The comb was further embellished with rilling along the side of each end. The surface was subsequently painted yellow with a mixture of yellow ochre and orpiment (yellow sulphide of arsenic), the latter pigment (identified by XRF) imparting a sparkle to the more sombre hue of the earth colour (Thompson 1956, 175–7). Orpiment was imported, chiefly from Asia Minor, but it was relatively cheap compared with other exotic pigments such as indigo and azure. Thus in the Great Wardrobe Accounts for 1350–52, where orpiment was listed among the pigments required for painting streamers and banners for the fleet of Edward III, it cost

only 6d per lb (Staniland 1986, 240). The painting and gilding of boxwood combs was forbidden among craftsmen working in Paris in 1324 since it was considered to be harmful to the hair (de Lespinasse 1892, 672). This was presumably because the colour was liable to flake off during use, and it can be seen as a wise precaution since the arsenic content of certain paints, particularly orpiment as used on the Swan-Lane comb, could eventually be fatal. This hazard was to some extent circumvented on the painted London comb since only the solid zone was coloured leaving the teeth plain.

The inscription on the comb, *vous* [. . . / . . .] *byen*, is a lover's motto or posy. The missing words have yet to be established, but it may be compared with the posy *nu si byen*, which occurs on the inside of contemporary gold finger-rings (Alexander and Binski 1987, 487 no. 658), and *je le done pour bien* on a boxwood comb possibly of late 14th-century date (Pinto 1952, 175–6 no. 10). The sentimental value of the comb is further emphasised by score marks or keying down the broken section of the comb, which suggest that it may have been repaired, but not very successfully in the long term since the fracture recurred before it was finally discarded.

Another wooden comb found beside the Thames in London, which is in private ownership, must have come from the same workshop as the previous example since it is stylistically so similar. It is inscribed on both faces with the posy *amorr placet* against a punched background and has an oakleaf carved between the words. No trace of paint remains but this is not an unexpected consequence of long-term burial in waterlogged conditions.

Ivory

1754   BC72   acc. no. 3817   (context 89)   ceramic phase 11   fig 249
Fragment with a convex end, guidelines for fine teeth on both faces and for coarse teeth on only (?)one face; h 70mm; 8 fine : 4 coarse teeth per 10mm.

Ivory was perhaps the most highly prized material used for combs in medieval England. Elephant ivory or walrus ivory was used according to what was available. Written sources indicate that by the 13th century the best quality ivory combs were purchased abroad, particularly in Paris. Thus, among various luxury articles procured for Edward I in Paris in 1278, were two combs of ivory for a sum of 32s 6d (Lysons 1814, 308). The *price* of these combs may be compared with the *value* of 4d placed on four combs of boxwood in a haberdasher's shop in London in 1378 (Riley 1868, 422), and that of 9s for a silver liturgical comb with gilded decoration, which was included in an inventory of vestments and church furniture compiled for St Paul's cathedral in 1245 (Sparrow-Simpson 1887, 468).

Double-sided combs of ivory from recent London excavations display none of the figurative ornament familiar from ecclesiastical pieces and are correspondingly much thinner in section. Part of a plain ivory comb was recovered from a 10th-century pit (Pritchard forthcoming, fig 3.82), while another from a late 14th-century deposit (ceramic phase 11) is distinctive for its thin cross-section and convex end (no. 1754, fig 249). This latter feature helps to distinguish it from small ivory combs of the two succeeding centuries, which are usually characterised by an elongated H-profile (MacGregor 1983, 262).

Cosmetic implements

The medieval person's concern with appearance extended beyond coiffure, clothing and jewellery. The range of cosmetic implements comprising various types of tweezers, toothpicks and earscoops show that the shape of the eyebrows, hairline, and beard, and cleanliness of nails, teeth and ears also received attention. This is underlined by literary descriptions; the Carpenter's wife in Chaucer's *Canterbury Tales* plucked and darkened her eyebrows (*The Miller's Tale*, Cawley 1975, 87, lines 3245–6), while the daughters of the Knight of La Tour Landry were warned against indulging in such vanities (Corson 1972, 79). A few toiletry articles, particularly tweezers, served a single purpose but others combined a dual function. Thus earscoops were frequently teamed with toothpicks or with tweezers and even, it appears, with pens (Ramsay, in Alexander and Binski 1987, 384 no. 424). Sets were also produced, which were presumably carried in a pouch or étui since no method of attaching them to a girdle was included in their design. Such cosmetic tools and sets were not a new introduction, for similar implements had been used in Britain from at least the late Iron Age. The functions remained the same, but the form of the implements was modified, which generally enables medieval examples to be distinguished from their forbears.

Like so many medieval accessories, copper and its alloys (bronze, brass and gunmetal) appear to have been customary for cosmetic implements in everyday use in 13th- and 14th-century London. These metals were apparently used indiscriminately, some implements and sets combining two different metals (nos. 1755 & 1756). Bone was also used but to a much lesser extent.

Sets

Cosmetic sets were found in deposits of the late-13th and 14th centuries (ceramic phases 9 and 11). They comprise three implements – a pair of tweezers, earscoop, and toothpick, which were riveted together at one end. The tweezers, which were made from two strips of metal soldered together at one end, are always the longest implement in the set, being roughly twice the length of the other two, which are placed on either side and fit neatly beside the arms of the tweezers extending close to the point where they divide. This was a new design feature of cosmetic sets produced in the late-medieval period and would have enabled them to fit into narrow étuis, similar to needlecases, rather than hanging freely from a chatelaine. The earscoops are similar in each set, and are flat rather than dished, but the toothpick could take at least three different forms.

The most common and simplest form of toothpick, when it was used in a set, was for the pick to taper to a point. It is represented by two examples from DUA excavations (no. 1755, fig 251 & no. 1757) and a further two in the Museum of London's collection (MoL acc. nos. 80.70/17 & 85.110/4). Another variation was for the pick to be shaped like a miniature sickle (MoL acc. no. 85.241/6), although none of this type has yet been recovered from controlled excavations in London. A third and more complex form is bifurcated with both ends differently shaped, one curving to a point and the other flat, thereby making it into a more versatile tool (no. 1756, fig 251). Part of a cosmetic set with a similar-shaped toothpick was recovered from the site of Woodperry, Oxfordshire, in the 1840s (JW 1846, 120, fig 9), and another from the deserted medieval settlement at Lyveden, Northamptonshire, which, like the Woodperry set, has lost its earscoop (Steane and Bryant 1975, 114, fig 43 no. 49).

1755 BWB83 acc. no. 222 (context 289) ceramic phase 9 fig 251
Copper/brass (AML) with lead/tin solder (MLC); the earscoop and toothpick are similarly decorated on the outside at the rivet end and have been finished on both sides with a file; the ends of the tweezers are bevelled on the outside; l of tweezers 67mm; l of earscoop 33mm; l of toothpick 26mm.

1756 BWB83 2760 (361) 11 fig 251
Brass/copper (AML) with lead/tin solder; one arm of the tweezers is broken off; the toothpick is bifurcated

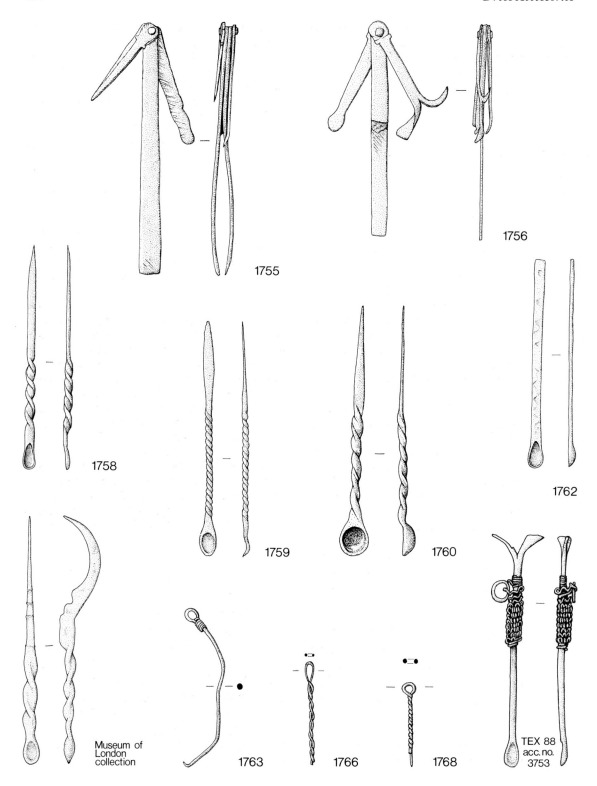

1755

1756

1758

1759

1760

1762

Museum of
London
collection

1763

1766

1768

TEX 88
acc.no.
3753

with one end curving round to a point and the other flat; the toothpick and earscoop are similarly decorated on the outside at the rivet end; 1 of tweezers 56mm; 1 of earscoop 31mm; 1 of toothpick 31mm.

1757 BWB83 2711 (328) 11
Copper alloy; toothpick only; 1 39mm.

Earscoops/toothpicks

Combined earscoops and toothpicks were produced from wire, sheeting, or square rods, in at least six forms. Four of these are represented from dated deposits in London. The most common form made from sheeting, which was recovered from 14th-century deposits (ceramic phases 10–11 and 11), has a scoop at one end and a flat, pointed pick at the other with a fluted shank in between (nos. 1758–61, fig 251). Analysis shows that brass and gunmetal were used, and an implement of this form, which was provisionally identified as pewter, has also been recorded from a 14th-century deposit in Southampton (Platt and Coleman-Smith 1975, 269 no. 1901 fig 246). The antiquity of this form of implement is uncertain although some of its characteristics can be traced back to the 5th century. A set of cosmetic implements on a wire ring from an Anglo-Saxon burial at East Shefford, Berkshire, for example, includes a very similar earscoop with a fluted shank, which is perforated at its flat end rather than being shaped into a pointed pick (Baldwin-Brown 1915, pl LXXXVII no. 2; Owen-Crocker 1986, 44 fig 36), and a silver cosmetic set on a wire ring which hung from the girdle of a richly attired lady, who was buried around the middle of the 5th century at Zweeloo in the Netherlands, consists of three implements all with fluted shanks including an earscoop (van Es and Ypey 1977, fig 7; Vons-Comis 1988, fig 3).

Another form of earscoop/toothpick has a sickle-shaped pick rather than one which tapers to a point (MoL acc. no. A17971, fig 251). An example made from gold without a fluted shank was placed in the tomb of Count Palatine Phillip Ludwig (died 1614) at Lauingen beside the River Danube (Victoria and Albert Museum 1980, 72–4

251 Cosmetic sets and earscoop/toothpicks: lower left MoL acc. no. 17971 (1:1)

no. 75a) and this suggests that the sickle form may be a slightly later development. A further form from the 14th-century has a straight bevelled end instead of a point and the shank is not fluted (no. 1762, fig 251).

Less robust earscoops and toothpicks were made from wire from at least the early 13th century (no. 1763, fig 251). They would have been extremely easy and cheap to make and must have been produced in quantity. A wire implement from Northampton and another from Sandal Castle have Z-twisted shanks and were finished by hammering the loop into a solid scoop and flattening one of the wires at the other end (Oakley 1979, fig 110 no. 78; AR Goodall 1983, 234 & 236, fig 2 no. 91). This wire form is not represented here probably because it became more common after the middle of the 15th century.

A sixth form of earscoop/toothpick, which was made from a square-sectioned rod is represented by a single example from London. It has a bifurcated toothpick, similar to that in one of the three-piece sets, and a shank decorated with transverse grooves (MoL acc. no. 84.341/6). Recent excavations at Thames Exchange in the City yielded an earscoop/toothpick of similar form only it is made from drawn wire rather than a square rod and is embellished with twisted wire decoration to which a small ring was fitted for attachment (TEX88 acc. no. 3753 fig 251). Another example of the latter form with twisted wire decoration was recovered from excavations at St Augustine's abbey, Canterbury (M Henig in Sherlock and Woods 1988, 214 & 216 no. 59 fig 69).

Type I – made from sheet metal, hammered into a scoop at one end and a flat pointed tip at the other, with a S-twisted shank.

1758 BC72 acc. no. 2802 (context 118)
ceramic phase 10–11 fig 251
Gunmetal (AML); four S-twists to shank; 1 60mm.

1759 BC72 2531 (79) 11 fig 251
Brass (AML); fifteen S-twists to shank; 1 61mm.

1760 BWB83 4478 (unstratified) fig 251
Copper alloy; five S-twists to shank; 1 66mm.

1761 BWB83 1910 (293) 11
Copper alloy; four S-twists to shank; curved tip; 1 68mm.

Type II – as above but with a bevelled, horizontal end to the toothpick and a plain shank.

1762 BC72 acc. no. 4146 (context 88) ceramic phase 11 fig 251
Copper (AML); l 55mm.

Type III – made from wire with one end bent into a loop and the other pointed.

1763 SWA81 acc. no. 2262 (context 2279) ceramic phase 7 fig 251
Gunmetal (AML); bent out of shape; shank decorated below loop with a short length of very fine wire S-twisted round it; l 55mm; d of wire 1mm; d of decorative wire *c*.0.2mm.

Type IV – made from copper-alloy wire, bent double and S-twisted leaving one end of wire generally slightly longer than the other.

1764 BWB83 acc. no. 1493 (context 108) ceramic phase 10
Incomplete and bent out of shape; surviving l 20mm; d of wire *c*.0.8mm.

1765 BC72 3213 (118) 10–11
l 29mm; d of wire *c*.0.75mm.

1766 BWB83 1414 (146) 11 fig 251
Hammered square along its twisted shank; l 22mm; d of wire, 0.8mm.

1767 BWB83 1375 (156) 11
l 22mm; d of wire 0.8mm.

1768 SWA81 761 (2097) 12 fig 251
Both ends neatly clipped; very worn round loop; l 27mm; d of wire *c*.0.75mm.

1769 SWA81 2164 (2115) 12
l 29mm; d of wire 0.9mm.

Earscoops/tweezers

Earscoops combined with tweezers were also made in a variety of forms in the 13th and 14th centuries, and they were produced in bone as well as base metal (copper, bronze and brass). The most common form in copper alloy, represented here by four examples, was made from a narrow strip of sheeting cut to a rounded shape at one end to form a scoop. The tweezer arms were formed by splitting the sheeting part way along the centre (fig 252). The sheeting was then folded into tube and the two edges soldered

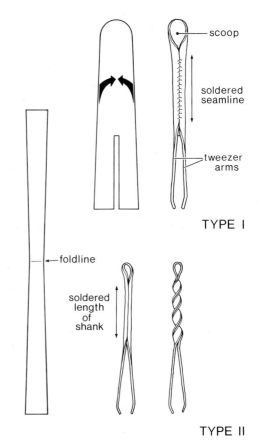

252 Two ways by which earscoop/tweezers were made from metal sheeting

together, leaving the seam open below a point which corresponded to the length of the opposing slit. One implement was reinforced round its shank with a band made from gunmetal (no. 1773, fig 253). This was soldered into position and does not slide up and down the shank, as it does on some other items tentatively interpreted as parchment clips or for handling gold leaf (AR Goodall 1981, 67 fig 65 nos. 10–11) and on a pair of tweezers, which may be Roman, from Colchester (Crummy 1983, 59 fig 63 no. 1876). An early manifestation of a fixed band on a cosmetic implement is that on a pair of tweezers dated stylistically to the 8th or 9th century from Reculver, Kent (Wilson 1964, 161 no. 62 pl XXXVIII). The opposite end of the implement is missing and the band would, therefore, originally have concealed the seam line.

An alternative method was to cut a longer and narrower strip of sheeting. Both ends were hammered to form the arms of the tweezers (fig 252). Next the strip was folded double so that it formed a loop at one end which could be used as an earscoop and, in addition, would have enabled the implement to be suspended from a ring or cord. Below the loop the sheeting was soldered on the inside, leaving the lower part open to form the tweezer arms, and immediately above the divide a reinforcement band was soldered (no. 1775, fig 253). An implement of similar form from Northampton appears not to have been soldered along its shank (Oakley 1979, fig 110 no. 74).

A bronze pair of tweezers and earscoop from an early 13th-century deposit (ceramic phase 7) in London also was not soldered after the sheeting had been folded and, instead of adding a reinforcement band, the shank was twisted in a Z-direction (no. 1774, fig 253). A similar cosmetic tool with a fluted shank was recovered from Waterbeach Abbey, Cambridgeshire (Cra'ster 1966, 82–3 fig 4b).

Double-ended tweezers and earscoops were also made from bone, which demanded greater skill to produce, although they apparently copied metal forms. A pair of bone tweezers and earscoop recovered from a late 14th-century deposit (ceramic phase 11) is decorated with lathe-turned bands of grooves, which were possibly inspired by reinforcement bands (no. 1777, fig 253). Its form is similar to others from London (eg Guildhall Museum Catalogue 1908, 122 no. 48 pl LII no. 4). A more unusual pair of bone tweezers and earscoop from 14th-century London (ceramic phase 9) has a fluted shank and a ring-and-dot pattern stamped along the arms of the tweezers (no. 1776 fig 253; Henig 1974, 198 no. 188 fig 40).

Type I – made from a piece of sheeting with a seam soldered along one side between the scoop and a tweezer arm; the other arm was formed by cutting a slit in the sheeting. The scoop is orientated at 90° to the arms of the tweezers.

1770 SWA81 acc. no. 427 (context 2018) ceramic phase 9
Copper alloy; perforated earscoop; one tweezer arm broken off and the end of the remaining arm angled inwards, decorated on the outside with two lines of zigzags; l 66mm.

1771 SWA81 428 (2018) 9
Copper alloy; one tweezer arm broken off and the end of the remaining arm angled inwards; a pattern of transverse grooves are engraved across the seam line; l 69mm.

1772 BWB83 3551 (355) 11 fig 253
Brass (AML); as preceding; l 69mm.

1773 BWB83 2675 (334) 11 fig 253
Brass (AML); the ends of the tweezer arms are angled inwards and bevelled on the inside; on the outside the arms are decorated with lines of opposed, punched triangles; a reinforcement band of gunmetal (AML) soldered round mid shank is decorated with diagonal grooves; l 82mm.

Type II – made in one piece from sheet metal folded double with a loop forming an earscoop at one end and widening out into two tweezer arms at the other.

1774 SWA81 acc. no. 2504 (context 2257) ceramic phase 7 fig 253
Bronze (AML); upper part of shank fluted with a Z-twist; tweezer arms angled inwards and very worn; l 101mm.

1775 SWA81 3379 (2139) 9 fig 253
Copper (AML); one tweezer arm broken and the other slightly damaged; shank soldered below loop and reinforced with a band also soldered in place; tweezer arms angled inwards; l 81mm.

Type III – made in one piece from animal bone (bone identified by James Rackham).

1776 CUS73 acc. no. 533 (context V,8) ceramic phase 9 fig 253
Cattle-sized shaft of longbone; one tweezer arm broken off; the remaining arm is gently bevelled on the outside and saw marks are visible on the inside. Both arms are stamped with ring-and-dot decoration. Spatulate scoop with fluted shank below which is a series of transverse ridges and grooves; highly polished surface; l 90mm; (Henig 1974, 198 no. 188 fig 40; MacGregor 1985, 100 fig 57c).

1777 BWB83 2677 (334) 11 fig 253
Cattle-sized shaft of longbone; highly polished; tweezer arms gently bevelled on the outside; spatulate scoop; shank decorated with three bands of four grooves; l 94mm.

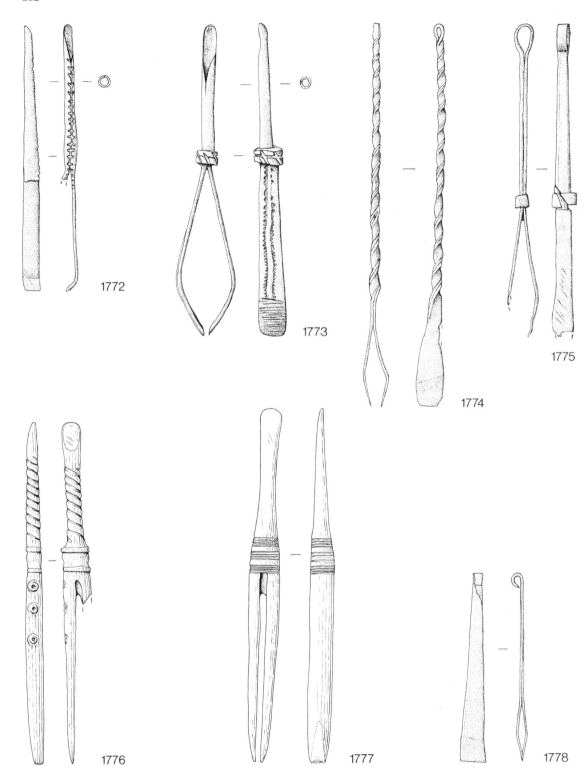

1772

1773

1774

1775

1776

1777

1778

253 Earscoop/tweezers (1:1)

Tweezers

Only two pairs of simple tweezers dating to the period covered by this survey have been recovered from recent excavations in the City. This suggests that double-ended implements and cosmetic sets were more popular as well as more practical. A pair of tweezers from an early 13th-century deposit is made from copper sheeting, which was partly slit, folded double and soldered at the middle of the shank, leaving two short arms at the wider end, while the opposite end was bent into a loop which could have served as an earscoop (no. 1778 fig 253). This is the earliest dated example from London of tweezers being made from sheeting folded in this manner. The other pair of tweezers is incomplete but traces of solder suggest that it could have been made in a similar way.

Medieval tweezers found on other English sites were usually made by folding a narrow strip of sheeting double (AR Goodall 1981, 65), which was also a Romano-British method. These tweezers are, therefore, not always easy to recognise as medieval unless they come from deposits lacking residual material, or are decorated with punched triangles typical of the medieval metalworker, as can be seen on examples from Eaton Socon, Bedfordshire (Lethbridge and Tebbutt 1951, 50–1, fig 1, no. 4) and Northampton (Oakley 1979, fig 110 nos. 75 & 76).

Made from sheet metal folded down one side and slit at the lower end; opposite side soldered above the arm opening:

1778 BIG82 acc. no. 2446 (context 3212) ceramic phase 7 fig 253
Copper (AML); the ends of the arms are angled inwards; hooked upper end; l 51mm.

1779 BWB83 4611 (286) 11
Copper alloy; part of one arm with the end bevelled on the outside; surviving l 48mm.

Needlecases

Needlework, especially embroidery, was a highly acclaimed female accomplishment in medieval Europe and it is not surprising, therefore, that needlecases were worn by women from chatelaines as a status symbol as well as for convenience. The tradition can be traced back in England to 6th-century Kent when women were often buried wearing them (Brown 1974, 152–3). Few needlecases have been identified from later-medieval deposits and their small size and the fact that many were made from organic materials has meant that a large number has perished. The five cases recorded from recent DUA excavations in London thus form an important group, particularly as they reveal that changes took place in the way that they were made and worn.

The earliest of the needlecases was recovered from a late 12th-century pit (ceramic phase 6). It was made from the longbone of a bird and is pierced in the centre of the shaft with two pairs of holes (no. 1780, fig 256). Through these holes metal rings would have been inserted to enable the case to be suspended from a chain or girdle and on which other implements, such as cosmetic sets and keys, could have been placed as well. The cylinder would have been plugged at either

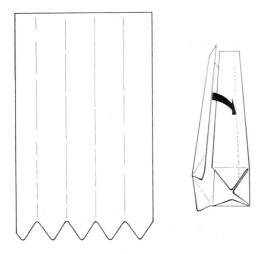

254 A method by which rectangular needlecases were made from metal sheeting

255 Copper needlecase with iron needle which was found inside it, no. 1784 (2:1)

256 Needlecases: lower centre MoL acc. no. 84.206/3 (1:1)

end to prevent the needles from falling out, or the needles could have been inserted through a piece of cloth which was then placed inside the case. The form of the case can be compared with earlier examples in copper alloy from many sites in north-west Europe, and also one in bird bone from Birka, Sweden (Graham-Campbell 1980, 22 no. 43). It is possible, therefore, that the bone case from London is a lot older than the date of the pit in which it was found.

The other cases, which were recovered from deposits dating to the late 13th and late 14th century (ceramic phases 9 and 11), are characterised by side slots and separate caps. One made from calf leather was catalogued in an earlier volume on scabbards in this series (Cowgill et al. 1987, no. 459). It is rectangular with a leather

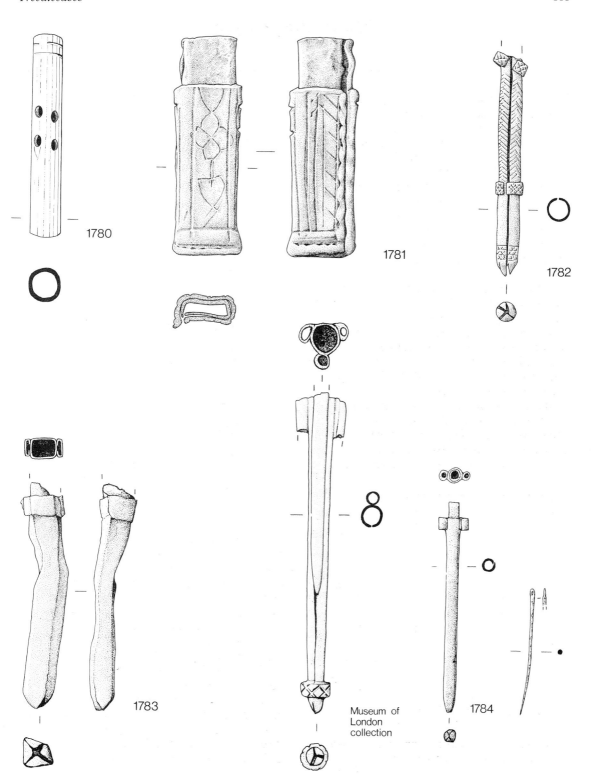

1780

1781

1782

1783

Museum of
London
collection

1784

lining, which was presumably glued into place, so that the lining projected above the edge of the exterior enabling a cap to fit on top; a quatrefoil is engraved on the front of it (no. 1781, fig 256). The narrow width of this case is in contrast to that of an elaborately decorated case of this type in the Roach-Smith collection at the British Museum (Roach-Smith 1854, 131 no. 650; BM MLA acc. no. 56, 7–1, 1901), which would have held larger implements, including perhaps a comb. Leather cases were, indeed, purpose made for a wide range of domestic items, for example spoons and quills, and all of these could be hung from a girdle (see fig 139B).

The three metal needlecases from recent excavations in the City were made from sheeting. The basic component was a thin, rectangular sheet from which four triangular segments were removed at one end (fig 254). Consequently, when the sheet was bent into the form of a tube the flaps could be pushed to meet in a point at the base and soldered together, thereby preventing needles from escaping. The smallest needlecase has an additional tube inserted into the mouth of its main cylinder (no. 1784, figs 255 & 256), which can be compared with the lining of the leather case. This device, by narrowing the opening, would have helped to limit the loss of needles by restricting the number that could be tipped out when the case was opened. To attach the needlecases to a girdle, a slot was soldered on either side of the main cylinder through which a cord or thong could pass. The size of slots on the smaller case would only have allowed a fine fibre cord to have been used, and traces of a linen cord are preserved in the side slots of a contemporary 14th-century tin needlecase recovered from the Thames waterfront at Billingsgate. A cap would have rested on top of the slots and complete examples in the Medieval Department of the Museum of London show that such caps usually had corresponding side slots, which would have helped to hold together the cap and container and would have allowed the cap to slide up and down. One of the metal cases catalogued here, which is broken along its upper edge (no. 1782, fig 256), has no side slots and may, therefore, have been carried inside a pouch.

Needlecases were sometimes designed to have more than one compartment, a characteristic which they shared with some knife sheaths. An example in copper alloy from Billingsgate shows a small tube soldered onto the main cylinder (MoL acc. no. 84.206/3, fig 256).

The number of needles contained in these cases would have varied according to size but the gunmetal case could have held at least six, and the smaller, copper case only two or three. This latter case, fortuitously, preserved a short iron needle inside, proving beyond doubt that such cases carried needles.

Bone

1780   MLK76   acc. no. 310   (context 1062)
ceramic phase 6   fig 256
Bird longbone (P Armitage); cylindrical with two pairs of holes positioned diagonally in the centre of the highly polished shaft; l 53mm.

Leather

1781   TL74   1942   (2332)   11   fig 256
Calf leather; cap missing; one slot on each side below the lining; l 58mm; internal w 10mm. (Cowgill et al. 1987, 154 no. 459).

Copper alloy

1782   BWB83   1911   (362)   9   fig 256
Brass (AML); cylindrical container with soldered seam. The lower end is serrated with the resulting four flaps meeting in a point at the base. Two strips of metal with cross-hatched decoration are soldered to the outside of the tube and between these a band of chevrons has been incised. Lower down the cylinder is a narrow band of cross-hatching. The upper edge of the case is broken and the cap is missing. Surviving l 59mm; d 6mm.

1783   BWB83   5927   (298)   11   fig 256
Gunmetal (AML); folded into a rectangular container and soldered along one side; the lower end is as preceding item; the cap is missing; an extra strip was soldered to each of the opposing narrow sides, near the top of the case, through which a cord or thong could pass and on top of which the cap would have rested; l 61mm; w 6–7mm.

1784   BWB83   367   (399)   11   figs 255 & 256
Copper (AML); as preceding, except that the container is cylindrical and a second tube was inserted at its open end; side slots circular in section aligned with the edge of the main cylinder; l 55mm; internal d 2mm. Iron needle made from drawn wire, head flattened and punched to produce a tiny eye; l 35mm; d 1mm.

Metallurgical analysis of the dress accessories

MIKE HEYWORTH

Introduction

A selection of medieval dress accessories recovered from excavations in London were analysed to attempt to reconstruct the pattern of alloy usage in the medieval period for these object types. Very little work has been undertaken on the identification of different alloys in use in this period and it was hoped that a comprehensive analytical survey of the composition of the dress accessories would reveal any patterns in non-ferrous metal usage both chronologically and for different types of object.

The analytical work was undertaken over a period of some four years, initially by Paul and Susan Wilthew and later by Mike Heyworth. During this time a large number of objects were analysed which form a representative selection of all the major categories of dress accessories. The majority of objects were made of copper alloys, although lead/tin objects and some gold and silver objects were also analysed. It was envisaged at the beginning of the project that a large number of analyses would be involved and it was decided to use x-ray fluorescence, a rapid, non-destructive technique that is readily available in the Ancient Monuments Laboratory. The analytical results obtained were qualitative rather than quantitative, but it was felt that they would provide an adequate summary of alloy usage for the dress accessories. Quantitative analysis would have involved much more effort and also some damage to the objects, which would have limited the number of analyses possible.

Analytical method

All the objects were analysed qualitatively by energy dispersive x-ray fluorescence (XRF) using a Link Systems Meca 10–42 machine. The primary radiation source was an x-ray tube with a rhodium target run at 35 keV, and the fluorescent x-rays were detected by a Si(Li) detector. The elements recorded were copper, zinc, gold, lead, silver, and tin.

Many of the objects consist of several parts and as far as possible each part was analysed separately. In many cases, however, this was not possible due to the size or shape of the object and consequently some results are ambiguous in that they are an average of more than one alloy. Where inlays or surface coatings were present both the bulk metal and the inlay or coating was identified if possible, but again the results are sometimes inconclusive.

Other than conservation treatment no surface preparation was carried out on the objects, and as XRF is a method of surface analysis the results will have been affected by surface contamination, corrosion and the depletion of elements from the surface that this can produce. The results should nevertheless give a reasonable indication of the alloys used in the production of the objects. This approximation should be better than for the majority of archaeological sites, as, in general, the objects were not deeply mineralised because of their relatively benign burial environment.

The XRF data for each element is presented as a ratio to the copper peak to allow easier comparison between analyses. In XRF analysis the peak heights for each element cannot be directly compared between elements as the height bears little relation to the proportion of that element in the object. Different elements are excited with varying efficiencies by the primary x-rays, eg tin is excited far less than zinc, so the peak heights will be a lot lower even when the amounts present are similar. A small selection of objects, of varying composition, were therefore analysed quantitatively with a Link Systems AN10000 energy dispersive x-ray analyser on a scanning electron microscope (SEM) using a 20 keV accelerating voltage and Link Systems ZAF/4 software. The data obtained from these analyses was used to roughly 'calibrate' the qualitative XRF data to obtain a more accurate definition of the alloys in use. The quantitative SEM analyses suggested that a suitable scaling of the element ratios could be applied to make them more comparable. Based on this information the zinc ratio has been left unscaled, the lead ratio has been multiplied by 2.5 and the tin ratio has been multiplied by 12. It is these scaled ratio figures that have been used in preparing the figures.

Data analysis

The analyses were split into three main groups: copper alloys, lead/tin alloys and other non-ferrous metals (mostly gold and silver). A separate data analysis methodology was devised for each group based on the differing number and level of alloying metals involved.

Copper alloys are mainly copper, with deliberate additions of tin, zinc and/or lead. It is necessary to take into account both the absolute and relative proportions of each alloying element in defining the alloy type (p 13ff). Brasses are mainly copper and zinc, bronzes copper and tin, while gunmetals contain significant amounts of both zinc and tin. Alloys containing large amounts of lead are described as 'leaded', whilst those containing lower, but still significant amounts of lead are '(leaded)'.

The relationship between the zinc and tin contents of the copper alloys analysed is shown in fig 257; one tends to increase as the other decreases through the period considered. The majority of the alloys have more zinc than tin, indicating that brasses and gunmetals were the alloys most commonly used in the manufacture of these dress accessories. It should be noted however that there are no separate clusters of points corresponding to different alloy names. The arbitrary divisions suggested by Bayley (p 14) cut through this compositional continuum so that objects of similar intermediate compositions can be described as different alloys, eg brass or gunmetal.

When lead contents are considered then a third dimension is added to the picture, which is best represented by using a ternary diagram (eg fig

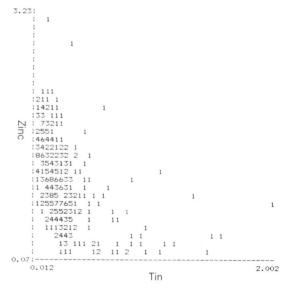

Fig 257   All copper alloys. Each number indicates the total of analytical results plotted in the area it covers

258). In this plot the nearer a point is to a corner, the higher the relative amount of the element present. It must be noted that as relative amounts are being plotted, an alloy containing 5% of both tin and zinc will appear in the same place as an alloy containing 10% of both tin and zinc. The ternary diagram shows that very few of the objects contain a significant amount of lead.

As the XRF data is not fully quantitative, the scatter of points on the ternary diagram is not exactly the same as would be given using fully quantitative percentage data, though the overall distribution is very similar. It is likely that, despite the scaling for different elements, the points are skewed towards the zinc corner of the diagram, hence the mismatch in comparison with fig 6.

The scaled element ratios were used in the assignation of alloy names to the analyses, and both absolute and relative ratio values were taken into consideration. When the individual copper-alloy groups are plotted onto ternary diagrams (see figs 259–261) some inconsistencies are apparent. This is mainly due to the ternary diagram only showing relative amounts, but is also a reflection of the arbitrary nature of the division of the compositional continuum into separate alloys. The means of the individual alloy distributions are well separated, but each covers a range of com-

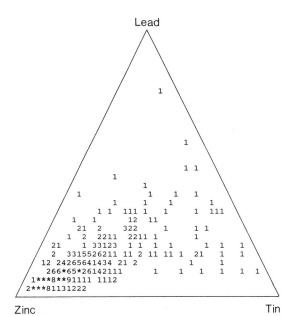

Fig 258   All copper alloys. Each number represents the total of analytical results plotted in the area it covers. Where there are more than nine results the position on the graph is marked by *

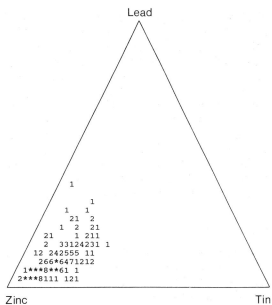

Fig 259   Brass alloys. Each number represents the total of analytical results plotted in the area it covers. Where there are more than nine results the position on the graph is marked by *

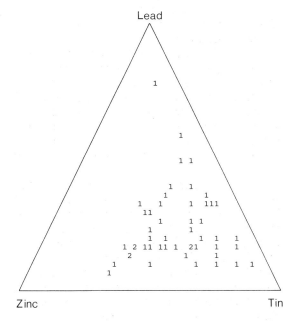

Fig 260   Bronze alloys. Each number indicates the total of analytical results plotted in the area it covers

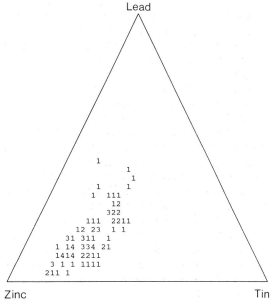

Fig 261   Gunmetal alloys. Each number indicates the total of analytical results plotted in the area it covers

positions which show some overlap between alloys. However, any overlap is not particularly significant in the description of the overall pattern of alloy types.

The lead/tin alloys are rather simpler to describe as only two elements are involved. A histogram of the lead:tin ratio for the lead/tin alloy dress accessories (fig 262) shows that it is possible to split the alloys into three main groups. The term 'pewter' is used to describe an alloy containing significant amounts of both metals, and other alloys are simply described as lead or tin, based on the main component of the alloy, although the object may also contain minor levels of the other element. The majority of dress accessories can be described as either tin or pewter (lead-tin), there are very few lead-alloy items that contain an insignificant quantity of tin.

Lead and tin were also used in the coating and soldering of some objects. Tin, or lead-tin, coating was often used as a cheap attempt to imitate silver items, though it was occasionally used on composite objects made of different metals to give a uniform appearance to the object (see buckle no. 457 and mounts no. 907, fig 63).

```
Midpoint   Frequency

0.05    t   67  *************************************************>
0.15    i    5  *****
0.25    n    3  ***
0.35         2  **
0.45    -    1  *
0.55         4  ****
0.65    p    8  ********
0.75    e   13  *************
0.85    w   13  *************
0.95    t    6  ******
1.05    e    5  *****
1.15    r    3  ***
1.25         1  *
1.35         0
1.45         2  **
1.55         0
1.65         1  *
1.75         0
1.85         0
1.95         0
2.05         0
2.15         0
2.25         0
2.35         1  *
2.45         0
2.55         0
2.65         0
2.75         0
2.85         1  *
2.95         0
3.05         0
3.15    -    0
 .           .
 .           .
 .      l    .
 .      e    .
 .      a    .
>9.75   d    3  ***
```

Fig 262   Tin/lead alloys: histogram of ratio of lead divided by tin. The cluster at the top of the histogram (with low Pb/Sn values) is the tin objects; the major group in the middle the pewter ones, and the three lead objects with very high Pb/Sn values are off scale at the bottom of the figure.

Tin or lead-tin coating was found on twelve copper-alloy objects of varying types. It was not always possible conclusively to identify any coating due to the presence of some tin and lead in the alloy and the lack of any surface preparation before an analysis. It is therefore possible that some coatings were not recognised, though all objects were also visually examined for signs of coating prior to analysis. Lead/tin solder was also used on a number of objects to hold together the separate parts; the majority were strap-ends and buckles which were often multi-part objects. Remains of solder were found on some mounts where it had been used to hold the mount onto a backing material.

The other non-ferrous metals identified amongst the accessories analysed were gold and silver, which were much less common. Several gold finger rings were analysed quantitatively by Paul Wilthew using the SEM analyser (using a 25 keV accelerating voltage) to assess the fineness of the gold used for their production. Quantitative results were obtained (using ZAF/PB software set up with pure element standards to process the spectra) for the concentrations of gold, silver and copper (see table 8 for results normalised to 100%). No surface preparation was carried out before analysis and the results may be subject to error due to contamination or corrosion of the surface. These effects will, if anything, have enhanced the apparent gold content of the metal.

Table 8   Quantitative analysis results for gold rings

catalogue number	area analysed	gold %	silver %	copper %
1610	hoop	74.7	14.4	10.9
	bezel	55.3	22.8	21.9
	collet	59.6	18.7	21.7
1611	hoop	44.0	28.8	27.2
1612	hoop	45.7	27.6	26.7
	bezel	45.6	28.5	25.9
1613	hoop	54.2	31.3	14.5
	bezel	54.6	32.5	12.9

The results suggest that two of the rings (nos. 1611 and 1612) were of similar composition, about 45% gold debased with about equal amounts of copper and silver. Number 1613 was somewhat purer (about 55% gold) and had been mainly debased with silver although it still contained about 15% copper. Both nos. 1612 and 1613 were in two parts and in both cases the analytical results were consistent with the two parts being of the same composition.

Number 1610 consists of three parts; the hoop, bezel and collet. The hoop is significantly purer (about 75%) gold than either the bezel or collet. The analyses of the bezel and the collet were not significantly different from each other (55–60% gold, debased with about equal amounts of copper and silver).

Two other objects, gold finger ring no. 1614 and the coating of silver-gilt mirror case no. 1718, were analysed qualitatively by XRF. Comparison with similar analyses of the gold finger rings that were also analysed by SEM suggest that the gold of both was relatively fine. The metal of the former is probably about 75–85% gold, whilst the coating on the latter is almost pure gold.

None of the silver objects was analysed quanti-

tatively but the seven silver objects analysed by XRF were of varying fineness. Comparison with silver objects of known composition have allowed some estimate of fineness to be attached to the silver dress accessories analysed. Three objects were relatively pure silver (ie over 90% silver): probable buckle no. 211, brooch no. 1334 and the pin of brooch no. 1337. Dress pin no. 1488 is heavily debased, with a silver content of about 50%, whilst the pin of brooch no. 1339 and the frame of no. 1337 were even less fine, with silver contents of about 40%. In the debased silver objects the main other element present was copper, though they also contained small levels of zinc, which suggests the silver was debased by adding brass to the metal.

Gold and silver were also used to coat the surface of a small number of objects, mostly brooches, buckles and strap-ends. Nine objects coated with precious metals were analysed; two of these were clearly mercury-gilded, but mercury was not definitely detected in the other

Variations through time

An attempt was made to identify possible changes in alloy usage from the mid twelfth century to the mid fifteenth century. The number of analyses for each ceramic phase and the metals represented are as follows:

ceramic phase	no. of analyses	copper	brass	gunmetal	bronze	lead	tin	pewter	gold	silver
6 (1150–1200)	24	9	4	5	1	–	–	3	–	1
7 (1200–1230)	26	5	3	4	4	–	5	4	–	1
8 (1230–1260)	33	3	11	4	2	–	2	10	–	–
9 (1270–1350)	147	13	55	40	14	–	8	12	–	–
10 (1330–1380)	16	–	8	3	1	–	3	1	–	–
10/11 (1330–1400)	4	–	2	1	–	–	–	–	1	–
11 (1350–1400)	275	15	125	46	29	2	22	19	3	5
12 (1400–1450)	113	3	51	12	6	–	27	9	–	–
unstratified	26	1	7	1	2	1	5	5	1	–
unphased	9	2	3	1	–	–	1	1	1	–
total	649	51	269	117	59	3	73	64	6	7

Element ratios for the copper alloys analysed from each ceramic phase are shown in figs 263 to 269 plotted on ternary diagrams. The proportion of the individual copper alloys in each phase is shown at the right (C = copper, G = gunmetal, Ae = bronze):

ceramic phase	no. of analyses	proportion of copper alloys
6	19	
7	16	
8	20	
9	112	
10	15	
11	215	
12	72	

cases, though it is likely to have been present. Brass mount no. 935 was coated with silver containing some mercury.

The larger number of analyses from some phases (particularly 9, 11 & 12) is a reflection of the larger number of objects found in deposits attributed to these phases. It is clear from these figures that copper and lead/tin alloys were used throughout the period from the late 12th to the early 15th centuries for the manufacture of dress accessories. The small number of objects in some of the earlier phases make any chronological variations difficult to show conclusively, but there does seem to be a greater proportion of unalloyed copper objects in the 12th and 13th centuries before brass objects became more common in the 14th century. There seems to be little evidence of any chronological variation in the use of lead/tin alloys with tin and pewter or lead-tin objects found in all phases.

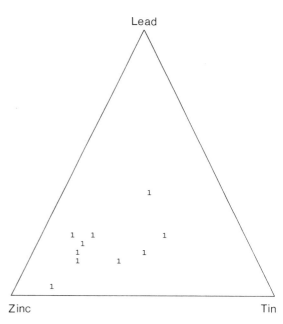

Fig 263   Copper alloys *c*.1150–*c*.1200 (ceramic phase 6). Each number indicates the total of analytical results plotted in the area it covers

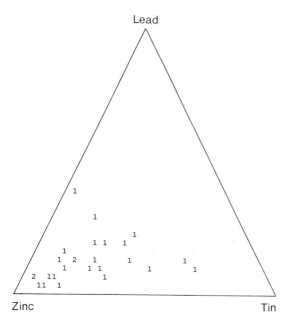

Fig 264   Copper alloys *c*.1200–*c*.1230 (ceramic phase 7). Each number indicates the total of analytical results plotted in the area it covers

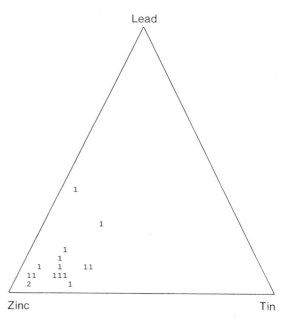

Fig 265   Copper alloys *c*.1230–*c*.1260 (ceramic phase 8). Each number indicates the total of analytical results plotted in the area it covers

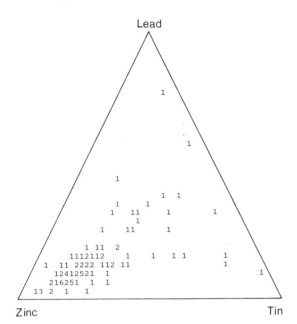

Fig 266 Copper alloys *c.*1270–*c.*1350 (ceramic phase 9). Each number indicates the total of analytical results plotted in the area it covers

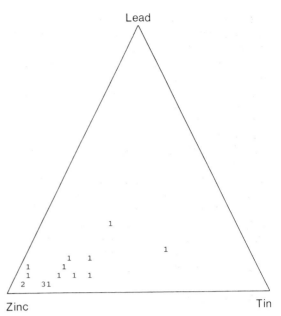

Fig 267 Copper alloys *c.*1330–*c.*1380 (ceramic phase 10). Each number indicates the total of analytical results plotted in the area it covers

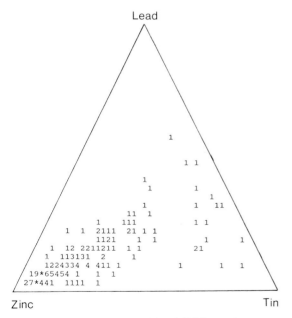

Fig 268 Copper alloys *c.*1350–*c.*1400 (ceramic phase 11). Each number represents the total of analytical results plotted in the area it covers. Where there are more than nine results the position on the graph is marked by *

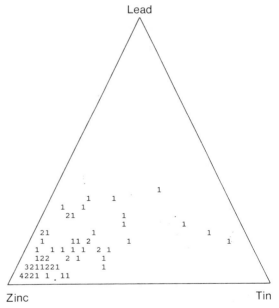

Fig 269 Copper alloys *c.*1400–*c.*1450 (ceramic phase 12). Each number indicates the total of analytical results plotted in the area it covers

Variations between/within object categories

A number of different object categories were included in the analytical programme to investigate whether any alloys were specifically associated with individual object categories.

The number of analyses of each object category included and the metals represented are as follows:

object category	no. of analyses	copper	brass	gunmetal	bronze	lead	tin	pewter	gold	silver
buckle	137	15	45	36	17	–	13	4	–	1
strap end	147	10	81	27	15	–	5	4	–	–
mount	116	13	40	19	6	1	30	5	–	–
brooch	57	3	4	13	4	1	1	27	–	4
button	18	–	5	2	5	–	5	1	–	–
lace chape	53	–	39	8	6	–	–	–	–	–
hair accessory	14	–	14	–	–	–	–	–	–	–
pin	20	–	13	3	1	–	–	1	–	2
bead	3	–	–	–	–	–	3	–	–	–
chain	2	1	1	–	–	–	–	–	–	–
finger ring	50	2	12	3	2	1	1	15	5	–
bell	27	1	8	1	–	–	15	1	–	–
mirror case	9	–	1	1	–	–	–	6	–	1
comb	2	–	–	–	2	–	–	–	–	–
cosmetic set	14	5	5	3	1	–	–	–	–	–
needlecase	3	1	1	1	–	–	–	–	–	–
total	649	51	269	117	59	3	73	64	6	7

For some object categories there does seem to be correlation with a specific alloy type, eg copper-alloy bells are predominantly brass with little or no tin or lead (though the majority of bells were pure tin). There are clusters of a limited range of compositions for copper-alloy brooches, buttons, and pins. Other object types, particularly buckles, mounts and strap-ends, are found in a much wider range of copper alloys, (lace chapes have a relatively wide variation within brass and bronze) often containing significant quantities of tin and less zinc. However, the object categories showing a greater variation in composition tend to be those objects which were analysed in greater numbers, and it is difficult to go further than to suggest the possible existence of a more restricted pattern of alloy usage for objects that were analysed in smaller numbers (this was due to their infrequent occurrence rather than any other sampling bias).

Variations in the metals and alloys found site by site were investigated, but no coherent pattern emerged; an archive text outlining ratios for the copper alloys analysed for each of the main object categories is held at the Ancient Monuments Laboratory (Heyworth 1989).

General discussion

The general picture which emerges from the attempts to correlate the pattern of alloy usage with the archaeological information regarding date, category of object and spatial distribution is that a range of alloys were available and widely used throughout the late 12th to early 15th centuries in London. Very few comparable analyses of similar objects of the same date are available from Britain, but those that are published (eg Brownsword 1987, 169–74) suggest that brass was the most widely used copper alloy, which fits well with the analyses of the London dress accessories.

The range of alloys between and within object categories suggests that the metalworkers were happy to use any available scrap metal, and had no particular requirements for pure metals or particular compositions. This was confirmed by a study of some buckles and strap-ends of composite form which include a forked spacer sandwiched between front and back plates. Whilst these particular objects are not of stylistically uniform quality, they are all very similar technically. The analyses of the objects showed that a range of alloys were used in their manufacture, and that again no specific alloy composition could be associated with these distinctive objects (see table 9). The range of alloy compositions used in their production reflects the overall pattern in that the majority are brass, though some have increased levels of tin, which put them into the gunmetal category and in some cases they could even be described as bronze. This same pattern of alloy usage is reflected throughout the dress accessories analysed.

Table 9.

Composition of buckles and strap-ends with forked spacers.

buckles

322	top plate = brass, bottom plate = brass, frame = bronze, loop = gunmetal
323	top plate = brass, middle plate = brass, bottom plate = gunmetal
324	top plate = brass, middle plate = brass, bottom plate = gunmetal, loop = bronze
325	plate = bronze, frame = gunmetal
326	frame = bronze, plate = gunmetal
330	plate = gunmetal

strap-ends

648	top plate = brass, bottom plate = brass, edge = lead-tin solder, knop = gunmetal
650	plate = brass
651	plate = (leaded) bronze
654	plate = brass
658	plate = brass
660	plate = gunmetal
662	top plate = brass, bottom plate = brass, edge = lead/tin solder
663	plate = brass
666	plate = gunmetal
668	plate = brass
669	top plate = bronze, middle plate = bronze, bottom plate = bronze
670	plate = brass
671	plate = brass
672	plate = brass
673	top plate = brass, middle plate = brass, bottom plate = gunmetal, edge = lead-tin solder?
674	top plate = brass, bottom plate = brass, edge = lead-tin solder?
675	plate = brass
676	top plate = brass, middle plate = gunmetal, bottom plate = brass
677	plate = brass
679	plate = brass
681	top plate = (leaded) bronze, bottom plate = bronze, knop = bronze
683	plate = brass

Conservation

ROSE JOHNSON

The conservation brief was:
- To advise on suitable storage for the finds from the time of excavation.
- The complete treatment of selected finds.
- The partial treatment of a larger group of material. This generally consisted of identification/analysis and possibly some removal of surface soil or corrosion obscuring details of construction or decoration.
- To advise on outside specialist analysis.

METALS

Selection and storage

Objects were chosen for full or partial conservation by the authors, curatorial and conservation staff. All iron was x-radiographed before selection. Limited resources generally mean that only a small proportion of objects, usually less than 10%, from excavations, are fully conserved. The proportion of conserved objects in the catalogue was greater.

After air-drying objects were individually packed in labelled polyethylene bags. Fragile finds were first packed in transparent polystyrene boxes using acid-free tissue paper for support. This standardised packaging system combines physical protection with high visibility and reduces physical damage caused by unnecessary handling. The same system was used for treated objects; an inert polyethylene foam (plastazote) which easily cuts to conform to the shape of the object was also used to support delicate finds.

Selected iron objects were kept in desiccated storage both prior to and after conservation. Excavated iron is often unstable, and further corrosion can occur if the relative humidity (RH) rises above $c.15\%$. A dessicated environment (RH $c.20\%$) is maintained by packing the iron in plastic freezer-boxes with air-tight lids with a bag of the desiccating agent silica gel. The RH is monitored by an indicating humidity strip placed inside the box so as to be visible through the translucent side. The silica gel is regenerated when necessary.

Examination and analysis

Visual

A stereo binocular microscope with a magnification range up to times 40, illuminated by a raking light, was the standard tool for examination. With this range of magnification a detailed study can provide a great deal of information about the condition and technology of an object.

X-radiography

The Conservation Department's Andrex x-ray machine was routinely used to record the shape and condition of many objects which were obscured by layers of corrosion. In addition, details of basic construction such as rivets, weld lines, solder, and decorative elements such as coating, engraving and inlay are visible on the x-ray plates. The presence of a tin coating on iron objects is often, though not always discernible on the plates. Occasionally removal of corrosion from both iron and non-ferrous metals revealed evidence of tin coating and gilding not observed on the plates.

Microchemical tests

The unfamiliar appearance of some of the metals from the waterlogged conditions initially caused some uncertainty about the identity of the metals present. Simple microchemical tests were used to differentiate between copper, iron, lead, tin and silver (Ganiaris 1985). Though these tests are by no means wholly reliable, when used in conjunction with microscopic examination they prove a useful preliminary guide.

Instrumental analysis

More-accurate analysis of metal composition, corrosion and decorative coatings was carried out where necessary by outside analytical laboratories, usually the Ancient Monuments Laboratory (HBMC), using various instrumental techniques – atomic absorption (AA), x-ray fluoresence spectroscopy (XRF), and x-ray diffraction.

Analysis of non-metallic components

Visual examination using stereo and polarising microscopy, microchemical tests, and measurement of physical properties, eg specific gravity, enabled preliminary identification to be made of non-metallic components such as gem-setting media and gem-stones. Outside expert analysis was often required to confirm results.

Treatment

Soil, concretions and corrosion were removed where appropriate using mechanical aids – scalpels, needles, wooden cocktail sticks, soft- and glass-bristle brushes, power pen and airbrasive equipment. The progress of removal was closely controlled by viewing the work through a stereo binocular microscope. Occasionally corrosion was removed by chemical methods or by electrolytic reduction. Where necessary metals were stabilised to inhibit further corrosion by well-established techniques, and then coated with an appropriate lacquer for protection. A detailed record is kept of the condition, investigation and treatment of each object. The x-radiographs also form part of the archival record of the objects.

Condition

The appearance and condition of metal objects from the anaerobic environment of these water-logged sites was both surprizing and sometimes deceptive.

Copper alloys

Objects ranged in colour from gold- to copper-coloured and were bright, shiny and apparently uncorroded, though closer inspection revealed etched surfaces. The degree of survival of surface detail is such that even metallographical

analysis is possible by observation of the surface (current research, D. Goodburn-Brown).

Many objects showed a characteristic dull gold-coloured 'bubbly' layer (colour pl 4C, lower part of object), sometimes thin and tenacious, more often a thicker crust of up to several millimetres, loosely attached to the underlying layer. Patches of iridescent colours were noted occasionally on this crust. The underlying layer was either the metal surface itself, or a black corrosion layer on the metal. The black layer, which also appeared on some objects without the gold crust, ranged in colour from brown-black to shiny blue-black and was soft and powdery, brittle or hard and tenacous (colour pl 4C, top part of object). The crust generally obscured shape and surface detail, though it sometimes faithfully mimicked surface contours. Beneath these layers the metal ranged in condition from sound to very thin and fragile. Its surface was again often bright and shiny though etched, fissured and pitted. The formation and composition of these sulphides has been studied (Duncan and Ganiaris 1987).

This dull-gold coloured layer was sometimes so smooth and thin that it was at first mistaken for gilding or some other artificially produced surface coating. Its presence on lead-tin objects caused some initial misidentifications (see colour pls 1E & F, and 6B & E).

Although microscopic examination and microchemical tests resolved most problems, some instrumental analysis was necessary. For example, the bright, silver-coloured shiny button (no. 1384, colour pl 7B) was initially thought to be either an intrusive modern object or of silver. Microchemical tests suggested that it was composed of tin. Later XRF and AA established that despite its colour, it is a high-tin copper-alloy. A dull-gold coloured mirror case (no. 1718, colour pl 12C) was first identified visually as copper alloy: XRF analysis at the Ancient Monuments Laboratory subsequently showed it to be gilded silver.

Iron

The condition of the iron items was very varied. Some objects were very well preserved, with an even blue/black-coloured surface patina. Others were very corroded, with large concretions obscuring their shape. Most objects fell between these extremes. They had patchy concretions which sometimes disfigured fine, black-patinated surfaces. Many objects had evidence of tin coating (colour pls 4G & 5A), both on the surface of the iron and in the corrosion layers. Even objects in apparently good condition were often very fragile. Despite the storage of the objects in desiccated conditions, some of the untreated iron shows signs of new or continuing corrosion. Small flakes and rust-coloured bubbles and blisters have been noted on a number of objects. The fine, black appearance of the ironwork does not always survive in desiccated storage. It has tended to alter to a dull-brown colour within a few years.

Lead, lead/tin alloys and tin

The different metals of these cast objects could not be distinguished visually. Many of them were in excellent condition. An even, dark-grey patina of lead sulphide on well-preserved metal was often only obscured by dirt. Other lead/tin alloy objects had the dull-gold coloured corrosion as described above for the copper-alloy objects (colour pls 1E & F and 6B & E). This layer was sometimes so thin and smooth that here too it was hard to believe that it had not been deliberately applied. As with the copper-alloy items a great deal of surface detail had survived, including casting flashes. Some objects were, however, in a poor condition; a hard, cream-coloured corrosion was present in pits and fissures. These objects were brittle and fragile.

Silver

Only six silver objects were treated. A thin and brittle, often tenacious dull-gold to black coloured corrosion crust was common. The underlying metal surface was often etched, pitted and very soft. Though the sulphide corrosion sometimes conformed closely to the shape of the object, it occasionally obscured fine detail, such as the inscription on brooch no. 1337 (colour pl 6C, shown after cleaning).

Settings

Several copper-alloy and lead-tin brooches, mounts and finger rings had been set with glass stones, some of which have survived (colour pls 4F, 6E & 7A). Simple microchemical tests on the white powdery setting media indicate the presence of carbonate. In common use at this time was either putty – a mixture of a drying oil and whiting (calcium carbonate), or a mortar – calcium hydroxide, which reacted with carbon dioxide to give calcium carbonate (AML). A lead-tin mirror case (no. 1710, colour pl 12B) retains the setting medium, which had been coated with black lead, together with traces of the glass.

ORGANIC MATERIALS

Objects made out of leather, wood and bone and textile fragments were preserved in the waterlogged layers. Fragments of these materials were also found in association with metals, eg leather between copper-alloy buckle plates and wound silk threads on both copper and iron wire decorations (nos. 1455 etc, figs 194 & 195).

Selection, treatment and storage

Once excavated, this material is very vulnerable to both physical change, shrinkage and cracking, and to further microbiological attack, eg fungal decay. It is also difficult and bulky to store in an untreated state for any length of time. For these reasons it was decided to conserve all the organic finds.

The wet wooden combs were often incomplete and very fragile, especially the teeth. The surfaces were soft and degraded; the cores stronger and less degraded. Some of the combs excavated in the early seventies had been allowed to simply air-dry and were brittle and fragile. The leather purses and straps were in generally good condition: brown in colour and soft though fragile and easily torn. Sometimes the leather had delaminated indicating a breakdown in structure during burial. Textiles were dark in colour, fragmentary and very fragile.

Objects were carefully washed and examined for evidence of surface decoration such as gilding or paint, for example traces of yellow pigment were noted on comb no. 1745. All wood and leather items were accurately drawn prior to treatment to provide records to monitor any shrinkage or distortion. Wood species were routinely identified by specialists before treatment. The conservation of wet organics has evolved greatly over the last fifteen years. The aim of all the treatments is to dry the material without causing excessive shrinkage and avoiding distortion (leather items shrink by up to 5%). The department routinely employs a range of pre-treatments suited to specific materials, followed by freeze-drying for leather, leather/metal composites (Starling 1984) and wood.

Wet textiles were carefully washed and allowed to air-dry. Chemical treatments were avoided whenever possible to limit interference with any subsequent analysis, such as the identification of tannins and dyestuffs.

After treatment the wooden combs were packed in the standard system, ie in clear polystyrene boxes supported by acid-free tissue or foam. Previously treated combs which had been stored in cardboard boxes were repacked using this system. Whilst providing good physical protection from handling, these boxes were sufficiently airtight to create a microclimate in which fungus thrived. The air-dried combs which had soil left between the teeth were particularly attacked. All the combs have been fumigated and repacked in acid-free boxes while investigations into more suitable storage continues. Treated leather is stored in perforated polyethylene bags supported by acid-free card.

Acknowledgements

In a work of this size and complexity the principal authors have been encouraged, helped and advised by a large number of colleagues and specialists. We gratefully record here our indebtedness and thanks to the following:

First, to colleagues and former colleagues at the Museum of London – Lynn Blackmore, John Clark, Jane Cowgill, Ann Davis, Gill Dunn, Tony Dyson (the DUA's editor) Hazel Forsyth, Helen Ganiaris, Dana Goodburn Brown, Francis Grew, Friederike Hammer, Penny MacConnoran, James Rackham, Kay Staniland, Brian Spencer, Peter Stott, Dominique Vaughan and Alan Vince. Conservation work was undertaken principally by Rose Johnson, and also by Heather Berns, Dana Goodburn Brown, Helen Ganiaris and Kate Starling, working under Suzanne Keene. Finds were fetched from store and much routine listing and checking was done by Joan Barker – who also undertook a large part of the typing of the script, Enid Hill, Joan Merritt and other volunteers, under the supervision of Penny MacConnoran. Wendy Garrett helped with the typing in the later stages of the project. Illustrations were drawn principally by Sue Mitford and Nigel Harriss (who with Anne Jenner undertook much of the work involved in laying out the figures) and by Nick Griffiths; students seconded from the Middlesex Polytechnic – Nigel Alleyne, Michael Bentley, Peter Crossman, Angelika Elsebach, Janice Iliffe, Rachel Lockwood, Terry Shiers, Rodenta Soprano and Anne Sutton – and volunteers – Gill Hale and Jennifer Harding – were also involved in the production of the drawings; all this work was supervised by Nick Griffiths and subsequently by Anne Jenner, who also drew the site plans.

Photographs were mainly taken by Jon Bailey and Jenny Bewick, as arranged by Trevor Hurst; Barrington Gray and his team, Marcus Leith and Torla Evans, were responsible for photography of items in the Museum of London's curatorial collections. Without the fieldwork by dedicated teams under the supervisors (listed in the discussion of the site sequences) this volume could not have been undertaken. Most of the excavations and post-excavation work, including the preparation of this volume, were funded by HBMC and its predecessor organisation within the Department of the Environment; the Swan Lane and Billingsgate watching briefs were mainly supported by the City of London Archaeological Trust Fund and the Museum of London Trust Fund, and the Ludgate Hill excavation was supported by the Norwich Union Insurance Group.

A grant of £10,000 from the City of London Archaeological Trust Fund has considerably reduced the price of this book.

We have also benefited from the kind advice and help of many individuals outside our own organisation:– Jan Baart, Justine Bayley, Duncan Brown, Marian Campbell, John Cherry, Dr Wendy Childs, Ian Eaves, Glynis Edwards, Blanche Ellis, Dave Evans, Mike Farley, Rowena Gale, Jane Geddes, Philippa Glanville, Les Good, Alison and Dr Ian Goodall, Olaf Goubitz, Roger Harding, Dr Vanessa Harding, Dr John Harvey, Captain David Horn, Marjorie Hutchinson, Dr Barry Knight, Nils-Knud Liebgott, Ronald Lightbown, Fritze Lindahl, Arthur MacGregor, Christine MacDonnel, Dr Sue Margeson, Tony McKenna, Michael Murray, Helmut Nikkel, Anthony North, Mike Ponsford, Alison Read, Tony de Reuck, Alma Ruempol, Peter Saunders, Prof Ian Shorte, Neil Stratford, Solene Thomas, Anneliese Streiter, Dominic Tweddle, HJE van Beuningen, Stephane Vandenberghe, Alexandra von Hohenastenberg, Claes Wahlöo and Erika Weiland. Profound thanks are due to the successive presidents (Roger Smith, Alan Stewart and Leigh Hunt), officers and members of the Society of Thames Mudlarks, including the ever-enthusiastic Tony Pilson, for the recovery of so many of the finds at the Billingsgate and Swan Lane watching briefs. Others who have contributed in various ways are acknowledged at appropriate points in the text. Special thanks are due from GE to Max Hebditch, John Maloney, Brian Spencer and Alan Vince for support at critical times, and to the field staff at the Swan Lane site and the Billingsgate watching brief. Our thanks also go to Corinne Barker, Dee Slater and Fred Stubbs of HMSO, who were most helpful during the final stages of preparing this volume.

Copyright for photographs included in this volume, for which permission to reproduce is gratefully acknowledged, is as follows:

Trustees of the British Museum – figs 212 (middle) & 242 (bottom) Bruckmann, Munich – frontispiece, fig 189 & colour pl 10

The Danish National Museum – fig 167 (bottom left)

Koninklijk Museum voor Schone Kunsten, Antwerp – fig 198

Maurice M Ridgway & Fred H Crossley – figs 159 & 214

Metropolitan Museum of Art, New York – fig 139

Reproduced by gracious permission of Her Majesty the Queen – fig 137

Royal Commission on the Historical Monuments of England – figs 20 & 132

Salisbury & South Wiltshire Museum – fig 173

Copyright of photographs of all items in the Museum of London's collections is held by the Museum's Board of Governors.

Bibliography

ADDYMAN, P V & HILL, D H, 1969 'Saxon Southampton: A Review of the Evidence, Part Two', in *Proc Hampshire Fld Club Archaeol Soc* **26**, 61–96

ÅGOTNES, A, nd *En Pryd for Sin Tid*, Bergen (Bryggen Museum exhibition catalogue)

AKERMAN, J Y, 1855 'Account of Silver Rings and Coins Discovered Near Worcester', in *Archaeologia* **36**, 200–02

ALEXANDER, J & BINSKI, P (eds), 1987 *Age of Chivalry, Art in Plantagenet England 1200–1400*, Royal Academy of Arts, London

ANON, 1803 in *Archaeologia* **14**, 275

ANON, 1979 'Objects of Copper Alloy', in Baker D et al. 'Excavations in Bedford 1967–1979', *Bedfordshire Archaeol J* **13**, 278–81

ARBMAN, H, 1940 *Birka, die Gräber*, **Tafelband**, Stockholm

ARMITAGE, K H et al, 1981 'A Late Medieval "Bronze" Mould from Copthall Avenue, London', Exhibit at Ballots, in *Antiq J* **61**, 362–64

ARMSTRONG, E C R, 1922 'Irish Bronze Pins of the Christian Period', *Archaeologia*, **72**, 71–86

ATKIN, M et al., 1985 *Excavations in Norwich 1971–1978 Part 2*, E Anglian Archaeol Report **26**

BAART, J M et al., 1977 *Opgravingen in Amsterdam*, Amsterdam

BAILDON, W P, 1911 'A Wardrobe Account of 16–17 Richard II, 1393–4', in *Archaeologia* **62** part 2, 497–514

BAILEY, K C, 1932 *The Elder Pliny's Chapters on Chemical Subjects*, part **2**, London

BAKER, D et al, 1979 'Excavations in Bedford 1967–1979', *Bedfordshire Archaeol J* **13**

BALDWIN BROWN, G, 1915 *The Arts in Early England* vol **4**, London

BAYLEY, J et al., 1984 'A Medieval Mirror from Heybridge, Essex', Exhibits at Ballots 2, in *Antiq J* **64**, part 2, 399–402

BAYLEY, J, forthcoming 'The Production and Use of Brass in Antiquity – With Particular Reference to Britain', in Craddock, P T (ed), *2000 Years of Zinc and Brass*, British Museum Occ Paper, London

BAYLEY, J & BUTCHER, S, 1981 'Variations in Alloy Composition of Roman Brooches', *Revue d'Archéométrie*, supplément

BAYLEY, J & WRIGHT, S M, 1987 'Metal Working and Miscellaneous Finds', in Wright, S M (ed), 'Much Park Street, Coventry: the Development of a Medieval Street – Excavations 1970–74', *Trans Birmingham Warwickshire Archeol Soc* **92** (for 1982), 84–88

BECKWITH, J, 1972 *Ivory Carvings in Early Medieval England*, London

BERESFORD, G, 1975 *The Medieval Clay-land Village: Excavations* at *Goltho and Barton Blount*, Soc for Medieval Archaeol Monograph **6**

BERGMAN, K & BILLBERG, I, 'Metallhåntverk', in *Mårtensson 1976*

BIDDLE, M (ed), 1990 *Object and Economy in Medieval Winchester*, Winchester Studies **VII** (2)

BINSKI, P, 1986 *The Painted Chamber at Westminster*, Soc of Antiquaries Occasional Paper **9**

BLAIR, C, BLAIR, J & BROWNSWORD, R, 1986 'An Oxford Brasiers' Dispute of the 1390s: Evidence for Brass-making in Medieval England', in *Antiq J* **66** part 1, 82–90

BLANCHARD, I S W, 1981 'Lead Mining and Smelting in Medieval England and Wales', in Crossley, D W (ed), *Medieval Industry*, Counc Brit Archaeol Res Rep 40, London, 72–84

BLINDHEIM, C et al, 1981 *Kaupang Funnene* I, Norsk Oldfunn **11**, Oslo

BOS, H et al, 1987 *Schatten uit de Schelde*, Markiezenhof, Bergen op Zoom (Netherlands)

BROBERG, B & HASSELMO, M, 1981 'Keramik, Kammer och Skor från Sju Medeltida Städer' (Fyndstudie), *Riksantikvarieämbetet och Statens Historiska Museer Rapport Medeltidsstaden* **30**, Stockholm

BROWN, D, 1974 'So-Called Needle Cases', in *Medieval Archaeol* **18**, 151–54

BROWNSWORD, R, 1987 'Technical Aspects of Individual Brass Letters', in Coales, J (ed), *The Earliest English Brasses: Patronage, Style and Workshops 1270–1350*, Monumental Brass Soc, London, 169–74

—, 1988 'An Introduction to Base Metals and their Alloys 1200–1700', *Finds Research Group Datasheet* **8**, Oxford

—, forthcoming, Appendix to chapter on copper alloys, in Blair, W J & Ramsay N L (eds), *Medieval English Industries*

BROWNSWORD, R & PITT, E E H, 1983 'Alloy Composition of Some Cast 'Latten' Objects of the 15/16th Centuries', *Hist Metall* **17** (1), 44–49

BRYANT, G F & STEANE, J M, 1971, 'Excavations at the Deserted Medieval Settlement at Lyveden, 3rd Interim Report', *J of Northampton Mus* **9**

BUDDE, R, 1986 *Köln und Seine Maler 1300–1500*, Cologne

BURY, S, 1982 *Jewellery Gallery Summary Catalogue*, Victoria and Albert Museum, London

—, 1984 *An Introduction to Rings*, London

CAL WILLS – *Calendar of Wills Proved and Enrolled in the Court of Husting, London*, ed Sharpe, R, 1889, part 1 (1258–1358); 1890 part 2 (1358–1688), London

CALLANDER, J G, 1924 'Fourteenth-Century Brooches and Other Ornaments in the National Museum of Antiquities of Scotland', in *Proc Soc Antiq Scot* **58**, 160–84

CAMERON, H K, 1974 'Technical Aspects of Medieval Monumental Brasses', in *Archaeol J* **131**, 215–37

CAMPBELL, M, 1987A 'Metalwork in England, *c.*1200–1400', in Alexander and Binski 1987, 162–68

—, 1987B 'Badge of Richard II', in Alexander and Binski 1987, 524

CAPELLE, T, nd 'Die Frugeschichtlichen Metallfunde von Domburg auf Walcheren', **1** & **2**, *Nederlandse Oudheten* **5**, Rijkdeinst voor het Oudheidkundig Bodemonderzoek, Netherlands

CAPLE, C 'Pins and Wires', in Mayes and Butler 1983, 269–278

—, 1986 *An Analytical Appraisal of Copper Alloy Pin Production: 400–1600*, unpublished doctoral thesis for the University of Bradford

CARRETERO, C H, 1988 *Museo de Telas Medievales Monasterio de Santa Maria la Real de Huelgas*, Patrimonio Nacional, Madrid

CAWLEY, A C (ed), 1975 *Chaucer's Canterbury Tales*, London

CEULEMANS, C, DECONNINCK, E & HELSEN, J (eds), 1988 *Tongeren Basiliek van O-L -Vrouw Geboorte* **I**, Textiel, Leuven

CHAMOT, M, 1930 *English Medieval Enamels*, London

CHENEVIX-TRENCH, C, 1970 *A History of Horsemanship*, London

CHERRY, J, 1973 'The Medieval Jewellery from the Fishpool, Nottinghamshire, Hoard', in *Archaeologia* **104**, 307–21

CHERRY, J, 1982 'The Talbot Casket and Related Late Medieval Leather Caskets', in *Archaeologia* **107**, 131–40

—, 1983 in Morris, M, *Medieval Manchester*, Greater Manchester Archaeological Unit, 77–78

—, 1985 'The Silver Brooch', in Shoesmith, R (ed), *Hereford City Excavations 3 The Finds*, CBA Research Report **56**, 21–24

—, 'Jewellery', in Alexander and Binski 1987, 176–78 etc

—, 1988 'Medieval Jewellery from Ireland: A Preliminary Survey', in Wallace, P & MacNiocaill, G (eds), *Keimelia Studies in Medieval Archaeology and History in Memory of Tom Delaney*, Galway, 143–62

CHRISTOPHERSEN, A, 1980 *Håndverket i Forandring, Studier i Horn- og Beinhåndverkets Utvikling i Lund c.1000–1350*, Lund

CLARK, J, 1988 (December) 'Some Medieval Smiths' Marks', in *Tools and Trades* **5**, 11–22

—, forthcoming *Horse Equipment* (Medieval Finds from London Excavations series)

CLARKE, H & CARTER, A (eds), 1977 *Excavations in King's Lynn 1963–1970*, Soc for Medieval Archaeol Monograph **7**

CLAY, P, 1981 'The Small Finds', in Mellor, J E & Pearce, T (eds), *The Austin Friars, Leicester*, Counc Brit Archaeol Res Rep **35**, London

CLAYTON, M, 1979 *Victoria and Albert Museum Catalogue of Rubbings of Brasses and Incised Slabs* (revised ed), London

COAD, J G & STREETEN, D F, 1982 'Excavations at Castleacre, Norfolk, 1972–77', in *Archaeol J* **139**, 138–301

COBB, H S (ed), 1961 *The Local Port of Southampton for 1439–40*, Southampton University

COLLIN, B, nd (*c.*1955) *The Riddle of a 13th-Century Sword-Belt*, Heraldry Soc, East Knoyle

COOK, A M, MYNARD, D C & RIGOLD, S E, 1969 'Excavations at Dover Castle, Principally in the Inner Bailey', in *J Brit Archaeol Ass* **32**, 54–104

CORSON, R, 1972 *Fashions in Makeup from Ancient to Modern Times*, London

COWGILL, J et al, 1987 *Knives and Scabbards*, Medieval Finds from London Excavations I, London

CRADDOCK, P T, 1985 'Three Thousand Years of Copper Alloys: From the Bronze Age to the Industrial Revolution', in van Zeist, B (ed), *Applications of Science in the Examination of Works of Art* **5**, 59–67

—, 1987 'Report on the Composition of the Ingots and Axle-Cap', in Meates, G W, *The Roman Villa at Lullingstone, Kent* II, Kent Archaeol Soc, Maidstone, 80–82

CRA'STER, M D, 1966 'Waterbeach Abbey', in *Proc Cambridge Antiq Soc* **59**, 75–95

CROWFOOT, E, et al., forthcoming *Textiles and Clothing* (Medieval Finds from Excavations in London series)

CRUMMY, N, 1983 *Colchester Archaeological Report 2: The Roman Small Finds in Colchester 1971–9*, Colchester

CUMING, H S, 1862 'On the Norman Fermail', in *J Brit Archaeol Ass* **18**, 227–31

CUNNINGTON, C W, CUNNINGTON, P E & BEARD, C, 1960 *A Dictionary of English Costume 900–1900*, London

— & —, 1973 *Handbook of English Medieval Costume*, London

DAHLBÄCK, G, 1982 *Helgeandsholmen, 1000 År i Stockholms Ström*, Stockholm

DALTON, O M, 1909 *Catalogue of the Ivory Carvings of the Christian Era, with Examples of Mohammedan Art and Carvings in Bone in the Department of British and Medieval Antiquities and Ethnography of the British Museum*, London

—, 1912 *Catalogue of the Finger Rings in the British Museum*, London

DANIELLS, M, 1979, 'Bedern Site', in *Interim* **6**/3, York Archaeol Trust 19–27

DAVIS, N (ed), 1971 *Paston Letters and Papers* 1, Oxford

DEPPING, G B (ed), 1837 *Réglements sur les Arts et Métiers de Paris Rediges au XIIIe Siècle et Connus sous le Nom du Livre des Métiers d'Etienne Boileau*, Collection des Documents Inédits sur l'Histoire de France ser **1**, Paris

DE LESPINASSE, R, 1892 *Les Métiers et Corporations de la Ville de Paris*, Paris

DE WITTE, H, 1988 *Brugge-Onder-Zocht*, Bruges

DIGBY, G W, 1963 *Elizabethan Embroidery*, London

DILLON (Viscount) & ST JOHN HOPE, W H, 1897 'Inventory of the Goods and Chattels Belonging to Thomas, Duke of Gloucester, and Seized in his Castle at Pleshy, County Essex, 21 Richard II', in *Archaeol J* **54**, 275–308

DOLLEY, M & SEABY, W A, 1971 (December) 'A Find of Thirteenth-Century Pewter Tokens from the National Museum Excavations at Winetavern Street, Dublin', in *Numis Circ* **79**, 446–48

DREWETT, P L, 1975 'Excavations Hadleigh Castle, Essex, 1971–1972', in *J Brit Archaeol Ass* 3rd series **38**, 90–154

DUNCAN, S & GANIARIS, H, 1987 'Some Sulphide Corrosion Products on Copper Alloys and Lead Alloys from London Waterfront Sites', in J Black (collator) *Recent Advances in the Conservation and Analysis of Artefacts*, Summer School Press, London, 109–18

DUNNING, G C, 1965 'Heraldic and Decorated Metalwork and Other Finds from Rievaulx Abbey, Yorkshire', in *Antiq J* **45** part 1, 53–63

EAMES, E, 1980 *Catalogue of Medieval Lead-glazed Earthenware Tiles in the Department of Medieval and Later British Antiquities*, British Museum, London

EGAN, G, 1985/86 'Finds Recovery on Riverside Sites in London', in *Popular Archaeol* **6** no. **14**, 42–50

ELLIS, B, 'Rowel Spurs', in Alexander and Binski 1987, 259–61

ERLANDE-BRANDENBURG, A, 1984 *The Abbey Church of Saint-Denis* **2**, The Royal Tombs, Paris

ERLANDE-BRANDENBURG, A et al., 1987 *Musée de Cluny Guide*, Paris

EVANS, J, 1921 *English Jewellery from the Fifth Century AD to 1800*, London

—, 1922 *Magical Jewels*, Oxford

—, 1952 *Dress In Medieval France*, Oxford

—, 1970 *A History of Jewellery 1100–1870*, London

FAIRCLOUGH, G J, 1979 *St Andrews Street 1976*, Plymouth Museum Archaeol Ser **2**

FAUSSETT, B, 1856 *Inventorium Sepulchrale* (ed Roach-Smith, C), London

FILEDT-KOK, J P (ed), 1985 *Livlier Than Life, the Master of the Amsterdam Cabinet or The Housebook Master c.a. 1470–1500*, Amsterdam

FINGERLIN, I, 1971 *Gürtel des Hohen und Späten Mittelalters*, Munich

FORD, B, 1954 (ed), *The Age of Chaucer, a Guide to English Literature* **1**, Harmondsworth

FORGEAIS, A, 1866 *Numismatique Populaire* **5**, 'Collection des Plombs Historiés Trouvés dans la Seine', Paris

FRERE, S, 1954 'Canterbury Excavations, Summer 1946' in *Archaeol Cantiana* **67**, 101–43

GALLOWAY, P, 1976, 'Note on Descriptions of Bone and Antler Combs', in *Medieval Archael* **20**, 154–56

GANIARIS, H, 1985 'A Portable Spot-Test Kit', in *Conservation News* **27**, United Kingdom Inst. for Conservation, London, 25–26

GEDDES, J, 1985 'The Small Finds', in Hare, J N (ed), 'Battle Abbey, The Eastern Range and the Excavations of 1978–80', *HBMCE Archaeol Rep* **2**, London, 147–77

—, & Carter, A, 'Objects of Non-Ferrous Metal, Amber and Paste', in Clarke and Carter, 1977, 287–98

GEIJER, A, FRANZÉN, A M, & NOCKERT, M, 1985 *Drottning Margaretas Gyllene Kjortel i Uppsala Domkyrka*, Uppsala

GERLACH, M (ed), 1971 *Primitive and Folk Jewellery*, New York

GIBBS, F W, 1957 'Invention in Chemical Industries' in Singer, C et al. (eds), *A History of Technology* **3**, Oxford, 678–708

GLANVILLE, P, 1987 *Silver in England*, London

GÓMEZ MORENO, M, 1946 *El Pantéon Real de las Huelgas de Burgos*, Madrid

GOODALL, A R, 1979 'Copper-Alloy Objects' in Smith, G H, 'The Excavation of the Hospital of St. Mary of Ospringe, Commonly Called Maison Dieu', in *Archaeol Cantiana* **95**, 137–45

—, 1981 'The Medieval Bronzesmith and his Products', in Crossley, D W (ed), *Medieval Industry*, Counc Brit Archaeol Res Rep **40**, London, 63–71

—, 'Objects of Copper Alloy', in Coad and Streeten 1982, 235–39

—, 'Non-Ferrous Metal Objects', in Mayes and Butler 1983, 231–39

—, 1984 'Objects of Non-Ferrous Metal' in Allan J P (ed), *Medieval and Post-Medieval Finds from Exeter 1971–1980*, Exeter Archaeol Rep **3**, Exeter, 337–48

GOODALL, A R & GOODALL, I H, 1977 'Copper-Alloy Objects', in Durham, B, 'Archaeological Investigations in St Aldates, Oxford', in *Oxoniensia* **42**, 148–52

GOODALL, I H 'Metalwork', in Drewett 1975, 138–46

—, 'Iron Objects', in Mayes and Butler 1983, 240–52

GOODBURN BROWN, D E, 1988 'Metalworking Tools and Workshop Practices: Interpretation of Worked Metal Surfaces by Silicone Rubber Moulds', in Olsen, S L (ed.), *Scanning Electron Microscopy in Archaeology* (Brit. Archaeol. Rep. S452) 55–64

GOUBITZ, O, 1987 'Calceology: A New Hobby: The Drawing and Recording of Archaeological Footwear', in Friendship-Taylor, D E et al, *Recent Research in Archaeological Footwear* (Ass of Archaeol Illustrators and Surveyors Technical Paper 8/Archaeol Leather Group), 1–28

—, 'Brugge op Grote en Kleine Voet Laat-Middeleeuws Schoeisel en Andere Lederresten', in de Witte 1988, 151–59

GRAHAM-CAMPBELL, J, 1980 *Viking Artefacts*, London

GREEVES, T A P, 1981 'The Archaeological Potential of the Devon Tin Industry' in Crossley, D W (ed), *Medieval Industry*, Counc Brit Archaeol Res Rep **40**, London, 85–95

GREW, F & DE NEERGAARD, M, 1988 *Shoes and Pattens*, Medieval Finds from London Excavations **2**, London

GRIFFITHS, N, 1986 Horse Harness Pendants, *Finds Research Group Datasheet* **5**, Coventry

—, 1989 'Shield-Shaped Mounts', *Finds Research Group Datasheet* **12**, Oxford

GROENEWEG, G, in Bos et al. 1987, 68–70

GROVES, S, 1966 *The History of Needlework Tools and Accessories*, London

GUIDO, M, 1978 *The Glass . . .*

GUIDO, M, 1978 *The Glass Beads of the Prehistoric and Roman Periods in Britain and Ireland*, Soc Antiq Res Rep **35**, London

GUILDHALL MUSEUM CATALOGUE, 1908 *Catalogue of The Collection of London Antiquities in the Guildhall Museum*, Library Committee of the Corporation of the City of London, London
(the 1905 edition is differently paginated)

HAEDEKE, H-U, 1970 *Metalwork*, London (translated Menkes, V)

HAMPE, T, 1896 *Katalog der Gewebesammlung des Germanischen Nationalmuseums* vol **I**, Nuremberg

HARBEN, H A, 1918 A Dictionary of London, London

HARTLEY, D & ELIOT, M M, 1931 *Life and Work of the People of England, The Eleventh to Thirteenth Centuries*, London

HARTSHORNE, A, 1891 'The Swordbelts of the Middle Ages', in *Archaeol J* **48**, 320–40

HARVEY, J, 1981 *Medieval Gardens*, London

HARVEY, Y 'The Bronze', in Platt and Coleman-Smith 1975, 254–68

HASSALL, M & RHODES, J, 1974 'Excavations at the New Market Hall, Gloucestershire, 1966–7', in *Trans Bristol Gloucestershire Archaeol Soc* **93**, 15–100

HATCHER, J & BARKER, T C, 1974 *A History of British Pewter*, London

HATTATT, R, 1987 *Brooches of Antiquity*, Oxford

HAWTHORNE, J G & SMITH, C S (translated & eds), 1979 *On Divers Arts, The Treatise of Theophilus*, Dover edition, New York

HEMP, W J, 1936 'Four Heraldic Pendants and Three Roundels', in *Antiq J* **16**, 291–94

HENDERSON, J, 1986 'Beads and Rings', in Tweddle, D, 'Finds from Parliament Street and Other Sites in the City Centre', *The Archaeology of York* **17/4**, 209–26

HENIG, M, 1974 'Medieval Finds' in Tatton-Brown, 1974, 189–201

—, 1975 'Medieval Finds' in Tatton-Brown, T, 'Excavations at the Custom House Site, City of London, 1973' part 2, in *Trans London Middlesex Archaeol Soc* **26**, 103–70

—, & WOODS, 1988 in Sherlock and Woods 1988, 201–31

HERTEIG, A E, 1969 *Kongers Havn og Handels Sete*, Oslo

HESLOP, T A 'English Seals in the Thirteenth and Fourteenth Centuries', in Alexander and Binski 1987, 114–17

HEYWORTH, M, 1988 'Analysis of Amber Samples from Sites in London', *Ancient Monuments Laboratory Report* **125/88** (unpublished)

—, 1989 'Analysis of Medieval Dress Accessories from London', *Ancient Monuments Laboratory Report* **87/89** (unpublished)

HINTON, D A, 1974 *A Catalogue of the Anglo-Saxon Ornamental Metalwork 700–1100*, Oxford

—, 1982 *Medieval Jewellery*, Shire Archaeology **21**, Princes Risborough

HOPSTAKEN, L, in Bos et al. 1987, 49–57

HORNSBY, P R G et al, 1989 *Pewter, a Celebration of the Craft 1200–1700*, Museum of London

HUME, A, 1863 *Ancient Meols: Some Account of the Antiquities Found near Dove Point on the Sea Coast of Cheshire*, London

HURST, J G, 1961 'The Kitchen Area of Northolt Manor, Middlesex', in *Medieval Archaeol* **5**, 211–99

JACKSON, S, 1986 'Objects of Copper Alloy', in Daniels, R, 'The Excavation of the Church of the Franciscans, Hartlepool, Cleveland', in *Archaeol J* **143**, 275–77

JOHNSON, R I, 1989 *Conservation of the Medieval Dress Accessories*, unpublished Museum of London Conservation Dept. report

JONES, J, 'Medieval Leather', in Tatton-Brown 1975, 154–67

J W, 1846 'Antiquities Found at Woodperry, Oxon', in *Archaeol J* **3**, 116–28

KING, D & KING, M, 1988 'Silk weaves of Lucca in 1376', in Estham, I & Nockert, M (eds), *Opera Textilia Variorum Temporum*, the Museum of National Antiquities Stockholm Studies **8**, 67–76

KUNZ, G F, 1973 *Rings for the Finger*, New York (Dover Edition)

LAMBRICK, G & WOODS, H, 1976 'Excavations at the Dominican Priory, Oxford', in *Oxoniensia* **41**, 168–231

LEGG, J W, 1890 'On an Inventory of the Vestry in Westminster Abbey, Taken in 1388', in *Archaeologia* **52** part 1, 195–286

LETHBRIDGE, T C & TEBBUTT, C F, 1951 'Excavations on the Castle Site Known as "The Hillings" at Eaton Socon, Bedfordshire', in *Proc Cambridge Antiq Soc* **45**, 48–60

LEWIS, J M, 1987 'A Collection of Medieval Artefacts found near Holywell, Clwyd', in *Bull Board Celtic Stud* **34**, 270–82

LIGHTBOWN, R W, 1978 *Secular Goldsmiths Work in Medieval France: A History*, Society of Antiquaries of London Research Report **36**, London

LINDAHL, F & JENSEN J S, 1983 'Skattefundet fra Slagelse 1883', in *Aarbøger for Nordisk Oldkyndighed og Historie*

LONGHURST, M H, 1926 *English Ivories*, London

LONGMAN, E D & LOCH, S, 1911 *Pins and Pincushions*, London

LOWERY, P R et al., 1971 'Scriber, Graver, Scorper, Tracer: Notes on Experiments in Bronzeworking Technique' in *Proc Prehist Soc* **37**, 167–82

THE LUTTRELL PSALTER, 1932 (Introduction by Millar, E G), London

LYSONS, S, 1814 'Copy of a Roll of Purchases Made for the Tournament of Windsor Park in the Sixth Year of King Edward I Preserved in the Record Office at the Tower', in *Archaeologia* **17**, 297–310

MACGREGOR, A (ed), 1983 *Tradescant's Rarities, Essays on the Foundation of the Ashmolean Museum 1683 with a Catalogue of the Surviving Early Collections*, Oxford

—, 1985 *Bone, Antler, Ivory and Horn, The Technology of Skeletal Materials since the Roman Period*, London

—, 1989 'Bone, Antler and Horn Industries in the Urban Context', in Serjeantson, D and Waldon, T (eds), *Diet and Crafts in Towns*, Brit Archaeol Rep **199**, Oxford, 107–28

MAGAGNATO, L (ed), 1983 *Le Stoffe di Cangrande*, Florence

MARGESON, S, 'Worked Bone', in Coad and Streeten, 1982, 241–55

—, 'The Small Finds', in Atkin et al. 1985, 52–67 & 201–13

MARSHALL, C & DE REUCK, A V S, 1989 'Buckles' (privately circulated – copy held at Museum of London)

MÅRTENSSON, A W (ed), 1976, 'Uppgrävt Förflutet för PK-Banken i Lund', *Archaeologica Lundensia* **7**

MÅRTENSSON, A W & WAHLÖO, C, 1970 'Lundafynd, en Bilderbok', *Archaeologica Lundensia* **4**

MARYON, H, 1971 *Metalwork and Enamelling* (5th ed), New York

MAYES, P & BUTLER, L A S, 1983 *Sandal Castle Excavations 1964–1973*, Wakefield

MEAD, V K, 1977 'Evidence for the Manufacture of Amber Beads in the City of London in 14th–15th Century', in *Trans London Middlesex Archaeol Soc* **28**, 211–14

MECKSEPER, C (ed), 1985 *Stadt in Wandel, Kunst und Kultur des Burgertums in Norddeutschland 1150–1650* **1**, Braunschweigisches Landesmuseum

MEYER, O, 1979 *Archéologie Urbaine à Saint-Denis*, Saint-Denis

MEYER, O et al., 1983 *Récherches Archéologiques Urbaines, Rapport 1982*, Saint-Denis

MEYER, O & WYSS, A, 1985 *Saint-Denis, Récherches Urbaines 1983–1985*, Saint-Denis

MILLS, N, 1983 (August) 'Medieval Finds from Bull Wharf', in *Treasure Hunting*, 5–10

MILNE, G & MILNE, C, 1982 *Medieval Waterfront Development at Trig Lane*, London Middlesex Archaeol Soc Special Paper **5**

MITCHINER, M, 1986 *Medieval Pilgrim and Secular Badges*, Sanderstead

—, 1988 *Jetons, Medalets and Tokens, the Medieval Period and Nuremberg* **1**, Seaby, London

MITCHINER, M & SKINNER, A, 1983 'English Tokens, *c*.1200 to 1425', in *Brit Numis J* **53**, 29–77

MOULD, Q, 'Leatherwork', in Queen Anne House site (Shrewsbury) Report, forthcoming

MULDOON, S & BROWNSWORD, R, nd. (*c*.1987) *Pewter Spoons and Other Related Material of the 14th–17th Centuries in the Collection of the Herbert Art Gallery and Museum, Coventry*, Coventry Leisure Services

MUSEO DE SANTA CRUZ, 1984 *Alfonso X*, Toledo

MUSTY, J et al., 1969 'The Medieval Pottery Kilns at Laverstock, Near Salisbury, Wiltshire', in *Archaeologia* **102**, 83–150

NATANSON, J, 1951 *Gothic Ivories of the Thirteenth and Fourteenth Centuries*, London

NEVINSON, J L, 1977 'Buttons and Buttonholes in the Fourteenth Century', in *Costume* **11**, 38–44

NEWTON, S M, 1980 *Fashions in the Age of the Black Prince*, Woodbridge

NEWTON, S M & GIZA, M M, 1983 'Frilled Edges', in *Textile History* **14, 2**, 141–52

NICOLAS, N H, 1846 'Observations on the Institution of the Order of the Garter', in *Archaeologia* **31**, 1–163

NOCKERT, M, 1985 *Bockstensmannen och hans Drakt*, Falkenberg, Sweden

NÖEL-HUME, I, 1970 *A Guide to Artefacts of Colonial America*, New York

NORTH, J J, 1975 *English Hammered Coinage* **2**, London

NORTHOVER, J P, 1982 'The Exploration of the Long-Distance Movement of Bronze in Bronze and Early Iron Age Europe', in *Bull Inst Archaeol, Univ London* **19**, 42–75

NOSS, A, 1985A *Draksølvet fra den Norske Samlinga i Nordiska Museet, Stockholm*, Norsk Folke-museum, Oslo (catalogue to exhibition)

—, 1985B; booklet of same title etc as preceding

OAKLEY, G E, 1979, 'The Copper Alloy Objects', in Williams, J H (ed), *St Peter's Street, Northampton, Excavations 1973–1976*, Northampton, 248–64

O'BRIEN, C, 1988 'Objects of Wood, Metal and Stone', in O'Brien, C et al., *The Origins of the Newcastle Quayside*, Soc Antiquaries Newcastle-upon-Tyne Monograph **3**, 104–08

ODDY, W A, 1981 'Gilding Through the Ages', in *Gold Bulletin* **14 (2)**, 75–79

ODDY, W A et al., 1986 *Romanesque Metalwork: Copper Alloys and their Decoration*, British Museum, London

OMAN, C, 1957 *English Church Plate 597–1830*, Oxford

OMAN, C C, 1930A *Catalogue of Rings*, Victoria and Albert Museum Dept of Metalwork, London

—, 1930B 'The Jewels of Saint Albans Abbey', in *The Burlington Mag* **57**, 81–82

OTTAWAY, P, 1985 'Horsing Around', in *Interim* **10**, 2, York Archaeol Trust, 21–28

OWEN-CROCKER, G, 1986 *Dress in Anglo-Saxon England*, Manchester

PALMER, N, 1980 'A Beaker Burial and Medieval Tenements in the Hamel, Oxford', in *Oxoniensia* **45**, 124–225

PAPWORTH, 1961 *Papworth's Ordinary of British Armorials* (reproduced from the 1874 edition), London

PAVRY, F H & KNOCKER, G M, 1957/8 'The Mount, Princes Risborough, Buckinghamshire', in *Rec Buckinghamshire* **16**, 131–78

PAYNE, A, 1987 'The Salisbury Roll of Arms, *c.*1463', in Williams, D (ed), *England in the Fifteenth Century* (Proceedings of the 1986 Harlaxton Symposium), Woodbridge

PERSSON, J 'Kammar', in Mårtensson 1976, 317–32

PINDER, W, 1952 *Der Naumberger Dom und der Meister seiner Bildwerke*, Berlin

PINTO, E H, 1952 'Hand-made Combs', in *Connoisseur* **130**, 170–76

PLATT, C & COLEMAN-SMITH, R, 1975 'Excavations in Medieval Southampton 1953–1969' **2**, *The Finds*, Leicester

POULTON, R, 1988 *Archaeological Investigations on the Site of Chertsey Abbey*, Research vol of Surrey Archaeol Soc **11**

PRITCHARD, F A, 1982 'Textiles from Recent Excavations in the City of London', in Bender Jørgensen, L and Tidow, K (eds), *Textilsymposium Neumünster, Archäologische Textilfunde*, Neumünster, 193–203

—, 1985 'Traces of Vanished Splendour – Medieval Textiles from London', in *Popular Archaeol* **6** no. 12, 28–33

—, 1988 'Silk braids and textiles of the Viking Age from Dublin', in Bender Jørgensen, L, Magnus, B and Munksgaard, E (eds), *Archaeological Textiles Report from the 2nd NESAT symposium 1–4 V 1984*, Arkaeologiske Skrifter **2**, Copenhagen, 149–61

—, forthcoming, 'The Small Finds', in A G Vince (ed), *Aspects of Saxo-Norman London* **2**: *Finds and Environmental Evidence*, London Middlesex Archaeol Soc Special Paper **12**

RADLEY, J, 1971 'Economic Aspects of Anglo-Danish York', in *Medieval Archaeol* **15**, 37–57

RAMSAY, N L, 'Stamp or Mould', in Alexander and Binski 1987, 387

RHODES, M, 1980 'Copper, Bone, Wood and Leather Items', 110–112 in Hill C et al., *The Roman Riverside Wall and Monumental Arch in London*, London Middlesex Archaeol Soc Special Paper **3**

—, 1982A 'A Pair of Fifteenth Century Spectacle Frames from the City of London', in *Antiq J* **62** part 1, 57–73

—, 1982B, 'The Finds', in Milne and Milne 1982

RIGOLD, S E, 1971 'Eynesford Castle and its Excavations', in *Archaeol Cantiana* **86**, 109–71

RILEY, H T, 1868 *Memorials of London Life in the Thirteenth, Fourteenth and Fifteenth Centuries*, London

ROACH-SMITH, C, 1854, *Catalogue of the Museum of London Antiquities*, London

—, 1857 *Collectanea Antiqua* **4** (privately printed) London

—, 1859 *Illustrations of Roman London*, London

ROBINSON, G & URQUHART, H, 1934 'Seal Bags in the Treasury of the Cathedral Church of Canterbury', in *Archaeologia* **84**, 163–211

RCHM, 1929 *London* IV *The City*, London

RORIMER, J J, 1972 *Medieval Monuments at the Cloisters, As They Were and As They Are*, Metropolitan Museum, New York (revised ed by K S Rorimer)

SABINE, E L, 1937 'City Cleaning in Mediaeval London', in *Speculum* **12** no. 1, 19–43

SAFFORD, E W, 1928 'An Account of the Expenses of Elenor, Sister of Edward III, on the Occasion of her Marriage to Reynald, Count of Guelders', in *Archaeologia* 2nd series **77**, 111–40

ST JOHN HOPE, W H, 1887 'On the English Drinking Bowls Called Mazers', in *Archaeologia* **50** part 1, 129–93

—, 1907 'The Episcopal Ornaments of William of Wykeham and William of Waynfleet, Sometime Bishops of Winchester, and of Certain Bishops of St Davids', in *Archaeologia* **60** part 2, 465–92

—, 1913 *Heraldry for Craftsmen and Designers*, London

SALZMAN, L F, 1923 *Medieval English Industries*, Oxford

SAUERLANDT, M, nd *Deutsche Plastik des Mittelaltern*, Dusseldorf/Leipzig

SAUNDERS, P, 1986 *Channels to the Past: the Salisbury Drainage Collection*, Salisbury and South Wiltshire Museum

SCHMEDDING, B, 1978 'Mittelalterliche Textilien in Kirchen und Klöstern der Schweiz', *Schrifter der Abegg-Stiftung Bern* **3**, Bern

SCOTT, M, 1980 *The History of Dress Series, Late Gothic Europe 1400–1500*, London

—, 1986 *A Visual History of Costume, the Fourteenth and Fifteenth Centuries*, London

SHARPE, R R (ed), 1912 Calendar of Letter-Books of the City of London, *Letterbook L*, London

—, 1904, —, *Letterbook F*, London

SHERLOCK, D & WOODS, H, 1988 *St Augustine's Abbey: Report on Excavations, 1969–1978*, Kent Archeol Soc Monograph **4**, Maidstone

SPARROW SIMPSON, W (ed), 1887 'Two Inventories of the Cathedral Church of St Paul, London', in *Archaeologia* **50** part 2, 439–524

SPENCER, B, 1969 (Spring) 'London – St Albans Return', in *London Archaeol* **2**, 34–35

—, 1980 *Medieval Pilgrim Badges from Norfolk*, Norfolk Museums Service, Hunstanton

—, 1982 'Pilgrim Souvenirs from the Medieval Waterfront Excavations at Trig Lane, London, 1974–76', in *Trans London Middlesex Archaeol Soc* **33**, 304–20

—, 1983, 'The Pewter Brooch', in Jarvis, K S (ed), *Excavations in Christchurch 1969–1980*, Dorset Natural History and Archaeol Soc, Dorchester, 81–83

—, 1984 'Medieval Seal-Dies Recently Found at London', Exhibits at Ballots 2, in *Antiq J* **64** part 2, 376–82

—, 1985 'Fifteenth Century Collar of SS and a Hoard of False Dice and their Container from the Museum of London', in *Antiq J* **65** part 2, 449–53

—, forthcoming 'Pilgrim Souvenirs' (Medieval Finds from London Excavations series)

STANILAND, K, 1969 'The Medieval "Corset"', in *Costume* **3**, 10–13

—, 1978 'Clothing and textiles at the court of Edward III, 1342–1352', in Bird, J, Chapman, H and Clark, J (eds), *Collectanea Londinensia, Studies presented to Ralph Merrifield*, London Middlesex Archaeol Soc Special Paper **2**, 223–34

—, 1986 'Court Style, Painters and the Great Wardrobe', 236–46, in Ormrod, W M (ed), *England in the Fourteenth Century*, Proceedings of the 1985 Harlaxton Symposium, Bury St Edmunds

STARLING, K, 1984 'The Freeze-Drying of Leather Pretreated with Glycerol', preprint for the 7th triennial meeting of the ICOM Committee for Conservation, Copenhagen

STATUTES OF THE REALM, **2**, 1826 London

STEANE, J M & BRYANT, G F, 1975 'Excavations at the Deserted Medieval Settlement at Lyveden, Fourth Report', *J Northampton Mus*, **12**

STOTHARD, C A, 1876 ed *The Monumental Effigies of Great Britain*, London

STRATFORD, N, 'Metalwork', in Zarnecki et al. 1984, 232–95

—, 'Gothic Ivory Carving in England', in Alexander and Binski 1987, 107–113

SWARZENSKI, H & NETZER, N, 1986 *Catalogue of Medieval Objects, Enamels and Glass*, Museum of Fine Arts, Boston

TAIT, H (ed), 1976 *Jewellery Through Seven Thousand Years*, London, British Museum

TATTON-BROWN, T, 1974 'Excavations at the Custom House Site, City of London 1973', in *Trans London Middlesex Archaeol Soc* **25**, 117–219

TEBBUTT, C F, 1966 'St Neots Priory', in *Proc Cambridge Antiq Soc* **59**, 33–74

THOMPSON, D V, 1956 *The Materials and Techniques of Medieval Painting*, New York (Dover edition)

THOMPSON, J D A, 1956 *Inventory of British Coin Hoards AD 600–1500*, Royal Numismatic Soc Special Publications **1**

THORDEMAN, B J N, 1939/40 *Armour from the Battle of Wisby 1361*, **1** & **2**, Stockholm

TODD, J M (ed), 1985 'Studies in Baltic Amber', *Jnl of Baltic Studies* special issue **16** no. 3

TREUE, W et al (eds), 1965 *Das Hausbuch der Mendelschen Zwolfbrüderstiftung zu Nürnberg* two vols, Munich

TRIBBICK, R, 1974 'The Metal Finds', in Sheldon, H, Excavations at Toppings and Sun Wharves, 1970–1972', in *Trans London Middlesex Archaeol Soc* **25**, 90–99

TRISTRAM, E W, 1950 *English Medieval Wall Painting, the Thirteenth Century*, Oxford

TWEDDLE, D, 1986 'Finds from Parliament Street and Other Sites in the City Centre', *The Archaeology of York* **17/4**, York

ULBRICHT, I, 1984 'Die Verarbeitung von Knochen Geweih und Horn im Mittelalterlichen Schleswig', *Ausgrabungen in Schleswig* **3**, Neumünster

USHER, A P, 1957, 'Machines and Mechanisms', in Singer, C et al., *A History of Technology* Oxford **3**, 324–26

VANDENBERGHE, S, 'Metalen Voorwergen uit Recent Archeologisch Onderzoek te Brugge', in de Witte 1988, 160–91

VAN ES, W & YPEY, J, 1977 'Das Grab der "Prinzessin" von Zweeloo und seine Bedeutung im Rahmen des Gräberfeldes' in *Studien zur Sachsenforschung*, 97–126

VAN WAATERINGE, W G– & GUIRAN, A J, 1978 'Das Leder von Lubeck, Grabung Konigstrasse 59' in *Lubecker Schriften zur Archaologie und Kulturgeschichte*, **1**, Frankfurt am Main

VCH, 1909 *Victoria Country History of London* **1** (Page, W ed), London

VEALE, E M, 1969 'Craftsmen and the Economy of London in the Fourteenth Century', in Hollaender, A E J and Kellaway, W (eds), *Studies in London History*, London, 133–51

VICTORIA AND ALBERT MUSEUM, 1980 *Princely Magnificence Court Jewels of the Renaissance 1500–1630*, Debrett's Peerage Ltd

VINCE, A G, 1985 'The Saxon and Medieval Pottery of London, a Review', in *Medieval Archaeol* **29**, 25–93

VONS-COMIS, S Y, 1988 'Een nieuwe reconstructie van de kleding van de "Prinses van Zweeloo"', in *Nieuwe Drentse Volksalmanak* **105**, 39–75 (151–87)

WARD-PERKINS, J B, 1939 'Bronze Belt-Chapes from London', in *Antiq J* **19**, 197–99

—, 1940 *London Museum Medieval Catalogue*, London

WATERER, J W, 1946 *Leather in Life, Art and Industry*, London

—, 1968, *Leather Craftsmanship*, London

WATERMAN, D M, 1959 'Late Saxon, Viking, and Early Medieval Finds from York', in *Archaeologia* **97**, 59–105

WEBSTER, L E & CHERRY, J, 1973 'Medieval Britain in 1972', in *Medieval Archaeol* **17**, 138–88

WEBSTER, R, 1975 *Gems*, London (3rd ed)

WESCHER, P, 1947 *Jean Fouquet and His Time*, Basle

WHITE, L (jr), 1978 *Medieval Religion and Technology* (Collected Essays), London

WHITING, B J (with Whiting H W), 1968 *Proverbs, Sentences and Proverbial Phrases, from English Writings Mainly Before 1500*, London

WIBERG, C, 1977 'Horn– og Benmaterialet fra Mindets Tomt', 202–13, in *Feltet 'Mindets Tomt'*, De Archaeologiske Utgravninger i Gamlebyen, Oslo bind 1, Oslo

WIDEEN, H, 1955 *Västsvenska Vikingatidsstudier*, Goteborg

WILMOTT, T, 1982 'A Medieval Armorial Brooch or Pendant from Baynard's Castle', in *Trans London Middlesex Archaeol Soc* **33**, 299–302

WILSON, D M, 1964 *Anglo-Saxon Ornamental Metalwork 700–1100*, (Catalogue of Antiquities of the Later Saxon Period I), London, British Museum

WIXOM, W D, 1988/89 'Medieval Sculpture at the Cloisters', *Metropolitan Museum of Art Bull* **46** no. **3**, New York

WOODS, H, 1982 'Excavations at Eltham Palace, 1975–79', in *Trans London Middlesex Archaeol Soc* **33**, 214–65

WORMALD, F, 1973 *The Winchester Psalter*, London

YOUNGS, S M et al., 1983 'Medieval Britain and Ireland in 1982', in *Medieval Archaeol* **27**, 161–229

ZARNECKI, G, HOLT, J & HOLLAND, T (eds), 1984 *English Romanesque Art 1066–1200*, Arts Council of Great Britain, London